communication and new media

To the future or to the past, to a time when thought is free, when men are different from one another and do not live alone—to a time when truth exists and what is done cannot be undone:
From the age of uniformity, from the age of solitude, from the age of Big Brother, from the age of doublethink—greetings!

Winston Smith, from George Orwell's 1984

They who control the data, control the world.

Bill Kirkley, Brisbane, 2005

communication and new media

FROM BROADCAST TO NARROWCAST

MARTIN HIRST and JOHN HARRISON

OXFORD
UNIVERSITY PRESS

253 Normanby Road, South Melbourne, Victoria 3205, Australia

Oxford University Press is a department of the University of Oxford.
It furthers the University's objective of excellence in research, scholarship, and education by publishing worldwide in

Oxford New York

Auckland Cape Town Dar es Salaam Hong Kong Karachi
Kuala Lumpur Madrid Melbourne Mexico City Nairobi
New Delhi Shanghai Taipei Toronto

with offices in

Argentina Austria Brazil Chile Czech Republic France Greece
Guatemala Hungary Italy Japan Poland Portugal Singapore
South Korea Switzerland Thailand Turkey Ukraine Vietnam

First published 2007

National Library of Australia
Cataloguing-in-Publication data:

Hirst, Martin.
Communication and new media : from broadcast to narrowcast.

ISBN 9780195553550.
ISBN 0 19 555355 1.

1. Communication. 2. Mass media. I. Harrison, John, (John Murray), 1952- .
II. Title.

302.2

Edited by Venetia Somerset
Proofread by Pete Cruttenden
Designed and typeset by Adrian Saunders
Printed in Hong Kong by Sheck Wah Tong Printing Press Ltd

FOREWORD

The American TV comic Jon Stewart got plenty of laughs at the 2006 Academy Awards ceremony when he described two of the year's best movies, *Good Night, and Good Luck* and *Capote*, as films about 'determined journalists defying obstacles in a relentless pursuit of truth,' and then added: 'Needless to say, both are period pieces.' In an age of media transformation, serious-minded journalism is becoming an anachronism that draws sniggers from TV comedians. In an age of digital, portable, and ubiquitous media, entertainment has replaced journalism as the primary content paradigm. In an age where many of the old media models are being marginalised or even destroyed, no-one can assert with authority what will happen next—except that it will be different.

So this is where we find ourselves: in the midst of a media revolution that allows comedians to draw laughs by describing the honourable pursuit of truth—the holy grail of journalism—as a period piece. And that's not even the worst of it, because the really important point to remember is that we're only part-way through this particular revolution. The replacement of 'old media' with digital media is still a work in progress, with the emphasis on progress. And that means many (if not most) of the assumptions being made about the shape of this unfolding communications revolution will be wrong. Traditional journalism may be dying, or not. Broadcast television may be replaced by personalised television, or not. Mobile telephony may become the media platform of choice for many consumers, or not. Citizen journalists may overshadow conventional journalists, or not. The new world of media may be more democratic, or not.

You don't need a PhD to comprehend the two certainties about these and most of the other predictions being made about the unfolding media revolution: change will continue and no-one knows where it will end. And when today's predictions are re-read in ten or twenty years' time, many of them will be laughable and only some will be right.

We have returned to what the American media culture commentator Kurt Anderson (*New York* magazine, 1 May 2006) describes as 'a new techno-paloozaical moment,' where 'once again, a critical mass of money guys and journalists and entrepreneurs are getting awfully excited, and the excitement is beginning to feed on itself.' Anderson describes the scene: 'There are the new social-networking services like MySpace and Flickr, with enough millions of users that a real network effect has kicked in. Blogs attracting significant audiences and advertisers. Money flooding into Web start-ups, and blog-conglomerates acquired for tens and hundreds of millions. The Nasdaq up 20 percent in the last year. Network TV migrating to podcasts, the collective Utopia of Wikipedia actually working, and follow-on "citizen media" entities (Digg, Newsvine) generating dreamy new visions of cultural transformation.'

This particular stage in the information revolution is different in style as well as substance. 'The vocabulary and doctrine are different,' says Anderson. 'To call a Web business a "dot-com" in 2006 would be the equivalent of calling a black person "colored." Rather, people thrill to ideas incorporating the "architecture of participation" and "collective intelligence" (like Wikipedia and Flickr), and companies with "lightweight business models" (Craigslist has eighteen employees).'

While it is clear that the technological force driving dot.com.2 is super-fast broadband Internet via cable or wireless, this book is far more interested in the social and political forces driving the revolution. And it is here that things are getting very interesting as the traditional media begins to lose its coveted role as the gatekeeper who directs the information traffic, only to discover that technology has begun to remove the gates.

No matter whether blogs become big or the Internet eats the lunch of traditional media, the democratisation of information has arrived. No longer is American journalism 'the business and practice of presenting the news of the day in the interest of economic privilege', as Upton Sinclair described it in 1928 (see page 86). No longer are the media barons in charge of the news agenda, and no longer can important information be supressed by agreement between a newspaper owner and a political leader. Just like the Wall that came down in Berlin and transformed democracy in Europe, the gates that have been removed from the media gatekeepers are responsible for transforming democracy of information.

But if you think the removal of rusty old gates will make this a uniformly good revolution, I'm not so sure. Of course the democratisation of media is a good development. And the disappearance of the gatekeeping elite won't be mourned. But this revolution is wreaking collateral damage, and not just commercially or financially. I am referring to the damage the Internet is inflicting on the best kind of public service journalism, especially in smaller democracies like Australia where good journalism has always been led a precarious existence because its appeal, by definition, is only to a small audience.

I fear for the future of quality journalism because its funding sources are now under sustained attack by forces which cannot be repelled. Much of the quality journalism you read in newspapers is actually paid for by the vastly profitable classified advertising that appears in other sections of those newspapers. Yet it is precisely that classified advertising—the funding source of the quality journalism produced by news staffs of hundreds of reporters and editors—which is the most threatened species in the new media business model. Why would companies with profit-focused shareholders continue to fund expensive quality journalism when their funding source of classified advertising 'rivers of gold' migrate to the Internet (as they are now doing with relentless frequency)? In two words: they won't.

This revolution, like most revolutions, will claim its victims. And if the institution of heavily-funded and well-motivated journalism is one of its victims, no amount of blogging or media democratisation will replace the void that will be created by downsizing serious journalism. Democracy itself will be the victim.

And in case anyone thinks that previous media upheavals haven't claimed victims, this book presents a list of the deceased:

- Talkies killed silent movies.

- Radio killed the piano player as a home entertainment.
- Television slowly killed the illustrated newspaper, most of the general interest magazines and most of the comic book industry.
- Radio and television slowly killed the afternoon newspapers.
- Television killed old-style radio programming, including almost all radio drama.
- The video camcorder killed the home movie camera.

The evolution from broadcast to narrowcast is unfolding faster than anyone could have predicted. Its genesis is technological, but its impact is sociological and political, driven in part by dramatic changes in demographics and in human behaviour.

But this is not just a revolution about delivering the same messages in a better way. The mode and content of the messages themselves are changing as the platforms that carry them change. Push is being replaced by pull. One-size-fits-all is being replaced by customisation. Mass media is being replaced by micro-targeted media. The traditional radio/television/newspaper broadcast model is now being challenged by a vastly superior technological delivery system—the Internet—which can slice and dice a mass audience into millions of mini-audiences. All of this, in turn, is creating new and entirely different content paradigms, just like the movie industry paradigm was overhauled by the introduction of sound, and the broadcast industry paradigm was overhauled by the introduction of vision.

If this all sounds confusing and unpredictable, it is. If it sounds energising and fascinating, it is. If it sounds threatening and potentially dangerous, it is. And if it sounds like a powerful exposition of Schumpter's famous description of capitalism itself—creative destruction—it is. Creative *and* destructive.

Eric Beecher

Eric Beecher is a former editor of *The Sydney Morning Herald* and book publisher. He is now the publisher of *Crikey*, Australia's leading independent news journal.

BRIEF CONTENTS

CONTENTS

PREFACE

Communication and New Media is an introduction to contemporary theories and views about mass communication and the mass media and how they are both changing their form and function in response to digtal convergence. We first need to explain why it's important to draw a distinction between mass communication and mass media: communication is the process of sending and receiving messages; the media are the means of communication and transmission.

It follows that many types of communication can take place using different types of media. 'Technological convergence' also means crossed signals or mixed messages and an increasingly fragmented media. A housemate on *Big Brother* uses his fifteen minutes of fame to launch a protest message about refugees in Australian detention centres; others are caught by hidden cameras while engaging in intimate personal communication. The news on television is another common form of communication, with more important and far-reaching implications than some harmless and mildly entertaining partial nudity from the bored and desensitised *Big Brother* housemates. Most of this communication is one way. Network news tells us about events in the world, or at least those selected for inclusion according to 'news values' that may or may not be transparent; we see only those segments of 'reality' captured by the *Big Brother* cameras that the producers deem to be 'entertaining' enough. Convergence of media technologies and forms is supposed to create more interactivity—but if this extends only to the expensive and ultimately pointless interaction of 'voting' for a housemate on *Big Brother*, it's not real interaction. For the media today, 'interactive' means that someone finds a way of tunnelling into your bank account.

Our approach to teaching, to learning, and to writing this book is also interactive. We are keen for you to respond as a reader. With an 'old' media form like a book, this is a little harder, but we've included questions, case studies, and exercises to assist your interaction with colleagues, classmates, and peers. *Communication and New Media* explicitly and implicitly binds together 'theory' and 'practice'. The embedding of theory and practice, one in the other, reflects the almost insoluble link between learning and action. This embedded approach most closely fits the pedagogical needs of tertiary courses in journalism, professional communication, and the creative industries more generally. More importantly, it is increasingly coming to be the required standard from employers who need graduates with emotional intelligence, curiosity, and an inquiring mind, and who are also aesthetically and ethically aware of the situations and contexts in which they will work. The integration of theory and practice also addresses two imperatives in higher education, which were always implicit but are now explicit:

- Graduating students must be able to demonstrate skills of critical analysis and independent thinking.

- They should cxhibit a strong foundation not only in ethical understanding but also in critical reasoning.

You might think it unusual that a textbook about mass communication and new media technologies would 'waste' valuable words on the esoteric subject of utopian and dystopian science fiction. But there is a purpose to our digressions. Ever since the Greek empire dominated the known word and was wealthy enough to employ full-time philosophers, human society has been interested in devoting resources to speculative wondering about the future. Plato's famous treatise *The Republic* is one of the earliest writings to embrace utopian ideals in contemplation of an almost perfect world that had yet to come to pass. Since Plato's time, and using his text as a template, political writers, social critics, and anti-authoritarian dissidents have employed similar means to promote their cause (Rothstein 2003).Often a mythological language and poetic-Socratic style was used to evade the censors, who would not allow a serious debate about unpopular government policies. As a result, we now have a rich tradition in literature that today is manifest in the science fiction writing of people like William Gibson, who can present the near and distant future in ways that show it is clearly derived from past and present conditions, both technological and emotional.

Finally, we hope that reading this text is an enjoyable and inspirational process for you. We have included many references to science fiction, particularly the genre known as 'cyberpunk'. This is a deliberate attempt on our part to make *Communication and New Media* engaging. But the serious side is that science fiction has a knack of making workable predictions about the future. In this instance we think 'cyberpunk' has some useful things to say about our digital future.

ACKNOWLEDGMENTS

We said to each other at the beginning of this process that 'blood is thicker than ink'. The fact that we can still say this now that *Communication and New Media* is finally published is a testament to our friendship as well as our collaboration. Our families and close friends deserve a mention for their patience and for putting up with our long absences from the dinner table while this book was in its formative stages.

Martin Hirst thanks everyone who helped keep him together, body and soul, while he was digesting the research and writing the text. In particular, his wife Tiffany White for love and encouragement; colleagues and collaborators in Sydney, the Blue Mountains, Melbourne, Brisbane, Perth and elsewhere. The team at DPC who didn't mind his disappearing act for weeks at a time. Sharon Bailey for personifying the links between Gonzo and Zen.

John Harrison would like to thank the usual suspects—friends and colleagues at the University of Queensland, and before that at Queensland University of Technology; in particular Mark Hayes, Bernard McKenna, David Rooney; Michael Bromley, Greg Hearn, and John Cokley; his students, especially those in Communication Skills New Media, who keep him honest; his children Caitlin and James, who keep him techno-functioning; and the dear Julie, who doesn't really believe in books, but who is enormously tolerant of their writing all the same.

The staff at Oxford have been outstandingly professional as always, generous in their comments and with their time, particularly Lucy McLoughlin, Tim Campbell, and our editor Venetia Somerset. To any one who's offended by our comments, we apologise; it's not personal. Thanks to all of our willing correspondents who provided helpful and compelling personal stories that do so much to enliven our text. Thanks also to Eric Beecher for providing the Foreword.

This book would not have been possible without the unconditional love of our cats and Orwell, the faithful hound.

ABBREVIATIONS

AANA	Australian Association of National Advertisers
AAP	Australian Associated Press
ABA	Australian Broadcasting Authority
ABC	Australian Broadcasting Corporation
ACA	Australian Communications Authority
ACCC	Australian Consumer and Competition Commission
ACLU	American Civil Liberties Union
ACMA	Australian Media and Communications Authority
ADMA	Australian Direct Marketing Association
AFR	*Australian Financial Review*
AFTRS	Australian Film, Television and Radio School
AI	artificial intelligence
ALGOL	ALGOrithmic Language
AOL	America Online
APC	Australian Press Council
APN	Australian Provincial Newspapers
APRA	Australian Performing Rights Association
ASB	Advertising Standards Bureau
ASCC	Automatic Sequence Controlled Calculator
ASIC	Australian Securities and Investments Commission
ASIO	Australian Security Intelligence Organisation
ASX	Australian Stock Exchange
AT&T	American Telephone and Telegraph
AWA	Australian Workplace Agreement
BASIC	Beginners All-purpose Symbolic Instruction Code
BBC	British Broadcasting Corporation
BSB	Broadcasting Services Band
CBS	Columbia Broadcasting System
CCD	Charge-coupled Device
CCTV	closed-circuit television
CEI	Charter of Editorial Independence
CEO	chief executive officer
CGI	computer-generated imagery
COBOL	COmmon Business Oriented Language
DARPA	(US) Defense Advanced Research Projects Agency
DCITA	(Australian) Department of Communications, Information Technology and the Arts

EBA	enterprise bargaining agreement
EDC	electronic digital computer
EFF	Electronic Frontier Foundation
ENG	electronic news-gathering
ENIAC	electronic numerical integrator and computer
FBI	US Federal Bureau of Investigation
FORTRAN	FORmula TRANslation
FTA	free-to-air
GIO	generalist intelligence officer
HCUA	House Committee on Un-American Activities
HDTV	high-definition television
HLL	high-level language
HSARPA	Homeland Security Advanced Research Projects Agency
IBM	International Business Machines
ICANN	Internet Corporation for Assigned Names and Numbers
ICT	information and communication technology
IFEX	International Freedom of Expression eXchange
IPO	Initial Public Offering
ISP	Internet service provider
IT	information technology
LAN	local area network
LP	long-playing
MANA	Media Alliance for New Activism
MEAA	Media Entertainment and Arts Alliance (formerly the Australian Journalists Association)
MIT	Massachusetts Institute of Technology
MITS	Micro Instrumentation and Telementry Systems
MJW	Mobile Journalist Workstation
MPPDA	Motion Picture Producers and Distributors of America
MUD	Multi-user domain
NGLT	National Gay and Lesbian Taskforce
NYSE	New York Stock Exchange
NYT	*New York Times*
OECD	Organisation for Economic Co-operation and Development
PBL	Publishing and Broadcasting Limited
PFF	Progress and Freedom Foundation
PKIU	Printing and Kindred Industries Union
PMG	Postmaster-General (Australia)
PRSA	Public Relations Society of America
RFID	radio frequency identifying
RSS	Really Simple Syndication

SBS	Special Broadcasting Service (Australia)
SLR	single lens reflex
SMH	*Sydney Morning Herald*
UNIVAC	Universal Automatic Computer
VDU	visual display unit
VJ	video journalist
WAN	World Association of Newspapers
wiki-	what I know is
WSJ	*Wall Street Journal*
WWW	World Wide Web

PART 1 POLITICAL ECONOMY, TECHNOLOGY, CULTURE, MEDIA AND CAPITALISM

> It's by using the technologies and pathways laid down by promoters of control that cyberians believe they must conduct their revolution. (Rushkoff 1994, p. 285)

American Douglas Rushkoff was one of the first journalists to explore the implications of cyberspace, back when it was still a largely experimental and somewhat mythical entity, before the days of Hotmail and Google. He interviewed many of the founders of the Internet and those first intrepid souls who believed it would bring about a utopian revolution, challenging the entrenched power of the mainstream media and giving ordinary people access to liberating technology. Today Douglas Rushkoff runs a consulting business that provides 'Gen-X' advice to 'baby-boomers' about computing and cyberspace issues and runs his own business from the website <www.rushkoff.com> (Mosco 2004; Rushkoff 2006). Douglas Rushkoff has certainly benefited from the information revolution. What about the rest of us?

We now know—with the benefit of ten years' hindsight—that such a dream, while real enough for the pioneers of cyberia, was ultimately mythic rather than actual. It was quickly overtaken by corporate giants keen to regain their profitable monopolies and to harness the new technology to an ever-expanding market for goods and services, both real and virtual. This first part of *Communication and New Media* begins to lay out the theoretical and analytical tools necessary to understand what upset the digital dreams of the early believers.

Throughout the book, the issues that arise in relation to aspects of the mass communication media are constructed in a definite set of social relationships that exist in a state of creative tension—what we call a dialectic of historical change. These ever-shifting relationships are primarily defined by the ways in which communication industries and practices are economically structured. These industries and practices are then situated in the broader political, economic, and ideological structures of society alongside the institutions of government and civil society. This is why we have decided on a political economy approach and why we have chosen to start with an explanation of the purpose, methods, and theories of what we mean by political economy. We are standing on the shoulders of giants in this regard and acknowledge the important contributions of four generations of communication scholars working in the political economy tradition (see Mosco 1996, 2004; McChesney & Schiller 2003).

In settling on this approach we do not intend to play down the importance of factors other than the economic. We see economics, politics, culture, and social attitudes (ideologies) as being entwined, much like the strands of a DNA double helix. Our argument (expanded in later sections) is that the economic organisation of society is itself a complex of social relations that determines all other relationships between people and between people and the commodities that society produces, through its economic base, to meet the needs and wants of its consuming citizens.

As well as outlining what we mean by a political economy of communication, these first few chapters also deal with the concept of the 'dialectic', which simply put is the process of change that marks out history by bringing together, in a state of tension, a range of social forces that interact and clash. Of course we also have to deal with some definitional issues, particularly what we understand by the term 'technology'. It is common sense to think of technology as objects, machines, and things, but what about the process through which they come into being? We answer this question in chapter 3 by suggesting that technology is not just about machines and commodities. Instead, we suggest, it is a process of linking useful knowledge and science to the ways in which society organises its productive (and destructive) relationship with nature and the material world. In other words, we incorporate our discussion of communications technology into political economy because it is impossible to remove technology from the mode of production.

The final chapter in part I concludes our theoretical discussion by outlining some working definitions of technology and incorporating them into the political economy approach to communication studies. In this chapter we focus on the dialectic of convergence and show how periodic crises and attempts to overcome them have shaped global capitalism in the late 20th and early 21st centuries. We argue that the technologies of communication, and indeed, the social relations of mass media and mass communication, are not immune from this process. In a sense, the current fixation on creative industries, the 'information' economy and 'knowledge' society reflect an intellectual and practical need for capital to come to terms with the economic crises of over-production and profitability, and with the political crisis of failing nation states.

The final sections of this chapter are our attempt to come to terms with the vexed question of determination and determinism in theoretical accounts of the digital revolution. We feel that many approaches tend to privilege the technological over the social and we argue that this is a mistaken and ultimately determinist view that does not account for the effects of the dialectic and mutual constitution.

This first section makes explicit our epistemology—our theoretical position—in debates about mass communication, the media and technology. We conclude that the current mode of development that is driving capitalism—an ever greater rate of digital convergence coupled with tectonic shifts in the relations and forces of production—is leading, almost inexorably, towards a narrowcasting form of mass media. In the rest of the book we do not refer to the *theories* of political economy, but we do apply its *methods* to develop and argue for our analysis of both the declining broadcast media and the emerging forms of narrowcasting. This theoretical first part underpins our discussion of the thesis that narrowcasting is an important signifier and crucial component of the developing surveillance society. It also makes it clear that we do not regard the surveillance economy (see part 4) as something distinct from capitalism; it is merely a new form of exploitation and hegemony.

1 DIGITAL FUTURES: HOW THE MOBILE PHONE HAS REPLACED THE TELEVISION

OBJECTIVES

This chapter introduces the themes of *Communication and New Media* and outlines the purpose of each section. Reading this introduction will familiarise you with the ideas we are discussing and the language we use to discuss them.

After reading this chapter you should be ready to tackle the topics in the main body of the book and have some understanding of why *Broadcast to Narrowcast* is structured in this particular way. In particular, we hope you will take the following from reading this introduction:

- how and why the book is written, and structured, the way it is;
- the idea that technology alone does not determine the shape of the future;
- how the means of communication—forms of broadcasting and narrowcasting—are socially determined by a range of complex factors that we can understand using, among other things, the tools of political economy.

KEYWORDS

> Keywords: 'the record of an inquiry into a *vocabulary*: a shared body of words and meanings in our most general discussions, in English, of the practices and institutions which we group as *culture* and *society*'. (Williams 1989, p. 15)

At the beginning of each chapter we will flag some of the keywords and concepts that you will encounter. In all cases, the keywords are defined in the text. However, if you are puzzled about a word or concept you see on this list, grab a dictionary, or check in our Glossary, or go to Wikipedia to read a working definition.

For example, the following terms will be prominent throughout the book: technology, convergence, analogue, digital, dialectic, utopia, dystopia, political economy, meme, mode of production, and mode of development.

We have tried to avoid jargon as much as possible, so the meanings we employ are usually the most common and logical. Some terms, like dialectic, meme, and mode of development, are of a more specialist nature and we have taken some time to work them into the text in an understandable way, but (we hope) without 'dumbing them down' and reducing them to clichés.

Digital futures

> During the past century the successive advances in technology have been accompanied by corresponding advances in organization ... In order to fit into these organizations, individuals have had to de-individualize themselves, have had to deny their native diversity and conform to a standard pattern, and have had to do their best to become automata. (Huxley 1965, p. 18)

Aldous Huxley wrote these prophetic words in a 1958 essay, 'Brave New World Revisited', which was a coda to his bleak but bawdy science fiction novel *Brave New World*, first published in 1932. *Brave New World* was a comic story of an imagined future in which the science of socially grading human beings had been perfected. On the surface the future world appeared to be perfect—particularly for those classed among the higher levels. For the nameless 'drones', it was less perfect. The equilibrium of the world is threatened by the arrival of a 'primitive' in the fashionable society of London. The central characters are forced to challenge their utopian view and the world is revealed as very authoritarian and dystopian.

Huxley felt compelled to add this epilogue because he was, at the time, 'a good deal less optimistic' than when he was writing the novel (p. 1). His optimism had been dented by the rise of totalitarianism in Europe (Hitler, Stalin, Franco, and Mussolini), the depression years, World War II, and the atomic bomb.

In the essay Huxley compares *Brave New World* to that other classic of nightmare totalitarianism, George Orwell's *Nineteen Eighty-four*. Huxley describes Orwell's work as 'a magnificent projection into the future of a present that contained Stalinism and an immediate past that had witnessed the flowering of Nazism' (p. 2). Huxley's *Brave New World* begins with a utopian promise, while the dystopia of Orwell's *Nineteen Eighty-four* is apparent from the beginning. Throughout this book we will refer to other works of futuristic science fiction and the ways in which they oscillate between utopian and dystopian views of the world. The novels and short stories we include here provide very appropriate windows into our own possible digital futures.

The major differences that Huxley saw between his work and Orwell's were on the question of how totalitarian states exercise their social control. In *Nineteen Eighty-four*, total control over the exploited population is maintained through surveillance, terror, and the fear of terrible punishment; in *Brave New World* control, no less totalitarian, is exercised through 'the more effective methods of reward and scientific manipulation' of individual minds (p. 3).

In both books the entire population is under constant surveillance and the methods of ideological manipulation are similar—the mass media play a central role in disseminating the regimes' propaganda. In *Nineteen Eighty-four* it was the telescreen: a two-way mechanism for instruction and surveillance that could never be turned off, while in *Brave New World* it was 'non-stop distractions of the most fascinating nature'. Huxley continues in order to draw a widely applicable conclusion, based on his observations of English society in the 1950s: 'A society, most of whose members spend a great part of their time … in the irrelevant other worlds of sport and soap opera, of mythology and metaphysical fantasy, will find it hard to resist the encroachments of those who would manipulate and control it' (p. 29).

A good example of the creative tension between utopian and dystopian dreams of the future is a short story by the Canadian sci-fi writer William Gibson, 'The Gernsback Continuum'. In this story a commercial photographer is recruited to take photographs of 20th-century American industrial architecture and as he moves around each location, he is reminded of a future that never was, a 'never never land' and 'the true home of uninhibited technophiles' (Gibson 1995, p. 38). At the same time, he notices that some of the buildings he's commissioned to photograph have 'a kind of sinister totalitarian dignity' (p. 40); others exude 'potent bursts of raw technological enthusiasm' (p. 41). In *Communication and New Media* you will find the same contradictions apparent in the new media technologies. On one hand, they hold the promise of a bright, abundant future; on the other is the threat of increased surveillance, even greater monopoly over resources, and greater control over our political selves—our citizenship. If this is beginning to sound all too uncomfortable and familiar, you have picked up the right book!

Aldous Huxley's essay on *Brave New World* is fairly pessimistic, but he does end it on a more positive note. In a concluding chapter called 'What can be done?' he argues that people can be 'educated for freedom', but society is, in his view, 'threatened from many directions' including overpopulation and the ever-present shadow of totalitarianism and psychological disease (Huxley 1965, p. 89). Today, we could also add environmental ruin;

seemingly endless warfare; expanding regions of poverty; the HIV-AIDS virus; the threat of a bird-flu pandemic; and the return of physical illnesses we thought vanquished long ago (tuberculosis among them). We have written this book as a university text for use in communications courses, but also because we, like Huxley, retain our optimism, while recognising the technological threats all around us. We believe, as Huxley did, that 'there is still some freedom left in the world'.

We couldn't agree more. The digital future is in your hands.

Keeping up with the future

> It's not like Big Brother, more like Big Mother ... Michael's the first kid on his northern beaches block to have a new child's mobile phone that doubles as a tracking device. (L. Williams 2006)

These days, 8-year-old kids like Michael in this newspaper story are likely to be more techno-savvy then the average 38-year-old adult. Mobile phones are no longer just phones—they are GPS tracking devices, video and still cameras, wireless Internet connections, and pocket calculators. In the United States all mobile phones are now fitted with GPS (global positioning system) and they are now also available in Australia. Does this make you feel that technology is moving too fast? Did you just get used to the CD Walkman and then discover you really should have an iPod? Perhaps it's a generational thing, but anyone over 40 could be forgiven for just sticking with their collection of vinyl discs and a turntable. Unfortunately, it's not possible to bury your head in the sand and it's not easy being the office technophobe (Snow 2005). The future is never far away and it does seem that digital technology is developing and changing at a rapid rate. But where is it going? Despite her self-confessed technophobia (fear of technology), journalist Deborah Snow is able to recognise the apparent contradictions invested in the latest wave of digital technologies:

> Yes, of course, the communications revolution ... has brought benefits ... but that's not to say we shouldn't, as individuals and as a society, take time to try to digest, then adapt to each wave of technological change before the next one breaks upon us. Trouble is, the pace of change has become so furious that catching breath between the waves is becoming nearly impossible. (Snow 2005)

A central argument of our book is that there are several possible futures associated with digital technologies. The process of convergence—the melding of one technology with another—produces a range of new hybrid technologies that can either make our lives easier, or as Huxley and Orwell warn, lead to a nightmare future of more effective social manipulation and control. The British writer and essayist Kinglsey Amis captures the utopia/dystopia dialectic well in his essay on trends in science fiction *New Maps of Hell*, written in 1960 when the promise of a bright technology-driven future was real, though overshadowed by the Cold War. He suggested that modernist science fiction often portrayed human society 'groaning in chains of its own construction' (Amis 1960, p. 66).

On the other hand the optimists believe that the future of technological abundance will supply all the information and techno-toys we'll ever need and perhaps some we don't. Haven't you always wanted a portable, digital ghost radar? We kid you not, the first such device, which can tell you if a ghost is evil or not, went on sale in Japan in April 2005 (Ghosts in the machine 2005). In a techno-positivist vein, some scientists are predicting that future technologies will even make it possible to radically re-engineer human DNA to 'blend ourselves with machines in unprecedented ways ... ranging from homogenised humans to alien-looking hybrids bred for interstellar travel' (Boyle 2005).

The technologically positivist future relies on the argument that technology somehow equals 'progress' and that once we've ironed out a few difficulties—like inequality of access—the world can look forward to eliminating the social ills of poverty, war, and pestilence. The Australian government's strategic framework document for the 'information economy' is clearly in the utopian camp when it asserts that successful adjustment to the new technologies will 'create a platform for long-term national competitiveness, the renewal of regional communities and stronger social cohesion' (DCITA 2004, p. 6). In this view, unemployment will be a thing of the past, and prosperity and democracy will flourish everywhere. In this future, the convergence that produces digital communications technologies is seen as a process that can expand democracy and shrink the world to what Marshall McLuhan called the global village. We will come back to McLuhan's ideas about the mass media and technology later.

The alternative future is less ideal. In this future the increasing role that digital technologies play in our everyday lives does not lead to abundance and world peace. Instead it moves us inexorably towards a totalitarian world state, similar to that envisioned by Huxley and Orwell, in which the divisions between the wealthy and the poor are as wide as ever and technology enslaves us to the machine. In this future digital technologies move from being communication-oriented to surveillance-oriented. What DICTA means by 'stronger social cohesion' is anybody's guess. Much like the ever-present telescreen, there will be 'no way of shutting it off completely' (Orwell 1988, p. 5).

Our primary directive—to quote another popular science fiction idea—is to show that, given the present state of converging technologies, particularly in the realm of mass communication, either future is possible. Technologies do not exist in a vacuum; they are imagined, invented, and implemented in an imperfect world of inequality and social divisions.

A secondary goal is to argue that the type of future we leave for our children and grandchildren will not be determined by the technology itself, but rather by the legacy of the social conditions in which these technologies are developed and exploited. Technology itself—as a series of intersecting scientific methods, discoveries, and practices, often embodied in 'things'—has no inherent social values. In fact the reverse is true: the values of the dominant societies on earth today will shape the ways in which communication technologies and practices of the present and in the future are invented, distributed, consumed, and controlled. We are as much interested in this social process of convergence as we are in the converging technologies themselves. The values we express through our relations with other humans and with nature will also go a long way to determining the uses for which current and future digital technologies are employed.

The first clue about how we might imagine the digital future is in the subtitle of our book, *From Broadcast to Narrowcast*, which illustrates in a single catchy phrase our central concern. In a nutshell, what we mean by this is that the age of mass broadcasting (we include print publishing in this) is perhaps coming to an end. Instead we are looking at a future of mass communication that involves highly targeted narrowcasting—the mass audience is split into its individual (atomic) particles, the single receiver-consumer. The first widely available technology that began what we believe is a seismic shift was the Internet. The mobile phone and the digital set-top box are the latest and perhaps more important technologies that cement in place the narrowcasting future. Our understanding of how digital technologies are changing our world will be developed using the theories and tools of political economy and, to some extent, cultural studies. We have taken a necessarily eclectic approach for two reasons. First, the historical scope of the book demands that we trace the connections—both forwards and backwards from today—between the new digital technologies and the technologies of the analogue age. Second, it is important to understand the broader social and cultural context in which these technologies exist. Their configuration and their uses are influenced by both economics and by the milieu in which they are brought into being, commercialised, and ultimately used as tools in our everyday lives.

The second important concern we want to discuss at length is the issue of technological convergence. We're not claiming that this is something brand new that no one's noticed before. Far from it. There are plenty of media sources and academic texts devoted to a discussion of digital convergence; indeed we've drawn on some of them for the ideas in this book. Where we differ from many texts is that we want to emphasise the social relations of convergence, rather than focus primarily on the gadgets, doodads, and digital devices that are becoming common. Of course no book about convergence and media could ignore the iPod, the Palm Pilot, and the digital camera; nor could it ignore 'podcasting' and the 'backpack journalist', which are revolutionising the ways we receive broadcast news and current affairs.

Another point of difference is our use of the dialectical method and a philosophical outlook—a worldview—that asks us to examine the interconnected and contradictory elements of technology as they exist in a social context. As we explain in chapter 2, the dialectic is found in nature, but it is also a driver of social change. It is a clash of ideas, but also a clash of social forces (Hirst & Patching 2005). More fundamentally it is the clash of social forces with the forces of nature. As the British materialist philosopher Alex Callinicos (1995, p. 158) puts it, the need to control nature through the implements created by technology 'is a constant in the history of the human species'. All human societies, from the primitive cave dwellers of the Stone Age to the sophisticated urbanites of the 21st-century sprawl, have harnessed nature in order to produce the means of their own social reproduction. Our approach is to focus not only on the technologies but also on these social and political impacts. Thus the theme *From Broadcast to Narrowcast* creates an explicit sense-making spine to the book, which draws on the authors' backgrounds as experienced media practitioners and their academic expertise in history, sociology, political economy, philosophy, theology, communication theory, and media technologies.

Structure of the book

The book is divided into four parts, divisions that logically follow our thematic approach under the banner of 'from broadcast to narrowcast'. We have situated our arguments within an historical and sociological continuum that allows us to track, discuss, and explain how the 'new' media both extend and eclipse the 'old' media, creating a new set of epistemological and theoretical problems for students of media and mass communication. Our approach is to embed discussion of the issues in coverage of communication industries and practices as they have been historically developed within the context of the mass media. In this context we will examine journalism, public relations, and advertising as professional practices and the print media, radio, television, and the Internet as independent but related means of mass communication. This is not a book about audience studies, which is a distinct field within the discipline of communication and media studies. But it is impossible not to mention audience, since this is the focus of so much effort on behalf of all media organisations. Our view is that the audience is made up of two distinct but integrated aspects: consumers and citizens. One of the central arguments that we make in these pages is that the transition from broadcasting to narrowcasting is also a transition for the audience. We move from being citizens to being consumers. This shift in perception and marketing is partly about further dissecting the commercial opportunities for exploiting the audience as a collective and as individual consumers. Narrowcasting is all about finding and exploiting the niche market.

This last point is one reason why we begin the text with an explanation of political economy, technology, and media cultures in fairly simple theoretical terms. We are keenly concerned with the social aspects of the convergence of digital technologies and this means a particular focus on the economic, political, ideological, and cultural structures, processes, and relationships that govern the ways in which technologies are inserted into the fabric of our society. After considering the history of technological change in this socio-cultural context we examine the ways in which governments attempt to regulate and control technologies and their end-users (individuals, organisations, corporations) through the application of legal sanctions and frameworks for mediation and regulation.

Part I: Political Economy, Technology, Culture, and the Myths of Cyberia

Part I establishes the outlook and the framework for the book and is the place for our more theoretical discussions. Its purpose is to outline the history of attempts to understand mass media and communications technologies and to present an overview of common theoretical approaches to the study of mass communication. The foundation of this part is several chapters that discuss the ideas of political economy in relation to media and communication studies. In part I we define and explain the role of the dialectic as both a social force and a set of relationships that determine the final shape, scope, and purpose of technologies. We argue that the impact of digital convergence can best be understood as a 'disruptive process of change' (DCITA 2004, p. 7) that affects many aspects of our daily existence. How we react to that change and to the transformations wrought by digital technologies will shape the world for the next hundred years. In this first part we also begin to explore some new ideas that help to make sense of convergence and the changing nature of digital communication technologies. We also take the opportunity to introduce a discussion of ideology and the role of the mass media in disseminating, reinvigorating, and renewing some of the social values that we take as commonsense and everyday.

Part II: Hot Metal to Hotmail: The (Recent) History of Mass Communication

In part II we discuss the concrete and historically developed communication industries of print, radio, and television over the past 200 years. Of course, these core industrial forms of mass communication are also constantly evolving and so our approach is to understand the development of mass communication from broadcasting to narrowcasting as part of an historical progression. We trace the development of modern industrial forms of mass media as deriving from more craft-driven and partisan 19th-century print media, through mass distribution of cheap newsprint, to radio and television broadcasting in order to establish the historical continuity between these forms and the new media form of narrowcasting.

In part II we also examine the history of mass communications from the perspective of state regulation, legal restraints, and the ethico-legal paradox that often exists when attempts to marry the law with ethical principles strike a contradiction. Our approach is to place the right emphasis on issues of media regulation, governance, and ethics within the context of issues and industries. It is our intention to highlight the ethical and legal dilemmas that the new communications technologies create for regulators such as the Advertising Standards Bureau and the Australian Communications and Media Authority.

Part III: The Emergence of Convergence: New Century, New Media

In part III we develop, in a systematic way, the argument that the shift to new digital media technologies is a continuation of an historical process of convergence that began with the lever and the wheel. In the way it presents today, digital convergence is the product of the economic, social, administrative, ethical, and political pressures exerted by the market economy and its in-built, almost manic drive to profits and thus obsolescence. This section explicitly links the mass communication industries of the 20th century with the new media forms of the 21st.

In this part we also introduce the idea of the techno-legal time-gap—that is, the existence of a delay in the regulatory process that means it is nearly always playing a catch-up game with the technologies and the ways in which they are deployed. While the phrase is our own, the concept is well recognised and it applies particularly to the digital and online worlds in relation to intellectual property rights, regulation in the global marketplace, questions of privacy and data protection, the integrity of data systems, and questions of cross-border jurisdiction in relation to matters such as defamation and copyright.

Part IV: From Broadcasting to Narrowcast: The Emergence of a Surveillance Economy

Part IV summarises and explains many of the trends we identify in the previous chapters under the general heading of 'surveillance'. Our argument is a simple one: the mass media and the infrastructure of mass communications have fundamentally changed in character because of the impact of convergent digital technologies. Communication infrastructure is rapidly becoming surveillance infrastructure. Electronic record-keeping tags every phone call and business transaction we make. The telephone companies (and by extension government agencies) know where we are, our movements are tracked by GPS-enabled phones, and all our financial transactions are electronically monitored. Our every interaction with the mass media is now logged and measured through set-top boxes and vast databases of personal information. In this final part we attempt to measure the impact of the Internet on political communication (Net-activism, political campaigning, electronic voting, and community media). We also recognise the important emergence of new, and somewhat 'alternative', forms of mediated communication such as 'indymedia' and bloggers.

It is becoming clearer every day that the transition from communication to surveillance is running parallel to the change from broadcasting to narrowcasting. In one sense they are almost the same thing. It is the ability to increase surveillance, particularly in the marketplace, that makes the transition from broadcast to narrowcast media so attractive to advertisers, marketers, media companies, and the telecommunications giants. There is a double helix of effects associated with the shift to a narrowcast media and this is manifest as one of the key contradictions of the information economy. At the same time as our personal privacy disappears and all space becomes, in effect, 'public', the public sphere for non-commercial communication is being privatised. This highlights one of our major themes: the notion of non-commercial, political citizenship is being eroded and replaced by the consumer-citizen. As we demonstrate throughout the text, what we have now is the media-saturated consumer, trapped in a shrinking public space that is prioritised by the narrowcast communications industry. Citizenship has been consumed by the voracious appetite of the market and the citizen is being replaced by an atomised, de-politicised cipher. In the digital age the credit card has replaced the ballot as the passport to 'freedom'.

Young voices, new perspectives

People like Tim Marshall, Bronwyn Adcock, Alex Graham, Billy Kirkley, Manuel Derra, and Linus Andersson are the voices of the future. Tim and Bronwyn are recent alumni of the journalism program at Charles Sturt University, but their careers have taken widely different trajectories since they graduated. Bronwyn is now a reporter on the SBS *Dateline* program and Tim is a successful journalist with the telecommunications trade publication

CommsDay. Alex graduated from the journalism program at the University of Queensland in 2002 and is now a reporter with ABC radio and television in Brisbane. They all have different experiences of the impact of digital convergence on their work and they've agreed to share their stories with us.

Manuel Derra lives in Munich and has been a huge fan of William Gibson's stories since his teens. He started the 'aleph' website in 1999 because he felt that there was not really a Gibson page worth discussing on the net. Manuel's site grew pretty quickly and is still fairly well updated; it has attracted five or six thousand visitors a month for the last few years. Manuel studied Japanese language and culture in Germany and has been to Japan twice for extended periods and also in 2005 for the Aichi world expo. He used to play in bands and is now working for a small music label in Munich; in his spare time he is a DJ. He is interested in the impact of the new technologies on our daily life, and also in all kinds of graphic and other design.

Linus Andersson is a PhD student in Media and Communication studies at the Baltic and East European Graduate School at Södertörn University College, Stockholm. His research interests encompass alternative media, media production and activism, globalisation, and social movements. His thesis will investigate media activism and alternative cultural public spheres in the Baltic States.

Bec Fitzgibbon lives in Hobart and is a professional magazine feature writer and photographer, specialising in underground pop culture, multimedia, art, design, and emerging artistic movements. Bec writes for a variety of mainstream women's fashion and culture magazines, as well as independent street presses. She also writes a column on pop culture for the Hobart *Mercury*. Bec's aim in writing is to bring to light aspects of Australian culture that are seen as 'underground'. She sees her role in exposing subcultures and counter-culture sentiment as a healthy contribution to mainstream media, and editors generally love her 'black sheep' lefty topics.

Billy Kirkley is a bit older than the others, 'Gen X' rather than 'Gen Y'. Billy is an Internet entrepreneur who runs his own web design and hosting company for many Australian and international clients. Like nearly everyone involved in online business, Billy suffered the crash, from 'dot.boom' to 'dot.bust'. Billy was broke, he paid out his now unprofitable contracts with long-term suppliers of server space and had nothing left. He had to start all over again. After pulling himself together, he began building and hosting websites for what he calls his 'more legitimate' clients. Now he runs a small empire with a healthy residual income stream.

Bronwyn Adcock is 31 years old, and has been working in journalism for more than ten years. Bronwyn graduated from Charles Sturt University in Bathurst with a Communications degree in 1995, and the following year began a cadetship at ABC Radio Current Affairs in Sydney. For the next few years she worked as a reporter for *AM*, *PM* and *The World Today*, *Four Corners*, Radio National's *Background Briefing* program, and in the ABC's Canberra Press Gallery bureau.

After taking a break overseas for about a year, Bronwyn returned to Australia and scored a job with SBS TV's *Dateline* program. For the first year she worked mainly as an interview producer, then moved on to video journalism, which is where she is today. In 1997 Brownyn was awarded the Andrew Olle Scholarship through the ABC. In 2004 she won two United Nations Media Peace prizes, one for a remarkable story exposing the detention of asylum-seekers on Nauru. Her story is given at p. 254. Her second UN prize was for a story in Zambia about genetically modified food aid. In 2005 Bronwyn won the prestigious George Munster Award for Independent Journalism for a story about Mamdouh Habib after he was released from Guantanamo Bay. Bronwyn been a finalist in the Walkley Awards three times, and a finalist in the Logies twice.

As the Asia-Pacific managing editor for Decisive Publications, **Tim Marshall** has spent most of the past ten years tracking the transformation of telecom networks into the multimedia delivery platforms we are starting to see today. He reckons it's been an interesting period, watching one of the world's largest infrastructure industries falling over itself to transform for the future. 'Today we are just starting to see some of the pie-in-the-sky promises of the dot.com boom becoming a reality and after years of stumbling,' Tim says. He believes that the next five years should hold some of the most exciting media access and delivery changes seen since the early days of the Internet. Tim works for *CommsDay*, a daily electronic news bulletin that covers the telecommunications industry. Its subscribers include industry leaders across the telecoms, ICT (information and communication technology) , and media industries, mainly at executive and management levels.

Like many of his peers, Tim regards himself as Generation X although he's conscious that his age cohort sits on the edge, and there's a hint of uncertainty in his response: 'Certainly we were eighties kids born in the early to mid-seventies and many of us still have quaint old habits like reading newspapers.' Tim thinks that the generational definition somehow seems to be become more relevant as we get older and we look for ways to define the younger ones and just how different they are from us.

Alex Graham says she always wanted to be a journalist: 'I just always knew it was what I would do,' she told us. Alex is in her mid-twenties and in 2006 had been working for the ABC for just over three years. She graduated with a BJ/BA from the University of Queensland and in 2002 and did a short stint with Channel 7 Mackay before winning a hard-to-get ABC cadetship.

Alex spent her cadet year with the ABC in Brisbane, and then spent eighteen months in the Beef Capital of Australia, Rockhampton in Central Queensland. She transferred back to Brisbane in late 2005 and now works as a 'bi-media journalist'—that is, she files for both radio and television, including working from the ABC's Parliament House office in Brisbane.

Alex says that as a uni student she did 'oodles' of work experience. This included working for most of her summer holidays at 7 Mackay (where she grew up). Alex says she also did work experience with the big commercial networks in Brisbane and some smaller radio stations.

In her discussions with us Alex talks about the technological difficulties of working outside the capital city in a state as large as Queensland. Despite the lack of 'state-of-the-art' equipment, she told us that she loved her time in the regional city of Rockhampton: 'I love doing stories with real people who aren't media savvy but have a story to tell you. I also believe it's important to report on issues outside of capital cities—especially in a state as decentralised as Queensland.'

As a former ABC radio and television journalist, PR operative and author **Neville Petersen** is the voice of age and reason. Neville started working for the ABC on leaving school in 1951. In 1953 he was appointed at the age of 18 to a position in the Sporting Department where he wrote regularly for on-air broadcast. In 1956 he joined the ABC Talks Department where he did some production work on major spoken word programs and also produced *News Review*, a key interview and eyewitness program, modelled on the BBC's *Radio Newsreel*.

After completing a part-time Sydney University degree in Arts, Neville worked for ABC Talks in Canberra, Melbourne, and Hobart before being posted overseas as the Assistant Manager Southeast Asia, where he collected material for Talks, travelling widely throughout the area. He returned to Australia in 1966 to be a reporter on *Four Corners* and in 1967 became the ABC's first representative in Japan. He returned to Sydney ABC TV news briefly before being appointed European News Editor, based in London, in 1971.

On his return to Australia in 1974 the ABC granted Neville a Postgraduate Scholarship tenable at Sydney University where he took an MA degree in Government. He continued this part-time while working as Senior TV News Reporter. The degree was completed in 1978. In that year he resigned from the ABC to join the University of New South Wales as Senior Public Affairs Officer.

In 1980, Sydney University offered Neville the position of Director of Information Services, a new position handling corporate and public relations and managing a range of publications. He left there in 1993 and joined the University of Western Sydney as a lecturer in Cultural and Media Studies. He has worked there in a full-time and part-time capacity ever since. A PhD degree begun at Newcastle University in 1998 has unfortunately been put on hold due his recent poor health. In our conversations with Neville he has provided some wonderful anecdotes about working with broadcast technologies over a fascinating fifty years in the 20th century.

We want to introduce these writers to you now because they each provide a fresh insight into many of the issues you'll encounter in this book. As you follow the text, you'll come across their comments in the form of short 'grabs' from interviews we conducted between October 2005 and March 2006. We asked them to comment on the themes of 'broadcast to narrowcast' and to relate them to their own experiences. Each of them has a unique perspective on how the digital revolution has impacted on their working and personal situation.

2

DIGITAL DILEMMAS: CONTRADICTIONS AND CONFLICT IN THINKING ABOUT COMMUNICATION

OBJECTIVES

After reading this chapter you will have a solid grasp of the important concept of the dialectic, both as a method of reasoning and as an organising principle that helps to explain how both technology and social relations are transformed over time by the process of integration and contradiction. In particular, you should focus on the following ideas:

- how the dialectic works as an organising principle and a process of transformation that drives the development of human society and the transitions from one type of social organisation to another;
- how to 'think' dialectically in order to understand the processes of historical development in relation to new media technologies;
- the ways in which the dialectic informs the theories and practice of political economy, and how the dialectic that binds information and communication can be explored to make sense of the digital revolution.

KEYWORDS
contradiction
dialectic
idealism
ideology
materialism
meme
vector

What is the dialectic?

> [C]ommunication and information are two sides of the same process, dialectically linked in mutual constitution. (Mosco 1996, p. 67)

Don't be put off by our introduction of a word you might not have seen before, or possibly don't understand. It's really quite simple. The word 'dialectic' describes a philosophical concept that means thinking systematically using a process of logic. From both Latin and Greek roots, *dialectic* describes the methods of discussion and debate and, in a similar way, 'the method of determining the interrelation of ideas in the light of a single principle' (Williams 1989, p. 106). The German philosopher Georg Hegel (1770–1831) first used the term in its modern sense to describe the process of resolving a contradiction between competing ideas—for example, explaining the relationship between God and man, which is what Hegel was trying to do. In *Communication and New Media* we are using the dialectic to investigate the movement of history in terms of media technologies—such as the transition from analogue to digital media production. As we explain in this chapter, the dialectic is the organising principle on which the forward momentum of society is based. It is the pervasive but often unseen logic of 'two steps forward, one step back' that marks the passage of time and the transition from one form of social organisation to another.

DIALECTIC

The idea that history is shaped by opposing forces. The predominant force, idea, movement, or paradigm (the thesis) is challenged by an opposing force, idea, movement, or paradigm (the antithesis), which results in a third new force, idea, movement, or paradigm (the synthesis). The synthesis, in turn, becomes the new predominant force, idea, movement, or paradigm (the new thesis), and the process begins all over again. The dialectic is the process of creation, and resolution of contradictions.

The Hegelian dialectic had three elements: the proposition (thesis); an opposite or competing proposition (antithesis); and the logical resolution of the tension between them (synthesis). Hegel used a simple example to explain his theory of the dialectic: an acorn contains the potential to become a strong oak tree and produce more acorns, but it order to do so, the acorn must disappear or *negate* itself. By a series of small incremental changes in quantity induced by the interaction of the living acorn with the soil in which it falls, the acorn becomes something qualitatively different: an oak tree. Water, ice, and steam provide another clear example: when the temperature of water is gradually reduced it remains in a liquid state until zero degrees Centigrade when it is transformed into a solid:ice. This new substance has many properties that water doesn't have. When water changes from a liquid to a solid it behaves differently. At the other extreme, heat water to boiling point and it becomes steam, able to resist gravity in a way that liquid water cannot (cited in Callinicos 1987, p. 59). Water contains the potential to be ice or steam, but in order to become either it must contradict (negate) its fluid state.

While Hegel resolved his contradictions through a belief in the unity of an Absolute Spirit (God), Karl Marx (1818–1883) and Friedrick Engels (1820–1895) recognised that the method of dialectical reasoning also had an application to the study of human history:

> All fixed, fast-frozen relations, with their train of ancient and venerable prejudices and opinions are swept away, all new-formed ones become antiquated before they can ossify. All that is solid melts into air, all that is holy is profaned, and man is at last compelled to face with sober senses, his real conditions of life, and his relations with his kind. (Marx & Engels 1973, p. 46)

Translated into more mundane language than that used in the *Communist Manifesto*, this means that the configuration of any social system is historically determined by the relationship between human beings and nature. Throughout human history this relationship has been mediated by technology (see chapter 4 below). In all societies this relationship is expressed through the organisation of production, which 'contains within it the contradictions that give it the potential for change' (Callinicos 1987, p. 75). Thus we can think of the dialectic as a process that proceeds along a series of 'fault lines' (Hirst & Patching 2005, pp. 2–5). These fault lines occur between things and events in nature, between the natural world and human society, and within and between the social formations created by humans—what we collectively call civilisation. The methods of political economy (discussed in chapter 3) work from the principle of the dialectic and dialectical thinking, which recognises that the real world is made up of both 'parts and a whole', organised in a 'concrete totality' that contains both 'integration and contradiction' (Mosco 1996, p. 33).

Alex Callinicos describes the operation of the dialectic in human society as a process of historical change over time, 'a spiral movement' in which each advance contains within itself an element of regression (Callinicos 1995, p. 152). The dialectic is a way of understanding the relationship between things through the ways they are connected and the ways that they also simultaneously contradict each other.

The dialectic of nature

> [T]he oak developed out of the acorn. It was, once, that acorn. Acorn and oak mark the beginning and end of the same process. (Callinicos 1987, p. 60)

As this example shows, the concept of the dialectic expresses itself as a process of contradiction and resolution that is originally found in nature. Charles Darwin's theory of natural selection, the development of complex organisms from simple cell structures, and the transformation of energy—from a lump of coal to radiant heat, for example—are all manifestations of the dialectic in nature, 'this incessant process of transformation from one form into another' (Engels 1976, p. 43).

At the basic molecular level of living organisms, the dialectic is expressed through the double helix of DNA, which is held together in a state of tension and contradiction. The relationship of individual genes and strands to each other is a dialectical process of interaction, mutation, and conflict. The very 'laws of nature' are themselves interactive in this way. At a social level, the condition of human existence is one of a dialectical relationship with nature. Nature can sustain us; nature can also harm us. In our efforts to maximise the benefits we extract from nature, we are also capable of doing extreme damage to the natural world. There is evidence of this all around us today. From oil spills on fragile sections of the planet's coastlines and a worldwide epidemic of asbestos-related deaths to the potential for a 'bird-flu' pandemic and a permanent disaster zone around the ruins of the Chernobyl nuclear reactor. Our interest is to examine the dialectic in its social manifestation. This is a necessary precursor to our discussion of mass communication and the dialectic that has created the historical shift from broadcasting to narrowcasting.

Living and working in a 'material' world

> Everything which sets men in motion must go through their minds; but what form it takes in their minds depends very much on the circumstances. (Engels 1976, p. 48)

Hegel conceptualised the dialectic at the level of ideas; it was Karl Marx and Friedrick Engels who transformed it into a theory of human development, change, and history. Marx and Engels turned Hegel upside down; Hegel's idealist philosophy became a philosophy for the real world.

Before proceeding it is important to clear up some confusion that surrounds the concept of materialism. Everyone has heard of someone described in a negative way as materialistic—that is, the person seems to be concerned with the pursuit of material wealth primarily for the sake of acquiring more of something than another person acquires. Materialistic people are often thought of as greedy and selfish. The pop star Madonna had a global hit with her song 'Material Girl' ('We're living in a material world and I am a material girl'). Indeed some people probably are greedy, selfish, and 'materialistic'. But our concern here is with another definition of materialism that has to do with our senses of sight, touch, hearing, smell, and taste.

IDEALISM

The opposite of materialism. Idealism is the worldview in which all manifestations of reality actually stem from the thought process of human beings, rather than from their material circumstances. For example: 'People are greedy, that's just human nature' is idealist thinking.

What we can see, touch, hear, smell, and taste are real things; they are material in that they are composed of matter. Material things have a concrete existence in the world. Even odours, which we sense with our nose but often can't see, are vapours and gases made up of molecules. They have substance; they can be weighed, measured, and contained. In this sense materialism is, like the dialectic, a concept of philosophy and theory, which seeks explanations of phenomena by reference to the solid, physical, and mechanical aspects of nature and life. Such explanations of the world have been around as long as philosophy itself, but became important in Western traditions from the 17th century as an alternative to the idealistic and metaphysical idea that human existence was created at the whim of a supreme being (Williams 1989, pp. 198–9). In the hands of Marx and Engels materialism also gained an historical character that argued for the determining role of human agency in the development of social formations. Historical materialism refers to the study of human societies that positions our interaction with nature—everything from stone tools to complex manufacturing—as the force that drives invention and adaptation. This is the sense in which the concept of the dialectic relates to another central concern of this book, technology:

> Technology reveals the active relation of man to nature, the direct process of the production of his life, and thereby it also lays bare the process of the production of the social relations of his life, and of the mental conceptions that flow from those relations. (Marx 1990, Vol. 1, p. 493 ff)

For Marx, the beginning of human history and our understanding of it is the collective and social organisation of production, which is reflected in the development of technology and in its application to the production process (Callinicos 1987, p. 85). First and foremost, from the viewpoint of historical materialism, the production process is a social endeavour and can only be properly understood when we ask the question: 'Who controls the production process?' It is the distribution of power within the production process that ultimately determines questions of ownership, access, and wealth (p. 87). This is an important foundation for the rest of this book because when we begin to analyse the political economy of the media, the question of ownership and control of the means of communication becomes a central issue.

In the modern capitalist economy the separation of ownership and control from those who are the direct producers and consumers, not just of the media but of all forms of production, is the key to all other social relations. What Marx realised was that exploitation and inequality in the distribution of resources and wealth were not inevitable and certainly not immutable. He

MATERIALISM

The philosophical mode of thought that suggests that events, situations, and relationships in the real, physical world determine, to the largest degree, human consciousness and thinking. Historical materialism, the method of Marx and Engels, posits the theory that human beings' interaction with nature creates the material conditions for the development of social structures and argues that the social force that drives historical change is the struggle between classes for control of the material world, in particular control over the means of production.

knew, through his observations and study of history, that the dialectic in human society takes the form of a constant struggle between the exploiters and the exploited and that under certain conditions such struggle could lead to the violent overthrow of one system and the creation of a new one in its place. He expressed this idea many times, perhaps nowhere more clearly than in these lines from the *Communist Manifesto*:

> The history of all hitherto existing society is the history of class struggles ... [I]n a word, oppressor and oppressed, stood in constant opposition to one another, carried on an uninterrupted, now hidden, now open fight, a fight that each time ended, either in revolutionary re-constitution of society at large, or in the common ruin of the contending classes. (Marx & Engels 1973, pp. 40–1)

You're probably thinking that this kind of incendiary talk is a long way from the topic of this book. But it's not that far removed at all. We now live in a world where the capitalist economy has extended its reach to every corner and crevice of the globe. It touches and shapes the lives of every being on the planet in one way or another through the 'rapid improvement of all instruments of production' and the 'immensely facilitated means of communication' (Marx & Engels 1973, p. 47). Further, we cannot ignore all the talk of 'revolution' that accompanies discussion of technology today. There are numerous instances of politicians, pundits, academics, and journalists embracing the term 'revolution' when it refers to digital convergence, information, knowledge, or other concepts. Each of these implies some form of social disruption and period of uncertainty, change, and instability in the economy, politics, and cultural life. Thus our interest in talking about social revolution is justified, particularly a revolution that has profound impacts on the mass media, because this is where our concern lies. It is through the means of communication at its disposal that the current ruling class—what Marx called the bourgeoisie—is able to maintain its political, economic, social, and cultural dominance. That is, to hold back social revolution. This control is maintained through the process of controlling the production process itself, but also through controlling the broader ideological ways of thinking that dominate society. Control of the means of communication (as a subset of the means of production) is also vital to the hegemony (see chapter 3) exercised by the ruling class. We can briefly characterise the ideological and political control exercised by the bourgeoisie as an attempt to control the dialectic of communication—the clash that Vincent Mosco recognised between information and communication.

Memes: The dialectic of information and communication

> [A] meme is a self-propagating unit of cultural evolution, analogous to the gene (the unit of genetics). Memes can represent parts of ideas, languages, tunes, designs, skills, oral and aesthetic values and anything else that is commonly learned and passed on to others as a unit. The study of evolutionary models of information transfer is called mimetics. (Wikipedia)

A *meme* is a thought or idea that spreads throughout society in an almost unconscious way. A meme is a small, transmittable lump of ideology—the ideas in our head that help us make sense of the world—that carries a particular set of social attitudes and directions about how we might think about an object, event, or social custom. A meme might be a catchy tune that becomes almost universal, or a trend in fashion that catches on to become widespread, almost before it's even recognised as a trend. The biologist and geneticist Richard Dawkins is credited with the first modern use of the word 'meme' in his book *The Selfish Gene* (written in 1976). 'Just as genes propagate themselves in the gene pool by leaping from body to body via sperms or eggs, so memes propagate themselves in the meme pool by leaping from brain to brain via a process which, in the broad sense, can be called imitation' (Dawkins 1989, p. 192).

MEME

A small but powerful chunk of ideological 'DNA' that carries ideas, meanings, trends, and fashions through both time and space via the process of mimetic (imitative) transfer. Memes can be generated by hegemonic or subversive social forces and are usually transported via the various communication vectors of the mass media, narrowcasting, and popular culture.

However, Dawkins' caution about biological determinism must be restated here; we cannot simply transfer an idea from biology to the study of human society. Our social systems are much more complex than termite colonies and our ability to remember and imitate the behaviour of others goes beyond simple genetic replication. Having said that, we find that the concept of the meme, when used cautiously, does help to explain how certain aspects of ideology appear to be naturalised as common sense and transmitted or mutated over space and time. We can see memes in the realm of fashion, such as hip hop and surf wear, that are transmitted globally via the vast networks of interconnected entertainment and leisure industries. Memes are also apparent in the transient popularity of musical styles and the use of slang by subculture groups that take on a worldwide acceptance one week, only to be replaced by new 'vogue' words in the next. As we shall see in the next chapter, memes also have a socio-economic function: they move cultural patterns through time and space and also make them vulnerable to commodification and appropriation.

Dawkins ascribed to memes patterns of replication similar to those found in genes. Thus we can talk of a meme pool as being analogous to the gene pool found in nature. Memes are the medium of cultural transmission, often at a much faster rate than that of genetic mutation and evolution in nature (Dawkins 1989, p. 189). But we can go a little further than this and argue that the mass media now play a key role in the process of mimetic reproduction and mutation. Thus a riff in a pop song may become a meme much quicker today because of the high-rotation airplay it receives on radio and television. Last year's hit tunes are appropriated as the soundtrack for this year's hip new commercials.

Memes have also been likened to viruses: a virus that infects a computer reproduces by a process of virtual cloning before jumping out onto the Internet to infect other machines. The Internet is important in the discussion of meme transmission for another reason. The speed and the anarchic architecture of the Internet can lead to the rapid circulation of a new meme and can, at times, create a paperless trail that legitimises information that is functionally unreliable and 'unchecked by reality' (Wikipedia). This is another sense in which we can relate the meme to the concept of ideology—the sense that ideology represents a 'false' consciousness tied to the 'social relations of domination' (Wayne 2003, p. 173). In this sense ideology wrongly naturalises 'social and historical relations' (p. 174) that are the product of the unequal power relationships of class society by making them seem normal and ahistorical. The popular media participate in the circulation of such ideological memes by mobilising our fears and desires—for example, through political propaganda and advertising—and causing us to respond at an emotional level in a way that neutralises any feelings of disquiet or anger and is 'conducive to the reproduction of exploitative social relations' (p. 174). We can see how the media's popularisation of the idea of the information society and the digital revolution as positive developments of benefit to the whole of society fits this model of an ideological meme. Mimetic transmission is the vector for the propagation of digital myths (Mosco 2004).

IDEOLOGY

A worldview based on principles or intuitions that may or may not be logical or internally consistent.

This sentiment is made explicit in Rushkoff's *Cyberia*, which is cheekily subtitled *Life in the trenches of hyperspace*. He describes a small underground magazine for hackers, *Mondo 2000*, which existed briefly in the early 1990s, as a 'meme' (a self-replicating idea); *Mondo 2000* was the 'media virus' (Rushkoff 1994, p. 289) that its adherents hoped would help cyberians spread their message of technological liberation. The magazine was loosely edited from a house in Berkeley, where the *Mondo 2000* collective accepted for publication 'whichever memes make the most sense at the time' (p. 291). When not publishing the magazine, the group spent its time 'discussing and embodying fringe concepts' (p. 292), and Rushkoff gushingly describes the 'Mondoids' as 'human memes' who 'depend on media recognition for their survival' (p. 293). The mythic meme that *Mondo 2000* seemed to be pushing most intently was a form of digital anarchism, at least according to one of its founders and leading lights, the unlikely monikered 'R. U. Sirius': 'The only thing we're pushing is freedom in this new territory. The only way to have freedom is not to have an agenda. Protest is not a creative act, really' (quoted in Rushkoff 1994, p. 294).

According to the Wikipedia entry on *Mondo 2000*, 'R. U. Sirius' was the pseudonym of Ken Goffman. Though no longer in print (it ceased publication in 1998), there are several websites that archive articles and other material from the magazine that can be accessed from Google. The magazine's former art director Heide Foley maintains her own website and blog at <www.heide.to>.

The story of the *Mondo* 'meme factory' is told at the end of *Cyberia* and it encapsulates the dialectic that generated some of early myths of the information revolution; it captures the energy that motivated the early hackers and amateur Internet enthusiasts and it also sounds a note of caution about the 'event horizon' that in 1992 appeared to be looming over mainstream and still non-digital society. Rushkoff signs off with the observation that 'Cyberia is frightening to everyone': 'Not just the technophobes, rich businessmen, midwestern farmers and suburban housewives, but most of all, to the boys and girls hoping to ride the crest of the informational wave. Surf's up' (Rushkoff 1994, p. 300).

The information revolution: Digital dialectic

> As [mainstream scientists] rely more and more on the computer, their suspicions are further confirmed: this is not a world reducible to neat equations and pat answers, but an infinitely complex series of interdependencies, where the tiniest change in a remote place can have systemwide repercussions. (Rushkoff 1994, p. 15)

The surf *is* up, but the dialectic of the digital revolution, which began with the counter-cultural anarchists of Cyberia, exerts its own influence once it is unleashed on the world. The 'Information Revolution' is the ideological and mimetic manifestation of a shift in the relations of production that has been under way within the capitalist mode of production for most of the past sixty years. There has been a seismic shift within the mode of development (see p. 45) of capitalism as we enter the 21st century. There is a new technological dialectic at play that, in the process of becoming dominant, is replacing the previously hegemonic industrial-technical relations and forces of production. It has also all but wiped out the emergent meme of techno-liberation that was planted by the Mondoids.

The emergent and subversive (to the old ways at least) technology meme entered the mode of production and the popular mind through the vector of important discoveries in science: computing in mathematics, the binary code, and the application of the resulting new technologies for miniaturising and mass-producing silicon microchips. By the 1970s, computing technologies were deeply embedded in industrial and commercial applications. Investment in the new technologies went, first of all, back into the machinery of manufacturing and other production—plant and equipment. As we've noted in chapter 5 with the development of the Internet, much of this research and development work was funded by governments for military purposes and later commercialised. This has led, in the past ten to fifteen years, to the gradual displacement of the anarcho-technical meme espoused by 'R. U. Sirius' and the cyberians. The emerging meme is much more controlled and commercial; it is the meme of the 'knowledge society' and it is heavily supported by both governments and companies who invest in the digital communication technologies.

This new meme began to circulate during the second wave of digital development, beginning in the late 1970s, with the widespread application of these new technologies to consumer goods. This process is ongoing, and has been boosted by the rapid improvement and convergence in digital technologies. Historically, since the 1950s we can trace it something like this: the home radio (the first wireless instrument of civil communication) followed by hi-fi records; television; stereo; videotape; FM radio; personal computers; satellite TV; laser-read CDs and DVDs; digital peripherals; home entertainment centres; wireless applications; broadband; and the 'wired' lifestyle. At each historical stage we can also trace the mimetic messages along the lines of 'radio will replace newspapers', 'television will replace radio', and 'video killed the radio stars'. Today's version is more sophisticated; it suggests that these various media will coexist with the Internet and wireless communication for the foreseeable future.

We are now roughly at the forty-year mark in terms of the silicon chip thesis (the current technology meme) within the mode of development that is now driving the capitalist mode of production. The speed of mutation in this meme has been phenomenal. We can see this if we compare it to the time-frame of the Industrial Revolution, which took a hundred years to 'mature', a century marked by the classic cycle of booms and slumps identified by political economists as the inevitable dialectical nature of capitalism. On a longer time-scale, social scientists have retrofitted a technology meme to various points in history: the 'Bronze Age', the 'Iron Age', the age of steam, the epoch of the railway, and, more recently, 'Fordism' and 'post-Fordism' relating to the predicted but not yet realised end of industrial manufacturing. We always say 'But someone has to make the Playstations'. In our view, manufacturing is still a crucial and central element of the global capitalist system; we are not yet fully immersed in the world of so-called 'immaterial' commodities. In 50 years' time things may be very different.

The silicon chip and digital convergence in technologies of communication, broadcasting, computing, and mass media now play a key role in the mimetic reproduction of the capitalist mode of production on a number of levels. But in order to be effective—like viral marketing campaigns—there must be a cost-effective way for the memes to be transmitted. The easiest way is through transmission vectors, which work much like routes of infection: a susceptible individual or individuals are infected and then the virus can travel freely between hosts. This is easy because in most cases the vectors are themselves the means of communication and they are, for the most part, owned, operated, and controlled by individuals and corporations with a strong vested interest in circulating mimetic codes favourable to their interests.

VECTOR

In medical science a vector is the pathway or pathways open to pathogens to infect a population. For example, infected chickens may be a vector for avian bird flu to infect humans. In communication studies a vector is a pathway or pathways open for communication, in particular the transmission of ideology via mimetic transfer and mutation.

Vectors: A circuit for the viral transmission of mimetic code

> We live every day in a familiar terrain: the place where we sleep, the place where we work, the place where we hang out when we're not working or sleeping. From these places we acquire a geography of experience. We live every day also in another terrain, equally familiar: the terrain created by the television, the telephone, the telecommunications networks crisscrossing the globe. These 'vectors' produce in us a new kind of experience, the experience of telesthesia—perception at a distance. (Wark 1994, p. vii)

Australian cultural studies scholar McKenzie Wark describes 'vectors' as the globally pervasive routes of communication that have come to dominate and interpose themselves between us and the real world of materiality. Our experience of important events is felt only from a distance; we cannot possibly all be in one place at the same time to 'see' things for ourselves. We rely on the communications media to keep us in touch with relatives, friends, and trends. More importantly, we rely on the news media to help us make sense of bigger and more fundamental events and issues.

In the early work on memes and mimetics it was assumed that the transmission of the social coding they contained was simply from human brain to human brain. Ultimately this is because the ability of a meme to attract and hold our interest and attention—its appeal to new hosts—is a survival technique that works to assist the replication of the meme. This may well have been how the earliest memes were transmitted through oral traditions, such as throughout Indigenous Australia and in other parts of the world; literally, by word of mouth, through stories and songs, but also in iconographic representations—drawings of mythical creatures and scenes from the Dreaming. With the advent of technologies that mediate our interaction with the natural world, however, the transmission vectors became less personalised and more collective in their targeting. A central thesis of *Communication and New Media* is that we are now seeing a further change as the mimetic targeting employed by media companies and advertisers becomes more focused on individual consumers.

The most important of the mimetic vectors in the past hundred years have been the parliamentary/presidential style of civil society and the development of a highly commercial and now globally dominant, media-dependent popular culture. With the onset of digital convergence we are once again noticing a move back towards individual targeting and the narrowing of vectors. For instance, a mobile phone is now an individually targeted vector for the transmission of all sorts of information, including memes based on popular culture. We will look more closely at ideology and politics in the digital world in chapter 15. A key theme when talking about vectors is that they are not necessarily themselves neutral or value-free. A vector itself may be hegemonic or subversive. For example, television is almost always, and by its very social nature, a hegemonic vector. The garage-rock music scene that spawned bands like the Ramones, the Clash, and the Sex Pistols in the 1970s was a subversive vector in the beginning and created punk music. It's important to add, though, that the mimetic qualities of punk music were eventually mutated by exposure to other memes and their rerouting through the dominant vectors of popular culture controlled by record companies.

Wark argues that our view of the world is conditioned by the distancing effect of the mass media, and that information only reaches us via the well-established vectors built around information technologies. In a sense we are disconnected by this experience, or as Wark succinctly sums it up: 'We no longer have roots, we have aerials' (1994, p. x).

Thus there is a tension between our physical experiences—going to work, coming home, hanging out—and what they tell us about the world around us, and the mediated view presented via the externally (to our lives) controlled vectors of mass communication.

One important aspect of this emerging and powerful dialectic is that it has fundamentally altered the vectors by which the mutating and mutable social memes are transmitted to new hosts and reinforced or modified in existing hosts. Just a quick reminder, in case you've forgotten, that we are the hosts for these memes.

In the case of digital media, the technologies themselves are often the vectors, though we also see them generated by clever marketing campaigns and government policies; for example, this statement from a 2004 discussion paper on Australia's potentially fantastic digital future: 'Australia's vision for the information economy is where government, business and society are all connected, can participate with confidence, are open to innovation and can collaborate to maximise the economic and social benefits' (DCITA 2004, p. 23).

The Microsoft Corporation has also expertly crafted its message of digital prosperity for all through the generation of an ideological position it calls 'digital inclusion', which it describes in glowing terms as 'a core part of our business strategy and a cornerstone of our ongoing efforts to empower people around the world through information and communication technology' (Microsoft, n.d.).

As the contemporary dominant mode of development within capitalism, digital convergence has created more powerful vectors by adding speed, variety, and interactivity. Traditional industrial-media vectors for the mass distribution of memes were the newspaper, radio, and television. Each of these has been enhanced in various ways by their attachment to, and interaction with, digital media forms.

Convergence as a dialectic

> Stated in the most dramatic terms, the accusation can be made that the uncontrolled growth of technology destroys the vital sources of our humanity. It creates a culture without moral foundation. It undermines certain mental processes and social relations that make human life worth living. Technology, in sum, is both friend and enemy. (Postman 1993, p. xii)

Neil Postman was a technological pessimist who described the effects of technology on our lives as both a 'burden and a blessing; not either-or, but this-and-that' (p. 5). In fact, Postman argued, technology, if it is not properly understood and consciously managed, can alter the meaning of words we take for granted: 'freedom', 'truth', 'intelligence', 'fact', 'wisdom', 'memory', and 'history' (p. 8).

This process of technologies converging and changing how we think and how we view the world happens because tools, while they may appear as innate and useful objects, are actually the result of a social process of invention and application. Therefore, 'embedded in every tool is an ideological bias, a predisposition to construct the world ... to amplify one sense or skill or attitude more loudly than another' (p. 13). We are representing this technical and social process as the 'dialectic of convergence'. This has perhaps never been more important than it is today because technology is now pervasive in a way that it has not been since the early days of the Industrial Revolution. At the same time, we seem to take for granted the idea that digital technologies bring with them continuous improvements to make our work easier and our leisure time more enjoyable, and they may even connect us with virtual friends who can enrich our lives. This is the ideological bias that Postman is warning us about. We should note the fact that Neil Postman wrote this at a time when digital convergence was a new and largely experimental field and before digital technologies became so common.

There has always been convergence in technologies, whether in manufacturing, transport, or communication. Technicians and scientists are always looking for ways to improve 'things', and entrepreneurs are always looking for ways to make a buck. Put science and commerce together for any length of time—especially if commerce is the stronger partner—and convergence for profit is often the result. In fact it was the convergence of preceding technologies that eventually led to the development of the computer, a process that began in the 19th century with the eclectic British inventor Charles Babbage (see chapter 5 for our discussion of Babbage and his 'difference engine').

A number of other inventions had to come into existence and manufacture before the computer became a feasible proposition. It would need advances in electrical circuitry, the telegraph, the telephone, and the development of the 'and/or' logic of Boolean algebra. The next big advance did not occur until the 1930s when the English mathematician Alan Turing showed that it was theoretically possible to build a problem-solving machine that had, in a sense, 'artificial intelligence'. Within a decade of this discovery, John von Neumann had invented the first machine that became known as a computer (Postman 1993, p. 110).

Even today, however, we are some way off having machines with true artificial intelligence—that is, machines that can exchange thoughts with a human in the form of a conversation. Artificial intelligence, or AI, is a staple in science fiction, and in a small tribute to Alan Turing, William Gibson has created a fictional police agency, the 'Turing Registry', to prevent AIs from becoming too independent. In *Neuromancer* (Gibson 1993 [1984]) three Turing agents attempt to stop Case from releasing the AI Wintermute from its core computers.

The hegemonic technology meme is now delivered through new technologically enhanced transmission vectors. It has mutated into a dominant force within the current mode of production. The cultural meme of the 'information revolution', in its dialectical interaction with the mode of production, has created for itself new vectors to aid its transmission and take-up by the general population. Many of these new vectors take the form of narrowcasting—targeting individual consumers with a variety of commercial messages, often disguised in cheap forms of popular culture, such as promotions for *Big Brother* or other television and music products. It is our intention to discuss these developments in some detail in later sections of the book, but first we have to describe and explain the methods of analysis we are using. In this opening chapter we have referred freely to concepts such as mode of production, ideology, technology, and political economy. In the next two chapters we will explain these terms and ideas in greater detail and this will lay the theoretical foundation for the rest of the book.

WHAT TIM RECKONS

In a broad sense, telecom convergence is being driven by the technology that's available today. Some of the things we're seeing now have been in development for decades, and Internet-based systems offer strong enhancements to many legacy services (radio, film, video). But there is little doubt that the actual pace of convergence is being driven by economic imperatives. Infrastructure owners are being forced to buy systems that not only prepare them for the converged future, but also allow them to launch an array of new services on the fly to make up for slowing revenues in their traditional areas of business.

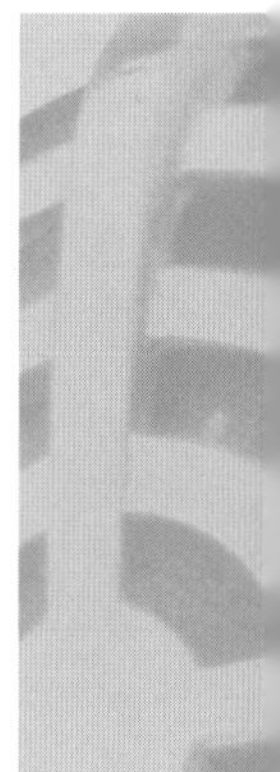

KEY POINTS

The key points from this chapter are:

- The principle of the dialectic means that there are forces (theses) and counter-forces (antitheses) operating not only in the natural world but also in human society, which interact to produce a new force (synthesis), which in turn becomes the next thesis.
- The notion of 'the material' and the way in which the question is asked of who owns the technologies of production is fundamental to any understanding of economics, and, in particular, of media and communication in modern capitalist societies.
- The concepts of *memes* and *vectors* can be applied to assist our understanding of media and communications. In the age of narrowcasting, audience members are individually targeted for media content and are constituted as consumers rather than citizens.

CLASS DISCUSSION

1 Can you think of examples that illustrate the process of thesis–antithesis–synthesis in the dialectic of everyday events in the world today?

2 What are the key vectors for the transmission of digital memes today? For example, are they present in newspapers and magazines, in the electronic media, and in computer games?

3 How does our use of the term 'materialism' differ from what we might consider the 'commonsense' definition that informs Madonna's 'Material Girl'?

3

THE POLITICAL ECONOMY OF COMMUNICATION AND MEDIA

OBJECTIVES

After reading this chapter you will have an understanding of the importance of *political economy* in shaping the various theories of the mass media and technology that are in circulation today. This chapter also introduces some of the key historical and contemporary theorists in communication and media studies who have influenced our own study of the complex technological, economic, political, social, and cultural changes that have created a narrowcast world.

The chapter will help you to come to terms with the following material:

- the key concepts in the field of communication and mass media studies and their application to the theory of broadcast to narrowcast;
- an insight into some of the key theorists of mass media and mass communication;
- knowledge of the fundamental aspects of a political economy approach to mass communication and media technologies;
- the concepts of 'base' and 'superstructure' and 'communication capital'.

KEYWORDS
capital
commodity
globalisation
hegemony
labour
mode of development
mode of production
political economy
relations of production

The political economy of communication

> Any media business has two products to sell: its content (to readers and viewers); and its audience (to advertisers). (King content 2006)

A political economy approach to the business of media helps to explain the dual nature of media as both content (information and entertainment) and commodity (product). In this chapter we will explore the production of these commodities: the content (news, information, and entertainment) and audience (the object of much media studies focus). One of our key arguments in this book is that the media audience today is fragmented; it is simply not the homogeneous mass audience of the television age. Marketing and audience research techniques have become very sophisticated and the focus is much more on the individual consumer than it was even a decade ago (in the mid-1990s). For the major players who dominate the global media industries today, the ability to repackage content and to cross-promote it over several delivery platforms is underpinned by digitised commercial surveillance. One key aspect of this process is the management of the 'brand' through cross-promotion and targeting specific consumers in order to win and retain sales (Murray 2005).

This chapter is crucial to the historical discussion of communication technologies developed in later chapters; these survey the communication and media landscape as it existed at the end of the 20th century and the changes that will see them into the 21st. Our thesis is that the old divisions between print and broadcast media are breaking down as a result of digital convergence, with the corollary that there is also commercial convergence between the 'old' and the 'new' media forms. As a consequence, the largest and most powerful media companies, such as those owned by global citizen Rupert Murdoch, are moving away from their single-business model towards vertically and horizontally integrated giants that straddle everything from newspapers to satellite television, the entertainment industry, the Internet, and telecommunications (Mathieson 2005).

In the late 1980s, American communications scholar Ben Bagdikian wrote a groundbreaking analysis of media monopolies that has been reissued many times since. He paints a bleak picture of the ability of the global communications cartels—loose associations of giant corporations that control markets through their sheer size and ability to cooperate to commercial advantage—to penetrate the social landscape: 'Aided by the digital revolution ... the communications cartel has exercised stunning influence over national legislation and government agencies, an influence whose scope and power would have been considered scandalous or illegal twenty years ago' (Bagdikian 1997).

At the time, he was writing mainly about America and American companies, but today many members of the communications cartel are based in Europe, Asia, and even Australia. The interlacing of national companies with the global economy and elements of the nation-state has advanced even further in the last decade.

This is the process of commercial convergence (Mosco 2004) and the reason why Ben Bagdikian wrote about the increasing monopolisation of the communication media. We believe that this process of integration of communication and media capital can best be understood using the tools of political economy. Much of the recent debate on media policy in Australia, while ostensibly about technology and the technologies of convergence, is really about control: who controls our media? A political economy approach to such a debate is enlightening.

Why political economy?

> To approach communication without political economy is similar to playing the piano wearing mittens. (McChesney 2000a, p. 115)

Robert McChesney, an influential American communications scholar, is an important figure in the study of the political economy of communication and media. He is explicit about the link between the study of communication as an academic discipline and the public-political role of the mass media in working for or against democratic principles. He consistently argues that communication scholars have a 'crucial role to play' in advancing the agenda of democratic politics (McChesney 2000a, p. 110). This is one reason why a political economy approach has been marginalised in the study of mass communication in the last twenty years. The dominant discipline today in media studies is the populist relativism of postmodernism and cultural studies, with its emphasis on the *text* and the audience (see, for example, John Hartley's *Popular Reality*). According to McChesney, cultural studies appears to be uninterested in the 'structural factors' that influence and determine the types of content produced and consumed via the media marketplace. In contrast, these are the very issues that political economy seeks to address, understand, and influence. Ultimately, cultural studies adopts a conservative view; much like mainstream economics and studies of communication policy, it ignores the broader links between economics and politics and the specific connections between corporations and government. These mainstream and ideologically conservative disciplines favour the existing relations of production based on the false premise that the 'market and the broader social situation' represents 'the best of all possible worlds' (McChesney 2000a, p. 110). Thus inequitable relationships of class and power, which determine who controls media production, are assumed to be at most a benevolent fact of life, or they disappear from analysis altogether.

A political economy of mass media challenges these assumptions by pointing out that market forces are the product of a particular history and set of circumstances that feed a dialectic of conflict and uncertainty. To do this it looks at the issues of concern to economists—price; demand; supply; and the structure of local, national, and global markets—but it adds to the mix the study of cultural, ideological, political, and social forces. According to leading media studies scholar Vincent Mosco (1999, p. 104), a political economy approach is motivated by 'standards of social justice' and a keen moral philosophy. Thus it is obliged to present a broader view that takes into account a range of influencing factors and the dialectical ways in which they interact. A political economy of media questions several aspects of the whole phenomenon: the structure of the communications industry; issues of ownership and control; the ideological messages that are overtly and covertly positioned within the content; the history and application of technology; delivery systems and platforms; and the cultural contexts that surround both production and consumption.

POLITICAL ECONOMY

A theory of social economics which argues that knowledge and analysis of ownership and control of economic entities is a useful, indeed, essential means of understanding. Political economy can be based on a class analysis or some other taxonomy, such as institutional form.

Chapters 8 and 12 on regulation, ethics, and governance use the political economy approach to describe and analyse these mechanisms of control in terms of ownership, content, and impact on audience. Political economy is also crucial to part IV of the book, which outlines our theoretical approach to the study of the new surveillance media. Recent research, such as the writing of the influential media sociologist Manuel Castells, throws up some interesting questions about the future of mass communication and about the future itself. While we focus on the rise of the surveillance economy in the final pages of the book, it is time now to unpack the concept of economic convergence that goes hand in hand with convergence in the realm of digital technologies.

Selling eyeballs: The production and consumption of an audience

> The newsroom managers did not apologize for doing what they believed was absolutely necessary. 'Our job is to sell eyeballs,' one executive producer told me. 'And without them, we're out of business.' (Ehrlich 1997, p. 308)

Matthew Ehrlich interprets this executive's 'eyeball' comment to mean 'deliver audiences to advertisers' (1997, p. 308)—in a nutshell, to deliver a profit on their news, information, and entertainment broadcasts. The media production process has an unusual relationship with its market. It is not a simple matter of putting 'ideas' into the public 'market' so that price can be determined by 'supply and demand'. All media outputs are clearly commodities in a capitalist society. Newspapers are sold, magazines have a cover price, and the electronic media are increasingly looking to narrowcast marketing to realise a profit, but the real commodity that the media 'sells' is its audience, and the real customer is the advertiser. This is one reason why advertising executives took a keen interest in the March 2006 reforms to the media ownership and the future digital 'roadmap' outlined by Communications Minister Helen Coonan (Sinclair 2006). We take up this issue in detail in chapter 12.

Following the political economy approach, we can move on to examine the conflicted relationship between the media and audiences by unpacking the duality and contradictions of the consumer-citizen. The news media provide us with a window on the world and an intellectual framework for understanding what's going on around us. But we have to question the completeness of this picture and the validity of many of the opinions we encounter. There are many mechanisms in place that the media use to edit and frame news, including 'agenda-setting' and 'gate-keeping' (Berkowitz 1997), which work to reduce the scope of what items make it into a newspaper or broadcast bulletin and also the range of viewpoints that are given credibility and space.

The media corporations are interested in what you want; they want to be able to sell you to as many advertisers as they can and they want to minimise the waste—they're not interested in selling you to an advertiser whose products you will never buy. This is the main reason that radio and television ratings are so important and it is why the vast consumer databases full of information captured at the point of sale (credit card details, demographic profiles, tastes in music, video, and films, and a host of other relevant data) are an important key to profitability in the world of media convergence. These databases also raise important issues about individual privacy and lead us to talk about the techno-legal time-gap in chapter 12. Basically the concept of the techno-legal time-gap refers to the time-lag between the introduction of new media technologies, their commercial application, and regulations to control them.

A second important key to profitability in the digital media world is control over content—that is, control over access to the vast libraries of content (entertainment and information) that have been built up over the past fifty years. According to the editorial in a January 2006 issue of *The Economist* ('King content' 2006), the share price of 'old' media companies fell behind the market leaders on the American stock exchange's S&P 500 index. At that time, the market value of Google was equal to the combined worth of Disney, News Corporation, and Viacom, three of the global 'old' media giants. On the upside, it is these same media companies that today control huge amounts of video and film content that can be repackaged, digitised, and marketed via the Internet. The *Economist* predicted that 'old media will command audiences for many years yet'. The magazine also noted that 'old media is now investing in digital media in earnest', having learnt the lessons of the dot.com crash of 2000. What we see in this small example is the economic convergence of what were once distinct commercial entities: media content providers such as the film studios of

Hollywood, newspaper publishers like News Corporation, and the distribution networks (telephone companies, Internet service providers [ISPs], and cinema chains). How do we make sense of this process and what does it mean? These are the issues that we shall address, and to do so we will use the tools of political economy.

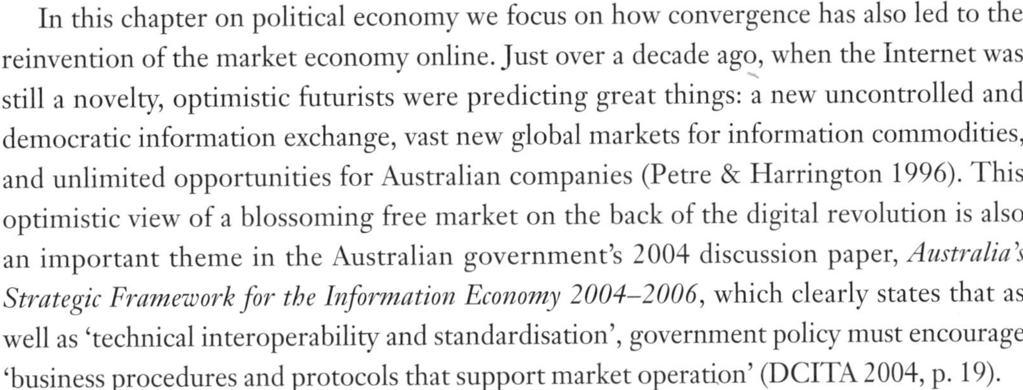

WHAT TIM RECKONS

The emergence of universally available and increasingly personalised media will have a major impact on media and telecommunications over the coming decade, just as they have over the last twenty years. Both sectors are still unsure how it will all work out. Media companies are struggling to define their core values and the telcos are still attempting to become content brands in their own right. Barring hype and misguided investment, technology is the easy part. A much greater challenge is the cultural change needed inside these organisations to transform the way they address their markets.

In this chapter on political economy we focus on how convergence has also led to the reinvention of the market economy online. Just over a decade ago, when the Internet was still a novelty, optimistic futurists were predicting great things: a new uncontrolled and democratic information exchange, vast new global markets for information commodities, and unlimited opportunities for Australian companies (Petre & Harrington 1996). This optimistic view of a blossoming free market on the back of the digital revolution is also an important theme in the Australian government's 2004 discussion paper, *Australia's Strategic Framework for the Information Economy 2004–2006*, which clearly states that as well as 'technical interoperability and standardisation', government policy must encourage 'business procedures and protocols that support market operation' (DCITA 2004, p. 19).

But as the authors of *The Clever Country?* noted, the scramble to join the digital revolution led to a global 'merger and acquisition feeding frenzy' (Petre & Harrington 1996, p. 13) as the old media companies competed to get a toehold on the Internet. The 'old media' model of free-for-all competition has simply been transposed onto the new digital platform. Today, the 'frenzy' is ongoing. Among telephony customers there are high rates of 'churn' as people change from plan to plan, persuaded by aggressive telemarketing campaigns out of India, to add the latest features to their mobile phone. Trevor Barr (2000, p. 26) noted in an early review of the information revolution, *newmedia.com.au*, that by the end of the 1990s members of the global telecommunications cartel (only a handful of major companies) had undertaken a series of acquisitions and mergers of 'unprecedented financial magnitude'. This was done as a preparatory manoeuvre in anticipation of the convergence we see today in media companies and technologies. Nearly a decade later, the situation is no different.

In early 2006, when the Japanese Internet company Livedoor got into financial difficulties and its chief executive was charged with fraud, investors began sniffing around for bargains. One newspaper described the situation as 'vultures' circling the stricken company (Sanchanta 2006). Today the acquisition and mergers frenzy is driven not so much by the initial enthusiasm of individual firms eager to reach new markets as by competition between already giant global firms to shut out new players and to carve up the digital world for their own super-profits. In 2005 the global public relations market was worth nearly $US4 billion and it was dominated by a handful of British and American mega-corporations ('Do we have a story for you!' 2006). In 2005, Rupert Murdoch spent $US1.4 billion on three Internet companies to create Fox Interactive Media, making one of the biggest players in online content management ('Old mogul, new media' 2006). In 2006 the Walt Disney corporation bought the successful animation studio Pixar; Google launched in the huge Chinese market and the share market was still hot with media stocks. The French media multinational Vivendi paid $1.5 billion to increase its holdings in the Universal Music record label in February 2006. The seller was the Japanese electronics manufacturer Matsushita. The company made a strategic decision to concentrate on the production of digital media devices, including plasma TVs and digital cameras (Turner & Jones 2006). Our colleague and friend Phil Graham correctly describes the stock market scramble for commercial control over digital media technologies as providing 'global capital with the means to create specialised knowledge monopolies' (Graham 1999). In the following chapters we explain why this is happening and what it means.

A brief history of political economy

> Political economy has an historic commitment to praxis, or the unity of research and social intervention. (Mosco 1999, p. 104)

Vincent Mosco is absolutely right to say this; that is why we have chosen to write from a political economy perspective. We are also aware of the poor reputation that political economy enjoys in the wider field of media studies today. However, our view is that while cultural studies has a lot to offer, it has abandoned some of the important insights about production and the broader economy that political economy provides. As McChesney (2000a, p. 110) notes, cultural studies seems more concerned with text than with the social relations in which it is produced and understood.

A political economy approach to the study of mass communication is not a new one. It has been around as an academic discipline for more than thirty years and it has provided a useful set of analytical tools for those interested in examining historical trends in the mass media (Schiller 1999). In fact the discipline of political economy is itself more than 200 years old. In a wide-ranging review of the field, Vincent Mosco (1996, p. 39) suggests its roots are in classical Greek philosophy. It first rose to prominence during the early years of the Industrial Revolution when economists came to terms with the rise of capitalism as the global system of production and exchange. The general principles of political economy were formulated by the Scottish economist Adam Smith (1723–90) in *The Wealth of Nations*, published in 1776. A key element of Smith's writing was to formulate a theory of the division of labour. He noted that a manufacturing operation would be more productive if the production process was simplified and each worker concentrated on a single task (Marshall 1998, p. 604). As an emerging discipline, political economy also became an ideology that would benefit the emerging bourgeois class of manufacturers and traders based in the great cities of Europe; they would see it as an attempt to rationalise the transformation of the world from a feudal to a capitalist mode of production using 'abstract laws, codified in mathematical form' (Mosco 1996, p. 40).

Today, with global capitalism clearly entrenched as a system built on competition, war, and crisis, economic theory is fundamentally different and based on the false assumption that markets will always find their point of equilibrium under conditions of perfect competition. Modern theories, such as monetarism, supply-side economics, and, more recently, the theories of neo-liberalism that underpin the ideological armoury of many Western nation-states, are the descendants of neo-classical economics (Bullock & Trombley 2000, p. 572).

Classical political economy was the subject of Karl Marx's extended study that resulted in the publication of his three-volume work *Das Kapital* (*Capital*) in the late 19th century. Marx's critique of political economy challenged Smith's assertion that the surplus value created through the commodity production process was merely the result of entrepreneurial spirit. Instead Marx refined Smith's labour theory of value by noting the exploitative nature of capitalism and arguing that the entrepreneurs (capitalists) expropriated surplus from the workers who laboured to produce it. According to the political economists who came before Marx, inequality was no more than an accident of birth, but Marx showed that exploitation of human labour power was a built-in feature of the capitalist system of production.

Marx argued that the way a society organises the production of its life-supporting goods and commodities will in the long run determine what that society looks like: how it organises its civil affairs and how it thinks about life, the universe, and everything in between. He also made the point that it is the political economy of a society, in particular its use and abuse of productive technologies, that drives history—what in some circles is called 'progress'. As Marx noted, the capitalist mode of production exists and renews itself through a constant process of combined and uneven economic, technological, political, and social development:

> … [by] uninterrupted disturbance of all social conditions, everlasting uncertainty and agitation … by the rapid improvement of all instruments of production, by the immensely facilitated means of communication draws all, even the most barbarian nations, into civilisation. (Marx & Engels 1973, pp. 45–7)

Marx wrote *Capital*, his most famous work, at the time of the Industrial Revolution, a process that took over a hundred years to complete. We are now experiencing a new industrial revolution: a revolution in digital technologies that will have the same profound effects on how we think and act as social animals. That is why an understanding of political economy is so important. We need it in order to understand the process of convergence and the new revolution that is reorganising the very foundations of the global economy into what many call the 'information' or 'knowledge' society; or what Phil Graham (2002) calls 'hypercapitalism'. Today the tradition of a political economy of media takes as its starting point many of the ideas of Marx, and theorists who write on the political economy of mass communication are often described as neo-Marxists (Murray 2005). This tradition is a development of the post-World War II period and, unlike the Marxism of Marx's time, it has become an academic rather than an activist theory (Bullock & Trombley 2000, p. 573). This last point is relevant because, for the approach that we take, political economy is not just a means of understanding the world. We are not alone in taking this view in relation to the mass media. Robert McChesney makes this very point in the preface to one of his books: 'The point of *Rich Media, Poor Democracy* is not merely to interpret the world, but to change it' (McChesney 2000b, p. xiii).

Like McChesney, we believe in the activist, as well as the explanatory, power of a political economy approach to mass communication. We share his view that once an understanding of the unequal structures of media power is gained, it is logical to look for ways to shift the balance in favour of a more equitable and democratic system.

Political economy methodology

> All the debates around the new media essentially turn on the extent to which this technology integrates into, alters and/or comes into friction with the social relations of capital. (Wayne 2003, p. 39)

Mike Wayne makes an important point about political economy with this statement: the central focus of analysis is not the technology itself, but the crucial social relationships that surround it and govern how it functions. Technologies do not come out of thin air, ready formed. As we outline in chapter 4, new technologies are created out of the convergence of existing technologies and within specific sets of conditions that are at the same time economic, cultural, political, and ideological. It is the dialectic—the frictions inherent in these ever-changing social relationships—that creates the dynamic for new technologies to emerge, often in response to a perceived economic or social need, or in response to a particular crisis. Political economy unpacks these dense social conditions in order to explain how and why particular communication technologies are 'invented' at certain historical points in the life-cycle of an economic and social system. Thus, using the methods of political economy, we are able to situate the global digital revolution (if that's what it is) in the context of information globalisation. As the communications academic Trevor Barr (2000) notes, political economy asks a number of key questions when addressing the rise of digital communication technologies in the 21st century: 'who and what is driving these changes, and how; whose interests are being served; and who benefits?'

There are several important elements to a political economy approach because unlike conservative and classical economics, it does not start from a normative model of how things *should* be, but rather from how things *actually* appear to be. The starting point is the world around us, not just an econometric computer simulation of a market operating under laboratory conditions. Tim Anderson (2003, p. 136) calls the idea that the world presents itself as an impersonal and unified market for goods and services 'one of the great propaganda myths of the last [20th] century'. He goes on to argue that this is because mainstream economic theory starts with an ideal model and then mysteriously removes the key relationships of power that we see around us every day. On the other hand, Anderson writes, 'political economic analysis has an important task to draw out ... moral debates, while maintaining a critical engagement with "economic" argument' (p. 137). Using this reasoning we are able to draw out some logical principles that inform a political economy approach:

- The analysis must examine the interests of power (both economic and political). Political economy recognises that inequality will lead to a dialectic of conflict and struggle over resources (Mosco 1999, p. 104).
- A political economist will ask relevant questions; in particular, 'Who benefits?' and 'Which interests are advanced?' (Anderson 2003, p. 143). Political economy has a particular focus on the concentration of ownership and control of resources (Mosco 1999, p. 105).
- There is no pretending to be philosophically neutral, but all positions and arguments are treated on their merit. Political economy distinguishes between ideologically motivated argument on the one hand, and opinion based on an analysis of the facts on the other. It seeks the answers to questions about influence and power.
- Political economy emphasises the importance of structural factors such as the way that production is organised. It questions the size, scope, and geographic spread of markets for goods and services.
- Political economy looks at the conflict between capital and labour that dialectically envelops the creation of value and it challenges the assumption that governments are neutral in their handling of economic issues.
- Political economy is interdisciplinary and seeks to understand how power is embedded in both the forces of the market and cultural forces in the 'micro-relations of social life' (Mosco 1999, p. 104).
- Reflecting its historical links with the Marxist tradition, political economy recognises the continuing relevance of a class-based analysis of economic and political realities—what Anderson (2003, p. 140) calls 'Marxist economic sociology'.

When we begin to apply these principles and methods of inquiry to the field of mass media and communication studies, we have to make them relevant to the media landscape today. This is done by narrowing the focus to concentrate on the ways in which media and communications 'systems' are connected to wider social structures and social forces. A political economy of communication begins with a number of questions:

- How do media and communication systems influence the political structures of society?
- How are media and communication systems economically organised, owned, and controlled?

- What is the role of advertising in the economic, social, and cultural landscape of the media?
- What is the relationship between media form (print, radio, television, multimedia), technology, and content?
- How have media industries changed over time and what are the social forces that have shaped and driven this change?
- What are the social forces that shape the content of media messages, whether news and current affairs or drama and entertainment?
- How does the audience react to media?
- How do government policy, law making, and regulation influence the behaviour of media companies and the content they produce?

According to McChesney, these questions lead to political economy's emphasis on 'structural factors and the labour process' and the role they play in the 'production, distribution and consumption of communication'. He argues that political economy may not answer all the questions to everyone's satisfaction, but it does provide the 'necessary context' for nearly all subsequent research in the field (McChesney 2000a, p. 110). The questions that political economy attempts to answer are concrete, grounded in what we call the social relations of production, distribution, and consumption. However, before tackling these issues it is important also to look at some of the more abstract concepts that support this approach. We begin with two abstract concepts that are often hidden from view in more traditional approaches: *value* and *capital*.

Value, capital, and the media

> Historically speaking, innovations in communication technologies have invariably coincided with ruptures in social relations ... technologies and social relations have mutually determinative and constraining effects upon each other. (Graham 1999, p. 3)

This mutually determining and constraining bond between the social relations of political economy and media technologies is how the dialectic is played out in the digital economy (Mosco 2004). This dialectic is also aligned to the ways in which the abstract concept of value is created, distributed, consumed, and stored at the economic level (the base of society) and how social power is also produced, exchanged, and exercised in the civil society (superstructure) that rests on the economic base. In the capitalist society we inhabit today, media industries operate on very similar value lines to the rest of the economy, with one important difference: the media industry produces commodified meaning. Thus there are two types of value produced in this economic exchange: one is purely commercial, measured by rates of profit and the value of capital invested; the other is more social, political, and attitudinal—what we might call the ideological effects of media. The duality of the media commodity reflects this economic and ideological value (Hirst & Patching 2005, p. 55). It also reflects the basic principle of political economy—the fact that every commodity has a dual nature. It has what Karl Marx called a 'use value' and an 'exchange value'. The use value of media commodities is informational; it is for entertainment, for the transfer of useful information (in news and documentaries), or for the circulation of ideologies—what we refer to as 'churning'. By this we mean that the use value of, for example, an item about politics on the evening news provides a certain amount of factual information (politician X did Y with consequence Z). But at the same time, it provides an ideological context and meaning that reinforces the prevailing power structures of the system. In effect, the news media 'churns' ideologies to keep them refreshed and relevant, and able to keep alive the dominant mythologies that inform ideological memes (Mosco 2004). This is an aspect of what Robert Rutherford Smith (1997, p. 332) calls 'the transmission and reinforcement of the myths of our time'.

On the other side of the duality, an exchange value is roughly equivalent to what, in mainstream economics, is called 'price'; that is, the value of one commodity expressed in terms of an amount of other commodities, or more commonly in a capitalist society, in terms of money. Money is the abstract form of exchange value in which the value of one commodity is measured against all others. A litre of petrol is worth about $1.20; an average car is worth $36 000, which makes it 30 000 times more valuable than a litre of petrol. As Marx wrote in volume one of *Capital*, commodities are the social form of the exchange of labour and they have a dual nature because 'they are at the same time objects of utility and bearers of value' (1990, Vol. 1, p. 138).

We take as our starting point the important principle outlined by Marx that human labour is the source of all value in society. This abstract idea is called the labour theory of value. By this term Marx meant that the value of a commodity is equal to the value of the labour time consumed in its manufacture. Marx's famous collaborator, Friedrick Engels, was among the first political economists to make the point that the development of human labour is a key marker of social history: 'Labour is the source of all wealth ... But it is even infinitely more than this. It is the prime basic condition for all human existence, and this to such an extent that, in a sense, we have to say that labour created man himself' (1975).

LABOUR and LABOUR POWER

Terms from political economy that refer to the actual process of work that humans undertake in their interactions with technology and nature (the means of production) to produce the means of subsistence and the necessities of life. Within any given social formation or economic system, the forms that this labour takes are determined by the relations of production. Within the capitalist economy of the 20th century (and today), labour takes a commodity form in which its price (wages) is determined not on the principle of a fair day's pay for a fair day's work, but by the power of capital to impose conditions of exploitation on the labouring classes.

To illustrate this point, let's examine a small example from Marx's own writing: gold and diamonds are valuable, but only because they have been dug out of the ground, refined, and manufactured by actual living workers. The value of these commodities is high because it takes a large amount of human labour time to process the raw materials into something useful. 'Yes,' you might argue back, 'but surely the mining machinery and all the technology that goes into producing gold and diamonds is also very expensive and this must surely add to the value of the end product.' If you thought this, you would of course be right. But what lies behind this simple appearance is the fact that the mining equipment, smelting furnaces, and jeweller's tools used in the transformation of raw materials into gold and diamond jewellery (for example) are also the product of human labour. In one of the small jokes that are scattered through *Capital*, Marx notes that if we could transform carbon into diamonds 'without much labour', the value of diamonds 'might fall below that of bricks' (1990, Vol. 1, p. 138). Marx notes that as an abstraction, a commodity is nothing more than the expression of *congealed* labour—that is, the total value of all the labour time that has gone into its production.

Marx made a further distinction between what he called *living* and *dead* labour. Living labour is that direct labour time of workers that is consumed in the process of producing a commodity, whether an expensive ring from Tiffany's or a media commodity such as a newspaper, magazine, CD, DVD, or movie. Dead labour is that labour time embodied in the technological commodities that are also used in the production process. A simple way of understanding this is to use an everyday example; for instance, the Apple iPod.

COMMODIFICATION

The process of turning non-commercial material—goods, services, ideas—into saleable products or commodities.

An iPod is a sophisticated piece of modern commodified digital electronics. The use value of an iPod is its ability to entertain us while we're mobile and its connectivity (ability to connect to other electronic devices). It contains a tiny but powerful silicon chip, some soldered electrical circuits, a power source, some knobs and dials, an LED screen, and a small amplifier. Each of these elements is the product of hours and hours of work by Apple inventors and technicians. Thus they individually embody a huge amount of human labour time. Once the technology of the iPod was perfected, Apple was able to work out a way to mass-produce them using state-of-the-art factories loaded with expensive manufacturing technology. The plastics for the cases had to be extruded through special die-cast machines; the tiny circuits had to be cut into the silicon and placed on a small motherboard; all the additional components had to be built and assembled. Much of this work is done by other expensive machines, each containing a giant store of Marx's *congealed* labour time.

Somewhere along the iPod assembly line, more humans had to become involved, doing the jobs that cannot yet be done by machine, probably including final assembly, testing, and packaging of the iPods in their boxes, ready for shipment to stores worldwide. Each single iPod then contains the value added at points along the production line; the expensive manufacturing equipment transfers a small amount of its stored value (congealed labour) to each iPod as it passes along. So, too, the human workers involved in running the machines, packing, shipping, and selling the iPods add a little bit more. The value of the iPod then represents a fraction of the value of all the dead and living human labour that has gone into its manufacture. At some point, the accountants at Apple would have done their sums and worked out an exchange value (price) for the iPod by averaging out the total labour time involved in producing say 100 million.

If commodities are stored value and that value is the product of human labour, then how do companies like Apple make a profit from the sale of their iPods? This is the question at the very heart of Marx's political economy, and to answer it we must briefly explore a third dimension of value—what in political economy is known as *surplus value*. In very simple terms, surplus value arises in the production process when the total amount of labour embedded in a commodity is greater than the price paid for that labour. Thus, for part of the day, workers are working effectively only for their employer. Mike Wayne describes the process with a neat metaphor: 'Like an evil spirit capital then moves from the body of labour whose power to labour it activates, and into the commodity labour has produced only to then leave this material body when it is exchanged so that its use-values can be consumed' (Wayne 2003, p. 11).

Part of this surplus value that accrues to capital and capitalists is used for their own personal consumption (lifestyles of the rich and the famous) and part of it is reinvested in capital and new labour in order for the process of accumulation to continue. The ability of capital to extract and consume this surplus value through its unequal exchange with labour (flesh-and-blood workers) is a benefit of the social, political, and ideological power that it has over 'what, where, why, when and how commodities are produced' (Wayne 2003, p. 13). Importantly, it is also the basis for the inherently and structurally antagonistic class relationship between workers and capital.

CAPITAL

For Marx and for the discipline of political economy, capital refers to the accumulation of value, usually expressed in terms of money, that accrues from the exploitation of labour during the production of commodities in a particular set of production relations. In neo-classical economics the term is stripped of any notion of exploitation and refers to the exclusive right of the monied class to own and control the means of production.

Political economists have been aware of a tendency within capitalism for the general rate of profit to fall as the amount of congealed dead labour stored in technological goods rises. Put simply, this means that every new piece of productive machinery and the development of the technologies that support it will contain more embedded human labour time than previous models. Thus the organic composition of the piece of technology—the ratio of labour power to nature involved in its design, engineering, manufacturing, and marketing—rises. This eventually creates the conditions for economic crisis.

These crises are periodic and ongoing; they are a constant feature of the capitalist mode of production. They are also one of the key social forces driving change: the mode of development within the capitalist production process. As Wayne explains, political economy views the concept of mode of production as a 'master category' that maps the 'fundamental social and technological antagonisms and priorities of an epoch'. We also like his definition of mode of development as the 'particular configuration of technology and social and cultural relations' that exist in a mode of production and cause it to change over time (Wayne 2003, p. 127).

Communication and media as both 'base' and 'superstructure'

> The media are both a business, an increasingly important site for capital investment, accumulation and employment, and a producer of ideas, values and so on. (Wayne 2003, p. 132)

It is this duality of the communications industry that causes political economists to ponder over the location of the media: is it part of the economic or the civic structures of society? The twin concepts of 'base' and 'superstructure' are the foundation of Marxist political economy. 'Base' refers to the economic realm of production and 'superstructure' refers to the rest of civil society (culture, politics, and ideology) that 'rests' on the base. However, this conceptual distinction has been critiqued as being 'economist'—that is, by asserting that the base determines the superstructure, political economy privileges the economic relations of production over and above those of culture. It is also one source of the tensions between political economy and cultural studies (Wayne 2003, p. 132). As Mosco (1996, p. 45) points out, many critics of Marx believe 'he did not carry the social analysis of capital far enough'. In a famous essay, *Base and Superstructure in Marxist Cultural Theory*, the British pioneer of media political economy, Raymond Williams, argued against a rigid view of Marxist political economy in which the concept of the economic base meant 'a strong and limiting sense of basic industry', at the same time defending a more dialectical alternative. The relationship between base and superstructure, he argued, was 'always in a state of dynamic process' (Williams 1980, p. 34).

This is very much the position that we adopt and it helps to position social and economic relationships of 'integration and contradiction' that drive change, including, we believe, the digital revolution. Base and superstructure are not architectural forms, or rigid categories, which Williams rightly argues would constitute a 'dead end' if used as a framework for studying the 'economics of modern cultural activity' (p. 35). In the same vein, Williams argues that the concept of superstructure must be 'revalued' away from 'a reflected, reproduced or specifically dependent content', and towards 'a related range of cultural practices' (p. 34). For Williams and for the Marxist tradition of political economy today, the argument about base and superstructure can be summarised in the famous aphorism 'being determines consciousness' (p. 35). In this sense, according to Williams, to talk about base is to talk about 'the primary production of society itself ... the material production and reproduction of real life' (p. 35).

We can see from this that there is no 'Chinese Wall' between base and superstructure. So why separate them at all? The important reason is to identify the source of value in Marxist economics at the level of *forces* and *relations* of production, which in the capitalist economy means the production of the commodity form and the reproduction of alienated labour. For Williams this allows, using his analogy, the piano *player*, as well as the piano *maker*, to be considered workers since they both, in their way, contribute to the creation and circulation of surplus value. They also, therefore, both contribute to the reproduction of the conditions of their own lives, within a capitalist system. Williams dismisses as ridiculous the idea that the piano-maker is 'base' and the piano-player 'superstructure' (p. 35).

Andrew Milner's *Cultural Materialism* draws our attention to the crucial theoretical conflict over base and superstructure in Williams' work. At its heart is a rejection of a determining role for relations of production in the relationship between base and superstructure. Milner writes of 'the central but false tenet of virtually all hitherto existing Marxist cultural theory, that of a determining base and a determined superstructure' (Milner 1993, p. 69).

Milner's otherwise excellent appraisal of Raymond Williams agrees with his rejection of the 'economic structures' of the base determining 'all other social life' (Williams 1980, p. 101). Williams and Milner apply the term 'cultural materialism' to their theoretical break with Marxism on the question of base and superstructure. Milner indicates that for Williams this was a necessary response to already existing postmodern cultural forms, which were a by-product of advanced capitalism and a response to radical changes in the social relations of cultural process (Williams 1980, p. 245; Milner 1993, p. 67). In response we would ask: are these changes really a radical departure from the normal process of capital accumulation and regeneration? Our brief answer is 'no'.

Williams argues that the commodification of cultural production reaches its peak with the arrival of postmodernism, and that in this period art forms and popular entertainments become 'debased forms of an anguished sense of human debasement' (Williams 1983, p. 141). While we agree with Williams up to this point, we do not support Milner's qualification that this phenomenon is 'unamenable to analysis in terms of any base and superstructure metaphor' (Milner 1993, p. 68). Instead, we argue that the general features of a 'postmodern' cultural landscape can be explained quite easily by reference to the political economy of communication and the work of media scholars who continue to explore the field. For writers like Mosco (1996, p. 80) and Wayne (2003, pp. 128–31), the dividing line between political economy and cultural studies is fluid and permeable, and they should inform each other in a process that Mosco calls 'mutual constitution', which can be characterised as the dialectical interaction of ideas between the two. One way of incorporating this idea into our analysis is to look at the ways in which two basic concepts of political economy—mode of development and mode of production—exist in a dialectic state of mutual constitution; how they impact on each other to drive the changes in both technology and in the social relations of the communications industries. These antagonistic and mutually constitutive changes take place in both the realm of the economic (the base) and in the realm of ideologies and cultural activity (the superstructure).

Mode of development and mode of production

> A new society emerges when and if a structural transformation can be observed in the relationships of production, in the relationships of power and in the relationships of experience. (Castells 1999, p. 360)

In his monumental three-volume work on the dawn of the Information Age, Manuel Castells argues that the digital revolution has fundamentally transformed modern life. In order to show this is true, we must be able to observe fundamental changes in the mode of production—a 'structural transformation' of the ways in which production and distribution are periodically reorganised to rejuvenate the unequal transfer of value from labour to capital. The various formulations of 'information', 'knowledge', and 'digital' economy that are now in common use signal that some change has occurred. The questions remain 'How much change?' and 'Why?'

We can begin to answer these questions using Castells' neat and useful theoretical distinction between the important concepts *mode of production* and *mode of development*. It is useful because it gives us the tools to understand and explain when, why, and how what we are calling the 'surveillance economy' (see chapters 13 and 14) began to appear and become the dominant form of economic activity within the *capitalist mode of production*. Before outlining the evidence and arguments for the surveillance economy in part IV, it is worth giving a brief explanation of Castells' arguments in favour of differentiating a mode of production from a mode of development. Castells uses this neo-Marxist taxonomy in order to distinguish between the social relationships of production (the mode of production) and the 'technological arrangements through which [human] labor works on matter [nature] to generate the product [commodities]' (Castells 2000, p. 16), which constitutes the mode of development.

MODE OF PRODUCTION

A mode of production is the way that human society organises its productive relationship with nature in order to provide the means of subsistence that allow a society to function and reproduce itself. A mode of production exists historically as the sum total of the relations of production that govern how society is organised economically, socially, and politically. Modes of production are usually named after the dominant social relations of an epoch. For example, slavery, feudalism, capitalism, and socialism are social structures based on particular modes of production.

To understand this process we first have to define what we mean by mode of production. The phrase refers to the defining features of the economy: the methods and means by which new value is created, collected, circulated, and reinvested within a specific set of social relations. It is also, as Mike Wayne explains, more than just machinery and factories and banking; it involves both capital and labour, which are simultaneously *both* forces and relations of production: 'As a category, the mode of production is composed of two concepts that amount to the *master couplet* of Marxian theory. These two concepts are the forces of production and the relations of production. Together these two concepts compose the mode of production' (Wayne 2003, p. 38).

The growth of the money economy, in the form of lending (usury), had a 'revolutionary effect' on pre-capitalist modes of production in that it 'destroys and dissolves' hitherto dominant relations of production (Marx 1990, Vol. 1, p. 732). Gradually, over centuries rather than decades, the mode of development characterised by a monetary exchange value for commodities engulfed all previous modes of production and the modern capitalist economy was born. As Yves de la Haye (1980) argues, money was an important means of communication as well as exchange because it allowed manufacturing and the trade of commodities to be generalised from the local to the global scale. The rise of money as a universal exchange value, he argues, thus creates capitalism as the first 'information' economy. This process was clearly manifest during the Industrial Revolution, which began in the 18th century based on the developing technology and social relations of the machine age (Marx 1990, Vol. 3, p. 494), and was assisted by the simultaneous rapid expansion of the means of communication (Marx 1990, Vol. 2, p. 164). The power of the capitalist mode of production and the modes of development nested within it 'gradually dismembers and absorbs' all previous modes of production, though not in a 'linear and consistent' way (Wayne 2003, pp. 12, 131). This process is characterised by the combined and uneven development of the dialectic that within the capitalist mode of production today is playing out in the contradictory interplay of two modes of development: 'informationalism and industrialism respectively' (p. 132).

Each particular mode of production is defined by the element that is 'fundamental' in defining productivity within the production process. Thus, in a mode of production that is characterised by agriculture, productivity increases are brought about by an increase in the labour force, or in the fertility or area of land under cultivation, or by a technological change that results in more efficient use of the human labour power, such as a better plough. In the industrial mode of development, such as that which led to the Industrial Revolution, the key sources of greater productivity are the introduction of new energy sources—steam, oil, and electricity—and the ability to 'decentralize' the use of these energy sources 'throughout the production and circulation processes' (Castells 2000, pp. 16–17). We could add that new technologies that take advantage of these new power sources might also make a difference.

MODE OF DEVELOPMENT

The mode of development in any mode of production will determine how the economy is shaped by what Castells (1996, p. 16) calls the 'technical relations of production'.

When we apply this analysis to Castell's information economy thesis, we see that the process of technological innovation and adoption can never be mapped as a smooth graph of ever-growing prosperity. Social systems expand, thrive, and disintegrate for reasons to be found in the ways they organise production and reproduction, not in the technologies they employ. Callinicos (1995, p. 177) mentions a number of examples of pre-modern (pre-capitalist) societies that collapsed because their methods of production (their ways of interacting with nature) created local ecological disasters from which they never recovered. Modern economists going back to Adam Smith recognised this phenomenon as being a dialectical process of combined and uneven development, within individual societies and between societies separated or defined by geography and by methods of organisation.

If the digital revolution has led to similar significant and fundamental changes within society, we can expect to see concrete manifestations of this in the relations of production. The transformation of relationships of power and experience must be premised on these organic changes within the realm of political economy. In other words, the mode of production (base) must first be transformed so as to support change in other, dependent social relations (superstructure). Mosco (1996, p. 91) has also provided useful insights into this process of what he calls 'structural transformation' by highlighting the dialectical nature of change and identifying the social forces that simultaneously promote integration and division among the large communications monopolies. There is some support for this proposition in Castells' outline of the birth of the information economy.

Castells presents some strong evidence that the first use of the term 'information society' was in Japan during the 1960s, at a time when the Japanese government was struggling to come to terms with the place of its national economy in the world market for resources and commodities. At the time a number of government agencies and private think-tanks recognised that Japan had to shift its economic base from industrial production to information industries. This change introduced a new logic of development into the Japanese economy, through the diffusion of emerging information technologies and shifting the centre of economic power away from resource-intensive manufacturing into 'intelligence-intensive production and exports' (Castells 1999, p. 242). This, according to Castells, was the first instance of a new 'mode of development' being consciously introduced—through government policy—into the global system of capitalist production. It was in the process of analysing this change that Castells reached a definition of what he calls the 'information society': 'An information society is not a society that uses information technology. It is a specific social structure, associated with, but not determined by, the rise of the informational paradigm' (p. 242).

RELATIONS OF PRODUCTION

The social ties that bind together the elements (labour, technology, nature) that constitute a mode of production. The relations of production determine how various technologies and labour processes come together to produce goods and services and to reproduce themselves.

Castell's main argument in *The Rise of the Network Society* is that capitalism is now in a new era where the mode of development has shifted from the industrial to the 'informational', where the source of productivity increases lies in 'the technology of knowledge generation, information processing, and symbol communication'. He adds that the 'action of knowledge upon knowledge itself' is 'the main source of productivity [increases]' (p. 17).

In Castells' analysis this is a fairly benign development at one level, and he suggests that the core performance principle around which the information economy is organised is 'the accumulation of knowledge' and 'complexity in information processing' (p. 17). This appears to deny the centrality of the social relations on which the system is organised: the accumulation of capital and the therefore necessary extraction of surplus value from an economically exploited working class. We have some disagreements with Castells on the question of what is driving the so-called information economy on this ground. If, as Castells maintains, the mode of development characterised by informationalism is active within the capitalist mode of production and merely represents a change in technological emphasis (from industrial technologies to digital information technologies), how can he then assert that the 'pursuit of knowledge and information' is the key characteristic of the system?

It is not credible to believe that capitalists, individually or collectively, would suddenly jettison the *raison d'être* that has served them so well for three centuries, in favour of mere knowledge. Knowledge is only useful to capitalism if it contributes to the productivity of human labour, leading to a consequent increase in surplus value and/or the circulation of surplus value so that profits flow into the bank account of the capitalist.

Our view is that the process of digital convergence—the mode of development that is revolutionising production and disturbing the social conditions we experience daily—follows the pattern identified by Marx and Engels. It is, in a sense, an inevitable historical movement of technology and social relations, locked in an embrace of contradiction, uneven development, and creative tension. As we move through this book, this theme will be further amplified and explained, in particular in the final section. Political economy also recognises the importance of understanding society beyond the economic sphere. It therefore also ventures into political theory. In our case this is an important consideration if we are to understand the full range of social forces that impact on convergence and on various cultural and political manifestations of the digital revolution. If we briefly turn our attention to these issues, we can begin to unpack the relationship between social power (hegemony) and the media (communicative practice).

Hegemony and communicative practice

Within the field of communication and media studies there is ongoing debate about the role and place of communicative activity—is it part of the economic base, or part of the social superstructure? The commodification of communication places it within the realm of the economic; it is an element of the circulation, accumulation, and distribution of value in a capitalist economy and thus part of the base. This point is further illustrated by the importance of communication and ICTs in the international division of labour that marks the period we call globalisation. As Mosco (1996, p. 95) points out, ICTs and the communication process help capital to manage international operations, to respond to changing market conditions, and to 'overcome space and time constraints' in order to maximise control over the international value chain of production, distribution, marketing, and consumption.

HEGEMONY

A term popularised by Antonio Gramsci to describe the domination of one social class by another.

GLOBALISATION

The mistaken and outdated notion that economic development proceeds best on the basis of a single worldwide market dominated by the United States and, to a lesser extent, Europe, who source materials and labour from anywhere in the world at the lowest possible cost.

This still leaves the question of how communicative practices relate to and exist within the superstructure. To answer this, Raymond Williams refers us to the notion of 'hegemony': the laws, constitutions, theories, ideologies, and social institutions that express and ratify the domination of a particular class (1980, pp. 36–7). Hegemony is a term brought into the discourse of political economy by scholars who read and absorbed the writing of the Italian journalist and Marxist theoretician Antonio Gramsci (1891–

1937). In Gramscian terms, hegemony refers to the active process of a dominant social class winning the support of subordinate classes for its continued rule. Hegemony implies that the subordinate classes in a sense *agree* to be governed by a class whose interests are in reality opposed to their own. Gramsci wrote extensively from an Italian prison in the 1920s on how popular literature, education, the legal system, and the links between Church and State all contributed to the process of manufacturing consent (Forgacs & Nowell-Smith 1985; Forgacs 2000). Hegemony is the result of the political power of ideological memes to normalise the dominant economic and social interests of the ruling class as the 'commonsense' thinking and as 'active forms of experience and consciousness' that seem to apply to all people (Williams 1989, p. 145). Hegemony disguises the real underlying inequalities (in economics, culture, and politics) that characterise class-structured societies, and it is legitimised through the prestige attached to the professional intellectuals and the institutions that embody the dominant social relations (Holub 1992, p. 25). Hegemony is created when the subordinate classes *internalise* the mental structures of dominance imposed on them by the ruling elite. Communicative practices are simultaneously part of both the base and the superstructure because hegemonic ideas are expressed through the duality of the information-communication commodities produced by the mass communication industries. This is Mosco's 'mutual constitution' at work and also what Renata Holub calls 'directed cultural production'; in particular, she refers to news commodities and the news media as one of the 'most dynamic' parts of the ideological structure that creates and sustains hegemonic thought (p. 104).

Hegemony is not all-encompassing, however, and as Gramsci and his followers argue, it is open to contestation by the social and cultural practices of the subordinate classes. In this sense there is a contestable social space that is open to counter-hegemonic social forces associated with the classes that are economically and ideologically subordinate to the ruling class. Williams (1980, p. 38) suggests that the concept of hegemony must also allow for 'variation and contradiction', 'alternatives and its processes of change'. Like other social phenomena, hegemony is constructed with a dialectic at its core; it can be contested, challenged, and even overcome under the right circumstances.

Thus when we consider hegemony, the cultural and ideological superstructure, like the base, is not a structure at all but a set of processes for 'social training'. The purpose of this mimetic ideological process is the 'continual making and remaking of an effective dominant culture', but a dominant culture that can tolerate (within limits) 'alternative meanings and values' that are at times incorporated, at others left alone (Williams 1980, p. 39). It is a central element of political economy of communication that the contradictions, gaps, and tolerances are the very spaces in ideology that oppositional or counter-hegemonic ideas and social forces might choose to occupy. In the mass media these spaces are the operational results of the dialectic stresses and contradictions that operate within the daily newsbeat and competition for 'front page' exposure. Wayne (2003, p. 176) characterises this as the news media treating individual stories with a 'contradictory amalgam of common sense and good sense, rational critique and ideology'. Importantly, this is not a fixed relationship; it is mutable through forces acting on what we might call the *emotional dialectic* of the front page.

Milner (1993, p. 56) rightly notes the importance of Gramsci's contribution to Marxism, political economy, and cultural theory as the reintroduction of dominance and subordination into a debate about culture and cultural production. In a sense, he argues, this solves the base–superstructure problem in favour of what Raymond Williams called a 'dialectic ensemble' (Williams 1983, p. 110; Milner 1993, p. 56). This is very similar to Mosco's point about the mutual constitution of contradictions within the economic and cultural realms of capitalism.

In *Keywords* Williams refers to the Gramscian concept of hegemony as both political domination and 'a more general predominance ... a particular way of seeing the world and human nature and relationships' (1989, p. 145). An ideology becomes hegemonic when it gains a certain amount of general acceptance and when it is naturalised as the general emotional attitude of an epoch and alternatives are, for the most part, precluded. Counter-hegemony is introduced as a social force to be created by an 'emergent' (Williams 1980) new class or other cultural group within the society in which an existing hegemonic elite holds sway. To put this another way: to become hegemonic an ideology must have great mimetic momentum and able to travel through several key vectors.

It is here that Williams issues the challenge that hegemony and counter-hegemony show the superiority of 'cultural materialism' over economically determinist Marxism (Milner 1993). Hegemony does this by including 'cultural as well as political and economic factors in its analysis of social forces' (Williams 1989, p. 145). Williams suggests that changes in culture can be a 'decisive factor in radical change of any kind, including many kinds of change in the *base*' (p. 146, emphasis added). Interestingly, he refers his reader to his notes on 'determinism' in his closing statement on hegemony, and we shall return to this idea in our discussion of digital determinism and the myths of the Information Age below.

Hegemony, subversion, and mimetic mutation

> Democracy and freedom will be the theme of every broadcast and editorial ... Meanwhile the ruling oligarchy and its highly trained elite of soldiers, policemen, thought-manufacturers and mind-manipulators will quietly run the show as they see fit. (Huxley 1965, p. 91)

This is precisely the process of hegemony; it is the dominance of a particular set of ideologies that benefits the ruling group, but gives the mass of the ruled the feeling that they are really quite well off. Hegemony is the dominance of one group over another, through either physical coercion (as in Orwell's *Nineteen Eighty-four*), or through the dominance of its ideas or ideology (as in Huxley's *Brave New World*). We can think of hegemony as what Herman and Chomsky (1988), in the classic text on the political economy of the mass media, called the 'manufacture of consent'. The concept of hegemony has two elements:

- the use of coercion by the 'predominant economic group' through the institutions and the 'state apparatuses of political society' in order to maintain its rule;
- the use of the 'microstructures of the practices of everyday life' to produce (manufacture) the consent of the subordinate group (Holub 1992, p. 6).

Marx and Engels invoke a very straightforward definition of hegemony when they talk about the rule of one class over another: 'What else does the history of ideas prove, than that intellectual production changes its character in proportion as material production is changed. The ruling ideas of each age have ever been the ideas of its ruling class' (1973, p. 72).

Importantly, this is not a fixed relationship; it is mutable through forces acting on the emotional dialectic. In a sense an emergent or oppositional dialectic is 'counter-hegemonic' and can 'pull' ideologies in contradictory directions.

To understand how hegemony can be a shifting set of relationships, we take our cues from Daniel Hallin's allied concept of *consensus*, *limited controversy*, and *deviance*. We find Hallin's work useful because it allows us entry to a discussion of dominant ideologies without having to refer too often to arcane language and sources. It is also useful to us because it is directly about the role of the mass media in spreading dominant and emergent or subversive memes of ideology. Our explanation is more expansive than Hallin's, taking in the concept of memes and linking it explicitly to the process of the emotional dialectic.

Hallin's concept of spheres of consensus, limited controversy, and deviance was developed to help him explain why the American mass media seemed to turn on its government over the conduct of the war in Vietnam in the 1960s and 1970s. In his example Hallin is talking about television journalism, but the idea fits ideology more generally. He describes each of the spheres in the following terms:

> **Consensus**: At the centre is the sphere of consensus, the region of 'motherhood and apple pie' and taking in the ideas that are not regarded 'by the journalists and most of society as controversial'.
>
> **Limited controversy**: The sphere of limited controversy lies just beyond the boundaries of consensus. For journalists this is the 'province of objectivity'; for Western liberal-democratic society it is 'the region of electoral contests and legislative debate … defined primarily by the two-party system … as well as by the decision-making process in the bureaucracies and the executive branch' of government.
>
> **Deviance**: This lies outside the sphere of limited controversy and is the realm inhabited by 'political actors and views which journalists and the political mainstream of the society reject as unworthy of being heard' (Hallin 1989, pp. 116–17).

Thus hegemonic ideas exist in the sphere of consensus and also dominate the sphere of limited controversy. Many counter-hegemonic ideologies begin life in the sphere of deviance and migrate into the sphere of consensus through mimetic mutation. A good example is Gay Liberation. Until the 1960s the idea that homosexual men and lesbians could be accepted in mainstream society was totally abhorrent to most people. The famous 'Stonewall' riots in New York began to change all that when gay men and their supporters fought back against police repression of their nightclubs. The ideas of revolutionary socialists and anarchists, however, remain firmly in the sphere of deviance. When was the last time you heard a Trotskyist spokesperson quoted in a news story? Chances are it was never, unless it was someone being given a tiny space to awkwardly defend 'violence' against the police at a demonstration.

McLuhanism: A meme for our time?

> It has sometimes been said that Marshall McLuhan's most impressive achievement is his reputation. (Miller 1971, p. 1)

Marshall McLuhan is one of the most influential North American media theorists of the 20th century. McLuhan was Canadian by birth, but spent some years as an academic in Britain before becoming famous and popular in counter-cultural America of the 1960s and 1970s. He was born in 1911 and died in 1980, so he did not experience the full effects of digital convergence in his lifetime, but his study of the 'electric process' of the broadcast media and its '*decentralizing*, *integrating* and *accelerating* nature', makes him an interesting pioneer in convergence studies (McLuhan & Zingrone 1997, p. 2). A brief discussion of McLuhan is also warranted to further our understanding of the transmission and mutation of ideological memes that were generated in the 1960s by McLuhan's work on the mass media.

Despite the sometimes dense and perhaps ultimately senseless prose, McLuhan's arguments have been popularised and some of them are now deeply embedded in popular culture. McLuhan understood, like his contemporary, pop artist Andy Warhol, that in the media age a good 'image' is invaluable, and he was able to reduce his complex ideas to simple 'dramatic mottos' (Miller 1971, p. 7). Two of the most important of these aphorisms, or popular metaphors, are the well-known saying 'the medium is the message' and the idea that we now inhabit what McLuhan famously described as the 'global village'. These terms are now common representations of digital mythologies. By tracing how these mimetic terms have become embedded in popular consciousness and how they have all but lost their original meanings, we can address the question of how ideas are transmitted through the media, how they mutate, and how they come to be interpreted differently in different times and places.

Marshall McLuhan was a complex man. Deeply conservative and quite religious by nature (Miller 1971), in later life he became a devout Catholic, but in appearance and manner he was outwardly very radical. In the 1960s this appearance of radicalism generated an audience for McLuhan's ideas and he gathered a large following at a time when many younger people were questioning society in general and the mass media in particular. His interest in television was wide and in 1964 he published a classic text, *Understanding Media* (McLuhan 1967), about the relationship between the audio-tactile nature of television and the pleasure people get from reading ancient manuscripts. According to Miller (1971, p. 121) this is an eccentric theory that is easily discredited, but McLuhan*ism* has undergone something of a revival in the last few years, with some of his most famous works being reprinted and several appreciations and critical studies published. This revival underlines the viral force of memes, which in McLuhan's case have been in infective circulation for nearly forty years.

Despite the staying power of the McLuhan memes and according to one of his most stringent critics, Jonathon Miller (1971, pp. 124–7), McLuhan overlooked the destructive features of the mass media, those that actually undermine any sense of a global 'village' community. McLuhan wrote that television is a 'cool' medium—it allows more interpretive and thinking space for the audience. Instead, argues Miller, television increases the daily alienation of human beings, one from another, by showing them a view of the world that is removed from their daily lived experience. The electronic mediation of events via the mass communication process has the effect of distancing the viewer 'from the scenes he is watching' (Miller 1971, p. 126). According to Miller's critique of McLuhan, audiences may well be global, but they are 'cut off from the pain, heat and smell of what is actually going on', and events happen 'in some unbelievably remote theatre of human activity' (p. 126). We are all familiar with this phenomenon, even if only unconsciously. Think back to your reaction in March 2003 when we saw 'embedded' reporters travelling with the American and coalition troops on their way to Baghdad. We certainly knew that there was a war going on in Iraq, but it was sanitised and we got no sense of the death and destruction that befell the Iraqi forces and the many civilians caught up in the conflict. One Australian journalist described the heavily censored and controlled media presence as 'Operation Mushroom' (Callinan 2003). Several 'embeds' have themselves described how they only saw limited aspects of the Iraq conflict and had no sense of the overall campaign, despite being on the frontlines with American and coalition forces (Ayres 2005).

Marshall McLuhan was able to harness his understanding of the subliminal nature of marketing to enhance his own reputation; at the same time, his work also led a movement to dissect advertising messages through the influence of his book *The Mechanical Bride* (1951). *The Mechanical Bride* is subtitled *The folklore of industrial man*, and it attempted to capture the mythic and mimetic function of advertising in 1950s America. Like other McLuhan publishing ventures, this book also attempts to subvert the linear progression of a printed work by using techniques of pastiche, montage, and fragmentation—in a style very similar to that practised by postmodernism today. McLuhan reached the unsurprising conclusion that the folkoric function in 20th-century America was performed by the mass media, not by poetry or music or education. McLuhan's mission was to turn the forms that advertising used to promote the selling of cheap mass-produced goods against themselves; to educate people to read through the mimetic messages and to understand the contradictions that could be exposed by semiotically unpacking them (Lovink 2002).

McLuhan was also one of the first academics to write on postwar popular culture in the 1940s and until his death in 1980. He claimed he needed to understand the culture of his students to communicate with them. Perhaps this is the first attempt to bridge the generation gap! In the early 1960s he established the first Centre for Culture and Technology at the University of Toronto, which, according to legend, was at first just his office, but rapidly grew into a larger and more well-known organisation as McLuhan himself gained notoriety and became a 'sort of minor communication industry unto himself' (Norden 1997, p. 235).

Misreading McLuhan

> McLuhan's famous distinction between 'hot' and 'cool' media referred to the different sensory effects associated with media of higher or lower definition. 'Hot' media (radio, photography, cinema) are more full of information and allow less involvement of the user; 'cool' media (telephone, cartoons, television) are less full of information and allow much greater sensory participation by the user. (McLuhan & Zingrone 1997, p. 3)

This would seem to present a problem for us, or perhaps for McLuhan's theories, in the age of convergence. How do we explain the cross-pollination that occurs between McLuhan's 'hot' and 'cool' media when the telephone is converged with a camera and a radio or audio format? Further, into which of McLuhan's categories should we place the computer? According to sympathetic but critical readings of McLuhan, he was equivocal when it came to seeking any positive values in either print or broadcast media. But it seems that in the end he felt that print was a more civilised medium that would save society from the barbarism of television (Goodheart 2000). Perhaps a little harshly, Eugene Goodheart, writing in *Partisan Review*, remarks that McLuhan has 'little to offer' to a study of the Information Age. He adds that the distinction between 'hot' and 'cool' media 'does little to illuminate the uses and abuses of the Internet' (Goodheart 2000). His techno-positivist approach—with occasional blasts at the horrors of television—means that McLuhan has, in Goodheart's words, 'effectively abdicated the role of social or cultural critic'. This may be the case, but because the aphorisms 'global village' and 'medium is the message' have been colonised by ideology and continue to circulate widely in mimetic viral form, his works are still available and it would not hurt if you were to read them for yourself. A quick search on Google will reveal over 270 000 hits on 'Mechanical Bride' alone, some a little weird, but all interesting. In the way of memes, 'Mechanical Bride' has even been adopted as the name of a song by a band called The Gourds. McLuhan's fascination with communication technologies—he saw them as either an 'extension' to or an 'amputation' from the human body—prefigures a lot of the hype about so-called 'virtual reality' that inspired the denizens of Cyberia in the 1980s. With this in mind, in the next chapter we turn our attention to questions about technology. What is it? How do we use it? Where does if fit in our political economy of communication?

KEY POINTS

The key points from this chapter are:

- the idea of 'political economy': that media content is also a commodity for consumption. A political economy approach liberates us from looking only at the technologies, or the content, and gives focus to questions of ownership and control;
- the centrality of the notion of 'production' in a political economy approach to mass communication;
- the contribution made by Marx, the political economists and neo-Marxists, McLuhan, and Castells to our understanding of mass communication;
- the concepts of 'value', 'capital', 'hegemony', 'emotional dialetic', 'base' and 'superstructure', and 'communication capital'.

CLASS DISCUSSION

1. Do you have a sense of being part of a global village? Write down some of the mediated interactions you have with people; that is, interactions which are not face to face.
2. What are the technologies you use for these interactions?
3. Have the technologies you have used changed much in the past three years?
4. When you receive your mobile phone bill, do you ever think about the contribution you are making to the profits of your telephony supplier, or is your focus on what you can do with the technology—text, send pictures, videos, receive email, etc?

4

MEDIA AND CAPITALISM: THE ROLE OF TECHNOLOGY IN PRODUCTION AND COMMUNICATION

OBJECTIVES

This chapter opens our discussion of the technologies of mass communication and the ways in which they are slowly morphing into the means of narrowcasting. After reading this chapter your understanding of our political economy approach should be deepened as we show, by example, how it can be used to understand and investigate the history of technological change and convergence. In this chapter we hope to show how economic forces interact in a process of combined and uneven development (the process of the dialectic) to drive both technological change and our socio-cultural adaptation to that change process.

Our main objective here is to outline how new technologies are introduced into society, not as an abstract and external force, but as a direct result of the social history of development, production, and our communication needs. In particular, we look at the following ideas and arguments:

- The actions of human beings, using the tools created by technology to interact with and change the natural world, are the key determinants of both the present and the future.

- Throughout history it has been human agency—people socially interacting with new ideas and technologies—not the technologies themselves, that has been decisive in forcing the pace of change.
- Technology is not just things, but rather a complex interaction of ideas (knowledge) and objects (tools) that exist and function in socially determined contexts for socially determined reasons.
- There is a contradiction, expressed through the dialectic, between the forms of technology and the social relations that govern their application.
- The social relations that define a mode of production and modes of development are perhaps more important than technology in shaping our future.

KEYWORDS

capitalism
contradiction
convergence
means of production
technology

What is technology?

> Technology … the knack of so arranging the world that we need not experience it. (Max Frisch, *Homo Faber 1957*, cited in Partington 1997, p. 146)

This is a very dark view of technology and one that, at first glance, doesn't seem wholly accurate. But how accurate is it? A person with Frisch's disposition today might argue that the development of virtual realities and sensory devices that can simulate 'real' experiences in the brain takes us away from experiencing the world itself. We know that our view of the world is mediated and partly distorted by the mass media today. What do we mean by our phrase 'the world itself'? In short, the world we inhabit is both a natural and a social environment. Technologies mediate our interactions with nature and increasingly, in our media-saturated culture, our interactions with each other. As you will remember from our arguments in previous chapters, we see the world as a material thing—it is open to our senses and nature provides us with the things we need in order to survive. The development of technologies, over tens of thousands of years of thinking, experiment, and convergence, takes place within the social environment. This social world increases in complexity as societies learn from the past and imagine new ways of doing things—new ways of interacting with nature.

TECHNOLOGY

1) An object, or system of connected objects, that can be used in a productive process to provide a practical solution to a problem. 2) A process of incorporating knowledge into the production process; in capitalist systems this takes a distinct commodity form.

A clear, concrete example is the manipulation and modification of the basic building blocks of all living matter: the short, almost invisible strings of sugar, carbon, and acid of the DNA double helix that make up our genetic coding. Evolution is the long process of organisms changing through their interaction with the physical environment and so genetic mutation is a natural thing. Today the social environment (which includes technologies) is such that we now have the knowledge and the means to push genetic mutation at much higher speeds. Unfortunately, we see examples every day that indicate our control over this process is incomplete and fraught with dangers. In November 2005, the news told us of experiments conducted in Australia to modify the genetic code of the humble pea; this was done to make pea plants more resistant to a weevil that reduced the profitability of crops. The CSIRO scientists who had been working on this project for ten years abandoned their research when testing showed that the genetically modified peas caused an inflammation in the lungs of mice that were made to eat them in the laboratory. The driving force behind this 'science' was not just an attitude of 'Let's see if we can', but rather a response to the demands of pea growers for a higher-yielding crop.

Perhaps we should start with a simple definition and one that might give us a sense of what we know of technology ourselves. Here's one from the Collins dictionary:

> **technology** *n*. **1**. the application of practical or mechanical sciences to industry or commerce. (Hanks 1990, p. 1338)

But that's only the first entry; the second and third are about technology as 'the methods, theory and practices' relating to such applications and 'the total knowledge and skills available to any human society'. There's no getting away from it. Our definition of technology must have room for the idea that it embodies the skill and the labour of human beings and our ability to harness and shape aspects of the material world into things that are useful to us.

On another part of the definitional spectrum, *Roget's Thesaurus* (1979, p. 252) uses the noun form of *technology* as a possible synonym for *skill*. This is an interesting proposition. For example, 'Have we got the skill to do the job?' is often a subtext in the question 'Have we got the technology to do that?' Implicit in any definition of technology is an appreciation of the skill of those who have imagined, created, and explained how it will work, and those who have shaped it to suit our human purposes. This meaning is also present in this definition offered by the Penguin edition of the Macquarie dictionary:

> **technology:** *n*. the branch of knowledge that deals with science and engineering, or its practice, as applied to industry; applied science. (Delbridge 1990, p. 645)

There's technology and there's also alternative technology, defined as follows in the Oxford dictionary of new words:

> **alternative technology:** *n*. technology deliberately designed to conserve natural resources and avoid harm to the environment, especially by harnessing renewable energy resources. (Tulloch 1992, p. 14)

There's another entry in the Macquarie that has the same *techno* roots as technology. The word is *technocracy* and it has a decidedly Orwellian tone to it:

> **technocracy:** *n.* [the] theory and movement advocating control of industrial resources and reorganisation of the social system based on the findings of technologists and engineers. (Delbridge 1990, p. 645)

Those in charge of such a system were to be known as *techno*crats, a play on *aristo*crats—the keepers of knowledge and power in feudal times. Interestingly, the Delbridge entry notes that technocratic theories and movements were active in the early 1930s, at the time when fascism in Europe was beginning to flex its own technocratic muscles. German manufacturing was being made 'efficient' through the gradual reintroduction of slave labour into the economy, and Italian trains ran with military precision.

The etymologies, the linguistic roots, of techno-related words are easily found in the simple *techno*, which is traceable back to the Greek words *tekhnologia* meaning systematic treatment and *tehkne* or skill (Hanks 1990, p. 1338). According to Raymond Williams' *Keywords* (1989, pp. 315–16), technology also has a linguistic root in the Latin *technologia*, with a similar meaning to the Greek. We can also trace the word as it evolves even further. New meanings are created in language all the time—nuance and inflection added in response to new uses for old things and ideas. A recent one is *technophobia*, a fear of technology. Our editor knows someone who describes herself as a 'technoklutz'. The opposite of technophobe is *technophile*, which describes those who can find no fault with technology and believe that there is a technological 'fix' to just about every problem that humans encounter in their interactions with the material world and with each other. Neil Postman has some fun satirising what he sees as the overly optimistic view of technophiles: 'They gaze on technology as a lover does on his beloved, seeing it as without blemish and entertaining no apprehension for the future. They are therefore dangerous and to be approached cautiously' (1993, p. 5). Another modern word from the same roots is *technobabble*:

> **technobabble:** *n.* jargon or gobbledegook that is characteristic ... of computing and other high technology areas ... [sounding] like so much nonsense to those who are not 'in the know'. (Tulloch 1992, p. 22)

There's also the pure *techno* now attached to a style of urban music and its subgenres: *techno-funk*, *techno-fusion*, *techno-pop*, and so on. The common factor, according to Sara Tulloch (1992, p. 284), is 'making heavy use of technology (such as synthesised and sampled sounds, electronic effects) ... a synthesised, technological sound and a dance beat'.

One more *techno-* word we came across recently deserves a short mention: *technopath*. This appeared in Indra Sinha's *the cybergypsies*, an interesting story of the author's engagement with some of the first inhabitants of the cyberworld, and he uses it to describe the computer-savvy generators, collectors, and launchers of Internet viruses with 'links to every major partisan group in the virus underground'. The implications are clear from the root of the second part of the word: a *technopath* is someone who displays pathological (anti-social) behaviour in the same way as a sociopath displays behaviours which indicate a disregard for the 'normal' rules of a given society. The *technopaths* are 'the people who write cancerous code and send it out into the world to mutate other people's data' (Sinha 1999, pp. 2–4). They have little or no regard for the social rules of the cyberworld. Later Sinha comes across other *technopaths* who enter large multiplayer game sites. This group likes to randomly and violently kill other characters in the game. Not very sociable at all! *Technopaths* may also exhibit anti-social (or at least anti-establishment) behaviour in their real-world relationships too.

There's no doubt that many people would consider hackers to be technopaths. The US military spends more than $1.5 billion a year to defend against hacking attacks. In 1999 a four-star general became the first American chief of cyber-defence (Schwartau 2000, p. 21). The first technopath-hackers were the 'phone phreaks' of the 1970s who discovered that they could use simple computers to hack into the US phone system. 'Just by sending tone down the line, nothing else, it was possible to take total control of the internal network of the telephone company—for free—and call anywhere an operator can' (Draper 2000, p. xiv). Technology journalists Katie Hafner and John Markoff (1991) tell the stories of three pioneer hackers and their 'gangs' in *Cyberpunk: Outlaws and hackers on the computer frontier*. In the late 1980s the stories they relate were being lived by the hacker underground, which was working on the fringes of what was considered legal and ethical. They were making money 'buying, selling and stealing information' (Hafner & Markoff 1991, p. 9). In the emerging surveillance economy this lucrative trade is reserved for the data corporations and has been legitimised by weak privacy laws and international protocols that have created the market on a more sustainable basis. The same technology used by the early hackers—albeit with more sophistication built in—now feeds a global industry worth billions of dollars (O'Harrow 2005). The technology has been harnessed to the emergent digital mode of development to create a new profitable niche in the global media economy.

So far we've been looking at technology almost as a way of being or thinking and the practice of doing things with this technical knowledge. One element that's missing from our definitions so far is any concept of technology as a 'thing' itself—technology viewable as an everyday object with a physical form. Tulloch's definition comes closest with the reference to using technology to create techno music. In this context we can see how the concept of technology as *tool* or *instrument* begins to form. The technology *is* the synthesiser. Techno-music became popular in the mid-1980s when, for the first time, smaller and more powerful synthesisers became available to musicians. The keyboard interface and array of mixing channels combined elements of the piano and the studio 'desk', allowing musicians to experiment with a wider variety of 'sounds' and effects.

It is easy to see an electronic musical instrument as a *piece* of technology, but what do we say about a bus, a washing machine, a tractor, or a personal computer? In what ways do these things represent or embody technology? Each of them assists us with a daily task in our lives: a means of getting somewhere (public transport), meeting a personal need (clean clothing), finishing a job (ploughing the field), or communicating with colleagues and friends (sending and receiving email). Or doing practically anything else in our lives.

Now that we've got this far, let's pose a question: what is technology considered to be today? All of us are aware of it in the world—it's everywhere. 'New' technology is emerging almost weekly. Can a state-of-the-art vacuum cleaner be considered to be a *piece* of technology, or the result of the *process* of technology?

To consider this question we have to explore the following propositions:

- Technology involves the application of knowledge to act upon the world in a systematic way through the human labour process using the tools and raw materials available under existing social conditions.
- Technology is based on specialist practices, for example engineering, and is organised to accomplish big, important tasks.
- As a set of practices and as a way of organising and harnessing 'knowledge', technology is also a set of social relations. This includes aspects of how it is distributed and controlled in particular societies; how it is managed, produced, and consumed; and where it has the most impact and does it add to, or subtract from, the well-being of the society that employs it.
- Technology is most often the application of scientific methods in an industrial or commercial or business context. This is an obvious common sense when we look at the world around us: we all use technology in a variety of formats and contexts every day.
- Technology has the appearance, most of the time, of an object, a piece of equipment, a tool, or an instrument.
- Today we most often come across technologies in the form of consumer goods (from cars to MP3 phones); we are also confronted with technology in our homes, classrooms, and workplaces. The common view today, in our opinion, is that technologies appear to us in the form of consumer goods (commodities).
- Encouraged to consume endlessly, we see technology as an infrastructure of objects and processes (laser disc readers in our DVDs) that can enrich our leisure time, as well as make our work easier, cleaner, and more enjoyable.
- All of this enthusiasm for 'new' technology is closely linked to what is popularly known as the 'information revolution'.

Many commentators in the popular media and a number of communications scholars place the physical manifestations of technology at the forefront of their analysis of what we commonly call the 'information', or 'knowledge', economy/society. As we argue later, this is a technologically determinist argument and it's an incomplete picture of the world. To understand the new digital technologies and the attendant process of convergence, we must also investigate the social relations surrounding and in many ways shaping the digital revolution.

In an everyday sense, we often define technology as an object, or system of connected objects, that can be used in a productive process to give a practical solution to a problem.

Given this definition, a technology can be something as simple as a stone axe or even a branch of a tree used for leverage.

At a more theoretical level, technology is also a process of thinking and design, involving a range of problem-solving skills that we normally associate with science. However, as the Collins dictionary reminds us, this form of technology is often applied in the context of industry and commerce. That is, it is linked to a definite set of social relationships that signify a particular historical epoch. Was there technology before the historical period of industry and commerce? Of course there was. We might consider it to have been primitive technology, but every human society must harness its available technologies (knowledge and resources) in order to survive and prosper and to benefit from a productive interaction with the natural world.

Technology and society

> By combining twentieth-century computer technology with nineteenth-century time-and-motion studies, the McDonald's corporation has broken the jobs of griddleman, waitress, cashier and even manager down into small, simple steps. (Garson 1988, p. 37)

This small example of how the giant American fast food chain, McDonald's, was able to insert new technology into its rigid division of labour illustrates the process of the dialectic—combined and uneven development—within the economic confines of the capitalist mode of production. The use of such labour-saving devices and processes in the workplace is one important aspect of the relationship between technology and the social system. The debate about the relationship between technology and the broader society makes an excellent starting point from which the developing issues of media convergence can be examined. Technology does not exist in a social vacuum. The rate of inventiveness in a society is in direct proportion to its level of social development. A degree of social cooperation is necessary to use even simple tools for everyday jobs (Marx 1990 [1867], p. 452). Hunter-gatherer societies could invent the technology of simple tools for farming or animal husbandry only when they had reached a certain size and level of linguistic and social integration. But no one would suggest for a minute that such primitive social organisation could have produced the internal combustion engine, aeroplanes, space travel, or the microchip.

The more complex human society becomes, the more technology comes to provide humans with their 'instruments of labour'. Karl Marx wrote: 'it is not what is made, but how and by what instruments of labour, that distinguishes different economic epochs' (Marx 1990, Vol. 1, p. 286). For example, it is not the use of coal per se that determined progress in the Industrial Revolution, but rather improvements in how the coal was mined, transported, crushed, and burnt thus creating new applications for coal-fired technologies. The rapidly developing smelting technologies of the massive iron and steel blast furnaces of the 19th century required more efficient production of ever-greater amounts of coal. The general advance in production processes, science, and technology during the Industrial Revolution was so widespread because the social logics of the mode of production—capitalism—demanded that everyone keep up or be swallowed up by the juggernaut of 'progress'. Following Marx, political economy argues that technological change is cumulative, but always under the influence of the prevailing social conditions that determine how the necessities and luxuries of human existence are produced, distributed, and consumed.

CAPITALISM

An economic system based on private ownership of the means of production (capital) and the private accumulation of profits. Capitalist ideology is based on the idea that an unfettered free market is the best way to deliver increased wealth and prosperity for all. The operation of capitalist systems is often characterised by distortions arising from excessive government regulation and intervention, monopoly and oligopoly, plutocracy, low wages, and hyper-consumerism. Capitalism is a class system in which two contending classes (labour and capital) are engaged in a constant struggle over the distribution of the production surplus (surplus value).

Marx made a further intriguing observation about the complex and contradictory relationship between society and its instruments of labour. He noted that without the application of human labour power, the tools themselves would lie idle: 'The use and construction of certain instruments of labour ... [are] characteristic of the specifically human labour-process ... an appropriation of what exists in nature for the requirements of man' (*Capital*, vol. 1, pp. 286–90, cited in Callinicos 1987, pp. 84–5). Some might dispute this today when it appears that full automation of production is not only possible but also likely in the very near future. But of one thing Marx was very certain: no new social value can be created only by machine-labour (technology). Economic value is determined by the expenditure of human labour power, always in its social context.

In the second volume of *Capital*, Marx took his arguments about social relations one step further by writing that it was the process of interaction between the means of production and the relations of production that created the most tension and exposed the biggest contradictions in any given society. That is why Trevor Barr (2000, p. 28), writing about the new technology of the information revolution, can highlight the obvious 'paradox' of convergence and divergence in the global information economy. This dialectic takes the form commercial consolidation (fewer and larger telecommunications giants) and an expansion of the goods and services offered to feed our limitless commodity fetishism. Convergence and its side-effects are not limited to the digital revolution; it is a constant in the social history of technology.

Technologies and convergence: A brief history

> Thus civilisation and mechanical progress advanced hand in hand, each developing and being developed by the other, the earliest accidental use of the stick having set the ball rolling, and the prospect of advantage keeping it in motion. (Butler 1967, p. 163)

This is a passage from the fictitious *Book of the Machines*, which appears in long tracts in Samuel Butler's utopian/dystopian story *Erewhon* (written in 1872). Through this story Butler's purpose was to appeal to Victorian England's middle class to abandon the Industrial Revolution. Butler believed that industrial society would eventually lead to humanity being enslaved by machine intelligence. In the utopian society of Erewhon all machines had been destroyed in an agrarian counter-revolution against industrialisation. We mention this here to illustrate the point that the 'love-hate' relationship between humans and technology has been around for a long time.

CONVERGE

To converge means to come together. In the context of communications technologies this means the *coming together* of telecommunications, computing, and broadcasting into one electronic system or field. The key to this modern form of convergence is the microprocessor—the computer chip. Convergence is both a technological and an economic-social process that proceeds dialectically and via a series of contradictions.

In fact, as we suggested in the chapter on political economy, the features of any particular mode of production are dialectically fluid over time. It is the mode of production—the specific ways in which labour and technologies of production combine—that determines the overall complexion of any particular society: 'The specific manner in which this union is accomplished distinguishes the different economic epochs of the structure of society from one another' (Marx, *Capital*, vol. 2, pp. 36–7, cited in Callinicos 1987, p. 86).

When we begin to unpack this statement it becomes clear that in any stage of human history, the technologies—the means of production—are constantly developing in ways that seem to correspond to the socially determined needs, ambitions, and values of those groups and individuals who 'own' them. As Marx outlined in *Capital*, the use of machinery was introduced to reduce the labour-time necessary for the production of commodities—in other words, to increase the productivity of labour (Marx 1990, Vol. 3, p. 467). Manuel Castells makes a similar argument about the introduction of digital machines into the production process in the information economy. The motive is an increase in productivity, but not just for its own sake—the ultimate reward for capitalists is 'profitability and the growth of their stocks' (Castells 2000, p. 94; see pp. 77–99). This information requires that our definition of technology includes the social relationships—sets of economic, political, and cultural links or influences—that contextualise its history, its present, and its future. So now we can outline a clear understanding of technology that will serve us as we explore the landscape of the digital revolution.

CONTRADICTION

A state of tension or conflict between two ideas or social forces that indicates two opposing sides to an issue or idea.

In order to fully explain the social dynamic of technology, however, one further detour is necessary. It is important to understand the process of social development—that is, of societies and of history—as a series of contradictions, conflicts, and resolutions. The tool for this job is the philosophical concept of the dialectic. We can now put this term together with our definitions of technology to create a useful analytical concept: the *dialectic of technology*.

The dialectic of technology

To come to grips with the role that convergence increasingly plays in our lives today—the so-called 'digital revolution'—it is necessary to bring together the dialectic and our definitions of technology. The first step is to explain the concept of technology as a means of production. In plain English this means that technology is first and foremost the physical means—the tools and machinery—with which a society can produce what it needs to survive and prosper. Importantly, tools and machines are not simply the physical instruments of labour; they also embody knowledge and congealed labour—the work that has gone into their development, construction, and deployment.

MEANS OF PRODUCTION

An ensemble of the available technologies and natural resources that combine with human labour and within specific forms of social relations to form what political economy calls the mode of production.

As we've seen, advances in the technological base of society occur within a complex matrix of social conditions and in turn impact on them. The discovery that round objects will roll down a slope led eventually to the technology of the wheel, but it took thousands of years for this simple idea to be literally harnessed to a horse in order to create the cart, or horse-driven buggy. This point of convergence first needed the domestication of wild horses and the development of more complex tools and technologies—the saw, the chisel, and the wood plane; the tanning of leather from animal skins; and the application of the principles of levers. Each of these things could only happen under certain conditions of human existence, each more complex than the preceding ones. On their own, carpentry, the domestication of animals, and the development of simple mechanics enabled the societies that employed them as productive technologies to become wealthier. In turn, a part of this wealth could be then used for the further intellectual development necessary to provide the next breakthrough. This is the dialectic of technology in action.

The dialectic of technology is one of the determining influences on development of the productive forces that takes place within a mode of production. The likelihood of future mutations in the dialectic of technology is ultimately a product of the complex daily interaction and conflict between the social relations of production and the forces of production.

The forces of production are not just the physical means of production (human labour power and nature). The forces of production are themselves the engine for a most powerful dialectic: the interaction between human labour power and the natural world and the contradictions that the process of mutual constitution forces to the surface.

The dialectic of technology determines how new forms of convergence emerge and are put to use within a mode of production. However, as digital convergence has become one strand of the emerging dialectic of technology in the 21st century, it must have its opposite. We have chosen to use the term 'fragmentation' to represent divergence as the state of 'oppositeness' to convergence. We will examine the process of 'fragmentation' in detail in later chapters. To conclude we will simply say that fragmentation is the process that produces the phenomenon of narrowcasting. As the technology of digital media comes together, one of its most significant impacts is to split the collective audience into autonomous, individual consumer-citizens.

Another manifestation of the contradiction between technological convergence and market fragmentation is the subjugation of social relations to the relationship between individuals and *things*. As we were drafting this text we were surprised at the number of our friends, colleagues, and students who implicitly understood technology to be defined by common commodity forms; that is, objects in the everyday world around them. For example, we commonly think of a computer or a digital camera as a piece of technology. This objectification of technology serves the purpose of deflecting our attention from the social aspects of the commodity and towards valuing the object for what it is and does and what it says about us (an expression of our personality or social position). Karl Marx called this the fetishism of commodities and he added that within any particular mode of production this would take a particular form. One of the most recognisable and oldest memes that contains the fetishism of objects is religious practice centred on the worship of iconic relics and symbols.

The objectification of technology

> Digitization expands the commodification of content by extending opportunities to measure and monitor, package and repackage entertainment and information. (Mosco 2004, p. 156)

The digital revolution has extended the commodification of our social and spiritual life even further than industrialism. In fact political economists argue that our love of commodities is more powerful than religion because they have a materiality that 'presents itself directly' to our senses more powerfully than religious belief (Mosco 1996, p. 143). In relation to our love of gadgets—mobile phones, iPods, and so on—we have described this as 'technology fetishism', after the Marxist concept 'commodity fetishism'. Marx describes commodity fetishism as the way that the actual social relations of a commodity—the fact that is the product of human labour locked in an unequal dialectic with capital—takes on 'the fantastic form of a relation between things', obscuring the social aspects of its production: 'I call this the fetishism which attaches itself to the products of labour as soon as they are produced as commodities, and is therefore inseparable from the production of commodities' (Marx 1990, Vol. 3, p. 165).

This fetishised relationship between consumers and commodities arises because of the process of alienation: the goods produced appear to be independent of the labour that produced them and they come to the market in the form of things owned by capital. There is no direct exchange between producer and consumer; exchange is mediated by money, transforming the production process into a 'complete mystery', and the true value of the commodity is 'withdrawn from view' (Marx 1990, Vol. 2, p. 303). Through the global use of money as the medium of exchange, there is 'further distortion' of the true relations of production; capital appears as an independent force, 'a mere accessory' to the production process: 'The fetish character of capital and the representation of this capital fetish is now complete' (Marx 1990, Vol. 1, p. 516). In the digital world of endless consumption and planned obsolescence, this fetishism is transposed onto the technology-commodity.

This is most clearly expressed in the positivist versions of the digital society, which in their most extreme form give rise to digital fetishism. The positivist idea is of a benign information society in which the gradual replacement of human labour by machines results in increased leisure time and creativity for the masses. One Japanese guru of this movement even described it as 'Computopia' (Holub 1992, p. 175). Computopia represented an idealised view of the information society and, according to some critics, became a plank of Japanese economic policy (Dyer-Witherford 1999; Castells 2000). It is this process of fetishising the products of technology, rather than explaining the process, that generates the 'need' for all of us to be electronically up to date—to have the mobile phone with the MP3 player and camera built in. It is also one of the dialectics of technology that sees the marketing of this 'need' in lock-step with the manufacture of new, bright, shiny, and attractive commodities, such as expensive mobile 'lifestyle hubs':

> If your mobile phone does not boast a one-megapixel camera or an MP3 player, you have a lot of catching up to do ... [T]he advances were designed to lead consumers towards a new age in mobile telephony in which handsets become more than communications devices or playthings and are transformed into 'lifestyle hubs' ... able to meet consumers' entertainment needs ... as well as their financial obligations. (Dudley 2005)

As all of us are too painfully aware, these mobile 'lifestyle hubs' create their own financial obligations. The headline on this thinly disguised promotional piece in the Brisbane *Courier-Mail* was 'Dial your own future'. According to reporter Jennifer Dudley, many of the new-generation phones on offer in 2005 'took multimedia convergence to a new levels'. A few pages further on in the same edition of the *Courier-Mail* is a regular feature called 'Place and Time'. It features ordinary folk on the streets of Brisbane answering a question of the day. In this edition the question was: 'Did you buy your mobile phone because of the gadgets on it?' The responses are an instructive snapshot of opinions that also reflect the age and generation gap between 'digital immigrants' and 'digital natives':

> Adam (39): 'No. I bought mine out of necessity to keep in contact with my wife and kids. It has a camera in it that I've never used.'
>
> Jayne (18): 'I got a new phone as part of a home broadband package. I use the camera but only for fun. I definitely could get by without it.'
>
> Myles (17): 'Yes. I bought it because it has a video camera and video talk. I also use the Internet on it.'

> Elizabeth (48): 'No. My husband bought one for me because he thought I needed one. I think the technological advancements are good enough.' (Place and Time 2005)

This is the dialectic of the digital future.

The economics of convergence

> In the postwar era, particularly in the past 25 years or so, there has been a rapid and intense restructuring of global production and the international state system. These stunning and often bewildering changes signify an unfolding dialectic of grand proportions, offering hope for the preservation of public discourse but also the appearance of a more homogenous and authoritarian world order. (Sussman 1999, p. 85)

We have seen how these tendencies, Sussman's 'unfolding dialectic of grand proportions', have played themselves out over the past decade. As we discuss in chapters 13 and 14, the events of September 11, 2001 signalled an unprecedented change and a dangerous shift towards what Gerald Sussman feared in 1999: the appearance of a more authoritarian world order. The rapid and intense restructuring of global production that Sussman suggests is at the heart of this process has been keenly felt in the media and communications industry. The process has been driven by a series of convergences, some technological and others more social in nature. We argue that technological convergence is itself the end product of important social and economic forces, in particular the process of commercial convergence.

Commercial convergence

> By collating ever more detailed subscriber profiles from individual media product databases, conglomerates are able to track and categorize users, charging premiums for the sale of these groups to advertisers seeking highly specific niche audiences. (Murray 2005, p. 424)

Commercial convergence is driven by and in turn contributes to trends in digital delivery and content convergence. Simone Murray (2005, pp. 415–16) calls this 'synergistic convergence' and it involves the constant 'recycling' of product (content) across all the delivery platforms and communications channels that the media company has control over. This is clearly evident in the ongoing mergers, takeovers, and buyouts that have characterised the past 15–20 years of growth and change in the broadly defined creative industries. There are many examples available, but two that are easily identifiable and representative of the trend are News Corporation and Disney. These two global giants have 'multi-platform content strategies' (Murray 2005, p. 416) at the core of their business planning to help them dominate the mediascape today. They are also prime examples of the privatisation and corporatisation of what was once previously public space and what were once public texts.

Murray gives the example of the Fox Studios precinct near Centennial Park in Sydney. This complex, built on previously public space that was the Royal Agricultural Society's showground and the iconic home of Sydney's Royal Easter Show, has become a 'content cocoon' (Murray 2005, p. 416) where the vast product range of News Corporation entities is for sale. The Disney Corporation maintains several similar theme parks around the world, including one in Paris. The mediated experiences on offer at Disney World are a 'seamless illusion', what Neal Stephenson (1999, p. 50) calls a 'magic mirror', reflecting the world back to visitors 'better than it really is'. Former journalist Carl Hiaasen is best known for his gritty crime fiction stories, but he's also a campaigner against the Disney Corporation, which he describes as 'Team Rodent'. Disney is one of the most integrated media and entertainment companies in the world, offering consumers an endless variety of products and experiences, but where control is the 'signature ingredient' (Hiaasen 1998, p. 69). Visitors to Warner Brothers' Movie World on the Queensland Gold Coast are presented with a similar experience: the rides, the merchandise, and larger-than-life cartoon characters are all Warner Brothers creations, based around their movies and cartoons.

But what Stephenson noticed on his trip to Disney World in the late 1990s was that the Disney characters, such as Peter Pan, Winnie the Pooh, and Alice in Wonderland, were totally divorced from their literary origins. He realised that the original books on which the Disney versions are based were not available in the Disney World bookshops. The Disney characters seemed to him to be more wholesome and suitable for the family-oriented Disney audience, against which the texts 'seem deeply bizarre, and not wholly appropriate for children'. By contrast, the kid-friendly Disney World is a 'Sensorial Interface' providing a 'neatly packaged executive summary' of the texts on which the commodified Disney characters are based (Stephenson 1999, pp. 50–3).

Simone Murray got a similar feeling from her visit to Fox Studios Australia where content from Fox and other News Corp subsidiaries is 'fashioned into commodities' that carry the message of News branding. This emphasis on brand loyalty leads to the 'complexities and nuances' of individual texts being 'subordinate to their role as portals to News Corporation content and services as a whole' (Murray 2005, pp. 416–17).

These examples highlight the convergence of content and platforms made possible by the digital revolution. But Murray also identifies two 'preceding and interrelated' aspects of convergence: ownership and technology (p. 417). The commercial convergence really began sometime in the 1980s, before the technological revolution, and it was kicked off by the ideological push for deregulation of the global market. This led to fierce competition between the largest fifty or so media corporations and the eventual whittling down of the pool to a handful of around ten mega-corporations by the late 1990s. Once these commercial structures were in place, the remaining oligopoly companies were in a position to take advantage of the digital technologies. They were able to store, copy, and manufacture copies of their product (videos, television shows, music, movies) through 'inter-operable systems'

(Murray 2005, p. 418) that allowed the content to be transferred from one delivery system to another quickly and at relatively low cost. Neal Stephenson maps a similar trajectory for the global computing industry as it grew from the 1970s on, and two rival monopolies rose to dominate the market. One is Microsoft, which has managed to corner the global market for operating systems and consumer software for PCs. The other is Apple, which built its fortune on the manufacture of a unique hardware system (MacIntosh) and has now become one of the largest suppliers of personal computing and entertainment hardware in the world. These new vectors and new information technologies can be harnessed for public good and the benefit of humanity, or they can be used to further control, atomise, and oppress us. One future is utopian, the other darkly dystopian. Humans have the unique capacity to imagine how they might want their future to look and there is an interesting history of such imagining informing a genre of writing that goes back hundreds, if not thousands, of years. In the modern world, we call most of this imaginative writing 'science fiction'; in earlier times it was known as 'utopian' literature. It appeared in novels and in political tracts translated from the early Greek. We can even say that the early chapters of Genesis—the Creation and Fall—is a parable that illustrates the dialectic between utopia and dystopia. We will return to this theme, but now we turn our attention to one manifestation of a utopian view of technology, what we call 'digital determinism'.

Digital determinism: A postmodern commodity fetish

At the height of the dot.com boom in the 1990s and right up till the dot.com bust in the final years of the last century, many media theorists and Internet pundits were saying some pretty foolish things about the new digital technologies and their capacity to fundamentally alter our world. If you believed only half of what you read at the time, the Internet and peripheral communications technologies would deliver a wireless utopia.

While we don't disagree that digital technologies can provide the capacity for 'an age of technological abundance' (Barr 2000, p. 29), the utopia that the proponents of the digital revolution saw in this promising future has yet to be realised. It is the same promising future that proponents of postmodern media studies could also see, illuminated by the blue glow of millions of PCs, iPods, mobile phones, and MP3 players. It was an information future where connectivity, networking, and downloading meant a level playing field. In this scenario the dirty factories of late capitalism are replaced by the green and clean knowledge economy, based on cultural diversity, accessibility, and trendy gonzo niche marketing (Hirst 2004). This leads to our second argument, that digital determinism is also a variant of the cultural determinism of postmodern theory. This is a tendency in postmodernism to play down the 'darker side' of capitalism in favour of an 'effervescent enthusiasm' for manifestations of suburban popular culture within a pluralist regime of 'sliding signifiers, simulacra and spectacle' in which anything and everything can be celebrated and economic divisions of class can be ignored (Dyer-Witherford 1999, pp. 58–9)

It is postmodernist cultural theorists such as John Hartley who ultimately fall back on a 'cultural determinist' position that is as flawed as the model of economic determinism they seek to criticise. Hartley's position is based on the false and misleading assumption that: 'Culture—the discursive, media, knowledge-producing and sense-making sphere of life—*might itself determine* such matters as class, conflict and the state' (Hartley 1996, p. 276, emphasis added).

Digital determinism is another aspect of the technology fetishism of postmodern theory and shares many of the attributes of Hartley's cultural determinism. We take the position that digital determinism and cultural determinism are variants of the same technological determinist ideology and that they both exist as a result of reification—the process of developing ideologies out of the relations of production as seemingly independent of them, as 'objective' and somehow outside human intervention. This overlap between digital and cultural determinism is displayed in a unique way by a speech by Howard Finberg at the opening of 'Newsplex', a 'prototype newsroom of the future':

> [T]here is no single culture that resides in our media organizations ... [T]here are competing cultures: for example the clash of visuals versus the written word is a cultural quarrel. Convergence actually increases the complexity of cultural relationships within a newsroom, within a company, and within the corporate boardroom. (Finberg 2002)

The title of the speech was 'Convergence and the Corporate Boardroom', and 'convergence' has rapidly become the digital utopians' code word for the digital revolution in mass communication, journalism, and the media. Finberg's speech displays aspects of the reified view from the media boardroom when he discusses what he calls the 'social suppression of the radical potential of new technology', and adds, 'You could just call it denial.' As we mentioned earlier, the radical meme of the digital revolution has been co-opted into the boardrooms of Wall Street and the 'big end' of town.

Writing during the heady days of the dot.com boom in the late 1990s, but unfortunately published on the cusp of the crash, Australian media theorist Trevor Barr also falls into the trap of digital determinism: 'If there is any aspect of contemporary information society that is clearly revolutionary it is the technical capability, reach and intelligence of information networks' (Barr 2000, p. 29).

This is what we call the 'digital utopia' formulation; it invests the hardware with the agency of radical social change inherent in the use of the term 'revolution'. It is a big call to make and one that is, in our view, unsustainable in the face of the growing digital divide, the gap between the information-'rich' and the information-'poor', which, ironically enough, seems to follow the same territorial patterns as other indicators of growing gaps in the distribution of social and individual wealth, such as income, ethnicity, education, healthcare, and life expectancy.

A number of issues in the debate about emerging communication and news technologies in the digital age impinge on the question of 'determination'. Do aspects of one particular element in an equation have an overly determining effect on others? In other words, can one element, such as 'technology' or 'culture', have more importance in determining the ensemble of emotional attitudes that constitute an ideology? For instance, can the economic relations of production determine in a fixed sense all other social relations? Philosophically, this is an important debate in media studies as a whole. It rages between those who reject any form of determination in social relations and accuse Marxists of being 'economic determinists' and others who believe that many aspects of cultural studies and postmodern theory are predicated on their own forms of technological and cultural determinism. In short, the pejorative 'determinism' or 'determinist' implies the *mistaken* privileging of one element over another. No one, it seems, wants this accusation and insult hurled at them or their work. We prefer Mosco's formulation of 'mutual constitution'.

Instead of the promised utopia of digital connectivity, it's business as usual for the international media corporations. The links between digitised media corporations and the general fund of global capital have also been strengthened; international alcoholic beverage producers now control movie and music studios as they seek both vertical and horizontal integration in the leisure market (Wayne 2003, pp. 64–6). According to the World Association of Newspapers (WAN), audiences for web-based news have increased by over 350 per cent since 2000, while the circulation of printed copies globally was down across the 208 countries surveyed (BBC 2004). The association's annual report, covered by BBC News online, mentioned the 'digital revolution', 'ceaseless technological change', 'financial constraints', and 'the need to redefine relations with readers' as the greatest challenges: 'For editors and journalists, the challenge is to identify what aspects of this [digital] revolution they should invest in, and what is potentially dangerous for the profession, speakers at the WAN congress agreed' (BBC 2004).

The problems with technological determinism are twofold:

> The common feature of technological determinism is that it levers technology, its development, implementation and effects out of the social relations in which they are embedded, thus a) marginalizing or removing the social relations from analysis and b) ascribing powers and characteristics to technology which are the result of social relations between people, rather than properties intrinsic to things. (Wayne 2003, p. 40)

The essential attribute of technological determinism in the current period is its total reliance on digital technologies for its arguments and prognosis. In a sense it is a subspecies—digital determinism. It is a view that sees the 'abundance' of digital recording devices, in particular the digital video camera, combined with the networking power of the Internet, as somehow being themselves agents of social liberation. In some cases the proponents of this new 'revolution' in communication are themselves in denial about their own determinism. Take, for instance, the American journalism educator and theorist John Pavlik:

> I propose that although convergence is happening, it is neither inevitable nor necessarily good. I do not offer a technologically deterministic view of new

> media. Rather, I assert that convergence merely holds the promise of a better, more efficient, more democratic medium for journalism and the public in the twenty-first century. (Pavlik 2000, p. xiii)

In Pavlik's view convergence and the arrival of new technologies are a fulcrum for the leverage of change in journalistic and media content, context, processes, and production values. Despite his denial of digital determinism, what Pavlik does claim is that media convergence 'holds the promise' that it can transform journalism into a 'more democratic' medium. This, too, is a mantra of the digital determinists and a promise that remains unfulfilled. As well, he argues, the new (technology-driven) media encourage a 'realignment' in the pattern of relationships between reporters and editors, between editors and owners, and between news organisations and audiences. There is certainly a degree of realignment as we discuss below in our comments on the changing reportorial community (see chapter 11), but what John Pavlik and others who have been seduced by the hype surrounding digital media don't see is the dialectical constraints that limit the utopian elements of their vision and insert a decidedly dystopian tint to their rose-coloured video screens.

Before proceeding to explore the utopian and dystopian possibilities of the new communication technologies, we want to outline a brief history of the traditional media in terms of its technological, commercial, and social development over the 20th century.

WHAT TIM RECKONS

There are certainly concerns for the traditional media companies about how they can make money in the converged and commoditised future. Interestingly, most of Google's moves away from its web search roots are being driven by investors keen to see it lock in guaranteed revenue streams. Given its heritage in usability and content aggregation, Google will be a major player in the mainstream media world, but I doubt it can become a monopoly. It will share the market with groups such as eBay, Amazon, or even the Catholic Church—in short, anyone that can maintain communities of users and can deliver them targeted content and services.

Content is nothing without distribution. At present we lack the physical infrastructure needed to deliver on the promises of converged media, such as video-on-demand or mobile video telephony. But it's on the way. The next challenge is building the business case for the virtual distribution system and how content companies might choose to market their material.

In theory, the Internet users of the future should be able to access anything they want, direct from the source. More likely, the mass market will obtain content from a trusted brand acting as a middleman between it and the content generators. Traditional media companies need to establish whether they will be content producers or distributors.

KEY POINTS

The key points from this chapter are:

- 'New' technologies are not new; technological development and technological change have been part of the human experience since the beginning.
- Technology does not occur or exist in a vacuum; it has always had social implications.
- Like the term 'technology', the term 'convergence' has a long history, and is in fact the key means by which technologies change; technological change is a dialectical process in which convergence creates divergence and 'fragmentation'.
- The positive and negative aspects of technology are dialectically aligned and can be found in nearly all digital commodities, as well as within the social relations of digital production systems.

CLASS DISCUSSION: TECHNOPHOBE OR TECHNOPHILE?

1 Draw up a continuum line with technophobe and one end and technophile at the other.

  (a) Think about your own position somewhere along that line and be prepared to defend it in a discussion.

  (b) Where do you think most people fit between technophobia and technophilia? Why do you think the majority subscribes to the view you suggest they have?

  (c) Where do technomania and technobabble fit on this spectrum?

2 What term could you use to describe the midpoint where it is possible to have what we might call a 'sensible' view of the pros and cons of technology?

3 What would you imagine is a good definition of a 'technoklutz'?

PART 2

HOT METAL TO HOTMAIL: THE (RECENT) HISTORY OF MASS COMMUNICATION

In part II our first task is to outline a short history of the mass media and mass communication. We want to concentrate on the last 200 years, but the story is much older than that. For the sake of convenience and to follow a logical historical progression, we have divided the chapters in this part according to the individual media type: print, photography and film, and radio and television; our final chapter in part II examines the ways in which analogue media have been regulated and the ethico-legal framework in which they operate. At the same time, this structure allows us to develop the arguments about the complex social relations and the tension—the dialectic—that draws old and new into conflict.

Each chapter discusses a particular set of technologies—the combination of science, the means of production, and the social relations of work and exchange—within our broader framework of process, regulation, ethics, and institutions. The sequence of chapters is also logical because by demonstrating the historical development of individual technologies, we can trace the important links between them. The pace and sequencing of scientific research, commercialisation, and eventual mass production relies on extension and continuous modification of existing technologies, as much as it does on totally new ideas. For example, the interactive and highly graphic nature of Internet communication relies on our deeply embedded understanding of print, photography, video, and audio technologies.

Increasingly our computers are also televisions, newspapers, research libraries, video archives, and shopping malls. This is convergence in action. Old technologies are rarely abandoned entirely; more often than not they are merely modified, recycled, and plugged in to newer modes.

What is important and consistent within our historical account is the paramount importance of social context in determining the ultimate form and purpose of communication and broadcasting technology. An historical narrative relies on our understanding of what was happening broadly in societies in which important new technologies began to emerge. It is therefore necessary to 'read' the history of technological development, innovation, and convergence in the mass media in the context of economic, political, and cultural events and trends that occur in combination with advances in social applications of new means of production and communication.

OBJECTIVES

After reading this part you will have some understanding of the following:

- how the mechanics and aesthetics of mass communication are derived from the principles of more traditional arts and crafts, such as engraving, painting, printing, photography, theatre, recording musical performance, and cinema;
- how patterns of communication are established in relation to social conditions and needs and how they tend to follow similar paths to that of global economic expansion and investment;
- how modern newspapers, magazines, broadcasting, and mass communication began to develop their modern industrial form, following dramatic economic, political, and social changes in 19th-century Europe and the 'New World';
- the links and relationships between the technologies of the mass media and the social relations of mass communication.

5 FROM GUTENBERG TO GLOBAL NEWS: A BRIEF HISTORY OF THE PRINT MEDIA

OBJECTIVES

This is not a comprehensive history of the print media, instead it provides several snapshot examples to illustrate the general points. It is highly unlikely that human society would be as advanced as it is today if printing had not been invented. According to Anthony Smith, printing, which became widespread in the 15th century, was 'the first revolution in the means of communicating information' (1980, p. 7). After reading this chapter you will begin to understand the importance of communications technology as a means of enabling humans to transform the world. Without printing, the spread of scientific knowledge would have been immeasurably slowed and it is unlikely that many of the major discoveries that we today regard as commonplace would have occurred. The objective of this chapter is to cover the following material:

- an historical overview of printing and why it is important as the first mechanical means of mass communication;

- how the printed word was at the heart of convergent media technologies, and the role printing still plays today;
- how the publishing industry today can be considered a form of broadcast mass media and how it is also affected by the growing trend towards narrowcasting in all types of media;
- an appreciation of the historical links between the commercial mass media and other important social, technological, economic, and political changes from the 19th to the 21st centuries.

KEYWORDS

broadsheet
font (or typefont)
killer application
tabloid (compact)
typeface
typography

Print culture

In the James Bond film *Tomorrow Never Dies* (1997), the villain is media mogul Elliott Carver (reputedly based on Rupert Murdoch). Carver engineers a conflict between China and Britain timed to coincide with the launch of his new global satellite TV network. He tells his editors:

> 'Hold the presses ... we have the perfect story with which to launch our satellite news network tonight. It seems a small crisis is brewing in the South China seas. I want full newspaper coverage! I want magazine stories! I want books! I want films! I want TV! I want radio! I want us on the air 24 hours a day ... and a billion people around this planet will watch it, hear it and read about it on the Carver media group. There's no news like bad news.' (*Tomorrow Never Dies* 1997, Scene 5)

Aboriginal rock art in Kakadu National Park in northern Australia is a long way from the high jinks and high tech of a Bond film, but Nourlangie Rock is an example of one of the earliest and most enduring forms of mass communication: mixing muds to make paint, and making messages out of the mud by applying it to a hard, durable surface where it could be witnessed by all who came by.

The ancients had mass communication, but their forms of mass communication were limited to those who could gather in one place. Thus the plays of Euripides could only been seen in amphitheatres such as those of Corinth or Ephesus; the stone obelisks of the Babylonians and Egyptians stood in the sand beside the great rivers; and Homer's tales of Troy were passed down by oral transmission—stories sung and told and retold, before finally being written down about 750 bc.

It is not until the invention of moveable type and the printing press that communication media became independent of their site of production. Until this point, the Aboriginal art remained fixed on the rock face, the Greek tragedies were restricted to the amphitheatre, and the Babylonian obelisks remained rooted in the sand. Even books, which were produced by the arduous process of copying by hand, tended to remain where they were created. In the 7th century ad, monks from Iona, in Scotland, established a priory on Lindisfarne Island in north-eastern England. Here they produced one of the great treasures of the Anglo-Saxon world, the Lindisfarne Gospels, by hand. But only those who visited this windy isle, just south of the border between Scotland and England, could see and read these Gospels for themselves. While medieval books did travel to some extent, the advent of printing brought a new independence to the written word.

So modern mass communication is the liberation of the communication form from its place of creation. As time has passed, the place of production has become even less important to the form of communication. In the 19th century, if you lived in the Torres Straits, and you wanted to read *The Times*, you waited for months until it was delivered, by ship, from London. In the 20th century, you had *The Times* delivered, again in hard copy, by air freight, from London a day or so after publication. In the 21st century, you, the reader, can access *The Times* online anytime, and you can access regular news updates through the day or night. In the September quarter of 2005, *The Guardian* newspaper printed 404 187 hard copies for circulation to its customers, and claimed a readership of 1 215 000. In the same quarter, the *Guardian Online* had 12 261 601 unique users on its website. This is ten times the readership of the print edition, and thirty times the readership of the print circulation.

We understand the modern print media today as newspapers and magazines, what we generally call periodicals: daily newspapers, the news weeklies, reviews, and monthly magazines, journals, and digests; there is usually a defined interval or 'period' between publication dates. Most of you are probably also aware that the worldwide market for printed periodicals is fluctuating: niche magazines come and go; the number of daily newspapers is falling. Age differences in readership are also telling. The baby-boomer generation, now in their early fifties to late sixties, are the last great newspaper-reading generation. Gen-X, adults who are now in their mid-thirties, and anyone younger are unlikely to be regular newspaper readers.

The variety and scope of glossy magazines now aimed at younger markets has never been greater, but some would argue that the real 'choice' is between brands rather than ideas or ideologies. In the early years of the mass circulation print media the separation between readers was more likely to be along political lines, since newspapers and other periodicals were more partisan, propagandistic, and overtly proselytising.

The changes in culture of the mass print media over the last hundred years are profound and fascinating. The shift from agitational party press to capitalist conglomerate mirrors and documents the trajectory of the 18th- and 19th-century revolutionary bourgeoisie into the moribund and corrosive edifice of capitalism today.

Gutenberg

It was Johann Gutenberg (*c.* 1398–1468) who developed the machinery that today has become the modern printing press. While primitive forms of printing had been developed in China and Korea before Gutenberg's time, in 1452 the German metal and stone smith began the print run of 200 copies of what became known as the Gutenberg Bible.

The development of printing had a number of immediate cultural effects. It encouraged literacy, it disseminated ideas more rapidly, and it fostered greater standardisation of texts, which had previously been copied by hand. Gutenberg's Bible was based on the Vulgate, the Latin translation of *c.* 380 ad. The expansion of the technology of printing also had a profound effect on the intellectual and political order of the day. The Protestant Reformation, which began in 1517 with Martin Luther's rebellion against the Roman Catholic Church, destroyed the pre-eminent position of that institution in Europe. Not only did printing allow people to read the Bible for themselves, and in their own vernacular, but the availability of printing presses also enabled the Protestants to print posters, handbills, and other propaganda to promote their cause. Early attempts to publish the Bible in English had been resisted by the ecclesiastical authorities. William Tyndale was burned at the stake in 1536 for his efforts.

Newspapers, first in the form of 'news books' and then as 'news sheets', were published by entrepreneurial printers who saw these evolving forms of publication as a way of selling more printing. As Sigfrid Steinberg notes, the social impact of mass printing was even more profound:

> Down to the end of the seventeenth century, both literacy and leisure were virtually confined to scholars and 'gentlemen'; during the eighteenth century, the commercial middle class and especially womankind acquired a taste for reading; and the introduction in the nineteenth century of compulsory school attendance even widened the circle of potential readers. (Steinberg 1961, p. 228)

Newspapers were characterised by diversity of content and periodicity of appearance. It was in Basel in Switzerland in 1566 that the first prototypical newspapers were published. From the earliest days, the aim was to entertain and inform (Steinberg 1961, p. 240).

While the Egyptians and others in the ancient Middle East used papyrus to make a primitive form of writing paper, it was in China over 2000 years before the present that paper-making became a highly sophisticated art. Chinese paper-manufacturing techniques reached Europe by way of trade with the Arab world between the 5th and 10th centuries ad. Unlike the Chinese, who used tree pulp, the Arabs used rags as the base for their paper. By the end of the 13th century, paper-making processes had spread to Germany, where the first mill was built at Nuremberg in 1390. The development of printing technologies placed huge demands on rags as a source of paper, but it was not until 1843 that the use of wood pulp for paper manufacture was patented. In the first part of the 19th century all the processes of hand manufacture were mechanised. The second half of that century brought advances in the web width of the paper manufactured, which paved the way for web offset printing, and the fast, efficient production of daily newspapers. Even industrialised paper production retains something of its origins as art: paper is made in various weights or thicknesses, in various textures, colours, and sizes. The commercialisation of printing on cheap, mass-produced paper was an important engine of economic and cultural change from the 14th to the 19th centuries.

Journalism and the Age of Revolution

The traditions of media freedom we hold dear today were hard won in Britain during the 17th and 18th centuries as governments tried variously to license and tax newspapers, tax advertising, and suppress the reporting of Parliament. It was only after repeal of the Stamp Act in 1855 that newspaper design as we know it became possible. Daniel Defoe, (1660–1731), best known now as the author of the novel *Robinson Crusoe* (published 1719), is sometimes called the father of modern journalism. A prolific pamphleteer and propagandist, Defoe was also a satirist, who savaged the attitudes of the Anglican establishment. For this he was arrested and imprisoned. Between 1704 and 1713 he produced a periodical called *Review*, at first weekly, then tri-weekly, upon which his reputation as a journalist is based.

Defoe was an indefatigable proponent of the freedom of the press, as shown in his *Essay on the Regulation of the Press*:

> ALL Men pretend the Licentiousness of the Press to be a publick Grievance, but it is much easier to say it is so, than to prove it, or prescribe a proper Remedy; nor is it the easiest Grievance to Cure. To put a general stop to publick Printing, would be a check to Learning, a Prohibition of Knowledge, and make Instruction Contraband: And as Printing has been own'd to be the most useful Invention ever found out, in order to polish the Learned World, make men Polite, and encrease the Knowledge of Letters, and thereby all useful Arts and Sciences; so the high Perfection of Human Knowledge must be at a stand, Improvements stop, and the Knowledge of Letters decay in the Kingdom, if a general Interruption should be put to the Press. (Defoe 1704)

The relatively modern institution of journalism as we know it had its beginnings in the radical pamphleteers of the French and American revolutions of the 18th and early 19th centuries. News sheets were circulated to inform an active citizenry and they struggled against the 'tax on knowledge' that many European governments imposed on the news magazines of the 17th and 18th centuries. As Irene Collins wrote in her introduction to *The Government and the Newspaper Press in France 1814–1881* (1959), 'Liberty of the press has long been one of the most cherished freedoms', a freedom that Frenchmen came to enjoy (within limits) after 1819: 'The [French] press laws of 1819 settled for once and for all that newspapers were entitled to as much liberty as books, and that liberty could not be regarded as compatible with the use of censorship' (Collins 1959, p. ix).

This monumental struggle for 'freedom of the press' is well documented, but in England and the new world, freedom from the newspaper tax was quickly replaced with a press beholden to the interests of the rich and powerful bourgeoisie that came to own it (Hollis 1970; Walker 1976; McQueen 1977; Bowman 1988; Williams 1989; Schultz 1994, 1998; Engel 1996; Hartley 1996; Williams 1997).

As Kevin Williams points out, the history of journalism and the news media can only be fully appreciated if one takes into account 'the countervailing pulls on the mass media' exercised by public opinion on one hand and 'powerful institutions in society' on the other (1997, p. 5). Dennis Cryle's (1997) case study of status among journalists in colonial Australia and Cyril Pearl's excellent *Wild Men of Sydney* (1977) are two examples of histories that factor this contradiction into their narrative accounts. However, the modern newspaper could not exist without the convergence of other industrial technologies of mechanical printing.

Typography, telegraphy, telephony, and photography converge to make 'news'

The typefonts in our word processors—such as Arial, Garamond, and Times Roman—have a 500-year history. There are four different classification of type: serif, sans serif, script or manuscript, and display, although there is some debate among the aficionados of typography about the boundaries of the classification system (Bringhurst 1992). Within each of these basic classifications, typefonts are grouped in families. So a common serif typeface such as Times Roman will have medium, bold, italics, extended, and condensed forms, all of which are part of the Times Roman family of fonts. A *serif* typeface is defined as one having flourishes or curls on the ascenders and descender of the letter; whereas a *sans serif* typeface is one without such adornments—sans meaning 'without'.

TYPEFACE, FONT, OR TYPEFONT

The characteristic styling of the letters of the alphabet, particularly through the ascenders and descenders of individual letters, to create a particular look. Serif (with curly bits) and sans serif (without curly bits) are the two main forms of type. Fonts can also be rendered in bold, italic, condensed, and extended forms.

Eric Gill (1882–1940) was an artist, sculptor, calligrapher, and graphic designer. He is best remembered for the Gill Sans typeface produced in the mid-1920s, which was based on the sans serif lettering style developed by his teacher Edward Johnston. Gill Sans was the typeface chosen for the signage on the London Underground. In the 1930s Gill created a series of sculptured works for public buildings, most notably for Broadcasting House, home of the BBC in London, and the League of Nations building in Geneva.

Across the Atlantic, typographer M. F. Benton (1872–1948) studied engineering at Cornell University, then joined his father in the American Typefounders Company, where he produced some 180 different fonts, including Franklin Gothic and Century Schoolbook. He also reinterpreted the classic faces of Bodoni and Garamond.

Changing styles in art and architecture are reflected in typography. The Bauhaus school of design, with its philosophy of integrating art and engineering, flourished in Weimar Germany. Led by architect Walter Gropius and designer Herbert Bayer, the Bauhaus influenced architecture, industrial design, and typography with its simplicity of form and clarity of line, not just in Europe but also in the United States. The typefonts developed by the Bauhaus School are needless to say, exemplars of sans serif type design.

TYPOGRAPHY

The study, or the art, of understanding and creating typefonts.

The Industrial Revolution brought changes in printing and pre-press technologies, such as Koenig's steam-powered press (1814), Hoe's rotary press (1846), and Mergenthaler's Linotype machines (1885), innovations that sped up the production of all printed material. It was, however, the convergence of printing with two other technological innovations, the electric telegraph and the photograph, that gave rise to mass circulation newspapers in the late 19th century. The railways, of course, also played a key role in the distribution of the popular new mass medium. We will examine the history of industrial journalism by briefly looking at Australian, British, and American examples.

Print journalism in 19th-century Australia

In the 19th century, Australian newspapers were very much the province of the individual proprietor, who was usually the main writer, editorialist, and printer. What few contributors they had were drawn from the ranks of 'educated men' with a background in the Church or an English university education. But there was also public disquiet about the lack of professionalism, even at this time. One publication, the *Victorian Review*, advocated that a Chair of Journalism be established in an Australian university 'to train up a race of journalists impressed with the responsibility of the profession they embraced and competent to discharge the function they would be required to perform' (*Victorian Review* cited in Lloyd 1985, p. 19).

There were very few reporters as such on the early colonial newspapers. In the main they were managed and produced by the owner with the help of one or two compositors, a clerk, and a small team of printers (Mayer 1968, p. 188). The colonial newspapers, like those in England, were divided politically and tended to attract, as their owners and patrons, men who had political ambitions. Henry Mayer provides a long list of colonial politicians who either owned or wrote for the major newspapers of their day. As he notes, being associated with a newspaper was 'one road to political success' (p. 189). By the 1870s more newspapers were employing reporters, but their status in colonial society was fairly low. According to some accounts of the time, journalists were lacking in morals, learning, and self-respect. Colonial journalists had an 'ambiguous' status according to Mayer: 'It seems to have been taken for granted by most writers that journalists were not just "ordinary" workers. Yet they did not seem to fit into the picture of a profession, and certainly did not earn professional rewards' (Mayer 1968, p. 191).

There seems little doubt that in colonial Australia working for a newspaper in any capacity, but particularly as a reporter, was seen by many as a 'disreputable profession'. This was particularly so until the latter years of the 19th century when changing production routines began to improve both the professional standing and the public reputation of news workers (Cryle 1997b). But this respectability also had its price. The colonial journalist came to be regarded in much the same light as a clerk or scribe, 'using skills similar to those of other white-collar workers', many of whom regarded their working assignments as 'temporary and tedious, rather than as the pinnacle of their careers' (Cryle 1997a, p. 6).

When the founder of the journalists' union, Bertie Cook, became a journalist in about 1890, newspaper reporting was more a craft than a profession. Lloyd describes the conditions as 'irregular entry, lack of formal training, absence of professional standards, existence of strong newspaper craft unions, paternalistic proprietors and editors'. At the time, the Australian newspaper industry was barely ninety years old (Lloyd 1985, p. 15).

By the end of the 19th century Australian journalism had largely outgrown the image of the Bohemian and the wild colonial boy, no doubt because of the greater discipline required of the commercial newsroom. While a formal cadet system did not exist, there was some on-the-job training and it was widely accepted that to be a journalist one had to have natural abilities and that formal education was a secondary requirement (Lloyd 1985, p. 29). In 1913, the reporter Henry Gullet described recruitment to Australian journalism as a haphazard process 'of unofficial selection and individual solitary impulse which it is scarcely possible to define ... certainly it did not involve much efficiency in the sort of education imparted by schools' (p. 29).

Up to a point, Lord Copper: Media magnatism (*sic*)

Some of the most famous mastheads in newspaper history were launched in the last decade of the 19th century, and the first decade of the 20th. The rise of the popular press in the late 19th century brought with it the beginning of a long and dishonourable tradition of media proprietors interfering in, and influencing, politics. Alfred Pearson (1866–1921), who founded the *Daily Express* in 1900, strongly supported Joseph Chamberlain's policies on free trade, organising the pro-free trade Tariff Reform League in 1903.

Lord Northcliffe (Alfred Harmsworth 1865–1922), co-founder of the *Daily Mail*, was a kingmaker in the British governments before and during World War I. He advocated conscription at the outbreak of World War I and criticised Lord Kitchener, the Secretary of State for War and a hero in the classic Victorian mould, describing Kitchener's death at sea in 1916 as a stroke of good fortune for the British Empire. He used his papers to successfully campaign against the wartime Prime Minister H. H. Asquith, whose replacement David Lloyd George then invited Northcliffe (as a Member of the House of Lords) into the Cabinet to silence him. Northcliffe refused. His brother, Lord Rothermere (Harold Harmsworth 1868–1944), did accept appointment as Air Minister in 1917.

Yet Rothermere was even more extreme than Northcliffe in his views. He published the fake Zinoviev Letter in the days before the 1924 British general election, which led to the defeat of the incumbent Labour Government led by Ramsay McDonald. He supported the policy of appeasement in the 1930s, and an infamous article in 1934 praised the British fascists led by Sir Oswald Mosley. Rothermere did not tolerate being contradicted. He was satirised by Evelyn Waugh (1903–66) in *Scoop* (1938) as the media magnate Lord Copper, whose staff when they disagreed with him would utter the now immortal phrase, 'Up to a point, Lord Copper' as a way of softening their criticism (Waugh 1943, p. 41).

Then there was the Machiavellian Lord Beaverbrook (1879–1964). Born Max Aitkin, he was a Canadian thruster who, having made his fortune in Canada, moved to Britain in 1910, where he acquired the London *Globe* and a knighthood, and soon after secured a seat in the House of Commons as a Conservative. There he ingratiated himself with successive players in the British Cabinet, notably Bonar Law and Lloyd George, the radical Liberal who later ennobled him in 1916. Beaverbrook served briefly as Minister for Information in 1918. Conveniently for those in power, Beaverbrook had purchased the *Daily Express* in 1916, founded the *Sunday Express* in 1921, and acquired the *Evening Standard* in 1929. Beaverbrook promoted his papers along the lines pioneered by Harmsworth at the *Daily Mail*, but politics was his metier. He subsequently served in Churchill's national government Minister for Aircraft Production (1940–41), Minister of Supply (1941–42), Minister of War Production (1942), and Lord Privy Seal (1943–45) during World War II. Beaverbrook was a campaigning proprietor who argued that the weight of media-led public opinion could change public policy. As history shows, his campaigns of the 1930s in support of King Edward VIII, and on imperial free trade, failed.

Across the Atlantic William Randolph Hearst (1863–1951) was, like Beaverbrook, a newspaper owner who dabbled in politics. San Francisco-born and Harvard-educated, Hearst took over the San Francisco *Examiner* in 1887, and expanded it into a nationwide empire of publications. His infamy, however, came from his tenure as editor of the New York *Journal* in the lead-up to the Spanish American War in the late 1890s. Indeed, it is arguable that the Spanish American War would not have occurred without Hearst's jingoism. In 1903 he was elected to the US Congress for two terms as a Democrat, proposed himself as the Democratic nominee for President in 1904, and then unsuccessfully contested the mayoralty of New York in 1906. He then formed his own party to promote his candidacy for mayor, unsuccessfully. Hearst is best known to popular culture for providing the character of Charles Foster Kane in the 1941 screen classic *Citizen Kane* directed by Orson Welles, and featuring Welles as Kane. Nominated for nine Oscars, and winning only one (Best Screenplay), the film made the Hollywood smart set uneasy, and Hearst's own papers were forbidden to mention it (Swanberg 1961; Nasaw 2000).

The Brass Check

> Journalism is one of the devices whereby industrial autocracy keeps its control over political democracy ... Not hyperbolically and contemptuously, but literally and with scientific precision, we define Journalism in America as

> the business and practice of presenting the news of the day in the interest of economic privilege. (Sinclair 1928, p. 222)

Upton Sinclair's view of American journalism in the 1920s is not very flattering, but it is close to what we might call the 'political economy' view adopted in this book. To unpack this, and to understand what it means for the reportorial community today (see chapter 11), we have to understand Sinclair's position and where it came from. Sinclair's study of American journalism, first published in 1920, was called *The Brass Check*. The title is a reference to the token issued to a customer in a brothel. Sinclair argues that American journalism in the first part of the 20th century had been prostituted to the service of big business. With the obvious caveats about geographic and cultural differences, Sinclair's analysis is broadly applicable across the capitalist world for the time he was writing *The Brass Check*.

Upton Sinclair (1878–1968) was a muckraking journalist and political activist who rose to fame and notoriety in the United States upon publication of his novel *The Jungle* in 1906. Though it was presented as fiction, *The Jungle* was an exposé of the harsh lives of meatworkers in the Chicago stockyards. Sinclair was a prolific writer and social campaigner. Over his life he wrote ninety-two books and twenty-nine political pamphlets, many of them, like *The Brass Check*, self-published because the commercial publishers had blacklisted him (McChesney & Scott 2003). Sinclair was also a utopian socialist and in 1907 wrote a play called *The Millennium: A comedy of the year 2000*, which was published as a novel in 1924 (Sinclair 2000). The story begins with a cataclysmic event—the detonation of a nuclear 'radiumite' bomb that kills the entire world's population, except for eleven people. This small group then sets about building a utopian commune just outside New York. The plot is very similar to Sinclair's own life; he attempted to establish a utopian commune that failed spectacularly when the group's compound burned to the ground in a disastrous fire.

When Sinclair was preparing material for *The Brass Check* it was a time of rapid change and political turbulence, and socialists were a significant force on the American (and indeed the world) political landscape. Two revolutions in Russia (1905 and 1917) brought the politically motivated working class onto the world stage. Working-class militancy was on the rise and the capitalist class was panicked into responding, usually with violence, but always through the propaganda arm of the ruling elite—its newspapers and later radio stations (McChesney & Scott 2003). Of course, by the 1960s the Western world was enjoying a postwar economic boom and consumerism was the new ideology of social compliance. By the mid-1960s journalism has lost all the radical potency of the inter-war years and journalists, by and large, were complacent in their social attitudes—the owner had the right to set the news agenda and the system of free enterprise was endlessly promoted as the pinnacle of social organisation.

Things were vastly different at the beginning of the 20th century. Newspapers were still fairly progressive and partisan as they had been in the 19th century and no single newspaper was able to dominate the market as it might today. For example, for many years the Australian Labor Party published a daily paper in Sydney (the *Daily Mail*) that was eventually sold to the Packer family and then to Rupert Murdoch. Thus Sinclair was writing at a time when there was upheaval and change. The newspaper market began to act like most other markets and ownership became more concentrated. The number of published titles fell and advertising became the largest source of revenue. By 1920 newspaper publishing had become big business (McChesney and Scott 2003, pp. xv–xvii). This shift towards monopoly and oligopoly led to what became known as the 'crisis' in American journalism. It was, in essence, a struggle between those, like Sinclair, who believed in progressive 'muckraking' journalism that championed the cause of the downtrodden against the rise of monopoly capitalism, and those like Joseph Pulitzer and Randolph Hearst, who promoted the salacious, bawdy, entertaining, and less newsworthy 'yellow' journalism. According to McChesney & Scott in their introduction to a 2003 reprint of *The Brass Check*, 'The hallowed obligation of the democratic press to accurately report public affairs was brushed aside by a wave of gimmicky features, fakery, and hysterical headlines' (p. xvii).

It was the working out of this dialectic—excessive commercialism struggling with and against the tradition of the muckrakers and progressive journalists—that eventually led to the development of what we might now call 'professional' journalism. It was a time when a reporter's training became based on the creed of objectivity and on the ideology of pluralism—of course within the unchallenged context of a free market for ideas. There were no American journalism schools in 1900, but by 1915 they were well established at major universities right across the nation. There were two university courses for journalists in Australia by 1921, at the University of Western Australia and the University of Queensland. McChesney and Scott argue, and we'd agree, that the rise of professionalism in American journalism at this time was a response to the so-called yellow journalism and also to the critique of left-wing writers such as Sinclair and others about the 'corruption, dishonesty, and class bias of journalism'. This critique was a direct challenge to the power of the press barons of the day; 'professionalism' was their 'tame' solution (p. xix).

We can also make some comments about the role of newspaper technologies in the great changes that were taking place in the years before and just after World War I. Apart from the telegraph and a limited telephone network, there was little equipment around that would allow the reporter to gather much material from the relative comfort of the newspaper office. Instead, the reporter had to rely on personal observation and face-to-face interviews. This meant that the journalist was much closer, geographically, emotionally, and socially, to his or her sources. It was this physical, economic, cultural, and political closeness that produced reporters like Upton Sinclair and made them active radicals. As the technologies of newsgathering gained a hold in the newsroom, the distance between reporters and their sources increased. Newsgathering became much more about the transfer of information from similarly equipped centres of influence—the government bureaucracy and the large commercial firm—than a process of gathering from observation and discussion with ordinary people out on the street. The development of national newspaper chains and the reduced influence of purely 'local' papers also contributed to this process (an example of commercial convergence). Thus, while the shifting technologies were important, the most decisive shift was a social one: reporters were no longer part of the audience they *reported for*; they were much more closely aligned to the interests they *worked for* and more likely to share the worldview of the proprietor. As Upton Sinclair laments in *The Brass Check*, the bias in the modern press became pro-business and anti-labour. Sinclair called this the 'Empire of Business' and argued that it exercised four types of control over journalism in newspapers and magazines: 'First, ownership of the papers; second, ownership of the owners; third, advertising subsidies; and fourth, direct bribery. By these methods there exists in America a control of news and of current comment more absolute than any monopoly in any other industry' (Sinclair 1928, p. 241).

Katherine Graham and the *Washington Post*

Not all newspaper proprietors in the 20th century were as craven as Hearst or Beaverbrook and their cronies. Katherine Graham (1917–2001) was the publisher of the *Washington Post* as the Watergate scandal engulfed Richard Nixon's presidency in 1973. Under Graham, and her executive editor Ben Bradlee, the *Post* published the Pentagon Papers—a secret history of the Vietnam War prepared by the US government—and revelations about the Watergate break-in by investigative journalists Bob Woodward and Carl Bernstein. Graham became owner, and publisher, of the *Post* upon the death of her husband Phillip, who suicided in 1963. Her memoirs, *Personal History*, published in 1997, were awarded a Pulitzer Prize, particularly for her frank account of her husband's mental illness. The work of the *Post* was celebrated in the 1976 film *All The President's Men*, in which Robert Redford and Dustin Hoffman play Woodward and Bernstein. Perhaps ironically, Graham doesn't make an appearance in the film, with all the moral courage being focused on the character of Bradlee, a former White House correspondent for *Newsweek*, and a friend of President John Kennedy. Actor Jason Robards won a Best Supporting Actor Oscar for his portrayal of Bradlee. Of her own role, as the proprietor in the Watergate coverage, Graham wrote in 1997:

> I have often been credited with courage for backing our editors in Watergate. The truth is that I never felt there was much choice. There was never one major decisive moment when I, or anyone, could have suggested that we stop reporting the story. Watergate unfolded gradually. By the time the story had grown to the point where the size of it dawned on us, we had already waded deeply into its stream. Once I found myself in the deepest water in the middle of the current, there was no going back. (Graham 1997, p. D1)

While Graham's concept of proprietorship is one of supporting editors in the professional judgements they make, Rupert Murdoch is the obverse: an interventionist proprietor encouraging an editorial group-think across his empire.

Citizen Murdoch

> In any account of the information wars at the turn of the millennium, the question is what to make of Rupert Murdoch. On the one hand Murdoch is the archetypal modern media mogul, whose history illustrates the broad changes that have transformed the way the world communicates. Yet Murdoch is also a one-off. He has had a singular impact in the shaping and reshaping of the world's media industries for the last half century. (Chenoweth 2001, p. xiii)

In Jeffrey Archer's novel *The Fourth Estate* (1996), one of his characters, Keith Townsend, is obviously based on the international media mogul Rupert Murdoch. Townsend begins his newspaper career on a provincial paper in Australia, moves his operations to London and eventually into the American market—just like Murdoch. The novel's other protagonist, Armstrong, is a thinly disguised caricature of the late British newspaper baron and rogue Robert Maxwell.

In the 1940s the fictional Keith Townsend spends time apprenticed to another publisher where he observes: 'Surely in the end, however massive a paper's circulation was, the principal aim should be to make as large a return on your investment as possible' (Archer 1996, p. 150). This is a principle that Rupert Murdoch has firmly endorsed. He built his global media empire from humble beginnings—one afternoon newspaper in Adelaide. Now he is one of the most influential and powerful individual media owners on the planet. In the 1960s he was quick to buy into the young Australian television industry and also acquired Festival Records at a time when the pop music scene was about to burst open with fresh new talent and the spending power of affluent young baby-boomers. In the 1970s Murdoch expanded his newspaper empire by establishing the first national daily general newspaper in Australia and buying the *Daily Telegraph* from the Packer family. At the same time he began acquiring newspaper assets in Britain, further enhancing his reputation as a smart and ruthless businessman.

Famously, in the 1980s Murdoch took on the powerful British union movement by shifting his newspapers from their traditional home in London's Fleet Street to the decaying industrial suburb of Wapping. After a protracted battle, which included huge picket lines outside his factory, Murdoch won. He is credited with turning around declining profitability in the British newspaper industry by embracing new technology and downsizing his workforce of journalists and printers.

After this success Murdoch moved into the American media market and cemented his position as a global giant in the news and information business. He has acquired film studios, and satellite television assets, and has secured a foothold in the lucrative Chinese media market through his ownership of newspaper, magazine, and broadcasting assets. Murdoch's business acumen and success mark him as an important figure in the history of global communication industries in the 20th century. He appears regularly in our account and is now one of the key players in the transition from broadcasting to narrowcasting. In his public pronouncements, Murdoch appears to be keenly aware of the power of digital technologies and equally keen to ensure that News Corporation remains at the front line of change and chance.

The end of Fleet Street: Industrial processes win over craft

> [T]he shop floor at the *Express* was overmanned by a ratio of three to one, and … while wages made up its largest outgoings, there could be no hope of a modern newspaper group being able to make a profit. In the future someone was going to have to take on the unions. (Archer 1996, p. 150)

Archer's fictional account is closely modelled on exactly what Rupert Murdoch did with his English newspaper production when he moved it from the traditional home of English newspapers, Fleet Street in London, to Wapping in 1986. In the process of moving *The Times* and the *Sunday Times* to London's docklands area, he locked out the journalists' union with the full support of then Prime Minister Margaret Thatcher.

In the novel, journalists on the *Globe* newspaper complain to Keith Townsend about the poor working conditions in the new plant, prompting Archer to write: 'Once they were inside, few of them cared for the production-line atmosphere, [or] the modern keyboards and computers, which had replaced their old typewriters' (Archer 1996, p. 421). Murdoch's Wapping plant was the first newspaper office in the world to be fully computerised.

British journalist and author Raymond Snoddy wrote of how Murdoch's 1986 move to Wapping helped develop and entrench a competitive ideology and a feeling of distrust among the journalists who worked there. He notes that this was a direct result of the changed working conditions, which had destroyed collegiality in the newsroom: 'Most of the unions were left outside the gates at Wapping. Journalists were able to enter their copy directly into computer terminals, and, after editing on screen, their articles were automatically turned into print by a computerised typesetter' (Snoddy 1992, p. 14).

In what has become a Murdoch signature move, he was able to enlist the support of conservative British prime minister Margaret Thatcher in his battle with the unions. Thatcher provided a heavy police presence on the picket lines to help Murdoch's vast army of scab labour to get the newspapers out. Today Murdoch is close to political leaders of all stripes and maintains these friendships through mutual favour-calling. What was that about 'life imitates art'? Murdoch's eventual success at Fortress Wapping created a climate in which other newspaper proprietors turned on their own journalists and printers. Robert Maxwell sacked one third of his workforce and so did United Newspapers, publishers of the *Daily Express* and other papers (Snoddy 1992, p. 14).

The computer revolution in newspaper production

> As with the Teletypesetters of the 1920s, new technology seemed at first to threaten the sovereignty of editors; it performed functions behind their backs,

> as it were, and thwarted lines of discipline and control that held the fabric of the newspaper's social organisation together. Gradually they came to see the new techniques with different eyes. The real problem in applying computer science to the newspaper industry was that of breaking down habitual attitudes and methods within the newspaper organisation itself. (Smith 1980, p. 95)

The Wapping experiment created an unstoppable trend in newspaper production—the introduction of computing power to replace journalists, typesetters, and printers. It is unthinkable that anyone could run a newspaper today without computers. There has always been a virtual mountain of technology behind and embedded in the modern printing press, and it is most obvious in the newspaper industry. Much of it is of a heavy, industrial nature: printing presses are jocularly known as 'beasts' because of their size, the noise they generate, and their generally troublesome nature when something goes wrong. They are still giant and expensive pieces of machinery today, though they are controlled by microprocessors with very little human intervention. It is fair to say that in modern newspapers, computers are now doing thousands of functions that were previously done by hand. Anthony Smith's *Goodbye Gutenberg* (1980) details the industrial history of newspapers and the bulky, manual setting of type. Desktop computers and local area network (LAN) connections have all but eliminated setting and design of pages by hand. Copy is keyed in by the journalists themselves, stored electronically in queues, and edited via another terminal. Plates for the press are composed electronically and 'photographed' direct to the laminated plastic sheets that have replaced the cradles of linotype and hot metal. Thanks to Citizen Murdoch, the newspaper business today is a good example of digital convergence as Hotmail has replaced hot metal as the most common means of communication.

The future of newspapers: Circulation and credibility

The first issue we should consider here is the future of the newspaper as a medium for the delivery of news and information in competition with broadcasting and the Internet. All newspapers are sustained by advertising revenue. 'Rivers of gold' was the description given to the classified advertising revenue streams of *The Age* and the *Sydney Morning Herald*, but the flight of advertisers to the Internet has newspaper executives worried. In 2005 newspaper advertising grew only 4.38 per cent, while in the same period Internet advertising grew by 59.7 per cent (Sinclair 2005). This has forced newspapers to reconsider their online strategies as audiences and therefore advertising revenue (measured by eyeball 'reach') migrate to the Web (MacLean 2005b). Rupert Murdoch has acknowledged not taking the Internet seriously until recently. In a widely reported speech in April 2005, he told the American Society of Newspaper Editors:

> Scarcely a day goes by without some claim that new technologies are fast writing newsprint's obituary. Yet, as an industry, many of us have been remarkably, unaccountably complacent. Certainly, I didn't do as much as I should have

> after all the excitement of the late 1990s. I suspect many of you in this room did the same, quietly hoping that this thing called the digital revolution would just limp along. Well it hasn't ... it won't ... and it's a fast developing reality we should grasp as a huge opportunity to improve our journalism and expand our reach. (Murdoch 2005)

Later in 2005, Murdoch repeated these comments at a shareholder briefing for News Corporation and admitted that Internet advertising was 'hitting newspapers hard' (McGarry 2005). In the United States, the highest circulation newspaper is *USA Today* with approximately 2.2 million subscribers (30 June 2005). The *Wall Street Journal* has 2 million and the *New York Times* 1.1 million subscribers. The influential *Washington Post* has 750 000 and *Newsweek* 3 million. In the United Kingdom, the London tabloid the *Sun* has the largest circulation with 3.2 million, followed by the *Daily Mail* with 2.3 million and the *Daily Mirror* with 1.7 million. Daily papers with a circulation of under 1 million are the *Daily Telegraph* with 0.9 million, the *Daily Express* and the *Daily Star* with 0.8 million each, *The Times* with 0.68 million, the *Financial Times* with 0.4 million, and *The Guardian* with 0.36 million.

In Australia, national newspapers have a short, even chequered, history. Murdoch founded *The Australian* as a national daily in 1964, prefiguring the emergence of a more vibrant Australian nationalism later in the decade. Originally based in Canberra, the paper was soon moved to Sydney when Canberra's dismal weather hampered production and distribution. The current circulation for *The Australian* is approximately 130 000 (Monday–Friday). Other papers with a national outlook such as Fairfax's *Australian Financial Review* (circulation 85 000 at 1 July 2005) struggle (national weeklies and monthlies likewise). Even the venerable *Bulletin* (established 1880) has outlasted the *National Times*, the *Independent*, and *Nation Review* (Kirkpatrick 2005, p. 7).

Metropolitan newspaper ownership in Australia is dominated by Murdoch's News Ltd, and by John Fairfax. Rural Press and Australian Provincial Newspapers (APN) are second-string players, especially in regional newspapers. In Sydney, the market is dominated by the News Ltd tabloid the *Daily Telegraph* with a circulation of just under 400 000 (M–F). Circulation of the Sunday edition, the *Sunday Telegraph*, is over 700 000. The *Sydney Morning Herald*, a broadsheet, circulates 214 000 (M–F).

In Melbourne, the News Ltd tabloid *Herald Sun* (550 000 M–F) is the highest circulating newspaper in the country. The Fairfax-owned broadsheet *The Age* has a circulation of 196 000 (M–F). In Brisbane, a one-newspaper town, the *Courier-Mail*, the News-owned broadsheet turned 'compact' (Lehmann 2005a), has a circulation of some 200 000 (M–F). Decentralised Queensland also has a strong regional press, with the News-owned dailies the *Gold Coast Bulletin*, the *Townsville Bulletin*, and the *Cairns Post*. APN owns dailies in the other regional centres. In Adelaide, the *Advertiser*, a tabloid owned by News, has a circulation of 200 000 (M–F). In Hobart, the *Mercury* reaches a circulation of 50 000. In the nation's capital, the *Canberra Times*, owned by Rural Press, struggles to break the 40 000 mark (M–F). In Western Australia, the *West Australian* has a circulation of 210 000 (M–F). Globally newspaper circulation has been in steady decline for some years; diversity suffers as a result.

The second issue facing newspapers is that of credibility. In the US, a report by the Pew Centre found that two news organisations share the top spot in terms of print news credibility (Pew Research Center for the People and the Press 2004, p. 24). The weekly news magazine *U.S. News & World Report* and the *Wall Street Journal* are viewed as highly credible by 24 per cent of those who are able to rate them. In previous polls, the *Wall Street Journal* stood well above the rest of the pack, but that is no longer the case. Credibility ratings for the *WSJ* have plummeted in recent years. In 1998 and 2000, 41 per cent of those able to rate it said they could believe all or most of what they read in the *WSJ*. That number fell to 33 per cent in 2002 and now stands at 24 per cent.

BROADSHEET

A newspaper format in which each page is approximately A2 size. Traditionally regarded as an upmarket form to distinguish it from tabloid, which is A3 and downmarket.

TABLOID (COMPACT)

A newspaper format based on a page size approximately A3. Traditionally associated with journalistic practices such as beat-ups, sensationalist reporting, and photographs of semi-naked women on page 3. Also pejorative term used to describe poor-quality journalism in any medium.

Most of the other print sources tested in the poll receive similar ratings for believability. *Time* magazine is viewed as highly believable by 22 per cent of people familiar enough to rate it, and the *New York Times* gets a 21 per cent rating. *Newsweek* and *USA Today* rate at 19 per cent; that is also the rating respondents give to their own daily paper. The Associated Press is viewed as highly credible by 18 per cent of Americans who can rate it.

Ratings for *Time*, *Newsweek*, and *USA Today* have fallen somewhat in recent years. Ratings for local daily newspapers have fallen more sharply. In 1998, roughly three in ten (29 per cent) of those able to rate their local newspaper said they could believe all or most of what it said. That declined to 19 per cent in the most recent survey. Entertainment and tabloid news sources receive the lowest ratings overall. Just 7 per cent of those who can rate it say they can believe all or most of what they read in *People* magazine, and even fewer (5 per cent) find the *National Enquirer* highly believable.

Two-thirds of Australians do not believe newspapers to be a fair and accurate source of news, according to an opinion poll conducted by Morgan Research in 2004 (Morgan 2004). Only 25 per cent of respondents said newspapers in Australia accurately and fairly reported the news. The poll was taken by telephone of 621 people over the age of 14. This is consistent with other research by Morgan—an annual survey of honesty and ethics in the professions—which shows that newspaper reporters consistently rate more poorly than television journalists and talkback radio hosts for honesty and ethics. Of the newspapers, the Murdoch-owned tabloids the *Herald Sun* and the *Daily Telegraph* were most mentioned for their inaccuracy and unfairness. Newspaper editors—in this case, Andrew Jaspan of the *The Age*—respond:

> If you listened to some armchair experts newspapers are an endangered species. Their argument goes along the lines like this. Circulation has been generally declining worldwide since the 1970s. Advertising revenue is under threat because of the rapid expansion of the Internet. Costs are up and staff numbers are being squeezed in newsrooms around the world—even illustrious papers like *The New York Times* [have] had to shed staff. There is greater competition for eyeballs than ever before. Life is busy and complicated. People simply don't have the time to read newspapers people say, and so on it goes.
>
> The clear advantage that quality papers like *The New York Times* and *The Age* have in this new media era is that they are trusted brands. They stand for credibility, independent journalism, free of conflicts of interest, publishing fearlessly in the public interest. Research is showing that readers will always migrate to trusted sources of information wherever that is. Fiddle with that at your peril. Newspapers have a great future. But they will only survive—in print or online or any other channel—if they continue to meet and exceed the expectations of readers. (Jaspan 2005)

Perhaps with subconscious irony, Jaspan's closing phrase echoes the long-running promotional campaign of the Murdoch-owned Brisbane *Courier-Mail*, until December 2005 a tabloid wolf printed in broadsheet sheep's clothing. Editor David Fagan said the move to a 'compact' format was a natural progression for the *Courier-Mail* to make it 'readily accessible and easy to read' (quoted in Lehmann 2005a). Jaspan's substantive point holds out little hope for newspapers—and their online offshoots. In the hours after the London terror bombings in 2005, people did reach for the sources they regarded as most credible—the BBC and CNN online sites received record hits. Newspapers have to reinvent themselves as media available 24/7, not just on the lawn at dawn.

There have been many predictions that the digital age means not only the end of newspapers as we know them, but of books as well. This is an argument about the future of the printed page. Here's how sci-fi writer Neal Stephenson envisioned a paperless bureaucracy in his novel *Snow Crash*:

> Just workstations and chairs. Not even any desktops. Desktops encourage the use of paper, which is archaic and reflects inadequate team spirit. What's so special about your work that you have write it down on a piece of paper that only you get to see? … When you're working for the Feds everything you do is the property of the United States of America. (Stephenson 1992, p. 263)

Futurists in the 1980s happily predicted the demise of paper (Toffler 1981, p. 32). Other, more recent commentators, like Jason Epstein writing in the *New York Review of Books*, take a different view:

> But a significant market for books read on screens has not yet emerged, and in my opinion this may never become the major mode of distribution for books on line. The more likely prospect, I believe, is that most digital files will be printed and bound on demand at point of sale by machines—now in prototype—which within minutes will inexpensively make single copies that are indistinguishable from books made in factories. These neighborhood machines for making paperbound books can, like ATMs, be placed wherever electricity and supplies of paper exist—whether in Kinko's, Starbucks, or high school and university libraries and residence halls, to name only a few possible sites. (Epstein 2001)

A number of attempts to produce an electronic book have been made. None of them have been, as yet, a killer application. We will revisit arguments about the supposed 'death' of the traditional print and broadcast media in chapter 16, but first, to continue our review of analogue digital media we take a look at the development of still and moving pictures.

KILLER APPLICATION

A computer application that revolutionises the use of the computer system and renders redundant (kills off) previous applications. Spreadsheets and word processing were the original killer applications; Internet browsers and search engines are another example. The search is always on for the next 'killer app'.

KEY POINTS

The key points from this chapter are:

- that technological change is continuous; that new technologies continue to create new syntheses, even in the oldest of the mass media: print;
- the role played by print in promoting liberty and democracy, and the manner in which plutocracy inhibits the promotion of liberty;
- that issues of circulation and credibility have challenged the dominant agenda-setting function of the print media.

FAIRFAX SHREDS MAGAZINES

In July 2005 the Fairfax group began restructuring its financial news operations in preparation for the mooted launch of a $10 million online project, *AFR Desktop*. Four finance titles were to be scrapped and merged into the *Australian Financial Review* as lift-out sections. According to a report in the *Weekend Australian*, the titles were no longer attractive to advertisers and Fairfax management was 'reluctant' to invest in marketing the titles (Boreham 2005).

As part of the restructure, print-based jobs would be cut and those that remained would migrate to the new web-portal. In the same month Japanese researchers announced the invention of bendable electronic paper that could display images but used only tiny amounts of power. In a media release the Fujitsu electronics company claimed the material had the characteristics of paper and could preserve images without distortion, even when folded. Fujitsu said electronic paper would be a great medium for advertising and planned to commercialise it in 2007 (Frugal e-paper nears reality 2005).

CLASS DISCUSSION

1. Given the shrinking market for journalists and the number of journalism students, are you giving any consideration to an alternative career?
2. Do you expect newspapers to completely disappear during your lifetime? Why?
3. Are you comfortable with print media?
4. How much online news are you consuming daily? Weekly?

TIMELINE FOR PRINT

1440	German Johann Gutenberg invents movable type.
1455	Gutenberg prints his first book, a Latin Bible.
1475	William Caxton prints the first book in English: *The Recuyell of the Historyes of Troye*.
1704	Daniel Defoe publishes the *Review*, covering European affairs.
1772	*Morning Post* launched.
1785	*Daily Universal Register* founded; changed its name to *The Times* in 1788 and is now Britain's oldest surviving newspaper with continuous daily publication.
1793	The *Pennsylvania Evening Post* becomes America's first daily newspaper.
1796	Lithography, a process enabling printing of images invented by Alois Senefelder.
1803	The *Sydney Gazette and New South Wales Advertiser*, Australia's first newspaper.
1806	First use of illustration in *The Times*.
1812	Friedrich Koenig invents the steam-powered cylinder press.
1817	*Scotsman* launched.
1821	*Manchester Guardian* founded by John Edward Taylor.
1822	Mechanical typesetting invented by William Church.
1827	Samuel Morse founds the *Journal of Commerce* in New York.
1835	Charles-Louis Havas launches Agence Havas; later AFP news agency.
1842	*Illustrated London News* launched: first fully illustrated weekly publication.
1843	*Economist* founded.
1843	*News of the World* launched.
1846	*Daily News* launched, edited by Charles Dickens.
1846	Richard Hoe patents the first rotary press.
1848	Associated Press newsagency founded in New York.
1849	Paul Julies Reuter uses carrier pigeons to fly stock market prices between Aachen and Brussels.
1851	*New York Times* launched.
1851	Reuters News Agency opens in London.
1854	*The Age* founded in Melbourne by John and Henry Cooke.
1855	Repeal of the Stamp Act in Britain opens the way for the production of low cost, mass-circulation newspapers.
1856	Syme family buys *The Age* for £2000.
1862	Reuters aligns with American Associated Press.
1863	William Randolph Hearst born.
1865	Web offset printing invented.
1873	Typewriter invented.
1877	*Washington Post* founded.
1880	First photographs appear in a newspaper.
1883	Reuters uses 'column printer' to transmit messages to London.

TIMELINE

1892	Herman Ridder buys the leading German-language newspaper in the USA, *Staats-Zeitung*.
1895	Hearst buys *New York Journal* for $US180000.
1896	*Daily Mail* launched by Harmsworth (later Lord Northcliffe).
1900	*Daily Express* launched.
1901	Electric typewriter invented.
1903	Charles Landon Knight buys the Akron (Ohio) *Beacon Journal*.
1903	*Daily Mirror* launched by Harmsworth.
1905	William Randolph Hearst unsuccessfully runs for Mayor of New York City.
1907	National Union of Journalists founded in UK.
1911	First award for Australian journalists ratified by the Arbitration Commission after a successful case by AJA.
1921	Wirephoto, the first electronically transmitted photograph, introduced.
1922	Death of Lord Northcliffe, founder of tabloid journalism.
1922	McClatchy family launches the Fresno *Bee*.
1922	*Reader's Digest* launched.
1923	*Time* magazine launched.
1927	Reuters introduces the teleprinter, forerunner of the telex.
1927	AP news picture service commenced.
1932	Times Roman typeface first used in *The Times*; also first colour photograph in *The Times*.
1933	Penguin Press introduces the paperback book.
1935	AAP—Australian Associated Press founded as a cooperative news agency owned by 14 cooperating newspapers. First chairman Sir Keith Murdoch.
1936	*Life* magazine founded.
1939	Reuters moves to Fleet Street.
1939–44	AFP operated by as a French language anti-Nazi propaganda unit from London.
1941	*Citizen Kane* mythologises the life of William Randolph Hearst.
1943	Frank Gannett establishes national news service in the USA.
1944	AFP becomes publicly owned.
1946	AP launches first sports news wire service.
1951	Death of William Randolph Hearst aged 88.
1952	Rupert Murdoch inherits the Adelaide *News* and the Adelaide *Sunday Mail*.
1953	*Playboy* magazine launched.
1959	News agencies United Press and International News Service merge to form UPI.
1959	*Manchester Guardian* becomes *The Guardian*, based in London.
1960	Murdoch buys Cumberland Newspapers and Sydney's *Daily* and *Sunday Mirror*.
1964	Murdoch launches *The Australian* as the first national newspaper.
1966	*The Times* bought by Canadian Roy Thomson.
1967	*Rolling Stone* and *New York* magazine launched.
1969	Murdoch takes over *News of the World* and launches the London *Sun*.
1969	Knight Newspapers and Ridder Publications both go public.

1972	Murdoch purchases the Sydney *Daily Telegraph* and *Sunday Telegraph*.
1973	Murdoch expands into the USA: purchases *San Antonio Express and News*.
1973	Reuters introduces monitoring of financial markets.
1973	*Washington Post* wins a Pulitzer Prize for reporting the Watergate scandal.
1974	Ridder and Knight merge to form Knight-Ridder Newspapers.
1977	Murdoch buys *New York Post*, *New York* magazine, and *Village Voice*.
1980	News Corp formed.
1981	Murdoch takes over *Times* and *Sunday Times* in London.
1982	Gannett launches *USA Today*, the first newspaper published simultaneously in several cities, via satellite.
1982	*Mail on Sunday* launched: the first photocomposed national newspaper in Britain.
1982	Hearst Corp sells Boston *Herald-American* to Murdoch for $1 million.
1984	Robert Maxwell buys the Mirror Group.
1984	Ill-fated float of Reuters on LSE and NASDAQ.
1985	*Daily Telegraph* bought by Conrad Black.
1986	Murdoch takes on the British print union and moves to Wapping.
1986	News International moves all national titles to its new plant at Wapping.
1986	*Today* launched by Eddy Shah, first national colour newspaper.
1987	Maxwell launches *London Daily News*: first attempt at a 24-hour newspaper in Britain. Publication ceases within a few months.
1987	Murdoch takeover of Herald and Weekly Times group, which includes Queensland Press, publisher of the *Courier-Mail*; purchases the *South China Morning Post* and publisher Harper & Row.
1987	Ill-fated attempt by Warwick Fairfax Jnr to privatise Fairfax.
1987	*Today* bought by Rupert Murdoch.
1988	McClatchy goes public.
1988	Knight Ridder buys Dialog Information Services for $353 million, from Lockheed.
1990	*European* launched by Robert Maxwell. Ceased publication on 14 December 1998.
1990	John Fairfax Holdings goes into receivership.
1991	Hearst Corp takes a 20 per cent stake in cable sports broadcaster ESPN.
1991	UK Press Complaints Commission replaces the UK Press Council.
1991	Tourang consortium led by Conrad Black successfully bids for the remains of Fairfax.
1991	Death of Robert Maxwell.
1992	Knight-Ridder establishes *Detroit Free Press Plus*, an online newspaper.
1995	In Sweden, the Modern Times media group launches the world's first *Metro* newspaper, a free newspaper for commuters now published in 64 editions in 91 cities.
1996	Knight-Ridder launches 31 news websites based around its daily newspapers.

TIMELINE

1997 Hearst Corp broadcasting merges with Argyle television assets to form Hearst-Argyle Television.

1999 Daily Mail group launches London *Metro* for commuters—in opposition to the Scandinavian product.

1999 Hearst-Argyle goes digital and buys 30 per cent in Internet Broadcasting and Geocast Network Systems.

2000 Knight-Ridder New Media renamed as KnightRidder.com, renamed Knight Ridder Digital a year later.

2001 Melbourne *Express*, based on the European Metro model of a free giveaway newspaper, launches and folds within a year.

2001 Conrad Black renounces his Canadian citizenship; subsequently made a member of the British House of Lords, following the well-trodden path of fellow Canadians Max Aitken (Lord Beaverbrook) and Roy Thomson (Lord Thomson of Fleet).

2002 Capital value of Reuters falls to £1.4 billion.

2003 Fairfax buys New Zealand's Independent Newspapers Ltd for $1 billion.

2003 Conrad Black resigns as CEO of Hollinger, and is subsequently sued by the Hollinger group for $200 million.

2004 London *Times* switches to tabloid format.

2004 *Washington Post* buys *Slate* online magazine from Microsoft.

2005 *New York Times* buys About.com for $US410 million.

2005 Gannett becomes the largest-circulation newspaper group in the USA.

2005 Reuters buys Action Images sports photo agency.

2005 Fairfax pays $38.92 million for Internet dating site RSVP.

2006 Trade-Me, a NZ based Internet site, purchased by Fairfax for $625 million.

2006 Phillips announces the prototype of a screen-based electronic book.

2006 Knight-Ridder sold to McClatchy for $US4.5 billion.

2006 Hearst-Argyle takes 20 per cent interest in financial service firm Fitch Ratings for US$592.

2006 AAP launches AAP Message Connect—business to business communication service via fax, email, SMS and voice.

6

INDUSTRIAL LIGHT AND MAGIC: A BRIEF HISTORY OF STILL AND MOVING PICTURES

OBJECTIVES

After reading this chapter you should understand:

- why the discovery of photography was important for the development of all other forms of mass media;
- how photography harnesses scientific breakthroughs to useful and not-so-useful social purposes, and, in particular, why the camera has always been a good example of the application of convergent technologies;
- how the technology of moving pictures and synchronised sound is a required element of convergence because it is still the 'standard' in terms of capturing the images and audio from the 'real' event or performance;
- the relationship between cinema, social identity, and the state, and the global influence of 'Hollywood' as a synonym for American culture and values.

KEYWORDS

analogue
camera obscura
celluloid
digital
half-tone
photogravure
pixel

From 'camera obscura' to pixeltopia

The reproduction of images, first on paper, then on film, and now in digital form, has defined mass communication almost as much as the invention of the printing press. The ability to distribute these images—still, then moving—in printed forms, in celluloid form, over the telephony network, and through the air, in various non-digital and digital wireless forms, continues to transform our culture. We start here with still photography, and look at the way the still image has etched its way into our understanding of both ourselves—through the family album—and our world.

ANALOGUE

A mechanical technology used to transmit sound, light, temperature, position, or pressure. Perhaps best described as a wave that is measured by variations in time and amplitude during transmission, rather than by the binary system (zero or one), which is the basis of digital technology.

DIGITAL

Electronic technology works using binary code to store and transmit data using only two states: 'positive' and 'non-positive'. These conditions of either 'on' or 'off' are represented by two numbers (digits), 'one' and 'zero'. Digital technology is primarily used with new communications media, such as mobile phones and satellite and fibre optic transmission.

The second part of this chapter outlines the history of motion pictures from the days of the short, silent, one-reel comedy to the global movie industry of today. In the first instance films were made without an electronically recorded soundtrack, and later film stock was manufactured with a special stripe that allowed synchronised sound to be recorded alongside the images. These apparently simple technical innovations, and early examples of technological convergence, have had a profound effect on our culture, leading to what some have called the Hollywood-isation of the world: the complete control of the production and distribution 'value chain' by the major studios (Cousins 2004, p. 397). This influence, and the values it exemplifies, has been strongly challenged in the early 21st century by a resurgent Islam.

In March 2005, Kodak, the multinational communications equipment manufacturer, launched an advertising campaign for its latest digital camera. The creatives at the company's advertising agency came up with the catchy hook 'Welcome to Pixeltopia'. The idea behind this slogan is that this new digital camera is so advanced that it will transport the user to some imagined utopian future. There's no doubt that digital cameras are easy to use, almost foolproof, and less expensive in the long run, but not everyone has benefited from the switch from film to pixels.

PIXEL

A dot that is the smallest single identifiable element of an image or picture. The greater the number of pixels per square inch (PSI), the clearer the image will reproduce.

In September 2004, 600 workers at Kodak's Coburg (Victoria) film manufacturing plant lost their jobs, victims of the digital revolution in photography. Paul Taliana, a 25-year veteran of the Coburg factory, told the media that despite years of resistance, he had finally bought a digital camera for his family:

> 'I had held off and I was hoping others would too,' he said yesterday.
>
> 'It's only since I have been using it that I realised it is also much more convenient, and the cost is lower because you don't have to get every single picture developed, just the ones you want. And you can touch (them) up.' (Quoted in Fraser & Speedy 2004, p. 6)

The Taliana family, despite enjoying their digital camera, was devastated by the plant closure. Paul, his wife Connie, two of their children, and his cousin all worked for Kodak. The company's Australian chairman, John Allen, described the closure as a 'very sad day', but said that consumers were to blame: '"These closures have been caused by the fundamental change in consumer behaviour driven by the increasing popularity of digital photography," he said. "It's a very sad day but I think on the site here it's understood that this is a technology-driven change"' (quoted in Gooch & Leyden 2004, p. 1).

A year earlier, the parent company that owned the Coburg factory, the US-based multinational Eastman Kodak, had announced 6000 job cuts worldwide in response to a drop in profits of $A250 million. It had lost a further $A135 million by the end of 2003 and told the media that profits on its Australian operations had fallen from $A56 million in 2000, to $A41 million in 2001, and down to just $A615 000 in 2002 (Gooch & Leyden 2004, p. 1).

On the upside, the Photo-Imaging Council of Australia told the *Australian Financial Review* that the boom in digital camera ownership had led to 14 000 new jobs in sales and service across Australia (Skulley 2004, p. 8). The paper also published a chart showing that worldwide sales of digital cameras, released on the mass market in mid-1999, had grown steadily from around 5 million to 50 million a year. An *AFR* columnist wrote that the decision to close Coburg was 'simply a multinational taking the most politically palatable way to downsize in the face of a seismic shift in its market'. He added, 'the world is changing fast and, faced with closing one of its plants, Kodak has simply chosen the least painful option' (Roberts 2004). However, the workers' union representatives disagreed, arguing that the work was being sent overseas to Kodak plants in France, South America, and China (O'Connor 2004, p. 5).

While coverage in the Melbourne papers was sympathetic to the sacked workers, an editorial in the *Weekend Australian* pointed out that in 1989 the Labor government had given Kodak $A60 million to keep the Coburg plant operating, but that 'nobody except union leader Doug Cameron' was arguing that more federal funds be spent on keeping the film plant working. The reason, according to the editorial, was simple:

> And there is nothing anyone can do about it, because people will never stick with inferior technology just because it provides jobs. The computing revolution ended the typist's trade as word processing revolutionised office productivity … Where once the typing pool was a big employer of semi-skilled labour, now there are call centres. And as digital voice recognition technology improves, these in turn will disappear.

So if any of you are considering a career in call centre management—a growth industry in 2005—perhaps you'd better think again. Not that you'll get any sympathy from the leader writers at the *Weekend Australian*. The editorial about the closure of Kodak continues:

> This is an excellent outcome. Technology is the foundation of Australia's 3 per cent-plus annual rate of productivity improvement, which makes the economy bigger and generates more jobs for us all … None of us can know for sure how we will take and transfer our happy snaps in 15 years' time. But it's a fair bet the technology will have changed. (*Weekend Australian* 18–19 September 2004, p. 18)

There is a salient point in this otherwise unsympathetic editorial: the uncritical belief in technological progress—even a technological revolution—as a foundation for economic growth. Technological determinism (see chapter 4) is an important issue throughout this book and we will return to it often. The technology of capturing lifelike images through a lens and imprinting it on a stable medium for others to see has changed more quickly and impacted more directly on other media and technologies than almost any other we can think of. Welcome to Pixeltopia.

Silver nitrate to silicon chips: The technology of photography

The original 'camera obscura', invented in Europe in antiquity, was simply a darkened box with a pinprick hole in one face, but the image it generated on the opposite surface was inverted. This created technical and ethical dilemmas for the early experimenters in photography: how to correct for imperfections in the image yet still record a 'true' facsimile of the objects in the viewfinder. Until the late 18th century, the camera obscura was used to project images on walls and other flat spaces, as an aid to drawing. By the mid-1850s the technology had developed sufficiently to promote a boom in studio photography.

CAMERA OBSCURA

An ancient form of reprographic technology. Using a pinhole or lens, a lighted image is projected from outside, into a darkened room, allowing the external image to be reproduced on the opposite wall. It is suggested that some of the Old Masters who achieved such fine detail in their paintings were assisted by a camera obscura.

During the late 19th century one of the uses of photography was to record social inequity and anthropological information. Edward S. Curtis (1868–1952) exposed some 40000 negatives in his mission to record the life and culture of Native Americans between 1895 and 1928. His work, published in a 20-volume limited edition, is an astonishing mixture of art and anthropology. In Australia, Dr Walter Roth, a medical doctor who was Northern Protector of Aboriginals, was also a keen photographer who used his camera in support of his anthropological investigations. Of course, the invention of the still camera and the mass production of photographs also kick-started the pornography industry. Indeed, there has been considerable debate about the extent to which anthropological photography descended into Victorian pornography. Today, the camera is still one of the most important tools for the generation of Internet pornography, one of the least savoury examples of convergence.

After 1900, still photography moved in two directions. Manufacturers of cameras and film, while attempting to improve the quality and standards of equipment and materials for professional photographers and cinematographers also converted the still photograph and the still camera into consumer commodities. In 1900 the consumer-friendly Kodak Box Brownie camera was released; in 1906 colour film as well as panchromatic black-and-white film became available. In 1914 German optics firm Leitz developed a camera using the now standard 24 × 36 mm still frame as well as sprocketed 35 mm movie film. In 1928 Rollei introduced the Rolleiflex twin-lens reflex producing a 6 × 6 cm image on roll film. Advances in film were slower. It not was until 1936 that Kodachrome, a multilayered colour film, was developed.

World War II promoted technical developments in cameras, such as the 35 mm single lens reflex (SLR) camera, which were commercialised in the postwar period, with products from Hasselblad and Pentax (1947) and Zeiss (1948). The SLR became the standard camera for amateur photographers before the digital age. The Nikon F came in 1959, Polaroid film and cameras in 1963, and the Kodak Instamatic also in 1963. In 1973 came the C41 colour negative process, which increased the affordability of colour snaps and led to the opening of photo labs in every mall, and one-hour photo processing—a concept quite alien to the digital camera user. So one of the relics of the 20th century is the family photo album, allowing succeeding generations to see what their forebears looked like. The popularity of digital cameras—and the ease with which data is disposed of—may mean that it is the 20th century from which we retain the more enduring images. By 1983 Kodak was marketing photo-storage on disks and a decade later it launched PhotoCD. The days of photographic film were numbered and soon to be over.

WHAT BILLY RECKONS: ANALOGUE VERSUS DIGITAL PHOTOGRAPHY

There is actually a limit to analogue photography and interestingly enough digital photography's probably surpassed the limits of analogue. With analogue photography, depending on the size of the film stock, even 35 mm, you're still limited by the grain.

And you're limited to the size of enlargement you can get before the photo starts falling apart, grain by grain. And now the digital CCD chips are getting to the same quality of resolution that 35mm film is at. So it's actually at a crossover point now and digital is starting to move ahead.

The difference is that pixels are square and grains are fairly random because they're crystals. So they can be different shapes and sizes. But in terms of the picture, a pixel and a film emulsion crystal are similar; each is a single piece of data.

Film's got a warmness about it, it's got a certain colour, it's got life. And every different emulsion has its own life and its own unique properties depending on how you treat it. For example, shooting in a hot or a cold environment. If the film stock's new or old, it's got a different life about it. With film you're dealing with something that's almost organic and living. So every photograph you take on film is going to be different. You can't really know exactly what the result's going to be like until it's processed. On the other hand, with digital you know the result straight away and you can manipulate it and you can see the changes from that manipulation as they take place. You get a much faster result. If you're taking a still life with analogue film, you'd be shooting Polaroids first to get an idea of what result you're going to get and then shoot the film. Then you have to take it to the lab, process it and then look at the results. So it could be up to a 24-hour process just to see the results come back.

If anything, digital photography's made the process a hell of a lot faster and you can get really good, consistent results. It takes a lot of the guesswork out of it.

From my point of view this takes some of the fun out of photography. The other thing that it's taken out is the knowledge that goes into the photograph. When you're dealing with film and emulsions and film stock speeds, paper stock and lighting, and everything like that, depending on how you light the subject and the emulsion and the film and everything you use, you can get different results. And you learn that from experience—using it over and over again. Whereas with digital it's pretty cold. But then you change your white balance in the lighting and camera settings and then you go for the different types of results you want. For example, you might white-balance on a slightly warmer piece of white material, or paper.

So digital does take some of the fun out of it, but fortunately I think the designers of a lot of the digital equipment, Kodak and Fuji for instance, have gone into chip manufacture and wisely looked at the fact that the chips are the replacement for the films they were producing. So the knowledge behind the chips still has that film knowledge built in and a lot of the tools that are being used still have that film knowledge built in too.

So it's actually moved the 'knowledge' required for good photography from the photographer's head and into the computer and I think a lot of operators today don't understand what it is they're doing when making adjustments in the computer environment, or the reasons behind those adjustments.

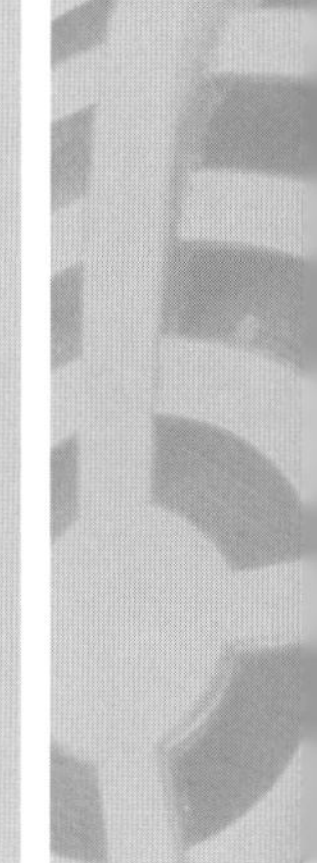

Most of my career as a photographer was analogue, but really for me the transition to digital was a sort of halfway house. I still shot on film and then scanned the image. From that point onwards instead of doing the manipulation of the image in a film lab, you did it on a computer. That was the first transition, and that was when I really started to notice that there are differences between film and digital.

But for me, the real transition was an economic decision. It was far cheaper to do the manipulation, do the changes, do the edit on a computer than to do it in the film lab, or print it in the lab and do the changes and then make the decision. You were printing on paper and spending on film and chemicals, so it was quite expensive. So it was an economic transition; it was cheaper to do what we wanted to do on a computer and in business you're always pushed to be saving money.

Pictures on paper: *Illustrated London News* and *Life* magazine

The *Illustrated London News*, a British weekly newspaper, was founded in 1842 by Herbert Ingram, a printer. Successive innovations and the convergence of printing and photographic reproduction technologies enabled the paper to thrive. In 1860 hand photo-engraving was employed, and half-tone blocks were used from the mid-1880s onward. The half-tone process enabled the company to launch three new mastheads, the *Sketch*, (1893), the *Sphere* (1900), and the *Tattler* (1901). The photogravure process was first employed in 1911. Victorian and Edwardian England—the centre of the British Empire—gave Ingram and his successors the opportunity to showcase the Empire in all its glory. Illustrative of the publication's continuing imperial connections is the fact that it published a special edition in 2002 commemorating the life of Elizabeth, the Queen Mother, a project on which work had begun in the 1970s.

HALF-TONE

A series of black and white dots used to simulate grey in the reproduction of black-and-white images. The more dense the black dots, the more dark that section of the image; the more frequent the white dots, the lighter that section of the image would be when printed.

PHOTOGRAVURE

A mechanical method of printing images whereby a negative of the image is transferred to a printing plate by means of an acid etching process. This process enabled the widespread publication of photographs in newspapers, magazines, and books.

Across the Atlantic, in 1880, 24-year-old George Eastman established the Eastman Dry Plate Company in Rochester, New York and in the same year, the first half-tone photograph was published in the New York *Graphic*, an imitator of the *Illustrated London News*. Eight years later came the first Kodak camera, complete with 20-foot roll of paper, enough for a hundred 2.5-inch diameter circular pictures.

It was in *Life* magazine that the art of photo journalism flourished weekly from 1936 to 1972. Founded by *Time* magazine proprietor Henry Luce, it complemented the quintessential weekly news magazine with its large-format, quality paper, and eye-catching art and design, to say nothing of the content, which ranged from political action to pin-up girls. *Life* magazine was to photo journalism what *60 Minutes* was to become to television—a flagship, a populist pulpit, and an exposition of the craft, as well as the source of some of the iconic images of the 20th century. Declining circulation shut *Life* down in 1972, and various attempts have been made to resuscitate it. From 1974 to 1978 it was quarterly, and monthly from 1978 to 2000; then it shut down again until revived in 2004 as a weekly newspaper supplement.

Life's mixture of celebrity, politics, and lifestyle journalism (sound familiar?) is illustrated by three covers taken at random from the early 1950s: Dean Martin and Jerry Lewis tap dance on the 13 August 1952 cover with a plug for an inside story on 'What to do about germ warfare?'. 'Marilyn Monroe: the talk of Hollywood' features on the 7 April 1952 cover, with a story inside headlined, 'There is a case for interplanetary saucers'. John F. Kennedy, then a Senator from Massachusetts, and his bride to be, Jacqueline Bouvier, are the cover feature for 20 July 1953, under the heading 'Senator Kennedy goes a-courting', with barefoot Kennedy aboard a sailing boat. Already the myth of Camelot was being spun. The inside story plug is for 'Outdoor Cooking: How and What to Grill'—BBQs in the burbs, fifties style.

In a recent essay in *American Journalism Review*, journalist Bill Barol chronicled the impact of *Life* magazine on the United States and its self-perception over three decades:

> This is what I know about the world in the years before I was born: In the 1930s foreign governments were either clearly friendly or overtly hostile, and always quaint in their otherness. The early 1940s rumbled with the sound of faraway trouble drawing near. In the war years Americans were plucky and defiant, kept their chins up, learned to rivet, saved scraps of soap. The late '40s were years of privation, but a peculiarly American kind in which the new car and the new radio and the long-promised television were not yet in reach, but would be soon. And in the '50s they were, in quantity. The '50s were years of unimaginable abundance, years in which large Caucasian families regularly gathered in the sparsely landscaped yards of their brand-new tract homes to arrange in neat rows exactly a year's worth of canned soup, sewing materials, dungarees and bed linens.

He continued:

> The reason I know all this is that I read it in *Life* magazine. It's a cliché to think of *Life* as The Great American Magazine, but it was, and the ways it portrayed America are now largely the ways in which we think of America when we look back. Its reach was so vast and deep that it's not at all clear: Did America shape *Life*, or did *Life* shape America? (Barol 2002)

Perhaps a better way to phrase the question would be: Did *Life* shape America through its images, or did America shape the images of *Life*? *Life*, of course, was not the only famous

American picture magazine. *National Geographic Magazine* (later abbreviated to *National Geographic*) was first published in 1888, its distinctive yellow border making it a landmark publication. Unlike *Life*, *National Geographic*, the magazine of the National Geographic Society, has flourished, now being published in over twenty-five languages and spawning a subscription television channel (another instance of commercial convergence). The *Geographic*'s pictures are not without political impact. Its remarkable 1985 cover photograph of Afghan refugee Sharbat Gula, by photographer Steve McCurry, and her subsequent story, were a powerful political statement.

Playboy magazine was launched in 1953 by Hugh Hefner, a purveyor of soft porn. Photographs of nude women were the magazine's staple, even though it attempted to claim some of the intellectual high ground by way of news-making interviews with major celebrities such as Jimmy Carter, Ayn Rand, Jean-Paul Sartre, Ralph Nader, Orson Welles, Marshall McLuhan, and Martin Luther King Jr. Although an early adopter of Internet technologies, circulation of *Playboy*'s hard copy edition has been harmed by the advent and easy accessibility of online pornography. *Playboys*'s 2006 launch in Indonesia was plagued by a backlash from Muslim fundamentalists, despite the fact that the bunnies draped inside were clad. Another lifestyle magazine, *Rolling Stone*, was founded by Jann Wenner in San Francisco during the 1967 'summer of love'. Making the cover of *Rolling Stone* was a sign of arrival in the world of popular music. While *Rolling Ston*e was famous for its photography and stable of photographers such as Annie Leibowitz, it was also renowned for its longtime celebrity writer, 'Dr Gonzo' himself, Hunter S. Thompson (1937–2005). In 2006 *RS* celebrated its thousandth issue.

Ansel Adams and the great outdoors

San Francisco-born Ansel Adams (1902–84) was regarded by many as the greatest landscape photographer of the 20th century. Adams photographed the mountains, hills, valleys, forests, and streams of the western United States from the mid-1920s onwards. Much of his work celebrated the beauty of the National Parks, Yosemite, and the High Sierra. Interestingly, these landscapes were also the setting for many of the westerns being produced in nearby Hollywood such as *High Sierra* (1941) and *Treasure of Sierra Madre* (1948). On the centenary of Adams' birth, critic Adrian Searle wrote in *The Guardian*:

> The world in an Adams photograph is filled with variegated shadow and tone, crisp texture and radiant light ... [H]e also saw nature, and its relation to the flat, bounded plane of the photograph, in terms of shapes, tonality, graphic variety and detail. The lyricism of his work is tempered by a great deal of artifice, his images manipulated by the use of lens filters and work in the darkroom. He makes you invent colour where there is none, and feel immanence where no feeling is. (Searle 2002, p. 12)

When the camera goes to war

> Photography was first devoted to portraiture and landscape, but it did not take long for enterprising practitioners to glimpse the possibility of using it to bring news images to the public. War was always news, and so very quickly after the invention of wet-plate photography, which could be used, if with some difficulty, away from the studio, photographers began to take their apparatus to theatres of war. (John Keegan, cited in Knightley 2003, p. 6)

In the 1850s when the British army was fighting a disastrous campaign against Tsarist Russian troops in the Crimea, a photographer was commissioned to take photographs, but not of images likely to disturb the British public. According to the celebrated Australian correspondent and author Phillip Knightley (2003, p. 12), the work of Royal photographer Roger Fenton 'established the axiom that although in most cases the camera does not lie directly, it can lie brilliantly by omission'. Despite his self-censorship—he apparently refused to take photographs of the dead after the ill-fated and fabled charge of the British Light Brigade—Fenton's work was recognised as an important contribution to war artistry.

The US Civil War (1861–65) brought images of death and destruction to a wider audience. Taking cameras in covered wagons on to the battlefields, Matthew Brady and his associates exposed some 7000 negatives of this conflict. His 1862 exhibition *The Dead of Antietam* was controversial, but it exposed audiences to the raw reality that war is about killing people, in the same way that, a century later, television pictures of the 1968 Tet Offensive in Vietnam would have a profound effect in provoking anti-war opinion in the United States (Hallin 1989).

The problem was that until after the American Civil War, printing technology lagged behind photography—there was no reliable method of transferring the photographic image to the printed page. But, according to Knightley (2003, p. 13), by the beginning of the 20th century 'the camera had arrived and its development, although slow and spasmodic, was now unstoppable'. When, through the process of convergence, the newspaper printing press caught up with photography it created a new wave of interest in the work of photographers. Dramatic incidents caught in the glare of a newshound's flash became the staple of the 1920s 'yellow press' in America and established the tradition of tabloid news 'splashes' on the front page of the daily paper; only a short time later these gave rise to the now infamous 'paparazzi'.

Henri Cartier-Bresson (1908–2004) was a journalist—a journalist who used a camera. He travelled the world extensively with his simple kit: a 35 mm SLR camera with telephoto lens. He began as an artist influenced by surrealism, but after a year in the Ivory Coast, mounted a photographic exhibition in New York and Madrid in 1932. Detained during the German occupation of France, he escaped, and covered the liberation of Paris in 1944 as a photo journalist. In 1947 he founded Magnum Photos in Paris with fellow photographers Bill Vandivert, Robert Capa, George Rodger, and David Seymour, who met up again in Paris after its liberation. Capa was instrumental in driving the agency (Kershaw 2002).

Magnum was, and still is, an international photographic cooperative owned and operated by its members. The name came from the 20-quart bottle (or bottles) of champagne the quartet consumed at their reunion. Cartier-Bresson then spent three years in India, Burma, Pakistan, Indonesia, and China (during the last six months of the nationalist Kuomintang regime and the first six months of the People's Republic of China). He subsequently covered North America, India, and Japan for Magnum. In 1968 he refocused his energies on painting and drawing.

Robert Capa has been described as one of the greatest war photographers of the 20th century, though his reputation has also come under question for a controversial photograph taken during the Spanish Civil War. The photograph, of a Republican soldier at the moment he is hit by a fascist bullet, has subsequently been alleged to be a fake (see, for example, Knightley 2002, pp. 227–30). On 24 May 1954, Robert Capa died in a lonely field in Vietnam after stepping on a mine while trying to get 'one more' photograph. According to his biographer, Alex Kershaw (2002, p. 255), the Magnum Agency is a continuing testament to Capa's brilliance and persistence, though the heyday of photo-journalism was the 1940s and 1950s before 'television usurped the still image as the primary medium' for news images.

Fashion, celebrity, and the paparazzi

Cecil Beaton (1904–80) was a celebrity photographer in that not only did he photograph celebrities but he was also a celebrity himself, perhaps best known for his photographs of the British royals. He worked in film production in the 1950s and 1960s: *Gigi* (film, 1951), *My Fair Lady* (stage, 1956; film, 1964), and *Coco* (1969), and was a prolific publisher of his artistic output. His work included *The Wandering Years* (1962), *The Happy Years* (1972), *Memoirs of the 40s* (1973), and *The Unexpurgated Beaton: The Cecil Beaton Diaries as He Wrote Them, 1970–1980* (2003, ed. H. Vickers). His photographic work continues to be shown in retrospective exhibitions, although there is some argument that his best work was in film production design, for which he won several Oscars. Like Cartier-Bresson, he was influenced by the surrealists; unlike Cartier-Bresson, his principal interest was not in the image in the viewfinder, but in the image behind the viewfinder—the photographic artist himself.

Despite suggestions that his portraiture was facile, shallow, and created in the darkroom, through his photography of the German bombing of England, Cecil Beaton, like the famous American radio journalist Ed Murrow (see chapter 7), made an impact on American public opinion that pushed the United States into World War II in 1941. Perhaps his most powerful image was of a child injured in the bombing—3-year-old Eileen Dunne, pictured bandaged in a hospital bed. The photo made the cover of *Life* magazine in September 1940.

Vanity Fair: Celebrity

Helmut Newton (1920–2004) was one of those photographers whose work bridges photography, art, erotica, and even pornography. Berlin-born Newton was an apprentice photographer before fleeing Germany in 1938 for Australia, where he worked as a freelance photographer, mainly for European fashion magazines. In the late 1950s he began working for *Vogue* and moved to Paris in 1961. His work was immediately controversial, and he was accused of sado-masochism:

> Newton transformed his models into odalisques and icons, acting out dark and often erotic fantasy tableaux set in a world of hedonistic luxury. Lounging in anonymous hotel rooms, or stalking the streets in stilettos, naked beneath their furs and jewels, they represented a race of glacial, alpha females, and it is their potency that has driven Newton's creative and emotional energy for more than 60 years. (Hickman 2003, p. 52)

His model-muse was June Brunell, who he met in Australia in 1947 and later married, and who is a consistent figure in his photographs in the decades that followed. June took the professional name of Alice Springs and began her own career as a photographer in 1970. In 1975 Newton's first exhibition at the Nikon Gallery in Paris was a commercial success, and in the following year his first volume of photographs, *White Women*, was published. Newton photographed celebrities, most notably artist Salvador Dali and the actors Michael Caine, Catherine Deneuve, Jodie Foster, and Isabella Rossellini. Newton loved to photograph people with power. In his autobiography, published in 2003, he acknowledged his enjoyment in photographing Margaret Thatcher. Christine Hickman wrote in a *New Statesmen* review, 'Even Margaret Thatcher turned him on. She hated her unsmiling portrait, which now hangs in the National Portrait Gallery in London. Helmie loved it. "She looked like a shark," he says' (Hickman 2003, p. 53). Newton's archives are in Berlin and before his death he was reconciled with the German homeland he fled as a refugee in 1938. Helmut Newton was not technically a paparazzo, but his influence in fashion photography is certainly evident in our fascination with images of celebrities in compromising positions.

Paparazzo! Capturing the lifestyles of the rich and famous

> No Jewish mother would choose a career as a paparazzo photographer for her boy. For a start, it's not good for the health. It combines the dangers of the quick knockout in a street fight with the more insidious risks to the constitution of long hours hanging about outside, interspersed with quick bursts of action when your quarry comes into sight. Then there's the social kudos of the job. A guy who jumps out and photographs people when they're least expecting it doesn't seem to win the same respect from the public as, say, a bank manager or an accountant, which is what my mother would really have liked me to be. (Young & Moulsdale 1989, p. 4)

Richard Young is a famous British paparazzo photographer. He's taken his share of illicit shots, but he's also been allowed to photograph many celebrities and boasts of his first-name friendships with many of them. While it may be a 'good life' for the photographers involved, why do the rest of us get such a vicarious pleasure from the voyeuristic consumption of their photos?

The term *paparazzi* comes from the name of a character in Fellini's 1960 film *La Dolce Vita*. Paparazzo (played by Walter Santesso) was a Vespa-riding news photographer who worked with Marcello (played by Marcello Mastroianni), the world-weary gossip columnist with ambitions to be a novelist. Thus the paparazzi are the photographers, often freelance, who photograph celebrities, preferably at moments when those celebs would prefer not to be photographed.

A fad for photographs and advertisements featuring pale, skinny models with dark sunken eyes and fine, blow-away hair gave rise to the term *heroin chic* in the 1990s. The advertiser most prominently associated with this style was Calvin Klein. In 1997, the death of a prominent fashion photographer from a heroin overdose and a public chiding of the fashion industry from President Clinton (Wren 1997, p. A22) saw advertisers and fashion editors back off heroin chic, and return to images in the rag trade of tanned, healthy, well-fed models pictured outdoors with no grunge in sight. When waif-like model Kate Moss, perhaps the face of heroin chic, was photographed snorting cocaine by paparazzi in 2006, the backlash from the industry and the public sent Moss into rehab and saw advertisers cancelling contracts. However, Moss was quickly rehabilitated as her image is a valuable commodity and powerful inducement to buy among the fashion-conscious.

Today magazines that feature candid paparazzi shots of celebrities are among the biggest sellers on the newsstands and supermarket checkouts. In October 2005, *Woman's Day* was selling 515 776 copies per issue; *New Idea* 402 038; *New Weekly* 195 889; *Who Weekly* 159 058; and the relative newcomer, a spin-off from the British edition *OK!*, was selling 74 671 a month. After market research showed that celebrity photos attracted readers, *Who Weekly* boosted its 'Star Tracks' section from ten to twenty pages (MacLean 2005a). In 2005, the celeb-gossip market was growing at around 10 per cent a year compared with the general magazine market growth of just 2.9 per cent. In the 2004 calendar year some $A236 million was spent on celebrity-focused magazines and according to the managing director of News Magazines, Phil Barker, the market is still expanding: 'People can't get enough celebrity and the more incarnations there are, the happier they are,' he told *The Australian* (Sinclair & MacLean 2005). Media commentator Mark Day says the gossip magazine industry is fuelled by a 'celebrity boom built on human curiosity,' but he argues that it is a poor cousin to real journalism, a point that Phil Barker is happy to agree with: 'It's an entertainment product created by journalists ... [and] part of the entertainment industry ... We've all got to make money in the end, and these titles do that' (quoted in Day 2006).

While newspapers and serious journalism appear to be languishing, gossip magazines that pride themselves on having no articles longer than just a few hundred words, most considerably shorter (photos and captions mainly), are thriving. If Day is right, these magazines tell us a lot about ourselves and our media consumption habits in the age of narrowcasting: it would seem that we have short attention spans and a healthy appetite for prying into the lives of the rich and vacuous. As we shall see, there's also a trend developing to turn us into amateur paparazzi—snaps taken with mobile phones or domestic digital cameras are now finding their way into gossip magazines and, in particular, onto online news sites and blogs. Channel 7 is even encouraging viewers to send in photos and videos of newsworthy events taken on their mobile phones.

From film to digital: Digital photography in the public domain

When terrorists bombed the London Underground rail network in July 2005, some of the most dramatic vision of the event came from passengers who captured pictures on their mobile phones. Such sources, some media commentators said, epitomised the rise of the 'citizen journalist'. Others like Mark Glasser at Annenberg School of Journalism at the University of California asked: were those quick with the camera phone 'citizen journalists' or 'citizen paparazzi'?

Citizen paparazzi is not really a new concept, and the proliferation of cameras has continued unabated since the first point-and-shoot 35 mm cameras took off, right through to cheap digital cameras. But while a few amateur photos might have made it into print magazines in the past, now the Internet is awash with photos and video taken by amateurs. As the term 'citizen journalist' becomes part of mainstream thought—spurred on by entrenched media outlets and relatively new start-ups—what role do these outlets play in encouraging or reining in paparazzi behaviour?

Digital photographic technology and the advent of digital cameras in mobile phones have brought their own dilemmas, and authorities in a number of jurisdictions are now moving to legislate against photography in public places—such as on beaches, and in pool and gym change rooms. Such moves have implications for news photographers, who until now have had no restrictions, except possibly those of taste, on their activities in public places. In November 2005 the federal Attorney-General, Phillip Ruddock, announced he was considering introducing laws to prevent the unauthorised photographing of children in public places, and Surf Life Saving Australia proposed its own ban on people snapping shots of young lifesavers on the beach without permission. Many sporting clubs had by then already introduced similar bans at netball and other junior sporting events (Clark 2005).

Certainly the technology of photography has come a long way from its origins in the 19th century when the subjects had to stand still. We will now consider the technology of moving pictures and the cinema, which from the early 20th century began to transform leisure time—entertainment moved out of the home into the cinema and a new industry was created. As we shall see, like most enterprises in the capitalist economy, it soon developed into a virtual monopoly, dominated by American products.

Moving pictures: Celluloid to pixels

> The house lights went down; fiery letters stood out solid as though self-supported in the darkness. THREE WEEKS IN A HELICOPTER. AN ALL SUPER-SINGING, SYNTHETIC-TALKING, COLOURED,

> STEREOSCOPIC FEELY. WITH SYNCHRONISED SCENT-ORGAN ACCOMPANIMENT.
>
> 'Take hold of those metal knobs on the arms of your chair,' whispered Lenina. 'Otherwise you won't get any of the feely effects.'
>
> The Savage did as he was told. (Huxley 1965, p. 128)

This passage from Aldous Huxley's *Brave New World* was written in 1931 when the cinema was still a fairly new industry. The 'feelies' prefigure 3D glasses, Dolby surround-sound, and digital effects, but 'the Savage' begins to get the sensations in his own body, mimicking the action he's sees on the screen—two actors kissing: 'The sensation on his lips! He lifted a hand to his mouth; the titillation ceased; let his hand fall back on the metal knob; it began again … and once more the facial erogenous zones of the six thousand spectators in the Alhambra tingled with almost intolerable galvanic pleasure. "Ooh …"' (p. 129).

The technology to create this virtual sensation would not be invented for another fifty years, but the early cinema was remarkable enough. The technology of cinema is the story of technical advances that enhance the filmgoers' experience. The key innovations have been the advent of sound—the talkies in the late 1920s—the introduction of colour in the 1930s, and the use of digital effects to create special effects from the 1970s.

Sound, colour, and movement

The first moving pictures ever recorded on film were silent, which, according to Mark Cousins (2004, p. 18), added to their ephemeral appeal and ensured that the birth of the movies was a truly international phenomenon. This idea is confirmed when we examine the invention of moving film and the first 'movie' cameras: it occurred almost simultaneously in the UK, Europe, and the United States in the last years of the 19th century (pp. 19–27). In the first years of the 20th century the modern film industry was born as the early silent movies took on a more narrative form and began to tell stories, rather than just examine the marvels of the medium. Techniques of lighting and editing also developed a more 'artistic' style in this period. By 1912, the Hollywood star system was in place 'in all its extravagant, tawdry glory' (p. 43).

CELLULOID

Based on the natural polymer cellulose, celluloid is a form of plastic, from which film was originally made in pre-digital times. The word has also become a shorthand way of describing the world of film and its ephemeral character.

The Jazz Singer (1927) is sometimes regarded as the first talkie, but it is largely silent, with Al Jolson making comments in and around his songs. But this new technique proved popular with audiences, and cinemas became more popular. According to Mark Cousins (2004, p. 118), in the first year after sound became widely available an extra 10 million cinema tickets were sold in the United States. It's also interesting to note, in the light of the success of the 'Bollywood' film industry today, that in the 1930s over 200 films a year were being produced in India (Cousins 2004, p. 123). The gangster flick *The Lights of New York* (1928) was the first film made with sound from beginning to end. The film is poorly plotted, the actors are clearly unaccustomed to film speech, and the film still used the story cards so familiar to silent audiences for scene-setting. One interesting by-product of the talkies was the demise of actors who looked good in silent movies but whose accents grated when they spoke. Stars such as the Italian Alfonzo Guglielmi were expendable in this system. From 1921 to 1925 he was the toast of Hollywood, but he died at the age of 31 and his headstone carried his stage name, Rudolph Valentino. He was the sort of foreign actor who could never be acceptable in an Anglophone Hollywood that 'eroticized and idealized' a constant parade of 'beautiful, immature, expendable stars' (Cousins 2004, p. 135).

The introduction of colour was far more variegated. The looming threat of television—still in black and white—prompted innovations such as Technicolor (1932), Cinemascope (1953) by 20th Century Fox, and Panavision (1959). While the 70 mm format has existed since the earliest days of film, most movies are shot on 35 mm film; one of the exceptions is Spielberg's *Close Encounters of the Third Kind* (1977), in which most of the film was shot on 35 mm but the special effects in 70 mm. The wide sandy vistas of David Lean's *Lawrence of Arabia* (1962) shows the 70 mm format to advantage, and there was a trend from the 1950s onwards to use the 70 mm format because of its superior soundtrack. The advent of digital sound put an end to that and the last feature film made entirely in the 70 mm format was Kenneth Branagh's *Hamlet* (1996).

Early days: New York and *The Great Train Robbery*

While Hollywood, California, is the location most associate with the motion picture industry, the earliest films were made on the east coast of the United States, in New York, New Jersey, and Delaware. Perhaps one of the first narrative films was Edwin Porter's 10-minute, 14-scene, black-and-white *The Great Train Robbery* made in 1903, which prefigured many of the cinematic techniques that later audiences would find commonplace, including the spatial jumps made possible by sequential editing to collapse time but retain a chronological structure (Cousins 2004, p. 38). In the final scene, the gang leader fronts the camera and fires directly into it. More than a century after the film was made, the technique can still surprise the viewer. Porter was a photographer who had worked for the inventor Thomas Edison. He directed, filmed, and edited the picture, which was based on a recent real-life event. The film used no name actors—the Hollywood studio system was several decades away. In the early years of the film industry, most movies were shot like stage plays—the action being filmed from front on. It wasn't until the late 1920s, when *The Jazz Singer* ended the era of the silents, that the 'classic' age of cinema began to emerge (p. 112).

Early Australian film

In 1900, the Salvation Army in Australia produced what may be considered the world's first documentary, *Soldiers of the Cross*. Mixing photographic slides on glass plates with fifteen short action sequences, the film was produced by Herbert Booth, a son of the movement's founders William and Catherine Booth. It was essentially religious propaganda, described by Booth as designed to 'incite Salvationists and all Christians to a holy life and fearless service' (Long & Sowry 1994, p. 63; Kyte 2002, p. 250). Remnants of the film are held in the National Screen and Sound Archive in Canberra. In the first decade of the 20th century, the Salvation Army's Limelight Department was the dominant producer of film in Australia.

Between the making of *The Story of the Kelly Gang* in 1906 and 1931, some 260 feature films were made in Australia, only a quarter of which survive in full or in part. The two great directors of the first phase of the Australian film industry were Charles Chauvel and Ken G. Hall.

Hall (1901–94) was a journalist turned film publicist, who successfully tried his hand at directing in the late 1920s and became head of the Cinesound studio. Hall had success with a series knockabout bush comedies characterised by strong Australian accents, based on the Dad and Dave stories by 'Steele Rudd' (Arthur Hoey Davis 1868–1935): *On Our Selection* (1932), *Grandad Rudd* (1935), *Dad and Dave Come to Town* (1938), and *Dad Rudd, M.P.* (1940). His more dramatic work, such as *The Silence of Dean Maitland* (1935) and *Tall Timbers* (1937), was also authentically Australian.

Hall's *Kokoda Front Line!* (1942), a documentary filmed by renowned war cameraman Damien Parer, became the first Australian film to secure an Academy Award. As American exhibitors took over the Australian film distribution and promotion business after World War II, demand for Australian features declined and Hall found a new vocation with the advent of television in Australia after 1956.

Charles Chauvel (1897–1959) is best known for his World War I epic *40,000 Horsemen* (1941) about the exploits of the Australian Light Horse in Palestine, filmed in the sandhills of Kurnell on the shores of Botany Bay. During World War II Chauvel made a number of war films, the most famous of which was *The Rats of Tobruk* (1944) featuring Chips Rafferty, an Australian actor who became the stereotypical Australian for Hollywood. Chauvel also made *In the Wake of the Bounty* (1933), which launched the career of a less stereotypical Australian, the Tasmanian-born actor Errol Flynn. Chauvel's *Jedda* (1955), the first colour film made in Australia, was controversial not just because of its storyline of interracial conflict, but because Aboriginal actors played the main roles.

Prior to the revival of the Australian film industry in the 1970s, several Australian actors made their names in Hollywood, principally Errol Flynn and Peter Finch. After making *In the Wake of the Bounty* (1933), Flynn's Hollywood career took off with *Captain Blood* (1936). He subsequently appeared in *The Charge of the Light Brigade* (1935), *The Adventures of Robin Hood* (1938), *The Dawn Patrol* (1938), *Dodge City* (1939), *The Sea Hawk* (1940), and *Santa Fe Trail* (1940). Flynn had a reputation as a Hollywood hell-raiser through the 1930s, but his career stalled during World War II when he was charged with rape, though acquitted. Like Marlon Brando later, Flynn's lifestyle ruined his health; his aptly titled autobiography *My Wicked, Wicked Ways* was published shortly after his death.

Cinema and the state 1: Eisenstein and Stalinism

Just as Hollywood, and indeed Bollywood, has made cinema subservient to national aspirations, so too did the so-called revolutionary cinema of Russia, after the Bolshevik Revolution of 1917. The centre of this new cinematic style was the Moscow film school, led by a former fashion designer, Lev Kuleshov. The central metaphor for this group of young filmmakers was the rise of the 'machine' and their mission was to make propaganda for the Bolshevik revolution (Cousins 2004, pp. 102–5). This is most vividly seen in Sergei Eisenstein's *Battleship Potemkin* (1925), which commemorated a revolt by the ship's crew in 1905 during the first Russian revolution against the Tsar. Eisenstein's contribution to film technique lay in his use of montage, an editing of scenes for effect. While under the influence of Stalinism, the ideology of Soviet filmmaking was deemed to be 'socialist realism', a form of reductionism in which the artistic medium served the purposes and values of totalitarian state power; in short, propaganda. Eisenstein (1898–1948) was nonetheless able to demonstrate a mastery of cinematic technique. The most famous sequence in *Battleship Potemkin* is the scene set on the Odessa Steps. This is how Oscar-winning film historian Chuck Workman described the sequence:

> This baby carriage—the baby screaming, the mother dead—lurching down Russia's Odessa Steps during the 1905 revolution. The scene is intercut with hundreds of other shots: soldiers killing townspeople, horrified faces, marching feet, crowds of people rushing towards the sea, the army in pursuit, guns firing, bayonets raised, screaming, running, dying. Sergei Eisenstein can probably be called the greatest filmmaker of the silent era, his startling and unique images edited in a complex and inspired counterpoint. (Workman 1993, p. 37)

The sequence is all the more powerful when it is remembered that *Potemkin* is a silent film. Eisenstein made other films: *Strike* (1925); *October* (1927), a film commemorating the tenth anniversary of the Bolshevik Revolution, distributed in the English-speaking world as *Ten Days That Shook The World*; *The General Line* (1929, released as *Old And New* in the United States); and *Alexander Nevsky* (1938). During a hiatus in the United States and Mexico between 1929 and 1932, he failed to make it in Hollywood when David O. Selznick at Paramount rejected his ideas for a film, but he shot a huge volume of footage in Mexico, later edited and released by others as *Que Viva Mexico!* (unfinished) (1930–32), *Thunder Over Mexico* (1933), and *Eisenstein in Mexico* (1933). He returned to the Soviet Union when Stalinist paranoia was at its height, and was not permitted to make films again until 1935. A theoretician of film as well as a filmmaker, Eisenstein became engaged in now arcane debates about film theory that thrived in the 1930s in the Soviet Union and were subsequently published in English. His last cinematic work was a series, *Ivan the Terrible* (1945–46), which was unfinished when he died in 1948.

Cinema and the state 2: The Hollywood Ten and McCarthyism

It wasn't just in Stalinist Russia that filmmakers were encouraged to be propagandists. In Hollywood, the inevitable commodification of movies meant the commodification of one of its major inputs: actors. This expressed itself in the star system. But not everyone in Hollywood was a star and the subject of public adulation. In 1947 a Committee of the US House of Representatives, the House Committee on Un-American Activities (HCUA), led by ultra-conservative Senator Joseph McCarthy, began investigations into alleged left-wing influences in the movie industry. The immediate postwar period—the beginning of the Cold War—saw a fear of communism whipped up by both religious and political protagonists in the United States, Britain, and Australia. Ten of the Hollywood figures interviewed by the HCUA refused to name others who might have had left-wing views or associations, citing the Fifth Amendment to the US Constitution, which precluded self-incrimination. Mainly writers, the Hollywood Ten, as they became known, were convicted of contempt of Congress and jailed. They, and up to several hundred others, were blacklisted by the studios and were forced to write under pseudonyms, work outside the United States, or move out of the industry. They included Ring Lardner Jr (1915–2000) who later scripted the classic anti-war film *M*A*S*H* (1970), and Dalton Trumbo who won Oscars for *Roman Holiday* (1953) and *The Brave One* (1956), which he wrote under assumed names. After the blacklist was abandoned Trumbo scripted *Spartacus* (1960) and a number of other films.

The persecution of the Hollywood Ten was part of a wider wave of anti-communist sentiment in postwar America, which followed the invasion of Eastern Europe by the USSR at the end of World War II and the beginning of the Cold War. Both J. Edgar Hoover, Director of the FBI, and Senator Joseph McCarthy, as well as Roman Catholic priests such as Father Charles Coughlin, were active and unscrupulous anti-communist crusaders. Michigan-based Coughlin conducted a weekly radio program from 1926, in which he railed against the evils of communism. The name given to this phenomenon is McCarthyism, and Australia was not immune, with Prime Minister Robert Menzies unsuccessfully attempting to ban the Communist Party in 1951 and establishing a Royal Commission into alleged communist influence in Australia. He was aided in this task by groups within the Australian Labor Party led by a lay Catholic, B. A. Santamaria. The 'Groupers', as they were known, split from the party in 1957. Mass media played a significant role in promoting anti-communist hysteria; McCarthyism was about the importance of mass communication in promoting and maintaining the dominant ideology. This is why the HCUA investigation into Hollywood was aimed at writers. How does this differ from the Soviet Union's policy of 'socialist realism' in film and the arts pursued under Stalin in the 1930s? It doesn't. Both are fundamentally undemocratic and totalitarian in intent. There are similar risks in the 21st century in the demonisation of Islam and young Arabic men. In all these instances, the role of the judiciary in undermining basic freedoms of expression and association, and failing to assert the rule of law to protect basic liberties, makes them part of the apparatus of the surveillance society. Filmmakers have often taken their social responsibilities seriously, pushing them into a dialectical conflict with the studios and the distribution system.

The Australian film renaissance

In a sense, the revival of the Australian film industry in the late 1960s and early 1970s owes as much to the British director Nicholas Roeg as it does to an emerging nationalism that began to break down the 'cultural cringe', in which Australians regarded themselves as second-class British subjects. Roeg's film *Walkabout* (1971) was one of the first to mythologise the Australian outback through the story of two young white children who are forced to journey through the bush after their father shoots himself while on a family picnic (Cousins 2004, p. 361).

The 1970s were a golden age in Australian film. In the 1960s few films of note were made in Australia. Those that were made—*On the Beach* (1959), *Summer of the Seventeenth Doll* (1959), *The Sundowners* (1960), *They're a Weird Mob* (1966), and *Age of Consent* (1969)—had major overseas input by way of featured actors and financing. *On the Beach*, based on the novel by Australian writer Neville Shute, deals with a slowly dying world in a post-nuclear apocalypse. It was directed by Stanley Kramer and features Gregory Peck, Ava Gardiner, Fred Astaire, and Anthony Perkins. John Meillon is the token Australian presence, though Graham Kennedy has a small uncredited role. Set around Melbourne, the film was shot around that city, giving rise to the possibly apocryphal comment by Gardiner that Melbourne was a perfect place to make a film about the end of the world. *The Sundowners*, directed by Fred Zinnermann and based on the book by Australian novelist Jon Cleary, featured Deborah Kerr, as well as Robert Mitchum, Peter Ustinov, and the token local talent Chips Rafferty. *Age of Consent*, featuring an acerbic James Mason and a nubile Helen Mirren, is really a British film set on the Barrier Reef. Whether it be Melbourne, Alice Springs, or the Great Barrier Reef, Australia in the 1960s was a giant outdoor movie set.

In the late 1960s and early 1970s the Australian film industry underwent what has been termed a 'renaissance', encouraged by government funding. Whether a renaissance can be said to begin with the production of raucous, boisterous, comedic romps, some of which verged on soft porn films, like *Stork* (1971), *Alvin Purple* (1976), and then *The Adventures of Barry McKenzie* (1972) and *Barry McKenzie Holds His Own* (1974), is debatable. However, these films provided work and experience not only for Australian actors but for Australian producers such as Phillip Adams, directors such as Bruce Beresford, and writers such as Barry Humphries, all of whom were involved in the Barry McKenzie sagas. A quarter-century later, Stephen Crofts described it this way:

> Ockerism drew its strength from an array of discursive forces. Emerging at a moment of uncoupling from Empire, it both disavowed the insecurities of national identity and asserted an Australian self versus its British other more virulently than was possible before or after. Its vulgarity was catalysed by the

> suddenness of the liberalisation of censorship from the draconian to the normally democratic. *Adventures* confirmed the fledgling cycle of ocker comedies ... as major box office successes, and ... decisively called attention to the rebirth of the Australian feature film production industry. (Crofts 1996, pp. 123–4)

Ocker comedies were not the sole product of the revival. The 1970s produced a series of classic Aussie pictures including *Picnic at Hanging Rock* (1975), *Sunday Too Far Away* (1975), *Caddie* (1976), *The Devil's Playground* (1976), *Don's Party* (1976), *The Fourth Wish* (1976), *The Last Wave* (1977), *The Picture Show Man* (1977), *The Chant of Jimmie Blacksmith* (1978), *Newsfront* (1978), *The Last of the Knucklemen* (1979), *Mad Max* (1979), *My Brilliant Career* (1979), *The Odd Angry Shot* (1979), *'Breaker' Morant* (1980), *Gallipoli* (1981), and *The Man From Snowy River* (1982). At the heart of the revival were Australian directors, of whom the most prominent were Peter Weir, Gillian Armstrong, George Miller, Fred Schepisi, and Bruce Beresford. They not only used the Australian landscape in a distinctive fashion, but they also prodded and probed Australia's soul, in the process developing local acting talent such as Mel Gibson, Jack Thompson, Judy Davis, and Bill Hunter.

This second wave of Australian films was fostered by state-funded film bodies. In 1978, the Australian government decided to promote investment in Australian films by giving such investments preferential tax treatment, under what became known as Rule 10B (1978) and subsequently Rule 10BA (1980) provisions of the *Income Tax Assessment Act (1936)*. Well intentioned, the tax rules proved a creative disaster, with an enormous volume of rubbish produced, such as the horror film *Razorback* (1984) featuring a giant (mechanical) feral pig. Cash, not creativity, became the determining factor, although some films of merit were made. Changes were made to the system in 1988, ostensibly to stop rorting by investors who would otherwise have invested in pine nut plantations or emu farms, and the national government established the Australian Film Finance Corporation. In 2002–03, the latest data available, 25 000 Australians were employed in the film industry, which contributed some $A2 billion to GDP in the same period (DCITA 2005). In 2005, the Australian government again reviewed the taxation incentive provisions, in the face of growing industry and public anxiety that the Australian industry was failing (Chenoweth 2003; Quinlivan 2003; Boland 2004; Galvin 2004; Hughes 2004; Teichmann 2004; Molitorisz 2005).

For all the support governments might offer national film industries, all will remain niche markets as the global juggernaut that is Hollywood sucks up the creative talent worldwide like a subterranean monster in the worst ever B-grade horror flick. In 2004 Australian films were only 1.3 per cent of the $A900 million box office takings in cinemas, which had fallen from 9.5 per cent in 1986. Of some billion dollars invested in Australian productions by the Australian Film Finance Corporation since 1988, it has only recouped around $A240 million. Many Australian films never realise a profit and the last big international hit for an Australian film was *Shine* (1996), the story of dysfunctional but brilliant pianist David Helfgott, who was played in the film by Geoffrey Rush (Chalmers 2005). However, some commentators retain their optimism. Writing in the *Weekend Australian* in October 2005,

Lawrie Zion could see some light at the end of the tunnel. He credits the turnaround to the release of some adult dramas that attract an older audience, instead of trying to play Hollywood at its own 'slick mainstream' game (Zion 2005). Sometimes the talent is crushed in the monster's embrace, and sometimes the talent falls in love with the monster—what a great plot line for a movie!

Digital effects

The creation of computer-generated imagery (CGI) techniques allowed a blend of live and drawn action to appear seamlessly on the screen for the first time and was used to great effect to create the 'liquid metal' character of the bad-guy assassin in *Terminator 2: Judgment Day* (1991). At the same time, digital technology was also being examined as a means of creating even more commercial convergence in the film industry. In 1992, *Bugsy* (directed by Barry Levinson) was the first full-length feature film to be transmitted electronically from the Sony studios at Culver City to a cinema in nearby Anaheim (Cousins 2004, p. 457).

There can be no doubt that digital techniques have altered the creative language of cinema, including the use of 360-degree pans and seamless zoom shots. It has also created an interesting blend of Eastern and Western styles, such as 'wire fu'—the use of thin wire supports and harnesses to shoot seemingly impossible fight-action sequences—and also the use of Japanese 'anime' styles and sensibilities in mainstream films such as *The Matrix* (1999). *The Matrix* is also interesting as a series of films and the use of multimedia platforms to fill in pieces 'missing' from the cinema releases (Cousins 2004, pp. 459–60). The use of digital effects has moved from the sci-fi of George Lucas in *Star Wars* (1977) to the fantasy world of Peter Jackson's *Lord of the Rings* (2001) trilogy. Just as Tolkien created new languages to tell his story (appended in *Lord of the Rings*), so Jackson has created a new language for film, which can be seen in Jackson's remake of *King Kong* (2005), as well as in the *Matrix* films (1999–2003), in the *Star Wars* prequels (1999–2005), and in *The Lion, The Witch and the Wardrobe* (2005).

Leading the digital effects revolution since 1977 has been the George Lucas-owned company Industrial Light & Magic. The company has won fourteen Academy Awards for Best Visual Effects and received seventeen Scientific and Technical Achievement Awards. In 2001, the Steven Spielberg film *Artificial Intelligence* used a real-time interactive on-set visualisation process that allowed actors to move around virtual sets. Perhaps ironically, the use of such technologies is prefigured, as part of the story, in the film *Wag The Dog* (1997) where a White House spin doctor and a Hollywood producer create a conflict with Albania in a studio, in order to win a presidential election.

Bigger than *Ben Hur*

The global influence of Hollywood is one of the commercial success stories of the twentieth century, and it exemplifies the advertising maxim that to sell a product, you must engage and entertain the audience. The product? The American way of life and its ethic of consumerist materialism.

Formation of the Motion Picture Producers and Distributors of America (MPPDA) in late 1921 and early 1922 provided the stage from which the American film industry could colonise the world. As Hiroshi Kitamur tells it:

> During the mid 1920s, (Will) Hays and Frederick L. Herron, the head of MPPDA's Foreign Department, orchestrated the industry's trade plans and formed close ties with the State and Commerce Departments, which backed the industry under the slogan 'trade follows the film.' This corporatist collaboration with Washington enabled Hollywood to finesse quota restrictions, tax laws, and content regulation overseas. The interwar years ultimately rewarded the U.S. film industry with high commercial returns. (Kitamur 2005, p.237)

Not that this push was without resistance. In France, art house cinema flourished, celebrating both the cerebral and the provincial, against the popular, mass-produced product of Universal, Paramount, United Artists, and Disney. In Britain, filmmakers like Korda and Rank tried to co-opt Hollywood to sustain the British film industry.

More recently the resistance has come from the Muslim world. According to Mateen Elass, an American theologian with extensive links into Saudi Arabia:

> The international marketing of Hollywood sex, scandal and slasher movies paints a lurid picture of American life for the sheltered Third World. The fact that reruns of *Dukes of Hazzard*, *Dallas* and *Baywatch* are played around the world lead those who have never been in American homes to assume that illicit sex, fast cars, guns and intrigue are the daily menu of average American lives.

Elass continues:

> The U.S. is seen worldwide by religious Muslims as the primary exporter of immorality, particularly through entertainment channels. Many Muslim governments have sought to stem the flow of cinematic corruption into their country through censorship, but with the advent of satellite dishes and other technological advances this is becoming impractical. (Elass 2006)

Nonetheless, the MPPDA is still influential. It has led the global war against film piracy, a piracy made possible by convergent technologies, and Hollywood studios still dominate theatres, controlling about 75 per cent of the global distribution market, and 44 per cent of the global box office.

Of course, the cash flow from movies doesn't stop when the movie ends on the big screen. In what is known as the 'windows of exhibition', a film has a life next as a DVD or video release, then on pay television (in a variety of saleable forms including hotels and airlines), then to free-to-air television, where it can be syndicated for endless re-runs. Each window generates more cash, albeit in diminishing quantities.

Princeton sociologist Miguel Angel Centeno reported that United States films have 93.1 per cent share of the market for first release movies in the United States; 80.6 and 81.41 per cent in the English-speaking markets of Australia and Britain respectively, 67 per cent in Spain, 59.7 per cent in Italy, and 51 per cent in France (Centeno 2005). That means that in Australia, local and non-US films, mostly European films, capture only 20 per cent of the market. There is little evidence that these statistics have changed significantly; indeed convergent technologies have in fact linked the windows more closely.

The long-anticipated *Superman Returns* was not released in cinemas until mid-2006, but as much as a year before it was available diehard fans were being encouraged to follow progress of the movie's production schedule via the Internet. Director Bryan Singer was posting video blogs showing daily scenes from the set. Peter Jackson did a similar thing while making (or remaking) *King Kong* in New Zealand (Tedmanson 2005).

While this might seem a generous gesture by the studios and directors, the reality is that they know that advance publicity and glimpses of 'behind-the-scenes' footage will drive ticket sales and increase the box office profits of the film. According to one film school lecturer, the weblog format works well for cult films with a strong fan base, but it is becoming increasingly popular as audiences become more familiar with blogs and with watching videos over the Internet. AFTRS lecturer Mark Pesce told *The Australian*'s Sophie Tedmason (2005) that he had linked to Peter Jackson's *King Kong* blog site so that students could watch the director at work.

Hollywood today is a long way from the perceived golden age of the 1940s and 1950s; it is the global centre of a highly profitable culture 'industry' that is integrated vertically and horizontally and closely tied to other sectors of the economy (Wayne 2003, see pp. 61–86). The tendency today is for every scrap of 'value' to be wrung from a film property, through cross-promotions, spin-offs in television, and other forms of entertainment—games and toys, for example. Profitability, not artistic merit, drives the film industry today.

In *Die Another Day* (2002), James Bond drives an Aston Martin, wears an Omega watch, travels British Airways with Samsonite luggage, drinks Finlandia vodka in his martinis, and listens to a Sony stereo. Eleven companies reportedly spent $20 million on advertising products related to the film. 'The Bond franchise is one of the pioneers of product placement,' Jeff Chu wrote in *Time* magazine in 2002 when the film, and its associated brands, were launched. As far back as *Dr No* (1962) the Bond film producers were product-placing Pan Am airways, Red Stripe beer, and Smirnoff vodka. Chu's analysis of *Die Another Day* continued:

> Some publicity-hungry firms pay for screen time. But far more product placement actually works on barter. For example, Ford provided several Aston Martins (for Bond), Jaguars (for the bad guy Zao), Thunderbirds (for Jinx—the inevitable Bond girl), Range Rovers (utility vehicles), spare parts, and technical help. That in-kind contribution saved EON millions in production costs ... In return, Ford will get invaluable screen time for its vehicles. Millions more in

> promised movie tie-in promos from the carmaker will also cut the ad budgets of the distributors—MGM in the U.S. and Fox overseas. (Chu 2002)

Perhaps most insidious of all is the use of tobacco in movies targeted at the teen market (Dulroy 2002, p. 5).

Conclusion

Convergence, of course, means that instead of going to the movies, the movies can come to you. But that has been happening ever since the advent of broadcast television. In the digital world, however, you need a giant plasma screen to get the best experience in order to watch the 21st-century equivalent of the ancient Roman circus—live sport: where the video referee is an electronic Caesar high in the stands, offering a digital thumbs up or thumbs down. It is that arena—television—and its technological proving grounds—telegraphy and radio—to which we now turn.

KEY POINTS

In this chapter you will have examined:

- how both still and moving pictures have entertained rather than informed;
- how the state can suborn the cinematic medium;
- the struggle for an Australian national identity through cinema against the global dominance of American cultural capital through Hollywood, posing the question: what does narrowcasting mean for mass communication forms such as cinema?

TIMELINE

CELLULOID TO PIXELS: TIMELINE FOR PHOTOGRAPHY AND CINEMA

1816 Nicéphore Niépce combines the camera obscura with photosensitive paper.

1826 Niépce creates a permanent image.

1834 Henry Fox Talbot creates permanent (negative) images using paper soaked in silver chloride and fixed with a salt solution; then positive images by contact printing onto another sheet of paper.

1837 Louis Daguerre creates images on silver-plated copper, coated with silver iodide and 'developed' with warmed mercury—the Daguerreotype process.

1841 Talbot patents his process under the name 'calotype'.

1851 Frederick Scott Archer develops the 'wet plate' photography process.

1853 Nada (Felix Toumachon) opens his portrait studio in Paris.

1854 Adolphe Disderi develops *carte-de-visite* photography, making professional portrait photography popular and accessible.

1861 Colour separation process is developed by Scottish physicist James Clerk-Maxwell.

1861–65 Mathew Brady and colleagues cover the American Civil War, exposing 7000 negatives.

1871 Richard Leach Maddox, an English doctor, proposes the use of an emulsion of gelatin and silver bromide on a glass plate: the 'dry plate' process.

1880 First half-tone photograph published in the *New York Graphic*.

1880 George Eastman, aged 24, sets up Eastman Dry Plate Company in Rochester, New York.

1888 First Kodak camera.

1891 First telephoto lens.

1895 First portable camera and first public screening of projected film by the Lumière brothers in France.

1899 Edwin S. Porter begins work at Edison as a filmmaker.

1900 Kodak Brownie box roll-film camera introduced.

1900 The Salvation Army in Australia release *Soldiers of the Cross*, which contains silent movie footage and slide-projected images.

1901 First cinema opens in Britain.

1902 Vivaphone, Chronophone, and Kinetophone synchronise sound and film. Georges Méliès, a magician-turned-filmmaker, introduces innovative special effects in the first real science fiction film, *Le Voyage Dans La Lune*, a narrative fantasy of long shots strung together, punctuated with disappearances, double exposures, and other trick photography and elaborate sets.

1903 Porter directs *Life of An American Fireman* and *The Great Train Robbery*, the first fictive film form.

1905 The first 'Nickelodeon' opens in Pittsburgh. The name derived from 'nickel' (5 cent piece), the price of admission, and 'odeon', the Greek word for theatre. The opening film was Porter's *The Great Train Robbery*.

1906 Panchromatic black-and-white film and high-quality colour separation colour photography. Stuart Blackton makes the earliest surviving example of an animated film: a 3-minute short or cartoon called *Humorous Phases of Funny Faces*. The *Story of the Kelly Gang* marks the beginning of the Australian film industry.

1907 East coast producers go west in winter as Los Angeles provides cloudless skies, varied locations, low humidity, and lower labour costs. The entertainment industry trade magazine *Variety* publishes its first film review. Bell & Howell develop a reliable film projection system.

1908 D. W. Griffith shoots his first film, *The Adventures of Dollie*, for Biograph studios in New York City. By 1908 more than 5000 nickelodeons span the USA and the daily audience exceeds 2 million Americans. The Motion Picture Patents Company becomes the first attempt to create a film monopoly, known as 'the trust'; the Company tries to shut out non-members with threats and intimidation.

1909 The first permanent film studio established in Hollywood by the Selig Polyscope Company.

1910 Thomas Edison demonstrates a talkie using his kinetophone technology. The now-forgotten Florence Lawrence, known as the 'Vitagraph Girl', was the first 'movie star' created by the Carl Laemmele studio.

1912 Motorised movie cameras supersede hand-cranked machines. The first true 'fanzine', *Photoplay*, spawns the celebrity-gossip magazine culture. First *Keystone Cops* film released. Herbert Kalmus begins experimenting with colour film processes and establishes the Technicolor company.

1913 Griffith goes independent. The name 'Hollywood' becomes the official title for the west coast film industry, which is now bigger than that in New York. John Randolph Bray's first animated film, *The Artist's Dream* (aka *The Dachshund and the Sausage*), the first animated cartoon made in the USA by modern techniques, was the first to use 'cels'—transparent drawings laid over a fixed background.

1913 Live theatre owners discover cinema. Movie palaces are born. Audiences flock.

1914 35 mm film developed in Germany by Oscar Barnack at Leitz.

1914 Mack Sennett hires silent comedy genius Charlie Chaplin.

1917 Nippon Kogaku K.K., later Nikon, established in Tokyo.

1919 The first *Felix the Cat* cartoons are created.

1920s The birth of German expressionism.

1923 Walt and Roy Disney start an animation studio in LA.

1924 Leitz markets the 'Leica', the first high-quality 35 mm camera.

1925 Charlie Chaplin's film *The Gold Rush*.

1925 Sergei Eisenstein's *Battleship Potemkin* establishes film montage technique.

1927 Jolson's *The Jazz Singer*, the first popular 'talkie'.

1927 Movietone offers newsreels with sound.

1927 The Academy of Motion Picture Arts and Sciences is founded. German film-maker Fritz Lang releases the first science fiction film, *Metropolis*.

TIMELINE

1928	First Mickey Mouse cartoon.
1928–29	Talkies begin in earnest.
1929	Twenty-four frames/second established as sound motion picture camera standard.
1930	Photoflash bulb invented.
1931	Development of strobe photography by Harold Edgerton.
1932	8 mm film introduced for home movie buffs; the precursor technology for home videos and citizen journalism. Technicolor comes to the movies as Herbert Kalmus develops an optical and dye three-colour process.
1934	Fuji Photo Film founded.
1934	Hayes Code begins a regime of movie censorship.
1935	AAP Wirephoto service launched.
1935	Kodak releases Kodachrome colour film *Becky Sharp*, the first all-colour feature-length film. German film-maker Leni Riefenstsahl releases *Triumph of the Will*, glorifying Hitler and the Third Reich, but displaying new modern techniques of cinematography.
1939	One of the most popular films of all time, *Gone with the Wind*, starring Clark Gable, is released. Audiences are stunned by the full range of mechanical and optical special effects on display.
1940	Charlie Chaplin's *The Great Dictator* pokes fun at the Nazis and the Italian fascists at the start of World War II.
1941	*Citizen Kane* experiments with flashback, camera movement, and sound techniques.
1944	Charles Chauvel's *Rats of Tobruk* released to celebrate an important allied victory in World War II. Australian actor Chips Rafferty briefly becomes an international star.
1947	Henri Cartier-Bresson, Robert Capa, and David Seymour start the Magnum picture agency. House Committee on Un-American Activities investigates alleged communist influences in Hollywood, leading to the blacklist. The Polaroid camera invented by Dr Edwin H. Land.
1952	Stereoscopic 3-D films spark brief interest—a fad. The Hollywood star system starts to fail as James Stewart signs an independent contract.
1953	Fox develops CinemaScope, a proprietary wide-screen projection technique. Other studios follow with Panavision and Visavision.
1955	The first Australian colour film, *Jedda*, directed by Charles Chauvel, tells the controversial story of love in an Aboriginal community and stars unknown Aboriginal actors.
1958	Number of drive-ins in USA peaks near 5000.
1959	Nikon F camera introduced.
1960	Screenwriter Dalton Trumbo—one of the Hollywood Ten—wins an Academy Award for *Spartacus*.
1970	Canadian filmmakers invent giant projector IMAX system.
1971	Indian movie industry produces 433 films, making it the largest in the world—Bollywood is born.
1972	Cable TV starts in Pennsylvania.
1973	C-41 colour negative process introduced.
1975	George Lucas founds Industrial Light & Magic.

1975 Sony markets the first Betamax VCR viewer and recorder, followed by JVC with VHS. The release of *Picnic at Hanging Rock* confirms a renaissance in the Australian film industry.

1976 Dolby stereo sound movies introduced.

1977 *Star Wars* and *Close Encounters of the Third Kind* are released, the first of a new generation of films using special FX.

1985 Murdoch buys 20th Century Fox.

1992 Pacific Bell and Sony demonstrate digital cinema with *Bugsy*.

1992 Kodak introduces the PhotoCD.

1993 An IMAX 3D digital sound system goes into a New York theatre.

1993 Kodak and Apple release the first digital still camera.

1994 The release of *Pulp Fiction* begins era of the 'postmodern' film and marks Quentin Tarantino as an important director/screenwriter.

1995 CD-ROMs are able to store a full-length feature film.

1995 *Toy Story* becomes the first completely computer-generated feature film.

1997 Kodak launches the first point-and-shoot digital camera.

1998 DVDs are introduced.

1999 The first of the *Matrix* trilogy is released.

2000 *Blair Witch Project* becomes a hit through viral and web marketing. Ang Lee's *Crouching Tiger, Hidden Dragon* marks the coming of age of Chinese-language cinema in the Western mainstream.

2004 Computer-generated visual effects win an Oscar for *The Lord The Rings* trilogy.

2005 Viacom buys Dreamworks.

2006 Viacom spins off some media assets to form CBS Corporation. Disney buys Pixar.

7 TELEGRAPHY, THE TALKING WIRELESS, AND TELEVISION

OBJECTIVES

From this chapter you will begin see the importance of convergence in the development of the technological forms of the broadcast media based on a combination of sound and image. In particular, this chapter emphasises the development of electronic sound and picture recording using both analogue and digital technologies. The chapter makes the following key points:

- the importance of research and innovation in general science that creates the technological and technical platform for the emergence of mass media and mass communication;
- how the historical timelines of scientific discovery and commercial application are dialectically related;
- how the industrial development of mass-produced and miniaturised components interacts with the social development of mass communication;
- the important economic links between mass production, the emerging electronic mass media, and mass marketing;
- how the technologies of broadcasting and the cultural forms of radio and television are dialectically related;

- the importance of the British BBC model in the development of government-funded national television systems;
- how television news brought together elements of performance from radio and newsreel films but then lost its way.

KEYWORDS

broadcasting
podcasting
public service broadcasting
radio
reality television
telegraphy
television

Telegraphy

The basic technology behind telegraphy was the electromagnet, first demonstrated in 1825 by British inventor William Sturgeon, and enhanced for use in long-distance communication by Joseph Henry, an American, in 1830. It was Samuel Morse (1791–1872) who successfully commercialised these inventions. In 1835 he developed Morse code, which imprinted dots and dashes on paper; in 1843 the first long-distance electric telegraph line was built from Washington D.C. to Baltimore; and in the following year the first 'news' transmitted by electric telegraph reported the nomination of Henry Clay as a candidate for president. So before the middle of the 19th century we can see the balance of technological innovation shifting from Britain to the United States. The basic scientific discovery occurred in Britain, but its technological application and commercialisation happened across the Atlantic. This shift had important implications for the future of broadcasting.

TELEGRAPHY

The transmission of data over purpose-built data lines (copper wires) using Morse code, developed in 1835.

The involvement of the US government in seed-funding the diffusion of this technology was crucial in what Peter McMahon (2002, p. 380) has described as the 'golden age' of 'liberal capitalism'. In 1843 Congress provided the $30 000 required for the 38-mile line from Washington to Baltimore. It is a myth that in a free-market economy the market somehow produces the scientific knowledge that can be commercialised. The reality is that the key technological innovations that have occurred in the United States in the past 150 years have been state-sponsored; as we shall see, the Internet was developed out of Pentagon R&D funding, and NASA's exploration of space is state-funded. McMahon (p. 383) argues that the telegraph was a key technology in the development of the global system of nation-states based on what he calls the 'industro-military' tendencies of 19th-century capitalism. It was certainly important in the rapid industrialisation of the United

States facilitated by the new (privately owned) communication technologies. For example, the Western Union company was established in 1851, running cable alongside railway lines, linking the east and west coasts of America via a transcontinental telegraph line a decade later.

By 1866, Europe and North America were connected by cable, India in 1870, Japan and China in 1871, and in 1872 in Australia, the Overland Telegraph Line was completed connecting the colonial capitals with Europe via Darwin and a submarine cable to Java (McMahon p. 381). The line ran from Port Augusta in South Australia to Darwin, along a route that had been surveyed by the explorer John MacDouall Stuart only a decade before. Charles Todd (1826–1910), the South Australian Supervisor of Telegraphs, who drove the project, messaged upon its completion in August 1872:

> WE HAVE THIS DAY, WITHIN TWO YEARS, COMPLETED A LINE OF COMMUNICATIONS TWO THOUSAND MILES LONG THROUGH THE VERY CENTRE OF AUSTRALIA, UNTIL A FEW YEARS AGO A TERRA INCOGNITA BELIEVED TO BE A DESERT. (Cited in Taylor, 1980)

Technological refinements to telegraphy followed. Automatic, as distinct from manual, transmission began in 1914, teleprinters in 1925, prototypical fax machines in 1927, and in 1959 telex machines, which enabled parties to communicate directly without the intermediary of an exchange. Perhaps what is surprising about telegraphy is its longevity, in the face of competition from the telephone after 1877. The advent of data transmission via computers over the telephony system was the climate change that turned telegraphy into a dinosaur.

Yet during its brief time telegraphy played in important part in the newsgathering process; it was satirised by Evelyn Waugh in his novel *Scoop*, first published in 1938 as the Italian army was gearing up to invade North Africa, and based on the author's experiences as a war correspondent for the London *Daily Mail* in Abyssinia (Ethiopia) in 1935. The protagonist, foreign correspondent William Boot of the *Daily Beast*, regularly receives unintelligible cables from his editor: 'PRESUME YOUR STEPTAKING INSURE SERVICE EVENT GENERAL UPBREAK' (Waugh 1943, p. 106). The telegraph was as important in military affairs as it was in commerce as war became increasingly systematised in the late 19th century (McMahon 2002, p. 384). In *The First Casualty*, Philip Knightley (2002, p. 44) suggests that the telegraph created the golden age of war correspondents at the turn of the century because reports could be sent from the front lines within days, instead of weeks or months.

Telegraphy was a binary technology—messages were relayed in Morse code, using dots and dashes to form words—and as such is a proto-digital technology that established economic and social patterns into which the digital technologies that followed fitted seamlessly. In an interesting early case of the techno-legal time-gap (see chapter 12), the first transnational cooperative to regulate the telegraph was not established until 1865, more than thirty years after the first transmissions (McMahon, 2002, p. 382). It was a technology that assisted the rapid expansion of modern imperialism by facilitating commercial transactions over great distances, and the telegraph was an important component of the global infrastructure needed to build the emerging system of mass industrial development. In the same way that theorists today, such as Manuel Castells, argue that the new 'information' economy is a necessary adjunct to globalisation, the telegraph established a 'new global information code' that facilitated the circulation of capital (in the form of money) and economic control (in the form of imperialism) (McMahon 2002, p. 380).

Making airwaves: The development of commercial radio

> That [radio] broadcasting should develop as a capitalist enterprise, a vehicle for advertising and commercial expansion is not surprising ... What is curious is the sequence of steps by which it became so, the twists and turns which took the medium out of the hands of the state and the military and emphasised its universal entertainment value as against its long-distance communication role. (Lewis & Booth 1989, p. 30)

Peter Lewis and Jerry Booth are talking about the birth of the commercial radio industry in America between the end of World War I and the start of World War II. In that period of twenty years the radio moved from being a tool for law enforcement and military command to being one of the most widely accepted domestic appliances, services, and social routines of the 20th century. Today we take radio for granted. It's on while we drive to work or uni; it's on in the background at work. Radio is even available over the Internet. But radio, like the telegraph, was initially a commercial medium; as a 'communications and control' technology it was used in the coordination of international shipping and other forms of transport. At first, radio's inventor, Guglielmo Marconi (1874–1937), backed by the British and Italian governments, attempted to retain a monopoly over marine communications, but the Germans baulked at the idea and in 1912, after the 'unsinkable' *Titanic* did sink in the North Atlantic, oceangoing vessels were required to carry a radio transceiver as a uniform safety measure (McMahon 2002, p. 385). Guglielmo Marconi was granted the world's first patent for wireless telegraphy (Morse code sent via radio signals, rather than copper cable) in 1896, and in 1897 formed a company to market the new technology. Ironically, Marconi had been supported in his endeavours by the British Post Office, but severed his relationship with the organisation when it became clear that it thought the new invention had no real purpose (Weightman 2003, p. 33). After a series of trials over shorter distances, Marconi made the first intercontinental radio transmission, from Cornwall to Newfoundland in 1901 (Nobelprize.org 2005).

RADIO

Transmission or broadcast of sound by wireless or a device for receiving such transmissions. An abbreviation of radio broadcasting, which is the intentional and programmatic broadcasting of information via a radio broadcasting station dedicated to that purpose.

Copper wire to iPods: Changing technologies of sound recording

Where would we be today without the ability to electronically reproduce sound? Most of us probably have an iPod and used to have a CD Walkman. But music wasn't always that portable. The first sound-recording equipment was very bulky and cumbersome. It also produced very weak signals and there was no stereo!

In 1877 Thomas Edison (1847–1931) produced one of the earliest mechanical devices for reproducing recorded music, the phonograph, which played from cylinders. A decade later the gramophone came on the market and used flat discs to hold the recording.

The first electromagnetic tape-recording and playback system was publicly available in 1935. In 1948 the first modern long-playing (LP) discs were developed and ten years later the first stereo system was introduced. The short-lived eight-track tape cartridge was introduced in the mid-1960s, but was killed off by the tape cassette in the early 1970s. Compact discs were first marketed in 1982 and were initially very expensive. In the 1990s Sony developed the minidisk recorder and player and as compression techniques improved and convergence in digital technologies began to move quickly, MP3 files made their first appearance in 1997. The iPod was released onto the market in 2003 and has quickly replaced the transistor radio and the CD walkman as the mobile music source of choice with many young people.

Today consumer music technology is making another great leap forward, which will make CDs appear so last century. We take up podcasting in a later chapter; for now we want to make the general point that the technology for reproducing music in the home or car has come a long way in just 120 years. The next step is to have music stored on hard drives, or downloaded from a subscriber network. Now, music subscriber networks are teaming up with the British rail network to allow commuters to download music to their MP3 player from platform-mounted vending machines (Shedden 2004).

VALVES TO CHIPS: MARCONI SHARE SCANDALS

One of the giant names in radio and electronics, Marconi, has fallen on hard times. The company takes its name from the Italian inventor Guglielmo Marconi, who was experimenting with electromagnetic techniques for broadcasting in the late 1900s. After World War I, Marconi was among those working towards the transmission of the spoken word to a large and dispersed audience—the first moves towards broadcasting. Marconi is credited with being among the first to design and build radio technology in the 1920s, and from that point on the development of broadcasting (both radio and television) was fairly rapid (Thompson 1995, pp. 78–9).

Today the Marconi company does a lot more than build radios: it is one of the world's leading networking technology companies. Unfortunately, in 2005 it suffered a major setback when British Telecom gave contracts to eight of Marconi's international competitors for the £10 billion ($A24.5 billion) refit of its British network (Wray 2005).

The problems facing Marconi are indicative of the global nature of information technologies within the world economy. The companies bidding against Marconi for the British Telecom contract were headquartered in France (Alcatel), Japan (Fujitsu), China (Huawei), Germany (Siemens), Sweden (Ericsson), and the United States (Ciena, Cisco, and Lucent Technologies). Marconi already had in place an international marketing agreement with Huawei and according to Wray's *Guardian* article, financial analysts were expecting the Chinese company to buy Marconi's British assets.

The share market reacted to Marconi's bad news by cutting almost 40 per cent from its price and the company said that up to 2000 jobs could be cut from its research and development operations. According to London's *Financial Times* (Pesola et al. 2005), Marconi could find itself the target of takeover bids, or even facing extinction. It has become too small to compete successfully in the global market.

Radio and all that jazz

In 1920 radio station KDKA in Pittsburgh, Pennsylvania became the first commercial radio station in the world. Just as World War II gave impetus to the development of emerging computer technologies, so World War I had stimulated technical developments in radio. It was, however, the convergence of the phonograph, and later the gramophone, with the technologies of radio transmission that gave commercial radio broadcasting its biggest boost. If Britain emerged from World War I decimated, then the United States, which had funded the war, now dominated the world economy. The 1920s—the Roaring Twenties—was a time of prosperity. It was the Jazz Age, and the trumpet and the sax could soon be heard coast to coast. By 1922, there were over 600 licensed commercial radio stations in the United States. In 1927 both CBS and NBC radio networks were established. From an activity that was a hobby before and during World War I, radio in the 1920s became big business. However, as Robert McChesney notes, the hobbyists did not give up without a fight and commercial radio was initially unprofitable (2000b, p. 199). The first attempts at regulation came with the introduction of the Federal Radio Commission in 1927, and one of its first acts was the allocation of commercial licences that favoured the big companies.

The stimulus for this expansion was, in part, Marconi's arrival in the United States in 1899, where he established a subsidiary of his company. This stimulated intense competition and a number of American companies—AT&T, Westinghouse, and General Electric—acquired patents for important aspects of the emerging radio economy (Lewis & Booth 1989, p. 207). In 1912 the American government began issuing radio licences and a number of universities began to broadcast—weather bulletins in Morse code! The Radio Corporation of America was formed in 1919, in part to prevent a complete monopoly over radio by the American navy and to keep amateur experiments in check (p. 207). Attempts by the university sector to establish a national radio network modelled on the BBC (see below) failed because many of its backers felt it would be politically difficult to achieve (for more of this history see McChesney 2000b, pp. 189–225).

BROADCAST

To broadcast means to scatter (cast) widely. In this sense broadcasting is clearly linked to the concept of publishing in the print media. The message (program) is published (broadcast) to a wide audience via electronic signals originating from a single source. Radio stations and free-to-air television services are the most common forms of broadcasting today.

'This is the BBC': The public service model

Unlike the United States in which free enterprise flourished—creating a market—the United Kingdom developed a public service model of radio broadcasting. The British government retained control of wireless broadcasting and instituted the BBC—the British Broadcasting Corporation—as a 'public service' network (Lewis & Booth 1989, pp. 208–10). By 1927, the various corporations interested in radio broadcasting, and most certainly in the production and sale of sets on which radio broadcasts could be received, had been allowed to pursue their commercial interests, and were succeeded by a national corporation responsible for the production of radio content. The BBC was funded by a licence fee on every receiver—first radio and later television. The driving force behind the BCC and its philosophy of public service broadcasting was Sir John Reith (1889–1971). Reith ran the Corporation until 1938, leaving his mark on its character. Indeed, some would say that he moulded the BBC on his own character: high-minded, elitist, and exacting (Lewis & Booth 1989). For Reith, broadcasting was about creating and preserving cultural capital; it was about education and edification, not entertainment. Such values could only prevail in a broadcaster untrammelled by the need to fund itself by selling airtime to advertisers. It was a model that served the country well in its darkest hours. The Australian Broadcasting Corporation (ABC) was modelled on the BBC and for many years enjoyed an independent existence. Under the government of John Howard the ABC's independence has been repeatedly threatened, most recently by the appointment of well-known conservatives and the decision to abolish the staff-elected representative on the governing board, a move described as a 'cynical, cage-rattling provocation' by former ABC senior producer David Salter (2006).

PUBLIC SERVICE BROADCASTING

A broadcasting regime funded by the citizens—the public—by taxes or other means of public subscription such as licence fees. Such broadcasters, of which the BBC is the definitive model, have a charter obligation to address certain audience needs. The ABC is one such broadcaster; other examples are PBS in the USA and NHK in Japan.

Fireside chats: Roosevelt and Churchill

On assuming the presidency in the Great Depression, Franklin Roosevelt used the medium of radio initially to reassure his people, to sell his New Deal policies, and later to gather support for the US entry into World War II. Known as 'fireside chats', these thirty talks between 1933 and 1944 enabled Roosevelt, a Democrat, to avoid the gatekeepers of the mass media—who were largely Republican—and appeal directly to the people. A number of his speeches make the point. In his address of 9 December 1941, following the Japanese attack on Pearl Harbor, Roosevelt said:

> To all newspapers and radio stations—all those who reach the eyes and ears of the American people—I say this: You have a most grave responsibility to the nation now and for the duration of this war.
>
> If you feel that your Government is not disclosing enough of the truth, you have every right to say so. But in the absence of all the facts, as revealed by official sources, you have no right in the ethics of patriotism to deal out unconfirmed reports in such a way as to make people believe that they are gospel truth. (Roosevelt 1941)

No matter what we might think of this today, Roosevelt's strategy was obviously successful. He was elected to office for four successive terms, and died in office in 1945 in the closing stages of the war.

During World War II, the BBC proved a valuable part of Britain's defence infrastructure (Lewis & Booth 1989, p. 209). Its shortwave service was used as a conduit for the Resistance movements on the Continent, and for British operatives behind enemy lines. But the most memorable function of the BBC was the reporting and broadcasting of morale-maintaining speeches by Prime Minister Churchill.

Before the war, when in opposition, Churchill had used BBC Radio to criticize the British government for its policy of appeasement and its failure to prepare for an inevitable European war against fascism. His particular concern was the lack of adequate air defences. On assuming office in 1940, Churchill, like Roosevelt before him, used the medium of radio in defence of the realm. Churchill was an orator the like of whom we shall not see again. He was meticulous in his preparation, memorised his text, and practised his delivery. Nearly all of the speeches were made first on the floor of the House of Commons, reported on radio by the BCC, and then only later broadcast by their author. Such was the case with one of his most famous utterances, known as 'We shall fight on the beaches', delivered first on 4 June 1940 when the threat of a Nazi invasion of Britain was greatest. Here is an excerpt:

> We shall go on to the end, we shall fight in France, we shall fight on the seas and oceans, we shall fight with growing confidence and growing strength in the air, we shall defend our island, whatever the cost may be, we shall fight on the beaches, we shall fight on the landing grounds, we shall fight in the fields and in the streets, we shall fight in the hills; we shall never surrender. (Churchill 1940)

The BBC retained its monopoly over broadcasting in Britain after the war, but the introduction of television in 1954 saw the first commercial broadcasting introduced when the Conservative government gave a licence to ITV. The BBC could not keep pace with the changing tastes of its younger audience, who were beginning to enjoy greater freedoms, including rock'n'roll music. This led to the first successful experiments in what became known as 'pirate radio' (Lewis & Booth 1989, p. 209).

Pop, rock, and pirate radio: Radio Caroline

On Easter Sunday in 1964, a revolution began to rock radio in the UK. With the opening words, 'This is Radio Caroline on 199, your all day music station', the two unknown announcers then played the Rolling Stones' 'Not Fade Away'. The originator of Radio Caroline was a well-to-do Irish pop promoter, Ronan O'Rahilly, who, as the UK pop revolution of the 1960s swung into full gear, was unable to get airplay for his artists on either the state monopoly, the BBC, or on the offshore commercial competition, Radio Luxembourg. The solution: equip a ship with a radio station, register it under a flag of convenience, anchor it in international waters offshore from major population centres, and blast away. It was called Pirate Radio, and it took off. The name Radio Caroline came from a *Life* magazine image O'Rahilly had seen of JFK's daughter playing at her father's feet in the Oval Office while the business of state was transacted over her head. That was Radio Caroline: at play while the heavyweights debated. It was not until 1970 that the BBC's monopoly on radio was broken.

In Australia, a youth-oriented radio station, 2JJ, was established in Sydney in 1975 by the ABC. In the late 1980s the station went national on the FM band and became 'Triple J'. While it has never really enjoyed the success of its commercial counterparts, Triple J has been an important element in the Australian radio scene, particularly through its fresh, young approach and the 'homegrown' musical talent it has 'unearthed'. In 2006 the ABC announced that Triple J would develop its brand through a series of weekly television shows, aggressively marketed podcasts, and a 'youth culture' magazine (MacLean 2006). Triple J has been able to take advantage of digital convergence to relaunch itself to a new audience as its diehard fans from the early years move on to other media outlets, such as the ABC's local network or the more upmarket 'Radio National', which features more spoken-word content (Meade 2005), and the 'adult-pop' FM networks (MacLean 2005c).

Talk radio: Technology of mass populism

In the 1970s and 1980s radio listeners abandoned the AM band for the higher technical quality of the FM band. In the 1990s, however, the AM band bit back with talk radio. Talk radio relies on telephone calls from listeners and the strong—often outrageous—opinions of the presenters. The presenter can then bounce his or her own views against those of the caller. Aided by regulatory changes in the United States in 1987, radio stations were able to be more partisan in the presentation of opinion. One of the most opinionated was Missouri-born Rush Limbaugh, who has a weekly audience variously estimated at between 14 and 20 million listeners. After working in music radio, Limbaugh came to prominence in Sacramento, California, moved to New York, and was syndicated nationally from 1988. In addition to taking calls from listeners, he has made extensive use of email in generating content for his show.

In Australia, Limbaugh had his imitators, who are, in the main, politically conservative yet populist presenters. Bob Francis, on 5AA in Adelaide, got into trouble in October

2005 for suggesting his listeners 'smash the judge's face in' over a bail application in a child pornography case and in another incident he called an 81-year-old woman a 'dickbrain' when she rang to defend alleged terror suspect David Hicks (McGarry 2005). The Sydney radio market is dominated by two of the best-known talk-radio hosts, Alan Jones and John Laws: Jones at breakfast and Laws after 9.00 a.m. In recent years, both have run foul of the media regulator, the Australian Broadcasting Authority (now ACMA), for their failure to adequately distinguish between opinion and paid advertising (Hirst & Patching 2005). In December 2005 Alan Jones boasted that his radio program had helped inspire anti-Muslim riots in the Sydney beachside suburb of Cronulla. Despite their populism and conservative opinions, politicians like to use talk radio hosts as a way of communicating directly with their constituencies. It was on the John Laws program that Paul Keating made his famous 'banana republic' remark in 1986. John Howard has made more use of talk radio than any of his predecessors, again with the intention of bypassing the gatekeepers of print and current affairs television, to speak directly to his constituency, a constituency that overlaps considerably with the Jones/Laws audience demographic.

Broadcast to podcast

> Podcasting might sound like something farmers do with peas but a fast-increasing number of devotees know better ... (even the Pope has a podcast). (Dudley 2005)

There's a short note of wry humour in this opening line from Jennifer Dudley's report about the birth and growth of podcasting. The term 'broadcast' itself has agricultural roots—seed was 'broadcast' into the ploughed field. But podcasting today is one of the most important forms of narrowcasting and it exemplifies the paradigm shift in media as a result of digital convergence.

Podcasting—the word is a combination of 'iPod' and 'broadcasting'—first became publicly available in 2004 as a way of linking audio to weblogs and according to Dudley's research it has become the new wave in Internet downloads. A podcast allows the user to time-shift radio broadcasts that are posted on the Internet by downloading them to an MP3 player and listening at their own leisure. The software can also be programmed to automatically check websites for updates and new download material.

PODCASTING

A digital audio technology that enables listeners to download material from the Internet for time-shift listening using a digital media player. Also possible with video.

Like many innovations in computing, podcasting began as an alternative to the large commercially oriented broadcasters, but it has become a feature on the websites of mainstream broadcasters. In Australia both the ABC and the Austereo networks were quick to jump on the podcasting bandwagon. The ABC's Nick Bron says it won't affect the traditional radio audience, but rather will provide an extra service: 'I don't think existing radio listeners are going to throw away their radios. The existing audience will download a program because they want to listen to it again or because they missed it, but the potential for expanding the audience is huge' (ABC spokesman Nick Bron, cited in Dudley 2005).

In the context of commercial radio, podcasting is about building listener loyalty and having it reflected in the all-important ratings surveys. However, there is some doubt over just how popular podcasting might become because one of the main attractions for younger listeners in particular—music—presents problems for the initiators of the podcast. Current copyright laws for recorded music make it difficult and expensive to obtain the relevant permissions to podcast music. This highlights one of the continuing contradictions in digital convergence: the time-lag between the technology and the regulatory and legal frameworks in which it operates. We will cover this issue in more detail in chapters 8 and 12, but according to Michael Anderson, chief executive of Austereo: 'The issue of digital rights is a nightmare and the technology is moving far faster than companies and the legislative capacity to deal with it and there will always be some frustration because of that' (cited in Dudley 2005).

The regulators and licensing agencies, such as the Australian Performing Rights Association (APRA), are examining how they might respond to podcasting. But resolution of the issue will be complicated because the copyright on recorded music is spread across the writers, artists, and record companies who hold the rights to the physical recording. According to a pioneer of podcasting in Australia, Mick Stanic, niche spoken-word programming is likely to be the main feature of podcasting for the foreseeable future: 'We'll never kill radio and the intention is not to kill radio. What we're doing is offering a whole new bundle of material when listeners want it' (cited in Dudley 2005).

Podcasting is just one cultural form of digital radio. Australian networks are keen to move onto a digital platform because it will allow them to broadcast a greater range of material with better sound quality. Under the federal government's 'digital roadmap', radio stations will be given free access to some parts of the digital spectrum to provide services such as streaming weather and traffic reports, or information about the music being played. It is likely that there will be a long lead-time before analogue radio signals are switched off as digital is seen as a 'supplementary' rather than a 'replacement' technology (Day 2005).

This raises a question about the delivery of audio over the Internet, either by streaming, podcast downloads, or RSS (Really Simple Syndication) feeds: is it still radio? Undoubtedly it retains some of the features of radio—music and spoken word—but it presents a new set of issues concerning culture and political economy. The commercial model for successful podcasting and other forms of digital (non-radio) delivery have yet to be worked out fully and perhaps it's too early to tell if these new forms will actually replace radio completely. In our final chapter we provide a short discussion about the supposed 'death' of old media technologies as new ones come along: is it true that video killed the radio stars, and will podcasting kill the video stars?

WHAT I RECKON: NEVILLE PETERSEN ON THE GOLDEN AGE OF RADIO AND TELEVISION

In the 1960s and 1970s a journalist was someone who worked for a newspaper. Radio and television people were not rated at all. We were treated with some disdain as not being 'real journalists'. I must confess to realising that I had a lot to learn working side by side with distinguished foreign journalists overseas. To this day there are old-timers in the ABC who do not regard me as 'a real journalist' because I did not attend journalism training school and had joined News from the hated Talks department. For my part I was very keen to demonstrate that television journalism had its own strengths. It was hard to do this, however, as long as were expected to concentrate on filing stories by teleprinter in the same way as print journalists. This lasted until the early 1970s.

Was there a golden age of radio? Yes, in Britain, the US, and Canada during World War II. Voice reporting and the technologies involved in allowing war correspondents to go to air and to record 'actuality' (sound recorded in the field) reached a level undreamed of in 1939. Australia unfortunately was not part of this because of the News restrictions on interviewing politicians and on the use of actuality. Unfortunately, after the war all three countries retreated back to dreary 'factual' accounts until spurred on by the emergence of Ed Murrow's *See it Now* on CBS. This in turn led to a new style of TV news and current affairs reporting in the late 1950s. Radio jumped onto the bandwagon. By the mid-1960s BBC radio news and current affairs had made radio once more a major vehicle for the discussion of issues.

When I arrived in London in 1971, things had improved markedly in that TV news was receiving greater priority. They had just appointed a full-time cameraman to the London office, Les Seymour, so clearly we were to use him to the full. In Tokyo I had been dependent on the Visnews cameraman, Bob Nakai, who had many other commitments. Seymour and my five reporting staff in London, who worked for both news and current affairs, were involved in film stories continuously, in both Europe and Britain. We did stories for *Newsreel*, *Weekend Magazine*, and *This Day Tonight*. The daily Visnews satellite connection for feeding news to ABC and commercials did not start operating until mid 1974, just after I left London. When that happened there was much greater emphasis on getting same-day footage of breaking stories for TV news. Prior to this all film was shipped by air, but we were able to package a growing number of softer stories before shipment in London using local studios.

Television's golden age, I believe, was the period 1960 to around 1975. The flowering of the genius of Hugh Carlton Green, BBC Director-General, produced for the first time an era of drama and comedy in which the interests of the working man and woman were addressed. Elites and those in authority were called to account. Satirical current affairs (like the BBC program *That Was the Week That Was*) was ground-breaking, as was election coverage and, in Australia, current affairs programs such

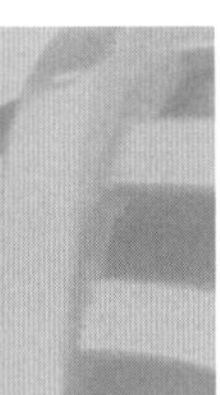

as *Tonight* and *Panorama*. The quality of *Steptoe and Son, The Avengers,* and *Callan* in this period has never been surpassed. The ABC was years behind, but eventually followed with *Four Corners* and *This Day Tonight* in current affairs and *The Mavis Bramston Show* in comedy/satire.

Television, technology, and cultural form

> Much of the great popular appeal of radio and television has been due to this sense of apparently unmediated access. The real mediations will have to be noted, but again and again they are easy to miss. What is offered is a [television] set with a tuner and a switch; we can turn it on or off, or vary what we are receiving. Throughout its history there has been this popular sense that broadcasting is a welcome alternative to the normal and recognisable social order of communications. (Williams 1978, p. 132)

Did you know that Australia's famous awards for television, the Logie, was named after the Scotsman who invented television? Even though television has only been commercially successful for a little over fifty years, John Baird (1888–1946) made his discoveries before World War II. In his dystopian novel *Brave New World*, written in 1932 but set hundreds of years into the future, Aldous Huxley makes use of the television as if it is part of everyday life. There is a Bureau of Propaganda by Television and a television factory at Brentford, near London. Television is the product of convergence in technologies (audio and film recording; the development of broadcast transmission and, later, video), but it is also a cultural convergence that has cannibalised other forms of media, including the stage and music hall variety show, radio news bulletins, film, and drama (Hall 1996).

A tall, engaging, and well-spoken Welsh intellectual called Raymond Williams (1921–1988) was one of the first Western academics to explore the technology and the cultural forms of television in the 1960s and 1970s. He was also a political radical, a Marxist, and a supporter of left-wing causes. He was very active in the British nuclear disarmament movement, like many other great thinkers of his day. Williams' pioneering analysis of the early days of the BBC and later commercial television in Britain explores a wide range of issues. In a series of books and essays, he developed important and clear insights into the contemporary British TV scene. But importantly, he went further than that. His insights predate and predict the very elements of television today, even the so-called 'reality' television that has colonised our screens so effectively over the last ten years.

In *Television: Technology and cultural form* (1978), Williams begins by emphasising the importance of studying cause and effect—the dialectic of contradiction and creative tension—within the relationship between 'technology' and 'a society', 'a culture', and 'a psychology'. He says these connections are both 'theoretical' and 'immensely practical'. Understanding cause and effect, he says, is the key to asking the right questions about technology. These questions include: how it is used; the institutions that bring it into being, manage, and employ it; the impact it has on patterns of work, consumption, and leisure; and the content and form of the medium (Williams 1978, pp. 9–10).

TELEVISION

An electrically powered box of valves, clips, tubes, vacuums, and wires, used mainly for home entertainment, and occasionally for receiving information from a number of central sources known as television broadcasters.

Williams was interested in television because he saw that society generally had come to believe that after just twenty years television had gained widespread acceptance and that the medium had 'altered our world' (p. 11). Television did appear to have had the effect of changing the world forever, but like us, Williams was keen to make the important distinction between those versions of the argument that were technologically determinist and those that understood technologies within a process of change that is 'in any case occurring or about to occur' (p. 13). At the same time Williams is critical of what he calls the 'symptomatic' view of technology, where change is caused by events and processes outside the realm of scientific discovery and innovation. This view, he argues, is just as sterile as technological determinism; it is an early form of the cultural determinist argument. The flaw in both cases is that technical innovation and 'science' are seen as value-free neutral activities that would take place regardless of social circumstances: 'technology is then as it were a by-product of a social process that is otherwise determined' (p. 12). To escape what he saw as a determinist 'trap', Williams introduced the concept of 'intention' to the dialectical process of 'research and development': technology is developed consciously 'and designed with certain [productive] purposes and [social] practices already in mind' (p. 14).

This insight became clear for Williams in his study of television because it was a technology developed with a clear purpose in mind. Governments, bureaucrats, and business leaders had all learned important lessons over the 150 years of the print media and after nearly forty years of radio. The mistakes of the past, and the successes, would greatly influence the way in which the technology of television delivered the consequent social impacts that Raymond Williams identified and we are still experiencing today. Television shapes us both as consumers and as citizens in a clear demonstration of mutual constitution.

Television, the market, and citizenship

> Television is fascinating ... Television fascinates because it embodies the culture it depicts. In a genuine sense, television is culture today: capricious, intemperate and absorbed by a near-religious devotion to consumption. (Cashmore 1994, p. 2)

Without mass consumption there would be no free-to-air commercial television and without the ability of television to influence consumption there would be no market for mass-produced consumer goods. There is no doubt that television today exists in, for, and of the market: commercial 'breaks' in programming of up to nine minutes; promos and trailers for upcoming programs interrupting dramatic moments; and the endless 'brought to you by' and 'proudly sponsored' tags that intrude over the end of programs and credits (Wayne 2003). Now we also have the endless urging and cajoling of presenters and voice-over artists encouraging us to love or hate the housemate, the 'wannabe', or the potential lovesick millionaire enough to call the convenient voting hot lines ($0.55 per call, with parent's permission).

Ellis Cashmore (1994, p. 3) compares television to the internal combustion engine—both 'have changed us immeasurably'. The TV industry is an interesting mirror that reflects the dominance of the military-industrial-information complex in 20th- and 21st-century economic life and popular culture. It brings together all the techniques of mass production—a soap opera like *Days of our Lives* is run like a giant factory operation—with the generation of a slow-acting, sweet-smelling, and potent cultural nerve gas as a happy and coincidental by-product.

The key cultural form of television is determined by the social relations of capitalist production: television is dominated by market relations and by the need to sell both programs and viewers to advertisers (McQueen 1977; Ehrlich 1997). This dominant economic function of television (and all commercial media) sits in dialectical tension with its public service role as a communication resource that promotes 'public dialogue' (Groombridge 1972, p. 240). Television has definitely been the mass medium of the broadcast age and the arena for both entertainment (mass culture) and for political participation. In this climate, what passes for public service broadcasting must also be good for business (Phelan 1991). Increasingly, this has seen control over programming decisions pass from the media firm to the advertiser, through co-productions and branded formats (McChesney 2000b, p. 41). These commercial links are only going to expand and strengthen as a result of digital and commercial convergence (Mosco 1996, pp. 106–7). The French philosopher Pierre Bourdieu puts a slightly more postmodern spin on the same issue: 'With television, we are dealing with an instrument that offers, theoretically, the possibility of reaching everybody. This brings up a number of questions' (Bourdieu 1998, p. 14).

For Bourdieu the questions conjured by this hypothetical possibility of reaching everybody revolve around the content and the purpose of the broadcast: 'Is what I have to say meant to reach everybody? Am I ready to make what I say understandable by everybody? Is it worth being understood by everybody? You can go even further: should it be understood by everybody?' (pp. 14–15).

Typical of his postmodernist 'type', Bourdieu's questions reveal that he is at the centre of his own universe. Instinctively he knows his audience is limited, by interest and perhaps education. But like an elitist scholar, he can dismiss the rest: 'Is it worth being understood by everybody?' The practical limit—that access to television is limited by the economics of availability—can be ignored in this hypothetical world. But there is one important insight in Bourdieu's comments: in the real world of television these very questions—or variations on them—are asked every day about every programming decision in every television network around the globe. There is control and censorship of the material that is broadcast on television. In a sense television's expression of deviant values or attitudes is monitored by the power of economic censorship: 'there is so little job security in television and radio [that] there is a greater tendency toward political conformity' (p. 15). While this infrastructure of control is very real and invested in the private corporations and government agencies who deal with the regulation of broadcasting, Bourdieu (p. 16) points to 'many kinds of anonymous and invisible mechanisms' through which television has become 'such a formidable instrument for maintaining the symbolic order'. We can see this process very clearly at work in television news broadcasts where our forms of citizenship and participation are mediated.

Television makes news

Television news values are those of the commercial world. The views of the world's richest men (and a few women) are widely covered as if they are gospel. On some networks on some days it is hard to tell where the marketing ends and the news begins. Commercial current affairs programs are constantly spruiking wonder cures and marvel diets one week and then attacking them as 'shonks' the next. Never mind, there's always a new product just around the corner, in time for the next ratings season. John Langer (1998) describes this as 'tabloid television' that focuses on bad news stories, leavened with entertaining stories and material that reaffirms the values of the market economy.

EDWARD R. MURROW AND THE ADVENT OF BROADCAST NEWS

Ed Murrow (1908–65) was born of Quaker stock and grew up in the state of Washington. At Washington State University he paid his college fees by working as a lumberjack in the forests of the Pacific north-west. There he encountered the Wobblies, the militant Industrial Workers of the World. His introduction to radio came in 1930 when as a student union activist in New York he co-produced the University of the Air program for the nascent Columbia Broadcasting System—CBS. Murrow never forgot his background in forestry.

Having joined CBS in 1935, Murrow arrived in London in 1937 with a brief to act as a talks producer. Radio news, as Murrow was to shape it, and as we experience it today, did not exist. But at the outbreak of war in Europe, CBS began coverage of what Winston Churchill memorably called 'the gathering storm'. Murrow recruited American newspaper reporters in Europe and put them to air. One of his finds was the Berlin-based William L. Shirer (1904–93), whose journalistic and historical accounts of the rise of the Third Reich still make chilling and compelling reading (Shirer 1959). When Great Britain entered the war, German bombers hit English cities at night during what was known the Blitz. Murrow broadcast from outdoor locations, from rooftops, from the burning streets, and from among the ruins and unexploded bombs. His signature opening was 'This ... is London'. Murrow is credited with building support in an isolationist United States for Britain's struggle against fascism. More than that, he is credited with fashioning broadcast news in its purest form.

In the postwar period Murrow was to take up the fight to the anti-democratic US Senator Joe McCarthy, and to engage CBS head William Paley over the intrusion of entertainment into broadcasting. No doubt his wartime experience in England predisposed him to a public service model of broadcasting. He won his battle against McCarthyism; and as we know from watching television today, he lost the battle with Paley. Perhaps it was no coincidence that Paley served in psychological operations on the staff of General Dwight Eisenhower in World War II. In 1961, Murrow was appointed to head the US Information Agency by President John F. Kennedy.

ENG: Videotape and the nightly news

> Television news editors refer to ENG … with a familiarity that suggests it has been around since television began, yet it is only one development in a rapidly developing business … Electronic news gathering is a three word name for a process which may use a variety of different equipment, but all of them begin with a television camera. Americans and Europeans developed video cameras, but the Japanese miniaturised them and made them versatile tools for gathering news. (Masterton & Patching 1990, p. 68)

In the same way that other technologies we've discussed so far contain their own contradictions, which are usually expressed in socially constructed and contextualised ways, magnetic image recording on videotape also developed dialectically. Importantly, from the 1980s on, videotape replaced film in nearly all areas of television production. The first area of high impact was in news production. ENG stands for 'electronic newsgathering' and when it was first proposed and introduced there was an immediate and hostile reaction from camera operators, editors, and other staff associated with film and television production.

The television news genre first developed out of combining techniques from radio's live presentation (the news reader) with intercut 'package' pieces pre-recorded by reporters in the field (Winston 1993). At first, field reports were shot on 16 mm film, which then had to be processed into a negative and a positive before it could be edited for broadcast. It was simple enough if the pictures were to accompany a reader's voice-over, but if a reporter's soundtrack was to be added, or other sound effects, then the whole piece had to be cut together. In the early days of television news it was impossible to record synchronous sound, so the reporter would write a piece to be read by an announcer—the 'reader voice-over'.

Even when the technology improved to allow the recording of an audio track on a magnetic strip attached to the film stock, it was cumbersome, expensive to process, and time-consuming to edit (Masterton & Patching 1990, pp. 66–8). Thus deadlines were set very early in the afternoon. There was often a wait of at least an hour while the film was put through the lab. If the piece had to be sent anywhere it was usually done physically, leading to further unplanned delays and cutting further into the deadline. Video was meant to change all that.

Today the situation is vastly different: television news is now global and almost instantaneous; the 'news clock' never stops and it is possible to see 24-hour news channels on cable or satellite television in almost any major population centre on the planet. Globalisation is a product of both technological and commercial convergence and it has permanently altered the process of the production, dissemination, and consumption of news (Gureveitch et al. 1991). The constant among all this change is that news broadcasts on commercial television must remain profitable. In order to maintain profitability, the cultural form of television news has been radically altered over the past twenty years. Globally, news operations have been 'downsized' and news values have been shifted from 'hard' news to 'softer' and 'lifestyle' stories. The other benefit (to the corporate owners) is that celebrity stories and a concentration on dramatic incidents, such as crashes, natural disasters, and crime, is hardly likely to create any controversy that can upset the all-important advertisers (McChesney 2000b, p. 54). In short, television is moving away from being a public service information provider to being a medium designed purely for entertainment.

Television and entertainment

> True specialist television offers a range of programs to please the average discerning viewer. This is in the tradition of broadcasting. Some say the age of narrowcasting spells the end of specialist TV. Does it? (Williams 1996, p. 49)

Robyn Williams doesn't think so, though from his vantage point as a respected ABC science journalist and self-confessed television 'junkie', he recognised that within twenty years of writing these words the television landscape would have changed again. Williams is also a television nationalist. His argument is that the short-term views of the late 1990s, driven by the global drive for profitable investment in the means of communication, 'may well have destroyed' the local Australian television industry by 2020 (p. 59). Even though investment in new television has declined steadily over the previous decade, it is clear today that television is still the preferred medium for information and entertainment in every society where it has established itself as a viable industry. Increasingly, television is being dominated by a small group of powerful conglomerates that offer a small amount of localised programming within a dominant stream of international (mainly American) entertainment (McChesney 2000b, p. 106). It seems that this global stream is now overwhelmingly a mix of crime and legal dramas (with the occasional medical soap opera thrown in) and so-called reality television. This is very nicely parodied by the cyberpunk author William Gibson.

Cops in trouble

> There was a woman there from *Cops in Trouble*, which had been Rydell's father's favourite show ... Rydell lay there thinking about all the times he and his father had watched *Cops in Trouble*. 'What kind of trouble we talking here?' he finally asked.

> The woman just smiled. 'Whatever, Berry, it'll probably be adequate.'
> He squinted up at her. She was sort of good-looking. 'What's your name?'
> 'Karen Mendelsohn.' She didn't look like she was from Knoxville, or even Memphis.
> 'You from *Cops in Trouble*?'
> 'What you do for 'em?'
> 'I'm a lawyer,' she said. Rydell couldn't recall ever actually having met one before, but after that he wound up meeting a lot more. (Gibson 1993, p. 11)

Berry Rydell is an important character in several of William Gibson's books, introduced in *Virtual Light* (1993). He meets the woman from *Cops in Trouble* while he's lying in hospital, injured in a shoot-out with fugitives while on patrol for the Los Angeles police. He's a cop in trouble and the woman is there to get his story for her program. Unfortunately, he doesn't make the cut and is bumped from the show by another cop in trouble—a policewoman who, according to a production assistant on *Cops in Trouble*, was 'balls out telegenic' (Gibson 1993). There are not (yet) any shows on television quite like *Cops in Trouble*, but there are plenty of 'reality' programs that feature police surveillance footage. There was a whole crop of them a couple of years ago—all those crazy stunts involving highway patrolmen stopping stupid drunks, or high-speed chases through narrow streets. It's not too far-fetched to argue that by making the use of surveillance footage humorous in the context of these shows, the police are in fact trying to normalise the use of surveillance and dashboard-mounted cameras in their cars. The most common format is one in which viewers derive their pleasure from watching the discomfort of others—those caught in the glare of surveillance entertainment.

The unreality of reality TV

> Reality TV is also life-changing in the sense that 'former reality show contestant' has almost become a career in itself. (Murphy 2006, p. 143)

What exactly is reality television? It turns the mundane into the extraordinary; ordinary people into instant celebrities. One thing is clear about it: there's very little actual 'reality' involved. As soon as a television camera and the enormously expensive process of production are involved, the spectacle loses its most important connections to the 'real'. It is structured, scripted, and edited according to the wishes of the producers, and their motive is really selling the program to advertisers. When you actually turn off the television and think about it, it's perfectly obvious that so-called reality television is in fact a series of carefully constructed game shows. Most of them—in fact all of them that are not documentary in style—are competitions: *Survivor*, *Race around the World*, the *Idol* series, *Joe Millionaire*, *Outback Jack*, *The Biggest Loser*, and so on. The people involved—let's call them contestants—are in it for the fifteen minutes of fame and the million bucks on offer.

The worldwide phenomenon of *Big Brother* is a case in point: a pre-packaged franchise with heavily scripted plot twists and rules (Murphy 2006). It's entirely appropriate that the Australian version of the show was shot on a set constructed inside one of the nation's best-known theme parks, Dreamworld on Queensland's Gold Coast. What's real about taking a dozen or so unrelated individuals, with nothing in common, except a desire to be 'seen', and putting them in an artificial 'domestic' environment with fifty hidden cameras and microphones. For a start, this is not how most of us live our 'real' existence. Then there's that endless parade of meaningless tasks—where's the meaning in spending an entire day waiting to catch a watermelon before it smashes on the pool deck?

REALITY TELEVISION

A genre of television drama that purports to be a 'fly on the wall' rendering of the activities of non-professional actors in contrived situations. More easily understood as a postmodern form of 'game show' genre.

We can then add to the unreality by getting the public to systematically eliminate 'housemates' after watching them 'perform' in carefully edited 'highlights' shows. *Big Brother* is essentially an elaborate and slightly interactive game show. The next twist, the *Joe Schmo* show, goes even further. The 'real' contestant knows he's in a *Big Brother*-style household and is competing to stay inside, but everyone else in the 'house' is an actor, paid to make life hell for the unlucky 'Joe'. It may be slightly amusing and entertaining, but it's not real.

Taping and editing shows like *Big Brother* in the short time-frame available to the producers—getting on air within twenty-four hours—would not be possible without the current generation of digital technology. The physical layout of the house, with its hundreds of metres of hidden corridors, is not suitable for large, bulky cameras. The wireless microphones that each housemate is required to wear and the fixed cameras in the showers, toilets, and garden are all products of the digital revolution in television technology.

Social commentator David Chalke is probably right when he argues that the audience for *Big Brother* has the 'attitudes of classical adolescents' (quoted in Coultan 2004, p. 29), but it's not rocket science to think so. For the generations that have grown up with up to forty hours of television watching a week for fifteen, twenty, or thirty years, the effect has been essentially what we might call 'brain rot'. The values of entertainment television—fame, novelty, and endless, mindless fun—have become dominant. In the same article market researcher Neer Korn describes the effect as 'numbing down'. She says of the television generations, 'They have numbed down, completely numbed down' (quoted in Coultan 2004, p. 29). It's not surprising really because like all game shows, *Big Brother* is about conspicuous consumption and escapism. The message is simple:

> Forget your alienation, forget the world's problems. Just watch the show and we'll make you feel better. Take comfort in your television because in the next series it could be you in the house competing for a million bucks and, if you're lucky, you could get a part in a TV soap like *Neighbours*, or end up on a celebrity diet show.

Fat chance, eh *Big Brother*? This is a show where the communications technology of the looming surveillance society has been put to good use—generating revenue and creating new markets for cheap consumer goods. But the Australian series of *Big Brother* in 2005 and 2006 pushed the boundaries too far, and offended the sensibilities of the moral minority. After complaints to the Australian Communications and Media Authority about undisguised raunchiness on the program, Channel 10 was found to have breached the Commercial Television Industry Code of Practice and gave undertakings to improve the content classification process in future. The furore also drew attention to the fact that the Queensland government was giving a subsidy to the producers, to provide employment in the industry. The up side for Channel 10 was the additional free publicity for the show generated by the public debate. In July 2006 Prime Minister Howard called for the show to be axed in response to an alleged sexual assault in the house.

Reality television shows are all about advertising. Sponsors on *Big Brother* donated whitegoods and stereos to the house and housemates got a sponsor's car when they were evicted. Even more insidious is the way these show force viewers to reach into their own pockets through so-called participation. That is to say, audience members can vote for evictions (*Big Brother*) or their favourite performer (*Idol*, *Starstruck*, etc.) by calling in to an advertised number or SMSing to another one. The fine print at the end of the show explains that this can cost upwards of 50 cents a vote.

Why do we constantly tune in to game shows on television? With very few exceptions we've got no chance of winning a prize ourselves and the only sure thing is that we're unlikely to know any of the contestants. It's not as if we really have to care about the winners and the losers. On the ABC the game shows are mostly stupid, or based on science, or both. And the ABC prizes are even crappier, cheaper, and less useful than on the commercial networks. Yet for over sixty years game shows with big brand prizes that are heavily promoted to contestants and the home audience have been a popular staple of nightly prime-time viewing. With shows that offer huge cash prizes, such as *Who Wants to be a Millionaire?* (who doesn't?) the odds against winning are probably less than those of pulling a major jackpot on the pokies with your last dollar. The odds of getting picked to go on such a show maybe even less.

One of the first Australian game shows was *Pick a Box*, hosted by Bob Dwyer and his wife Dolly. Like many that followed it on Australian television, *Pick a Box* was a direct copy of British and American versions, including the famous catch-cry 'The money or the box?', to which members of the audience would respond with competing calls, in an attempt to influence the contestant.

Just as sucker fish feed off the shark, the *Big Brother* franchise has been a boon for mobile telephony companies. The Australian show's consistent breaches of the broadcasting regulations have not only helped the flagging ratings, but also provided the opportunity for the regulator to prove its worth:

> The new chief of Australia's media regulator yesterday vowed to 'sharpen up' investigations into risqué television programs, admitting the probe last year into the Ten Network's *Big Brother Uncut* took too long. Chris Chapman, chairman of the Australian Media and Communications Authority, said the regulator realised there was a 'need for more dynamic responses'.
>
> Federal Communications Minister Helen Coonan has foreshadowed wider powers for the ACMA to crack down on the standard of controversial programs. (Lehmann 2006, p. 8)

The regulator has also been slow to require the owners of Network Ten to remedy breaches of the foreign ownership laws. Majority-owned by the Canadian operator CanWest, which holds 57.5 per cent of the stock (but only votes 15 per cent of the total stock) since 1992 when it bought Ten out of receivership from Westpac, the network has been in breach of the foreign ownership laws. Late-night nudity, it seems, is more of a threat to the public interest than overseas ownership. As we shall see in the next chapter, regulating content has been consistently prioritised over regulating ownership and control.

CASE STUDY: *GOOD NIGHT AND GOOD LUCK* (2005)

The surprise movie hit of 2005 was George Clooney's *Goodnight and Good Luck*, the bio-pic story of the American journalist Ed Murrow (see above). If, when viewing *Good Night and Good Luck*, you substitute the word 'terrorism' every time the word 'communism' is spoken, you will see why this film as been praised as a parable of our own times. George Clooney as screenwriter, director, and the supporting character CBS producer Fred Friendly has zoomed in on the contradictions within our contemporary political culture. It is, wrote A. O. Scott in a *New York Times* review, 'a passionate, thoughtful essay on power, truth-telling and responsibility' (Scott 2005, p. 1).

It is the story of how American journalist Ed Murrow took on the power and influence of Senator Joseph McCarthy, who ran a campaign looking for communist influence in the United States in the early years of the Cold War. Australia, too, went through a period of McCarthyist hysteria with Menzies calling a Royal Commission into Soviet espionage in Australia in 1954 (Manne 1987).

Murrow had made his name as a CBS radio reporter and producer in Europe before and during World War II where his dramatic eyewitness reports of the German bombing of London stirred his American audiences. His sign-off 'Good night and good luck', gives the film its title. He made the shift to television after the war, and from 1951 to 1958 was presenter of the prime-time current affairs show *See It Now*, a weighty precursor of *60 Minutes*: 'it unfolds, cinéma-vérité style, in the fast, sometimes frantic present tense, following Murrow and his colleagues as they deal with the petty annoyances and larger anxieties of newsgathering at a moment of political turmoil' (Scott 2005, p. 1).

The film is a polemic that promotes the Fourth Estate paradigm of journalism, and addresses questions of journalistic independence and integrity. If ever there was a golden age of broadcasting, it was the 1950s. Political scientists like David Putnam, who are concerned about the decline in social capital in the United States, speak of the 1950s as the time when the 'cocooning of America' began—directly as a result, he suggests, of the diffusion of television (Putnam 2000). The politically subversive effects of television—news footage of body bags coming home from Vietnam—lay in the future.

As art, the film is artless in its seamless interweaving of the black-and-white actuality of Senator McCarthy with the rest of the film. The entire film is shot in black and white, and the news footage from the 1950s is indistinguishable from the scripted drama.

The other message from this film is that television has a civic responsibility to inform and educate for democracy, not just to entertain. The film is framed by an address Murrow made in 1958 to the Radio and Television News Directors Association where he criticised the television industry as being 'fat, comfortable and complacent', and the medium as 'being used to detract, delude, amuse and insulate us' (quoted in Edgerton 1992, p 86). Eddie McGuire take note.

Finally, there is a suspicion that Clooney as the *auteur* of the film has taken a subversive delight is showing how much smoking was part of television culture in the 1950s. In these politically correct times, one is more likely to see a condom on television than a cigarette. In the 1950s, television presenters used smokes as a prop. David Strathairn as Murrow is a master in using the cigarette to add both gravitas and cool to his performance.

Conclusion

In 2006 Australia celebrated 50 years of television. In that time the form and content of programming has changed and the free to air model is under threat from 'pay per view' and Internet-based TV-like series. The 20th century was the age of television, but the future of broadcasting is uncertain. The major Australian TV networks are suffering financially as advertising revenues drop and costs keep rising. The only certainty is that after 50 years, most of the programming on TV is still crap.

KEY POINTS

In this chapter we have reviewed the history of radio and television through the 20th century and discussed how the shift towards narrowcasting and digital convergence is reshaping both the technologies and the cultural forms of broadcasting. In particular, we touched on the following:

- how the development of broadcast technologies follows the now familiar pattern of technological and commercial convergence;

- how television is a 'hybrid' cultural form that borrows from many earlier forms of media and entertainment, such as the theatre;
- how the technology and the political economy of television are moving the medium away from the 'public service' model of broadcasting towards being mainly an entertainment medium.

CLASS DISCUSSION

1. Is television news losing its audience appeal and are the days of the charismatic network anchor over?
2. How important is television news in your media consumption patterns today?
3. Look at recent financial statements or business news stories about network television. What's happening economically?

TIMELINE FOR TELEGRAPHY, TALKING WIRELESS, AND TELEVISION

1793	The Chappe brothers establish the first commercial semaphore system between two locations near Paris.
1843	FAX invented by the Scotch physicist Alexander Bain.
1844	Telegraph invented by Samuel Morse.
1856	Western Union formed by six men from Rochester, NY.
1858	Transatlantic submarine cable laid connecting Europe and the USA.
1861	Transcontinental telegraph line across the USA completed.
1872	Australia is connected to Britain with completion of the Adelaide to Darwin Overland Telegraph Line.
1876	Edison invents the electric motor and the phonograph.
1876	Telephone invented by Alexander Graham Bell.
1887	Flat record, a horizontal disc developed by Emile Berliner, replaces Edison's cylinder.
1890	Herman Hollerith gets a contract for processing the 1900 census data using punched cards. His firm named IBM in 1924.
1896	Marconi patents wireless telegraph.
1901	Guglielmo Marconi sends first transatlantic wireless signals on 12 December.
1903	Marconi transmits a radio signal from USA to England.
1904	E. F. Alexanderson's alternator boosts radio signals.
1906	Lee deForest invents the vacuum tube.
1906	Phonograph records may be 6⅔", 7", 8", 10", 11" 12", 13¾", or 14" wide.
1906	The jukebox is invented in Chicago.
1906	Marconi company experiments with radio transmission across Bass Strait.
1907	Bell and Howell develop a film projection system.
1907	De Forest broadcasts music from phonograph records.
1909	Charles Pathé creates the newsreel.
1909	Marconi and Braun share Nobel Prize in Physics for wireless development.
1910	Amalgamated Wireless Australia (AWA) formed.
1915	Wireless radio service connects USA and Japan.
1918	The first direct shortwave radio message is sent from England to Australia.
1919	Radio Corporation of America (RCA) is formed.
1920	In England, Marconi creates the first short-wave radio broadcast.
1920	KDKA Pittsburgh becomes the world's first commercial radio station.
1921	First radio broadcast of a sporting event (Dempsey v. Carpentier heavyweight championship prize fight) takes place.
1921	Wirephoto—the first electronically transmitted photograph is sent by Western Union.
1922	First radio advertisement is broadcast in the USA.

TIMELINE

1922	The BBC begins radio broadcasting.
1923	Audience measurement company A. C. Nielsen is founded.
1923	Commercial radio broadcasting commences in Australia.
1923	Reuters uses radio to transmit news.
1924	First US presidential campaign broadcasts. Coolidge buys $US 120 000 in advertising.
1926	US corporate giants RCA, General Electric, and Westinghouse combine to establish NBC.
1926	NHK Japanese Broadcasting Corporation is founded.
1927	NBC begins a second radio networks, NBC Blue, later ABC.
1927	Philo Farnsworth assembles a complete electronic TV system.
1927	US Radio Act declares public ownership of the airwaves.
1928	John Logie Baird beams a television image from England to the USA, followed by first scheduled TV broadcast in the USA.
1929	CBS founded by William S. Paley.
1929	First magnetic sound recording on plastic tape takes place.
1929	Car radio is invented.
1929	William Randolph Hearst founds newsreel production company Metrotone News.
1932	Australian Broadcasting Commission (ABC) is established.
1932	British Broadcasting Corporation (BBC) begins broadcasting television four days a week.
1933	Frequency Modulation (FM), a static-free method of transmission, is released.
1934	'High-fidelity' records are first advertised.
1934	Federal Communications Commission—the US broadcasting regulator—established.
1935	Tweeter and woofer reduce loudspeaker distortion.
1936	Canadian Broadcasting Corporation (CBC) goes on air.
1937	NBC uses truck for ENG newsgathering in New York.
1938	Orson Welles' broadcast of H. G. Wells's *War of the Worlds* creates panic in the USA, as listeners believe aliens have invaded. Broadcasting regulations are subsequently amended.
1938	*World News Roundup* radio program starts on CBS.
1940	CBS demonstrates colour television in New York.
1940	For phonograph recording, a single-groove stereo system is developed.
1940	Regular FM radio broadcasting begins.
1940	WNBT New York, the first commercial television station in the USA, commences transmission.
1941	The ABC *Argonauts* revived as a national children's program on the ABC, after a trial in Victoria 1933–35.
1942	*Kindergarten of the Air* starts on ABC Radio.
1942	First Australian Broadcasting Act.
1946	Broadcasting Act amended to require ABC to broadcast Parliament when in session.

TIMELINE

1947 ABC's independent national news service is established.

1947 Seven US east coast television stations begin regular programming.

1948 Broadcasting Act amendments result in direct funding by Commonwealth rather than from licence fees.

1948 Australian Broadcasting Control Board (ABCB) is established.

1948 LP ('long playing') records, running twenty-five minutes per side replace the old four-minute standard 78 rpm.

1949 Emmy Awards for television begin.

1949 RCA offers the 45 rpm record and player.

1950 *The Adventures of Superman* television series starts on NBC.

1950 First pay per view television in USA begins.

1950 A. C. Neilsen uses people meters to track television audiences.

1951 Colour television is introduced in the USA.

1951 Ed Murrow's *See It Now* starts on CBS.

1951 The Nagra tape-recorder adds precision, quality sound to silent cameras.

1952 Twenty-two million television sets in the USA, up from 1.5 million in 1951.

1952 Sony markets a miniature transistor radio.

1953 Television Act establishes ABC as the national television broadcaster.

1955 ITN is established, breaking the BBC's television monopoly.

1955 First issue of *TV Guide* magazine is published.

1955 Fairfax gains commercial television licence ATN-7.

1956 First ABC television broadcasts in Sydney, Melbourne, Brisbane, Adelaide, Perth, and Hobart. Ray Dolby, Charles Ginsberg, and Charles Anderson of Ampex develop the first videotape recorder. Frank Packer gets Sydney commercial television licence (TCN-9). Herald and Weekly Times launches Melbourne commercial television station HSV-7.

1957 Commonwealth Inquiry into FM broadcasting is held.

1957 Fairfax-controlled television station ATN-7 begins broadcasting.

1959 Reg Grundy Productions starts.

1960 Nine television network established when Frank Packer buys 62 per cent of Melbourne station GTV-9.

1960 Sixty million TV sets in the USA, up from 1.5 million a decade before.

1961 FM stereo broadcasting approved in the USA by the FCC.

1962 Telstar, the first international communication satellite, makes its first transmission.

1962 Marshall McLuhan's *Gutenberg Galaxy* is published.

1963 CBS and NBC TV nightly news expand to 30 minutes in colour.

1963 Ansett Transport Industries (ATI) gains Channel 0 (later 10) licence in Melbourne.

1964 Global satellite transmission of the 1964 Tokyo Olympics.

1964 Pirate radio challenges BBC Radio monopoly.

1964 First domestic VCR released.

TIMELINE

1964 Ansett buys 49.9 per cent of TVQ-0 Brisbane.

1965 Marshall McLuhan's *Understanding Media is* published.

1966 First television pictures from the moon are broadcast. First satellite television signals are exchanged between UK and Australia.

1967 First movies are available on video for home use. US Congress creates the US Public Broadcasting System (PBS).

1968 Two hundred million television sets worldwide. *60 Minutes* starts on CBS.

1969 RCA SelectaVision plays pre-recorded video cassettes, but cannot record. *Sesame Street* made by the Children's Television Workshop is first broadcast. Sony launches 3/4" U-Matic, the first videotape cassette editing system.

1970 First talkback radio is broadcast in Boston.

1972 Sony's Port-a-Pak (portable video recorder) signals the start of the camcorder revolution. HBO begins cable TV. Murdoch buys 46 per cent stake in Sydney's Channel Ten.

1973 ABC begins colour broadcasts.

1974 First ABC shop is opened. Death of Frank Packer, Australian newspaper and television mogul. Associated Press launches AP Radio Network.

1974 ENG (electronic newsgathering) equipment introduced. In England, the BBC transmits Teletext data to TV sets. Whitlam government abolishes radio and television receiver licences.

1975 First ABC 24-hours-a-day rock station 2JJ, later Triple J launched. Colour TV starts in Australia.

1976 First ABC-FM Stereo radio broadcasts. Murdoch buys a stake in Ten Sydney. ABCB Australian Broadcasting Control Board replaced by Australian Broadcasting Tribunal (ABT).

1978 Special Broadcasting Service formally established, assuming responsibility for 2EA and 3EA.

1979 AUSSAT established. First video rental shop opens.

1980 SBS television begins broadcasting. 0-10 Network re-badged as Network Ten. FM radio commences in Australia. Ted Turner launches CNN.

1983 Pay-TV operator Broadcast & Communications (Broadcom) listed.

1985 Lowy's Westfield Corporation buys 20 per cent stake in Northern Star, which will eventually give it control of Network Ten. ABC Radio 1 network renamed Metropolitan network; Radio 2 renamed Radio National.

1985 Murdoch becomes a US citizen to buy more American media outlets.

1985 Cable Shopping Network is launched in the USA.

1986 Fox Broadcasting Company is established.

1986 News sells stake in Network Ten Holdings to Westfield.

1987 Packer sells Nine network stations in Sydney and Melbourne to Alan Bond for around $1 billion. Fairfax sells Seven network television stations in Sydney, Melbourne, and Brisbane to Skase's Qintex group.

1989 Aggregation of regional television begins. ABC's Triple J radio network is launched. *The Simpsons* premieres. Sony buys

TIMELINE

Columbia and Tristar for $US 3.4 billion.

1990 BSkyB is formed after Sky merges with British Satellite Broadcasting. Westpac bank puts receivers into Network Ten. Packer regains control of Nine network's Sydney, Melbourne, and Brisbane stations for around $250 million.

1991 News Corp sells some print assets to stay afloat and fund its broadcasting empire.

1991 *Special Broadcasting Service Act* 1991 authorises commercials on SBS television.

1992 Canadian television operator CanWest buys control of Network Ten for $245 million using complicated ownership structure. Australian Broadcasting Authority established under the *Broadcasting Services Act* 1992 to regulate Australian media. Digital AM radio broadcasting is tested. Pay TV starts in Australia. Sony releases the mini-disc, a recordable magneto-optical disc.

1993 Sky, the first satellite TV channel, launched in the UK by News. Murdoch buys a controlling interest in Asian satellite television service, Star TV. Pay-TV operator Australis lists on the stock exchange. Australian Broadcasting Corporation is established by *Australian Broadcasting Corporation Act* 1983.

1994 DirecTV launches first digital TV service via satellite. Packer buys 15 per cent of Optus for $318 million. AP ALLNEWS Radio 24-hour radio news cast begins. Radio HK, a 24-hour Internet-only radio station, is launched.

1995 Kerry Stokes takes a 20 per cent stake in Seven Network. Murdoch's News Ltd and Telstra launch the Foxtel pay-TV joint venture. Sony demonstrates a flat-screen television set.

1996 Australian Competition and Consumer Competition blocks a merger between Foxtel and ailing Australis.

1997 Telecommunications deregulation in Australia begins. DVDs go on sale.

1998 Australis goes into receivership; some licences and assets acquired by TARBS. Packer gains a 25 per cent stake in Foxtel. V-chips go into television sets.

1999 US television networks start broadcasting a digital signal.

2001 Digital television broadcasts start in Australia. Southern Cross buys Sky Network and radio talkback stations 2UE and 4BC from Lamb family's Broadcast Investment Holdings for $90m.

2003 News Corp buys DirecTV.

2004 TARBS goes into receivership.

2005 Kerry Stokes' Seven Network sues other FTA and pay TV operators over the failure of his pay TV sports channel. The Australian Broadcasting Authority (content and licensing regulator) and Australian Communication Authority (spectrum management regulator) are merged into ACMA (Australian Communications and Media Authority).

2006 Australian government releases plans to ditch the 1987 cross-media and foreign media ownership restrictions. Media mogul and Australia's richest man, Kerry Packer, dies—lauded as a man with the common touch.

THE GOVERNANCE, REGULATION, AND ETHICS OF MASS COMMUNICATION MEDIA

OBJECTIVES

If understanding ownership is one of the keys to understanding the content of mass communication and new media, then understanding how both ownership and content are regulated by the state is central to an approach to media based on political economy. In this chapter we explore how traditional mass communication media have been regulated.

Upon completion of this chapter you will understand:

- the corporate and legal framework on which the regulation of mass communication is based;
- the nature of ethical practice and decision-making as it applies to traditional mass communication media;
- how there is often a time-lag (the techno-legal time-gap) between the introduction and commercialisation of a new technology and the rules that govern its use and potential or actual *misuse*;

- the ways in which ethics and law are often contradictory and exist in a dialectical relationship that manifests as what we call the ethico-legal paradox.

KEYWORDS

ethico-legal paradox
ethics
governance
regulation
self-regulation

Citizen Murdoch: A law unto himself?

Rupert Murdoch, the Australian-born global media magnate, always returned to the city of Adelaide to hold the News Corp annual general meeting—for sentimental reasons, he said. As the only remaining asset after the dismemberment of his father's media holdings, Adelaide's afternoon daily *News* was the first paper in Rupert's empire, although it closed down in 1992. In 2004, Murdoch moved his corporation to Delaware in the United States, claiming that incorporation in the United States gave him better access to capital. But was the real reason that challenges to his corporate governance practices irritated and annoyed the septuagenarian media mogul? A former editor of the Fairfax-owned *Australian Financial Review*, Allan Kohler, wrote:

> It's not Australian, there's no dividend worth mentioning, it's a corporate governance disaster run as Rupert Murdoch's family company with his kids in key jobs and his mates on the board and it's giddily volatile. But they (super fund managers) couldn't afford not to own it because it has such a big influence on the index benchmarks. (Kohler 2004, p. 22)

The cheeky corporate governance activist and Internet publisher Stephen Mayne of Crikey.com claimed it was his questions at the News Corp AGM and his standing for election as a News director in 2002 that provoked Murdoch's ire. Delaware reportedly had less onerous corporate governance requirements, but strong representations by American investors—in particular, several powerful superannuation funds—meant that Murdoch was unable to take full advantage of Delaware's generosity.

The move to list on the NYSE as well as the ASX was hailed by the claque of News Ltd commentators as a stroke of genius by Rupert Murdoch. 'It's GOOD NEWS week', ran *The Australian*'s Media section headline: 'The Murdochs came to town this week to announce the biggest media news story in a decade' (Schulze 2004, p. 17). Terry McCrann's column was headed, 'Murdoch follows a 21st century path. News's US listing should be a model not a problem' (McCrann 2004, p. 32).

Rupert Murdoch can virtually do as he pleases with his own business, though, like other capitalists, he is duty-bound to increase shareholder value along the way and to turn a tidy profit. Murdoch's actions in shifting the base of his operations 'offshore' from Australia can be seen as a case of jurisdiction shopping—that is, seeking the most favourable location, subject to local laws, to conduct business. What Murdoch and News Corporation did is not illegal. It doesn't actually even really break any 'golden rules' of ethics. As we shall see, this is perhaps because the legal system itself—and the specific rules governing the operation of the media—are designed to facilitate the capitalist business process, with minimum intervention from the courts, or government. That is, until something goes wrong!

Media law and ethics

The laws and regulations surrounding mass communication and new media are extensive and complex, and, unlike the laws of the ancient Medes and Persians, are constantly changing. This is partly because regulation always lags behind innovation, and partly because it is the product of the legal framework itself: media law is based on what we call the 'common law'. In this chapter we examine the legal and ethical structures, rules, and procedures that govern how the media operate. Our focus is on history and analogue media. We tackle the new ethico-legal paradox created by digital media in chapter 12.

So who governs the media, old and new, who regulates the people who run them, and who ensures that the people who work in them uphold the law and ethics of media? The answer to this rhetorical question should become clear as you work your way through this chapter. But first, it is necessary to unpack some of the complexities surrounding issues of legal and legislative regulation, codes of ethics and codes of practice, and governance regimes, both internal to media companies or public organisations and those imposed from outside, either by law or by mutual agreement.

Our discussion will cover the regulation of the economic entities of the media, or what we might call commercial governance issues, and also the laws and ethics that cover content issues in mass communication and new media. In particular, we will examine the way media organisations in Australia, and those who work for them, are governed and regulated by external bodies, and how they govern and regulate themselves. The key concepts to understand in this section are governance, regulation, co-regulation, and self-regulation, as well as law and ethics. We will start with media law because the legal system creates an overarching framework for systems of regulation and self-regulation and it also creates the conditions in which ethico-legal paradoxes can occur.

All media content is subject to laws that regulate matters such as defamation, privacy, and copyright. Commercial media operators are also subject to the Corporations Law and the *Trade Practices Act*, laws restricting ownership of media assets by foreigners, and laws placing restrictions on cross-media ownership. Most Australian media law texts are really designed for journalists and so spend most of their time discussing case law and statutes that affect the journalist in his or her daily routine—defamation, contempt of court, acceptable and unacceptable methods of newsgathering, and secrecy and privacy. This is not a media law textbook, so our aim is to provide an overview of some law and ethics that relates to journalism specifically, but also to describe the legal context in which media institutions operate. This is far more complex because media companies are subject to a range of commercial law—such as the *Trade Practices Act*—and also to many forms of government regulation—like the Broadcast Services Act and the Foreign Investment Review Board.

REGULATION

The legislative, but more often sub-legislative, regimes that govern organisations.

General laws covering the media

Since the 1970s there has been a raft of laws that have had an impact on the way media professionals go about their work. These include laws on privacy, whistle-blowing, and freedom of information. The advent of new regimes of national security laws in the United Kingdom, the United States, and Australia after the September 11 tragedy also have the capacity to inhibit media scrutiny of government security agencies. In a number of jurisdictions that do not have a long tradition of commitment to democratic values and the rule of law, censorship of the media, old and new, remains a significant barrier to the development of an informed civic culture and a vibrant public sphere.

The legal regulation of the media in the English-speaking world upholds the notion of free and independent media, although in Australia there is no constitutional machinery that guarantees freedom of the media; it is instead 'recognized' by a 'variety of constitutional, international and administrative means' (Armstrong et al. 1995, p.1). This means that the protection of free speech in Australia is really subject to the interpretation of these various laws, statutes, and minor constitutional points by the court system. In one important case in 1994, *Theophanous v Herald and Weekly Times*, the High Court ruled that there is an implied right to free expression of political ideas in the Australian Constitution: the court determined that there is a reasonable level of 'protection' for material published that is relevant to the development of public opinion (Armstrong et al. 1995, p. vii). In 1997 another High Court defamation case, *Lange v Australian Broadcasting Corporation*, affirmed the Theophanous decision and extended the defence of qualified privilege. But the court also ruled that this was not an absolute privilege and would not override 'reasonably appropriate' laws (cited in Pearson 2004, p. 37).

In a political economy dominated by market forces, the rights of property take precedence over the rights of individuals. In terms of the ideology of unfettered property rights, both individual and corporate entities are treated 'equally' in terms of their status before the law. This in fact masks what is at its core a very unequal relationship between *property* and *person* when it comes to business-oriented legal and regulatory frameworks. Capital uses the legal ideologies of 'free' enterprise and the inalienable right to dispose of personal and corporate property unencumbered to bolster its laissez-faire approach to media law and regulation. Wealthy enterprises can factor the cost of expensive legal opinions into their business plan and they always approach things with a battery of well-armed lawyers ready to pounce. Throughout most of 2005 the Seven and Ten networks were locked in a legal tussle with the AFL and Channel Nine over the television rights to the 2007 national football competition. At the time it was credibly estimated that the overall legal bill, split between the parties to the dispute, would be 'at least' $A50 million (Lehmann 2005b).

In Australia, outside the general laws of commerce and investment, there is very little direct government regulation of the print media (see Armstrong et al. 1995: ch. 11). Only the usual laws of defamation are really applicable. Newspapers operate under a system of almost total self-regulation through the Australian Press Council—a situation that law professor Sally Walker (1989, p. 263) ascribes to the absence of more formal government intervention. However, both broadcast content and new media content are governed by an overarching regulatory framework set out in the *Broadcasting Services Act 1992*.

Until 1 July 2005, the broadcasting spectrum and the telecommunications infrastructure (the medium for narrowcasting) were governed by the *Telecommunications Act 1997*, mainly administered by the Australian Communications Authority (ACA) and the Australian Telecommunication Authority respectively. Until 30 June 2005, broadcasting and online content and ownership were overseen by the Australian Broadcasting Authority (ABA), with the ACA responsible for spectrum management. In 2005 these two agencies were integrated into the Australian Media and Communications Authority (ACMA). The regulation of competition in telecommunications is the responsibility of the trade practices regulator, the Australian Consumer and Competition Commission (ACCC). From this it is quite clear that there are two types of media regulation: one set of rules for content issues and a second, separate set of rules governing most of the economic and policy issues, such as ownership and control.

The chief constraints on the content of print media are those relating to defamation, contempt, copyright, obscenity, blasphemy, and sedition, which also apply to the broadcast media. The second set of constraints on the media are those on ownership, principally cross-media ownership laws that place restrictions on ownership of both print and broadcast media in the same market—the dimensions of that market being defined by the law. So in Australia, while there are no restrictions on the number of newspapers a proprietor may own, nor on the market reach of those papers, such a proprietor is not permitted to own broadcast media in the same market. The regulation of narrowcast media—which is a convergence of computers and telephony—has largely been subsumed under the regulatory regimes applied to broadcast media, though with some significant differences. We have devoted a chapter (12) to the discussion of the changing ethico-legal and regulatory environment in the world of narrowcasting and will have more to say on this matter there.

Forms of media regulation

> We have set the rules, the regulator is focused on enforcing the rules, as required, and we are now looking to the industry to get on and operate within the rules. However, the debate continues. (Coonan 2005b, p. 2)

As Communications Minister Helen Coonan said in a November 2005 speech to the telecommunications industry, 'one topic that never seems to leave the news these days is "regulation".' Regulation describes the laws and the associated legal and administrative structures that governments use to regulate a sector of the economy or society. So the term 'regulatory regime' is used to describe the overarching design, intent, and performance of the regulatory system. It is a reality of media regulation that globally, and on a local scale, print media and broadcast media are subject to regulatory regimes that are fundamentally different in purpose, scope, and effect.

To bring this chapter into the 21st century, it is probably important to mention regulation of the telecommunications industry in this context. The combination of digital and commercial convergence has pushed the telcos much closer to the traditional media companies over the past decade (Barr 2000). Importantly, both Telstra and Optus have interests in pay television and in the delivery of new content over the mobile phone networks. Many of their plans are already well advanced and we discuss them in other chapters—check the index!

To give you an idea of how quickly regulatory and legal changes are taking place in telecommunications, in 2005 the federal government passed five substantial pieces of legislation that, according to the Minister, will change the face of the industry in Australia (Coonan 2005a). One of those was to strengthen 'key consumer safeguards' by underwriting the investment of $A3.1 billion dollars in new telecommunications infrastructure, most of it digital. Regulations were reviewed to make the industry deliver 'real benefits' to consumers. This really meant a process of price-fixing by legislation to ensure that players other than Telstra can access the existing network and any future cables that comprise 'bottleneck infrastructure'. This was to be enforced by new powers to the ACCC (Coonan 2005a, p. 2). Another 'customer safeguard', but not mentioned in the Minister's speech, lest it upset her audience of bankers and telco honchos, was the introduction of a 'block call' list for phone owners to opt out of telemarketing lists (Heywood 2005). As you might expect in a world of self-regulation, the telemarketing industry attempted to block the new laws by offering a 12-month trial of an industry code of practice instead. The industry's peak council—the Australian Direct Marketing Association (ADMA)—proposed the trial in order to 'get the telemarketing calls right first'. It also seems that the government only acted in response to a private member's bill from ALP backbencher Anna Burke (Lebihan 2005b).

Broadcast regulation

Broadcast media regulation operates from the principle that the airwaves over which content is transmitted are a public resource that is licensed for predetermined periods to private and community organisations under certain conditions, and that those licensees should pay a fee to the public purse for the benefit conferred upon them. The conditions of broadcast licences have a number of requirements in relation to ownership, content (including advertising), and complaint resolution. The model under which the broadcasting industry is regulated purports to be that of co-regulation. Co-regulation means that the government sets up the broad parameters of regulation, and that the broadcasting industry is responsible for the development of codes of practice that provide the detail of regulation; these codes are approved and administered by the broadcasting regulator, the ACMA.

One of ACMA's predecessor institutions, the Australian Broadcasting Authority (ABA) singularly failed in this last task of effectively administering the codes, and allowed commercial radio stations in particular to make a mockery of the distinction between program content and advertising (Johnson 2000).

Complete regulation of a media outlet occurs in corporations established and owned by government, such as the ABC and the Special Broadcasting Service (SBS), which are both statutory corporations engaged in public broadcasting. Both of the national broadcasters are constituted by an Act of Parliament, which broadly sets the legislative framework, and they are funded by a direct government grant that is renewed each financial year. The SBS is also allowed to sell a proportion of its airtime to gain extra revenue. The theory is that these organisations operate at 'arm's length' from government and are 'independent'. However, the federal Minister for Communication controls appointments to the ABC and SBS boards and so political interference is never far from the surface. The ABC also has an editorial charter, which, in theory again, is an extra guarantee of editorial independence. There have been some spectacular breaches of the charter in the past, not the least of which was an attempt by some producers in 1994 to gain backdoor sponsorship for certain television programs. Two ABC staff members bravely blew the whistle and their careers suffered as a result (Hirst & Patching 2005, pp. 75–6).

Commercial and community radio, television, and online media all operate under the co-regulation model based on the conditions of their broadcast licence, which is supervised by a government agency, the Australian Media and Communications Authority. The public broadcasters ABC and SBS also have some accountability to the Authority, but their main legal framework for operation is an Act of Parliament. Until 2005 the Australian Broadcasting Authority looked after content and licensing and the Australian Communications Authority was mainly concerned with spectrum management. They were merged on the ground that such separation was unnecessary and unhelpful in a convergent world. At the time of writing it is too early to tell if the new body will actually be any good, and it has yet to be tested by a difficult issue.

Self-regulation

Self-regulation occurs in media industries such as advertising and newspaper publishing. The Advertising Standards Bureau (ASB) is an industry-funded body that receives, processes and adjudicates complaints about advertising in most media. The standard against which complaints are judged is the ASB Code of Ethics. Similarly, the newspaper publishers have an industry-funded self-regulatory body, the Australian Press Council (APC), which deals with complaints against newspapers. These types of self-regulatory operations are often regarded as little more than camouflage for the industry.

SELF-REGULATION

The governance of organisations and professions by those organisations and professionals without recourse to external authorities such as the courts.

One way that self-regulation occurs in some media outlets is through what are sometimes called codes of practice. A code of practice is a set of in-house rules that governs the conduct of the reportorial workforce, and there has been at least one case in Australia of a subeditor being dismissed for breaching a code of practice. Mark Pearson (2004, p. 343) notes that such codes often encroach on codes of ethics, carving out 'new ethical territory'.

A different form of in-house self-regulation is the so-called Charter of Editorial Independence (CEI). Charters are usually established by reporters as a 'firewall' between management and editorial and to protect them from owner or shareholder pressure (Pearson 2004, p. 343). These have no legal force outside the company in which they are drawn up, and sometimes very little force even inside them. Charters are usually found in the major newspaper organisations; in Australia the Fairfax company has the most visible CEI (for a discussion of the Fairfax CEI, see Hirst and Patching 2005). CEIs are normally negotiated between management and unions in a similar way to pay rises and conditions covered by an Enterprise Bargaining Agreement (EBA) or Australian Workplace Agreement (AWA). Since they have little or no legal weight, charters are usually only effective when the union involved is strong enough to enforce it. Self-regulation also occurs within specific media-related occupations when members of professional groups such as journalists, public relations practitioners, or other groups of media workers band together to establish a professional code of ethics. We take up this issue below in our discussion of media ethics.

Self-regulation is one of the enduring fault lines in any discussion of media law and ethics. For governments it provides an easy cop-out clause: 'Self-regulation remains a cornerstone of the Government's strategy because it is a flexible, responsive and transparent approach' (Coonan 2005b, p. 3). In July 2006 Prime Minister Howard called on Channel 10 to take *Big Brother* off-air to show its commitment to self-regulation. Channel 10, not surprisingly, refused. The central contradiction in self-regulation is between the public values of honesty, truth, fairness, and fair dealing and the self-serving, competitive, and anti-social drive for profits (Hirst & Patching 2005). This is a key dialectic that guides the political economy approach to law, governance, and regulation. It is particularly important in relation to the media because of the ethico-legal clash between its culturally valuable public service role—to provide an active citizenry with accurate and timely information—and its business function—the production, distribution, and selling of various commodities, including 'eyeballs'. There is no reason to believe it will change in a narrowcasting environment. As Minister Coonan put it, it will be business as usual: 'Emerging technologies and the pace of change in mobile telecommunications will continue to offer industry exciting new business development opportunities ... And I'm sure the industry and Government will work well together to tackle the regulatory challenges' (Coonan 2005b, p. 6).

Yes, Minister!

Governance

Governance is about how an organisation is run, the manner in which policies and decisions are made, and the principles on which they are based. Good governance is seen to be based around notions of accountability, transparency, and openness in matters of finance, appointment of directors and staff, relations with suppliers and customers, and legal compliance. Governance is about law and ethics. The characteristics of poor governance are a lack of transparency, cronyism and nepotism, unresponsiveness, and even corruption. Standards of governance can be applied to governments, but more often the context is corporate governance. Governance refers to the way corporate organisations, in particular corporations listed on the Stock Exchange, are run, although non-profit corporations are not excluded from the notion of corporate governance. In Australia there are several government and quasi-government bodies that play a role in enforcing (or not) governance regimes across the media industry.

GOVERNANCE

The rules, principles, and practices by which a corporate entity is constituted, organised, and managed.

Australian Securities and Investments Commission (ASIC)

ASIC is the government agency responsible for overseeing the Corporations Law. The law sets down minimum standards for corporate governance, and when legislated in 1990 represented a major advance in corporate governance standards in Australia.

There is a view among some institutional investors in Australia that Murdoch's News Corporation moved to incorporate in Delaware because of increasing criticism of its corporate governance practices in Australia, and signs that the increasing corporate regulation in Australia was going to place the company's practices under greater scrutiny. One institutional investor told the ABC's *7.30 Report* that News is a public company, run like a family company.

The Australian Stock Exchange (ASX)

Listed companies with interests in media are also required to abide by the listing rules of the Australian Stock Exchange. The principal rule is that in order to maintain the integrity of the market, there needs to be continuous disclosure of information that may have a material influence on the share price, and, of course, communication media play an important role in reporting to their audiences information given to the ASX. Communication professionals—investor relations managers—in such corporations need to be mindful of that principle, and there have been cases where non-adherence has cost investor relations managers their jobs.

Australian Consumer and Competition Commission (ACCC)

The ACCC attempts to ensure there is a level playing field between companies and between companies and consumers. The ACCC is shaping up to play a key role in arbitrating the mergers and acquisitions that are sure to follow the deregulation of media ownership laws. When Helen Coonan announced the changed media rules in March 2006, the *Australian*

Financial Review reported that many senior media players were unhappy that the ACCC might apply tough new market-penetration tests to the lucrative classified advertising value chain (Crowe & Shoebridge 2006b). To head off too much angst on the part of the moguls-in-waiting, ACCC chairman Graeme Samuel quickly said he would issue a discussion paper on his new views before the controversial cross-media ownership laws are amended (Crowe & Shoebridge 2006a). We'll have more to say about these new changes—Helen Coonan's long-awaited 'digital roadmap'—and the new regulatory dialectic they might impose on the emerging narrowcasting media, in chapter 12.

The ACCC also plays a major role in prosecuting companies for breaches of the misleading and deceptive conduct provisions of the *Trade Practices Act*. More recently, the Commission has not only prosecuted companies but has also included their advertising agencies in the court-enforceable undertakings it has sought from advertisers.

ABA–ACA merger

Consistent with its vision of a convergent media world, the federal government has amalgamated the broadcasting licensing regulator, the Australian Broadcasting Authority, with the broadcasting technology regulator, the Australian Communications Authority, in order to bring spectrum management responsibilities under one authority. The Department of Communications, Information Technology and the Arts produced two discussion papers, one in August 2002 and one a year later (DCITA 2002, 2003). Merger of the two authorities was announced in the 2005 Budget. While industry reaction to the merger was positive, following the appointment of former FTA TV executive Chris Chapman as head of the Authority, the risks are that the new Authority may be dominated by a philosophy of technological determinism—'we should do it, because we can'—and the enforcement weaknesses of the old ABA will be carried over into the new body.

The Australian Press Council (APC)

The Australian Press Council is the self-regulatory body of the print media and it embodies the public interest versus profit contradiction. It was established in 1976 with two main aims: to help preserve the traditional freedom of the press within Australia and to ensure that the free press acts responsibly and ethically. To this end, the Council will adjudicate on any complaint made by a reader who feels a publication has violated its principles in a specific instance. The relevant clauses of the Press Council's statement of (ethical) principles are that:

> Clause 3. Readers … are entitled to have news and comment presented to them honestly and fairly, and with respect for the privacy and sensibilities of individuals. However, the right to privacy should not prevent publication of matters of public record or obvious or significant public interest.
> Clause 6. A publication has a wide discretion in matters of taste, but this does not justify lapse of taste so repugnant as to be extremely offensive to its readership.

> Clause 7. Publications should not place any gratuitous emphasis on the race, religion, nationality, colour, country of origin, gender, sexual orientation, marital status, disability, illness, or age of an individual or group. Nevertheless, where it is relevant and in the public interest, publications may report and express opinions in these areas. (Australian Press Council 1996)

These principles tend to be dichotomous and are indicative of a cultural dialectic around 'privacy' and 'taste'. They also add an ethico-legal dialectic between personal privacy and the public interest. Privacy and sensibility are respected, unless there is an overriding public interest. References to matters such as sexual orientation are OK, as long as they are not 'gratuitous'. Publications have discretion on taste, so long as any lack of taste is not 'extremely offensive'. There is no guidance on how taste might be defined, or what constitutes bad taste in a pluralistic, secular, democratic society. Implicit in this principle is the notion that 'we can't define bad taste, but *we* know it when we see it'. When it comes to matters of taste, sensibility, and media morality, the Press Council, like many other committees and commissions established to determine the public 'good', favours a conservative view. This tends to define 'good' taste in terms of a narrow agenda and low tolerance for deviant or subversive ideas—particularly around sex, sexuality, and sexism (Vnuk 2003).

The common argument against the APC is that the industry is sitting in judgment on itself. In a balanced account, journalism professor Mark Pearson (2004, pp. 330–3) acknowledges the criticisms while arguing that the APC's overall performance has improved since 2001. The balance of its membership has been heavily weighted to the industry for most of its life. To be fair, the MEAA (Media, Entertainment and Arts Alliance) now sits on the Council, having been a founding member but withdrawing for more than twenty years and only rejoining a few years ago. But we can't resist quoting Mark Pearson's evocative description of the Press Council, though it's not necessarily his personal view: 'the Press Council appears to be destined to be perceived in many quarters as a high-profile, often vocal press freedom lobbyist wielding a mere feather when it needs to discipline one of its member publications' (pp. 331–2).

This is also an issue for other media regulatory bodies such as the Australian Advertising Standards Bureau, a self-regulatory industry body funded by large advertisers. Such bodies are left to their own devices to determine what they consider community standards to be. As the use of ethics codes in media organisations has proliferated over the past decade, there has been an emerging counter-view in the wider field of applied ethics that codes are not especially useful instruments for promoting integrity, and are in fact regressive instruments of social control (Kjonstad & Hugh 1995; Laufer & Robertson 1997; Maguire 1999; Schwartz 2000). This counter-view offers a radical critique of codes and goes much further than the discussion on the limits of codes by Black and others (Black 1985; Longstaff 1994; Black et al. 1995). In recent work (Mosco 1996; McChesney 2000b; Wayne 2003; Hirst and

Patching 2005), a political economy approach to ethics challenges the hegemony of the market model of ethics based on deeply embedded cultural, and social values of capital.

Advertising Standards Bureau

The principal body concerned with the regulation of advertising in Australia is the Australian Association of National Advertisers, formed in 1928. The primary concern of this body has been to preserve what it terms 'the right to commercial free speech'. This concern followed successful community pressure on governments to restrict the advertising of tobacco and alcohol, and the complete banning of tobacco advertising and promotion. Tobacco advertising was banned on radio and television in Australia from 1976 and print advertising (including outdoor) from 1995. The AANA code provides that advertisements will not be offensive, portray violence, or promote discrimination.

The regulation of advertising in Australia is undertaken under the umbrella of the Advertising Standards Bureau (ASB 2002). The Bureau has two boards: the Advertising Standards Board and the Advertising Claims Board, which operate under various sections of the Advertiser Code of Ethics of the AANA.

The Standards Board does not consider complaints that deal with questions of law, or are under litigation, or questions it regards as 'highly technical' or 'trivial'. Nor does it consider what the Bureau terms 'local advertising' or complaints covered by a specific industry code. AANA members account for almost 80 per cent of Australia's national advertising expenditure and include most of the nations biggest advertisers, media buyers, and agencies.

The rather peculiar notion of 'commercial free speech' came from the United States, where 'freedom of speech' is enshrined as constitutional right. There, attempts to ban advertising of tobacco have been challenged by both the advertising industry and the tobacco industry as denial of freedom of speech. The central issue is, of course, the extent to which the freedom of individuals to express opinions and the ability of corporations to promote its products for commercial profit are the same right. 'Commercial free speech' is an attempt to close the ethico-legal fault line between profits and public interest.

Co-regulation

Co-regulation is a popular policy position for governments seeking to withdraw from the regulation of industry and commerce. According to Gareth Grainger, a former deputy chair of the now defunct Australian Broadcasting Authority, 'Co-regulation does not mean no regulation. In Australia we believe that this approach provides a sound basis for government to work with industry on broadcasting, online and telecommunications issues as we advance confidently into the digital age' (ABA 1998). For example, the Code of Practice for Commercial Television, which includes advertising, represents co-regulation.

The Commercial Television Code of Practice contains a number of provisions relevant to advertising, including: the classification of commercials (G, PG, M, MA, AV); advertising of alcohol and gambling; cinema, video, and videodisc films and video; computer and CD games; community service announcements; advertising directed at children; and 'products of a particularly intimate nature'. These codes are cross-referenced to other codes such as the Advertiser Code of Ethics of the AANA, which advertisers are required to adhere to and to the Children's Television Standard.

What we have just described represents the situation as it was at the beginning of 2006. The common thread with self-regulation, even with a degree of legal and government oversight, is that it is dialectically challenged by the much stronger imperatives of media economics. Above all it is the relations of the market—the relations of production—that weigh most heavily on ethical practice and theory (Hirst & Patching 2005). We believe this is as true for PR, advertising, and the other commercial 'creative' industries as it is for journalists. Convergence is after all a social as much as a technological process. There is plenty of professional and cross-disciplinary blending of journalism and the 'dark arts', and most media people in the workforce today and tomorrow will make the switch. Key issues in technology and in the market are also converging across the media and communication industries. On the evidence to date we can say that the situation in Australia is similar to that in the United States, the UK, and most of the capitalist world: market forces are powerful, perhaps beyond self-regulation. The Press Council, Advertising Standards Bureau, the ACMA and the other government agencies involved are all caught up in a debate that doesn't seem to stop.

Media ethics

We most commonly understand media ethics as a set of informal rules that apply to reporters and editors and inform their day-to-day decisions about what is acceptable practice in newsgathering and what is acceptable to publish or broadcast in terms of 'taste' or other considerations (Hirst & Patching 2005). It would be a great day indeed if the media proprietors also announced that *they* would abide by the same ethical codes as journalists and other media workers. As opposed to the 'letter of the law' that prescribes and proscribes what is right (legal) and wrong (illegal), ethics is a more philosophical system of regulation that asks the 'ought' question. What ought we do? How ought we act in order to do what is right? There are three major approaches to thinking about ethics:

1 The approach based on principles of duty and responsibility, known as 'deontology'. A key aspect of deontological (duty-based) ethics is the prescriptive rule that we should always do what is right and responsible, even if the result of our actions is not necessarily the best.
2 The second approach is teleological and it is outcome-based. Teleological ethics are also known as consequentialism. A consequentialist ethic is one that focuses on getting an outcome that is right and good. Utilitarianism—the greatest good for the greatest number—is a form of consequentialist ethics.
3 The third form of ethical conduct is known as virtue ethics, which focuses on forming virtuous habits of character as the way of acting ethically. Virtue ethics is closest to the deontological system, but it is focused on the individual rather than on a collective sense

ETHICS

Ethics asks 'how ought we act?' and 'what is the right thing to do?', as distinct from 'what does the law permit us to do?' A concept little understood by many politicians and business people.

of duty and responsibility (Sanders 2003).

The traditions of ethical thinking can be traced back to the roots of our civilisations. The Ten Commandments of the Judeo-Christian tradition can be seen as one of the earliest forms of an ethics code, and it is to the Greek philosopher Aristotle that we owe our understanding of virtue ethics. In the eastern traditions, the Chinese philosopher Confucius developed a set of ethical teachings, which can be interpreted as either deontological or virtue-based. Paradoxically, the demise of Judeo-Christian dominance of our cultural institutions has coincided with a revived interest in applied ethics, not only deontology but also situational and virtue ethics, some of which draws heavily on the Christian tradition for its force.

Most of the discussion about media ethics has been about the ethics of duty and responsibility, as formulated in various codes of professional ethics adopted initially by journalists but also more recently by professionals in public relations, advertising, and marketing. While these codes make a good attempt to deal with the realities of the market economy, there is one issue that is a fault line common to all of them: the dialectical tension between law and ethics. In some situations the legal and ethical implications of a situation are aligned and in these cases the law will support a particular ethico-legal principle (Pearson 2004, p. 301).

But there are also many issues in communication and the media that throw into stark relief the rift that often exists between law and ethics. This is the point of ethico-legal rupture between what is legally acceptable and what is morally defensible. Both law and ethics presume to make judgments about what is the 'right' thing to do. Law prescribes in black and white what we may do and what we may not, and it lays down penalties for those who break the law. Ethics asks, 'How ought we act in a moral way, even if it appears to contravene a legal principle?' Inherent in these different ways of doing the 'right' thing is a paradox, or a contradiction, and it is this: sometimes, in order to do what is morally right, in order to do the 'right' thing ethically, it is necessary to break the law. This contradiction, often faced by journalists, is known as the ethico-legal paradox (Hirst & Patching 2005, pp. 197–8).

ETHICO-LEGAL PARADOX

The confusion that arises when an action is morally right, but legally wrong.

CASE STUDY: THE LEGEND OF DEEP THROAT: THE ETHICO-LEGAL PARADOX AT WORK

'As he recently told my mother, "I guess people used to think Deep Throat was a criminal, but now they think he was a hero."' (Nick Jones, quoted in Tacket 2005)

'Deep Throat' was the unknown government official who helped *Washington Post* reporters Bob Woodward and Carl Bernstein break open the story of the Watergate scandal that rocked the American political system in the early 1970s. Watergate eventually resulted in the resignation of US President Richard Nixon in 1974. In July 2005, a thirty-year mystery about the identity of the most famous anonymous source in the world was solved. W. Mark Felt, who was Deputy Director of the FBI at the time, identified himself as 'Deep Throat', ending three decades of speculation and intrigue.

Felt chose the glossy American magazine *Vanity Fair* to tell his story, which had been an open secret in Washington circles for some time. Nixon himself had suspected Felt was Deep Throat, though he didn't have the evidence or the political power to sack him at the time (O'Connor 2005).

Mark Felt broke the law in the interests of what he—and the reporters—saw as the exposure of criminal behaviour all the way to the Oval Office. As a high-ranking law enforcement officer, sworn to uphold the law, Felt saw it was his ethical duty to break the law, in the interests of a greater good. But not everyone agreed. Gordon Liddy, one of the men who served a prison term for his involvement in the break-in at the Democratic Party offices in the Watergate Building, said Mr Felt had 'violated the ethics of the law enforcement profession' by leaking information to the *Washington Post* (Harvey & AFP 2005).

This is the ethico-legal paradox. Mark Felt, whose grandson and family thought him a hero, found himself being accused of unethical and perhaps illegal behaviour for his actions. After decades of being honoured as the most famous whistleblower in US history, the disclosure of Felt's identity as the shadowy, cigarette-smoking government insider immortalised in the film *All The President's Men* sparked off a firestorm of debate. Leonard Garment, a lawyer in the Nixon White House, said that Felt's actions were dishonourable and called in question the justification for his whistleblowing because he had defied his 'sworn obligation to maintain security' (Harvey & AFP 2005).

The *New York Times* headline ran, 'Felt is praised as a hero and condemned as a traitor' (Seelye 2005). Nixon loyalists and conservative commentators condemned Felt while journalists and civil libertarians praised him. But Felt himself had repeatedly lied in the past when questioned about his relationship with Woodward and Bernstein and had refused to confirm he was Deep Throat when asked directly (Von Drehle 2005). In an ironic twist only confirmed after Felt's unmasking, at various times throughout the Watergate scandal Felt was given the job of tracking down the leaks that were damaging the President and his administration (Corn & Goldberg 2005).

Deep Throat's identity remained a mystery for more than thirty years, and Felt insisted on secrecy—repeatedly. Reviewing Woodward's book about his relationship with Felt, *The Secret Man* in *The New York Times*, Michiko Kakutani suggests that in 'today's media-bashing climate—when reporters' right to keep sources secret is under attack—could well inhibit sources like Mr Felt from stepping forward' (Kakutani 2005).

Deontology: An ethical philosophy of 'duty'

The approach to ethical decision-making determined by how we see our duty and what ethical principles and rules we subscribe to is termed deontology. Some of the long-standing ethical principles explicit in this approach are: 'Always treat others as you wish to be treated'; 'First, do no harm'; and 'Always act as if your action were to become a universal law of human interaction'. This approach to ethics has been criticised because of the rigidity and inflexibility of its principles, the argument being that there are times when a greater good can be achieved by abandoning a particular principle or duty.

Deontology, which comes from the Greek word *deon* for 'duty', is an approach to ethics in which our understanding and choices about what is right and what is wrong are determined by our duty—our duty to ourselves and our duty to others. The various deontological, or duty-based, approaches to ethics identify a variety of ways in which we can work out just what our duty ought to be. A duty is a responsibility to act in accordance with a particular principle, or in the interests of a particular relationship. There are three widely recognised approaches to the theory of duty or responsibility: the divine command theory, the classical theory of duty based on Immanuel Kant's two categorical imperatives, and the modern theory of Sir David Ross based on the idea that there exists a prima facie moral duty.

The application of the deontological theory into applied ethics is most clearly seen in the development of behavioural codes such as codes of ethics, codes of conduct, and codes of practice. Such codes set down the duties of those subject to the codes, and the principles by which they are expected to act, such as honesty, integrity, and fairness, and sometimes the rules through which those duties and principles are given effect.

Codes of ethics

Ethical principles and notions of duty are often expressed in codes of ethics, and such codes are used as the yardstick to determine what is ethical or unethical behaviour, or what is right and wrong. For those who practise professionally in mass communication—journalists, public relations practitioners, and advertising professionals—there has emerged over the past decades a plethora of codes to subscribe to. This is a worldwide trend, and most have been sponsored by professional associations or industry groups rather than employers of media hands. Media industry employers, however, have been prescribing codes of practice for their employees, some of which contain codes of ethics, or prescribe certain ethical behaviours such as declarations of the receipt of gifts or sponsored travel.

The journalism ethics codes deserve special attention. First, because of their longevity—journalists were developing codes of ethics decades before it became fashionable. Second, because many of the better ethics codes in journalism were developed by the trade unions covering journalists. In the United Kingdom, the National Union of Journalists Code dates from 1936; in Australia, the MEAA code dates from 1944 and it has been revised twice, most recently in the mid-1990s (Hirst 1997; Hirst & Patching 2005). Because journalism codes of ethics are in some countries regulated by the trade union, charges of breaching the code can only be made against journalists who are members of the union, and such charges can be abrogated simply by resigning from the union. The journalists code may well be deontological because keeping to it is an ethical duty of members of the association.

Teleology: Get the right outcome—or face the consequences!

A second approach to ethical decision-making is based on the idea that if the outcome of an action is good, then it is right. This approach to ethics has been criticised as promoting a philosophy that 'the end justifies the means', and a 'whatever it takes' mentality. Certainly, within the mass media, the rights of individuals have often been negated using the argument that the story was 'in the public interest', and that a greater good prevailed.

In *Primary Colors*, the novel of the 1992 Clinton presidential campaign (subsequently made into a film starring John Travolta and Emma Thompson), Henry Burton, the principled campaign aide, is ready to resign on the eve of the poll because he cannot tolerate the continuing lies and deceptions dominating the political process. Governor Stanton (the Clinton look-alike played by John Travolta) exhorts him to stay, arguing that descending into the gutter is acceptable and worthwhile, because upon attaining the prize, you can do 'good' and make history (Klein 1996). This is consequentialist ethics at its most stark and revealing.

The technical term for the outcome-based approach to ethics is 'consequentialism' or 'teleology'. Consequentialism simply means concerned with the consequences. Teleology comes from the Greek word *teleos* meaning 'afar'. The term 'consequentialism' was coined by Elizabeth Anscombe (1958) in the late 1950s. This approach to ethics is concerned with the outcome, the long-term consequences, the ultimate goal. For a consequentialist, the rightness of an action is considered only in relation to the consequences, or outcomes, it produces. In considering outcome-based ethical theories, we must first ask: what is the outcome we are seeking; what is our ultimate goal? Utilitarianism is a form of consequentialism that begins with the premise that all human beings seek happiness. In the 19th century, this idea of seeking happiness was theorised as the utilitarian ethic by the British philosophers Jeremy Bentham and John Stuart Mill. Utilitarianism seeks the consequence of the greatest good for the greatest number.

The 'third way': Virtue ethics

A third approach to ethics, which has currency in a growing number of areas of professional practice, is virtue ethics. Virtue ethics is exemplified by Alisadir MacIntyre's *After Virtue*, first published in 1984, although the notion of 'a fit and proper person' that underlies some of the broadcasting licence requirements may owe something to Aristotle. When we talk about moral virtues, what sort of things are we talking about? In general terms, we are talking about values like honesty, integrity, sensitivity, good judgment, and a sense of social responsibility. We are not talking about cognitive abilities like intelligence, nor are we talking about psychomotor skills like good hand–eye coordination or a well-muscled physique, although these may contribute to virtue. Aristotle made a distinction between intellectual virtues and moral virtues; the former he listed as intelligence, practical wisdom, understanding, and good sense.

How then do we define a moral virtue? One of the most important contemporary writers on virtue ethics, Alasdair MacIntyre, says virtues are 'dispositions not only to act in particular ways, but also to feel in particular ways' (1984, pp. 149–50). A disposition is a habit, so being virtuous means being disposed or habituated to act and feel in particular ways. Moral virtue is a state of being and doing wrought through experience, rather than a result of conscious, rational, cognitive decision-making.

The institutionalisation of ethics

Current best practice in ethics code design is towards shorter, more aspirational codes that focus on values rather than prohibitions, as two recent Australian examples show. In 1997, the Media, Entertainment and Arts Alliance undertook a revision of the Australian journalists' code under the guidance of Jesuit priest Frank Brennan (MEAA 1997). The outcome of that revision was a renewed focus on the values underpinning the code, as stated in the preamble: 'MEAA members engaged in journalism commit themselves to honesty, fairness, independence and respect for the rights of others.' However, revisions to the MEAA code of ethics were unable to resolve the dialectical tension between commercial imperatives and public interest. Instead it relies on an appeal to journalists to do the right thing (Hirst 1997).

The other recent code revision was that undertaken by the Advertising Federation of Australia (AFA 2001). This code one of the most refreshing documents of its type and worthy of publication in full:

> ... It's what we in advertising stand for
>
> **How To Behave**
>
> Every day we can be faced with ethical dilemmas. These guidelines will help you to do the right thing. Ethics can't be imposed. They have to grow from within each of us. And be understood by all of us.
>
> **What We Believe**
>
> 1 Stand up for what you believe is right.
> 2 Honour all agreements.
> 3 Don't break the law. Don't bend the law.
> 4 Respect all people.
> 5 Strive for excellence in everything you do.
> 6 Give clients your best efforts and advice, without fear or favour.
> 7 Look after your colleagues.
> 8 Compete fairly.

9 Think before you act.

10 Be honest.

Ethics and public relations

A number of writers on public relations regard ethics as the core of PR practice. Carl Botan, for example, stressing the increasingly strategic character of public relations, argues that 'a campaign intended to influence suggests a relationship, or a desired relationship, between the parties, and the ethicality of such campaigns is determined primarily by the values and relationships expressed in them, including how the target publics are treated' (Botan 1997, p. 189). But writers like Cornelius Pratt are not so positive and struggle to come to terms with the public relations industry's tarnished past, such as its role in supporting the tobacco industry, concluding that, 'at almost every stage of the tobacco wars, public relations was used precisely to attain goals which it was not professionally designed to accomplish' (Pratt 1997, p. 9).

For others in public relations, the discussion about ethics is tied up with the ongoing debate about the status of public relations practitioners as professionals. A commitment to ethics, and a commitment to the development and maintenance of ethical standards across the public relations industry, seem critical to practitioners' self-understanding and self-acceptance as professionals. For public relations academic Thomas Bivins, for example, serving the public interest is one of the defining characteristics of a profession. But, asks Bivins, how can a practitioner advocating a discrete point of view serve the interest of the greater public? Bivins is critical of the Public Relations Society of America (PRSA) Code of Professional Standards for the Practice of Public Relations for its failure to address such issues: 'as with many other professions and near-professions, formal guidance for practitioners of public relations is sorely lacking, even from their own professional association' (Bivins 1993, p. 117). Can similar comments be made of the Code of Ethics of the Public Relations Institute of Australia? Apart from a requirement to deal fairly and honestly in clause 1 of the Code, the remaining clauses are essentially a guide to business practice within the public relations industry with references to commercial confidentiality, representation of competing interests, contingency fees, injury to the professional reputation, and the practice of another member.

The application of codes, in particular their effectiveness and enforcement, has been even more problematic (Brooks 1989; Wright 1993). In both Australia and New Zealand, public relations institutes have encountered difficulties enforcing codes and sanctions in recent times. In one case, investigation of a complaint by the Institute's ethics committee was aborted and handed over to a QC (Espiner 2000a,b). Indeed, there is a growing body of literature critical of the use of codes, suggesting they are counter-productive (Farrell & Cobbin 1996; Schwartz 2000). All codes of ethics can be classified as falling at some point on a spectrum between prescriptive and aspirational (Farrell & Cobbin 2000). Monica Walle rightly makes the point that the five PR association codes she examined were 'posed in the negative'. She concludes that 'codes should include explicit directives … Only this way will the profession … begin to address its own poor reputation' (Walle 2003, p. 4).

The future of media regulation

If ethics and regulation were not complicated enough for old media, then new media bring a new raft of ethical and regulatory issues bouncing over the rapids, and the analogy of white water is appropriate. Amid the swirling currents of new technologies there are the rocks of new legal issues and the hard places of new ethical challenges. Mobile phones enable people to be in touch anywhere, any time—but should camera-equipped phones be banned from the change rooms of your local swimming pool? Some organisations, amid claims of adequate self-regulation, are taking matters into their own hands and banning photography under certain conditions in what are otherwise public places. Some state governments have also legislated to control photography in some parks and other venues, such as swimming pools (Clark 2005). The national benchmarking organisation, Standards Australia, issued a draft set of guidelines for the installation and operation of closed-circuit television cameras in public places, which covered privacy, training of staff, and data storage (Lebihan 2005a). The issue was politically framed as a response to a heightened threat of 'terrorism', but the impact is that CCTV is being 'enhanced' to promote greater 'security'. What it means is that we may have to get used to being closely watched most of the time, but as we see in chapter 13, sometimes CCTV can be badly abused by those who ostensibly 'control' the technology. There are also serious privacy issues raised by CCTV and other surveillance activities. The winner of the Australian Privacy Foundation's 2005 Big Brother Award, the 'Orwell', for being the 'greatest corporate invader' of privacy, was Telstra for its 'Employee Monitoring and Surveillance policy' (Vaile 2005). Perhaps the federal government should be nominated for an award for its new privacy-breaching laws that require banks and other companies to disclose information about their customers in relation to suspected terrorism activities (Davis 2005).

In a sense these 'technical' issues represent only a small fault line in the ethico-legal framework of new media, but digital and commercial convergence is already moving ahead of attempts to regulate it, on both a national and a global scale (see chapter 13). The sheer size and weight of the international media and creative industries are so important to the worldwide economy that to a great extent they write their own rules, or at least most of them. One of the other small but potentially very unstable cultural fault lines that intersects with the ethico-legal paradox is a shifting, postmodern dialectic of actual and literal truth (Spence 2006).

According to ethics researcher Edward Spence, the presentation of 'fiction' as factual 'truth' is becoming a 'pervasive but often undetected media phenomenon', for the simple reason that versions presented as 'truth' are good sellers. In a compelling remark he writes: 'Truth, like technology, works.' Interestingly, the uniform national defamation laws, progressively introduced around Australia in 2006, introduce the defence of 'contextual truth'. Michael Pelly (2006) described this as a defence 'which excuses those who get the majority of the story right'. Therefore, even the spin doctors 'present their fictitious messages of persuasion as truth', which presents a paradox for both PR/advertising and the audience. In the end this comes down to telling 'lies as truth' and is 'totally unethical and objectionable' (Spence 2006). We couldn't agree more. All we can add is that in the age of narrowcasting, marketing will be an even stronger and more subtle force and it will be deeply embedded in popular cultural forms, such as reformatted 'TV' experiences on a mobile phone screen 4 × 4 cm. It will be interesting to see if the regulators can keep up with the innovators.

CASE STUDY: MORE CASH FOR MORE COMMENT?

The 1999 cash-for-comment scandal involving John Laws, Alan Jones, and other radio talkback hosts is fairly well known. In this case study we examine the role of the then ABA in investigating subsequent allegations in 2002.

Complaints made by the Communications Law Centre, and aired on the ABC's *Media Watch* in October 2002, asked the ABA to investigate the compliance by Sydney commercial radio broadcasters Alan Jones and John Laws with the new disclosure regime imposed after the cash-for-comment investigations in 1999. Unlike 1999, when the investigation was public, the ABA determined this matter behind closed doors. Of particular interest was Jones' move from 2UE to 2GB, where he took up a shareholding in the Macquarie Radio Network, owners of the station. His breakfast program was sponsored by Telstra, who of course paid the station, and not Jones directly. In April 2004, the ABA found that this did not constitute cash for comment. Jones, it appears, has been able to circumvent the intent of the rules put in place to compel disclosure. The Macquarie Radio Network attempted, but failed, to injunct revelations by *Media Watch* that in December 2003 a draft ABA report did find Jones in breach. The draft report found that Jones denied or undermined alternative viewpoints on Telstra put to his program, and that his salary increase when he went to 2GB was partly because of his ability to attract Telstra sponsorship (ABC News Online, 2004b). ABA chair David Flint defended the Authority:

> [T]he draft report was prepared by a relatively junior officer and not approved by senior ABA staff. 'When experienced officers looked at all the evidence which we had and applied the standards and the codes, they came to the conclusion that you couldn't come to the sort of findings that had been made in the draft,' he said. (ABC News Online 2004b)

In Laws' case, in 2003 the ABA found that 2UE had breached the provisions of the Broadcasting Act on nineteen occasions when Laws did not comply with the disclosure requirements. In June 2004, however, the ABA announced that the Commonwealth Director of Public Prosecutions found there would not be a reasonable prospect of a conviction if the case proceeded. According to then acting ABA chair Lynn Maddock,

> 'The burden of proof in criminal cases is much higher than in civil cases and for a successful prosecution in this case it would have to be proven that radio 2UE engaged in the conduct with the requisite criminal intention.'
>
> The ABA has imposed a stringent monitoring condition on radio 2UE but would always be extremely reluctant to deprive the public of a popular service by suspending or cancelling the broadcaster's licence. (ABC News Online 2004a)

These are, of course, exactly the steps needed to make very clear to broadcasters the seriousness with which the ABA views such contempt for the regulatory process. The original complainant, the Communications Law Centre, made the obvious point that the Act needed strengthening.

The second major conclusion to be drawn is not about the opinionated and egotistical Laws and Jones hiding how they make a buck in a trashy Sydney sort of way, but the waywardness of Telstra's corporate governance practices. The corporation is still majority-owned by the Australian government, in trust for the people of Australia. The purpose of the Jones and Laws escapades is to improve the public image of Telstra to the point where the government can continue to privatise it. Telstra is using shareholders' funds—half of which belong to the Australian people—to engineer a change of ownership in the corporation, which is arguably not in the best interest of those very people. Corporate governance and perceptions of conflicts of interest is not something to which the former Telstra board chair, Bob Mansfield, was overly sensitive. If he had been, he would not have mooted the idea of taking over Fairfax, which would have left the Australian government as Telstra's majority shareholder in effective control of one of the country's major media companies.

- Examine some recent cases and new stories about the new ACMA. What sorts of issues have been coming up in relation to its performance?
- Research any other cash-for-comment incidents and see how they were handled by the regulatory authorities. Don't forget to examine jurisdictions other than Australia.

KEY POINTS

In this chapter we have examined the way legal regulation and ethical decision-making interact. There has been a brief discussion of the important legal and regulatory frameworks and the institutions that act as the 'guardians' of the public interest in these matters. We have explored:

- legal regimes governing mass communication media;
- governance authorities for mass media;

- the political economy of regulation and ethics;
- paradigms for ethics, including co-regulatory and self-regulatory regimes;
- an introduction to new concepts such as the ethico-legal paradox and the techno-legal time-gap.

CLASS DISCUSSION: REGULATION, GOVERNANCE, AND SELF-REGULATION

1. Can the legal frameworks and regulatory regimes move to match the pace of change?
2. Will today's institutions be capable of remaining relevant as the new cultural forms of broadcast and narrowcast media develop?
3. How will the culture inside these organisations and across the creative industries respond to new and changing ethico-legal paradigms?
4. Have self-regulatory bodies like the Australian Press Council and Advertising Standards Bureau done a good job?

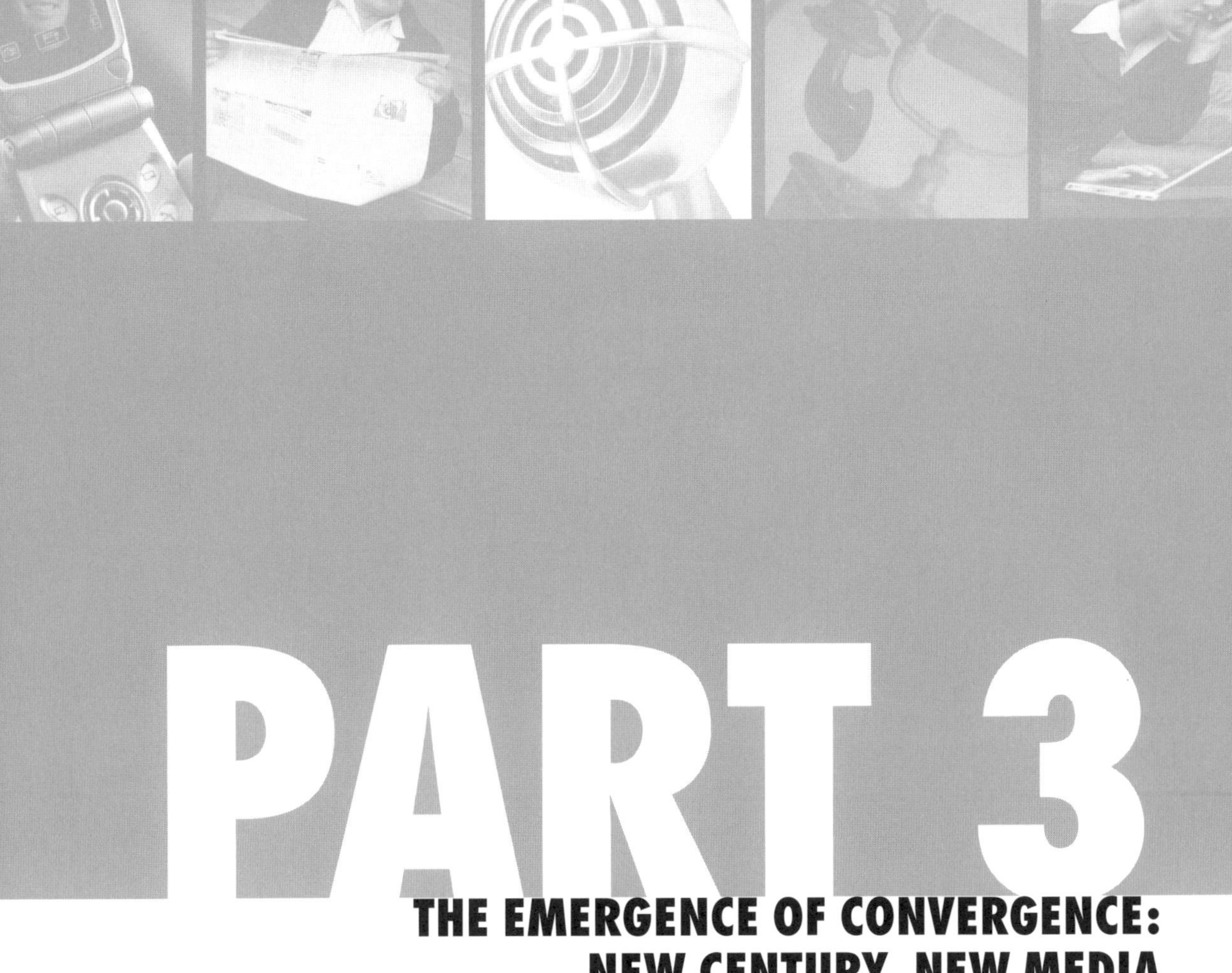

PART 3
THE EMERGENCE OF CONVERGENCE: NEW CENTURY, NEW MEDIA

OBJECTIVES

The chapters in this section explore the ways in which computers and media technologies have converged in order that we might further tease out the digital dialectic. We examine some myths of the digital age and the legal and regulatory regimes that are now struggling to cope with the transition from broadcasting to narrowcasting. It will, we hope, allow you to develop further insights into the issues raised in the first chapters. In particular, you could gain a greater understanding of:

- what we mean by 'convergence' when we're talking about the enabling and digital technologies of mass communication and the mass media;
- how the concept of 'convergence' is almost as old as technology itself, and how technological change must *always* and *only* take place in a social context;
- why we place as much, if not more, emphasis on the social conditions in which digital convergence takes place as we do on the technologies themselves;
- how the digital revolution has globalised economics, destabilised politics, and colonised popular culture and the dynamics of technology and social relations in both utopian and dystopian expressions of convergence.

KEYWORDS

convergence
digital revolution
globalisation
information society
knowledge society
narrowcasting

FROM CALCULATION TO CYBERIA: THE 2500-YEAR HISTORY OF COMPUTING

OBJECTIVES

> Every society is an information society. Throughout history, different cultures have adopted different modes of communication, but all are information societies of some kind ... The products of the convergence of communications have also meant that contemporary information society is highly dependent on information networks that can distribute images, data and symbols. (Barr 2000, p. 20)

Trevor Barr is right about society's dependence on images, data, and symbols. These have long been the elements of communication. Pictographs on the walls of Stone Age caves, Egyptian hieroglyphics, writing in many languages, and computer code are all tools of communication, each with their own technologies. This chapter begins to flesh out the concept of convergence that is central to the development of digital technology and also to the social conditions in which digital technologies develop. After reading this chapter you will have a better understanding of the following:

- the long and important history of mechanical and digital calculation that led to the modern computer age;
- what we mean by 'convergence';
- how the historical process of convergence has changed through time and why there are clear links between ancient, present, and future technologies;
- why convergence and globalisation are social processes, not just the product of technological innovation;
- the role of the dialectic—as a process of moving history forward—in the social relations of convergence.

KEYWORDS

bit

byte

mainframe

megabyte

Convergence: From calculus to computing

To converge means to come together. In the context of communications technologies we're talking about the *coming together* of several discrete technologies to create a hybrid technology. The keys to this modern form of convergence are the microprocessor—the computer chip—and the development of computing algorithms based on binary code. The technologies that are converging rapidly today are telecommunications, computing, and broadcasting (Ostergaard 1998, p. 95).

As convergence occurs at the level of technologies it does so within the context of mutual constitution that also has social impacts and consequences. One of the most important is really a *commercial convergence* between media content companies (television and radio networks, newspaper publishers) and transmission channels such as telephone cable networks. In the past decade this has begun to radically reshape the mass media landscape (De Bens & Mazzoleni 1998, p. 166; Barr 2000). The major international corporate players are now actively seeking to control the whole 'electronic distribution chain', from the production of content through to pay-per-access narrowcast delivery (Ostergaard 1998, p. 98). The consequence, according to Ostergaard (p. 95), is greater concentration of ownership and control and a situation where regulatory authorities are moving away from addressing questions of content towards the greater regulation of the technical means of delivery. We will return to this theme in chapter 12, but first a short digression is necessary. In fact we have to travel back in time some thousands of years to really begin a history of computing. Before 'computer' meant the machines as we know them today, it simply meant a person employed to do laborious and tedious additions, subtractions, and other sums. A 'computer' was a low-paid clerical worker who did calculations day in, day out.

From digits to digital: A brief history of counting, computing, and convergence

> Using a computer thirty years ago [1966], like piloting a moon lander, was the realm of a precious few schooled in the hocus-pocus needed to drive these machines sometimes with primitive languages or none at all (just toggle switches and blinking lights). In my opinion, there was a subconscious effort to keep it mysterious, like the monopoly of the monks or some bizarre religious rite in the Dark Ages. (Negroponte 1996, p. 90)

In 1996 Nicholas Negroponte was a digital optimist. He has now devoted his life to a charitable cause—ensuring that each child in third world countries has access to a laptop computer. At the beginning of the digital revolution he believed that computers would make life better for everyone—eventually. But it is his comment about the Dark Ages that draws us to this passage. The Dark Ages was a period from about 500 to 1000 AD in which it is considered that there was very little scientific advance and little in the way of what we might, today, call 'progress'. Of course this is a very 'looking backwards' viewpoint and through the 500 years of the so-called Dark Ages human life and history moved forward, though perhaps a little slowly from our perspective. In the vast scale of human evolution, 500 years is not a long time, but when it comes to the evolutionary history of computing, 500 years takes us a long way. In fact it takes us from the first mechanical calculator to the palm pilot. Leonardo da Vinci (1452–1519), the brilliant Italian painter, musician, sculptor, architect, inventor, and engineer, worked out the principles for a calculating machine, and a working model was built in the early 1970s from his drawings. Da Vinci was active during the Renaissance revival of art, literature, and learning, a time when modern science and important new forms of technology began to emerge from pre-modern ways of thinking. But to understand the real history of computing, we need to go even further back in time to ancient Babylon, 1000 BC.

In the primitive world, when it came to using objects to represent *numbers* of things, shells, bones, small stones, or seeds could have been used. That the word *calculate* is derived from the Latin word for small stone, *calculus*, suggests that pebbles or beads were the technology used in the first computing devices. By manipulating the beads or stones, it was possible with some skill and practice to make rapid calculations. At the same time, the Chinese were becoming very involved in commerce with the Japanese, Indians, and Koreans. They needed a way to tally accounts and bills, and out of this need the abacus was born. Other historical accounts suggest that the abacus may have been invented in Babylonia (now Iraq) in the 4th century BC (maxmon.com, n.d.-a). The abacus is the first true precursor of the adding machines and computers that would follow.

The abacus works by assigning a value to each bead, determined by its position: one bead on a particular wire has the value of 1; two together have the value of 2. A bead on the next line, however, might have the value of 10, and on the third line a value of 100. The abacus works on the principle of place–value notation: the location of the bead determines its value. In this way, relatively few beads are required to depict large numbers. The beads are counted, or given numerical values, by shifting them in one direction. The values are subtracted by shifting the beads in the other direction. An abacus is really a memory aid for the user making mental calculations, as opposed to the true mechanical calculating machines that were still to come.

Arabic numerals were introduced to Europe in the 8th and 9th centuries, and Roman numerals remained in use in some parts of Europe until the 17th century. The Arabic system introduced the concepts of zero and fixed places for tens, hundreds, and thousands, and greatly simplified mathematical calculations. It is not beyond the realm of possibility that the abacus, or a device very similar to it, was invented almost simultaneously in China and the Middle East, or that one followed on the heels of the other. It is consistent with the ways that commerce and trade developed and also with the principles of convergence and simultaneity. It is a common feature of human society that as it becomes more stable, wealthy, and complex, its inventiveness will also increase.

Aside from the abacus, early humans also invented numbering systems to enable them to compute with ease sums greater than 10. One such numbering system is the decimal numbering system, which is traceable to early Hindu–Arabic influence. This decimal system, with specific digits representing numbers from 0 to 9, came into general use in Europe and has survived to the present day.

From manual to mechanical counting

The abacus was a very simple counting apparatus. It is perhaps not even correct to call it a machine, though it did have a few simple moving parts. There was no mechanical power embedded in an abacus; it required the manipulation of the beads on the wire by hand. However, the invention of simple mechanical scales for weighing and measuring helped to move computational technology along. The progress of mechanical calculation was stalled for some time and had to wait for other technologies to catch up, including the development of mechanical clocks, gears, levers, and pulleys. It also had to wait for further advances in mathematics and other sciences, such as astronomy, chemistry, and physics. The primary advances were in mathematics because it was in this field—to help with complex calculations—that mechanical computational devices were of most value. At the same time, other philosophers and inventors were attempting to build mechanical devices to generate proofs of logic. Many of them, like the 13th-century Spanish theologian Ramon Lull, were attempting, through logic, to prove the absolute truth of statements in the Bible. Lull invented a series of discs that rotated around a common centre point. The discs were of various sizes and a series of words or symbols was printed on each. As the discs were rotated a series of logical sentences or equations would be assembled. Lull's most famous device, the *figura universalis*, had fourteen discs and could generate a vast number of possible logical sequences. The Lull device, though not a calculator or computer in a strict sense, did influence later generations of mathematicians, including Gottfied von Leibniz, who invented a mechanical calculator called a Step Reckoner in the 17th century (maxmon.com, n.d.-b).

The next big advances in computation took place in the same century. John Napier (1550–1617), Baron of Merchiston, Scotland, invented logarithms in 1614, which allowed multiplication and division to be reduced to addition and subtraction. A logarithm is simply a mathematical formula and it quickly became the basis for early, primitive attempts at programming mechanical calculators. In the early 1700s, Napier used algorithms to devise a series of complex multiplication tables, which were inscribed on strips of wood or bone and were a useful tool for mathematicians. This device became known as 'Napier's Bones' and was the precursor to the slide rule, which was invented in 1621 by William Oughtred (maxmon.com, n.d.-c). Like many of the early inventors discussed in this chapter, Napier was a child prodigy, entering St Andrews University at the age of 13 and combining his love of mathematics with religious fervour. This did not stop his critics from accusing him of being a Satanist, nor did his Christian beliefs prevent him from making an important contribution to science. His logarithms and mathematical genius are credited with helping to advance early astronomy and to have helped Isaac Newton in his breakthrough work on the theory of gravitational force (O'Connor & Robertson 1998b).

Two years later, a German mathematician and Lutheran minister, Wilhelm Schickard (1592–1635), built one of the first mechanical calculators in 1623; because it used a system of cogs and gears it was also known as the 'calculating clock' (wikipedia 2005a). The calculating clock worked with six digits, and carried digits across columns. It worked, but never made it beyond the prototype stage. When he invented the mechanical calculator, Schickard was a professor at the University of Tubingen, Germany, where he taught and conducted research in mathematics, astronomy, and surveying. Schickard corresponded with many scientists, including the renowned astronomer Johan Kepler, who used Schickard's calculator to help him work out the laws of planetary motion (O'Connor & Robertson 1996b).

The Pascaline, the first desktop calculator

The French mathematician, philosopher, and theologian Blaise Pascal (1623–62) built a mechanical calculator, the Pascaline, in 1642. It had the capacity for eight digits, but had trouble carrying numbers and its gears tended to jam. Pascal was 19 when he built the first machine to help his father, a tax collector in Paris. The Pascaline adopted the principles of the abacus but did away with the use of the hand to move the beads or counters. Instead, Pascal used wheels to move counters.

The Pascaline was based on a design described by Hero of Alexandria (2 AD) to calculate the distance a carriage travelled. The basic principle of his calculator is still used today in water meters and modern odometers. Instead of having a carriage wheel turn the gear, Pascal made each ten-toothed wheel accessible to be turned directly by a person's hand (later inventors added keys and a crank), with the result that when the wheels were turned in the proper sequence, a series of numbers was entered and a cumulative sum was obtained. The gear train supplied a mechanical answer equal to the answer that is obtained by using arithmetic.

This first mechanical calculator had several disadvantages. Although it did offer a substantial improvement over manual calculations, only Pascal himself could repair the device and it cost more than the people it replaced! (Dacles 2005) In addition, the first signs of technophobia emerged with mathematicians fearing the loss of their jobs due to progress (O'Connor & Robertson 1996a). The principle of Pascal's machine is still being used today, such as in the counters of tape-recorders and odometers. Pascal's machine was one of the first mechanical calculating machines. In 1674, Gottfried Wilhelm von Leibniz made improvements on Pascal's machine; it was now possible for the machine to divide and multiply as easily as it could add and subtract. As well as inventing the Step Reckoner, von Leibniz was also an advocate of the binary system of counting (0,1), which is a key feature of all modern digital computing (wikipedia 2005a).

The weaving loom and the steam engine: convergence aids calculus

> The computer is not as disjunctive from the early history of industrial capitalism as one might imagine; and to see computerisation alone as a new and quite distinct adjunct to surveillance is misleading ... This is well illustrated by the example of the work of Charles Babbage in the middle of the nineteenth century. (Giddens 1995)

When we examine the 17th-, 18th-, and 19th-century developments in mechanical computation it becomes clear very quickly that the Industrial Revolution and the digital revolution really began around the same time. It is also obvious that new inventions, like Pascal's counter, borrowed and built on technologies that had been around for some time, in his case a simple distance-counter that had been in use for over 1400 years. When we come to the 19th century, the crossover technologies that spurred research into mechanical calculation were the weaving loom and the steam engine. When the age of industrialisation spread throughout Europe, such machines became fixtures in agriculture and manufacturing.

In 1801, a French weaver, Joseph-Marie Jacquard, invented an automatic loom controlled by punch cards. With the use of cards punched with holes, it was possible for the Jacquard loom to weave fabrics in a variety of patterns. Jacquard's system automated what had, until that time, been an expensive job done by highly skilled weavers. The punch cards were made of a stiff pasteboard material and stacked at one end of the loom; each rotation of the spindle moved a new card into position against a series of push-rods that controlled the threads. The pattern of the holes allowed some rods to move and others to remain stationary, thus creating a pattern in the cloth. The punch cards were a simple control mechanism for the machine and acted like a primitive form of programming (wikipedia 2005a).

The British mathematician and inventor Charles Babbage (1791–1871) first conceived of a device to undertake mechanical calculus, which he called the Difference Engine, in 1820 or 1821. In 1827 he became the Lucasian Professor of Mathematics at Cambridge University, though he never taught, spending all his time working on prototypes of mechanical calculators. That he held this prestigious position is testament to his mathematical genius; others to hold the chair were Isaac Newton and Stephen Hawking.

At the time Babbage conceived of the Difference Engine, the calculation of logarithms and trigonometric tables (much used in astronomy and navigation) was done by hand. Teams of people, often called 'computers', would be assembled to perform the necessary calculations. It was very expensive and the potential for undetected human error to spoil the final results was high. The Difference Engine was designed as a massive steam-powered mechanical calculator to print astronomical tables and thus save time and money and to be more accurate (O'Connor & Robertson 1998a). It was intended to be fully automatic, even to the printing of the resulting tables, and was commanded by a fixed instruction program.

In 1823, with the encouragement of the Astronomical Society, Babbage was given a government grant of £1500 to begin work on the Difference Engine. By February 1830 the British government had put nearly £9000 into the project, but still there was no working machine. Four years later the government's investment had reached £17 000 and Babbage had sunk £6000 of his own money into work on the Difference Engine (O'Connor & Robertson 1998a). Babbage attempted to build a working machine over the next twenty years, only to have the project cancelled by the British government in 1842. However, the work Babbage had put into his device led to his next project, the Analytical Engine.

This was a mechanical computer that could theoretically solve any mathematical problem. Like the Jacquard loom, the design used punch cards to perform simple conditional operations. The idea of using punched card to store a predetermined pattern to be woven by the loom clicked in the mind of Charles Babbage. He spent many years working on a machine that would be able to perform all types of mathematical calculations, store values in its memory, and perform logical comparisons among values. He called it the Analytical Engine:

> Thus it appears that the whole of the conditions which enable a finite machine to make calculations of unlimited extent are fulfilled in the Analytical Engine. The means I have adopted are uniform. I have converted the infinity of space, which was required by the conditions of the problem, into the infinity of time. The means I have employed are in daily use in the art of weaving patterns. (Babbage 1864)

The work being done by Charles Babbage attracted international attention and he travelled throughout Europe talking to eminent scientists about the Analytical Engine. He had many supporters, including the Italian mathematician L. F. Menabrea, who would later become Prime Minister of Italy. Menabrea and Ada Lovelace wrote a lengthy description of Babbage's ideas and helped to cement his place in the history of computing.

Babbage spent more than a decade working on his invention, investing his own money in workshops and master toolmakers to make his design a reality, but in the end the Analytical Engine was never built. It lacked one thing—electronics. The technology at that time was not capable of building Babbage's dream because electronics was not yet known or even thought of. Electronics was the missing link in Babbage's analytical engine.

Augusta Ada Byron, the daughter of Lord Byron and the countess of Lovelace, met Charles Babbage in 1833. She described the Analytical Engine as weaving 'algebraic patterns just as the Jacquard loom weaves flowers and leaves'. Ada Byron Lovelace was a remarkable woman who competed very well in a male-dominated world. She no doubt benefited from her wealth and title, but that should not diminish her achievements in mathematics and computing. Her published analysis (Menabrea & Lovelace 1843) of the Analytical Engine is our best record of its programming potential. In it she outlines the fundamentals of computer programming, including data analysis, looping, and memory addressing. The Analytical Engine was a real parallel decimal computer that would have operated on words of 50 decimals and was able to store 1000 such numbers. If built, the machine would have included a number of built-in operations such as conditional control, which allowed the instructions for the machine to be executed in a specific order rather than in numerical order. As Giddens notes, Babbage did not succeed for want of trying but was defeated by the lack of appropriate technologies. He was, however, aware of the ways in which his mechanical devices could contribute to the profitability of the emerging industrial system of capitalism.

Before leaving Charles Babbage and the 19th century, it is worth noting that he was a respected economist as well as an inventor. He was able to make an explicit link between technology, the division of labour in the workforce, and the collection of surplus value by the capitalist in his book *On the Economy of Machinery and Manufactures*, written in 1834. He was one of the first theorists of the Industrial Revolution to predict the coming of thinking machines that could be taught to do complicated mathematical calculations, leading to improvements in productivity by adapting such machines to the industrial process (Rosenberg 1997).

The Difference Engine

> She let her gaze follow the steam-pipes and taut wires to the gleam of the Babbage Engine, a small one, a kinotrope model, no taller than Sybil herself ... Steam calculators were delicate things, temperamental ... In the stray glare from Mick's limelight, dozens of knobbed brass columns gleamed, set top and bottom into solid sockets bored through polished plates, with shining levers, ratchets, a thousand steel gears cut bright and fine. (Gibson & Sterling 2003, p. 24)

William Gibson and Bruce Sterling do an excellent job of reimagining the Industrial Revolution in the light of how Babbage's ambitious invention, a machine for storing and reading information, might have altered history. *The Difference Engine* is a 'what if' historical novel that asks, 'What would the Industrial Revolution have looked like if Babbage had succeeded in making a steam-powered computer, the Difference Engine?' A feature of the story that is of great interest to us is how Babbage's invention becomes a machine for the surveillance and control of the population, as well as a means of conducting commerce. Data about every individual is held in the 'government engines' and every person has an individual number. When this identifier is processed through the engine, it can print out the information on the person whose number is entered. In his convincing of Sybil join his shady scheme, Mick Radley tells her he knows of her own past as the daughter of a renegade who was hanged by the government; he adds that he can change her number and create a new identity for her:

> The cops and bosses have your number here, true enough! But numbers are only that and your file's no more than a simple stack of cards. For them as know, there's ways to change a number. (Gibson & Sterling 2003, p. 26)

The data is held in the Central Statistics Bureau, whose job is to assist the police to thwart an anti-industrial revolution led by the Luddites—a real political organisation that attempted to destroy capitalism by smashing all machines. In the fictional alternative history, Babbage is now Prime Minister and must put down the Luddite rebellion, which has engulfed London. The government succeeds in quelling the revolution. The story meanders around the lives of the main characters, and in the end the loop is closed; Sybil manages to disappear to France, Mick Radley is dead, and the industrialists are firmly entrenched through their control of the engines. However, the engines are in trouble themselves because they cannot be properly maintained and are slowly being overcome by grease and breakages in the gears.

The Book of the Machines

> How many men at this hour are living in a state of bondage to the machines? How many spend their whole lives, from the cradle to the grave, in tending them by night and day? (Butler 1967, p. 150)

It is also, at this point, worth reintroducing the writing of Samuel Butler, who, despite his Christian upbringing (or perhaps because of it), became an outspoken critic of 19th-century British morals and social customs. In his anti-utopian novel *Erewhon*, published in 1872, he savagely ridicules what he perceived as the mechanistic treatment of human life in Darwin's theory of evolution. While we might now see that Darwin was right, Butler's reworking of evolution in several chapters of *Erewhon* devoted to an argument against the advancement of machines provides an interesting insight into a disturbing 19th-century view of the future—our future.

In his 'translation' of the Erewhonian *Book of the Machines* Butler provides some startling insights into the future of machine intelligence. There are no machines in Erewhon, the inhabitants having been convinced by the author of the *Book of the Machines* that all mechanical devices, save for the wheel and the lever, should be destroyed. This industrial 'counter-revolution', some 200 years before the hero of the story (Higgs) arrives in the forgotten land, has left Erewhon in a state of arrested development and stagnation. In the chapters devoted to the 'translation' of the *Book of the Machines*, Samuel Butler lays out some interesting theories about the gradual but inevitable development of machine intelligence. The section culminates in the argument that machines will eventually enslave humans and therefore, to avoid this unpleasant consequence of science, they should be destroyed at once. At one point, there appears a reference to the work of Charles Babbage, which no doubt Butler would have been aware of:

> Have we not engines which can do all manner of sums more quickly and correctly than we can? ... Our sum engines never drop a figure, nor our looms a stitch; the machine is brisk and active, when the man is weary ... May not man himself become a sort of parasite upon the machines? An affectionate machine-tickling aphid? (Butler 1967, p. 148)

The arguments made in this 'translation' are quite sophisticated and for readers of *Erewhon* in the late 19th century, they would have been recognisable as a commentary on the role of mechanisation in the Industrial Revolution. Many of Butler's arguments about the dangers of humans becoming enslaved to machines are similar to those of Karl Marx who, when Butler was writing his satire, was busy working on the main ideas in *Capital*.

Take Butler's example of a railway engine driver who can choose to stop his locomotive 'at any moment that he pleases', but in reality can only do so 'at certain points which have been fixed for him by others' (p. 158). The locomotive driver has become a part of the machine and his will is not his own, it is owned by those who own the railway (the engine and the track it runs on). In volume 1 of *Capital*, Marx makes a similar point: 'the automatic mechanism is endowed, in the person of the capitalist, with consciousness and a will' (Marx 1990, Vol. 1, p. 527) that is outside the will of the worker. Like Butler's engine driver, labourers in the industrial factory are incorporated into the machine 'as its living appendages' and must work under conditions of 'barrack-like discipline' (pp. 548–9). Giddens (1995, p. 124), too, makes a similar argument, suggesting that the discipline of the factory was reinforced by the mass introduction of machinery, which in turn made mass surveillance of the workforce easier for the factory managers acting as agents of capital. Despite the hopes of Babbage and others, the Industrial Revolution itself did not directly produce a mechanical computer that worked to any great degree. But it did provide the impetus, both in terms of advances in technology and in terms of the social need for such machines, that was to culminate in the successful demonstration of practical computing in the first half of the 20th century. It was only some thirty years after Babbage's unsuccessful attempts to build the Analytical Engine, on the cusp of the century, that the first commercially viable mechanical calculator was patented and used as the prototype 'government engine' for crunching data about people.

Hole-punched cards advance mechanical computation

A further and more concrete step towards automated computation was made in 1890 when the American engineer Herman Hollerith (1860–1929), working for the US Census Bureau, first successfully applied Babbage's punch card technique to mechanical computing. The Bureau had taken nearly eight years to complete work on the 1880 census and feared that the 1890 census would take even longer. Hollerith began work on his tabulating machine in 1881 and won a competition sponsored by the Census Bureau (da Cruz 2004).

Hollerith adopted Jacquard's punched card concept. Census data were translated into a series of holes to represent the digits and the letters of the alphabet. The data were then passed through a machine with a series of electrical contacts that were either turned 'off' or 'on' depending on the position and sequencing of holes in the punched cards. These different combinations of off/on situations were recorded by the machine and represented a way of tabulating the result of the census. What came to be called the Hollerith Code is a set of computer punch cards or paper tapes of telex machines.

Surprisingly, Hollerith said he did not get the idea from the work of Charles Babbage, but from watching a train conductor punch tickets. Of course the big advantage he had over Babbage was the ability to apply the power of electro-magnets to the process, while Babbage had only mechanical force (like the Jacquard machine) and the possibility of steam as the driving power.

As a result of Hollerith's invention, reading errors were greatly reduced and work flow was increased in the Census Bureau. Importantly, stacks of punched cards could be used as an accessible memory store of almost unlimited capacity; furthermore, different problems could be stored on different batches of cards and worked on as needed.

Hollerith's machine was highly successful. It cut by two-thirds the time it took to tabulate the result of the census. It made money for the company that manufactured Hollerith's machine. And in 1911, this company merged with its competitor to form International Business Machines (IBM). From the 1950s onwards IBM has been a prominent name in computing and delivered the first mass-market personal computer in the 1970s.

Hollerith's machine, however, was strictly limited to tabulation. The punched cards could not be used to direct more complex computations (Hoyle 2004). Eventually Hollerith introduced a continuous strip of paper tape with punched holes; when these were passed over a metal drum the presence of a hole allowed an electrical circuit to be made and the machine would register the data that corresponded to that hole 'position'. A series of holes in combination could in this way be made to represent more complex data.

Hollerith also invented the first automatic card-feeder mechanism and the key-punch. He is also recognised as a pioneer of programming through the introduction of a switchable wiring panel to his 1906 Type I machine, which allowed it to perform different calculations without having to be rewired. Each of these innovations made a contribution to the rapid development of computing and information processing in the 20th century (da Cruz 2004). For example, the punch card technology was in use right up to the late 1970s (Bellis n.d.-a).

In the 1930s, a German civil engineer called Konrad Zuse (1910–95), who had already developed a number of calculating machines, released the first programmable computer designed to solve complex engineering equations. His first machine, the Z1, was built in his parents' living room and did not work very well, but it was the first binary machine to use a punched tape, rather than cards, and in that respect prefigured the modern computer. According to his own recollections, Zuse was working independently and had not been following the work of other inventors in the field: 'I started in 1934, working independently and without knowledge of other developments going on around me. In fact, I hadn't even heard of Charles Babbage when I embarked on my work' (quoted in O'Connor & Robertson 1999b).

Zuse pioneered the use of binary math and Boolean logic in electronic calculation. His second calculating machine, Z2, replaced mechanical with electrical components, but it was not completed because World War II interrupted his work. While in the German army, Zuse completed the Z3, which was controlled by perforated strips of discarded movie film. As well as being controllable by these celluloid strips, it was also the first machine to actually work on the binary system, as opposed to the more familiar decimal system. Zuse's work prefigured that of the English mathematician Alan Turing in that his machine was a 'general' computer, not one designed to undertake a specific individual function (Redshaw 1996). The Z3 was used by the German Aerodynamic Research Institute to work on problems in the production of military aircraft. The Z3 had over 2600 electrical relay circuits and when Zuse proposed to the German high command that he build a computer based on electronic valves he was told it was not necessary because Germany was close to winning the war! (O'Connor & Robertson 1999b) After the war Zuse continued to work on computing problems in the aerospace industry. In 1950 he established his own company, which was eventually incorporated into the giant Siemens electronics firm in 1967. In 1958 Zuse was up to Z22 in his series of computers. It was an early example of a computer that made use of transistors rather than valves.

Binary Code: One digit/no digit—on/off

Zuse's use of binary code was a big step forward in computing technology, particularly when it could be harnessed to an electrical circuit. The binary system is composed of 0s and 1s. A punch card with its two conditions—a hole or no hole—was admirably suited to representing things in a binary form. If a hole was read by the card reader, it was considered to be a 1. If no hole was present in a column, a 0 was appended to the current number. The total number of possible numbers can be calculated by putting 2 to the power of the number of bits (2^n) in the binary number. A bit is simply a single occurrence of a binary number—a 0 or a 1. Thus, if you had a possible binary number of 6 bits (2^6), 64 different numbers could be generated (2×2×2×2×2×2=64). Binary representation was going to prove important in the future design of computers, which took advantage of a multitude of two-state devices such card readers, electric circuits, which could be on or off, and vacuum tubes. Konrad Zuse is also remembered for his contribution to computer programming. In 1945 he invented a machine language called 'Plankilkul' and was able to design a chess-playing program (O'Connor & Robertson 1999b).

While Zuse was working on the German war effort, physicist Howard Aiken (1900–73) of Harvard University was working on similar ideas for his PhD. Like Zuse and others before him, Aiken wanted to build a machine that would take the drudgery out of the difficult and long mathematical equations that he needed to solve in order to get on with his important work in another field. Aiken fortuitously came across a few parts from Babbage's Analytical Engine that were in storage at the Harvard science museum and recognised that the technology of 1937 was developed enough to implement Babbage's concept (Ferguson 1998). With the combined effort of his colleagues in Harvard and IBM, the Automatic Sequence Controlled Calculator (ASCC) was finished in 1944; it cost $200 000 to construct. The ASCC machine weighed 35 tons, held 500 miles of wiring, and could complete an addition to 23 significant places in six seconds, while a division took around 12 seconds. Like Zuse and others, Aiken used punched paper tapes for instructions and punch cards for the data. IBM donated the machine to Harvard University and it became known as the Harvard Mark 1. Also like the Zuse machines, the Mark 1 was used in military applications, in this case to calculate the ballistic qualities of heavy-calibre ammunition (O'Connor & Robertson 1999a). The Mark 1 had over 760 000 parts and special built-in programs, or subroutines, to handle logarithms and trigonometric functions. It was the first in a series of computers designed and built under Aiken's direction between 1943 and 1952, ending with the Mark IV (O'Connor & Robertson 1999a; Hoyle 2004). Howard Aiken is also credited with establishing the first undergraduate course in computer science at Harvard (Ferguson 1998).

One further American researcher of note was working on computing and mathematics problems at the same time as Aiken and his colleagues at Harvard. He was the Hungarian-born John von Neumann (1903–57). Like several others we've met on this journey, von Neumann was a child prodigy who wrote his first published paper at the age of 18 and who completed, simultaneously, degrees in mathematics and chemistry. He is reputed to have passed his mathematics exams at the University of Budapest without attending any courses, while living in Zurich and completing a diploma in chemical engineering (O'Connor & Robertson 2003b). Von Neumann emigrated to the United States in 1930 and took up a post at Princeton University, where he pursued an interest in quantum mechanics. He quickly became interested in the work of Aiken and others and also met the British mathematician and computing theorist Alan Turing. During World War II von Neumann worked on the computing needs of the Los Alamos team that was to produce the hydrogen bomb (Lee 2002). After the war he retained close links to the American military as a member of the Armed Forces Special Weapons Project and then as a member of the Atomic Energy Commission (O'Connor & Robertson 2003b).

The key aspect of von Neumann's work on computer-related problems is the legacy of the computer infrastructure that is known as the 'von Neumann Architecture', which relates to the ability of the machine to store programs and data simultaneously, though in separate parts of its 'brain'. Before this, computers had to be physically rewired to perform different functions. For example, the Hollerith tabulator (see p. 197) used a plug board similar to a telephone exchange, and some machines were hard-wired for only one type of function. Using von Neumann's system, the machine could be much more flexible and could even be self-modifying in a limited way. Von Neumann contributed a new understanding of how practical, fast computers should be organised and built; these ideas, often referred to as the stored-program technique, became fundamental for future generations of high-speed digital computers and were universally adopted. The primary advance was the provision of a special type of machine instruction called conditional control transfer that allowed the program sequence to be interrupted and recommenced at any point, similar to the system suggested by Babbage for his analytical engine. If all instruction programs were stored together with data in the same memory unit, instructions could be arithmetically modified in the same way as data. Thus data was the same as program.

While we know this type of stored program as the von Neumann architecture, it is clear that there was some collaboration involved as similar designs were being developed by other scientists, some of whom were colleagues of von Neumann's at various American institutions. The stored-program concept quickly became the standard for prototype computers from the late 1940s onwards, and after World War II a number of discrete projects in the United States and the UK were using it (wikipedia 2005b). In the late 1940s and into the 1950s, von Neumann, Aiken, and others collaborated on several computing projects (Lee 2002). Von Neumann is remembered for his advocacy of the 'bit' as a measurement of computer memory.

With the success of Aiken's Harvard Mark-I as the first major American development in the computing race, work was proceeding on the next great breakthrough by the Americans. Their second contribution was the development of the giant ENIAC machine by John W. Mauchly and J. Presper Eckert. ENIAC, or Electronic Numerical Integrator and Computer, was developed for the Ballistics Research Laboratory in Maryland to assist in the preparation of firing tables for artillery. It was built at the University of Pennsylvania's Moore School of Electrical Engineering and completed in November 1945. The ENIAC is believed to be the first electronic digital computer. It had no moving parts, used about 18 000 vacuum tubes, and was able to calculate complex numbers in a few seconds. The vacuum tubes were quite delicate and had to be replaced frequently because they tended to burn out. Storage of all those vacuum tubes and the machinery required to keep them cool took up over 167 m^2 (1800 square feet) of floor space.

BIT, BYTE, MEGABYTE

A bit is the smallest unit of computerised data, either a zero or one; a byte is usually 8 bits; a megabyte is a million bytes.

The ENIAC was programmable and had the capability to store problem calculations using words of 10 decimal digits instead of binary ones like previous automated calculators/computers. Nonetheless, it had punched-card input and output and arithmetically had 1 multiplier, 1 divider-square rooter, and 20 adders employing decimal 'ring counters', which served as adders and also as quick-access (0.0002 seconds) read-write register storage.

The executable instructions composing a program were embodied in the separate units of ENIAC, which were plugged together to form a route through the machine for the flow of computations. These connections had to be redone for each different problem, together with presetting function tables and switches. This technique was inconvenient, and brings into question just how far ENIAC could be considered programmable. But it was efficient in handling the particular programs for which it had been designed. ENIAC is generally acknowledged to be the first successful high-speed electronic digital computer (EDC) and was productively used from 1946 to 1955. A controversy developed in 1971, however, over the patentability of ENIAC's basic digital concepts, the claim being made that another American physicist, John V. Atanasoff, had already used the same ideas in a simpler vacuum-tube device he built in the 1930s while at Iowa State College. In 1973, the court found in his favour and Atanasoff received the acclaim he deserved.

The breakthrough in Britain

> Perhaps the most remarkable feature of Turing's work on Turing machines was that he was describing a modern computer before technology had reached the point where construction was a realistic proposition. (O'Connor & Robertson 2003a)

While Aiken, von Neumann, and others were working at Harvard, over in the UK, the British mathematician Alan Turing (1912–54) wrote a paper in 1936 entitled *On Computable Numbers*, in which he described a hypothetical device that prefigured programmable computers: a 'Turing machine' (O'Connor & Robertson 2003a). The Turing machine was designed to perform logical operations and could read, write, or erase symbols written on squares of an infinite paper tape. This kind of machine came to be known as a finite state machine because at each step in a computation, the machine's next action was matched against a finite instruction list of possible states.

Turing's purpose was not to invent a computer, but rather to describe problems that are logically possible to solve. His hypothetical machine, however, foreshadowed certain characteristics of modern computers that would follow. For example, the endless tape could be seen as a form of general purpose internal memory for the machine in that the machine was able to read, write, and erase—just like modern RAM (random access memory).

The technologies of war

Like many of his contemporaries on both sides of the Atlantic, and in both the allied and enemy camps, Alan Turing served as a consultant to the armed forces. The military high command needed powerful machines for calculating complex problems, particularly for ballistics and range-finding. In Britain, Turing worked tirelessly as a government code-breaker and was involved with 'Colossus', a British computer used for code-breaking, that was operational in December 1943. For an enjoyable insight into the work of code-breakers during the Second World War we recommend Neal Stephenson's 'what if' novel

Cryptonomicon (2002). Most of the computing breakthroughs discussed in this chapter began life as military projects. The dialectic of war unleashes both terrible destruction and enormous investment in new technologies by combatant nations (IEEE Virtual Museum 2005).

The state and private enterprise have had a long-standing and fraught relationship with armed conflict. In the 20th century this relationship led to two major world wars and many smaller conflicts—from the Crimea to Suez, from Korea to Vietnam, and, from the 1990s onwards, Iraq. Governments have been willing to gamble with the lives of citizens and with the possible destruction of their entire civil and economic infrastructure in the pursuit of private profit and political strategic gain. The 20th century became the era of 'total war' and the global economy was built on the back of 'war economy' and a never-ending arms race (Shaw 1988, pp. 30–2).

Martin Shaw points to the complete industrialisation of warfare in the 20th century. This relies on the technological development of weapons capable of disrupting the enemy's production of armaments, breaking the distinction between civilians and combatants, and attacking the 'socio-economic infrastructure of the enemy'. These are the elements of 'total war' that led to the development of the giant bomber plane capable of laying waste to entire cities (Dresden, large sections of London, and many other cities in Britain and Europe) and of course the 'most important single military research project ever', the atomic bomb (Shaw 1988, p. 78).

While 'total war' gave the United States the impetus to complete the Los Alamos research project to produce an atomic weapon, it was an idea that first germinated in 1905 when Albert Einstein theorised that splitting the atom would release large amounts of energy. It was also Einstein, in 1939, who urged the American government to begin the top-secret 'Manhattan Project' that led to the hydrogen bomb. The project consumed an estimated $2 billion and employed over 120 000 people (IEEE Virtual Museum 2005). This is a good example of Shaw's dialectic of war. To build the weapon, a vast amount of capital was diverted from other needs. When the 'product' of the research was completed and used, it created even more horror and destruction—the levelling of the Japanese cities of Hiroshima and Nagasaki, resulting in tens of thousands of deaths and billions of dollars worth of destruction of infrastructure and productive capacity. Capital benfits from this destruction of value and profitability is restored through the reconstruction phase. The technological breakthroughs in electronics and computing coupled with the rebuilding of devastated cities and economies were the important contributors to the postwar boom in global capitalism from the late 1940s to the early 1970s.

Radar is another example of how rapid advances in technology occur during war. Radar was developed in Britain using vacuum-tube technology, but it was cooperation between British and American scientists working on microwaves that led to the building of about a hundred specialised radar systems before the end of 1945. Research into rockets and jet aircraft was also boosted by the need to 'weaponise' technologies in aid of the war effort.

The technology of the German V2 rocket, which the Allies captured at the end of the war, provided the scientific knowledge necessary to launch the 'space race' in the 1950s.

Today computers are part of almost every piece of military hardware, but they were not so important on the battle front during World War II. As we mentioned, many of the computers developed in the 1930s and 1940s did have military applications, such as working out trajectories and ballistics, and of course the code-breaking done in Britain would not have been so successful without the use of number-crunching computers.

In an interesting twist on the utopian/dystopian theme in science fiction, John Birmingham has written a series of 'what if' historical thrillers that illustrate the importance of technological advantage during wartime. The first book, *Weapons of Choice*, is subtitled 'World War 2.1', an obvious reference to the concept of versions that we are now so used to with software. It begins with an almighty technological clash when a multinational battle fleet from the 21st century is somehow catapulted back in time from 2021 to the year 1942, right into the middle of a US Navy task force headed for the famous battle of the Midway Islands. The multinational fleet had been testing a new weapon that was 'in essence, a teleporter ... designed to move a very small, simple warhead directly into the mass of a selected target' (Birmingham 2004, p. 18). The test fails and instead the fleet finds itself in a shooting match with the USS *Enterprise* (an aircraft carrier) and its armada of escort ships. After a brief but costly firefight between the vessels, both sides realise that the other fleet is, in a sense, an ally.

The multinational fleet then joins the Allied war effort against Germany and Japan. But the damage is already done. A number of 21st-century ships fall into enemy hands and so a new arms race begins. The vessels each carry an array of 21st-century technologies, from cruise missiles to reconnaissance drones and 'flexipad' hand-held computers. Some of these devices, plus eighty years of historical records from the ships' archives, are used by the Japanese and German generals to begin equipping their own forces.

In the second volume, *Designated targets: World War 2.2* (Birmingham 2005), the arms race begins in earnest, but the presence of the 21st-century fleet and its new information means that the course of history has already been altered. Japanese forces are landed in northern Queensland and General Douglas McArthur's forces must defend the 'Brisbane Line' against invasion. In a nice tilt at Silicon Valley, Birmingham has the 21st-century commanders establish a massive technology park just outside Los Angeles to begin a rapid build-up of new technologies. Unfortunately, the Germans (in cooperation with Stalinist Russia) and the Japanese are also pushing ahead with weaponising the technologies from their captured ships.

John Birmingham's books are novels, but like all good works of science fiction they are based on extrapolation from things that we know are happening—like the development of robotic soldiers, for example. In early October 2005 a driverless Volkswagen Touareg SUV called 'Stanley' collected a $US2 million prize for winning a race across the California desert sponsored by the US Defense Advanced Research Projects Agency (DARPA).

According to a DARPA media release, five vehicles finished the 131.6 mile (283 km) course, proving 'conclusively' that 'autonomous ground vehicles can travel long distances over difficult terrain at militarily relevant rates of speed' (DARPA 2005). The winning entry was designed and built by a team from Stanford University, which along with the other 'Ivy League' universities in America has had a long and fruitful relationship with the American defence agencies. The defence scientists were pleased with the result because in 2004 none of the entrants was able to complete a similar course. DARPA was the organisation behind the birth of the Internet (ARPANET) and also provided funding to build the deadly radar-evading Stealth bomber and the Predator military drone aircraft (Markhoff 2005).

Postwar computing

Following the technological and financial boost to computing delivered by the industrial-military complex during World War II, researchers in the United States continued their efforts to commercialise computers. Eckert and Mauchly left the Moore School of Engineering, where they had been academically successful, and started their own computer business. In an ironic twist of fate, their first client was the US Census Bureau, which fifty years early had launched Hollerith on the career that would lead to the founding of IBM. Eckert and Mauchly built the UNIVAC (Universal Automatic Computer) for the Bureau, but the effort nearly sent them bankrupt and the final cost was close to $1 million. They were eventually bailed out by the Remington Rand Corporation and went on to build and sell forty-six UNIVAC machines in direct competition with IBM (Bellis, n.d.-b). Throughout the 1950s computers became more and more accepted in commercial and bureaucratic applications and the IBM 'seven' series (the 701, 704, 7090) were successful, renting for around $15 000 a month. The company also maintained its ties with the US military and the 701 machines were used in atomic research, aircraft production, and the department of defence.

MAINFRAME

A term used to describe the large refrigerator-size computers that preceded the personal computer. The first commercial mainframe was the Univac, manufactured in 1951. The mainframe made a comeback in the 1990s as electronic commerce took off, and as networks-based systems became subject to hacking and virus attacks, as an efficient and secure means of performing high-volume transactions. IBM dominates the market for mainframe computers.

The invention of the transistor at the Bell Telephone company's laboratories in the mid-1950s was a breakthrough that converged with new computing machines to increase speed and reliability. The smaller and more reliable transistors replaced valves and tubes, the machines thus becoming smaller and more portable. In 1956 John Bardeen, William Shockley, and Walter Brattain won the Nobel Prize in physics for their invention.

The development of computer language in the 1950s also created momentum for computing. John Backus of IBM wrote one of the first high-level programming languages, FORTRAN (for FORmula TRANslation) in 1954 and it was commercially released in 1957 (Bellis, n.d.-b). A second type of computer language, called 'assembly language', was also being written at this time. Assembly language uses human words like 'add', but it has to be translated back into machine language—a series of zeros and ones (for 'off' and 'on')—before a computer can understand it. The third generation of code HLL (high-level language) uses human syntax and vocabulary, but must be translated for a machine to 'understand it'. The FORTRAN breakthrough really created the software industry as we know it today, and in 1993 John Backus won the National Academy of Engineering's Charles Stark Draper Prize for the invention of FORTRAN (Bellis, n.d.-b).

Solid circuitry to silicon chip

> What we didn't realize then was that the integrated circuit would reduce the cost of electronic functions by a factor of a million to one, nothing had ever done that before. (Jack Kilby, quoted in Bellis, n.d.-b)

There was literally a race between two men and two rival companies to come up with an integrated electronic circuit to replace transistors, resistors, capacitors, valves, and tubes. An integrated circuit allows an almost limitless increase in the number of circuits available for connection on one silicon 'chip'.

Jack Kilby of Texas Instruments and Robert Noyce of Fairchild Semiconductor both announced the development of an integrated circuit in 1959. In a clever commercial move, the two companies cross-licensed their technologies and created a global market now worth over $US1 trillion a year (that's a billion billion dollars). The original integrated circuit had only one transistor, three resistors, and one capacitor. Today they are much smaller and can hold about 125 million transistors (Bellis, n.d.-b).

In 1957, the IBM Corporation developed the IBM 704 computer, which could perform 100 000 calculations per second.

In 1958, a group of computer scientists met in Zurich and from this meeting came ALGOL (ALGOrithmic Language). ALGOL was intended to be a universal, machine-independent language, but they were not successful because they did not have the same close association with IBM as FORTRAN. A derivative of ALGOL—ALGOL-60—came to be known as C, which is the standard choice for programming requiring detailed control of hardware. After that came COBOL (COmmon Business Oriented Language). Developed in 1960, COBOL was designed to produce applications for the business world and had the novel approach of separating the data descriptions from the actual program. This enabled the data descriptions to be referred to by many different programs. Today there are tens of thousands of computer programs on the market and many thousands of applications that we take for granted. Software has become a global business in its own right.

Conclusion

In the Cold War environment, after World War II, the United States felt threatened by the looming technological superiority of the USSR, as demonstrated by the successful launch of the Sputnik satellite in 1957. During Eisenhower's presidency the Pentagon poured millions not only into the space race, but also into advanced computer research at major universities, such as MIT and Stanford. The Kennedy administration, elected in 1960, continued the policy. The first attempt to network two computers, in 1969 in California, crashed as the scientists entered the letter G, the third letter of the log in sequence (LOGIN) (Hafner & Lyon 2003, p. 152). It was an inauspicious start for a revolution that had been two and a half millennia in the making.

From the beginning of the 1960s, and on the foundations laid in the postwar years, computing began to take off at an exponential speed. At the heart of this growth was the silicon chip, which Mary Bellis describes as one of the most important innovations ever. Nearly all of our modern electrical products use some form of chip technology. Through the history outlined here we have discussed the first four generations of computers from the giant hard-wired punch card and tape machines of the Industrial Revolution to the transistor and solid-state circuit commercial machines produced by Remington Rand and IBM in the 1950s. We have also hinted at the close connection between the growing military-industrial complex and computing.

Until the 1960s computing had been a 'stand alone' application used mainly in industrial, military, and pure research settings. The next wave, which some suggest constituted a 'Golden Age' of computing, began when computers moved out of laboratories and military installations into the office, the home, and the classroom. In the next chapter we continue the story of computing by looking at the breakthroughs of the 1960s and the work of young American computer geeks like Steve Jobs and Bill Gates in places like the now-famous Silicon Valley in central California.

KEY POINTS

The key points from this chapter are:

- The critical insight to gain from this chapter is an understanding of the concept of 'convergence': that convergence is not a new idea, but is one of the key processes that underlies all technological innovation and change.
- The need and desire to develop 'thinking machines' has been an integral part of the human story since Neolithic times.
- Technological innovation and change cannot be adequately understood unless we understand the social context in which these changes are taking place.
- The process of convergence ensures that new technologies in the field of numerical calculation (computing) build on the insights, achievements, and failures of previous generations.

TIMELINE FOR A (MODERN) HISTORY OF COMPUTERS

1834	Gauss and Weber build the first electromagnetic telegraph, making electrical signals travel from one device to another.
1844	Samuel F. B. Morse demonstrates the Baltimore MD and Washington DC telegraph line.
1865	Nokia, in Sweden, operates its first pulp and paper mill.
1876	Alexander Graham Bell patents the telephone.
1877	Bell Telephone Company is formed.
1878	First commercial telephone exchange in the world opens at New Haven, Connecticut.
1878	First telephone directory, New Haven, with 21 listings is published.
1879	First telephone service in Australia is established in Melbourne.
1880	First telephone exchange is opened in Melbourne.
1885	American Telephone & Telegraph Co (AT&T) is founded.
1885	The Bell Telephone Company forms a new subsidiary, American Telephone & Telegraph (AT&T).
1889	Almon B. Strowger, a St Louis undertaker, invents the automatic telephone exchange.
1889	Invention of the coin-operated public phone; installed in a bank in Hartford, Connecticut.
1899	Name of Bell Telephone Company changed to AT&T.
1901	At federation 22 310 telephone subscribers in Australia.
1902	First telephone exchange is installed in Chicago.
1902	Telephone cable connects Australia and Canada.
1904	Telephone answering machine is invented.
1907	Melbourne to Sydney trunk telephone line is opened.
1912	First automatic telephone exchange in Australia.
1919	AT&T introduces dial telephones.
1924	The mobile telephone invented and installed in New York City police cars.
1927	First transatlantic telephone call, between New York and London.
1930	First London to Melbourne telephone call.
1937	British 999 emergency system established.
Late 1930s	German civil engineer Konrad Zuse develops the Z1 model computer, acknowledged as the world's first fully programmable computer using valves.
1939	Atanosoff and Berry develop the first electronic digital computer.
1941–44	Howard Aitkin and a team at Harvard develop the Harvard Mark 1 computer.
1943	First automatic interstate telephone exchange introduced in Philadelphia.
1945	Vannevar Bush defines hypertext language, the basis of HTML.
1946	First commercial mobile telephone service becomes available in St Louis, Missouri.

TIMELINE

1947 Bell Labs scientists John Bardeen, Walter Brattain, and Bill Shockley invent the transistor.

1949 CIRAC. First computer in Australia at CSIRO.

1950 The first microwave link between New York and Chicago opened.

1951 Remington Rand (a former typewriter and adding machine company) delivers the first commercial computer, the UNIVAC, made famous for matching couples on the reality TV show *People Are Funny* (NBC 1954–61), hosted by Art Linklater.

1952 UNIVAC predicts the winner of US presidential election on CBS TV.

1953 International Business Machines (IBM), later known as Big Blue, enters the computer market with its 701 EDPM model.

1954 IBM releases the FORTRAN computer programming language.

1957 Sputnik transmits the first radio signals from space.

1958 Defense Research Projects Agency (DARPA) founded. DARPA funded the development of the Internet.

1958 Jack Kilby and Robert Noyce invent the silicon chip, aka the integrated circuit.

1958 Laser invented by Bell Labs scientists Shawlow and Townes.

1958 SILLIAC and UTECOM time-sharing computers go live in Australia.

1958 STD Subscriber Trunk Dialling—dialling outside the local exchange area without operator assistance—begins in the USA.

1960 Theodore H. Maiman at Hughes Research Labs creates the first laser.

1962 Medlars, the Medical Literature Analysis and Retrieval System, one of the world's first computerised information services, opens in the USA.

1963 Eighty-one million telephones in the USA; 159 million worldwide.

1964 Douglas Engelbart invents the computer mouse.

1964 Picture phone on display at the New York World Fair.

1964 Touch dialling begins replacing rotary dialling.

1965 Car phones connected to rest of the AT&T terrestrial network.

1965 The first commercial communications satellite, Early Bird, launched.

1967 Two million telephones worldwide.

1967 Cordless telephones released.

1967 Toll-free number service begins in the USA.

1968 AT&T establishes '911' as the nationwide emergency telephone number.

1968 Intel founded.

1968 UNIX developed by Thompson and Ritchie at Bell Labs.

1968 Xerox PARC founded.

1969 ARPA Net—the first iteration of the Internet is switched on in California using packet switching technologies.

1969 Dialog computer database launched by Lockheed.

1970 AT&T establishes a commercial Picturephone in Pittsburgh.

1970	Chicago chosen as the test site for the development of cellular telephone networks.
1970	Fibre optics invented.
1971	First edition of the *UNIX Programmer's Manual* by K. Thompson and D. M. Ritchie.
1971	IBM introduces the floppy disk.
1971	Intel microprocessor released—first computer chip.
1971	Ray Tomlinson uses the @ symbol as part of an electronic messaging system on ARPA Net—email is born.
1971	Wang 1200 word processor released.
1972	5.25 inch floppy disks first appear.
1972	Atari founded by Nolan Bushnell and releases Pong, the first commercial video game.
1972	First Cray super computer.
1972	HP and TI release first electronic calculators.
1972	Motorola demonstrates the cellular telephone to the FCC. People can call each other without wires.
1973	Robert Metcalfe at Xerox in Palo Alto invents local area networking, via Ethernet.
1974	TCP protocol developed by Vint Cerf and Bob Kahn at BBN.
1974	US Justice Department takes AT&T to court for monopolistic practices.
1975	*Popular Electronics* publishes a cover story on the Altair 8800, which costs $397 in kit form and uses the Intel 8080 processor. The microcomputer boom begins.
1974–77	First PCs come to market: IBM 5100, Apple I & II, TRS 80, and Commodore.
1975	Bill Gates drops out of Harvard to pursue a career in software development.
1975	CompuServe first major ISP.
1975	Microsoft founded.
1976	Apple founded.
1977	Apple II released.
1977	AT&T rolls out the world's first commercial fibre-optic system.
1978	CDs released by Phillips and Sony.
1978	Video laser disk invented.
1978	VisiCalc, a spreadsheet program, becomes the first 'killer app'.
1979	First cell phone network in Japan.
1979	WordStar word processing software—the second 'killer app'.
1980	Animator Hanna-Barbera, begins computer automation of animation process.
1980	Donkey Kong released.
1980	First laptop computer.
1980	Number of computers in the US exceeds 1 million.
1980	Lotus 1 2 3 spreadsheet released.
1980	OECD formulates information privacy principles.
1980	Pacman video game released.
1980	The VCR is introduced by Matsushita. US sales of 40 000 in the first year.
1981	First cellular network licence awarded in the US to AT&T.
1981	IBM PC comes to market.
1981	Microsoft brings out the MS-DOS operating system.
1981	Sun Microsystems founded.
1982	Adobe founded.

TIMELINE

1982	AT&T agrees to break up of its monopoly, executed in 1984.
1982	Estimated 200 computers connected to the Internet worldwide.
1983	Apple Lisa released: the first commercial computer with a graphical user interface and mouse.
1983	Number of computers in the USA exceeds 10 million.
1983	Paul Mockapetris develops the Internet domain name system.
1983	Sony and Phillips release first CD players.
1984	First PDA released.
1984	Michael Dell founds Dell Systems selling computers by mail order.
1984	Enter the Apple MAC.
1984	Advent of 32 bit microprocessor and 1 mb microchip.
1985	America Online founded.
1985	First dot com domain name registered.
1985	Microsoft Windows.
1985	Microsoft, Sun Micro, and Silicon Graphics all go public.
1985	William Gibson coins the term 'cyberspace' in *Neuromancer*.
1986	Thirty million computers in the USA.
1986	GIF and JPEG formats announced.
1987	First global Internet worm infection.
1987	Integrated Services Digital Network (ISDN) introduced, making computer-to-computer data transfer faster and more efficient.
1988	Adobe Photoshop.
1988	Open Source Software Foundation formed.
1989	'Pocket' cellular telephone—the mobile phone—is introduced by Motorola. Goodbye to the brick.
1989	One million mobile phone subscribers in the USA.
1989	Four hundred and ninety-six million phone handsets worldwide.
1989	Australia connected to the Internet.
1990	Archie, the first Internet search engine, developed by Alan Emtage at McGill University.
1990	Electronic Frontier Foundation is founded.
1990	Tim Berners-Lee and colleagues at CERN in Geneva invent the World Wide Web, HTML, HTTP, and URLs.
1991	Four billion video cassette rentals in the USA.
1991	First PC-based video phones demonstrated by IBM and PictureTel.
1991	Philips introduces the Compact Disc Interactive (CD-I) player for music, and video.
1991	Recordable compact disc drivers, CD-Rs, reach the market.
1992	Ten million mobile phone subscribers in the USA; first SMS to mobile phones.
1992	Adobe Acrobat released.
1992	Mosaic web browser—eventually Netscape—released.
1992	US cable television revenues US$22 billion; 900 million TV sets worldwide, 200 million of these in the USA.
1993	Iomega zip drive released.

1993	MPEG-2 standard for digital television pictures adopted.
1993	*Myst* released, by 1998 the top-selling computer game of its time.
1993	Nokia sends text messages between mobile phones.
1993	The first digital mobile telephony network is established in the USA.
1993	Windows Internet Explorer (IE) released.
1993	*Wired* magazine launched in San Francisco.
1994	134 million PCs worldwide.
1994	Amazon starts selling books online.
1994	Banner ads first appear on the Internet.
1994	First Virtual establishes first online banking.
1994	Hewlett Packard combines printer, fax, and copier into one machine.
1994	Netscape Version 1 released.
1994	Pizza Hut starts taking orders on the Web.
1994	Real Audio allows audio listening in near real time.
1994	Yahoo search engine started.
1995	Twenty-five million mobile phones in the USA.
1995	Cable modems introduced.
1995	Netscape and Sun announce Java, an open, cross-platform object scripting language.
1995	Nicholas Negroponte's *Being Digital* published.
1995	Sony Playstation released.
1995	The Java programming language introduced.
1995	WebTV formed to combine television and the Internet.
1995	Wiki (What I Know Is...) developed by Ward Cunningham in Hawaii.
1996	Forty-six million mobile phone subscribers worldwide.
1996	DVD technology demonstrated.
1996	From Netscape: the cookie.
1996	Hotmail launched. Sold to Microsoft in 1998.
1996	Larry Page and Sergey Brin start Google.
1996	Motorola releases the 3.1 oz mobile phone StarTAC.
1996	Nintendo launches Super Mario home video game.
1996	Yahoo IPO.
1997	*Ask Jeeves* search engine launched.
1997	Australian Government sells of 33 per cent of the publicly owned telco, Telstra.
1997	Blogging begins.
1997	Google IPO.
1997	Nokia launches G2 mobile telephone technology.
1997	Philippe Kahn invents the digital camera phone.
1997	*Slashdot* website 'News for Nerds. Stuff that matters' launched.
1997	Streaming audio and video available on the Web.
1998	America Online surpasses 15 million members, launches AOL Australia, and is added to the S&P 500.
1998	AOL buys Netscape. Netscape publicly releases its code for Mozilla, an open-source browser.

TIMELINE

1998 Bluetooth wireless technology for personal area networks announced by Ericsson.

1998 First satellite phone call made over the Globalstar's system.

1998 ICANN established to regulate domain names.

1998 Microsoft anti-trust suit begins.

1999 Apple launches iMovie software on the iMac DV. It is later joined by iTunes, iPhoto, IDVD, GarageBand and iWeb, creating the iLife suite.

1999 Compaq creates the AltaVista Company.

1999 Global online population reaches 150 million.

1999 Motorola's i1000plus mobile phone handset integrated a digital phone, two-way radio and alphanumeric pager with Internet microbrowser, e-mail, fax, and messaging.

1999 Napster—first peer-to-peer file sharing software released.

1999 Second tranche (16 per cent) of Australia's Telstra sold off, leaving the government a 51 per cent shareholder.

2000 Digital camera phone Sharp J-SH04 comes to market.

2000 *Digital Copyright Act* in Australia.

2000 Napster & Bertelsmann AG partner to develop a membership-based music distribution system that would guarantee payments to artists.

2001 Merger of AOL and Time Warner.

2001 Apple introduces the iPod.

2001 Napster closes.

2001 Wikipedia—a free, user edited online encyclopaedia, launched by Larry Sanger.

2003 iTunes Music Store begins in the USA.

2005 US Supreme Court holds software distributors liable for copyright breaches. Australian courts follow suit in the Kazaa case.

2006 First live webcast from second smallest country in the world, Tuvalu.

2006 iTunes Music Store sells its billionth song.

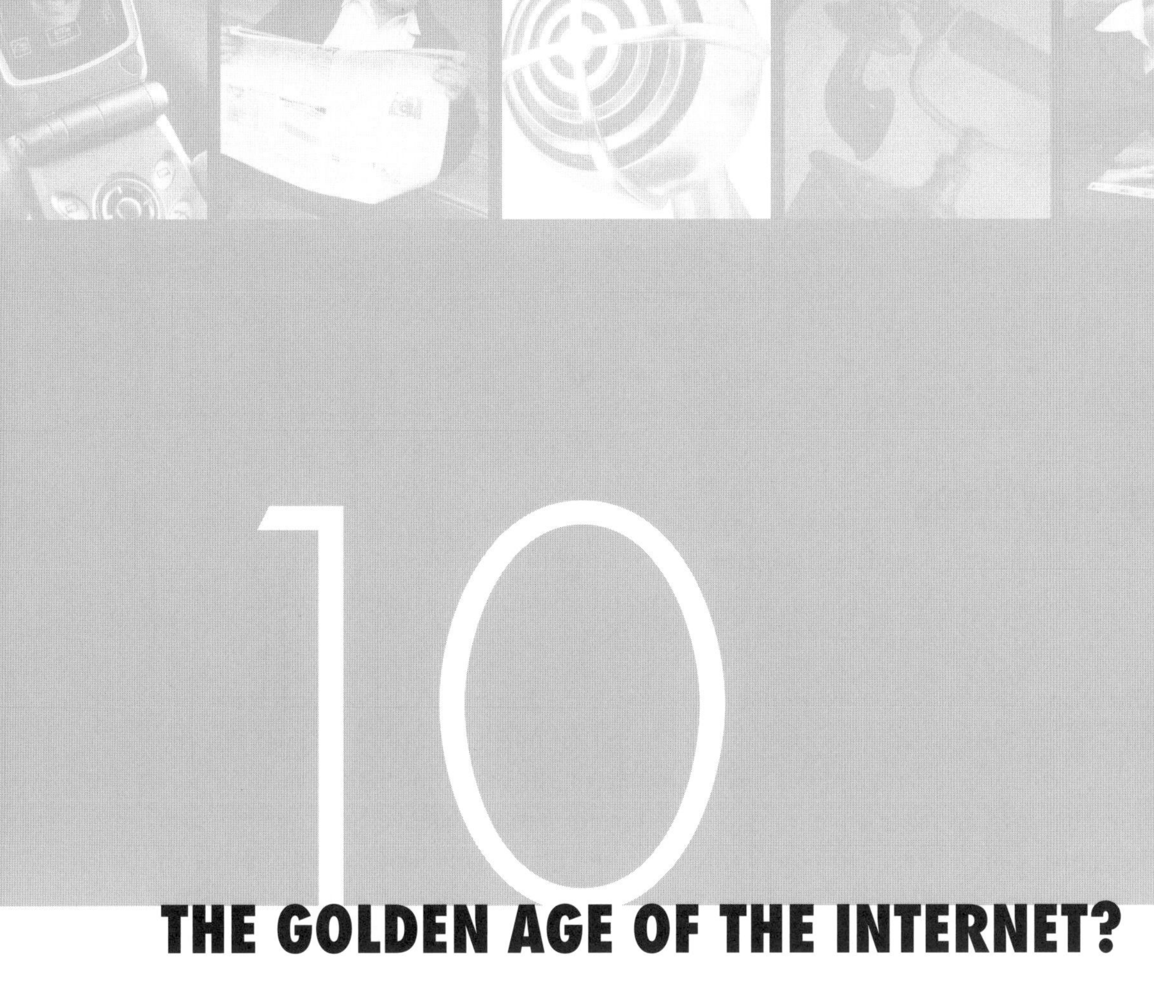

10 THE GOLDEN AGE OF THE INTERNET?

OBJECTIVES

After reading this chapter you will begin to form a fuller picture of where our argument is going. In particular, in this chapter we want you to consider the following:

- The development of the Internet, and of digital media, has occurred in phases that have their own distinct material features and their own mythologies.
- The dream of the Internet is very close to Marshall McLuhan's concept of 'global village', but the view that the Internet has had (or is having) a 'Golden Age' must be read in an historical context and with some scepticism.
- The reality of the Internet is limited by the same issues that create inequality in other areas of our lives: gender, money, power, colour, ethnicity, geographic location, government interference, and class.

KEYWORDS

cyberia
digital mythology

'digital sublime'
dot.com crash
'global village'
'Golden Age'
narrowcasting
new media
personal computer

Digital mythology

> As people once hailed the Telegraph Age, the Age of Electricity, the Age of the Telephone, the Age of Radio, or the Age of Television, we are now said to be in the Age of the Computer. (Mosco 2004, p. 2)

In this chapter we explore some of the myths about the Internet. We take as our starting point Vincent Mosco's argument about the 'digital sublime'. According to this idea, the digital revolution generates and sustains 'important myths about our time', which support the notion that we are experiencing an 'epochal transformation' that overturns our common beliefs about time, space, and power (Mosco 2004, pp. 2–3). These myths offer us an 'entrance to a new reality', which may be characterised by 'the promise of the sublime' (p. 3). We are particularly interested in what might constitute a 'Golden Age' for the Internet; how we might define it and how we might measure both its length (time-span) and its depth (how ingrained the ideological memes that deliver and support the idea may have become in our collective consciousness and in our culture). This means we have to situate our discussion of the 'Golden Age' historically: When did it start? Has it ended yet? How much further into the future might it extend?

DIGITAL MYTHOLOGY

The power of myth is that it contains elements of truth and seems to hold a timeless manifestation of an eternal and powerful entity. Digital mythology is based on the seemingly unstoppable power of technology to do 'good'.

These are enduring questions and opinion is divided. On one side are the pundits, 'armed with bits of bright shiny jargon' to convince us that there is a boundless utopia to be reached via the information superhighway. On the other, there are the 'oracles of doom' who 'see nothing but evil' (Moore 1995, p. xiv). It's interesting to see that this view is also strong in the more sociological writing about the economic, emotional, psychological, political, and cultural impacts (historical, present, and future-oriented) of the mobile phone, the Internet, and cyber-culture. Even as early in the digital revolution as 1995, which we estimate was probably about fifteen to twenty years in, humorous if somewhat jaded critics like Dinty Moore could see the potential for brain-burn, when there's just too much information: 'My head was a balloon about to burst, because all the information in the world is a wonderful thing, but I can only use so much of it. I had finally achieved true overload' (Moore 1995, p. 192).

Moore says the future of the Web will be like television but with thousands of channels, not just hundreds. The mouse will become just another remote control 'channel changer'. More optimistically, an important scholar of the Information Age, Nicholas Negroponte, was applauding the virtues of email in a way that seems lost in a more innocent age: 'E-mail affords extraordinary mobility without anybody having to know your whereabouts. While this may have more relevance to a travelling salesman, the process of staying connected raises some interesting general questions about the difference between bits and atoms in digital life' (Negroponte 1996, p. 194). Of course today every 'click' is monitored and every email leaves its electronic traces.

A couple of years earlier, Douglas Rushkoff was hanging out with and writing about 'Craig', one of the inhabitants of the emerging Cyberia: 'Instead of exploring the inner workings of a packaged video game, Craig was roaming the secret passages of the datasphere.' Rushkoff gets so caught up in his own tales of midnight raves and VR shows, smart drugs, brainiacs, and weirdos that he starts to believe some of the hype he's been picking up in the clubs and streets of San Francisco/Cyberia: 'To reckon with this technological frontier of human consciousness means to re-evaluate the very nature of information, creativity, property and human relations' (Rushkoff 1994, p. 25).

This is a fairly big claim to make about anything: that it means a complete makeover of human values and relationships. It is, nonetheless, a claim made fairly often about the Internet and about the digital revolution more generally. In this chapter, these claims will be explained and discussed, some in passing, some in detail. In each instance, evidence will be presented and challenged.

If there is a digital revolution going on, it is important to understand it and there are plenty of questions to get us started on a serious investigation. What are the issues? Who's behind it and who stands to gain from it? Are there winners and losers? Is one outcome or another inevitable? There are always optimists and pessimists—those for whom the glass is half full and those for whom it's only a few mouthfuls away from having to buy another round. When it comes to technology there are also many nuances in the positions of both optimists and pessimists. The same splits—over the benefits and pitfalls of technology, or over social outcomes from using it—appear in this chapter as we look at both sides of the argument.

The age of cyber mythology

Vincent Mosco writes about the myths of the Internet Age in his book *The Digital Sublime*, describing them as 'seductive tales containing promises unfulfilled or even unfulfillable' and an ideological battle between 'feeling' and 'reason' (2004, p. 24). Thus myths contain both positive and negative elements and when it comes to technological mythology there is both progress and regression; there is both material truth and hyperbole, caught up in a 'spiral of hype' (p. 25). Myths can also have a life of their own: they 'live' as long as they continue to give meaning to those who subscribe to them and as long as they have the ability to 'render socially and intellectually tolerable what would otherwise be experienced as incoherence' (p. 29). Myths also have a naturalising function: they ideologise certain elements and hide unpalatable truths that contradict the central purpose of mythologising—the elimination of 'complexities and contradictions' (p. 30). According to Mosco, the myths of the Digital Age demonstrate these values by shielding the *ideal* of cyberspace from 'the messiness of down-to-earth politics' (p. 31). This is done by a process of 'inoculation'—the admission that there are some (relatively minor) problems—in order to protect the myth from more substantial criticism. Inoculation is assisted by the complexity of digital knowledge environments where 'linguistic distortions' (a form of ideological meme generation) 'obscure and euphemise' the very reality 'to which they simultaneously refer' (Hearn et al. 2003, p. 233). The process of inoculation is further developed through the selective reportage carried in media vectors, what Mackenzie Wark calls an 'instantaneous global dialogue' that denies the existence of territorial location and in which events appear to be taking place 'on the surface of a strange new virtual geography' (Wark 1994, p. viii). Wark names this as 'telesthesia'—the distanciation of the audience/receptor from real events. Things appear to happen in a never-ending 'now', rather than as part of an historically date-stamped flow of events occurring at a particular place and time (p. 83).

Mythology also has another defence mechanism, the denial of history and the constant present of 'telesthesia' (p. 145). This process of denial is aided by the social 'dissolution' of the constraints of time and place that occurs within ideologies (Giddens 1995, p. 91). The ability of an ideology to spread via the mimetic virus of cultural DNA depends, according to Anthony Giddens, on the available 'storage capacity': 'the retention and control of information or knowledge' that brings with it control over 'social power' (p. 94). One power of myths, when seen in this light, is that they can blur the boundaries between 'before', 'now', and 'later'. What Giddens calls the 'time-space edges' are not clearly defined from one historical period to the next (p. 163). Techno-myths, supplemented by the vast storage capacity of digital media, have this ability to blur time-space boundaries, and they are able to generate the belief that what happened before the digital revolution is merely 'prehistory'. Thus, for those who believe in a Golden Age, its beginning, middle, and end points may shift in both time and space, though in a sense such inconvenient facts are irrelevant to the belief system and the purpose of the myth. In this mythic discourse, the Information Age is a product of a revolutionary 'rupture' with the past (Mosco 2004, pp. 34–5).

Like Mosco, we disagree with the illusion of historical dissonance that accompanies digital myth-making; the whole point of this book is to place convergence and digital technologies *into* an historical context. We agree with Mosco that there is a need for myth-busters to challenge some of the illusory statements that the cyber-boosters claim as digital truths.

In order to be propagated as mimetic ideology, myths need champions—carriers—who will spread the word through their public pronouncements, and the Internet has its share of hucksters, boosters, and proselytisers. Mosco describes Bill Gates as one of the most powerful myth-makers for the digital revolution, 'extolling the transcendent virtues of computer communication as a conqueror of both space and time' (2004, p. 36). In February 2006 Bill Gates was delivering this message at the World Economic Forum in Davos, Switzerland; in this instance the substance was that most companies could expect productivity growth of at least 5 per cent over the next financial cycle if they were prepared to use interactive electronic transactions (Gottliebsen 2006). Another powerful net guru is former US Vice-President Al Gore. In the mid-1990s Al Gore was spruiking the benefits of the 'information superhighway' as a cure-all for society's many problems. The main criticism of Gore's role in propagating mimetic myths about the Internet is not that they were far-fetched and have not yet been realised, but that by engaging with the myth and giving it legitimacy, Al Gore helped to make it seem real to those who were listening. During the campaign for the presidency in 1999 (for the 2000 election), Al Gore claimed to have had a role in inventing the Internet and he made what Mosco (p. 39) calls a 'pilgrimage' to Silicon Valley as a way of distinguishing himself from opponents.

The myth of the Golden Age also has champions in the media and Mosco describes Internet-boosting journalists as 'willing accomplices in the near adulation of cyberspace' (p. 43). These 'accomplices' are given plenty of space in newspapers and in other media; many of them are spruikers for the latest digital gadgets and they pop up regularly on lifestyle 'infotainment' programs. The *Australian*'s business columnist, Robert Gottliebsen, is a good example. In February 2006 he reported on the World Economic Forum and attended a session with '[o]ne of the greatest technology panels ever assembled'. He opens his report of their deliberations and pronouncements with a legitimating round of name-dropping: 'Bill Gates, Cisco [System's] John Chambers, Google's Eric Schmidt and Skype/Ebay's Niklas Zennstrom' (Gottliebsen 2006). Of course, the panel wowed the audience of 'surprised delegates' by unveiling a 'new paradigm in corporate technology' that will revolutionise business practices. Gottliebsen draws his own lessons from this and applies them to Telstra's business model, taking a subtle swipe at the way telecommunications in Australia is regulated. If things don't change, he says, then companies like Telstra are 'headed for the scrap heap'. The solution, according to Robert Gottliebsen, may not be the right one for consumers, but it must be based on the 'scenario' outlined by 'Gates, Chambers, Schmidt and Zennstrom'. Gottliebsen's column follows the myth-making template laid down by Vincent Mosco in that Gottliebsen 'wholly identifies with the corporate vision' with his opening line about the Davos meeting; then from his position of disinterested observer, who is 'more reflective' about the issues, he appears to 'rise above corporate self-interest', thus legitimising both his own opinion and that of Bill Gates and the other business leaders (Mosco 2004, p. 45).

Most newspapers also have dedicated technology reporters and many have lift-out sections like *Icon* in the *Sydney Morning Herald* or the three separate IT sections that appear each week in the *Australian—IT Today*, *IT Business*, and *ExecTech*. Typically, these sections are a mixture of product news (supplied by company media releases), tips, and hints like 'Damn that spam' (Stonehouse 2005), which provides ways to avoid an overflowing inbox and gives a review of anti-spam software products from the big providers.

A March 2006 edition of *IT Business* contains its share of boosterism, but it also plays the role of honest broker, echoing the need for online prophets to sprinkle the good news with bad in order to ensure protective inoculation. The lead article talks up the new trend of corporate blogging as an opportunity for 'the most monolithic' of corporations to appear 'more human and approachable to customers' (Jenkins 2006). Inside there is a case study of a company involved in the roll-out of voice-over-Internet technologies, a column about e-book technology, and a series of short news items. On page 5 there is a profile of a company information executive and an interesting article that takes up Al Gore's theme of an information superhighway with the twist that some cable companies are planning an 'express toll lane' ('Express tollway plan for net' 2006). The article outlines a plan by AT&T to offer a premium service to customers that will move their data over the network at a higher speed than non-premium content. This breaks one of the cardinal rules of the Internet: data neutrality, which means that no content is privileged when it comes to distribution over a carrier's network. This piece carries several mythic elements, apart from the opening line about Gore's naming of the information superhighway. It invokes the biblical story of David and Goliath to explain the principle of neutrality, but then switches to the myth of consumer benefit to explain why companies like AT&T are considering the premium service. But the core mythology embedded in the piece is the sanctity of free enterprise and the right of the cable companies to charge fair prices in order to make fair profits: 'Rather than passing the costs to consumers, they'd rather charge the websites taking up the most bandwidth' ('Express tollway plan for net' 2006).

In the end, the battle will come down to a political tussle in Washington DC, where legislators are split 'mostly along party lines'. This article normalises both capitalism and the decision-making process in government and places the argument on familiar terrain. It ends with a long quote from Republican Senator John Ensign that encapsulates both the substance and the mythic elements of the story: 'You do deserve a return on investment is the bottom line ... If we can't give them a return ... Wall St is not going to loan them the money to do this' (Express tollway plan for net 2006).

The *ExecTech* supplement of 14 March 2006 is typical of the genre. It contains a piece about the new BlackBerry hand-held device, a two-page review of the 'ultimate laptops', a piece reviewing Apple's home accessories that turn an iPod into a full-power stereo, a summary of features in three new notebooks, and a column called 'Double Click'. In the 14 March column, David Frith writes about wireless Internet connections using an anecdote about finding directions via a laptop while travelling in a car on a freeway north of Brisbane. The column ends with a typical piece of digital myth-making that puts consumers in the driver's seat when it comes to wireless technology: 'Stand by. The wireless connection business in Australia is about to become a battleground—hopefully one in which us punters will be the winners' (Frith 2006).

Frith's 'Double Click' column is a good example because it follows the pattern described by Mosco (2004, p. 43) of ascribing to the writer a 'higher degree of legitimacy' because it contextualises his comments with an anecdote that establishes his credentials: 'So there we were—a journo, a PR flack and an internet phone technology vendor—in a hired car charging up Brisbane's M1 motorway for a conference on the Sunshine coast …' (Frith 2006).

These full-colour newspaper supplements and the gadget promotion segments on television do not come cheap. The myth-making efforts of the mass media are supported by the advertising budgets of the major product suppliers that are deployed to build brand awareness and to spread the general message of the digital revolution: 'a new age has dawned and we must, in the words of Apple Computer, "think different"' (Mosco 2004, p. 42). There is, in effect, a particular mythic discourse at large that fits within and supports the process of social change that the digital revolution has created. This has particular relevance to the imagined representation of the information society, which is a projection of a 'possible state of affairs' (Fairclough *c.* 2000, p. 3). Norman Fairclough suggests that discursive language may play a more significant role in the socio-ecomomic changes wrought by digital convergence than it did in previous change: 'the neo-liberal political project of removing obstacles to the new economic order is discourse-driven' (p. 6).

The scope and penetration of the 'neo-political' agenda into digital myth-making is evident in the Australian government's *Strategic Framework for the Information Economy*, published in 2004. According to this document, successful adoption of digital technologies will create the conditions for economic growth, reinvigorate declining regional economies, and build 'stronger social cohesion' (DCITA 2004, p. 6). The emphasis is on the leading role that business will play and the framework offers the consumer-citizen little choice: 'Whether we want to or not, there is no choice but to continue to adapt' (p. 6). The price of failure is high, but the rewards of success are greater: 'If we succeed, a platform for growth and development will have been laid down that will underpin Australia's long term national performance' (p. 13). This particular element of myth-making, steeped in the rhetoric of the free market and community-building, is an example of the attempts by many governments to manage and promote the insertion of their national economy into the emerging new world order. The discourse of 'no choice' reinforces the myth of adapt or die 'on terms dictated by the allegedly impersonal forces of the market' (Fairclough *c.* 2000, p. 5).

At the same time, these 'impersonal forces' are attempting to gain leverage from the digital mythologies in order that they might appear more human and personable. Microsoft has promoted itself as a company that fosters 'digital inclusion' through its products and services: 'The true power of technology lies in its ability to empower people' (Microsoft, n.d., p. 3). Empowerment is a key element of the digital myth and a constant theme in the discourse of the Golden Age.

The collective noun 'digerati' has been coined to describe the main group of digital salesmen (and women) who endlessly promote the many benefits of the Internet and convergent new media technologies. Some are political figures like Gore, or business leaders like Bill Gates; others are intellectuals who have mastered the mythology and work out ways to popularise it through their writing and public appearances. A key figure in this group is Nicholas Negroponte, whom we've already met. We will return in a moment to

Negroponte's important work *being digital*, but first we must venture into the undergrowth because some of the most powerful myth-makers of the cyber age are the young misfits who, in the late 1980s and early 1990s, saw the Internet as a means of escape from the drudgery of daily life in the stifling analogue culture of late capitalism.

The now world-famous computer magazine *Wired* is to the 'digerati' of the Internet Age what *Rolling Stone* was to the rock generation. Both were originally published in San Francisco and both were trend-setting magazines that became 'must read' items for their audiences. One key purpose of *Wired*, though perhaps subconscious on the part of writers and editors, is the perpetuation of cyber-mythologies. This is illustrated by a series of articles in the December 2002 issue—a time when the world was still reeling from the 2000 01 dot.com crash—that argued for a 'new convergence' between technology and religion. One article by 'Editor-at-large' Kevin Kelly claimed that 'God is the Machine' and concluded that 'the universe is not merely like a computer, it is a computer' (cited in Mosco 2004, p. 14).

Our journey into and through the 'Golden Age' of the Internet begins with the utopian dreams and technological wizardry of the underground guerrilla armies of the digital revolution. Manuel Castells (2000, p. 49) documents the 'sprawling computer counterculture' associated with the 'aftershocks' of the 'libertarian/utopian' 1960s as a vital element of the dialectic of convergence. He cites the example from 1978 of how two Chicago students invented the first modem (the 'blue box') to send files over the phone so they didn't have to travel in a Windy City winter.

The Golden Age of the Internet

> High technology and high magic are the same thing. They both use tools from inner resources and outer resources. Magic from the ancient past and technology from the future are really both one. That is how we are creating the present; we're speeding up things, we are quickening our energies; time and space are not as rigid as they used to be; the belief system isn't there. Those who did control it have left the plane; they have been forced out because it no longer is their time. Those of us who know how to work through time and space are using our abilities to *bend* time and space into a reality that will benefit people the most.
>
> When Green Fire says all this to your face, believe it or not, it makes sense, especially in a Cyberian context. (Rushkoff 1994, p. 188)

CYBERIA

A play on the word Siberia—the frozen wastes of Russia—suggesting that the digital future is dystopian.

When reading that passage from Douglas Rushkoff's *Cyberia*, it helps to know that Green Fire is a modern urban witch—a psychic and probably into serious drugs. But Green Fire is typical of the characters inhabiting the San Francisco Bay area as it is described in Rushkoff's meandering, journalistic search for the optimistic roots of cyberspace in the late 1980s and early 1990s. To understand the origins of the sublime myths of the Internet, however, we have to go back a further twenty years, to the early 1970s. We ended the previous chapter deliberately in the 1960s when computing was just beginning to open up to its first serious commercial applications. The ubiquitous PC was still only a good idea and the silicon chip had not yet made the leap from the computer to the commodity of the everyday. The so-called 'Geek', the genius of the digital revolution, was not yet fully formed. In order for this to happen, like the larva of a butterfly, it had to find a safe place to rest in order to fortify and transform. This was as simple, so it turns out, as shifting from the university research lab to the safety of the family garage. Most of the geek chrysalis development took place in California, near the desert city of Paolo Alto—the place we now call 'Silicon Valley'.

Flowering in the desert: The Silicon Valley boom

In the previous chapter we outlined the history of computing from the earliest forms of digital calculation—literally, counting on fingers—to the development of the first prototypes of the modern computer in the early 1960s. We left that story at the time when the hi-tech industries located on the fringes of the California desert were beginning to take root. As we commented towards the end of that chapter, the development of 'machine language' and computer code has now developed into what Samuel Butler in the late 19th century predicted would become 'a speech as intricate as our own' (1967, p. 147). This development began in the 1940s, but did not really come to fruition until thirty years later in Silicon Valley.

In 1959, Ivan Sutherland demonstrated a program called Sketchpad on a TX-2 mainframe at MIT's Lincoln Labs. It allowed him to make engineering drawings with a light pen. An integrated circuit that cost $1000 in 1959 now costs less than $10. In 1968 Doug Engelbart demonstrated a word processor, an early hypertext system, and a collaborative application—three now-common computer applications.

Gordon Moore and Robert Noyce founded the giant silicon chip manufacturer Intel in 1968. The technology company Xerox (perhaps best known for its brand of photocopiers) created its Palo Alto Research Center, Xerox PARC, in 1969. Its mission was to explore the architecture of information. In the late 1960s, a Swiss computer scientist, Niklaus Wirth, developed the first of many computer programming languages. His first language, called Pascal, forced programmers to program in a structured, logical fashion and pay close attention to the different types of data in use. He later followed up on Pascal with Modula-II and III, which were very similar to Pascal in structure and syntax. Fairchild Semiconductor introduced a 256-bit RAM chip in 1970. It was on the back of these developments, innovations, and new products that Silicon Valley became a booming hub of the digital revolution. In late 1970 Intel introduced a 1K RAM chip and the 4004, a 4-bit microprocessor. Two years later comes the 8008, an 8-bit microprocessor.

1970: Intel inside

It was not until the mid-1960s that the third generation of computers came into being. These were characterised by solid state technology and integrated circuitry coupled with extreme miniaturisation. A series of events in the early 1970s can, with the benefit of hindsight, be seen as critically important to the myths of the Internet's 'Golden Age'.

In 1971 Bill Gates and Paul Allen formed Traf-O-Data and find a buyer for their computer traffic-analysis systems. In the same year Steve Jobs and Steve Wozniak were building and selling 'blue boxes' in southern California. The fourth generation of computers was characterised by further miniaturisation of circuit, increased multiprogramming and virtual storage memory.

In 1971 Intel released the first microprocessor, a specialised integrated circuit that was able to process four bits of data at a time. The chip included its own arithmetic logic unit, but a sizable portion of the chip was taken up by the control circuits for organising the work, which left less room for the data-handling circuitry. Thousands of hackers could now aspire to own their own personal computer. Computers up to this point had been strictly the preserve of the military, universities, and very large corporations simply because of the enormous cost of the machine, and then its maintenance.

In 1975, the cover of *Popular Electronics* featured a story on the 'world's first minicomputer kit to rival commercial models ... Altair 8800'. The Altair, produced by a company called Micro Instrumentation and Telementry Systems (MITS) retailed for $397, which made it easily affordable for the small but growing hacker community. The Altair was not designed for your computer novice. The kit required assembly by the owner and then it was necessary to write software for the machine since none was yet commercially available. The Altair had a 256-byte memory—about the size of a paragraph, and needed to be coded in machine code—0s and 1s. The programming was accomplished by manually flipping switches located on the front of the Altair.

PERSONAL COMPUTER

Also called mini-computer, or desktop computer, to distinguish it from mainframe computers and servers. PCs came of age in the 1980s, as a low-cost and accessible means of processing information.

Two young hackers were intrigued by the Altair, having seen the article in *Popular Electronics*. They decided on their own that the Altair needed software and took it upon themselves to contact MITS owner Ed Roberts and offer to provide him with a BASIC language which would run on the Altair. BASIC (Beginners All-purpose Symbolic Instruction Code) had originally been developed in 1963 by Thomas Kurtz and John Kemeny, members of the Dartmouth College mathematics department. BASIC was designed to provide an interactive, easy method for upcoming computer scientists to program computers. It allowed the usage of statements such as **print "hello"** or **let b = 10**. It would have been a great boost for the Altair if BASIC had been available, so Roberts agreed to pay for it if it worked. The two young hackers worked feverishly and finished just in time to present it to Roberts. It was a success. The two young hackers? They were William Gates and Paul Allen. They later went on to form Microsoft and produce BASIC and other operating systems for various machines.

Following the introduction of the Altair, a veritable explosion of personal computers occurred, starting with Steve Jobs and Steve Wozniak exhibiting the first Apple II at the

First West Coast Computer Faire in San Francisco. The Apple II boasted built-in BASIC, colour graphics, and a 4100-character memory for only $US1298. Programs and data could be stored on an everyday audio-cassette recorder. Before the end of the fair, Wozniak and Jobs had secured 300 orders for the Apple II and from there Apple's business has never looked back.

The TRS-80 was introduced in 1977 as a home computer manufactured by Tandy-Radio Shack. In its second incarnation, the TRS-80 Model II, it came complete with a 64000-character memory and a disk drive to store programs and data on. At this time, only Apple and TRS had machines with disk drives. With the introduction of the disk drive, personal computer applications took off as a floppy disk was a most convenient publishing medium for the distribution of software.

IBM, which up to this time had been producing mainframes and minicomputers for medium to large-sized businesses, decided that it had to get into the act and started working on the Acorn, which would later be called the IBM PC. The PC was the first computer designed for the home market that would feature modular design so that pieces could easily be added to the architecture. Most of the components, surprisingly, came from outside IBM, since building it with IBM parts would have cost too much for the home computer market. When it was introduced, the PC came with a 16000-character memory, a keyboard from an IBM electric typewriter, and a connection for a tape cassette player for $US1265.

This brief overview sets the stage for one explanation of the myth that says the 'Golden Age' perhaps began in Silicon Valley. This was not something that those at the epicentre were necessarily aware of. The seeds of the digital sublime were planted in desrt sands, but they now needed to be tended in order to flourish. This could only happen away from the hothouse atmosphere of Paolo Alto and when the PC had become more than just a geek toy. To sustain itself and spread, a mimetic myth needs a host organism—in this case a host community. Both of these conditions were met once the chip manufacturers found a way to increase the processing speed and memory-storage capacity and when a market opened up for the new 'thinking machines'. The host community for the myths of a 'Golden Age' were none other than Douglas Rushkoff's 'cyberians' and the cybergypsies—the early adopters of the new technology.

Geeks plus drugs: Is this the Golden Age of the Internet?

> Psychedelics appear to be a 'given' in Silicon Valley. They are an institution … the infrastructure has accommodated them. (Rushkoff 1994, p. 48)

According to Douglas Rushkoff, in the 1980s a list was circulating among the geek crowd alerting them to which Silicon Valley companies had a 'cool' attitude towards hard drugs and which ones insisted on urine-testing their staff. He asserts that in the heyday of the valley, when it was full of innovative young people, the 'industry leaders' would turn a blind eye to drug use among their employees because they knew that the 'psychedelics-using cyberians' were creating the 'computer revolution' at places like the Xerox PARC (Rushkoff

1994, p. 49). There was a clear 'tug-of-war' going on in Silicon Valley at that time: on one end of the rope the military-industrial complex and on the other end the 'heretics'—'pot smokers and psychedelics-users' (p. 50). But it wasn't just the geeks and nerds who were getting high and putting their extensive creative talents to work. Computers found their way very quickly into the remnants of the hippy underground.

Rushkoff's exploration of Cyberia in the Bay area of San Francisco led him to a secret world of designer drugs that were being manufactured and consumed in order to create a 'new designer reality' that more closely resembled the ideal utopian world that the cyberians were trying to create (p. 109). It also had a serious, political side. The cyberians were opposed to the tough American drug laws and saw their efforts as a way of developing a counter-offensive about 'good drugs and bad drug laws' (p. 145). The psychedelic and 'smart' drugs that the cyberians messed around with also had an intimate connection to their travels in cyberspace and their enthusiasm for 'virtual reality':

> Psychedelics and VR are both ways of creating a new, non-linear reality, where self expression is a community event … a kind of technological philosopher's stone, bringing an inkling of the future reality into the present … and an active, creative effort by cyberians to reach that future. (Rushkoff 1994, p. 84)

We are not, by mentioning this here, encouraging the use of psychedelic drugs. Our purpose is to show how, within the community of cyberians, the mimetic seed of the Golden Age idea began to take root. It was a utopian idea that grew out of the cyberian dissociation from, and dissatisfaction with, what was happening in the 'straight' and unconnected world around them. Many of the important carriers of the techno-meme of the Golden Age were people who had grown up in the Bohemian atmosphere of the 1960s and they appear—like the 'father' of LSD, Timothy Leary—in the pages of *Cyberia*. These characters tell Rushkoff again and again that Cyberia is a new frontier, a seismic tipping point for society at large and a fault line between the old society and the new. For the cyberians it is a struggle that involves generating a new reality very different from the constraining real world outside. It is a new consciousness that is all-embracing 'on a personal, theoretical, political, technological, or even spiritual level' (p. 92). But not all the trail-blazers on the frontiers of cyberspace were enhancing their experiences with illegal drugs.

Indra Sinha was an early traveller on the electronic frontier and described himself as a 'cybergypsie' in his book *the cybergypsies* (Sinha 1999). Sinha, in real life an advertising copywriter, began his exploration of cyberspace in 1984 when the Internet first became publicly available in the UK via a university network known as JANET. Like the cyberians, the cybergypsies were utopian, free-thinking, and disdainful of the commercialisation of the World Wide Web that was beginning to coalesce around them. The cybergypsies were pioneers of the online gaming world (one vastly different from today). They also haunted the early bulletin boards like FIDO and Shades, places

'GOLDEN AGE'

The idea that in looking back, there was a halcyon period in history in which everything was bright and beautiful.

where they could entertain each other and hold endless 'conversations': 'Cybergypsies like free-flowing, live, subtle interaction and internet chat is banal and brutish, compared with the range of expression afforded by Shades or the Fidonet bulletin board' (Sinha 1999, p. 59).

Unlike the Cyberians, Sinha and his cybergypsies mostly live out their drug fantasies at one remove—they didn't actually ingest any substances—but they felt a strong connection with 19th-century writers like Coleridge who indulged in a heavy opium habit. Their engagement with the online world of gaming, bulletin boards, and fantasy-reality takes place in an imaginary landscape, accessed via a modem and a telephone line: 'In cyberspace, for the first time, we create imaginary worlds which can truly be shared, in which each of us is fully present, with the power of free and spontaneous action' (Sinha 1999, p. 131).

The characters who inhabit the online world of the cybergypsies might seem a little quaint, or even downright weird, today, but fifteen years ago they were living out a fantasy of their own Internet 'Golden Age', complete with cyberspace marriages and honeymoons and even the odd pervert like 'Nasty Ned' who traded pornography from his bulletin board, long before it seemed to take over the Web completely. In this imagined community, says Sinha, the line between 'reality' and cyberspace appeared permeable and thin; they seemed to 'mirror one another' (p. 142). But, again like the cyberians, the cybergypsies also had a political side.

In 1987 Indra Sinha joined one of the first activist web-rings in the UK, Greennet, to campaign on behalf of Iraqi Kurds who had recently been attacked with poison gas by Saddam Hussein's troops in the north of the country. This quickly morphed into a real-life political campaign and when the Gulf war started at the end of 1990, Sinha began using Greennet to campaign against government censorship of news. The naivety of his optimism is obvious to us, but in 1991 it seemed that the Internet was a new tool that would herald a Golden Age of political openness: 'I became aware of the enormous power of the internet to subvert and nullify the attempts of governments, corporations and media moguls to stifle free speech' (Sinha 1999, p. 177). It is worth remembering that this was a long time before September 11, 2001 and the vast array of surveillance tools now available to monitor and censor Internet conversations (see chapters 13 and 14).

The third important group inhabiting cyberspace during its imagined Golden Age were the hackers. In a sense hacking preceded many of the more commercial developments we've been discussing, and in Internet mythology they hold a special and revered place. The whole intent of hacking was to mess with the system and to undermine the emerging commercial monopolies of the software and telecommunications cartels that were scrambling to make cyberspace like an online shopping mall.

Douglas Rushkoff tells the story of one hacker, 'De Groot', who had dedicated his life to creating the 'Global Electronic Village'. According to Rushkoff, De Groot was not 'just exploring the datasphere but actively creating the networks that make it up'. It wasn't just a hobby. De Groot was actively constructing the future from his equipment-crowded apartment (Rushkoff 1994, p. 51). The way Katie Hafner and John Markhoff (1991) tell the story, the early hackers began in the 1970s as 'phone phreaks'—able to crack into the circuits of the bulk telecom line carriers to make free phone calls. They didn't link up with the world of computers until the early 1980s, but they were already living on the edge of the law. The hacker culture of the first ten years of the digital revolution represented the 'demons' in the myth of the Golden Age. No doubt many of them were involved in criminal behaviour and many went to jail for their crimes, but their significance lies in the ways that they make us fearful of the new technologies. As Hafner & Markhoff comment, hackers are 'the new magicians' who have conquered their own fear of 'the machines that control modern life', the subject of occasional hysteria and 'sweeps' by law enforcement agencies (1991, pp. 11–12). But when all is said and done, are they a menace to society?

Hackers often see themselves not as criminals but as explorers in 'a remarkable electronic world'. In the early 1990s the rules of the road for the information superhighway were not clear and they are still being defined, refined, and rewritten today (see chapter 12). Hackers in the early years of the digital revolution represented, in true techno-myth fashion, the 'risks' of computer technology and also its 'allure' (Hafner & Markoff 1991, p. 12). The hacker mythology is also fed through the cyberpunk genre. For example, in *Neuromancer*, 'Case' and 'Molly' enlist the help of the 'Panther Moderns', a cross between a terrorist cell and demonic skateboarders: 'mercenaries, practical jokers, nihilistic technofetishists' (Gibson 1993, p. 75). 'Case' himself is a hacker, a 'cowboy hotshot', and a thief who displayed 'a certain relaxed contempt for the flesh', even for his own drug-damaged body (p. 12). Neal Stephenson has drawn similar characters in *Snow Crash* (1992) and they are regular players in many of Gibson's short stories.

WHAT MANUEL RECKONS: THE IMPORTANCE OF WILLIAM GIBSON

William Gibson has often expressed a certain unease with being labelled a 'cyberpunk' author, or even 'science fiction' author. He regards himself as an author of speculative fiction depicting developments in the society and technology of today; in his writing he explores the present from an 'odd' angle.

Many elements of the gritty and dirty world of Gibson's earlier works can be seen as a direct analogy to social phenomena Gibson perceived during the late 1970s and early 1980s: the overpowering influence of globalised corporations, the fear of economic and cultural domination by Asian countries (especially Japan), and the possible impact of emerging technologies such as computer and genetic engineering, to name a few. *Neuromancer* and its sequels take place in a dystopian future—not, however, in an attempt to predict a possible future scenario, but as a metaphor of how the author experienced reality during the time of writing.

In every period, Gibson had his fingers closely on the pulse of contemporary social phenomena and showed a keen sense of the *Zeitgeist*. Both the technologies employed and the characters appearing in Gibson's novels (be it cybernetically enhanced assassins or brand-allergic coolhunters) can be regarded as 'extensions' of each period—symbols of the possibilities and implications of the respective age.

Some ideas envisioned in Gibson's stories may become reality—some have already: think of the character 'Chia' in *Idoru* who buys a virtual designer's dress for an online meeting, something not out of place in our world of 2006 in which people spend hundreds of dollars for characters or properties in online games such as *Ultima Online*. However, as a counter-example, take the looming presence of the Soviet Bloc in the future world of *Neuromancer*. Gibson totally failed to foresee the rapid downfall of communism.

In the end, Gibson's stories cannot give us an outlook into the future, but they can provide an insight into the strange and fascinating world we live in today. Or, as Gibson once put it, most of the time the future turns out to be much more fantastic in reality than in writing.

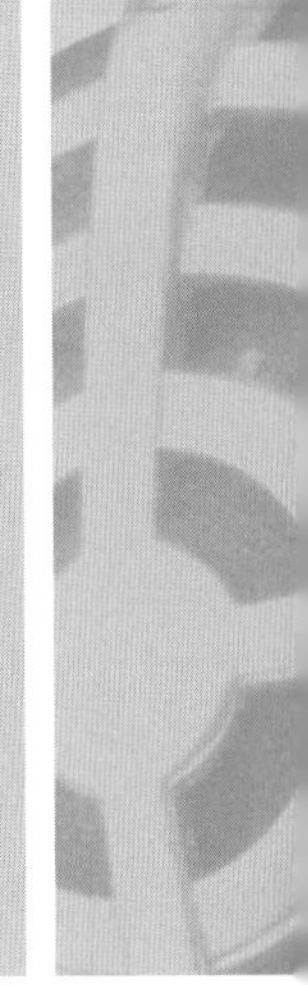

Being digital: A postmodern paradox?

> The information superhighway is about the global movement of weightless bits at the speed of light. (Negroponte 1996, p. 12)

Nicholas Negroponte's *being digital* is perhaps one of the most significant books to generate and argue strongly for the mythic representation of cyberspace and digital technologies. In the light of global advances in electronic eavesdropping and surveillance it is worth noting that his brother, John Negroponte, was for many years head of the US National Intelligence Service. Writing before the Internet and the connectivity of household appliances through the convergence process became common, Nicholas Negroponte was enthusiastic about the 'creative and new applications' that will become available on the 'information superhighway' (1996, p. 50). In 1996 the 'information superhighway' was, according to Negroponte, 'mostly hype', but he was confident that it would be 'an understatement about tomorrow' (p. 231) because a new generation of digitally savvy consumer-citizens was emerging 'free of many of the old prejudices' and 'released from the limitation of geographic proximity'. Negroponte concluded that digital technology would be a 'natural force' that could draw people into a sense of 'greater world harmony' as 'each generation becomes more digital than the preceding one' (pp. 230–1). This is a recurrent theme in the mythology of the Golden Age in which digital technology is described as 'the most potent tool of communication ever available to the individual' that will lead to 'a new empowerment' and even a return to the utopian 'pre-Gutenberg days'. Individuals will no longer be shackled by space or time, but rather a new global village will emerge in which 'one man's [*sic*] voice could reach as far as almost any other ('Talking to the World' 1999).

Negroponte's enthusiasm for the digital Golden Age is a futuristic version of the mythologies outlined by Mosco. It contains the same elements—the transcendence of time and place, and a belief in the positive impacts of thinking machines. For Negroponte the Golden Age will be the 'post-information' society, a time of 'true personalisation' of digital technologies that will know what you like, what you want, and what you need. The thinking machine of the post-Information Age will have the ability to remember our shopping preferences and to interact with us 'in the unfolding narrative of our lives' (Negroponte 1996, p. 165). In this version of digital nirvana, 'the transmission of place itself' will become possible.

This idea of spatial transmission has been taken up by a number of writers who share Negroponte's digital optimism and technological determinism. It is a feature of postmodern theories of communication and media, particularly around notions of the de-centred public sphere. Media scholar John Hartley articulates this position in his description of the postmodern public sphere: 'The postmodern (media) public sphere, which like suburbia itself is not a place at all, is the focus for the development of new political agendas based on comfort, privacy and self-building' (Hartley 1996, p. 157).

The theoretical foundations of postmodernism are heterogeneous and cover a range of positions, from French post-structuralism and the German critical theorists to Daniel Bell's 'post-industrial' society thesis, first published in *The Coming of Post-Industrial Society* (1973). At the core of postmodernism is an idea that the technological shift from analogue to digital has caused a profound shift in the social structures of society throughout the post-World War II period. A key vector for this shift has been the mass media—first the age of television and broadcasting and now the age of narrowcasting and the Internet. In this sense postmodernism is a 'periodizing concept' that marks the boundary in 'space and time' between an old order and a new social structure (Jameson 1998, p. 3). There are two key features of postmodernism, in Fredric Jameson's account, that help to explain the generation of techno-myths: the 'transformation of reality into images' and the 'fragmentation of time into a series of perpetual presents'. The effect of this is that society has 'little by little' lost its capacity to remember' and has lost its 'sense of history' (Jameson 1998, p. 20). In this way the myths of an Internet Golden Age can take hold and mimetically transfer themselves from host to host, thus sustaining the myth—keeping it alive in Mosco's sense. We can now suggest that the Golden Age of the Internet is a fluid concept; depending on the position you want to argue it is either over, or continuing, or just coming into being. Given the time-shifting qualities of the myth, all of these statements can be simultaneously true, depending on your point of view.

In the Australian context, Trevor Barr's *newmedia.com.au* represents the most cogent argument for a Golden Age scenario. It corresponds to what Barr calls 'phase two' of the Internet. Phase one was development from the 1960s to the early 1980s when most of the network was closed and only available for military and research applications. By the end of the 1970s the network was opening up and no longer only for 'military strategic' purposes (Barr 2000, p. 121). Phase two is marked by a cultural shift as the Internet becomes a more public space and 'a significant alternative or counterculture mode of expression' in which new 'grassroots electronic communities' emerge that would 'never' have been possible under old media rules (p. 122). This was a relatively short period according to Barr, and phase three—a period of rapid growth in home connection to the World Wide Web—began in the late 1990s and was marked by a commercial turn that transformed the information superhighway into a 'superhypeway' (p. 123).

Taken together, Barr's phase two and phase three scenarios represent the periodisation of the Internet's Golden Age. Like Negroponte, Barr believed that the Internet would effect a 'major change' in the processes of social interaction: 'In essence, cyberculturalists argue that this is the grassroots community interactive process in action, diametrically opposed to the centralised top-down broadcast model that has dominated the past 50 years of public communication' (p. 125).

A Golden Age in the virtual village?

Among the claims being made at the time, by Negroponte and others, was the prospect of 'utopian democratisation' and a new sense of community and an 'emergent electronic culture' (p. 126). While Barr is careful to note the sceptics who were then suggesting that the Internet might not deliver, he ultimately falls into the traps of mythology that we discussed earlier—time shifting, unfulfilled promise, and a blurring of the edges of historical time and space: 'In cultural terms, convergence has blurred our boundaries between reality and illusion, between our direct sensual world and illusion, and between the local and the global, potentially redefining our inner self' (p. 128).

Barr even predicts that Marshall McLuhan's much misunderstood 'global village' may now be a realisable dream. The Internet, he argues, will lead to 'more open and accountable' government because tyrants will not be able to suppress reform movements that can access 'the transactional space of the uncensored Net' (p. 129). This is a classic piece of techno-myth-making and as we'll demonstrate in the final section of this book, it is a promise that remains unfulfilled. To be fair to Trevor Barr, *newmedia.com.au* is not a simple homage to the Golden Age thesis; there is a very good chapter on the paradoxes that spring up to contradict the utopian visions of the new media world and he acknowledges that the shift from the analogue to the digital paradigm involves a period of 'considerable overlap' between the old and the new: 'At this stage in its evolution the Internet offers both promise and predicament as the dawning of a new communications era' (p. 144).

What Barr didn't know when he wrote these words was that the dot.com crash was just about to happen; in fact it coincided with the publication of his optimistic assessment. Less than a year later, a terrorist attack in New York and Washington DC would tragically impact on the lives of millions of people in the United States, Afghanistan, and Iraq. Within five years the citizens of Spain, England, Indonesia, and Australia would be among those caught up in a global 'war' not of their choosing. Many people, including the vast majority of the world's Muslim population, would be dislocated, angered, disturbed, frightened, and disoriented by the cycle of attacks, retribution, and revenge that has made the world a less

> **'GLOBAL VILLAGE'**
>
> A phrase popularised by the Canadian media sociologist Marshall McLuhan to describe the social effect of convergent technologies. In essence a global village would mean that we all get to know each other and interact in some utopian way, as was supposed to be the case in pre-industrial village life.

safe place for everyone. In such a climate of fear, distrust, and pain it is difficult to maintain the illusion of a Golden Age. Perhaps we're now moving into a new phase of development, one that is characterised by greater insecurity and greater surveillance. In the final section we will investigate the rise of the surveillance society in the age of narrowcasting. In the next few pages we want to close this discussion by looking at the two events that may very well signal the end of the Internet's 'Golden Age'.

The end of innocence on the Net: September 11, 2001

If there was a Golden Age of the Internet, we think it probably ended—officially—with the events of September 11, 2001. This was when the surveillance society kicked in a big way—you couldn't have cybergypsies wandering unsupervised all over the Internet when there might be terrorists lurking. From 9/11 there has been a gradual but continuous rise in the use of electronic surveillance, including of digital technologies; there has also been an erosion of civil liberties as governments tighten their controls over many aspects of life that were previously unregulated. In the final chapters we take up this discussion and outline what we are calling the surveillance economy that has grown to accommodate new security concerns. Having said that, there's another and slightly earlier end point to the 'Golden Age' that we wish to discuss—the dot.com crash of 2000. Until that point there had been dreams of a promising future for business on the Internet.

The tech boom and bust

From the mid-1990s until mid-2000, any company with .com after its name was a runaway hit on the world's stock exchanges. Thousands of new paper millionaires were created overnight and just as quickly it all melted away. Through the 1990s there had been an air of technological optimism around the Internet and it was thought that the new business models that sprang up in response to the declassification of cyberspace could not lose money. This turned out to be a serious miscalculation and it took several years for economic confidence in the World Wide Web to recover.

In early 2000, international stock markets came crashing down, the biggest collapse in value since 1987's 'black Friday'. According to the market-analysis website Investopedia.com, the high-tech stock index, the NASDAQ, fell a record 78 per cent. The site also fixes the dates of the dot.com crash as 11 March 2000 to 9 October 2002 (Investopedia.com). In one week between 7 and 14 April, 2000, American stock markets lost $US2 trillion dollars and Bill Gates' personal fortune fell by $30 billion in just a few hours (The Jobs Letter 2000). Though of course, you'd have to say he wouldn't really miss it!

DOT.COM CRASH

In the second half of the 1990s a significant number of computer companies 'went public'; that is, they listed on the stock exchange through a process known as an IPO (Initial Public Offering). In doing so, they created fabulous paper profits for those who owned the shares prior to the IPO. Those who cashed in their shares made huge profits. This was known as the dot.com boom. In late 1999 and early 2000, however, these stocks lost their allure and the market crashed.

The dot.com and telecommunications companies that had led the earlier confident rise in share prices took the hardest hits. Over the next two years (with September 11, 2001 right in the middle) a number of the start-up Internet companies, which on paper were worth billions of dollars, had disappeared entirely. Some of the giants of the copper cable and telecommunications cartel shed around 70–90 per cent of their stock values. Others, such as WorldCom and Global Crossing, were on the edge of bankruptcy; there were huge job losses right across the high-tech sector and corporate executives were dropping like flies in the face of investigations that showed they'd inflated share prices and profits to lure investors (Mosco 2004, pp. 4–5). Vincent Mosco makes a wry comment appropriate to the mythical power of the digital revolution: 'the only genuine break with history turned out to be the unprecedented collapse of a major industrial sector' (p. 5).

One of the biggest losers in the dot.com disaster was AOL Time Warner, which had formed through the merger of AOL (a new media company) and Time Warner (an old media conglomerate) only months before in January 2000. By March 2003 AOL's value had dropped 80 per cent below the merger value; Microsoft Corporation lost just over 50 per cent of its value and Intel 73 per cent. The Australian experience was much the same: Telstra's share price fell sharply and start-ups like One.Tel went under in spectacular fashion leaving angry employees, customers, and shareholders in their wake. One of the largest corporate scandals in Australian history ended with some of the leading players facing jail and huge fines for misleading the market and the regulators about the health of the company. Both Lachlan Murdoch and James Packer lost millions of dollars (of their fathers' money) in the deal. Before it fell apart, One.Tel had a paper valuation of over $6 billion; when it collapsed in June 2001 the company owed Optus more than $30 million in unpaid network fees (Kerr & Morrison 2001). In one exchange with the lawyers during a hearing into the collapse, young Mr Murdoch explained how young Mr Packer had come to his home in tears and apologised for getting the pair of them into the fine mess that was One.Tel (AAP 2005). Some senior officers in One.Tel had paid themselves bonuses of $7 million or more, but when the company went under, staff were left without their salary and entitlements. At the time of writing the corporate regulator ASIC was still pursuing One.Tel director Jodee Rich and the company's finance officer Mark Silberman for $92 million over the collapse.

Crisis? What Crisis?

The market crash of 2000 may well have been coming anyway—it might not have been just because the high-tech start-ups were inflating their values and hyping their prospects. Capitalism has always been prone to booms and slumps; this is one of the key dialectical fault lines in the system. Political economy tells us that the tendency towards periodic crisis is an inherent feature of commodity production in a capitalist economy because the average rate of profit falls when more capital is invested in a particular sector. This process—the product of an unplanned system of competition and corporate greed—wipes out any advantages that the initial investors may have had. The general collapse in profitability forces the weaker players out of the market and this process continues until some form of unstable and temporary equilibrium is found. Historically, this process has contributed to the centralisation and concentration of capital—the growth of cartels, oligopolies, and monopolies—as an inevitable consequence of the accumulation process (Callinicos 1987, pp. 128–39). This is precisely what happened during the 2000 dot.com crash: weaker and less stable companies went to the wall and those that survived got bigger as they absorbed the remains of their competitors' business.

As Investopedia.com notes in concluding its survey of market crashes over the past hundred years, 'regardless of our measures to correct the problems, the time between crashes has decreased'. A market crash often follows what economists call an investment 'bubble'—a time when there is plenty of money to be made and new investors are rushing in to grab a share of the action. The 'bubble' period for the new economy stocks based on digital technologies and convergence was probably from about 1996 to the 2000 crash, and over that period the NASDAQ index went from 600 to 5000 points. But the dot.com businesses were mostly empty shells; Pets.com issued a public share offering and raised millions of dollars in capital without even having a business plan or any income stream. At the same time, more start-ups began to imitate each other and by the time of the dot.com crash, Pets.com was facing stiff competition from a host of other pet-themed sites: 'petsmart.com, petfood.com, petstuff.com, petopia.com, and so on' (Andreas 2000). According to one investment advice website, most dot.com millionaires were under 30 and had no business experience: 'Never mistake a bull market for brains', it advises (Stock Market Crash! Net 2005).

In early 2000 there were signs that the dot.com bubble was going to burst (The Jobs Letter 2000). Joanna Glasner (2000) wrote in *Wired* magazine about the deflating Internet bubble just days before the NASDAQ demolition derby: 'The problem with a stock bubble is you never really know it is one until it pops.' Even then, in early April 2000 many digital analysts were talking down the prospect of a real crash, preferring to call it a 'correction' to the over-inflated market.

However, the crash was probably necessary to correct the ridiculous over-valuation of media and Internet stocks. One investment bank estimated that the high-tech stocks were overvalued by at least 40 per cent. From our perspective, *The Jobs Letter* offers a useful explanation of why the dot.com crash happened: 'How did things get so over-valued? Most of it has been put down to plain old hype and speculation. But there has also been a powerful new myth at work in financial circles: that the dot.com age is re-writing the basic laws of economics' (The Jobs Letter 2000). Karl Marx called the law of value one of the 'iron laws' of history, meaning it is difficult (if not impossible) to rewrite. From a political economy perspective, the dot.com companies were stopped by this law.

WHAT TIM RECKONS: THE DOT.COM CRASH

In 2000 the commercial internet was still new. People recognised its potential to transform the way we communicate and do business. Those same people needed investment and therefore needed some predictions—'traffic will double every 90 days' was a common refrain—to accompany their pitch. Clearly, the predictions were way out, but many of the underlying ideas that attracted attention are now becoming a reality and will continue to do so. Developers were arguably able to take stock and create a more 'open standards' technology environment, and there is now sufficient market penetration of some technologies to support new and innovative services.

At the same time, the dot.com boom also exposed a worrying failure by technology markets to learn from their mistakes. Despite the devastating fallout of dot.com mania, the telecom and media markets have had themselves in a tizz over succession of new innovations—WAP 3G mobile, so-called broadband, Wi-Fi, WiMAX, and now mobile TV and IPTV—infatuated with the thrill of the new, possibly to the detriment of the consumers who ultimately pick up the tab.

At localised level I'm increasingly confident that the world has recovered from the 2000 dot.com crash. Companies are starting to be creative again and the actual Internet and mobile phone population is large enough to generate some meaningful revenues. At a macro level it is almost there. Consolidation in the equipment and operator markets has reached its peak and new growth markets like India and China are delivering the opportunities needed to fuel employment. Has the world learnt from the dot.com crash? That is certainly another matter.

Was there ever a Golden Age and does it matter?

> The aftermath of the crash of 2000 is that the Internet has been brought back to the basics of business. It has been returned to the people with passion. It has been returned to the customers! (Roy 2000)

The dot.com crash did not dent the enthusiasm of the digital boosters too badly. By November 2000, Michelle Roy was predicting that it would all get better and soon. All that had to happen for the dot.coms to pick themselves up was to refocus on customer service. Roy remained confident, just months after everything went south at speed: 'The new economy is more of a new set of rules for businesses that have survived the test of time rather than a new paradigm for brand new companies ... Smart companies are still investing in their e-business development strategies' (Roy 2000).

Roy's vision was common among the people who'd been burned in the blaze of the dot.com crash. Information Architecture consultant Peter Moreville wrote, in November 2001, that the recovery from the crash would position high-tech companies for a more prosperous future: 'As we emerge from the ashes during 2001, we will begin to see signs that the Internet industry has come of age' (Moreville 2001). So the new economy came 'of age' in the aftermath of the crash of 2000 and while the remains of the World Trade Centre complex at 'ground zero' in New York were still smouldering—a Phoenix-like rise from the ashes of two spectacular disasters.

There's no doubt that the dot.com crash of 2000 dented the 'Golden Age' myth. We are perhaps yet to see if it turns Negroponte's dream of a future digital nirvana into a new technological nightmare of surveillance and cyber-malls. Alex Burns, writing in *Disinformation*, says the crash of 2000 caused many tech-analysts to question the 'social mantras' they had been 'long conditioned with': 'The dot.com disasters glaringly highlight the distance between the chimerical Digital Age and what economist Paul Krugman lucidly calls "the Age of Diminished Expectations"' (Burns 2001).

Despite the heartache and tears, it is hard to write off the digital myth altogether. It seems it is a necessary condition of the digital age that the myth continues to live in some form. Five years after the crash Chris Alden (2005) wrote in the *Guardian* that many survivors believed that the shake-out of Internet and other high-tech stocks was a good thing because it cleared the way for a more sensible approach to online business development and a more cautious attitude to the Internet on the part of investors and inventors. This remaking of recent history is part of the inoculation process of myth-making. This is a common view, and many commentators regained their optimism fairly quickly; the signs are now pointing to a resurgence in the digital economy on a more viable platform.

NEW MEDIA

A catchall phrase used to distinguish digital media forms from 'old media' forms such as newspapers, magazines, radio, and television.

As Vincent Mosco suggests in *The Digital Sublime*, the Internet and new media technologies really become 'important forces for social and economic change' when they move from being the 'sublime icons of mythology' and are no longer the source of 'utopian visions', but rather enter the 'prosaic world of banality' (Mosco 2004, p. 6). The real power of new technologies does not really emerge in the period when they are highly mythologised, but when they 'withdraw into the woodwork' (p. 19). Mosco calls this a shift to 'embodied physicality', such as when the microchip was successfully migrated from the mainframe to the desktop and then into a 'host of old and new devices' that could be commoditised, allowing the power of computing to grow, 'while withdrawing as a presence' (p. 21).

This is, in our view, the phase of digital convergence we are now in and perhaps have been in for the past five to ten years. There is a certain 'taken-for-grantedness' about digital media today. It is no longer a thing to be in awe of, or to fear. Digital devices are now commonplace, part of the everyday experience of most people. People in their twenties today (and younger) know very little about the pre-digital world (at least from direct experience). Digital technologies are now socially, economically, and culturally embedded in our daily lives. We are living in this 'new' economy with 'new' media all around us. It may or may not be a new (or enduring) Golden Age, but there's no question that it is now the paradigm for almost everything we do. As we shall explore in the next chapter, at the heart of this new paradigm is the process of convergence that has brought the computer and the media together and dispersed the banal power of the microchip into almost every piece of technology that we interact with in the home, the workplace, and the classroom, and when we are relaxing or being entertained. In particular we investigate how digital technologies are undermining the very idea of professional journalism and shifting the boundaries of what we call the 'reportorial community'.

WHAT BILLY RECKONS: DOING BUSINESS ONLINE

From what I was doing with the photographic library, word got around that we were building websites and we were doing e-commerce and, you know, we were making the impossible possible. I was trying to keep a low profile, because the banks weren't very keen on electronic commerce, but through my business I met people who would fantasise about stuff. They'd heard about the Internet and how great it was going to be, and how people could pay for things over the Net and it's all electronic and it's all automatic. They were sort of being romantic about it, and I would say, 'Oh yeah, well I can do all that, it's easy.' And from that point I was getting people asking, 'Can you do it for us?' So we were using the same system that we'd developed to begin processing payments for other people.

It was like 'frontier land' and I felt like a bit of a cowboy. And I certainly felt the fun of it because it was breaking new ground. And it was new, but that was the great thing about it. You could do no wrong and I certainly got an insight into, for instance, the way Thomas Edison must have felt when he was inventing the light bulb. There was this wonderful thing that you knew was going to work and you could see the potential in it. And, and it was like, 'Oh, wouldn't this be a great idea?' And that was sort of how the whole dot.com thing blew up and fell down. A lot of people had a lot of great ideas, it's just that some of them weren't economically viable. But everything I looked at was whether or not you could make money from it. Not fantasy money, but real money, right now. I asked myself, 'Did what I was wanting to do fulfil a need that was already there, but was not being met?'

Getting into building and servicing web servers was something that came from the interest of our clients. I had always known about the joys of residual income – people paying rent, over and over again. So when you supply a service, the money just keeps coming in. I discovered this could work with the hosting of websites, not just building them.

Look, it all comes from my own sheer laziness. I want to make as much money as possible, doing the least amount of work. Each step along the way was less work and the same amount of money, or more. When it came to hosting, as long as the thing operated, and worked, and ran smoothly it was fine. The secret behind it is to always have extremely good technicians who will act fast when there is a problem.

It's nothing new really. It works the same in the real estate market. Instead of selling physical real estate, I'm renting out digital real estate.

KEY POINTS

The key points from this chapter are:

- the prevalence of technological 'boosterism' as an important element of digital mythologies;
- the role of Silicon Valley as the incubator of consumer-directed digital technologies;
- that the Golden Age of the Internet—if it ever existed—ended with the dot.com crash of 2000 and the terrorist attacks on the Twin Towers in New York and the Pentagon on September 11, 2001, ushering in the age of digital surveillance;
- digital mythology continues to generate the memes of an Internet Golden Age that has shifting spatial and temporal boundaries.

CLASS DISCUSSION

Is there an enduring myth of a digital 'Golden Age'?

1 In this chapter we have outlined some of the mythology that surrounds digital technologies, particularly the Internet, and we have described what may be the most enduring myth as the Golden Age. Do you agree with this analysis?

(a) In your view, what are the enduring myths of the Internet and digital technologies today?

(b) Are we still caught up in the myths of cyberspace and the existence of a Golden Age?

(c) If you were to consider the time-frame, what would you point to as the beginning, middle, and end points of the Golden Age mythologies'?

(d) Are many of the so-called Internet myths circulating today linked to marketing or advertising?

Crash or shake-out?
What was the impact of the dot.com crash of 2000?

2 In this chapter we have commented on the impact of the dot.com crash that wiped out billions of dollars of value from dot.com companies. Today it's fair to argue that the digital economy has recovered. Do you agree?

(a) Did the dot.com crash 'clean out' some badly performing, or under-prepared companies? In hindsight, was this a good thing?

(b) Do you think the dot.com crash has contributed to the growth of cartels and oligopolies in the digital economy?

(c) When will the next boom-slump cycle create problems for the digital economy?

(d) What can economies and companies do to insulate themselves from a boom-slump event?

(e) What is the impact of cyclical crises on consumers, workers, and shareholders in the information economy?

(f) Has the globalisation of the information economy made it stronger, or more prone to crises?

11

WHO'S A JOURNALIST NOW? THE EXPANDED REPORTORIAL COMMUNITY

OBJECTIVES

This chapter seeks the answers to a number of questions, the most important perhaps being: who or what is a journalist in the convergent media world? After reading this chapter you will have a better understanding of how the Internet, mobile media-enabled technologies, and the shifting social relations of news production and consumption have impacted on what we have begun to call the 'reportorial community'. In particular, in this chapter we discuss the following points:

- how the demarcation lines between journalists, non-journalists, and audience-participants are dissolving, and how this is affecting the production and consumption of news in the 21st century;
- how the definitions and roles of journalists have changed over the past hundred years in response to changing technologies and changing social conditions;

- what we mean by 'the reportorial community' and, in particular, how 'eyewitness' accounts and interventions in the newsgathering process have been enabled by new media technologies;
- what we mean by 'citizen-journalist' and the debates around the impact so-called 'non-professional newsgathering' is having on the old media;
- what this means for the future of published and broadcast news and information.

KEYWORDS

backpack journalism
blogging
citizen-journalist
participatory journalism
reportorial community

Who's who in the digital zoo?

One of the key advances people mention when they talk about the good things that the Internet brings is that anyone can now be an author and publisher. The cost of renting a small shopfront on the World Wide Web is negligible—at least for the average middle-class person with an income and access to a computer and phone line.

A key theme in this section is to address the ways in which the new media are changing the relationship between the producers and consumers of what is broadly defined as 'news'. Throughout the 20th century the functions, character, and class position of journalists all over the world have undergone almost continuous and extensive change (Hirst 2001, p. 262; Oakham 2001; Pavlik 2001; Hargreaves 2003). It's also fair to say that the modern public relations industry was established by news reporters and editors who saw they could make more money by advising companies and governments. There has always been an unsteady professional relationship between newsgatherers and spin doctors. We often ask our students if the relationship is symbiotic or parasitic: who is feeding whom? The new media content providers—whether reporter, marketeer, or PR professional—all hold interesting and relevant positions within the mass media and communications industries of the 21st century. It is important in this context, and in the context of alternative forms of narrowcast media, to have some understanding of the changing character of what we call the reportorial community and the ways in which these changes have 'disrupted' journalism's traditional focus and practices (Meadows 2001).

REPORTORIAL COMMUNITY

Those who 'report' in a variety of media, old and new, using traditional journalistic genres and forms: the news story (written inside and outside the inverted pyramid); the feature story; the radio news report; the television news report; the 'live cross'; the documentary; the online news story, etc.

Citizen Kane to Citizen Journalist?

> Citizen journalism will not make institutional journalism redundant or irrelevant. It is a challenge to the authority of the traditional media, not an alternative. It will make traditional journalism stronger, better, more responsive. Sceptics tend to make you lift your game. (McDonald 2005, p. 14)

One of the most volatile fault lines cutting through the world of new media is just who gets to define, shape, edit, and present that bit of content known in the old mediaspeak as *news*. Recent events, such as the July 2005 terror attacks in London, have brought to public attention the existence of what has become widely accepted as the 'citizen journalist'. It is therefore important to examine the professional, emotional, economic, and cultural impacts of the power-shifting that has accompanied the widespread introduction of new, affordable, and reasonable-quality means of media production. Can everyone be their own editor and reporter?

CITIZEN-JOURNALIST

A person who is not attached to a media organisation, who witnesses an event, and then provides an account of that event, normally using traditional and new journalistic forms. Distinguished from an eyewitness by the nature and form(s) of their account.

In this chapter we examine the recent blurring of boundaries between 'professionals' and those who 'write' about the news. There are really two dynamics at play in this chapter: on the one hand, the rise of the so-called citizen journalist, and on the other, the changing face, work, and nature of traditional journalism as the old media silos of print, radio, television, and online break down even further. We should start with some historical accounting and the observation that for more than a hundred years the primary demarcation between reporters and amateurs has been the economic relationship (wages and salaries) between the news worker and the employer. There has always been some argument about whether journalism is an art-form, a craft, or a profession—or even just another form of wage-labour. But there has been, until recently, a consensus that reporters, news photographers, and editorial staff were a distinct class of labour, defined by its relationship to both media outlet and audience. This chapter looks at the proposition that converging technologies are slowly but surely breaking down this distinction and blurring the boundaries of the community of reporters.

This issue is discussed briefly by Tapsall and Varley (2001, p. 4). They argue that it is important to have a clear definition of what a journalist is so that consumers of news can tell the difference between 'good news, bad news, and no news'. Their research, involving journalists from most major media outlets in Australia, drew some interesting self-definitions from respondents. In order of frequency, the definitions included: 'news workers, information workers, gatherers, reporters, entertainers, historians, researchers, explainers, probers and writers'. Less frequent responses included 'editors, communicators, story-tellers, producers and presenters' (pp. 5–6). One respondent, ABC radio's foreign editor Peter Cave, is quoted as saying that journalists are 'intermediaries' between audiences and sources and also a 'filter'. He adds, 'and that's where the danger lies' (p. 6). SBS journalist

Helen Vatsikopoulos says an important part of the definition is that reporters and editors analyse information and set events 'in context' (p. 6). The authors note that changing media technologies and changing patterns of media control, production, and consumption make a simple definition—such as a journalist is someone employed to report and edit the news—is no longer as valid as it used to be. From this brief definitional survey it's easy to see how the boundaries can be blurred when it comes to reporting, or information-sharing in an online environment. It also highlights a difficulty for non-journalists operating in a newsgathering and reporting role. We know that when it comes to reputable news sources, reporters and editors are filtering the news and putting it into their own contextual framework; we accept that filtering goes on, but can we be sure that the filtering and contextualising done by 'amateurs' is as rigorous, or reliable?

THE CITIZEN-JOURNALIST AT WORK

In July 2005 the *New York Times* (Carey 2005) published a story about a soon-to-be-released study of bisexuality in men. Controversially, the study, led by Dr J. Michael Bailey, claimed that there is no such 'condition' as bisexuality and that most men who identified as bisexual were in fact gay. The *NYT* reported even-handedly, quoting Dr Bailey, his co-researchers, and some of his critics. It seemed like any other science story; reporting another research study about sexuality. But within days, it was in the top five emailed stories on the *NYT* website. Almost immediately, the National Gay and Lesbian Taskforce (NGLT) condemned the *NYT* science section for carrying the piece without questioning the methods and motives of Dr Bailey. That news wasn't carried in the online version of the paper initially, but travelled around on Internet user groups, blogs, email alerts, and chatrooms.

The NGLT statement circulated widely and carried a link to fact sheets critiquing the report and its authors. The day after the Carey piece, 'Straight, Gay or Lying: Bisexuality Revisited', one newsgroup was already linking to and copying people into blogs and other sites that were critical of the bisexuality research. On AmericaBlog, 'Michael' in New York posted an angry piece questioning the research findings. He added, 'it took reader Kathleen to alert me to what the *NYT* should have known before presenting this study uncritically'. According to the blog, Bailey had been challenged over alleged misconduct and his suspect methods. Michael concluded his message by asking readers to question the newspaper by email and to insist it check allegations that Bailey was linked to racist organisations and had 'stepped down' from his chair in psychology because of ethics breaches in his previous work (Michael in New York 2005). Another posted message on the QSTUDY list encouraged readers to write letters to the media outlets such as the *NYT*, which reported the study uncritically. Is this a case of the 'citizen-journalist' at work?

Journalism in the 20th century: Craft or profession?

> Constantly successful achievement in journalism requires more judgments on more diverse problems over the working hours than any other occupation. (Rivett 1965, p. 23)

Throughout the 20th century, during what we might call the age of 'industrial journalism' produced for mass consumption like so many 'widgets', journalism and journalists changed their character. At the beginning of the century, and perhaps until the end of World War II in 1945, journalism was understood as a craft—a vocation to be learned on the job through a system of apprenticeships. The cadet reporter would learn from the master through observation, hard discipline, and patient practice of the art. As our opening quote from the illustrious reporter and editor Rohan Rivett suggests, to be a journalist, even forty years ago, was to be marked out from the ordinary. According to Rivett, journalism could be distinguished from 'every other vocation' by the diversity of the daily routine that demanded, in equal measure, skills, ingenuity, and flexibility on the part of the journalist.

No doubt there's some truth in this statement, but equally we could argue that it is the preciousness and self-absorption of the profession that leads to such statements about the special nature of the journalist and journalism. As we'll see, the definition of the skills may change and there may from time to time be more or less emphasis on 'professionalism' versus 'craft', but the essential ingredient in most definitions is that reporters and newsworkers are somehow 'different' and not like 'ordinary' folk. The work of journalism demands a particular 'type' of personality and dedication to the cause. But does it really?

The best way to tackle this question is to examine the situation historically. We pick up our story in the early years of the 20th century when 'muckraking' journalism (the good guys) and the 'yellow press' (the salacious, tabloid bad guys) were fighting for circulation in the United States (see, for example, our discussion of Upton Sinclair's *The Brass Check* in chapter 5). We can get a sense of the situation in Australia at the time Sinclair was writing from a number of sources, the most important being Clem Lloyd's history of the Australian Journalists Association (AJA), *Profession: Journalist*, and the first full-scale study of the Australian media system, *The Press in Australia* by the historian Henry Mayer.

The career journalist

> Top hats, frock coats and walking sticks had given journalists an air of respectability, but it was a dubious respectability, for the 'working journalist' ... was paid barely enough to live decently and keep a wife and family. (Sparrow 1960, p. 16)

Unionist and journalist Geoff Sparrow wrote the first account of the foundation of the AJA in its jubilee year (1960) and as he describes it, in the first half of the 20th century, news workers were 'slaves of the press'. As the union became stronger it was able to win better conditions for its members and the humble journalist began to climb the ladder of respectability, though some would question how far they've come in the last eighty years! (You can read more about the early years of Australian journalism in chapter 5.)

By 1960 the situation had turned around enough so that Geoff Sparrow could confidently write in his conclusion to *Crusade for Journalism* that journalism was 'the path that led to high places' for some (p. 148). Nevertheless, by the mid-1960s, a new generation of AJA leaders was telling young reporters that journalism remained a tough career to enter and to stick at: 'Journalism is a hard life. It can be exciting, but it can sometimes be boring. It can be frustrating too' (Crosland 1965, p. 39).

In the mid-1960s, the reporter's union, the Australian Journalists' Association (AJA), decided it was time to produce the first manual for young journalists. After gathering together a large committee of eminent reporters, subeditors, and editors, the union chose twenty-eight contributors to write on interviewing, writing, grammar, subediting, photography, cartooning, a variety of news 'rounds', and a chapter on journalists and the law. The General Secretary of the AJA, S. P. Crosland, contributed a chapter on the career of journalism. When he wrote this chapter in 1965, Sydney Crosland had been a journalist for thirty-four years and claimed to be 'still fascinated by the birth of the daily newspaper' (p. 38).

Under a subheading, 'Qualifications of the journalist', Mr Crosland talks about the long hours, the shift work, the lack of contact with family and friends, and the harsh social conditions that reporters and subeditors must endure, but he says very little about qualifications. The only concrete statement that refers to the necessary qualifications for a young journalist in 1965 is that 'you must have a great deal of curiosity'. He adds: 'you must like people and be interested in what they do' and you must 'be able to write … in a simple and lucid fashion and, above all, quickly' (p. 40). What a contrast with today when a typical job advertisement for a journalist will require at least an undergraduate degree, good 'communication skills', computer literacy, and much more. The educational requirement in 1965 was a good high school education. Most new reporters would be taken on as cadets—office juniors who would do a great deal of the routine work and assist some of the other reporters. Only rarely would a cadet be assigned to write a story on their own. A typical cadetship would last up to four years. But Mr Crosland had some words of criticism for the cadet system of the 1960s: 'If a word of criticism may be offered, it is that the present system does not go far enough in educating young minds for the responsibilities of reporting, explaining, and interpreting the news' (p. 43).

There were very few university places to teach journalism in Australia at that time, but Crosland comments that the American system is based on university education for would-be journalists and he proffers the opinion that 'it would be desirable to amalgamate the best features of both systems' (p. 43). There were, in fact, some universities that provided courses for journalists, but not in the study of journalism itself. Courses for journalists were similar to a generalist Arts degree today as it was felt necessary for reporters to have a good understanding of history, social sciences, perhaps politics or economics, and English literature. As this brief history shows, in the middle of the 20th century the paths that led to a career in journalism were varied and vastly different from those on offer today.

Len Granato's influential textbook for young journalists, written in the early 1990s, paints a very different picture of the motives that lead young people to a career in news reporting. Granato writes that they may believe some of the popular fictional accounts in which a reporter will solve a baffling crime; they may have had a high school English teacher who encouraged their writing skills, or they may seek the glamour of a life in television 'as another Jana Wendt'; finally they may want to be a crusading journalist using their writing to 'change the system and save the world'. According to Len Granato, these are 'misleading influences'; the real picture is much more mundane: journalism is a job with 'extreme satisfactions and extreme frustrations' (Granato 1991, pp. 1–2). By the end of the 20th century, however, the idea that journalism could be a good profession for an ambitious young man or woman was well entrenched: 'So what is a contemporary Australian journalist? ... Ultimately, the essence that distinguishes journalists from ... other information brokers might be the commitment to the public good and the notion of a responsibility that goes beyond self and employer' (Tapsall & Varley 2001, p. 17).

This is a reasonable definition of the 'professional'—a commitment to serving the public interest—but is it enough to separate a journalist from a blogger? After all, bloggers have ethics too! The view that journalism is a profession rather than a craft is a fairly modern one that has been conveniently moulded to fit changed economic and social circumstances. If a journalist can claim to be professional, he or she can move a few more rungs up the respectability ladder. We think it is fair to consider professionalism as a paradoxical ideology of journalism (Hirst & Patching 2005, pp. 32–3), but it retains a strong hold in the minds of many reporters and certainly over the consciousness of the general public.

As a former journalist and a journalism educator for more than twenty-five years, Len Granato felt the need to defend university training for young journalists in the opening pages of *Reporting and Writing News* and to argue for the important intellectual content that a broad tertiary education can add to the craft elements of reporting by providing a balance of theory and practice. This is important so that those entering the profession as young beginners can 'learn how to think, report and write like journalists' (Granato 1991, p. 4). In this passage he is making the important point that for some time there has been too much anti-intellectual thinking among senior journalists and editors. Implicit in this is the belief that journalism is a set of skills and attitudes that place reporters and news workers apart from the general population, in much the same way that a distinct set of knowledge and practices distinguishes a surgeon from his or her patients. If we would never think of trusting complicated surgery to a gifted amateur, why would we believe that anyone with a PC and a modem can suddenly become a journalist?

A decade later, in the second edition of his successful textbook *The Daily Miracle*, journalism educator David Conley notes that the entry requirements for journalism, and the people seeking entry to the profession, are rapidly changing. In particular, it is attracting people who are looking to enjoy a second or subsequent career. He says that 'more than ever', reporting and news work look like attractive options for postgraduate students who are already qualified in teaching, law, nursing, or another profession (Conley

2002, p. viii). Conley's book begins with a chapter called 'Journeys in Journalism' in which he surveys some common notions about what journalism is at the beginning of the 21st century and where it might be heading, particularly because of some of the technological changes we've been describing in this book. He also poses the important question that has really been the subtext of this chapter: What is journalism? This is how he puts it: 'Although journalism's popularity was beginning to decline slightly in the new century, a question remains: is journalism's popularity transforming it into an art, a craft, perhaps even a religion?' (p. 3).

While we can forgive a rhetorical flourish—journalism is not likely to reach the status of secular religion for some considerable time—the popularity of journalism and communication studies in universities has flooded the job market for reporters and increased the competition for scarce jobs. In this context it is legitimate to ask: What will happen to all the frustrated journalists who cannot find a job? Will they want to express themselves through other means, such as weblogs?

Interestingly, in the setting of our current concerns about how journalism and the profile of the journalist are changing, Conley sticks to a fairly conventional definition of journalism as an 'informative function' linked to a 'traditional watchdog role', serving the public interest and providing some entertainment to audiences (p. 23). There is, in this framing, a contradiction between the public interest and the commercial interest of the media organisations, which can ultimately interfere with the duties of journalism to inform and to educate.

The impact of technologies and convergence on the practices of journalism have certainly created changes, not least to the form of journalism and by implication journalism education. The traditional inverted pyramid of print journalism is shaped for the eye, not the ear, so it doesn't transfer very well to electronic media, and this is even the case with web-based news services where 'the front-line stories have more in common with radio and television' (p. 187). This change in content and form has consequences for journalists too: 'New-generation media means new-generation journalists' (p. 306). According to Conley this means that there is even greater pressure on experienced journalists, those being trained at university, and journalism educators to maintain the distinguishing features of the profession. The Internet, he argues, means that 'citizens do not need journalists in the way they once did' (p. 306). We are now seeing this being played out in a million everyday information transactions—emails, weblogs, and SMS instant messaging. In a recent article published in the *Australian*, David Conley (2006) argued for the accreditation of journalism courses in universities. Such a move would by definition preclude bloggers and amateurs from the category of journalists. Accreditation of training for reporters is a small step from the further regulation and licensing of journalists. This is not a new idea, but it has not really gained any 'traction' in discussions among reporters or journalism educators in Australia (Hirst & Patching 2005, see pp. 118–9). However, in some countries, including the UK and New Zealand, tertiary journalism courses are accredited and regulated by an industry body, usually composed of senior editors and educators.

Journalists and technology: An unhappy marriage?

The Australian author and journalist George Johnston painted a fairly bleak picture of a Melbourne newspaper office in the 1930s in his famous novel *My Brother Jack* (1964). The offices of the fictional *Morning Post*—most likely the Melbourne *Argus* where Johnston worked in the 1930s (Sekuless 1999, p. 89)—are described as 'warrens of little rooms and airless cubby-holes divided by frosted glass and mahogany', where the classifieds were composed and the accounts settled (Johnston 1964, p. 187).

Fifty years later, things were not all that different at News Limited's Holt Street headquarters in central Sydney. According to Tim Krause (1999) it was 'noisy, dirty, overcrowded, chockablock with deadlines and a Mahogany Row more interested, we thought, in profits than prose'.

If Krause was talking about 'yesterday', Johnston was writing about journalism at a time when the 'mechanisation' of news production in Australia was only beginning to catch up with the rest of the world. In the first half of the 20th century the teleprinter, the telephone, and the telegraph all had an impact on newsgathering, and not always for the better. In the latter stages of the 20th century it has been the digital revolution brought about by an expanding arms economy and the exigencies of the Cold War. We deliberately use the term 'impact' here because technology does not simply superimpose itself on a production process: it is consciously articulated through the social relations of production.

The age of globalisation began in effect 150 years ago with the 'cable' technology of the telegraph wire, which came to Australia in the 1850s. The news agencies have always been active players in the introduction of new technologies to newsgathering and dissemination. Reuters was instrumental in the laying of telegraph cable in the second half of the 19th century and one of the first to take full advantage of satellite technology in the 20th (Boyd-Barrett 1998, pp. 32–3). London *Times* senior reporter Raymond Snoddy (1992, p. 144) suggests the introduction of the telephone meant that journalists stayed in the office 'rather than getting out and meeting the people they're writing about'. Of course, in the late 20th century the fax machine and the Internet strengthened this tendency to gather news from the reporter's room rather than the street. Schultz (1998) reports studies that show up to 90 per cent of news is generated from media releases that are distributed by fax, or even on videotape (see, for example, Ward 1991; Zawawi 1994).

As technologies have changed, so too have the definitions and duties of journalists. This is not to imply that there is a smooth, one-to-one correlation between technology and journalism; the introduction and acceptance of new technologies into the field does not always go smoothly. Like any business, the commercial reality of journalism is that new technology often means a change in the way the work is managed; new and different skill-sets being required and in some cases a reduction in staffing levels.

For example, former ABC reporter Neville Petersen recalls that his time in radio was marked by successive attempts to come to grips with magnetic tape technology and the use of tape machines generally. Most of the work up to 1956 was done in studios, where large Byer 77 machines were manned by technicians from the Postmaster-General's

(PMG) department, which controlled ABC technical services at this time. Tapes were cut-edited using two of the Byer 77 machines; until this time no tape could be cut and spliced. This changed after the 1956 Melbourne Olympic Games when staff in ABC Radio Talks defied the PMG's department and cut and spliced tapes each night of the Games for replay. Neville says that it could not have been handled fast enough otherwise. From this point on, Talks was allowed to record and cut-edit material in its own offices. Neville Petersen was a pioneering television journalist at the ABC and he says that the introduction of new cameras in the 1960s was a difficult process that caused some sections of ABC news and current affairs to be radically reorganised.

WHAT NEVILLE RECKONS: EARLY BROADCASTING TECHNOLOGIES

If one went on a mission to record someone outside the studio, a PMG van and technician would have to be booked. This was expensive as well as time-consuming. There was a clear need for portable recorders. The PMG designed such a machine itself, the CEB recorder, which proved an absolute disaster. You had to put it on the ground and tip it on one side to be able to operate it. You could not use it while it was being carried. The mechanism, moreover, left a lot to be desired. A clockwork motor began to run down after 3–4 minutes and if recording any longer you had to start winding the motor, often while conducting the interview. The springs also broke very easily.

Around 1960, the Stellavox recorder was made available. I took the first one to Holland on a test-run trip in that year. It recorded on small (2–3 inch) tapes but was very compact, sturdy, easy to operate, and gave excellent sound. Its drawback was the short duration of the tapes, which ran at 7½ ips [inches per second]. The next step in upgrading was the issuing of reel-to-reel recorders to ABC overseas offices from about the mid-1960s onwards. This was a big advance. They allowed for longer recording times and were of professional quality.

My impression is that cassette recorders appeared in the late 1960s. They were ordered by News (not Talks) and were flimsy and gave poor quality. Sound technicians deplored their use. Much later, those of much better quality and built to last appeared in London and were used constantly in conjunction with other recorders.

In television in the late 1950s early mute footage for use in interview programs, such as *People*, which I ran, came from Bell & Howell and Arriflex cameras. When I joined *Four Corners* in 1966 they had introduced double system cameras, the Arriflex BL and Eclair, widely used overseas. News at this time did not favour shoulder-held cameras or the use of actuality sound and retained its huge Auricon sound cameras, which were too heavy to manipulate and considerably reduced their options in the filming of on-the-spot occurrences. By 1970, when I returned to Sydney, TV News had moved to single system magnetic stripe sound, using Arriflex BL cameras. But reporters were not trained to maximise their use. TV News used radio reporters.

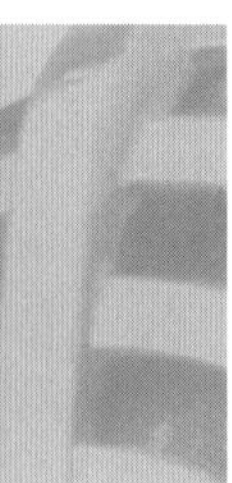

TV news really did not get into filmed news until the mid-1970s. *Four Corners* and *This Day Tonight* made all the running and made domestic news look stilted and trite by comparison. News was humiliated over this issue by program personnel who constantly urged it to change its ways. This was a crucial issue which led to the dismemberment of the News Division in 1983 and its takeover by Current Affairs.

A breakthrough study of technology, environment, and workplace design in the Australian context (Dombkins 1993) looked at the organisational structure of the *Sydney Morning Herald* as it was in 1962 and then compared it to how it is in 1992. Margaret Dombkins notes that over a period of thirty years, 'the role of the journalist has changed' and that journalists are necessarily 'multiskilled':

> The traditional mandatory shorthand, although still used, is not as essential [as in 1962]. News sense is still the main skill. Journalists now need word processing skills, not just adequate typing skills. Promotion is now based more on ability than seniority. Training has moved from the traditional craft-based training through the cadetship system to university training and a limited cadetship. (Dombkins 1993, p. 36)

When Dombkins did this study in 1992 the Fairfax organisation was in the process, once again, of updating its computer system for journalists and subs—with obvious knock-on effects for the blue-collar printing trades (plate-making and so on). She notes that computerised copy control 'provided owners and senior management with the power to control journalistic output', but adds that 'through industrial action' journalists were able to resist to a point, while productivity per journalist increased by 15 per cent (p. 48).

Rosslyn Reed takes a similar view of the Fairfax organisation. In her examination of the division of labour and the degree of managerial control over editorial outputs, Reed notes that professionalism 'and the autonomy it confers ... has eluded journalists except for short periods and in limited circumstances' (1999, p. 218). Reed insists on examining news technology and news production from the point of view of social relations, rather than the technological 'artefact': 'Itself produced by the social relations of production ... changes in the organisation and design of the work precede specific developments in technical artefacts which are premised on the subdivision of tasks in the detailed division of labour' (p. 219).

By the mid-1980s many journalists had come to admire the new technology because it gave them greater *professional* control over their copy (p. 222). But the gains of electronic copy-entry were not evenly shared. Reed concludes that journalists made small gains at the expense of printers as the new technology was introduced. The struggle over the introduction of new technology at the Fairfax papers in the 1980s resulted in both printers and journalists losing out. The printers' union opposed the introduction of computer terminals (VDUs) that allowed the reporters to enter their own copy into the production system and the journalists' union didn't support them. What journalists regarded as wins, mainly in the form of payment for re-use of material, has come back to haunt them, 'at the very time journalists had benefited from the industrial defeat of printers by newspaper proprietors' (p. 228). This indicates the contradictory nature of the emotional attitudes of journalists. The limits of professionalism confronted the reality of monopoly capitalism's tactics of divide and rule. At Fairfax there was also a generational divide between the older craft-style unionism of the printers organised in the PKIU and the younger, more white-collar journalists organised in the AJA. This age divide over the introduction of new technology has not gone away.

ABC reporter Alex Graham (2006) believes there's definitely an age divide when it comes to technology. She says that the fact that ABC radio in Brisbane still operates with tape decks and DCART is partly because a lot of older newsroom staff work off the mantra: 'If it ain't broke don't fix it.' According to Alex, people get comfortable with one type of technology and are then more hesitant to move with the times. She also says that some of the new technology available is still problematic and adds that in some instances management doesn't want to update radio kits if journalists aren't happy with what's on offer.

But what of the new digital technologies? They have been in use now in many newsrooms for more than a decade and they've had an enormous impact on journalism, both as a work process and as a social institution (Bowman & Willis 2005). There's a strong current of opinion that the Internet has radically changed the scope and practices of journalism because it accelerates the circulation of ideas and because of new technologies like open-source software and easy-to-use publishing tools for the Web. There's also a commercial angle: the 'old' media companies are losing revenue to online advertising and some search engine providers are now even considering an expanded and independent role as news providers (News to view from Yahoo 2005). The question for many is not so much whether the future is coming, but rather, now that it's arrived, can the mainstream media do anything about it? (Bowman & Willis 2005, p. 6).

Reporters and editors now have to be familiar with a new range of equipment and work practices, particularly in relation to producing news copy and items for online services (Pavlik 2001, p. 199). The Internet has become a new tool in the reporter's kit bag. In the United States it is used extensively for newsgathering and collecting copy. The trend in Australia seems to be following this pattern (Quinn 1998).

The rapid diffusion of hypertext has also challenged traditional models of journalism because it allows the multiple layering of information and links within an online text. This creates opportunities for new styles of narrative and news presentation (Flew 2005, pp. 87–8). John Pavlik takes a similar position and argues that the technology to create an 'omnidirectional view' of the world (360-degree photography, for example) is now available, but is being resisted by news organisations (Pavlik 2001, pp. 4–15). News, it seems, is no longer constrained by the limits of analogue technology, but rather by the social relations of news production, including traditions and training (p. 17), which may still be holding back digital media. As we've seen from the examples cited here and the experience of our contributing guests, the introduction and acceptance of new technologies is not necessarily without problems in the newsroom. Managerial concerns, the fears of entrenched older staff, and disputes over who can do what, as well as legitimate arguments about the possible and unforeseen consequences of the technology itself, all make change socially and culturally difficult at times.

And the future? According to John Pavlik, the next step in newsgathering technology is likely to be wearable computing devices. He says that initially these will be small and able to be clipped to belts or clothing, but he predicts that at some point miniaturisation will be so advanced that microchips could be implanted in the body, enabling journalists to access databases and 'internal computing power' (p. 199).

There are two important considerations to raise at this point: the first is the statement that the Internet makes us all journalists (Grossman 1999) and the second, a consideration of how these new media technologies have changed the profession and the practice of journalists. We will consider the first question later in this chapter, but for now we need to consider the rise of the so-called 'backpack journalist'; the one-person news crew, geared up and prepared for professional reporting in a multimedia world.

WHAT ALEX RECKONS: WORKING WITH A MIX OF TECHNOLOGIES

Despite the fact that minidisc technology is now available, most of the radio kits in the ABC's Brisbane newsroom are still tape-recorders. The reason for this is, quite simply, they never fail. They are bulky and awkward to carry—but they record beautifully every time! Their only downfall (it is the same for minidisc) is that you have to download that audio back into the computer-editing system when you return to work—and it is 'real time', so if you have twenty minutes of audio to dump it can be time-consuming.

We still edit in radio news using DCART—which is a dinosaur of a program, but once again, is very reliable and easy to use. Its one big downfall is that it records your audio in a straight line (with no sound wave) so you have to listen to where to make your edit marks—there is no visual guide.

With TV, we now edit with AVID (which is digital) but still record using analogue equipment. This again means that you need to download the grabs and vision that you need when you return to the office.

In my time in Rockhampton I worked mainly as a TV journo. The key difference in technology available in the regions is that my camera operator/editor didn't use AVID to edit. This meant we were cutting tape to tape. This system is a lot less reliable when you change your mind about the layout of a story and want to try adding bits in or take stuff out. It doesn't work. Generally we'd get around this by cutting what we could—and sending the out-takes to Brisbane (via satellite) where they would do the finishing touches.

Our biggest problem covering an area that stretched from Mackay to Bundaberg to the NT border was satellite points to uplink our stories. We had one in Rockhampton, and another in Longreach. But for towns like Emerald—which is a 3-hour drive from Rocky—it would mean driving there and back in a day and previewing your story in the car on the way home so it would make it to air. That would usually mean a 12-hour day to get a two-minute story to air!

For really big breaking stories—like Cyclone Larry or the tilt train derailment—the ABC does have a portable uplink which it brings in.

From my point of view digital technology has really made little difference to filing remotely. If we were on the road (for TV) we would take a portable edit pack—but you would still have to cut tape to tape. As I've mentioned sometimes, when our stories were filed back to Brisbane they could insert things using the AVID system, but really in the scheme of things this makes little difference.

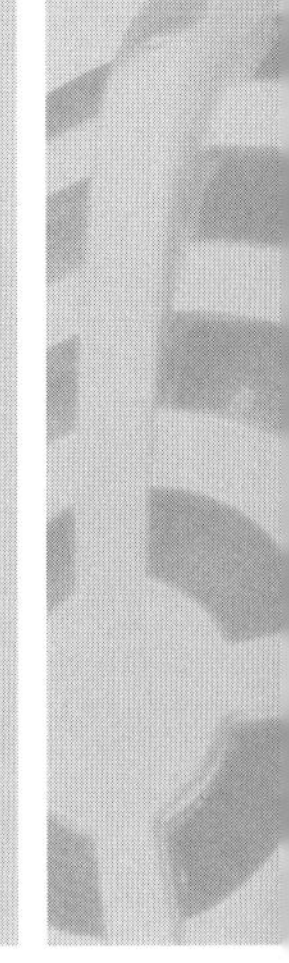

Backpack journalism

> I am a backpack journalist. I use a video camera as my reporter's notebook. I can put together multimedia stories that include video and audio clips, still photos grabbed from the video, as well as text. I can put together graphics information for Web designers. I can throw together a simple Web page. (Stevens 2002)

Jane Stevens describes herself as a backpack journalist and she is one member of a growing tribe of new, multiskilled reporters who are technologically equipped for a life of specialist reporting in the Information Age. At Columbia University's Centre for New Media, John Pavlik and Steven Feiner have created the first mobile workstation for the backpack journalist. The prototype Mobile Journalist Workstation (MJW) includes a 'wearable computer' with an audio and video display incorporated into a headset. Built around a computer bolted to a lightweight backpack frame, the MJW has a built-in camera, a Palm Pilot-style writing tablet, a GPS tracking system, and a wireless connection to the Internet. According to Pavlik and Feiner (1998), this kit provides the same newsgathering capabilities as a fully equipped newsroom, or a news crew in a small truck. More importantly, they suggest, the MJW makes possible 'new storytelling opportunities' and will 'transform print newsroom structure and management'. These are very large claims to be making about what is essentially a laptop hooked up to a cheap camera and mounted on an aluminium frame that can be easily carried on one's back. But it seems that there are compelling reasons—financial and practical—to believe that they may well be true, or at least in the process of becoming true.

BACKPACK JOURNALISM

The practice of a single journalist taking to the field equipped to report in all media forms: radio, television, print, online. Typically such a journalist would be equipped with a laptop computer, digital camcorder, and satellite phone: all items that can be carried in a backpack. Compare this with the baggage carried by a traditional television crew with lights, tripods, booms, reflector boards, monitors, and a picnic basket of pâté and red wine.

Computers and digital production suites are already common in many newsrooms around the world, whether print, broadcast, or online. In television, computerised digital editing suites have already cut the cost and turnaround time involved in preparing the traditional evening bulletin. They have the added advantage of facilitating the rapid upload of video stories to websites, allowing for multipurposing of the work of reporters. According to promotional material on the Apple website, workflows can be more easily managed and stories can be easily cut by editors with only a few hours training on their Final Cut Pro edit suites (Apple, n.d.).

The technology of backpack journalism is already in use in many television newsrooms. In March 2006 the ABC's *Four Corners* produced a remarkable story about the impacts of hardcore methamphetamine addiction on a group of people in Sydney. Reporter Matthew Carney (*The Ice Age*, ABC television, 20 March 2006) gained extraordinary access to the lives of his subjects, often spending days with them as they scored, got high, came down, and scored again. This access would be unthinkable with a full crew of camera and sound operators, producers, and assistants, but with Matthew shooting his own footage using a hand-held digital camera, the world of the addicts is exposed to a wide audience. In an example of how this new style of programming is eminently adaptable to the digital age, *The Ice Age* is available from the ABC's broadband Internet site for download. Unfortunately, the trend is not only fuelled by good news management or a desire to get reporters into once inaccessible places, but also by budget cuts. It is cheaper, and therefore more cost-effective, for organisations like the ABC to buy good-quality digital video cameras for its correspondents and send them into the field alone than to resource a full crew, particularly on overseas assignments: 'The new breed of ABC foreign correspondent ... [is] being asked to do more, for more people, and to do it faster and with more advanced technology' (Zuel 1999, p. 4).

At KTVX in Salt Lake City, Utah, the introduction of digital cameras and edit suites led to significant changes in job descriptions and work processing. According to the station's news editor, Chris George, 'anything that costs time is cut and everything that maintains or boosts speed is kept' (quoted in Apple, n.d.). The supporters of the trend to backpack journalism, like Jane Stevens, acknowledge that the technology speeds up organisational and structural changes in the newsroom. Stevens is confident that backpack journalists will be the frontline reporters of the future: 'So, in a few years, backpack journalists—or at least those who are familiar with backpack and converged journalism—will not only be the rule, they'll rule. And rock' (Stevens 2002).

The argument that news organisations must embrace the new technology and jump on the backpack bandwagon rests on the data that is suggesting that more and more consumers are accessing news and information via the Internet. In that environment, multimedia presentation is necessary to attract traffic and therefore the support of advertisers. On the other side of the equation, detractors argue that backpack journalists, because they have to do so much on their own, will end up as 'Jack of all trades, master of none' (Stone 2002). Martha Stone argues that it is not enough to provide the new lightweight equipment and send individual reporters out into the field. She says that the changes need to be strategically managed and supported in media organisations from the top down. The danger, according to Stone, is that the rush to provide a story that will satisfy the demands of very different media (print, broadcast, and online) will lead to 'mediocre journalism' because each aspect—writing, shooting the story, voicing the script, and editing the footage—is a specialist task. She argues that many backpack journalists are thrown into the field with little proper training in camera and sound operation. When backpack journalism was in its formative and experimental stages from the late 1990s to around 2003, it seemed an exciting, new, and cutting-edge technology. We are probably still in the early stages of the development of backpack journalists, and outside America there are very few journalism schools equipped to teach the new methods. In time we may see the new production techniques refined and embedded. The real question remains: can the skill acquisition and training regimes keep pace with technological development: and the commercial imperative for newsrooms to cut their budgets—to do more with less?

The video journalist revolution really began in television newsrooms—the light and easy-to-use cameras and laptop editing programs—but some supporters argue that the greatest impact will be felt in print newsrooms, which are most exposed to competition from web-based multimedia news presentation. Terry Heaton (2003) believes that the backpack journalist—he calls them independent video journalists—will turn broadcast news on its head, leading to 'reporter-driven' newsrooms that function more like a newspaper office. Heaton argues that the video journalist is a product of postmodernism and that it has significance 'far beyond the newsroom' because 'it opens the video news door to anybody'. This is what we might call a technologically determinist view: in Heaton's words, 'technology drives the train for video news'. This is an understandable but in our view mistaken position that Heaton explains on the basis of four conditions being met:

1 video streaming technology combined with available bandwidth so that the television and the computer can be run from the same source;
2 video-on-demand replaces the broadcast schedule (narrowcast replaces broadcast) as the way in which most people access television;
3 'point-of view' journalism becomes an accepted form of information programming;
4 Internet video news portal sites replace the network structure of news.

As Heaton suggests, at least the first three of these conditions are close to being realised and in the last couple of years the take-up of set-top boxes has certainly facilitated the technology of on-demand video journalism. Internet news portals have not replaced the networks to any large extent, though Internet-only news and commentary sites are gradually building brand recognition following the success of the gossip-oriented *Drudge Report*. The last big hurdle then might appear to be the non-technological condition outlined by Heaton: our willingness to accept opinion-driven point-of-view journalism. And, on the face of it, this is not such a big hurdle. There are many examples of the failing and falling credibility of the old-style (what the Americans call 'legacy') media.

CASE STUDY: NAURU STORY

A television reporter on assignment for SBS decides she wants to get close to a story about asylum-seekers detained on the tiny island of Nauru as part of the Howard Government's so-called 'Pacific Solution'. After several attempts to get into the detention centre legitimately without success, she decides to fly to Nauru on a tourist visa. The reporter was Bronwyn Adcock, and this is her story.

'At the *Dateline* office in Sydney we'd received a pretty reliable tip-off that there'd been a major incident in one of the camps on Nauru, and that the asylum seekers were now inside the camp on their own. We decided this would be a good opportunity to see if we could actually get inside the camp.

'At this point all travel to Nauru and access for journalists to the camps were prohibited.

'I flew into Nauru posing as a tourist. Once on the ground I started very discreetly asking around for information about the camp. A couple of people who knew the layout of the camps drew a few "mud-maps" for me, and one offered to show me the way to the fence. We went up through some pretty dense foliage to the edge of the camp, where I waited until one of the Iraqis inside wandered into earshot. After talking for a while they asked me inside and helped me crawl under the fence. I stayed in the camp for about five hours talking to the mainly Iraqi asylum seekers before I left by the same way.

'As the Nauru experience shows, being a VJ allows you to move around in a more unobtrusive way. You can film people and situations without being noticed by a lot of other people. This is handy for cases like Nauru, but it also helps, I've found, if you're filming people who aren't used to the media and TV cameras. If it's just one person and a small camera I think it can be less intimidating for whoever is being filmed, and they often relax pretty quickly and you get better material.'

Bronwyn would not have been able to complete this assignment if she had taken a full television crew with her. For a start, there was no way she would have been allowed into Nauru on a working visa; she had to pose as a tourist to gain access. Second, because she was alone and only carrying a small, easily concealed camera, she could be hidden inside the camp. Bronwyn's story is a good example of how enterprising young journalists can take advantage of the new technology to report on stories that would not otherwise be told.

Participatory journalism

> Any literate citizen in any corner of the globe who has a computer or mobile computing device with an internet connection can create his or her own interactive news media. (McKinnon 2004)

Digital media technologies have given form to a range of new information sources available on the Web. Any number of these can be grouped under the general heading of 'participatory journalism'. The Internet allows audiences to become more involved in stories, as commentators, sources, and even writers of the news in some cases (Bowman & Willis 2005). The term 'participatory journalism' may, however, be a bit misleading. The idea that anyone can now be a journalist is one of the enduring myths of the digital age. It is also to some extent a generational question. As a new generation of media consumers embraces a new form of 'news' that is 'interactive and subject to interrogation, engaging the emotions as much as the brain', older journalists 'shudder at this apostasy' (Hargreaves 2003, p. 220). This proposition leads Ian Hargreaves to challenge our definitions of a journalist. He asks if it is appropriate in the new media environment: 'Does it include news presenters, who may be actors rather than people trained in news? Does it include radio talk-show and tabloid TV hosts; does it include someone who sets up a weblog on the internet and shares information and opinion with anyone willing to pay attention?' (p. 227).

We know from his own account that radio talk-back host John Laws doesn't consider himself a journalist, at least when it's convenient to deny the tag (Hirst & Patching 2005, see p. 262). But Hargreaves' questioning does highlight the fault lines that are perhaps making a strictly professional definition of journalists redundant. Media theorist John Hartley (1999, p. 17) extends the idea of journalism a long way past the news media to include 'other factual and some fictional forms', even including marketing slogans written on the inside of beer bottle tops to entertain punters while they drink. In this postmodern context, Hartley argues, the modernist ideology of journalism and the professional practices associated with it 'simply cannot survive unscathed'(p. 27). The 'popular and postmodern' forms of journalism that John Hartley thinks are capable of democratising popular culture by broadening the participation of consumers can be found in cyberspace (weblogs, wikis, and personal sites) where the physical terrain of suburbia melts away into the 'mediasphere' (Hartely 1996, 1999). Dan Gillmor, the American founder of Grassroots Media Incorporated, also has a very positive view of the future media 'ecosystem'. He argues that 'if we're lucky', the electronic media will become a 'multidirectional conversation' using a 'distributional model' (Gillmor 2005, p. 11). These predictions may or may not come true, but one thing is clear—on the ground, young reporters and media-savvy individuals are taking up the challenge.

Freelance journalist Bec Fitzgibbon describes the casual participant in journalism as a 'common correspondent', which she says exists today because anyone can broadcast news online: 'we don't have to be journalists to make news these days.' According to Fitzgibbon, the camcorder has definitely democratised the media, as much as weblogs, livejournals, and indymedia (independent media) have. It seems today that do-it-yourself media are infused into every corner of the globe— the little people are making the big news:

> We've recently seen a reinvigoration of printed street zines in Tasmania (which I've written about for *The Mercury*); usually edited and published by late teens

> to mid-20 year olds, there's a distinct air of empowerment with new media for the youth, by the youth. We are all journalists today, definitely. I covet my freelancing magazine work. (Fitzgibbon 2006)

Another way of looking at the 'common correspondent' is the concept of the 'citizen journalist' providing 'user-generated' news that the mainstream media is beginning to take seriously (Bowman & Willis 2005, p. 7). If these new media forms are the work of amateurs, it makes any definition of journalism as a set of codified and structured practices almost meaningless. We have seen a proliferation of news-style sites established on the Web over the past decade, and blogs in particular have become very popular. Some blogs are written by journalists, but are they journalism? Blogs written by professionals in other fields often get quoted in news stories and in other blogs, but are they, strictly speaking, news sites? Then there are the estimated 8 million or so blog sites that are run by people who are definitely not journalists and who are not necessarily writing about professional issues in their area of expertise. Can we legitimately argue that these sites are 'news', or that their authors are working as journalists, even in an amateur capacity? Perhaps it's too early to give a definitive answer to these questions; we may have to reserve judgment for a bit longer. In our view, however, most blogs, wikis, and other amateur sites that contain 'newsworthy' material are not the product of journalism and most bloggers are not journalists. But there is no doubt that blogs are challenging traditional notions of journalism. Writing in the *Crikey* electronic newsletter, Guy Rundle (2006) noted that blogs can put the 'gatekeeper function' of traditional editors into some doubt.

We don't argue against blogs out of some sort of professional jealousy, or because we necessarily think that the current practices and social relations of journalism are all worth defending. But analytically, the distinction is an important one if we are to maintain any clarity about the terms of the debate. There is a certain kind of postmodern desire to describe anyone who posts information on a website for public viewing as a journalist, or potential journalist. We argue that this is an ahistoric and ultimately empty viewpoint.

New distribution systems, such as 'news on demand' and RSS feeds, are also impacting on journalism, but more particularly on traditional media outlets. It seems we are no longer tied to buying a morning newspaper, or sitting still in front of the television for half an hour in the evenings to get our daily news 'fix'. The development of podcasting and news alerts via mobile phones are changing the ways in which we consume news products.

Blog, blog, blog. Blog, blog!

> Weblogs are the mavericks of the online world. Two of their greatest strengths are their ability to filter and disseminate information to a widely dispersed audience, and their position outside the mainstream of mass media. Beholden to no one, weblogs point to, comment on, and spread information according to their own, quirky criteria. (Blood 2006)

Rebecca Blood is a blogger who has written a handbook on blogging, including a useful chapter on ethics where she makes the sound (in our view) distinction between commercial journalism and blogging: 'individual webloggers seem almost proud of their amateur status.' One of the key differences outlined on her site is that because of their commercial function (selling eyeballs to advertisers), journalists need a rigorous code of ethics. On the other hand, the unstructured and largely unmediated world of blogs is both a strength and a weakness (Blood 2006). The popularity of blogs means they are unlikely to go away quickly and we think it's good that Blood has published a handbook. There are other codes of ethics for bloggers that can be found online. The ones we checked all make this important distinction between blogs and journalism, which is not to deny that blogs are, as Blood says, important sources of news and information for many people.

Blogging is the new black! Just kidding—black is still the new black, but blogging is becoming trendy. We want to know: Who's got the time? Apparently at least one Sydney taxi driver who in April 2005 had one of his blogs published in a nationally circulating current affairs magazine called *Investigate*. Once the blog was published as a column in a magazine, does it make the cabby a journalist as well?

The wild, uncontrolled, and apparently democratic nature of the blogosphere has led some, like eminent American media theorist Jay Rosen (2005, p. 27), to hail blogs as the latest expression of a free press. He argues that blogging turns at least part of the media's power over to those who 'want to join the experiment and become, in some sense or another, part of the press'. Today blogs are more than just counterpoint news sites. They can be totally personal, like a diary, or places to express crazy ideas that some people will find amusing enough to return to. There is a certain degree of digital myth-making around the blogging phenomenon, perhaps created by the real challenge that blogs represent to journalism. As Shayne Bowman and Chris Willis (2005, p. 6) argue, the 'hegemony as gatekeeper' role of journalists is now threatened by new technologies and by audiences who are 'getting together' to set the news agenda. But we think it is easy, among all the hype, to overstate the case somewhat.

Writing your own news, however, is not so mundane as to escape the notice of Rupert Murdoch, himself the ultimate media baron. Murdoch was very quick to recognise the potential 'value-add' that bloggers and opinion-diarists could make to the growing online news and information market and therefore to advertising revenue. After brainstorming News Corporation's Internet strategy in February 2005 with his chief planners and executives (Schulze 2005), Murdoch went public in a well-publicised speech in April of the same year in which he admitted that News Corp had previously not known how to play online. His headline concern, in a speech to the American Society of Newspaper Editors, was to stop the 'leaching of significant advertising revenue' away from newspapers and into online classifieds and other advertising. Murdoch speculated that if Bill Gates was only half right in his estimate that online advertising would be worth \$US30 billion by 2010, 'we must be in a position to capture our fair share'. The way forward for News Corporation and the newspaper editors of America, Mr Murdoch told them, lay in 'providing virtual communities for our readers to be linked to other sources of information, other opinions, other like-minded readers' (Elliott 2005).

Whatever he may think of blogging, Rupert Murdoch claims to know a lot about the media industry and he thinks that linking his newspaper sites to weblogs will be good for business. He might be right, but according to some estimates there are around 8.5 million blog sites in cyberspace. Not even a media baron like Rupert could expect to own all of them. Blogs have sprung up from virtually nowhere in less than ten years to become the next big thing, at least until the next craze hits the Internet. Blogs have become important in the daily news-cycle for some mainstream media and they're certainly popular with readers. They create an open environment of information-sharing and the use of extensive hypertext links make them a rich source of information for those with the time and inclination to chase down alternative viewpoints. However, we agree with Rebecca MacKinnon when she writes that there are serious implications for what she calls an 'internet-driven de-professionalisation of news and information' that creates serious questions 'to many who study the relationship between media and democratic government' (MacKinnon 2004, p. 13).

Digital cameras and tourists create a big news story

> 'We are at the doorstep of a radically new kind of journalism, where in a sense every human being is becoming an assistant to a journalist just by virtue of having a [mobile] phone or other portable equipment,' said Paul Levinson, a media studies professor at Fordham University in New York. (*Washington Post* 2005)

This comment was made in the first days after the London bombings of July 2005. It was prompted by the fact that many of the initial images of the attack were SMSed to media outlets by people caught up in the attacks. Within six hours of the blasts the BBC had received over 1000 photos, twenty pieces of amateur video, 4000 text messages, and 20 000 emails from concerned citizens. The main evening news bulletin on the following day was a package of edited video sent in by BBC viewers (Sambrook 2005). The major news organisations took advantage of the consumer technology by soliciting images and video for publication on their news websites. But the question is, can these amateur 'assistants' to journalists really be counted among the newsgathers, or even as 'accidental journalists'?

Only two weeks after the bombings, the problems of relying on public eyewitness accounts as hard news were thrown starkly into relief when a 27-year-old Brazilian electrician, Jean Charles de Mendez, was shot execution-style by plainclothes London police who suspected him of being a potential suicide bomber. At the time of the shooting the news media reported that he was a terror suspect. The headline in the *Weekend Australian* was typical of most: 'Five police bullets end it all for train bomber who tried again' (Wilson 2005). The media accepted as fact the inference that Mr de Mendez was a potential suicide bomber, a view that was confirmed by eyewitnesses to the shooting, who had mistakenly described the man as a suicide bomber: 'A witness said the man had a bomb strapped to his body. "He had a bomb belt with wires coming out," Anthony Larkin told the BBC' (Wilson 2005).

Another eyewitness told the BBC that the man was 'Asian' and that he'd seen the shooting: 'One of the police officers was holding a black automatic pistol in his left hand. They held it down to him and unloaded five shots into him. I saw it. He's dead. Five shots, seriously he's dead' (quoted in Wilson 2005).

It was actually, the police admitted almost a week later, eight bullets and a terrible mistake. Mr de Mendez was not a terrorist; he was simply on his way to work. However, the BBC continues to solicit viewer input into its news and Richard Sambrook admits it is becoming part of the broadcaster's daily newsgathering work. He adds that the BBC believes it has a public service role to support members of the public to 'engage with the world' by becoming amateur reporters using the new digital technologies (2005, p. 14). Sambrook was the director of the BBC's global news resources when he made these comments, but there is a worrying edge to his enthusiasm. A massive restructuring of the BBC has cut around 3000 jobs and Sambrook argues that this money will be invested in digital technology. He predicts that the traditional model of 'channels and schedules' may well disappear over the next five years as the BBC prepares itself for the 'fully digital, [media] on-demand age'. This might sound like a fantastic adaptation to digital convergence, but as this example shows, with less well trained and alert staff in the BBC's newsrooms, more 'false positive' reports, like the terror 'suspect' who wasn't, will slip through. We question whether this is actually a good thing; Mr de Mendez is too dead to ask the question himself.

What of the future?

In 1967, the *New Zealand Herald* produced a 'manual of journalism' that opened with a chapter called 'The vocation of journalism'. Like many previous descriptions and definitions, the belief that journalism was a vocation relies on the idea that good journalists are 'born', not produced by this or that undergraduate program (Chappell 1967). How different it is today when it seems that anyone with a mobile phone or digital camera can be a reporter.

On the one hand we have 'citizen journalists': amateurs with video cameras who can supply material to the networks that privilege eyewitness accounts of important events. On the other we have what has become known as the 'backpack journalist': the news reporter who can work in different media and file print, broadcast, and online versions of their story direct from the field. From our survey we can draw the conclusion that the shape and boundaries of the reportorial community are changing. But it is not possible to say with any certainty if this is unequivocally a good or bad trend.

While for most, the Internet is just another useful tool, for an unfortunate few it can take over their real self and lead to a disturbing case of social dysfunction. A story in *Time* magazine (Reaves 2005), which was picked up by the tabloid current affairs programs in Australia, related the sad case of several young women who define their happiness by unhealthy weight loss. The *Time* article exposed a number of pro-anorexia websites and chat groups, some existing on the Yahoo! site, that promoted anorexia and bulimia through photographs and helpful hints on how to hide the disease from anxious parents. The *Time* editors thoughtfully provided a number of links to these sites in their online version of the piece, but by the time we went to check them out for ourselves, they had been taken down. Yahoo! closed the chat groups and in a media statement said it had done so because they had breached the company's policies of not using such groups to promote self-harm, or harmful behaviours.

We cannot reverse the trends of history, nor would we necessarily want to. But we can issue a note of caution about the mythical hype surrounding new digital technologies. The argument that podcasting, weblogs, and other forms of interactive information-sharing on the Internet will create a new and more democratic public discourse is seductive, but not all that solid. Certainly digital technology has the potential to reinvigorate democratic debate and certainly it challenges both the old media and our conception of what journalism is. At the same time, breaking down the practice journalism so that it is 'accessible' to everyone, anywhere, anytime, risks collapsing important theoretical and practical distinctions that still have a purpose. We are in favour of radically reforming journalism in a number of ways—increasing the rank-and-file control over newsrooms and exposing the contradiction between profits and public service are two—but we are not in favour of dissolving 'journalism' as a particular category of information management that is bounded by certain rules and conventions. In our view, to do so would be to destroy the possibility of a viable independent mass media capable of reaching vast numbers of people and mobilising them into action around their common interests. In the final section of the book we take up some arguments about the world of narrowcasting that seems about to take over from the age of broadcasting. We will also tackle, for a final time, some of the dangerous myths that surround emerging digital media technologies.

WHAT BRONWYN RECKONS: VIDEO JOURNALISTS

Video journalism is the backbone of what we do on *Dateline* (SBS television). Pretty much without exception, all stories we run are shot by video journalists. On the editorial front, I think we have an approach of selecting stories that are not being told by the mainstream media, or if they are already being told we try and look at them in a different way. We aim to provide a point of difference, which fits in neatly I think with the different 'look' you get from video journalism. Without a doubt *Dateline* pioneered the technique in Australia—and we are still the main users of this technique.

Working as a solo operator also gives you heaps of flexibility. You can change your plans quickly and move quickly if you feel the story is changing and something needs to be pursued.

It also lends itself to a certain 'style' that I think makes good TV and is unique—a very immediate, fly-on-the-wall telling of a story that brings the viewer right into the story. We often film things as they are unravelling, in almost video diary-type style, which allows the viewer to see events in a very raw, unscripted way.

I see video journalism as something that sits alongside more traditional video storygathering techniques. It is not something that would ever replace it. Traditional techniques also have their advantages over video journalism.

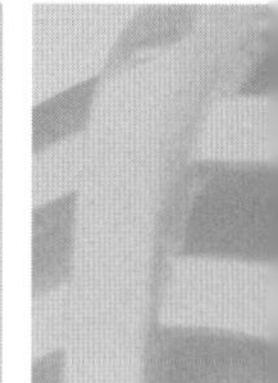

THE END OF THE NETWORK ANCHOR

In September 2004, as the US presidential election gained momentum towards the November polling day, the CBS network stunned Americans with a report claiming that President Bush had lied about his military service record. The report, on the flagship *60 Minutes* program, alleged that George W. Bush had skipped months of training in the Texas Air National Guard in the 1970s and was punished for failure to take a scheduled medical exam (Associated Press 2004). Within a week the CBS story was shown to be false and the network was back-pedalling in the face of mounting criticism for not checking its documents more thoroughly. The network had been hoaxed by its sources using forged documents. Most embarrassing for CBS was the fact that its mistakes were uncovered and denounced by Internet bloggers, not by its competitors among the networks. CBS put the documents backing its claims on the *60 Minutes* website, but within hours people were raising questions about their authenticity.

CBS was badly exposed by its failure to check the documents it received, and the network's enemies were quick to pounce. The network anchor, Dan Rather, who had for many years been the star news anchor and who had fronted the *60 Minutes* story, bore the brunt of the attacks. The comments of law professor and blogger Glenn Harlan Reynolds, published in the *Australian* newspaper, are typical of the heat that Dan Rather attracted:

> CBS, like most broadcast networks in the US—and, for some reason, just about everywhere else—is staffed by people who lean Left and who don't like Bush … Worse yet, they tend to talk mostly with people who share their beliefs. The result is an insular culture, rife with the prejudices of the New Class, which believes all sorts of absurdities and peddles them to the public in the sometimes honest, if often unfounded, belief that they are true. (Reynolds 2004)

We will take up the politics of this commentary in a later chapter, but the simple point (not well expressed here amid the rhetorical flourishes) is that CBS made a mistake and was caught out because of its rush to take advantage of the new technology. As Reynolds points out, it was the power of 'open source' journalism that brought the network undone. By posting the documents on its website, 60 Minutes was inviting commentary and leaving itself exposed. It didn't take long for several people to work out that they had been produced using a computer and a laser printer, 'rather than a typewriter and Liquid Paper' (Reynolds 2004) as they would have been if they were genuine products of the 1970s.

Questions

1 Is television news losing its audience appeal and are the days of the charismatic network anchor over?
2 Has the Internet made 'hoax' stories more prevalent and easier to expose?

CASE STUDY: CRIKEY.COM

In 2005, *Crikey.com*, which describes itself as a daily email with a supporting website that 'goes where other media won't go', was sold by its founder, Stephen Mayne, for $1 million. From humble beginnings in the spare bedroom of Mayne's house in suburban Melbourne in 2000, *Crikey*—an expressive colloquial euphemism for 'Christ'—had become in five years a hot new property. Its new owners, Private Media Partners, included former *SMH* editor Eric Beecher and former book publisher Di Gribble, both experienced media hands.

Crikey grew out of the website <jeffed.com> developed by Mayne and his mate Hugo Kelly during the 1999 state election in Victoria. Mayne was a former spin doctor for Jeff Kennett, Liberal Party premier of Victoria 1992–99. Before that he worked for News Ltd and Fairfax, at the latter on the *Australian Financial Review*.

While running *Crikey*, Steve Mayne also assumed the self-described role of 'shareholder activist'. His appearances—asking questions, standing for election as a director—at the AGM of Australian corporations such as News Ltd and AMP gave profile to his fledgling business. Mayne claimed that his interrogation of News Corp chair Rupert Murdoch over corporate governance issue at the News Ltd AGM in Adelaide—reported fully on *Crikey*—was responsible for Murdoch's decision to incorporate in Delaware in the United States.

But what business was Mayne in? *Crikey* describes its role and function this way:

> *Crikey*'s aim is very simple: to bring its readers the inside word on what's really going on in politics, government, media, business, the arts, sport and other aspects of public life in Australia. Crikey sees its role as part of the so-called 'fourth estate' that acts as a vital check and balance on the activities of government, the political system and the judiciary. (Crikey.com 2004)

In a puff piece celebrating *Crikey*'s first 1000 days, in October 2002, Sally Jackson wrote in the *Australian*:

> Mayne describes *Crikey* as a combination of journalism and activism, with an element of levity and gossip, which stays 'reasonably specific' to the worlds

> of business, politics, and media. 'We're looking at exposing society's power structures, to tackle those in power and put some sunlight on them.'
>
> But still nobody seems to know how to pigeonhole it. *Crikey* has been variously described as a rebel website, a watchdog website, and an activist website, and Mayne as a shareholder activist, a dissident journalist and, courtesy of 2UE radio presenter Steve Price, 'a turd'. (Jackson 2002).

However, it is not difficult to pigeonhole *Crikey*. It is a common new media phenomenon—part breaking news, part blog. It was *Crikey* that broke the story of Gareth Evans and Cheryl Kernot having an affair, after Laurie Oakes pulled his punches in the *Bulletin*, saying Kernot's newly published autobiography failed to acknowledge the biggest secret of her political life. Stephen Mayne justified *Crikey* naming names, saying: '*Crikey* only regarded it as an unsubstantiated rumour but [Laurie Oakes] has come out and effectively said, "[Gareth Evans] and [Cheryl Kernot] had an affair, which was pivotal to her defection and subsequent political failure"' (quoted in Walker 2002).

Crikey, however, does not represent an expansion of the reportorial community. Mayne, and Beecher also, are experienced print media journalists, as are many of their contributors. What *Crikey* represents is an expansion of the journalistic form, not the reportorial community. It is a form of narrowcasting. With less than 10 000 subscribers, and a larger audience of more casual readers, it will never compete with the *Australian* for circulation; but it will compete with the *Australian* and other dailies for influence.

Under Beecher's leadership, which promised a more 'professional' presentation, Mayne has continued to write for the site, while co-founder Hugo Kelly was sacked. Protocols governing corrections and rights of reply have been formalised. In Mayne's hands the site nearly went out of business when sued for defamation. Mayne's verdict on the new regime? 'The professional version of *Crikey* is far better than anything we produced out of the spare bedroom and all the subscriber numbers and reader surveys bear that out' (Mayne 2006).

Mayne has, of course, fallen for the fallacy that trips up all commercial advocates of a fourth estate model of the media: never mind the quality of the journalism; look at the circulation.

KEY POINTS

In this chapter you have been faced with the question: what constitutes the 'reportorial community' in an age of media convergence? In particular, we have examined:

- how what we are calling the 'reportorial community' is changing because of the impact of new technologies and new commercial methods in the mass media;

- the way contemporary journalism education defines and positions journalism;
- traditional, that is, 20th-century newsroom organisational structures;
- the emergence of backpack journalism, blogging, and citizen reporting, as forms of new media reportage.

12

THE TECHNO-LEGAL TIME-GAP: CAN THE LAW KEEP UP WITH THE DIGITAL REVOLUTION?

OBJECTIVES

In chapter 8 we discussed regulation, law, and ethical issues in the age of broadcasting. We noted that the emergence of digital media and convergence with communications infrastructure create new legal and ethical dilemmas and force change in the legal and regulatory environment. In this chapter we discuss some new and emerging legal and ethical fault lines in the age of narrowcasting. In particular, we examine:

- the way in which the wired world intrudes into all aspects of life—from the boardroom to the bedroom;
- the delay between innovation and the regulation of new technologies;
- the proposed changes to the regulation of digital broadcast technologies, and the deregulation of media ownership and control rules outlined by the Australian government in 2006;
- the debates about the legality and ethics of data-mining, hacking, and digital downloads.

KEYWORDS
ethico-legal paradox
techno-legal time-gap

Broadcast to narrowcast: An ethico-legal minefield

> A row is brewing over a new website that can publish details of celebrity sightings in [New York] within minutes—complete with a map pinpointing exactly where the star was spotted. (Williams 2006, p. 4)

A popular celebrity gossip website, Gawker.com, used the Google map of New York to trace the whereabouts of VIPs following up tips from celebrity-spotters. A harmless bit of fun? A new working tool for the paparazzi? Not so according to 'those who speak for the stars'; it amounts to an invasion of privacy. This is an interesting complaint because in New York, as in most jurisdictions, the concept of 'privacy' in 'public' places is not something that exists in law. However, we might argue that there's an ethical right to privacy, even for famous people whose whole existence and commercial value (celebrity-commodity) is based on their high recognition factor and popularity (Hirst & Patching 2005, pp. 174–6). This is a good example of an ethico-legal paradox in the regulation of new media, particularly the Internet. Such a paradox arises when the black-letter law is in conflict with, or 'greyed-out' by an ethical consideration (pp. 197–8). This is the dialectic that operates on the ethico-legal continuum: at one end is the finality of the law, while at the other is the personal and ideological dilemma that generates ethical fault lines of uncertainty within the supposed certainty of legal reasoning. The ethico-legal paradox is important in relation to the new digital media technologies because, for the first time, they allow things like the cyber-stalking example above to take place. Without the instant messaging capability of mobile phones, picture-SMS, and the online maps available from Google, Gawker.com would not be able to make its surveillance information available so quickly (within minutes according to the article) and interested gawkers would not have any way of connecting with the information without access to an Internet connection. This is just one example of the ethico-legal minefield exposed by emerging digital technologies.

ETHICO-LEGAL PARADOX
The confusion that arises when an action is morally right, but legally wrong or vice versa.

Media regulation in Australia: One step forward or a giant leap backwards?

> For the Government, the impact of digital technologies means the current regulatory settings, which are largely designed for an analogue world, risk becoming outdated … [I]f the Government doesn't act, then there is a genuine

> risk that Australia will become a dinosaur of the analogue age. (Coonan 2006 [Media Release, 14 March])

In chapter 8 we outlined the regulatory regimes that operated in Australia during the age of broadcasting. We pointed out that the federal government had been wanting to change aspects of the legal and regulatory system for some time. Finally in March 2006, just as we were finishing this book, the Communications Minister, Helen Coonan, issued a long-anticipated blueprint for a new regime of regulation that would operate in the expanding narrowcast environment. We have not had an opportunity to see exactly how this will be played out as the time-frame for most of the significant changes is over the years 2007 to 2012. No doubt by the time you're reading this there will be more certainty and indeed some changes may have already taken place. In the following section we intend only to outline the arguments that were raised in the first weeks after the digital media policy paper was issued in order to highlight possible trends and digital dilemmas that could be significant as the new regulations are rolled out over the next couple of years.

Background scan: Media reform—a long time coming

If, like us, you take an active interest in media events, the March 2006 reforms to cross-media ownership rules and the updating of the *Digital Action Plan* were long anticipated. Analysts, academics, consumer groups, and business leaders had been waiting almost ten years for the Howard government to make its move. Australian governments of all persuasions take a special interest in media law and regulation because they know that the individuals and corporations who dominate the national market are not to be treated lightly.

It is worth reviewing what some experts were saying about the need for and possible scope of media regulatory reform when the digital economy was much younger and less established than it is today. Legal scholar Jock Given (1998, p. 31) wrote that the argument about the transition to digital platforms for television has been 'public and violent', and it has been going on for more than twenty years.

In 1994 a group of academics at the Queensland University of Technology wrote a report (Hearn et al. 1994) outlining some possible future scenarios for the application of convergent media technologies within the 'communication infrastructure' as it stood then and how it might change and impact on the 'consumer economy'. The use of the term 'consumer economy' situates this report within the mythical spectrum, which takes existing economic forms as normative. For example, the authors have an uncritical view of the advertising industry; they argue that it 'informs consumers' and helps 'shape the evolution of new products', implying that it is a two-way model of communication. They also write that the mass media are the 'lifeblood of the consumer economy' because of their role in propping up 'entertainment and cultural industries'. Marketing and advertising, far from being an expense borne by consumers and hidden in the price of commodities, are 'integral to our current ways of communicating' (Hearn et al. 1994, p. 1). The mythic nature of the report is confirmed in a section that outlines the shifting ground of consumer capitalism:

- New information commodities make consumption 'less constrained by time and space'.
- New commodity forms allow consumers to 'exercise control' over the act of consumption.
- Consumption time is 'rationalised' within the domestic sphere and time becomes available for 'new forms of production'.
- Miniaturisation of electronic commodities creates 'new physical space'.
- Digital convergence creates 'compound commodities', opening up 'conceptual and physical spaces' for the creation of new consumer needs.
- Change is continuous and so is the 'exchange' of commodities, such as in subscription TV services where payments are made throughout the life of the contract, rather than in a one-off purchase.
- Styles change faster, creating 'aesthetic obsolescence', which in turn accelerates the rate of consumption and leads to 'greater plurality and diversity of commodities'. (pp. 5–6)

These ideas echo in a fairly precise way the core themes in digital mythology as outlined by Vincent Mosco and discussed in chapter 10. Despite this criticism, the report is a valuable historic artefact and an examination of its major concerns and recommendations gives an interesting window on the early development of policy research in the emerging digital world.

The starting point for the analysis in *The Information Superhighway and Consumers* is the taken-for-grantedness of the global capitalist society, which is ideologically normalised by the use of the term 'consumer capitalism' (p. 2). This system is based on an 'alliance' between producers and policy-makers (not on a conflict between workers and capital) and its major achievement has been 'sustained growth and stability'. On a global scale the economy is characterised by an emerging core of 'flexible economies' based on significant developments in the industrial application of information and communication technologies. A key question for Australia in this scenario is: How and when the necessary infrastructure will be built and who will pay for it? (p. 3).

When it comes to laying out a program of regulatory reform, the authors highlight four key issues:

- The public interest must be served in the 'efficient allocation' of spectrum and infrastructure because it is a 'national resource'.
- Social equity must be a concern to ensure access for all and a diversity of information.
- Communities, 'values', and 'aspirations' must be preserved. This raises the question of how regulators will address 'tolerance, stereotyping, diversity and social cohesion' in relation to targeted marketing strategies.
- The national interest is best served by the roll-out of a 'digital convergence infrastructure' and this should be stimulated by government policy. However, the authors note that establishing security and stability in the digital environment may be 'more problematic' than simply building the infrastructure. (pp. 8–9)

The report is based on discussions at a focus group-style forum in Sydney, which unfortunately does not provide much in the way of useful information. In the final section the authors return to the social and policy issues identified by participants in the forum in order to develop some conclusions. Seven key issues are identified as areas for policy work:

- problems arising from the commodification of identity;
- the social impact of 'antisocial fantasy products' such as violent games and online pornography;
- changes in the 'social fabric';
- shifting skill requirements in the information economy;
- shifts in 'time and psychological resources';
- problems arising from invasions of privacy and increased surveillance;
- the need to encourage the development of new consumer products and services. (p. 39)

The policy recommendations are not strong. For example, in relation to harmful online products the report suggests 'consideration of regulation, censorship, and taxation' as ways of controlling their distribution. The authors warn that increased 'fragmentation' is a corollary of increasingly targeted marketing (we discuss this in the final chapters). They suggest this fragmentation could lead to disruptive 'subculture rivalry' and 'social problems' as the 'national identity', which is encouraged by 'traditional media', is eroded or swamped by 'globalisation pressures' (p. 40). In relation to the changing nature of work and employment relations, the report says only that 'retraining and redeployment cost' must be factored into the pricing of infrastructure. There is a warning that new media could have a harmful impact on the learning abilities of children. On the other hand it could also lead to their 'more active and interactive engagement' with the media. Privacy must be protected and 'important protocols and etiquette' discussed before the new media infrastructure is opened up. Finally, there is a recommendation that more support be given to the creative industries through 'regulation', 'grants', and support for 'productive media products' in education and entertainment (p. 41). The report presents no other findings or recommendations, but it does contain one paragraph that highlights the complexity and the timelessness of the debate about media regulation:

> The question of which interests will ultimately be most powerful in operating the network is a fundamental issue yet to be fully realised. The current environment is wide open for exploitation and the role of the government or independent authorities will remain crucial. (p. 43)

As we have argued from the beginning, there is no vacuum when it comes to questions of economic power and control in relation to the operation of media resources. Despite the early dreams of a new, free (in both senses of the word), and democratic space being opened up by digital media technologies and the Internet, we have seen that the systemic tendency towards oligopoly and cartelisation of communication capital continues to operate. In some instances new monopolies have formed, such as Apple and Microsoft in computing, and Google and Yahoo in search engines. In other cases the 'old' media giants have formed alliances with the dot.com newcomers to tighten their grip through both vertical and horizontal integration in nearly all markets for information and entertainment goods and services. In this climate and under this pressure, how can a government react against these dominant and powerful interests, even if it wanted to?

A more recent and cogent view is provided by Trevor Barr in *newmedia.com.au* (2000). Barr is aware of the political economy arguments and devotes a chapter to 'Australia's media ruling class', though it ends rather optimistically with a question: 'With so many new choices along the superhighway, why worry about the old media conglomerates?' In 2000 the 'old' media moguls (the Packer and Murdoch families and the Fairfax group) were still firmly in control and 'entrenched in terms of their market share of audiences' (Barr 2000, p. 18). Nothing much has changed in the past decade.

As we've already noted, Barr is among the Internet true-believers and there is a technological determinist aspect to his position. He takes up the 'information society' argument and suggests there are several 'major forces' at work shaping: 'a new convergent communications era': globalisation; a re-evaluation of the role of the nation-state; a new ideological push for greater privatisation of government services; and the drive for deregulation (p. 21). Since the 1980s it has been the global nature of the market for telecommunications goods and service, linked to the convergence of digital media and the telephone infrastructure, that created the greatest pressures for reform and what Barr calls an international 'tide of deregulation' (p. 81). The Hawke government began the process in 1988 by restructuring the national phone and satellite carrier services, thus allowing Optus to enter the domestic mobile phone market. The *Telecommunications Act 1991* ended the Telstra-Optus duopoly and by 1999 there were thirty-one companies competing for the growing business of mobile phone connection (pp. 85–6). These changes were not the result of a clear policy setting, but rather the 'uneasy outcome' of 'serious conflicts' and government attempts to deal with competing 'vested interests' (p. 86). At the time, one of the biggest decisions was the partial privatisation of Telstra and a commitment to privatise the company fully in the near future. As Barr notes (p. 88), this created an unresolvable tension between the need to maintain profitability and the promise that deregulation would bring lower prices and other benefits to consumers. For the past decade this problem has haunted the Howard government and Telstra's share price continues to languish while its maverick American executives (aptly nicknamed the 'three amigos' for their allegiance to CEO Sol Trujillo) argue for even less regulation by government and threaten to cut dividends to shareholders because of over-regulation (Boyd 2006b). Telstra has become an important player in the media reform game because of its 50 per cent ownership of the Foxtel Pay TV service and because it is also looking to expand its capacity to deliver television-style services via its broadband network. On the same day that the government released the digital media discussion paper, Telstra's Sol Trujillo announced the company was in talks with Microsoft about using its software to stream content. A key aspect of any such deal would be to drive Internet traffic to Telstra's 'Sensis' advertising site, an important link in Telstra's business plan (Boyd 2006c). Telstra's terrestrial broadband network is an obvious delivery 'pipe' for new media.

Barr concludes that throughout the 1990s economic policy took precedence over social concerns in terms of deregulation of the telecommunication market. We can see the same forces at play in the plans to deregulate the mass media in the digital market, as the government's own discussion paper notes: 'it will become increasingly difficult to regulate the emergence of new players and new services' (DCITA 2006, p. 3). The tensions between the social needs of consumers and the commercial needs of the major industry players will not be easily reconciled. In the global world economy the nation-state has a difficult task in reconciling the divergent interests of consumer-citizens and its own home-grown capitalists, and this is further complicated by the need to remain part of the world system of international competition. This creates what Mike Wayne calls 'one of the most important social fault-lines in determining media and cultural policy' (2003, p. 101). This fault line remains as a result of the reform proposals put forward in March 2006.

Key changes proposed for media regulation

There are a number of key changes proposed in the government's discussion paper, and we've outlined them here for easy reference.

The moratorium on the allocation of new free-to-air (FTA) commercial licences expires on 31 December 2006. From 1 January 2007, the Australian Communications and Media Authority will be able to allocate new licences. New licences for FTA services delivered over wireless, satellite, and cable will also become available from 1 January 2007 (DCITA 2006, p. 4). This is difficult to reconcile with another announcement, that no new licences will be issued when the moratorium is lifted, nor in all likelihood until the end of the simulcast period in 2010–12. In fact the government will introduce legislation (no timeline is specified) to remove the power to grant new FTA licences from ACMA to 'the Government' (p. 7), thus opening the door for even more political interference in licence allocation. The government sees these changes as enabling new players to enter the market to develop 'television-like services', but the DCITA paper recognises significant cost-barriers to the entry of new providers because the reception infrastructure is not yet in place (p. 24).

Restrictions on datacasting transmitters will be lifted from 1 January 2007, allowing an expanded range of services such as subscription and narrowcasting television, including 'mobile television receivers' (phones). These new services will have access to the spectrum channels previously reserved for datacasting (p. 5). Suggested services on the newly allocated digital spectrum include 'religious, ethnic or home shopping channels or subscription TV' (p. 21). Mobile carriers will be limited to 'snack content', such as headlines, sport results, and music videos (p. 22). Columnist Peter Ruehl (2006) wrote that the idea of 'snack' television must be a concept devised by 'some media doof' to describe content-free programming by comparing it to the leftovers from 'last night's dinner'.

Two digital channels will be allocated 'as soon as practicable' in 2007 for subscription or 'niche "narrowcasting" services'. These services will not be allowed to replicate existing FTA content. Existing FTA providers can still use their allocated digital spectrum to provide complementary services, but they will not be allowed to control a datacasting transmission licence (p. 8). The changes mean that up to thirty new digital channels may eventually be available, but not for some time, though a limit of five is more likely (Norington 2006).

Decision-making power in relation to wireless, satellite, and broadband services will be transferred from ACMA to the government. There will be a 'public interest' requirement for these services, but no further detail has been provided on how the government might allocate the licences (DCITA 2006, p. 8).

Commercial FTA services using the Broadcasting Services Band of the spectrum (BSB), or operating at frequencies outside this spectrum, will be exempt from the media ownership and control provisions of the *Broadcasting Services Act 1992*. Newspapers are also exempted from these provisions (p. 9).

The anti-siphoning provisions (relating to coverage of major sporting events) of the *Broadcasting Services Act 1992* will be amended so that an FTA broadcaster must have acquired the rights, or the event must be delisted, before the rights become available to subscription TV providers. The government is proposing a 'use it or lose it' regime so that if an FTA broadcaster does not cover an event it is removed from the anti-siphoning list (p. 32).

When the simulcast period ends, FTA broadcasters will be allowed to use the digital spectrum for multi-channelling, subject to appropriate Australian content and other rules (pp. 28–9).

Quotas on the FTA broadcasters to program 1040 hours per year in high-definition TV (HDTV) will be lifted at the end of the simulcast period (pp. 31–2).

The most important and politically sensitive changes are concerned with media ownership and control. Rules limiting foreign ownership of broadcasting assets under the *Broadcasting Services Act 1992* are to be removed. At the same time, rules limiting foreign ownership of newspapers under the *Foreign Acquisitions and Takeovers Act 1975* will also be removed. The media will retain its designation as a 'sensitive sector' under the government's *Foreign Investment Policy* and foreign acquisitions will be subject to approval by the Treasurer (pp. 11–12). These changes are underpinned by what has become known as the 'voices rule'—in a metropolitan market there must be a minimum of five different media owners and in regional markets a minimum of four. Under the old rules there were twelve groups in Sydney, ten in Melbourne, nine in Perth, eight in Brisbane, and seven in Adelaide. The new rules would permit a single entity to own a newspaper, radio station, and television service in any one market, but not have an audience reach greater than 75 per cent of the nation.

There are some minor provisions designed to retain competition in smaller markets and provision for ACMA to allocate new radio licences in regional areas if required (p. 12). The government regards the current laws as unworkable in the digital environment and argues that they have limited the potential for growth and economies of scale. Their removal is expected to bring 'investment and innovation' to the Australian media market

(p. 38). However, Minister Coonan indicated that the cross-media and foreign ownership changes could be delayed if the major players do not accept her digital media agenda.

Any proposed merger of media assets under the new rules would remain subject to the *Trade Practices Act 1974*, and the Australian Competition and Consumer Commission (ACCC) will continue to assess mergers, takeovers, and other arrangements. According to some analysts, these changes put the ACCC in the 'front line' of attempts to retain diversity in an 'already concentrated' market (Fels & Brenchely 2006). ACCC chairman Graeme Samuel said that the Commission would re-examine how it defined markets and would look at mergers from the point of view of content and control of the distribution networks. Mr Samuels gave the example of classified advertising markets as one area the ACCC might look at when considering any proposal to merge media companies (Crowe 2006c).

The ACMA may get enhanced powers to respond to events and would be required to monitor licence conditions under the *Broadcasting Services Act 1992* (DCITA 2006, p. 13). The government argues that there is 'no compelling reason' for the restriction on foreign ownership to remain (p. 38).

Responses to the initial reform agenda

> Perhaps one of the most striking things about the overall package is that we see a lot of rhetoric in the ownership rules about new possibilities opening up, new investors coming into the industry, being able to do new kinds of things and, yet, when we turn over the page and get to the things about digital TV, we find the government still wanting to micro-manage a highly uncertain technology. (Jock Given, *7.30 Report* 14 March [ABC TV], 2006)

Jock Given is a law lecturer at the University of Melbourne and a former director of the Communication Law Centre. As well as appearing on the *7:30 Report*, he wrote an opinion piece for the *Sydney Morning Herald* in which he concluded that Australia would remain in the analogue dinosaur age as a result of the Coonan reform package. In particular, he argued that there would be a lessening of diversity, particularly on occasions when proprietors are exercising a 'direct interest'. He was also critical of the decision to remove the ACMA's power over licence allocation and give it to the government, saying the move was ripe for 'cronyism and corruption' (Given 2006). The national secretary of the journalists' union, Chris Warren, took a similar view, predicting greater concentration and less diversity, saying he expected a 'feeding frenzy' of mergers and acquisitions. He pointed out that a similar thing happened in 1987 after the last major round of media law reform when two of the three commercial FTA networks went into receivership along with the Fairfax group. Within weeks the nine network cut 100 newsroom jobs amid persistent rumours that it would soon be on the market. Warren also suggested that the number of media players in each market would fall to the new regulated minimum quickly: '"Obviously the result will be a significant consolidation … All the evidence points to a fall to the legal minimum"' (Norington 2006).

A more up-beat assessment came from the *Australian*'s media commentator, Mark Day (2006b). He wrote that complaints about a greater concentration of ownership and control were 'the rantings of deluded and embittered outcasts from mainstream reality'. His reasoning is pure digital mythology and is pegged to the argument that in the digital media power shifts from the 'proprietors of old' to the 'consumers of tomorrow', especially through the evolution of mobile platforms for news. It will be, he says, a future in which 'a thousand digital flowers bloom'. Of course we can expect this style of rhetoric from a loyal foot soldier for the News empire and he has his master's interests firmly in mind:

> [T]he incumbent media players will do what they've always done: follow the development of the most popular [digital] services and ultimately bid for their ownership. News Corporation ... is already on that path ... In the land of digital plenty, no one will be force-fed their information like a foie gras goose. (Day 2006b)

Day was also quick to pour cold water on the idea that the changes might lead to a round of mergers and acquisitions, arguing that the main players 'seem to have lost interest' in the idea (Day 2006a). There was a mixed reaction to Senator Coonan's announcement from the major media players. Overall, it's hard to see how they will lose out of the changes. Most will maintain their position, or at worst become part of a larger conglomerate. Perhaps Murdoch will buy Nine? Most of the existing large companies can see possible gains in the new climate, in particular the chance to own more than one type of medium in a market and the ability to attract new foreign investment (Murray 2006a). Peter Ruehl's humorous take is a reasonably accurate summation of what happened. He wrote that media deregulation in Australia seemed to revolve around protecting the vested interests of 'anybody named Packer or Murdoch' (Ruehl 2006). Of course, he was writing in the Fairfax-controlled *Australian Financial Review*, so he could afford to be cheeky. Some players welcomed the reforms, others were unhappy with some aspects, as outlined in the following summary.

Media stock share prices rose on the Australian Stock Exchange after the announcement and most commentators predicted there will be 'rationalisation' in the market when the changes are in place. The *SMH* political editor, Peter Hartcher (2006), described this as the 'real hot potato' in the package and the point most likely to stall implementation of the proposals. However, some market analysts said that there was little value in media stocks, and ABN Amro's Peter Shorthouse said that prices would fall, particularly if advertising numbers did not improve. A number of media stocks had dropped in value in 2005–06 and some in the market did not expect them to rise much more (Jury 2006). There was a consensus of opinion that the role of the ACCC would be increasingly important in the scrutiny of merger proposals and offshore acquisitions, particularly if they lead to market domination by one player (Crowe 2006b).

Publishing and Broadcasting Limited (PBL), the Packer family company that owns the Nine network and a stable of magazines, had lobbied against multi-channelling, but it will benefit from the government's decision not to introduce a fourth FTA channel in the foreseeable future. It gains because of the limited changes to the anti-siphoning rules and it could be a take-over target, or PBL might be interested in buying into the Fairfax newspapers. PBL is also moving some of its business into online gambling and has the cash-flow to enable it to make deals, in particular to encourage overseas investment in its online and gambling businesses (Hewett 2006).

News Corporation may bid for the new digital spectrum and is seen as a potential buyer for either Seven or Ten if they come on the market. A spokeswoman for News Corporation told the *Australian* that the company supports deregulation, 'provided the playing field is genuinely level' (quoted in Schulze & Lewis 2006). Analysts predict it might want to invest in a television network. News is also heavily focused on expanding its mobile phone and Internet assets globally (Hewett 2006).

John Fairfax P/L, the publisher of newspapers in Melbourne and Sydney, the *Australian Financial Review*, and several magazine titles, might be interested in bidding for one of the new digital 'snack' channels. It misses out on a television station because of the 'no fourth channel' decision and it could be a target for takeover when the cross-media and foreign ownership rules change. Fairfax CEO Ron Walker said the proposed changes were encouraging and indicated the company would be interested in becoming a digital television provider (Murray 2006b).

Seven welcomed multi-channelling and will benefit from the 'no fourth channel' decision. It is a potential takeover or merger target, too. A Seven official said the announcement contained 'a number of positive developments' (quoted in Schulze & Lewis 2006).

Channel Ten is majority-owned by a Canadian company and it could be on the market once the new cross-media and foreign ownership rules are in place. Ten opposed the multi-channelling option.

The radio industry was sceptical that the changes would enhance its move to the digital spectrum, but the main problem for them seemed to be infighting and disputes over the proposed new digital radio bandwidth. The FM stations want to use the 256 bandwidth, but the government had allocated the 128 band. According to a director of the Macquarie radio network, Mark Carnegie, broadband services and 3G mobile phones are steadily draining audiences from commercial radio. This was contradicted by the industry association, Commercial Radio Australia, whose chief executive, Joan Warner, was confidently predicting that digital radio would take off in Australia in coming years and would not 'cannibalise' existing radio markets (Lehmann 2006). One analyst predicted the Austereo company may be interested in buying a chunk of the Ten network (Cain 2006). Alternatively, Ten may want to buy Austereo. The Village Roadshow company owns 66 per cent of Austereo and analysts were suggesting this stake might be for sale and remains vulnerable to attacks from the DMG group and Australian Provincial Newspapers (APN News & Media) (Shoebridge 2006a).

Analysts were fairly unanimous that most change is likely to occur in regional Australia where smaller markets and struggling operators may look to grow by buying more assets, or sell out to a better offer. WIN TV is privately owned but affiliated to the Nine network and it is looking to expand its reach. In August 2006 WIN bought the small pay TV operator SelecTV. Southern Cross Broadcasting, a Ten affiliate, is considered a takeover target. APN News & Media owns the MIX radio network and papers in Queensland and New South Wales, and may be interested in buying the Seven-affiliated Prime network (Schulze 2006). The Prime CEO told the *SMH* that he welcomed the Coonan proposal, adding that there were still some 'controversial' issues around timing and the scope of the new digital channels (Murray 2006b). Rural Press chief executive Brian McCarthy expressed frustration at the proposal to have a minimum of four providers in regional areas, telling the *SMH* that it should be more than five in the cities and less than four in the regions (Murray 2006b). Mr McCarthy said that Rural Press might be interested in adding to its radio holdings and the WIN television group might buy some newspapers (Shoebridge 2006c).

Pay TV companies were generally unhappy that the anti-siphoning rules have not been abolished altogether and they feel they are disadvantaged because they do not get the right to bid for major sporting events. Foxtel chief executive Kim Williams has repeatedly described the anti-siphoning rules as the 'most draconian' in the world (quoted in Shoebridge 2006b). Free TV chief executive Julie Flynn said the complaint was 'meaningless' and that there was plenty of content available to the pay TV operators (quoted in Shoebridge 2006b). The subscription television industry is also worried about competition from broadband providers and Foxtel has moved into the market with its own content services in order to attract some of the consumers. MTV in Europe has been working with mobile phone companies to provide content for several years (McLean 2006).

The advertising industry welcomed most changes, but called on the government to move more quickly than the 2010–12 deadlines for conversion to digital, saying that the roll-out of multi-channelling and datacasting should happen much sooner. Advertisers were suggesting that there might be more concentration in media ownership, leading to similar developments in advertising as agencies sought to package up campaigns across several media platforms. Young & Rubicam executive Hamish McLennan told the *Australian* that Australia risked being left behind if new services were not introduced sooner than 2012 (Sinclair 2006). In general, the industry appeared confident that niche and target marketing would become more important in the advertising mix. One industry leader told the *Australian* that in a digital environment it is easier to know who you're talking to (Sinclair 2006). Outside the metropolitan areas, however, advertising agencies were less sanguine about the impact of the changes. One media buyer for an agency in Cairns told the *Australian* that he could not see the benefits of the changes flowing through to regional Australia (Wilson & Gerard 2006).

There were mixed reactions from politicians, including from some Coalition backbenchers. The ALP shadow minister for communication issues, Stephen Conroy, dismissed it out of hand and predicted the changes would lead to more concentration of media and would be a blow against 'diversity of opinion' (AAP 2006). Several National Party MPs and senators also voiced some opposition to changes that would affect rural and regional Australia. Queensland senators Paul Neville and Barnaby Joyce called for 'editorial separation' in regional newsrooms because they fear that mergers would mean less regional news and fewer news outlets. Senator Neville told the *AFR* that the principle should be adopted nationwide, but that it is particularly important in regional areas. He predicted that the government's changes would lead to a concentration of media ownership outside the capital cities and therefore separation of management and editorial functions would be a 'very important' issue (Crowe 2006a). Senator Joyce said that his main concern was that small business in regional areas would lose access to affordable advertising outlets (Lewis 2006). These comments make it hard for the government to move quickly and signal that the reforms may face some stumbling blocks in the Senate.

Editorial commentary on the proposals

One way to gauge the reactions of the media players is to see what is written in the major editorials. While these opinions cannot be taken as gospel, there is a tradition that editorial writers try to mould their opinions to those of the proprietors.

The *Courier-Mail* (News Limited, Brisbane) said that the market had already moved beyond the Coonan proposals and that the announcement elicited 'little more than a yawn' because the technology is years ahead of the law. However, the paper supported the idea that deregulation 'may mean greater diversity', which reflects Rupert Murdoch's opinion that young people in particular are now sourcing news, information, and entertainment from sources beyond the control of the media giants (O. Gibson 2006). The editorial ends saying that the government is 'a little like King Canute' and will be swamped by the incoming tide of digital technologies ('Media options are behind the times' 2006).

The *Sydney Morning Herald*, which has an open share register and does not have a dominant proprietor, was more hopeful: 'The bell has just sounded for a free-for-all in Australia's media industry' ('Media shackles start to loosen' 2006). The *SMH* said the changes recognise the fluidity of the market, both commercially and technologically, and acknowledge the importance of globalisation, but concluded that 'a lot more needs to be done'.

News Corporation's national circulation daily, the *Australian*, welcomed the reform proposals, but said they were overdue and that the government should move more quickly to implement them than 2010–12 ('Diversity is strength' 2006). The editorial said the old regime was 'needlessly restrictive' and was holding back the 'technological promise' of the media industry. It also noted that the changes could spark an 'upheaval' in media ownership and welcomed the winding back of anti-siphoning rules. The paper complained that even with most of the changes in place the media will still be shackled by 'over-regulation' that 'stifles innovation, diversity and efficiency' and argued that consumers will have more choice anyway because of the roll-out of new broadband services and the falling price of subscription TV services, since technology is 'running ahead' of regulation. The editorial asked a pointed question that reveals a little of News Corporation's desires, if not actual planning: 'So why should governments prevent newspaper companies from offering television services?'

Reforming the media: In whose interests?

> Even if one accepts that the Internet is to some extent the foundation of our current and future economic success, the important social questions remain: Who in the economy truly benefits? (McChesney 2000b, p. xxv)

This is a fundamental question when examining proposals to reform media law and regulation. In her comments on the day the federal government's new reform package was released, the Communications Minister made it clear who the main beneficiaries would be: 'it also presents significant opportunities to embrace new ways of doing business' (Coonan Media Release 14 March). The laws and systems of regulation that govern media industries are a good example of the mutually constituting dialectic between the base and superstructure of a society. Governments make laws that govern ownership and control of the mass media and regulate the content that can be carried over various communication channels. Rules around ownership and control are forms of property law, while content regulation specifies the types of material deemed 'suitable' for consumption by the reading, listening, and viewing audiences. The legal system is part of the superstructure—it has both overt and implicit political, cultural, and ideological content—but it also determines some of the economic forms and institutional arrangements in which the communication business functions. Thus a particularly important fault line in the dialectic of regulation and control is between the governance perspective adopted by regulatory agencies and enshrined in government policy, and the commercial interests of the media owners, who, naturally, want only what suits their business strategies for expansion and profitability. As Jock Given (1998, p. 64) notes, there has been little real debate involving the public; most of it has been conducted behind closed doors in Canberra and in the media boardrooms of Melbourne and Sydney. He argues that the language of 'public interest' has been 'largely evacuated' from discussions of government policy since the early 1990s. It certainly hasn't been reintroduced in the 2006 reform proposals!

While the rhetoric of government may be about encouraging diversity and competition, most analysts and newspaper commentators have recognised that the changes will in fact lead to greater concentration. Writing in the *Australian*, John Lehmann and Steve Lewis (2006) note in their opening paragraph on page 1 that the changes will start a 'flurry of takeover activity as moguls look to bulk up their business' with new acquisitions. The relaxation of foreign ownership rules led to speculation that large American companies such as Time-Warner and Viacom might be interested in Australian assets. In the same vein, the *Australian*'s business analyst, Michael Sainsbury (2006), wrote that the media already constitute a global business sector and that economies of scale are 'increasingly important'.

The rhetoric of consumer 'choice'

As we've mentioned in several places already and discuss more fully in the final section of the book, in the capitalist economy there is a close relationship between business and government. When a government undertakes a major piece of regulatory reform that affects a large and powerful business sector, it must be careful that it does not appear to be too hastily doing the bidding of the major commercial players. In order to cover its tracks, a government will engage with the rhetoric of consumer choice and will argue that the changes are necessary to ensure a greater level of choice. This language is clearly present in the Australian government's discussion paper on media reform options: 'For consumers, this means an ever-increasing number of new sources of information and entertainment.' Thus the proposed reform package must 'ensure the quality and diversity of services delivered to consumers' (DCITA 2006, p. 3).

As Robert McChesney notes, this consumer-choice rhetoric disguises the paucity of real democratic debate and is based on the techno-myth that digital communication technologies are 'inherently democratic' because they 'undermine' the real economic and political power of the current dominant media interests. He argues that the rhetoric is in fact 'either lies or half-truths', and that it removes any power that citizens may have been able to bring to bear in comprehending the changes and influencing policy (McChesney 2000b, p. 7). In a time of 'free market theology', like the present, consumers actually have 'less leverage than ever before' (p. 67) when it comes to influencing communication and media policy changes. It's only a small point, but it reinforces this larger one. The government allowed only four weeks for public consultation on the changes announced in March 2006, which gave consumer organisations very little time to formulate a response.

One of the key areas in which the government's reform agenda is premised on the illusion of greater consumer choice is the transitional arrangement in place to cover the period in which free-to-air television switches from an analogue to a digital-only signal. The transition period allows for FTA broadcasters to simulcast an analogue and digital signal for some time to 'assist industry' to make the 'necessary investment' and to 'encourage' consumers to make the switch (DCITA 2006, p. 4). It has been necessary for this encouragement to be in place because digital televisions are still fairly expensive and the take-up by Australian consumers has been slow. This is mentioned in the DCITA discussion paper, but only in vague terms: 'the take-up of FTA digital TV has not progressed at a level or pace to allow the switchover to commence in 2008 as originally planned' (DCITA 2006, p. 5). In other words, the industry needs more time to convince consumers to hand over large wads of cash for digital receivers or set-top boxes. The new 'switchover' date is to commence in 2010 to 2012 and is subject to progress on the Government's Digital Action Plan, 'the roadmap' (DCITA 2006, p. 7). As of December 2005, only 140 000 Australian households had a digital television or set-top box and retailers had more than a million digital TVs still in stock. Analogue televisions were still selling at more than twice the rate of digital sets in 2005. In order to convert the 14.5 million analogue sets to digital, more than 5000 set-top boxes must be sold each day to reach the 2012 conversion date (Burton 2006). The DCITA paper notes that Australia cannot afford to remain an analogue nation in the face of the global conversion to digital, nor can the dual analogue-digital broadcast system be maintained because it is expensive (p. 15).

Writing in the *Australian Financial Review*, academic economist John Quiggin (2006) argued that the reforms would not benefit consumers, describing them as a 'cosy deal' between the government and the existing monopoly players. He wrote that the public interest in diversity, choice, and competition had been 'disregarded' and that encouragement for consumers to switch to digital television really amounted to 'compulsion'. Communications academic Stuart Cunningham (2006) made the same point, arguing that the Coonan proposals were a response to 'big business lobbying' and of little benefit to consumers. He also noted there were no proposals to secure a role for Australian content and that the commercial FTA networks had been 'protected again' at the expense of innovative change that was already 'occurring in cyberspace'.

In general there appeared to be a consensus that the reforms were necessary, but overdue, and that they would not necessarily lead to benefits for most consumers. Some commentators were concerned that the media reforms were not more explicitly linked to the ongoing reform of the Australian telecommunications market. They argued that convergence, in particular of voice, data, and video, would make many changes redundant before they could be put in place (Boyd 2006a). A number of trials of datacasting and the freeing up of more spectrum to niche digital 'television-like' services seem to confirm this analysis, but as David Crowe (2006d) notes, there's a catch. Either the new service could be profitable, or it could also lead to money being wasted on 'technology that nobody wants'.

The media and telecommunications reform agenda in Australia has been on the political table for nearly thirty years, beginning with the deregulation of the national monopoly over phone services in the early 1980s. In 1986 the first shake-out of the media occurred after the then Treasurer Paul Keating introduced the cross-media rules preventing one company from owning a newspaper and a television network in the same market. The removal of this barrier is a key plank of the current reform package and as we've noted here, it is still an open question whether or not this will increase diversity as its supporters claim. Satellite television came to Australia in 1995, but the industry has struggled to gain momentum and it did not get the changes to anti-siphoning laws that it had been lobbying for. It seems clear from our analysis of the commentary that many of the important issues have not been resolved with the Coonan proposals. A key controversy, private profits versus public interest, has been an issue in the commercial media for most of the 20th century (Hirst & Patching 2005), and it seems likely that the same issue will be carried forward into the digital media field. Digital convergence makes it logical for telecommunications and media regulation to be considered together, but the reform package does not take this obvious step.

A decade ago, Jock Given proposed some simple priorities for a new regulatory regime for the digital media that would give serious consideration to public interest concerns. He suggested a system that would guarantee 'universal access' as the best way of ensuring public participation in the coming 'digital age'. His second point was 'diversity of institutions', including a properly funded public and community sector, which would create room for new players alongside the entrenched interests. In his opinion this would be a 'Good Thing'.

Finally, he recognised that the dialectical process of convergence also creates tendencies to both monopoly and the opening up of 'new spaces' that should make consumers wary of decisions to continue the old system of protecting the incumbent licence-holders (Given 1998, pp. 66–9). Unfortunately, at this point we have to conclude that this good advice has been largely ignored. The separation of content from platform—a key plank of the old policy—has been retained, prompting commentators to argue that Australia will be left behind in global trends in new media technologies and services. The ethico-legal fault lines that plagued the old media have not been closed and are set to open up further as digital media continue their technological march, two steps ahead of the regulators and government policy. In the following section we analyse how these issues are coming to the fore in relation to digital media and the Internet.

Who controls the Internet?

> While the Internet does not necessarily conform to state boundaries, mechanisms of geographic content control are increasingly being implemented. (Villeneuve 2006, p. 2)

There is a war of position being fought over digital regulation regimes and its existence helps to dispel the techno-myths that surround online communications. For example, the myth of the borderless Internet is exploded when we begin to examine the geographically bounded regulations being imposed by national governments 'seeking to assert information sovereignty over the Internet' (Villeneuve 2006, p. 2). A key front line in this global battle for control of the Internet was highlighted in October 2005 when some countries suggested that the United States relinquish its dominant position in favour of the United Nations. A number of countries, including the European Union, China, Iran, and Cuba, argued that ICANN (Internet Corporation for Assigned Names and Numbers), effectively a private not-for-profit company, should no longer have sole jurisdiction to allocate Internet addresses. Other nations, Australia among them, are supporting the retention of American control (Anderson 2005). An editorial in the *New York Times* summarises the American position:

> Some foreign governments are uncomfortable with the United States' controlling the nuts and bolts of the Internet … There may be a multilateral solution down the road, but right now it is in everyone's best interests to keep control of the Internet where it was founded, in America. ('Worldwide but Homegrown' 2005)

According the *NYT* editorial, any attempt to reduce US control would result in a 'balkanized [segmented and anarchic] Internet … leading to duplicate sites, confusion and a breakdown of the effectiveness of the global network' ('Worldwide but Homegrown' 2005). However, governments can still impose their own filtering systems at the national level; China is one country that routinely censors Internet traffic at its borders on the grounds of national security (see case study in chapter 13). As Nart Villeneuve points out, this raises significant concerns about levels of transparency, openness, and accountability that are operating under such strict filtering regimes because most of them are arbitrary, the result of government decree, or are implemented for reasons of political censorship. In most cases there is no right of appeal and the act of filtering is itself disguised because while websites may be accessible, sensitive content is blocked by URL-specific instructions (Villeneuve 2006, p. 9). Lawyer and software engineer Alan Anderson (2005), writing in the *SMH*, supported the US position, arguing that control of the Internet could not be left to a UN bureaucracy 'dominated by dictators and economic Luddites'. Despite the myth of borderless cyberspace, there are competing, complementary, and contradictory national regimes of control operating simultaneously to generate a complex regulatory framework. While such regulation is benign in some cases, in others it represents a significant attack on freedom of speech. This is a particularly important consideration when discussing politics in the cyber age (see chapter 15). As of July 2006 the US is still firmly in control and attempts to internationalise Internet regulation appear to have stalled.

A similar issue was brought to light in October 2005 when the Australian High Court ruled that a modified microchip that allowed users of Sony's PlayStation to override an internal security device was legal. The chip defeats the regional coding installed on the PlayStation and allows users to play games bought overseas, or copied from other sources. Sony argued that this was a breach of its copyright, but the High Court disagreed. The ruling could see a challenge under the Free Trade Agreement between Australia and the United States, which mandates stronger protection of intellectual property rights (Needham 2005; Priest & Crowe 2005).

As these examples show, the transition from broadcasting to narrowcasting and the growing importance of converged digital production and delivery platforms have created some significant problems and issues in forms of regulation for the media companies, for lawmakers, and for ethicists and experts. Not least of these is the techno-legal time-gap, the delay between law and regulation being put in place and the current capacity of the new technology to deliver new, unregulated services.

The techno-legal time-gap: An explanation

New technologies are constantly coming on stream, or being touted as the next 'big thing'. Often this is happening at the same time as moral, ethical, and political debates about whether or not the next 'big thing' is actually a good or a bad 'big thing'. Most likely the 'thing'—be it a new medical procedure or new business practice that takes advantage of the new technology as it becomes available—will be something about which society as a whole says 'OK, that's good, let's do it'. If that's the case, the law will soon be amended, or ethical and moral concerns will have been met. But there are times when the new technology seems fairly benign, or at least profitable, and there are no laws that actually forbid its introduction. It's also likely in such situations that existing laws don't adequately address the new 'thing' that the technology does or makes possible. There is, in effect, a legal vacuum. When such a situation occurs—regularly, it seems, with the new digital media technologies—individuals and companies will step in and begin to operate the technology without adequate safeguards in place. The 'mod chip' that overrides technical blocks on the digital copying of games is a good example of this. The chip's designer, Eddy Stevens, is free to continue selling the device until such time as a dispute under the Free Trade Agreement is lodged and resolved. This is precisely how the data-mining companies have been able to establish their multi-billion dollar industry over the past decade. They are free to compile and manipulate the data they gather until such time as the law is changed.

TECHNO-LEGAL TIME-GAP

The gap between the time a technology reaches the market, and the time it takes for legislators to regulate the socially undesirable aspects of that technology. At a minimum this is usually about two years.

The Australian government's digital media 'roadmap' (discussed above, page 271–282) is also another victim of the techno-legal time-gap. The technology that allows peer-to-peer file-sharing is already being used to download television programs to computer hard drives, and even though it is technically illegal, it appears to be beyond the law. In the United States and other countries, however, there are legal download sites that offer up-to-the-minute episodes of programs for around $3. An Australian company ReelTime Media has also launched a set-top box that connects a television to the Internet. ReelTime is offering episodes of television shows and movies for between $0.50 and $7.99. There are already televisions on the market (not in Australia) that use a wireless connection to take video feeds, and hand-held devices that do the same are on sale in electronics shops (Davidson 2006).

Privacy in the digital world

> Privacy is arguably one of the most important areas in which society and technology will affect each other in the coming years. (Connolly 2000, p. 49)

Physical privacy is something we take for granted. We close the door on the world around us when we arrive 'home' and in that environment we are safe from the prying eyes of neighbours and strangers. But we can no longer have that certainty when we enter cyberspace, via email or a web browser, or use a mobile phone. Privacy is both a legal and an ethical issue and dealing with privacy in the narrowcasting world presents us with a clear-cut ethico-legal paradox. Privacy in most cultures is perceived as a moral right, and is enshrined in legislation in some jurisdictions, but not in others. For online businesses there is the added dilemma that what might be legal and/or ethical in one jurisdiction or cultural setting will be regarded as criminal and/or morally offensive in another (Connolly 2000, p. 49). Legislation to allow consumers to 'opt out' of the endless cycle of telemarketing is an example of a law designed to protect individual privacy in the digital age. The federal government's 'do-not-call' register began operation in 2006 and it also requires telemarketers to give consumers access to information held about them. But it will not be easy to remove yourself from telemarketing databases—you must call the Australian Communications and Media Authority and tell them you want to be delisted (Heywood 2005).

To complicate things further, there appears to be a lack of uniform and accepted social control in the virtual world of the Internet (Hinduja 2004, p. 38). In fact, according to Sameer Hinduja, the paradox of privacy in cyberspace is that behaving normally increases the chances that your privacy will be invaded because the default settings embedded in the Internet automatically collect information. To avoid this, you must instead 'operate on the fringes of standard practice' (p. 39); that is, make yourself anonymous by using encryption and other software that can mask your identity and/or location.

The most persistent way that websites track visitors is via a small, unobtrusive piece of software called a 'cookie'. When you first visit a website, the server deposits the cookie on your hard drive; on subsequent visits the cookie is transferred back and forth to the server. The cookie is used to track your preferences when visiting that website, and some, such as remembered log-in details, can be relatively harmless. But cookies can also store and transmit information that goes beyond simple ID verification. Some of the collected information only has one purpose: the construction of a profile of the computer user. According to Hinduja (2004, p. 47), the problem is that consumers believe that their real-world privacy will automatically be respected in cyberspace, while companies dealing through the Web consider information provided (willingly or unknowingly) by the user is 'their annexed property' that can be commercially used without any further permission.

There is a history of contradiction and paradox in the relationship between privacy and communications technologies, what Connolly (2000, p. 49) describes as a series of 'high and low points'. When telephone systems were operated manually, particularly in small and remote communities, the local operator knew details of every call that was routed through her exchange and party lines meant that you could pick up a handset and listen in on the conversations of your neighbours. In the computing environment the analogy is the system administrator who can track your Internet and email use. A person in this position who lacks 'ethical discipline' can access 'forbidden knowledge' to deal unfairly with clients on their network (p. 49).

There is, in the digital world of narrowcasting, a reversal of the norms of public and private contexts. In this environment, normal ethical principles are eroded and displaced by 'purely economic' concepts (Hearn et al. 2003, p. 233). This paradox of the digital dialectic is played out through what Greg Hearn and his co-authors (pp. 231–45) describe as 'phenomenological turbulence' in the knowledge economy.

Privacy laws protect business not privacy

> Social control stemming from law in real space and the general public appears to be ineffective in curtailing some privacy-invading practices of online businesses. (Hinduja 2004, p. 50)

As we saw in the row about celebrity 'stalking' by the Gawker.com website, there is in this instance no clear argument about invasions of individual privacy. There are privacy laws in many jurisdictions, but around the world the experience of privacy advocates has generally been that when governments act to guarantee the privacy of individuals in cyberspace, the results are disappointing. For example, legislation in the United States to provide a level of privacy protection to bank customers actually allows banks to share the information they collect with other credit providers and insurance companies, or an associated business entity, as long as it is done for the purpose of carrying on business. Customers can choose to 'opt out' of the arrangement, but few take advantage of the offer. Opt-out clauses put the responsibility on the consumer. This reverses the assumption that corporations should protect privacy, rather than share personal information for commercial gain unless specifically requested not to. The basic contradiction highlighted by disputes about online privacy is about the ability of firms to do business. On one hand, the capitalist knowledge economy requires that commodified information be freely (at commercial rates) transferable between organisations and consumers; on the other, there is a presumed social and moral right of individuals to privacy, dignity, and anonymity. This issue is at the heart of attempts by governments and courts to fix some legal and ethical principles for online information transactions (Freeman 2005, p. 5).

Careful what you click for

> Like most material culture, the clickstream is becoming an asset, certainly to the individual, but in particular to the Internet industry. (Battelle 2005, p. 12)

A clickstream pattern is the digital trail you leave behind when you're surfing the Web. It is tracked via cookies and other methods that allow search engines to deliver targeted advertising to your browser by attempting to match what you were searching for. Before the days of net surfing, your clickstream was limited to movement around your hard drive or other storage devices attached to your PC; today, when you're online, your clickstream is a goldmine to both legitimate and illegitimate businesses on the web. From a consumer's point of view, there might seem to be advantages in trading a bit of privacy for the convenience of recommendations from a search engine that match our needs. For Internet business, 'search drives clickstreams, and clickstreams drive profits' (Battelle 2005, p. 12).

The 'ownership' of your clickstream and the related data that it generates is a tricky legal question at the moment, and one that illustrates the problem of the techno-legal time-gap. As John Battelle (2005, p. 15) points out, when it comes to deciding who owns the data and what our rights might be in relation to it, 'we just don't know'.

Computers have greatly increased the risk to individuals that their privacy will be compromised because of the speed and efficiency of networked systems in retrieving and analysing data. The commercialisation of the Internet in the past fifteen years has also led to a greater corporate reliance on personal data to refine advertising and marketing techniques at the heart of narrowcasting. The commodification of personal data is done for profit and often without regard for the privacy of individuals (Hinduja 2004, p. 49).

In the competitive world of global capitalism, efforts to instil the virtues of self-regulation on the Internet have also been ineffective. A new and largely unregulated business—the delivery of online customers to companies—has grown in the past decade without much self-control or legislative restraint. P. J. Connolly regards self-regulation of the data-collection and analysis industry as 'just too important to be left to the free market'; he adds that 'doing nothing' is not an option for businesses that are serious about online commerce (2000, p. 50). The laissez-faire attitude is slowly changing as the law attempts to bridge the techno-legal time-gap, but the online marketers are usually at least a few steps ahead of the regulators. New databases are being constructed and distributed almost daily; they are on the open market, available to the highest bidder. Some are legitimate; others operate in the legal shadows. The spread of these databases and the ability of data-mining companies to combine several of them into super-size information warehouses present what one American legal academic calls 'the ultimate Orwellian realization' because effective social control mechanisms 'to enforce corporate propriety' have not been established in cyberspace (Hinduja 2004, pp. 50–1).

While Hinduja's criticisms apply to the United States and many other parts of the world, the European Union has created tougher standards for data privacy; companies cannot share information with a third party without explicit consent. Thus non-European corporations operating in the 'nowhere' of cyberspace may be infringing EU regulations around data privacy when they engage in international online marketing, or even when performing a simple system back-up (Connolly 2000, p. 50).

Digging for gold: data-mining

> [M]y big concern right now is that legislation or regulation is potentially actually going to get in the way of all this happening. And obviously, it's going to impact the potential success of companies, as laws are passed that restrict the flow of information. (Charles Morgan, quoted in O'Harrow 2005, p. 70)

Charles Morgan is the Ferrari-driving CEO of one of the world's largest and most secretive companies, Acxiom. Morgan is one of the leading players in the data-mining business and his 'big concern' in 2000 was that the American Congress might pass information privacy laws that would cramp his business style. Acxiom and other companies like it, Esperion and ChoicePoint among them, rely on having almost unlimited and uncontrolled access to personal and public information about people to make their enterprise profitable. These data-mining companies sell their product—billions of records containing information about consumers—to banks, credit card issuers, retail outlets, and other businesses that need to know more about their customers' spending habits and credit rating than the customer might know themselves. Increasingly in the surveillance economy they are also doing business with governments around the world. Privacy laws that inhibit this flow of information between the data companies and their end-users are simply bad for business.

Perhaps Morgan need not have been so worried about how the American government might deal with his 'big concern'. According to investigative journalist Robert O'Harrow, US government agencies are among the biggest users of information provided by the major data-mining companies, for the simple reason that it provides a legal loophole: 'By outsourcing the collection of records, the government doesn't have to ensure the data is accurate, or have any provisions to correct it in the same way it would under the Privacy Act' (2005, p. 137).

This is how the American government uses its partners in the private sector to circumnavigate the law and exploit the techno-legal time-gap. In our view, digital data-mining is an issue that the law seems to have pushed under the carpet. In the final section of the book we examine how this new narrowcast-media industry is a key element of the surveillance economy and set to grow in coming years.

Piracy: Digital file-sharing and illegal copying

In February 2006 police in Switzerland and Belgium closed down the eDonkey peer-to-peer file-sharing network that was being used by an estimated million people to download video and music files in breach of copyright. John Kennedy, chairman of the International Federation of Phonographic Industries, said the closure of eDonkey was a 'significant breakthrough' in the entertainment industry's ongoing battle with Internet-based pirating of copyrighted product (Sherwin 2006). However, the fight to shut down peer-to-peer file-sharing and stamp out illegal downloading has been going on for the past decade and the pirates are able to stay one step ahead of the regulators. The recording industry in particular has argued for many years that Internet piracy costs it billions of dollars in lost profits, but in 2005 the world's leading music labels posted profits of $US1.1 billion from more than 420 million legal music downloads from legitimate websites. In this context, the same John Kennedy said that downloads from iTunes, Musicload, and MSN sites exceeded illegal downloads. He was also optimistic about the future: 'We expect this trend to spread as new and pioneering legal music distribution channels open up to consumers,' he told the world's media ('Tide turns against digital piracy 2006').

It had been tough for the music industry to get to this point and there are signs that the trade in pirated MP3s is still flourishing. In September 2005 the Rolling Stones' first studio album in eight years was available illegally on the Web before it was released in the stores. U2, Oasis, Eminem, and Radiohead are among the leading musical acts that have been victim to mass pirating of their material ('Rolled by Net piracy' 2005). Also in September 2005 the Federal Court in Sydney shut down the Kazaa website, which facilitated file-sharing between an estimated 320 million users, but analysts were not confident that this would put much of a dent in the illegal download market. Music industry experts were still claiming that pirate downloads were exceeding legal downloads by a ratio of 5:1 (Hayes 2005).

Illegal file-sharing began with MP3 music files, but it has spread quickly to newly released movies and even television programs. According to one industry study, by 2004 illegal downloading of television programs had increased by 150 per cent over previous years (Idato 2005). Consumers, it seems, are prepared to break the law in order to customise their music-listening and television-viewing habits. According to one study, Australians account for 15.5 per cent of all illegal television downloads and analysts say it is rapidly becoming a mainstream activity (Lee 2005).

But what is the real problem here? People were making illegal copies of records and tapes for many years before the digital revolution. Programs and hardware for CD and DVD 'burning' have been around now for ten years. Does it really cause any harm? According to reports in late 2005, the Australian government was considering amending the copyright laws to make 'fair use' copying of CDs legitimate. As we noted in chapter 8, this change was finally made in May 2006. A further question is raised by the techno-fixes employed by the major record labels and by Apple (makers of the iPod) to limit the availability of legal music downloads by regional coding and other security devices embedded on their websites and in the hardware. Perhaps Australian consumers are merely pawns in the international business planning of the major corporations. A song downloadable from the US iMusic site—which is not available in Australia—costs 30 per cent less than the same song downloaded from an Australian supplier. As Alex Malik (2005) wrote in the *Sydney Morning Herald*: 'faced with a partial digital music service and price gouging, who could blame consumers for taking the risk [of prosecution for copyright violation]?' This is a clear case of an ethico-legal paradox and one that is overlaid with issues to do with the commercial interests of some of the key players in the so-called information economy.

Conclusion

The argument that the wired world is a space for free expression is a myth, despite what we have described as the expanded reportorial community. There is increasing control of media content, in all its forms, and the technologies themselves make this possible. The craven way both News Corp and Google have capitulated to demands for content restrictions in order to operate in China shows that freedom of expression is a principle that can be traded away if there is enough financial incentive.

On the other hand, there is decreasing control over the ownership and control of media, old and new. The old media companies like News Corp, PBL, and Fairfax are now gobbling up new media enterprises that started in sheds and garages over the past decade. This challenge—increased content regulation, and diminished oversight of ownership and control—leads us to the final section of this book, in which we ask two questions: Have the digital technologies allowed the vision of a global village to become a society under high surveillance? and if this is so: What is the future of democracy, of discussion, debate, and dissent in a digitised world?

KEY POINTS

In this chapter we have explored:

- the built-in time-lag between innovation and regulation;
- key features of the proposed changes to Australia's media ownership and regulation systems, concluding that the 'reforms' are changes principally in the interests of the existing free-to-air broadcasters, and exposing the rhetoric of the free-market model as empty and false;
- important ethico-legal issues raised by digital technologies such as data-mining, hacking, and peer-to-peer downloading of content.

CLASS DISCUSSION

Reform and regulation

After reading the sections on media regulation in this chapter, consider the following questions:

1 Research the most up-to-date information on the progress of the government's reform agenda. How is it going compared with what the commentators were saying in March 2006?

2 Is it possible to close the fault line between the interests of business and the public interest?

3 What should the government do to move Australia into the digital media age?

4 How do young people feel about the old media? Have media habits changed significantly over the last ten years?

The techno-legal time-gap

1 Having read the section on the techno-legal time-gap, do you think it's a major problem?

2 How do you feel about illegal downloads and digital piracy?

3 Can government or industry do anything to close the time-gap?

Data-mining

1 Should governments do more to protect online privacy?

2 How do you feel about cookies lodging on your computer?

3 Is it possible to overcome privacy concerns to allow legitimate data mining for business applications?

PART 4

FROM BROADCASTING TO NARROWCASTING: THE EMERGENCE OF A SURVEILLANCE ECONOMY

OBJECTIVES

In this final section we are looking to the future, but our view is firmly anchored in what's happening today and builds on our historical survey in earlier chapters. This section is more speculative and gives an indication of what we think the direction is for media and technology as we progress into the age of narrowcasting. After reading this section you should have a greater understanding of what we mean by 'surveillance society' and 'surveillance economy'. In particular, the following concepts are important:

- the role of the media in legitimising the growing level of commercial and political surveillance over society;
- how the mimetic idea of 'Big Brother' has come to feature prominently in public debates about the surveillance society;
- how the current *mode of development* in the capitalist economy is driving elements of both the base and the superstructure in the direction of greater surveillance.

KEYWORDS

capitalism
globalisation
mode of development
mode of production
surveillance economy
surveillance society

13

I KNOW WHAT YOU DID LAST SUMMER: THE SURVEILLANCE SOCIETY HAS ARRIVED

OBJECTIVES

In this chapter we explore the parameters of the surveillance society. In particular, we will explain how the transition from broadcasting to narrowcasting is a symptom and an effect of increasing personal surveillance. After reading this chapter you should be familiar with the following:

- what we mean by surveillance society;
- how the shift from broadcasting to narrowcasting is symptomatic of the surveillance society;
- how the media play an important role in legitimising social surveillance.

KEYWORDS
information society
knowledge society
surveillance society

Big Brother in the 'big brown land'

> Like *1984*'s Winston Smith bombarded by Big Brother's propaganda on the telescreens, we have suffered this blizzard of Government advertising artfully crafted to convince us that less is more … but it matters not to this Government, for history can always be rewritten. (Carlton 2005)

Mike Carlton is one of a small number of Australian journalists who regularly criticises governments. In one of his weekly *Sydney Morning Herald* articles, headlined 'Big Brother rules the great brown land', Carlton criticises the government's anti-terrorism legislation, which he says 'frogmarches Australia down the road to tyranny' and he describes a new raft of industrial relations laws called 'WorkChoices' as 'a wonderful example of newspeak'. Carlton's opinions are obviously open to debate, but we have drawn your attention to this article for another reason. It is typical of the way that George Orwell's dystopian vision of the future, *Nineteen Eighty-four*, and the character of 'Big Brother' are commonly used to frame discussions about the world in which we live. Over the course of preparing this book we have collected quite a few newspaper clippings that make some reference to Big Brother—and we're not just referring to the TV show. It's a staple of newspaper subeditors (who often write the headlines) and it's becoming more common.

A small example from the *Australian*'s letters page in July 2005: 'Who trusts Big Brother to watch over us?' Here's another that has more serious implications: 'Smile, Big Brother is arresting you' (Daly 2005). The prevalence of Big Brother headlines might tell us something about the state of mind of most newspaper subs, but it's probably also an indication that the concept and image of Big Brother are alive and well in popular culture. In a sense, it has become mimetic and now has a viral capacity to spread and to influence how we frame events around us.

In 'Big Brother rules the great brown land', Mike Carlton's commentary begins: 'Orwell jumped the gun with the date, but everything else is moving along pretty much as he predicted.' In other words, we have arrived in the nightmare world of 'Howard's Oceania' (Carlton 2005); Australia has, in Carlton's view, become a surveillance society. Is Mike Carlton right? Unfortunately, it would appear so. For some confirmation, let's return to the Mick Daly piece in the *Courier-Mail*, 'Smile, Big Brother is arresting you'.

SURVEILLANCE SOCIETY
A society based on ever greater levels of physical and electronic surveillance of citizens.

The report is about a north Queensland police officer, Senior Constable Steve Murphy, who was investigated by the Police Ethical Standards Command for releasing secretly recorded video footage of his day on the 'beat' to the Channel Nine program, *A Current Affair*. It was not an offence under Queensland law for the officer to record his actions in chasing criminals, drug raids, booking drink-drivers, and interacting with suspects in the lock-up. Murphy defended himself by arguing that the videos were often useful in court in giving the magistrate and juries a chance to see the offender in a different light: 'It shows the magistrate what you, as an officer, have to put up with.' Murphy told *A Current Affair* (cited in Daly 2005). However, Bond University criminologist Professor Paul Wilson told the paper that he couldn't see anything positive in giving police video cameras: 'It would be a case of Big Brother gone mad for me. I don't think journalists or academics or anyone else would like to be filmed every second of the day. To do so would be morally and ethically wrong' (quoted in Daly 2005).

Morally *and* ethically wrong—a double whammy! Despite the objections of civil libertarians and ethical criminologists like Paul Wilson, we are under almost constant video surveillance while out and about in public. What's even more interesting is the cynical ways that surveillance footage is used by the media, whenever the opportunity presents itself. Programs like *A Current Affair* and *Today Tonight* (Channel 7) are always willing to show CCTV footage of convenience store or service station robberies—often when it has been released by the courts. Entertainment programs featuring police chases, car smashes, arrests, and interrogations are becoming more and more common, and newspapers are also willing to get in on the act whenever they can. Not only is the elusive Big Brother alive and well; he seems to have the ear of producers and news editors around the country. In this chapter we will begin to unpack the 'Big Brother' society and the growing evidence for the emergence of the surveillance economy that underpins it.

I spy with my little eye: Who was Big Brother?

> [T]he hostile figure melted into the face of Big Brother, black-haired, black-mustachio'd, full of power and mysterious calm ... Nobody heard what Big Brother was saying. It was merely a few words of encouragement, the sort of words that are uttered in the din of battle ... At this moment the entire group of people broke into a deep, slow rhythmical chant of 'B-B! ... B-B!'—over and over again ... a heavy, murmurous sound ... It was a refrain that was often heard in moments of overwhelming emotion. (Orwell 1948, pp. 16–17)

This is the only physical description we get of Big Brother, at the beginning of *Nineteen Eighty-four*. While we often think of BB as being modelled on Josef Stalin, it could be someone else. When Orwell was writing this novel, in the years immediately after World War II, another European dictator would have been prominent in the popular imagination; it's just as likely that his model could have been Adolf Hitler (black hair and moustache, power and mysterious calm). Given Orwell's anti-fascist and anti-Stalinist politics, it's more than likely an amalgam of the two 20th-century dictators, just as 'IngSoc' (short for

English Socialism) is a likely fusion of the National Socialism of the Nazis and Soviet-style *state capitalism* in the USSR. Throughout the book nobody ever sees Big Brother, but he is a constant presence on the telescreen and at the centre of all propaganda efforts by the Inner Party. Winston vaguely recalls first hearing of BB during the 1960s, but even then his daring exploits and marvellous achievements had been historically re-engineered until 'they extended into the fabulous world of the forties and the thirties'. Winston tries but cannot remember when the Party was formed, but BB had always been 'the leader and guardian of the Revolution since its very earliest days'—though he has no way of knowing how much of this legend was true and how much invented (p. 32). For Winston and the other characters in *Nineteen Eighty-four*, Big Brother had a powerful mimetic presence and helped cement the hegemony of the Inner Party cadre.

Orwell's fictional nation of Oceania—the 'newspeak' name for Britain—was a frightening rendition of a surveillance society. The telescreens never turned off and the Thought Police of the Inner Party were everywhere. When Winston is struggling to complete the compulsory morning exercise routine, led by a female party member barking through the telescreen, she berates him by name and number; a stark reminder that it is a two-way device and that she can see him: 'Smith!" screamed the shrewish voice from the telescreen. "6079 Smith W.! Yes, you! Bend lower please! ... You're not trying. Lower, please! That's better, comrade ... ' (p. 32).

In Oceania, children were enlisted in a youth organisation called the Spies, to spy on their parents and neighbours. When Winston and Julia leave the city to make love in the forest, they have to be careful—there are hidden microphones even in this remote and beautiful place; Big Brother, unseen, but all-powerful, is everywhere. There are some interesting parallels developing between the fictional world of *Nineteen Eighty-four* and the surveillance society of the 21st century.

There can be no doubt that we're living in a surveillance society and it's not just in Australia. There is a global shift away from the freedoms we have taken for granted in the past and away from an automatic presumption of privacy (Jensen 2004). Today it seems that the only place we can have any real *physical* privacy is in our own homes. But even there we cannot guarantee *electronic* privacy. The telemarketing calls, which never seem to stop, are used to gain information about us that we're not even aware of. Calls are recorded and analysed to prepare vast data files on our consumption and other habits (O'Harrow 2005). We are not safe from electronic surveillance if we log on to the Internet, watch cable TV, or use the telephone; someone somewhere has access to a record of that transaction. We are leaving electronic fingerprints all over the world, even from the privacy of a computer terminal in a bedroom, or home office.

Not only do we leave a trail all over the Internet, but there is also electronic spyware that attempts to lodge itself on our computers, unless we're protected behind a network firewall, or have up-to-date anti-virus software installed on our PCs. The situation is worse outside the four walls of our living spaces. In Western societies we have learned to accept a certain amount of surveillance and inconvenience in return for what we perceive to be the security offered by governments. Most people will put up with the minor irritation of longer queues and having their stuff searched at football grounds and airports, but the surveillance society does not necessarily respect local or national boundaries. As countries like China seek to move into the global economy, while retaining a strong grip on the actions and thoughts of their population, they are able to take advantage of digital surveillance technologies to retain their hold on political power. The case study in this chapter (Surveillance on the Chinese Internet) shows how the Chinese government is committed to expanding China's role in the world economy, while maintaining a totalitarian grip on civil society. We prefer to call such societies 'state capitalist' rather than socialist because their economies are similar in structure to those in the West, despite elements of state ownership of the means of production. Throughout the period that we were writing this book there was an almost daily update of growing electronic surveillance measures and deals between the regime in Beijing and international media/communications companies, like Google and Microsoft, who were prepared to accept controls over their products in return for access to the lucrative Chinese market.

Surveillance societies in the West

Since China has a state-run economy and a tightly controlled civil society, we might expect that its government would exercise tight control over all media, including the Internet. We might also think that Internet communication is perhaps not so tightly managed in the free-market economies of the West. But of course the term 'free market' is a misnomer and a piece of ideology rather than economic fact. Private control of the means of production in capitalist economies also requires a fair degree of government intervention—both in the economy and in the lives of citizens.

The myths of individual liberty and freedom, which derive from the French and American revolutions of the 18th century—the bourgeois revolutions—tend to disguise the autocratic and rigid class structure of capitalism. Participation in periodic elections in which we get to 'choose' representatives for Parliament or Congress, it is argued, guarantees these freedoms, but only so long as we agree to collectively live by the rules of the free-market mythology. Economic freedom means, in theory, that anyone could be Bill Gates or Rupert Murdoch. According to the myth we just have to be clever enough to make it as an entrepreneur. By working hard, saving, and getting a good education, it is possible for anyone to reach the top. To some degree all of us have internalised these mimetic surveillance mechanisms of private enterprise capitalism. Like many reporters working for the commercial media, we self-censor our hopes, dreams, and frustrations, believing that if we pay lip service to the myths we will be all right. The media and popular culture are saturated with these myths and, as we argued in chapter 2, the memes and viral patterns that these ideological myths create ensure their transmission from person to person, generation to generation. Anyone who attempts to argue against them is humoured for a while and encouraged to grow out of it. If that fails, they are shunned and ostracised. If that doesn't work then there's always the sedition laws to shut them up.

A nation of spies?

> In Collection your daily duties may involve:
>
> - Speaking with a variety of people, including members of the public who are volunteering information, as well as approaching people to help with our investigations.
> - The use of covert methods to obtain information, such as the recruitment and management of human sources. (ASIO 2005, Recruitment website)

In the bureaucratic weasel words of Australia's elite and secretive espionage service, 'recruitment and management of human resources' basically means becoming a spy master, like Tom Cruise in *Mission Impossible*, or 'M' in the James Bond movies. Are we being encouraged to become a nation of spies? Is this the beginning of an Amway-style pyramid selling organisation, where each of us recruits ten friends, who each recruit ten friends? One of the important developments that's gradually occurred in the post-Cold War world is that former spies and intelligence agents have been forced to retrain and now offer their services in a private capacity to the highest bidder (Maxwell 1998, p. 125). Now, in the face of growing 'terrorist' threats, state security services are expanding again.

In the wake of the September 2001 bombings in New York, and subsequent attacks in Bali in 2002, 2004, and London in 2005, the Australian government has, with the help of the states and territories, kept up a barrage of advertising to constantly remind us that there is a 'war' going on. The billboards, newspaper ads, and television commercials encourage us to report anything 'suspicious', such as unusual activity around public buildings, railway stations, shopping centres, and so on. Have you noticed any strange goings-on at a neighbour's house that might indicate a terrorist cell is meeting? We are told to look out for unusual packages that could be bombs, and leaving your luggage unattended at an airport can get you arrested. The Australian spy agency ASIO (Australian Security Intelligence Organisation) was given a huge increase in its budget and manpower capabilities in 2005, in response to the allegedly heightened threat of terrorism.

For most of 2005 and 2006 the newspaper careers and employment pages were filled with advertisements as ASIO attempted to recruit 'Generalist Intelligence Officer' (GIO) and other trainees in espionage, including IT graduates. A typical ad was captioned *We're looking for intelligent people to fill in the blanks*, over a facsimile of a letter on which the copy for the ad had been written, but with some of the words heavily blacked out. For example, the first line of the copy read: 'We're looking for people for a challenging career with ██████.' Further down, a whole paragraph is blacked out except for a few telling words: 'Daily work includes ████████████████ identifying threats ████████ ████████████████ and gathering intelligence ████████████ ████████████████████.'

The ASIO website contains a message strongly advising applicants not to discuss their intention to join the organisation with anyone, even members of their family. As well as encouraging this low level of deceit and dependency, it provides advice on what a generalist intelligence officer might do, once their year of basic training is finished:

> As a GIO you would use covert and sometimes intrusive, methods of investigation. Some of the more intrusive methods can only be used with the approval of the Attorney-General in the form of a warrant. Some of the methods we use which require a warrant include:
>
> - Interception of telecommunications.
> - Use of listening devices.
> - Use of tracking devices.
> - Access of information in computers.
> - Entry and search of premises.
> - Examination of postal articles.

ASIO has a professional responsibility to recruit new spies, but what about a bit of casual everyday spying? It's still illegal for most of us to tamper with Her Majesty's mail or break into people's houses and steal their undies, but if you need to know more about someone you've just met (or think is a spy/terrorist), no worries, just 'Google' them.

> **Google**: v. To search for the name of (someone) on the Internet to find out information about them. *New Oxford American Dictionary* (cited in Finnila 2005)

It could be argued that Googling someone is reasonably harmless; we've probably all done it to look for old friends and acquaintances that we've lost track of, but as Richard Finnila writes in Brisbane's *Courier-Mail*: 'It's rather like the modern-day equivalent of peeping over the neighbour's fence, only you can do it to anyone from anywhere without anybody knowing' (Finnila 2005).

That last bit's not quite right—your ISP has a record of the search and the results and the sites you visit from the Google search. And isn't perving over your neighbour's fence a gross breach of their privacy? It's a comment further down in Finnila's article that should start alarm bells clanging: 'Search engines, such as Google, have become the silent law enforcers—a huge modern-day threat to a criminal's ability to remain incognito' (Finnila 2005). Is Google.com the new home of Big Brother?

Googling has become so common—over 6 million Australians use it regularly to access more than 8 billion websites—that there are now rules of etiquette for people who use it to check out potential dates. Apparently you shouldn't tell your date that you Googled them because it might seem that you don't trust them. People can also be embarrassed by information available via Google—the Internet is not always reliable or easily checked for accuracy and it stores information for a very long time. It pays to remember that information on the Internet has a long half-life. According to librarian Belinda Weaver, 'It's like plutonium, it can follow you around for a long, long time' (quoted in Finnila 2005). It is no coincidence that the ASIO website lists the Internet as one of the non-covert sources that a GIO might use in the endless hunt for terrorists under the bed.

However, it's not just a problem that you might be 'fingered' as a potential terrorist through the traces you leave behind on the Internet. From the late 1990s a number of civil liberties groups have been raising doubts about the protection of personal privacy in cyberspace. Today the political police are not the only ones interested in your surfing habits, and private data companies are busily building files on tens of millions of Web users to produce detailed consumer profiles. This is one sense in which we can begin to theorise the surveillance economy: the very fact of surveillance and the results of data-mining have become valuable commodities in the information economy. The millions of bytes of data can then be sorted and resold to companies keen to better target their marketing strategies, assess the value of their customers, and adjust their products accordingly (Boukhari 1998).

Michel Foucault and the surveillance society

The French philosopher and sociologist Michel Foucault is credited with some of the first modern writing on the rise of the surveillance society. In his 1979 book, *Discipline and Punish*, Foucault argued that by the turn of the 19th century, modern Western capitalism had become a punitive society that relied on prisons and repression to keep populations under control. Discipline and power rose together in the form of the state apparatus, but governments do not only rely on violence to secure compliance. It was possible, Foucault argued, to police society through regimentation, surveillance, and categorising or differentiating the population into a hierarchy.

This system was perfected in the prison system, where a regime of total surveillance could be instituted and where, to a degree, the prisoners became self-regulating because they could never be sure that they weren't being watched. According to Foucault, the prisoners internalised the surveillance, a system of control that 'enables the disciplinary power to be both absolutely indiscreet, since it is everywhere and always alert, and absolutely discreet, for it functions permanently and largely in silence' (1979, p. 177).

A second instrument of power that features in Foucault's writing on discipline and punishment is the use of the examination, which has three functions:

1 to classify objects and people according to some visible means or arrangement;
2 to situate people within socially and ideologically determined fields of 'normal' behaviour or performance;
3 the documentation of an individual's 'progress' or 'condition' through meticulous record-keeping.

This allows individuals to be described and analysed, compared, and, more importantly, corrected if there is deviation from the acceptable norms or standards (Foucault 1979, p. 190). The racial and psychological profiling techniques that are now popular with law enforcement agencies as a way of identifying potential terrorists are based on these classification techniques that work on all types of gathered data; from phone records to library borrowing transactions, emails, and credit card purchases. The technical, digital means of gathering, sorting, classifying, and building a profile from available data now exist to elevate surveillance abilities 'to the level of the science fiction sublime' (Lewis 2003, p. 341).

In the thirty years since Foucault wrote *Discipline and Punish*, we have seen the technologies and techniques of surveillance and profiling moved out of the prison system and applied systematically to civil society. Foucault argued that the generalising of modes of surveillance beyond the prison walls has created the social and psychological condition in which all citizens are simultaneously the guards and the guardians. Foucault was not aware of the power of digital technologies when he made these observations, but it is clear today that the convergence of communication and surveillance technologies has made the task of total coverage much easier. According to some estimates, more than 26 million CCTV cameras were installed around the world in 2003 and the market was growing at between 40 and 50 per cent each year (Farmer & Mann 2003, p. 36); by 2006 that number had grown to well over 60 million. There are now databases in existence that can handle vast amounts of information about individuals and run pattern recognition programs that look for suspicious activity. Even mildly critical observers are worried about what they see in the future. Maureen Dowd, a columnist with the *New York Times*, says that the US government's attempt to create an all-encompassing, all-seeing database of its citizens is an 'attempt to create an Orwellian "virtual, centralized grand database", which could put a spyglass on Americans' every move, from scanning shopping, e-mail, bank deposits, vacations, medical prescriptions, academic grades, and trips to the vet' (Dowd 2003).

The Pentagon has argued that no one need fear this new powerful database—it is justified as a safety precaution in the face of a perceived terrorist threat. However, Foucault might argue that as power extends its influence and ability to carry out more complex surveillance actions, it also invents new applications for its new powers. Thus as models of deviant behaviour (such as a possible propensity for school violence or terrorism) are identified, or created through the application of technology and technique, the disciplinary and punishing powers are increased and further deployed (Foucault 1990, p. 42).

The media's role in naturalising the surveillance society

There is a kind of scaremongering journalism associated with terrorism and the supposed breakdown of society's moral codes that is very common in the tabloid newspapers, among talk-back shock-jocks, and on the commercial current affairs programs on television. On most days the local news is dominated by crime stories and by hysterical urgings for all of us to contact 'Crime Stoppers' and to report suspicious activity. In academic literature this is known as the generation of 'moral panics' and often they're hard to avoid if you're at all interested in reading the newspaper or watching television. The perceived threat of terrorism has created its own forms of moral panic journalism (see Hirst & Schutze 2004a,b). In addition to moral panic in the news, there are crime dramas on television on most nights of the week, usually two in a row and sometimes on all the commercial networks at the same time. In June 2003 there was an average of nine police/legal or crime dramas on television during peak evening viewing times, and in September of 2003, an average of seventeen. In October 2005 there was an average of twenty prime-time police/crime and legal dramas. One Sunday evening on Channel Nine you could watch three in a row: *CSI: Crime Scene Investigation*; *The Closer*, and *Real Crime*. Then on Tuesday, another episode of *CSI: Crime Scene Investigation* at 8:30, followed by *CSI: New York* at 9:30. On Wednesday there's *CSI: Miami* at 8:30 and *Without a Trace* right after. In March 2006 the number had dropped slightly to thirteen crime dramas in the average week. On Channel 10 you could watch variants of the popular *Law and Order* show and Nine was still showing *CSI* in a double episode on Tuesdays. There's an element of what we might call forensic voyeurism about this type of television and it bears little or no relationship to what's actually happening in the real world. It's no wonder we feel tense all the time.

Surveillance in our daily lives is also naturalised in other ways, most prominently by so-called 'reality' television programs, which are really only game shows, as we discussed in part I. *Big Brother* and *The Mole* are two prime examples, but now there is a new style of show gaining in popularity. The most common one in Australia is *Border Security*, which takes the surveillance cameras of the show's producers behind the scenes at Australian airports as drug-smugglers and other would-be 'pests' are caught and investigated by ever-vigilant customs officers (Murphy 2006). It wasn't always like that. Through the entertainment value that these so-called 'reality' television programs generate, the very act of surveillance is naturalised and we see it rendered in contexts that appear to reduce the intrusive and invasive nature of what we're seeing. In the case of *Big Brother*, our discomfort at essentially perving on the housemates is abated by our knowledge that they're in the house/studio voluntarily. In *Border Security*, our comfort is maintained by knowing (or at least by trusting the camera to show us) that the people being interrogated and searched are somehow 'bad'. They are either 'foreign' or they've probably done something 'wrong'—whether it's drugs or some other contraband they're smuggling, or they're making an attempt to somehow enter 'our' space without the requisite approvals. We see the surveillance as being somehow normalised and morally acceptable in these terms and it helps to blunt our suspicion of monitoring activities.

Surveillance is normalised in other ways, too, by the media. You've probably seen CCTV footage of a convenience store or service station hold-up on the nightly news. Do you ever wonder how and why this material gets into the hands of the television stations? The simple answer is that the police routinely hand it over; it's widely seen as a 'public service' role for the media. It works the other way, too. Television stations are often compelled, or volunteer, to hand over footage to the police, particularly of demonstrations when the police need to identify 'ringleaders' or individuals who commit 'violence'. In one famous American case, the Tampa (Florida) police department used crowd footage shot at the 2001 Super Bowl (the grand final of the American football season) and face-recognition software to record the images of 72 000 fans. After matching the faces against a database of known criminals, nineteen faces in the crowd were identified as 'known troublemakers'. Robert O'Harrow described this as an 'Information Age experiment' in which the Super Bowl crowd were unwitting guinea-pigs and the Tampa stadium the giant 'petri dish' (2005, p. 178).

We can also look at some historical reasons why the mass media are willing accomplices in building the surveillance capacity of the digital technology. There has always been a murky grey area between journalists and the intelligence community. After all, at a technical level (of skills, technique, and targeting) there is very little difference between a reporter and a secret agent (except that reporters don't usually kill people).

The celebrated case of the infamous British double agent H. A. R. (Kim) Philby is well known to most journalists: Philby was a British war correspondent who later ran the counter-intelligence branch of the Secret Intelligence Service and was eventually outed as a long-serving member of the Soviet spy agency the KGB (Knightley 2002, p. 244). This is an extreme case and the best known, but there have been other situations, both before and after Philby, of news reporters blurring the line between their public role as seekers of the truth and a more clandestine role as a conduit of information to governments. The Australian journalist Wilfred Burchett was widely believed to be working 'behind the scenes' during both the Korean and Vietnam conflicts, gathering and passing on unofficial intelligence. In Burchett's case he was working for the 'enemy' of the day—though many other correspondents were grateful for his tips as the censorship imposed by the Allies meant they were getting little news from their own side. Burchett was also accused of working openly for the KGB, the Chinese, and other 'communist' governments during the Cold War, claims he has always denied (Burchett 1981). In May 2006 the German government admitted that it had retained reporters as spies, including some from leading daily newspapers. There has always been a quitly acknowledged and furtive relationship between journalists and security services.

When discussing the news media's role in normalising overt and extensive surveillance, we must also look at the factors of 'self-censorship' and the journalistic reliance on 'official sources'. For example, a 2004 article in the *Economist* actually made the argument that the advent of miniaturised digital technologies such as the mobile phone, coupled with increased data storage capabilities on PCs, meant that surveillance was being 'democratised'. The source for this idea was 'security guru' Bruce Schneier. He told the *Economist* that 'surveillance abilities that used to be limited to governments are now, or soon will be, in the hands of everyone' (quoted in 'Move over, Big Brother' 2004). Bruce Schneier is the founder and chief technical officer for an information security company called Counterpane Internet Security Inc. and the author of several books including *Beyond Fear*. According to the book blurb (which you can read on Schneier's website www.schneier.com), *Beyond Fear* is a commonsense and practical guide to help you and your family to 'think sensibly about security' to 'enhance security at home, at the office and on the road'. In other words, it plays to the very fears that have been created by alarmist media coverage. In a neat twist, the self-promoting website also completes the media-hype circle: 'Described by *The Economist* as a "security guru" … '. There's a link from Schneier's website to the company he founded—'the world's leading protector of networked information'. Counterpane sells its 'managed security services' to many government agencies and a company media release of 13 January 2006 quotes Schneier: 'We are committed to creating state-of-the-art, adaptable security solutions that deliver comprehensive protection at a reduced cost.'

A simple Google search shows that Bruce Schneier is hardly a disinterested source for the *Economist*. The 'security guru' is not an independent commentator but heads a company that markets and sells security software and has a direct commercial interest in promoting a 'democratic' surveillance society. O'Harrow makes several such connections between security industry leaders, journalists, and government agencies in his excellent account of the surveillance society *No Place to Hide*. The argument that putting low-cost surveillance equipment into the hands of consumers somehow 'democratises' the surveillance society is, in our view, just another myth of what Vincent Mosco calls the 'digital sublime'. It creates the false sense of 'widespread popular empowerment' that grows without substance in a 'spiral of hype' (Mosco 2004, p. 25). It's also perhaps not surprising that the *Economist* (in this and other examples we've cited) has leapt on the bandwagon of the digital sublime. Mosco discusses the work of a senior editor at the *Economist*, Frances Cairncross, whom he says has 'sounded a mythic triumphalism' about the ability of the Internet to transcend geographic space and the ability of surveillance to promote 'massive improvements in crime prevention' (Mosco 2004, p. 86). The *Economist* is a conservative publication aimed at the global business elite, and as a senior writer with the magazine, Cairncross sees global business spearheading a new crime-free, peaceful world. She also sees the world being, with business at the helm, a more democratic place. The provision of new communication and media technologies will free consumers, who will gratefully become 'less susceptible to propaganda': 'Bonded together by the invisible strands of global communications, humanity may find that peace and prosperity are fostered by the death of distance' (Cairncross 1997, p. 279, cited in Mosco 2004, p. 87).

'DIGITAL SUBLIME'

Vincent Mosco uses the phrase 'digital sublime' to suggest the power of digital computing and digital technologies to apparently transcend the everyday (the 'banal') by seeming to be everywhere and able to satisfy desire or instil fear and to impress with an overwhelming presence.

In the cynical world of journalism and public affairs, this rhetorical style is rudely known as 'boosterism'. Cairncross's position is also redolent of digital determinism: the means of democratising surveillance is the consumer gadgetry of mobile phone-cameras, digital still and video cameras, and broadband Internet connections. In 2004 over 180 million phone-cameras were sold worldwide, compared with under 50 million film cameras and around 65 million digital cameras. So what are people going to do with them? Take photos of course. In an article headlined 'Move over, Big Brother', the *Economist* attempted a humorous tagline at the end, but perhaps this is more significant than the writer thought: 'Increasingly, it is not just Big Brother who is watching—but lots of little brothers' ('Move over, Big Brother' 2004).

The most obvious cases of journalistic self-censorship occur during wartime, when 'operational security' is used as a catch-all phrase to prevent the release of sensitive or embarrassing information. Military commanders often rely on the deep loyalty of individual reporters in order to use them as a conduit for propaganda (willingly or unwillingly). This has become particularly important since September 11, 2001 as the 'war on terror' has unfolded and the 'enemy' is often no more than a nebulous threat, or vague organisational structure that is hard to pin down (see, for example, Seymour Hersch's *Chain of Command* for an account of events since 9/11). The media's support for the 'terror frame' of analysis often goes unquestioned and unchecked and there's an unwritten assumption that if the government says something is so, then that's what should be reported (Hirst & Schutze 2004a,b).

This has certainly been the case in the United States, where both government and corporate support for new and invasive forms of surveillance technology is strong. The American media has been very supportive of claims—often not backed by evidence—that the new surveillance technologies (face identification, data-mining, and suspect profiling) are going to save lives and protect freedom. They have been less inclined to investigate what's really going on, a process that the American Civil Liberties Union believes is building the 'infrastructure of a surveillance society' (O'Harrow 2005, pp. 137–8). Governments around the world have now been arguing for more than four years that the terrorist attacks in New York and Washington D.C. in September 2001 have created a new security-insecurity paradigm. This is a situation promoted by mainstream media that play on ignorance and fear, which the large private data-collection and analysis companies have been keen to exploit and in which governments were willing to seek new powers and roll back historical restraints on their surveillance capabilities (pp. 11–33). September 11, 2001 will certainly be long remembered as the day the world 'turned', and one of the important stories to be told is how it led to the surveillance society.

When too much surveillance is barely enough: 9/11 is the tipping point

> The potential for the abuse of surveillance powers has also risen sharply due to a dramatic post-9/11 erosion of legal protections against government surveillance of citizens. (Stanley & Steinhardt 2003, p. 9)

Just six weeks after the attack on the World Trade Centre and the Pentagon in September 2001, the American government legislated a revision of the US surveillance laws. According to a report by the American Civil Liberties Union, *Bigger Monster, Weaker Chains: The growth of an American surveillance society*, the new laws, known as the Patriot Act, 'vastly expanded' the government's power to spy on its own people while at the same time it reduced judicial and other 'checks and balances' on those powers. The report argues that the events of

September 2001 were the tipping point that allowed the FBI to 'roll back unwanted checks on its powers' (Stanley & Steinhardt 2003, p. 9). Of course, we are not trying to suggest that there was no surveillance prior to 9/11; to do so would be absurd. The point is that we have moved beyond what has been historically considered adequate surveillance.

The American government was quick to seize on the 9/11 attacks to push hard for new domestic and international surveillance powers (Twight 2001; O'Harrow 2005); Australia, Britain and many other countries were quick to follow suit. According to Charlotte Twight's report for the Cato Institute, published within a month of the attacks, the moves by the US Congress to seek extra surveillance powers represented a perversion of its 'most fundamental mission': protection the of individual privacy and liberty of Americans (Twight 2001, p. 1). However, this did not seem to worry too many Americans; news polls consistently showed support for increased surveillance and even civil liberties groups were caught in a bind. On the one hand they supported moves to catch the 9/11 conspirators; on the other they were worried about the implications of lifting the lid on biometric scanning and other security measures (Steinberg 2001). Many privacy experts and futurists recognised the double edge of the surveillance dialectic. A senior member of the Institute for Alternative Futures wrote early in 2002 that surveillance may make for more political and commercial 'transparency' in American society. He also supported a form of surveillance-democracy—making the captured images from CCTVs in public places available to everybody to download to personal storage devices. But there's a downside too: a fear that giving governments too much information could be used as a means of control over citizens, 'especially those with different beliefs or ideas' (Rowley 2002).

In July 2005 the *New York Times* reported that the US Federal Bureau of Investigation (FBI) had been collecting documentation on civil rights and anti-war protest groups in what the American Civil Liberties Union (ACLU) claimed was a 'pattern of political surveillance against critics of the [George W.] Bush administration' (Lichtblau 2005). According to the *NYT* article, the FBI claimed that the surveillance activities were to 'prevent disruptive and criminal activity', not 'to quell free speech'. But what the disclosures show is that so-called anti-terrorism agencies are being used by governments to spy on citizens, not because they pose any terrorist threat, but simply because they are against the government in power.

Surveillance in public places: Just a counter-terrorist measure?

> State government security guards have made video tape compilations of people having sex in public places, including South Bank and the Queensland Cultural Centre. (T. Thompson 2005)

According to Tuck Thompson's security guard sources, Geoff Schultz and David Schneider, a small group of their co-workers at Brisbane's South Bank have for years been secretly recording couples having sex in cars and on the grass, and also nude models used in life drawing and other activities at the Queensland Cultural Centre. Their tools of trade? Closed-circuit television cameras and monitors in the security room: 'One whistleblower security guard said there was a competition to see who could zoom in closest to the action, with the record being 2m' (T. Thompson 2005).

Another bit of harmless fun, sexual perversion, or a dereliction of duty? According to the *Courier-Mail* story, the allegations are being denied, but Schultz and Schneider claim to have seen guards watching the tapes at work. This might be an extreme case, and it could still turn out to be an urban myth, but it doesn't change the fact that there are thousands of CCTV cameras in CBDs and major centres all around the world and someone must be keeping an eye on them. In another case in Tampa, Florida (home of the Super Bowl), another surveillance merchant wanted to catch the eye of the police department and he offered them the use of his expensive equipment for a trial. Robert O'Harrow was given a tour of the complex in 2003 and watched as the camera held frame on a woman using an ATM machine while the computer equipment scanned her face for a match against known criminals in the police image database. O'Harrow admits there was something 'acutely voyeuristic' in watching the woman, who was 'oblivious' to the surveillance. As she walked away from the ATM the police followed her movements on other cameras. The detective who was escorting O'Harrow on this visit seemed unconcerned: '"Police officers are human beings. When there is a pretty girl walking by, I am not going to tell you that the officers don't look at her through the cameras," he said ... "They are not looking in bedroom windows, they are looking in public places"' (O'Harrow 2005, pp. 179–80).

There are many types of surveillance going on all around us. Some forms, such as CCTV cameras in public places, are fairly obvious, even if they're hard to avoid and some people tend to take no notice, even when they *are* committing an offence. In July 2005 a young man was caught on several CCTV cameras as he went on what the *Sunday Mail* called a 'one-man crime spree' in the suburb of Oxley (Alexander 2005). Apparently oblivious to the cameras, the man stole items from a newsagent and was confronted by a shop assistant; he then tried to steal from another store and was confronted by the owner who let him go, but called the police. A *Sunday Mail* photographer was on the scene in time to snap a shot of the guy stealing a drink at a fish and chip shop and to get a couple more of him being arrested a few moments later at Oxley railway station. A couple of days after the *Sunday Mail* story, the Wednesday edition of the *Courier-Mail* carried an alarming story, 'Cameras track youths during rampage' (Chilcott-Moore 2005). This story, from police sources, was illustrated by still shots from a CCTV camera at Brisbane's South Bank train station showing two young men who were allegedly involved in several assaults and a stabbing on the previous Saturday night. A detective involved in the case recounted how a gang of between five and seven young men had been picked up on several CCTV cameras as they made their way from the city to South Bank via the Goodwill bridge. Along the way several of the group tried to pick fights with other young men. Eventually, the group managed to find a victim and stabbed 17-year-old 'Fetuao' in the neck, chest, ear, and arm. This story appeared as the main item on the weekly 'crime stoppers' page in the *Courier-Mail*, which is also sponsored by Channel Nine and radio station 4BC. Anyone with information is encouraged to phone the police 'crime stoppers' hotline ('Police use videotape in search for gang' 2005).

If the physical surveillance of CCTV and cops with lapel cameras isn't enough, there's also almost constant electronic surveillance, too. Every time you use EFTPOS or a credit card or your mobile phone it leaves a small electronic signature. Each transaction can be logged and archived and none of it is safe from Big Brother's prying eyes. The Australian government's anti-terror legislation, introduced in October 2005, allows police and security agencies to access documents and electronically stored information about people or groups they believe may be suspect 'whether or not a terrorist act has occurred or will occur'. The legislation sets out the categories of information that officers are able to collect: details of bank accounts and transactions, details of travel plans or trips taken, and telephone records. There are also stiff penalties applied if someone refuses to provide the documents or files. This is an overt, if slightly aggressive, form of surveillance and, if you ignore the gross breaches of civil liberties in this and other sections of the anti-terror laws, it could be argued that such measures are 'necessary' to 'protect' us from terrorist attacks.

An ID card system back on the agenda

> Trust alone will be no foundation for imposing a national identity card on Australians and a full debate on a corresponding Bill of Rights will be essential to its acceptance ... The idea is not in itself repugnant if government is prepared to recognise that identification can easily turn to surveillance and that would be an un-Australian activity. (Coates 2005)

In the aftermath of the London bombings in July 2005, the debate about Australia adopting a national identity card system was revived. The Hawke Labor government made an initial push for an 'Australia Card' in 1987, but it was not popular with the general public. According to Roger Clarke, one of the privacy advocates credited with helping kill off the Australia Card in 1987, the public might well be too cynical to believe that new technologies could protect their interests (Wardill & Heywood 2005). In 2006 legislation to formalise an Australian identification card was proposed and it was anticipated that they would be in place by sometime in 2008. However, by July 2006 it seemed there was little political enthusiasm for the scheme in the face of public hostility.

The debate was reignited by Prime Minister Howard and he was quickly supported by Queensland Premier Peter Beattie and various other parliamentarians. But it appeared that at least an equal number of high-profile politicians and others were just as strongly opposed to the idea. Barrister Stephen Coates was quick to point out that the Australian Constitution does not offer sufficient guarantees of personal and political freedoms to allow for the nation's leaders to plead 'trust us' when it comes to legislating for an ID system. He also highlighted the contradictions and the techno-legal time-gap between the capability of surveillance technologies and the framework of regulation that could guarantee the technology was not misused by private interests or governments: 'this information-age also has created a need to protect us from misuse of our information and it is this issue which should be central to allowing access via an identity card when "investigators" delve into our private lives' (Coates 2005).

A number of ID card opponents raised their concern that the 'war on terror' was being used as an excuse to increase surveillance of the general population, including by the introduction of an electronic identity card. One interesting objection was that a centralised database of identity information could become a lucrative target for identity fraud and other aspects of organised criminal activity. In an interesting juxtaposition of news that again highlights the dialectic of the front page in action, the lead story in the *Courier-Mail* on the day that the Australia Card debate began to take off was headlined 'Banks lose millions in Net fraud' (Lekakis 2005). According to an internal bank document quoted by the newspaper, the industry was 'under siege from criminals', who can use sophisticated software, such as worms, viruses, and fake websites, to capture the personal details of customers. The banking fraud story was clearly linked to the ID card issue through the placement of a teaser for the stories inside under the tag line 'ID card may increase risks'.

In an editorial on the same day, the *Courier-Mail* made its opposition to a national ID card system clear by insisting that it could not be justified as a weapon in the 'war on terror'. The paper's opposition was stated on two interesting grounds:

> [M]uch of the public disquiet over the Government's attempts to strengthen Australia's security and intelligence capabilities has centred on what such changes mean for civil liberties and the right to privacy ... There is another reason ... history suggests that governments cannot be trusted not to abuse such a system. ('Identity card not part of war on terror' 2005)

Surveillance in the workplace: Necessary discipline?

Walk down any street in a major city; go into any convenience store, bank, or shopping centre and you'll be on camera. If you carry a mobile phone and are in range of a transmission tower, you can be traced. Trains, buses, airports, major road junctions, freeways, and schools are now under the watchful eye of Big Brother. But what about less obvious forms of electronic surveillance, for instance in your workplace?

In fact, it is legal in New South Wales for bosses to spy on their staff under the NSW *Workplace Surveillance Act*, as long as it's done properly; this means giving employees adequate notice that they are under surveillance and having an adequate policy on Internet use for office workers (Lebihan 2005). In order to watch your every move in the workplace, read your emails, trace Internet traffic to your machine, or put a tracking device in the company car, an employer has to give two weeks' notice. On the upside the NSW legislation makes it an offence for employers to block Web access to a union website (O'Malley 2005).

In the cyberpunk story *Snow Crash*, L. Bob Rife, the corrupt preacher and 'cable monopolist' who is pushing mind-altering drugs to turn people into slaves, boasts about the surveillance he is able to carry out over his workers for what he calls 'unacceptable lifestyle choices'. He uses audio and video bugs in their apartments to spy on them and, in his words: 'We're working on refining our management techniques so that we can control that information no matter where it is—on our hard disks or even inside the programmer's heads' (Stephenson 1992, p. 108). In the same story, another character who works for what remains of the United States federal government is regularly subject to lie detector tests to monitor her loyalty to the organisation. While this is a fictional account of a dystopian near future—a bit like *Nineteen Eight-four* really—there is plenty of evidence to suggest that similar levels of surveillance are practised today.

In 2005 the San Francisco-based Electronic Frontier Foundation (EFF), a consumer privacy group that covers the Internet and related issues, announced that it had cracked a secret code that is covertly attached to documents printed on many commercially available colour laser printers. The Foundation confirmed a story from the previous year in *PC World* magazine that quoted an employee of the Xerox company saying that microscopic yellow dots were printed onto sheets processed through its machines.

The EFF said that they had verified that the dots, visible with a magnifying glass and a blue light, gave details of the printer's serial number and the time a document was printed. The *Washington Post* article that laid out the details began with a rather curious opening sentence: 'It sounds like a conspiracy, but it is not' (Musgrove 2005). Mike Musgrove might not think it's a conspiracy theory, but it sure does sound like one. Further into the piece there's an acknowledgment from the US Secret Service that it knew all about the secret markings, but justified them on the grounds that it's a crime-busting measure, not an invasion of privacy: '"It's strictly a countermeasure to prevent illegal activity specific to counterfeiting," said a [Secret Service] spokesman, Eric Zahren. "It's to protect our currency and to protect people's hard-earned money"' (quoted in Musgrove 2005).

A Xerox official gave much the same answer, saying the company was just helping the government, but that did not satisfy the EFF. Spokesperson Seth Schoen drew an interesting comparison with efforts in the former Soviet Union to collect samples of all typewriter fonts so that the government could track down the writers of dissident pamphlets: '"It's disturbing that something on this scale, with so many privacy implications, happened with such a tiny amount of publicity," Mr Schoen said' (Musgrove 2005). Disturbing, but not, in the context of the surveillance society, uncommon. We only have to look at what's happening in China to understand the global reach of surveillance, not just as a technique of control but as an entrenched way of running both the economy and society (see the case study below).

There's another complex layer to the world of electronic surveillance: counter-measures and counter-counter-measures. There are commercially available software programs that can be installed on PCs to eliminate traces of files that you might not want anyone else to see. Apparently they are very popular and retail for around $US150. Enough copies of *Evidence Eliminator* are sold to make the company that manufactures it millions of dollars a year in profits. A free 'shareware' version called *Eraser* is apparently downloaded more than 2.5 million times a year. However, the availability of file-deleting software has led to what the *Los Angeles Times* calls a 'high-tech arms race' that is often played out in courtrooms. In one high-profile case a suspect was charged with possession of child pornography and with 'trying to make the incriminating files disappear' (Barrie-Anthony 2005).

This *LA Times* feature is interesting because it reveals just how much forensic surveillance of computers is now undertaken by law enforcement agencies and private companies like the Chicago-based Navigant Consulting group and companies like Deloitte & Touche Forensic Investigation Services. According to one source quoted in the article, in 2000 there were about 1000 forensic computer analysts in US law enforcement; by 2005 the number had grown to around 20 000. It seems unlikely, on the present level of anti-forensic software, that every trace of every incriminating photograph, email, or document can be eliminated. If you're connected to a server system, via the office, or through an ISP, the chances are even less because the records can reside in these other places, not just on your hard drive. Even if you can wipe all traces—thumbnails, references in other software, or other files—and overwrite the evidence, you may not escape the forensic file hunters. It can be evidence of guilt and an offence in itself to remove, or to have been presumed to remove, evidence that might be of value in a criminal prosecution: 'Whether or not overwritten data is ultimately recoverable, in courtrooms the use of anti-forensic software is often enough to imply guilt or invite steep sanctions. Even if the software works as planned, each program leaves a unique footprint that is easily identified by investigators' (Barrie-Anthony 2005).

The digital battle lines

There are clearly emerging battle lines over the future of the surveillance society, and we've already seen a number of skirmishes, but the fight is uneven.

On one side there is government and business, whose interests are clearly aligned, even though they don't always agree. There is consensus on this side that surveillance in the workplace is an employer's right and that political surveillance of suspected evildoers is a right of government. They also agree that the marketplace can deliver to government massive amounts of data and still conform to expected privacy standards. This is more of a myth than a reality, but it is a useful myth because it secures a profit for the data-miners and it allows governments to argue that they are doing no more than what is accepted in the marketplace. This group also pushes the line that market surveillance (digital market research) is merely a tool to assist companies to deliver tailored customer service. And, one day, pigs might fly!

On the other side we have citizens, sometimes but not always conscious of the fact that their rights are under threat and being eroded. Occasionally an individual will get upset and push for change, such as when medical privacy is invaded by direct marketing materials and you begin to wonder how you got onto this particular mailing list.

There are several important, though poorly resourced, organisations fighting back. In the main they have a civil liberties focus. One is Britain's Information Commissioner, Richard Thomas. He has spoken out against invasions of privacy, the danger of gathering too much data for identity cards, and establishing a database of every child from birth to age

18. In an interview with the *Times* in London, Thomas expressed his concern that Britain might 'sleepwalk into a surveillance society' and warned that giving governments too much freedom to collect information on citizens could lead to a police-state ('Beware rise of Big Brother stare, warns data watchdog' 2004). Similar warnings are being issued by privacy watchdogs and consumer groups all over the world. The question is: Who's taking notice and what are we going to do about it?

Every email you send, every phone call you make, every book, video, or DVD you borrow, every opinion your express in a blog or a chatroom, every Sizzler salad you select, every uni course you pass or fail, every red light you run, every financial transaction you make, every time you use an ATM, every time you leave or return to the country, every visit to your doctor, every time you park your car, walk through a shopping centre—all this 'data' of daily life is now captured, and available for dissection. Has surveillance—rather than communication—become the central function of our digital technologies?

CASE STUDY: SURVEILLANCE ON THE CHINESE INTERNET

> China's decision to impose further restrictions on internet communication illustrates that the country's economic rise is not being paralleled by a greater tolerance towards freedom of speech. (Rosen 2005)

This opening line from Danny Rosen's comment piece in the *Australian* neatly highlights the dialectic at work in the creation of a surveillance society. As China's state capitalist regime is opened up to the globalising world market, there is a tightening of political surveillance over the population, not, as the laissez-faire theories of economists would have us believe, an accompanying rise in political freedoms. In the lead-up to the 2008 Olympic Games in Beijing, the Chinese government is trying to liberalise its rhetoric and tone down the more authoritarian aspects of its global image. To this end a discussion paper on the future of democracy in China was released in 2005. However, the document *Building of Political Democracy in China* makes a case for continuing one-party rule into the foreseeable future. According to Western experts, China is desperate to find a home in the global economy, but cannot afford to open up its political institutions too much. Peter Goff has highlighted how the dialectic is affecting the use of the Internet in China. There is a contradiction between the regime's desire for economic growth and securing China's place in the world economy, and its fear that allowing too much electronic freedom for citizens will undermine its authority: 'The dilemma for the Government is that while the internet is needed to fuel economic growth, the uncontrolled flow of information it brings could undermine one-party rule and the leadership's conservative approach' (Goff 2005).

According to the Chinese Human Rights Watch group, more than sixty people are in prison for expressing unwelcome ideas over the Internet. Amnesty International and other human rights groups say there are tens of thousands of Chinese police officers whose function is to monitor Internet traffic. Internet cafés are regularly raided or closed down if patrons are found to be surfing on 'inappropriate' sites. It seems that the Chinese government is prepared to go even further in controlling what its citizens can think and think about. In October 2005, *Newsweek* correspondent Melinda Liu ('Big Brother is talking' 2005), wrote about how the Net police are now actively participating in chatrooms to put the government's line on controversial topics: 'The aim is not simply to stifle dissent or to control the free flow of information, but increasingly to shape public opinion in cyberspace' (Liu 2005).

In September 2005 the Chinese government issued a new set of 'Web rules' to complement the thirty or so that have been promulgated since 1994. The rules require news postings to be 'healthy and civilized', they outlaw content that might incite 'illegal assemblies, associations, marches, demonstrations or gatherings that disturb social order', and ban content that might help an 'illegal civil organization' (Xhinua News Agency, quoted in Liu 2005). News sites and weblogs are allowed to promote only pro-China views and, according to the new Internet rules, they must register with the government as news organisations in order to operate at all (Rosen 2005).

Western technology companies are complicit in much of the censorship and surveillance on the Chinese branch of the web. It has been documented that some firms have been putting content filters in place on Chinese servers at the urging of the government. In 2004 a Chinese journalist, Shi Tao, was arrested and charged for comments he made about Taiwan. He was caught because Yahoo! gave details from his email account to the authorities (Rosen 2005). In June 2005, the global free speech organisation the International Freedom of Expression eXchange (IFEX) reported that Microsoft was among the multinational companies hoping to gain commercial favour with the Chinese regime by supplying software that made it easier for authorities to track dissidents over the Web. Amnesty International says that such assistance to the government in efforts to stamp out dissent is a violation of the UN covenant covering Human Rights Norms for Business, which requires firms to 'ensure that the goods and services they provide will not be used to abuse human rights' (cited in IFEX Communique 2005).

Questions

After reading this case study, consider the following questions:

1 Why shouldn't the Chinese government be able to control what its citizens do with the Internet?

2 Why should Amnesty International criticise Microsoft and the other companies who are trading in China. Aren't they just protecting their own business interests?

3 Check recent newspaper and other reports for further information on control over the Internet in China. Has the situation become better or worse for Chinese 'netizens'?

4 Is China's attitude to controlling the Internet any different from what we might see in Australia or other Western countries?

KEY POINTS

The key points in this chapter are:

- The idea of 'Big Brother', which first came to infamy in George Orwell's 1948 novel *Nineteen Eight-four*, and the subsequent appropriation of the phrase as the name of a tacky reality TV show, which in at least one jurisdiction has repeatedly beached broadcasting standards.
- 'Big Brother' has become a useful mimetic metaphor for describing, normalising, and criticising the surveillance society.
- The manner in which communication technologies are beginning to exercise surveillance over citizens, and not promote liberty, with a plethora of examples of how this is happening.
- The evidence points to the fact that, if we're not already living in a surveillance society, we soon will be.

CLASS DISCUSSION

1 Does knowing that surveillance CCTV systems are everywhere in public places make you feel safer, or less safe? Why?

2 Is Foucault right to think that the increase in surveillance has led to a situation where everyone is both gaoler and inmate?

3 Do you find it disturbing that we are being encouraged, like the young Spies in *Nineteen Eighty-four* or like young ASIO recruits in 2005, to check up on people we meet using a popular Internet search engine?

4 How much 'junk mail' do you receive from companies trying to sell you their products?

5 Do you wonder how they got your name?

6 Have you ever tried to get yourself removed from a marketing database?

7 Do you agree with the authors that the media have played a role in normalising and legitimising an increase in surveillance through the types of programming mentioned (*Big Brother*, crime shows, etc.)?

8 Would you agree to participate in an 'Information Age experiment' like the one conducted at the Tampa Super Bowl? Why?

14

THAT'S THE WAY THE COOKIE RUMBLES: A SURVEILLANCE ECONOMY

OBJECTIVES

After reading this chapter you will have an understanding of the ways in which a surveillance economy may be emerging as the new mode of development in the global capitalist economy. In particular we hope you become familiar with the following:

- the subtle but important differences between a surveillance *society* and a surveillance *economy*;
- how the subliminal myths surrounding the supposed 'death' of old media forms and technologies are related to the process of mutual constitution that underlies a surveillance society and creates the conditions for the growth of a surveillance economy;
- how euphemisms such as 'knowledge' or 'information' economy disguise the level of commercial surveillance at the heart of economic and social relations of production;
- where the surveillance economy has come from and some suggestions about where it is heading.

KEYWORDS
creative industries
search economy
security economy
surveillance economy

A *surveillance economy,* the key to a surveillance society

This chapter outlines our current thoughts on what might constitute a surveillance economy and how the transition from broadcasting to narrowcasting may contribute to the development of the surveillance economy. By looking at how surveillance is now constituting itself as an important element of the global economy we can further our understanding of how the economic base and the cultural-social superstructure are dancing the dialectic of Vincent Mosco's 'mutual constitution'.

SURVEILLANCE ECONOMY

The idea that the dominant forces in an economy are those to do with surveillance; that research and development in an economy has a focus on surveillance or security technologies; that capital investment in technologies is in the area of surveillance; that recurrent budgets in both the private and public sector make increasing provision for surveillance; that employment growth is related to surveillance and security; and that continuing surveillance of the citizenry and border protection are key imperatives in economic and social discourse.

In the previous chapter we outlined some of the ways that the emerging surveillance economy is becoming visible as an element of the emerging surveillance society—for instance, in the use of video and electronic surveillance in the workplace. The previous chapter also laid out the contours of the new surveillance landscape that is having an impact on our cultural, social, and political institutions. This would not be possible, we believe, without some similar changes in the economic base. In this chapter our aim is to show how a new mode of development—one that relies heavily on search and surveillance techniques, made possible by digital convergence—is slowly but steadily reshaping the global economy. We hope to demonstrate that our theory of the surveillance economy is more than idle speculation by documenting how the transition from broadcasting to narrowcasting is constituted by and helps to further develop aspects of surveillance that are now embedded in the economic foundations of global capitalism. We first need to clarify the important distinction between a surveillance society and a surveillance economy. It's not just a matter of semantics, but rather an important theoretical distinction.

A surveillance society

In a surveillance society there is a high degree of what we call 'social surveillance', by which we mean general surveillance for the purpose of keeping the peace, preventing and detecting crime, and maintaining social order (political surveillance). It is possible to have a surveillance society without a surveillance economy, but a surveillance economy can only develop in societies that have already 'accepted' a high degree of social/political surveillance over ordinary life.

Ever since the first nation-states and governments were alienated from the majority of the population, rulers have felt the need to carry out daily surveillance of citizens. When the authority of governments is vested in economic and military power, cloaked in a fog of democratic myth and illusion, there will always be a suspicion in the minds of the governing elite that someone, somewhere is hatching a conspiracy to overthrow them. This is why in English common law and in most judicial systems there are crimes of sedition and treason, often with very severe penalties, up to execution by hanging or firing squad.

Governments feel the pressure created by the contradictions that abound in the daily lives of their citizens. On the one hand, there is the myth that the power of governments is legitimised through popular elections; on the other, the reality of a system in which voting is, for most people, a ritual of choosing the lesser of two evils (see chapter 15). Our experience tells us that no matter who is in power, in pretty much any country in the world that calls itself an electoral democracy, the rich get richer and the poor get done over. People are not stupid and they are aware of this glaring fault line. On the other hand, most don't think there's anything that they can do about it. This is because of the strong ideology of self-surveillance and political compliance that has a viral hold on consciousness. It's also a function of the rhetoric that everyone gets a 'fair go'; that anyone can be on top of the pile if they climb the 'ladder of opportunity'; that we all 'aspire' to be just like those rich, white middle-class confections that we see every day in Television-land. Nationalism and patriotism are also strong mimetic codes in most hegemonic systems of ideology based on the geographic borders of the nation-state (Jensen 2004). These memes have become even more important during the current historical phase—the so-called 'war on terror'—and they are ever-present in most media discourses.

The myth is a society of equals and opportunity where failure is the result of individual fault. The reality is eight-hour shifts in factories, shops, and offices; rising taxes; less and more expensive health care; fewer teachers in public schools; the privatisation of roads, airports, and telecommunications infrastructure and other utilities; and the rob-the-poor-to-feed-the-rich principle of so-called 'user pays'.

A surveillance economy

> Security's third trade-off may involve globalisation an[d] technological change. It is not clear ... whether globalisation is compounding or extenuating the problems associated with the security economy. One can identify a race between two effects of globalisation. (Bruk 2004, p. 115)

The Paris-based global club of rich nations, the Organisation for Economic Co-operation and Development (OECD) published a report in 2004, *The Security Economy*, which examines the economic consequences of the changed world situation since September 2001.

The framework of the report is to define and outline the types of issues that have begun to emerge from the convergence of technologies and the perceived security crisis induced by the now global 'war on terror'. What the OECD blandly describes as the *security economy* is what we're calling, with much more purpose, the *surveillance economy*.

The definition of the security economy provided by Barrie Stevens (2004, p. 8), discusses the sharpening focus on security issues and the growing demand for 'security-related goods and services' that has given rise to 'a wide and varied range of economic activities in both the government domain and the business sector'.

For now we can suggest that in a security economy, the very act of surveillance has become part of the economic relations of that social formation. By this we mean that some surveillance functions have become commodified and that in general terms there is a specific set of surveillance functions that support the economy and shape its development. This includes the commodification of both privacy (or lack of it) and personal identity. Mosco (2004, p. 170) identifies one of the dialectics at work as being 'the struggle for personal privacy', which is also a struggle 'against the expanding commodity'.

In a surveillance economy, commodified surveillance is not just for the purpose of maintaining good order and weeding out trouble-makers, though that still occurs. Surveillance is used to shape and manage consumption patterns and there are physical and psychological/emotional manifestations of this in many of the commodities we take for granted today.

One example is the bar codes on products that are routinely scanned at the checkout in nearly all stores and shopping centres. These codes are used to track the merchant's stock and when tallied at the end of trading help to manage the restocking of shelves and the reordering of stock through the supply-chain all the way back to the manufacturer. This is a fairly benign use of bar codes and it's easy to see how it increases the efficiency of supply-chain management. It might also be seen as a boon for customers because it means your store is unlikely to run out of your favourite items. The manager always knows when the stock is running low. In fully automated systems the central computer can even alert the supplier and generate an automatic order for regularly stocked items.

But the bar code has other, less benign uses. Have you ever entered a competition that required you to send in the bar codes from a product—to collect ten or more bar codes and post them off as the cost of entry into a draw to win fabulous prizes? By entering such competitions and by passing on your carefully hoarded bar codes you are giving the marketing company that's running the competition valuable information about you and your shopping habits. By matching bar codes to your personal details, the marketing company knows where you bought the products, what batches they came from, and the period over which you purchased the products. This can help them work out your spending habits and to assess your value as a 'loyal' customer for that particular product. As a by-product of this process (collateral damage?), your name is entered into a vast database alongside your customer profile. This will then be used to further target marketing material at you and it may even be sold to other companies looking for people like you. This is one way that you end up on the mailing or phoning list of a company you've never dealt with before, but who will send you unsolicited advertising for years to come, or who will ring you at the most inconvenient time of the day to see if you're interested in buying what they're selling. The humble bar code may, however, soon be a relic of more benign times. The development of small radio frequency identifying (RFID) chips could make them redundant. According to O'Harrow, several US-based retailers are experimenting with implanted RFID chips in a range of consumer goods, including groceries and clothing. Once these tracking devices become common there is seemingly no limit to their application: 'virtually everything in the universe could be labeled with a tag containing a unique [identifying] number' (O'Harrow 2005, p. 286).

Consumer profiling has become a multi-billion dollar industry worldwide in the past decade. This would not have been possible without digital convergence. Personal digital data (everything from personal details to photographs, shopping habits, bank transactions, credit history, medical records, and criminal convictions) have become a very valuable information commodity.

Convergence and surveillance: From broadcast to narrowcast

> The revolution in urban surveillance will reach the next generation of control once reliable face recognition comes in. (*Earth Island Journal* 2001, p. 34)

The report to the European Parliament that contains this claim was published in 1998. Today, face-recognition software is a reality and along with other biometric surveillance and monitoring technologies it is already in use. In the United States the Bi-Lo grocery chain is using digital fingerprint technology to verify customers' ID. One of the leading companies in this field is BioPay LLC of Herndon, Virginia. As O'Harrow suggests, it is a name like 'something out of a cyberpunk novel' (2005, p. 175). The top-secret National Security Agency in Washington DC is also using face recognition to track employees and control access to its secure computer network (p. 176).

Governments spying on their citizens has been going on for a long time. It's been a fact of political life for centuries. Before the advent of telephones and listening devices, surveillance and spying had to be done at close quarters and in a directly physical way. The development of transistors made wire-tapping easier because the device could be smaller and less obtrusive; the spy was also at one remove physically and therefore safer. Satellite technology increased the global reach of the spy agencies and exponentially increased the amount of data that could be sampled, stored, and retrieved. The digital stage and even greater convergence has again exponentially increased the amount of surveillance and the volume of information that can be monitored. What is also interesting from our perspective is that many of the same technologies that are used for surveillance are also used in the media to perfect and reproduce the techniques of narrowcasting.

The electronic storage of phone records, text messages, and emails means that data is also retrievable at greater distances of time and space. This echoes what Thompson (1995) calls the distanciation of communication. We now have distanciation of surveillance. This phenomenon of distancing the watcher and the watched has led a professor at the prestigious Massachusetts Institute of Technology (MIT) to argue for a refined definition of surveillance in the age of convergence. Gary T. Marx (2004, p. 20) says the new definition should include 'the use of technical means to extract or create personal data'. This new definition (which adds to, not replaces, traditional definitions) takes into account that it's not just the 'watching' that constitutes surveillance today, but the additional things that can be done with the data once it's in a digital form. New methods of manipulation and matching make the data far more valuable, to both governments and corporations. According to Marx, the new means of digital surveillance can 'extend the senses' of the watcher, but also provide the watcher with 'low visibility' or even make them 'invisible' to the target; for good measure he adds that such surveillance is likely to be 'involuntary'. Data collection is also likely to be automated, 'relatively inexpensive', mediated 'through remote means', and available in real time. Further, he adds that it is 'more comprehensive' and can include 'multiple measures' (Marx 2004, p. 24).

One interesting and slightly disturbing aspect of the convergence of video technologies with wireless transmission is that many consumers are unwittingly inviting unwanted surveillance into their lives when they purchase home-security video units. In many cases these units operate on low-frequency wireless transmission of the signal back to a video monitor or computer. With the right antenna, anyone can intercept these signals from nearby. When people install these systems to increase their sense of personal security, they are unknowingly giving away their privacy.

This is an example of inadvertent intrusion that is created by flaws in the consumer products that push the surveillance economy into our homes on the pretext of increasing personal security. But this is not the only way we become ensnared in the surveillance economy. We are confident in our argument that suggests that the very transition—from broadcasting to narrowcasting—at the heart of our book is also an important vector for distribution of the mimetic code that replicates the ideology of a surveillance economy and allows it to enter our minds in a way that almost becomes standard operating procedure. In other words the narrowcasting media is an important site for the transmission of ideas which begin to normalise and hide the effects of surveillance below the level of our conscious thought.

Why do we call it a surveillance economy?

There are many theories, descriptions, and names for the current configuration of the global capitalist economy, but do they all fundamentally point to the same thing? The naming of an object, event, or trend is important because the act of naming implies a range of opinions and views about the thing being described. We don't have the space here to launch into a full-scale discussion of the differences in the naming practices that have given us such terms as 'knowledge' and 'information' society or economy. Instead we offer a brief overview and some arguments as to why we prefer to call it a 'surveillance' economy/society.

The knowledge economy

> [T]he concept of 'knowledge societies' offers a holistic and comprehensive vision with a clear development-oriented perspective that captures the complexity and dynamism of current changes in the world. (Briet & Servaes 2005, p. 3)

For the purpose of this review, we have joined 'information' and 'knowledge' economy/society as their definitions are close and the issues are similar in relation to both. According to Briet and Servaes (2005, p. 3), a knowledge society is based on four key principles that encompass social well-being and development: 'freedom of expression'; 'universal access to information and knowledge'; 'respect for human dignity'; and 'cultural and linguistic diversity'. These are admirable principles, but when we examine the reality of the global economy we quickly see that adherence to and action around these principles is hard to measure and hard to find (see, for example, Gwynne 2005). According to Wikipedia (2006b), the concept of a knowledge economy first came to prominence in New Zealand and was popularised by Peter Drucker in his book *The Age of Discontinuity*, first published in 1969. The driving forces for change that lead to the knowledge economy are globalisation, the intensity and density of knowledge embedded in economic activity, and the connectivity of information and communication technologies. The 'knowledge economy', or the 'information economy', is named as the 'network economy' by Manuel Castells. The 'network economy' is based on the 'network enterprise'. A network enterprise is one that is able to process knowledge efficiently, adapts to the changing landscape of the global economy, is flexible and innovative, and, above all, 'transforms signals into commodities by processing knowledge' (Castells 2000, p. 188). For Castells and others, the global media and the associated 'creative industries' are at the core of the network society and the knowledge economy (see, for example, Hartley 2005).

CREATIVE INDUSTRIES

A collective noun that refers to a range of activities and professions associated with media production in the information or knowledge economy. The creative industries include print, radio, and television production; literature and poetry; theatre and film; public relations; journalism; and marketing and advertising.

A fairly straightforward definition of the knowledge economy simply recognises that technology (and the knowledge that is embedded in technological objects) is a factor of production. This has been obvious to political economists for over a hundred years, but it seems that capitalist economics only discovered this idea in the 1980s when an economist called Paul Romer published work proposing that neo-classical economics change its view. In this view 'knowledge' is reinterpreted as a 'basic form' of capital and the argument is put forward that economic growth is driven by the 'accumulation of knowledge' (Ernst & Young 1999).

In our view this is an ideological argument and it arose mainly in response to the onset of a periodic crisis in profitability and accumulation within the global capitalist economy following the oil crisis of the late 1970s. In a sense the argument presented by neo-classical economists is basically that capital must appropriate as many forms of knowledge as possible in order to commercialise them (what the theory names as the creation of 'intellectual capital') and thereby resist the tendency to crisis for a little bit longer. Governments around the world were quick to seize on the knowledge economy argument in order to secure a commercial and competitive advantage for their own 'national' bits of capital. For example, the British Department of Trade and Industry argued in 1998 that 'the generation and exploitation of knowledge play the predominant part in the creation of wealth' (cited in Ernst & Young 1999). The key word in this passage, from our perspective, is of course 'exploitation'! The ideology of the knowledge economy is also technologically determinist and relies on ICTs in particular to sustain itself: 'Learning means not only using new technologies to access global knowledge, it also means using them to communicate with other people about innovation.' The digital-mythic nature of the knowledge economy mantra becomes clear in the following passage: 'With the advent of information and communication technologies, the vision of perfect competition is becoming a reality' (Ernst & Young 1999). As our political economy approach shows, there is no such thing as 'perfect competition' in the global capitalist economy—there are only winners and losers. The knowledge economy does not shift the balance in favour of the losers; it merely reorients the goalposts and changes the rules to ensure the winners continue their lucky streak. This imbalance cannot be ignored in knowledge economy theory. As Briet and Servaes (2005, p. 5) acknowledge, addressing the 'digital divide' is a key question and the gap 'will not easily be reduced'. A further important link between definitions of the knowledge or information economy and our preference to call it a 'surveillance' economy is provided by the growing importance of industrial espionage and security. As we noted earlier, this is recognised by governments and inter-governmental agencies like the OECD, which are beginning to name the 'security' economy and talk about it.

The 'security' economy

> In recent years security has taken a prominent place on the political and corporate agendas. Organized crime, terrorism, disruption of global supply chains, and computer viruses have raised people's awareness of the risks they face in today's world. (OECD 2004)

According to the OECD discussion paper *The Security Economy* (2004), the market for security goods and services is worth over $US100 billion a year and growing at between 7 and 8 per cent each year. The report supports measures to expand the security economy and acknowledges that commercial and political surveillance is increasing. The only cautionary note is that governments and corporations must ensure that surveillance and security are not misused 'Big Brother fashion' (OECD 2005). We can trace some of the historical outlines of the security economy back to George Bush's 'State of the Union' address in January 2002. In that speech President Bush made explicit links between the war on terror and the American economy and signalled the largest increase in defence spending in over twenty years (CNN.com 2002). As result of this unprecedented defence budget, the US Department of Homeland Security now has a mandate to specifically examine security economy issues and to ensure that communications and data storage infrastructure is secured against terrorist threats. In 2004 the department received nearly $US40 billion in funding and the National Science Foundation got over $US300 million for research into secure network technologies (Jackson & Welsh 2003). In March 2006 a Florida-based company got a $US40 million contract to build secure networks for the US National Security Agency as part of a 'crypto-modernization' project to harden ITCs (Beizer 2006).

SECURITY ECONOMY

The OECD uses this term as a polite way of describing what we define as the surveillance economy. The security economy has grown exponentially over the past decade in response to heightened risk assessment, particularly the threat of terrorism on a global scale.

The Department of Homeland Security is also encouraging further investment in security technologies by private companies. In a speech to the American Chamber of Commerce in Singapore, Homeland security chief Michael Chertoff said that new tracking and surveillance requirements for global shipping should be a private sector responsibility (Lippowicz 2006). In a highly unstable environment the protection of intellectual property becomes paramount in securing a competitive edge. Hence data security and encryption services are among the fastest-growing sectors in the economy. According to the Computer Science and Telecommunications Board of the US National Science Council, cryptography is an essential element of the security society: 'In an age of explosive worldwide growth of electronic data storage and communications, many vital national interests require the effective protection of information' (Computer Science and Telecommunications Board 1996).

We think that 'security' economy is a better description than 'knowledge' economy because surveillance and security are key aspects of the new relations of production, consumption, and the political-ideological framework of the network society. This is obvious in what Tilman Brük describes as the 'fifth trade-off' at work in the security economy: '*Security* versus *freedom* and *privacy*'.

> ... the political decision [is] about the balance of civil rights, privacy and individual freedom versus the possible need to curtail these rights in the pursuit of more security. Internet, computing, mobile and wireless technologies are highly vulnerable to security attacks. *At the same time*, these technologies can be used to monitor movements, usage and profiles of individuals or goods—*both those of consumers and those of potential perpetrators of crimes*. (Bruk 2004, p.117, emphasis added)

In a 'security' economy the methods of surveillance are much more deeply entrenched in the production and consumption process. Surveillance is, in effect, at the heart of all economic functions and dominates the whole fabric of society. A surveillance economy is a particular stage, period, or epoch in the development of the global capitalist system. It is also an interesting stage of capitalist economic development because of the close economic and political ties that are developed between capital and the state. O'Harrow's analysis contains many examples of how the growth of the security economy has been encouraged by huge grants from the American government to private companies to help them develop new technologies, such as face recognition, RFID chips, and other types of surveillance and data-mining capabilities. The Bush government created the Homeland Security Advanced Research Projects Agency (HSARPA) along the same lines as DARPA (the agency that built the precursor Internet) to boost research into economic security and surveillance measures, and a senior official in the Department of Homeland Security was explicit in encouraging private investment in a meeting with security industry contractors in 2003.

> 'We want you to recognize the economic opportunity that homeland security represents. It is important for all Americans to remember that when the terrorists struck on September 11 2001, one of their goals was to cripple the U.S. economy. We must remember this and change our mindset to make protecting the homeland a mission that moves our economy forward.' (Michael McQueary, quoted in O'Harrow 2005, p. 298)

In our view, the security economy and the surveillance economy are pretty much the same thing. But we have alluded to one important consideration: the security economy is driven almost entirely by government initiatives that draw in private capital by a process of research grants, commercialisation of results, and competitive tendering. The security economy draws the interests of the state and capital ever closer, further undermining the free market mythology. The security economy, while an important developmental stage of capitalism that highlights the close relationship between state and capital, is only half the picture. There is a purely commercial side to the surveillance economy that has been explored in a recent book called *The Search*, which has the interesting subtitle: 'How Google and Its Rivals Rewrote the Rules of Business and Transformed Our Culture' (Battelle 2005).

The 'search' economy

> As we root around in the global information space, search has become our spade, the point of our inquiry and discovery. (Battelle 2005, p. 12)

John Battelle calls it the 'search economy' because companies like Google recognised a business opportunity in cyberspace and turned it into the fastest-growing business in the history of the media. It was worth $4 billion in 2004 and is estimated to reach $23 billion by 2010 (p. 34). The main reason for this, according to Battelle, is that marketing and advertising executives have realised that search engines provide an efficient way to capture and exploit new leads and 'marketing leads are the crack cocaine of business' (p. 34). This has led to further commercial convergence between media content providers and search engines, particularly if they are capable of storing an individual's search history for later reference. According to the industry magazine *EContent*, advertisers see this as a valuable 'add-on' service. It becomes even more important if the advertiser is able to 'follow' a prospective buyer as he or she jumps from site to site (Smith 2005). The concept of the search economy is gaining a foothold to the extent that the *Wikipedia* site now has an entry for 'Google economy', which it defines as 'the concept that the value of a resource can be determined by the way that resource is linked to other resources. It is more complex than search ranking, and broader than interlinked web pages, though it draws meaning from both' (Wikipedia 2006a).

SEARCH ECONOMY

Battelle uses this term to describe the economic relations of production that seem to permeate capitalism in the early years of the 21st century, epitomised by the ubiquitous presence of Google on the World Wide Web. Bartelle coined the term to emphasise how so much of what constitutes commerce today relies on some kind of search function, particularly forms of electronic commerce.

Battelle paints a convincing picture of a digital future (which incidentally is not far away) in which our television and Internet habits will be constantly under surveillance by automatic means to push the most appropriate (in terms of what we are likely to purchase) advertising content directly at us. He argues that this changes the whole point of online marketing so that it is no longer merely a conduit for advertising but becomes, in his words, a new and effective 'sales channel', which fundamentally changes the economics of marketing in the digital domain: 'In the near future, it's quite possible that researchers tracking advertising by medium will have to fold television revenues into interactive [online]—they'll often be one and the same' (Battelle 2005, p. 171).

The America where Hiro Protagonist resides in Neal Stephenson's novel *Snow Crash* is a good, though obviously fictional, example of a surveillance economy. In Hiro's world the functions of government, including surveillance over citizens for the purpose of maintaining good order, have been farmed out to various franchises that compete against each other, economically and militarily. It is, in a funny way, another example of state-capital integration because all the firms and franchises are actually now constituted as sovereign nations. Only one organisation, the 'Feds' where Y.T.'s mother works, claims any jurisdiction over what used to be the physical space of the continental United States. Instead the Columbian drug cartels, the Mafia, and the Yakuza carve out their own little nation-states on the highways and in all the suburbs.

Hiro is a freelance spy for the 'Central Intelligence Corporation' and he gets paid when someone accesses the information, 'intel', that he loads into the CIC's database, the 'library'. The CIC and other agencies, nation-states, and franchises also hire a particular type of spook known by their slang nickname, 'gargoyles'. Like the backpack journalist we met in part II, the gargoyle is wired up for intelligence-gathering:

> Gargoyles represent the embarrassing side of the Central Intelligence Corporation. Instead of using laptops, they wear their computers on their bodies, broken up into separate modules that hang on the waist, on the back, on

> the headset. They serve as human surveillance devices, recording everything that happens around them. (Stephenson 1992, p. 115)

For any number of reasons, but mainly the ones outlined above, we prefer the term *surveillance* economy to some of the others. It is more honest about the core values and processes that are driving it. Surveillance is something concrete that we can see, hear, smell, touch, and taste, particularly with our senses 'working overtime'. On the other hand, terms like *knowledge* and *information* economy are less tangible and seem benign. Euphemisms like *security* make it sound a lot safer than it really is.

Surveillance in the market: Buying and selling identity

> As Google ventures deeper into the mainstream areas of media and advertising, many of the reigning powers there are watching with a mixture of fascination and fear. (Pfanner 2006)

We most often associate surveillance with a Big Brother-type state apparatus. It seems that governments will spy on citizens in order to maintain the peace—in other words, to maintain social control and to keep their power over the dispossessed. For most people this doesn't appear to be a problem. As the old saying goes: 'If you've done nothing wrong, you've got nothing to fear.' And the FBI claims it only monitors a small percentage of the American population and that it has checks and safeguards to stop the system from being abused.

Unfortunately, we know from American history and from the history of Special Branch police files in Australia that police agencies with powers to spy will almost always abuse those powers by indiscriminate wire-tapping, physical spying, or undercover surveillance. But what about the prospect of even more commercial surveillance?

What about media and market-based surveillance of our spending, eating, shopping, banking, entertainment, and other habits? Most of us are blissfully unaware of the snooping that private data companies are doing in our lives and we probably just chuck unwanted direct mail materials in the bin. However, to the companies involved, data-mining is a lucrative source of income and it puts them at the heart of the surveillance economy to the extent that Robert O'Harrow (2005, p. 266) says data-mining is at the core of the 'security-industrial complex'. The supporters of free-market data-mining argue that they are only trying to satisfy consumer demand. Bob Weintzen of the US Direct Marketers' Association says his members are simply trying to service the needs of the market and he justifies this by noting that we live in the 'information age'.

The sad truth is that today it's harder to be anonymous, not only from political surveillance, but also from market surveillance. Campbell and Carlson (2002) suggest that there has been a shift in thinking as we've moved into the information economy. They call this new paradigm the 'commodification of privacy' and say that it has weakened our resistance to surveillance marketing. Privacy has been reconceptualised so that it is no longer seen as a social right or a civil liberty to be exercised by consumers; in the surveillance economy it has become a means of exchange. It has also become what Foucault described as a form of self-discipline and self-surveillance through the unwritten contract that we are assumed to have signed when visiting websites, watching cable television, or using email. In a sense we expect to be watched, even though we cannot see the watchers; we must accept this surveillance in order to participate in the narrowcasting world, such as when we do our banking, make a purchase, or view an online news site: 'Surveillance has become automated, so that it is now the individual within the marketplace that often initiates the process of data gathering through such mundane activities as visiting an ATM, calling [1] 800 numbers, or making purchases with a credit card' (Campbell & Carlson 2002, p. 589).

Mining the consumer's mind

To make sense of all this volunteered data, a new industry has developed inside the emerging surveillance economy—data-mining. Like all aspects of capitalism, it is rapidly growing into an oligopoly with a handful of giant multinational firms dominating the global market. The inequality of power in the capitalist market system compels us to deal with the data-miners because it is the producers and suppliers, not the consumers, who decide the terms of the contract. In many cases the transaction that results in the delivery of consumer information to the data-mining companies is concealed behind a veneer of consumerism. We willingly comply with requests for personal information online in the (mistaken) belief that we will ultimately benefit from disclosure through the gaining of convenience and access to a range of otherwise unobtainable commodities. According to Campbell and Carlson, we are 'impelled through enticement' and compelled through the threat of exclusion to participate in a 'carefully constructed illusion' of a partnership between consumers and producers. We are never allowed to know the uses to which the personal information we hand over will be put (p. 590–1).

Three of the biggest data-miners are ChoicePoint, Axiom, and Experian. And now these companies are entering into commercial arrangements to sell data back to the US government, the FBI, and the CIA. No doubt the Australian authorities are interested. It will be interesting to see which of these large multinationals wins the tender to manage the introduction of ID cards in Australia. ChoicePoint collects, collates, and merges data from many databases, and managing director Howard Saffir says that it is his patriotic duty to sell this information back to the US government to help it sift out suspicious behaviour and map profiles of suspected terrorists. US Attorney-General John Ashcroft argued that the FBI should have access to ChoicePoint's data mines so that it can build comprehensive dossiers of potential terrorists by checking everyone's credit card, travel, and other habits to pinpoint likely suspects for further investigation. The FBI says it only targets criminals, but privacy advocate Chris Hoofnagle says that digital convergence brings with it new risks to privacy. Mike Polime, FBI agent, says the FBI's data warehouse is a necessary anti-terrorism tool in the post-9/11 environment. He argues that this does not infringe privacy, it just removes the ability of people to remain anonymous. Our acceptance of data-mining seems to be based on a misplaced trust in corporations and governments and relies on the market myth of consumer sovereignty. In reality we surrender control over our personal details for little or no benefit.

Google—and ye shall find

> Besides looking for new market segments like [the] local, search companies and new start-ups are focusing on several innovative approaches to monetizing your clickstream. (Battelle 2005, p. 37)

Only in the digital age of the surveillance economy could somebody happily spend their working day dreaming up new ways to monetise your clickstream! John Battelle is a founding editor of the cyber age's most influential magazine, *Wired*, so he's been involved in the online business world since the early days of the Internet. In his powerful book *The Search*, he outlines a large shift that is under way in the field of consumer marketing. In 2005, he believed that the shift was still in its 'early stages' (Battelle 2005, p. 167).

According to Battelle's research, Google and other search engine companies keep tight control over the complex mathematical formulae (algorithms) that determine the results of a search. By keeping track of the number of hits and by carefully screening the keywords and other text on a website, search engines can prioritise the order in which the 'organic' links are displayed on a results page. By periodically adjusting its secret algorithms, Google and the other large players can alter the order in which websites are ranked in a search. Google argues that it has to constantly update the algorithm to beat the efforts of spammers and scammers to cheat the search engine by creating false leads that boost a website's rating and push it to the top of the ranking list. Battelle draws the conclusion—vigorously denied by Google and the others—that this is done in order to maximise the revenue that search engines can generate from paid advertising: 'that it helped Google's business can't really be disputed' (p. 165).

There can be no doubt that Google's business planning has been successful. When it listed on the stock exchange in August 2004 the share price was $US85; in January 2006 it had reached a high-water mark of $US471.63. However, the stock was hit by a small shockwave in February 2006 when a Google executive said that the company felt that the new technology boom was over and that there would be few new innovations that could boost advertising revenue. Google's share price fell to $US362.62, a drop of 7 per cent (Hansell 2006). To counteract share market nervousness, Google quickly issued a clarifying statement indicating that the company was seeking 'other ways to monetize the business'—that is, to get more dollars out of the 'clickstream' by setting up direct payment systems for its classified advertising business; expanding its video-on-demand service; looking at using the phone system as well as the Web to connect buyers and sellers; and investing in a wireless Internet system. As the *New York Times* pointed out, despite this hiccup in its share price, Google stock was (as of 1 March 2006) still worth around $US107 billion and it was still the world's 'most valuable media company' (Hansell 2006). In fact, Google had become the world's largest media giant back in mid-2005 when its market capitalisation was only $US81.4 billion and its share price a paltry $US293.12. By comparison, Google's nearest competitor in the search engine business, Yahoo!, had a market capitalisation of just $US52.3 billion (Mathieson 2005).

It now seems that all of cyberspace and other narrowcasting media are ripe for commercialisation and commodification—most of it based on the 'search and surveillance' model established by Google and the other search engine providers to attract both searchers and advertisers. Even the blogosphere, that once sacred democratic corner of the Web, is now attracting big bucks from advertisers. In June 2005 ninemsn (a joint venture between Australia's Nine TV network and Microsoft) launched its own blog site and signed up luxury car brand Volvo as one of its first advertisers. But some bloggers are wary of the commercialisation of their territory and there have been cases of companies using blogs as a form of viral marketing—they pay people to create and populate blogs with praise for the company and its products, without acknowledging that they are linked (Canning 2005).

Is Silicon Valley today like Detroit in the motor age?

> Has the technology industry—a big and undeniably important slice of the [American] economy—become a business whose best days are behind it? In other words, is Silicon Valley turning into Detroit? (Lohr 2005)

Steve Lohr's article reports that several leading investment companies in the United States, including Goldman Sachs, have begun to view the digital revolution and the growth of hi-tech companies at the heart of the computing industry (Silicon Valley) as just another business cycle on the 'ladder of economic evolution' that creates similar opportunities and threats to those generated by traditional business cycles, such as the boom-slump cycle in the motor industry (Detroit). This is an interesting point that confirms our analysis, and the comparisons with the car industry are also instructive.

There is not the space in this chapter to explain fully the arguments sustaining a view that we are now in a 'post-Fordist' phase of capitalism, or, indeed, that post-Fordism represents a fundamental break with capitalist relations of production. In simple terms the Fordist/post-Fordist debate centres on methods of industrial manufacturing and the circulation of capital through the global economy that were initially based on the production model devised by Henry Ford (founder of the Ford Motor Company of Detroit) and new information-rich production methods that revolutionise, or move beyond, Henry Ford's old model (as signified by Silicon Valley). John Mathews, a leading theorist of the post-Fordist movement in Australia, defines Fordism as a system of 'mass production, assembly line techniques and scientific management' that is complemented by mass consumption, 'various forms of the welfare state', and 'collective bargaining' (Mathews 1989, p. 27). This model was capitalism's dominant mode of development during the post-World War II period, at least until the 1980s. At that point, Mathews argues, a new process of innovation and specialisation within manufacturing began to mark a shift to what he calls 'neo-Fordist' production. However, this was only successful for a short period before it ran into the limiting constraints of the Fordist economy (p. 33)—that is, it fell victim to the same cyclical process of booms and slumps that characterises the capitalist system worldwide. Fordism was a production system characterised by 'large integrated companies whose market dominance is secured with support from the [nation-] state', in return for the state providing some guarantees of economic and political stability (Mosco 1996, p. 109).

Post-Fordism was supposed to eliminate these systemic barriers to growth and profitability through a massive redesign of the production process that placed a greater reliance on skilled labour and knowledge transfers from workers to the production process, rather than the routine and monotonous assembly lines that were pioneered in Henry Ford's Detroit car plants. A key aspect of this shift was the integration of computing into the production process. Post-Fordism, at least in theory, was a global system of 'specialized production' for 'highly segmented markets' and decentralisation of production into 'networks of flexible producers' (Mosco 1996, p. 109). Mosco discusses the application of this approach to the media industry, but concludes that despite the obvious structural changes, there is 'little evidence' to support the post-Fordist argument that production has been decentralised into smaller networks. In fact, he argues, the media firms who do 'negotiate the process of structural transformation', have emerged 'all the more powerful' (p. 109) and can 'control the circuits of [capital] accumulation' (p. 74). Theories of post-Fordism are often linked to theories of the information or knowledge economy and share some of the same ideological flaws.

For example, as we discussed in the earlier chapters on political economy, attempts to replace living labour power with dead and congealed labour embodied in production machinery will also eventually hit the wall built on the inevitable dialectic of the labour theory of value: once the value stored in the machinery is transferred to new commodities it is effectively used up and has to be replaced. Productivity increases that are snapped up by the early innovators and that give them an advantage over their competitors are generalised throughout the economy and no longer provide the extra value and profits that prompted their initial introduction. This process has been observed in the communication industries by Mosco and others, and, rather than a more democratic and consumer-friendly media, the result has been precisely a shift to narrowcasting, resulting in 'customized media products for increasingly fragmented audiences' (p. 75).

Post-Fordists like John Mathews seem unable to grasp the significance of Marx's labour theory of value when advocating a strategic alliance between capital and labour to revitalise the economic system. Mathews (1989, p. 146) calls this 'flexible accommodation' and believes it would lead to a democratisation of the labour process. However, despite more than twenty years of post-Fordist development—in both production technologies and in labour relations—it is clear that the experiment did not deliver the promised reforms. Instead there is now an even greater international division of labour in manufacturing, in hi-tech industries, in the world's dominant media, and in the global services economy. While a small group of mainly middle-class technology workers have benefited from higher wages and more day-to-day control over their individual labour, the mass of unskilled or semi-skilled workers has also increased.

These changes are also at the core of what Castells (2000, p. 176) refers to as the 'network enterprise', which is based on 'horizontal' lines of control and dynamic processes rather than the 'vertical bureaucracies' that characterised Fordist production models. Castells' description of the network enterprise is accurate enough, but does it represent a fundamental break with the dominant production relations of capitalism? According to Castells, the network society is clearly marked by a changed strategic focus and greater global integration of production and circulation, and it maximises the competitive advantage provided by the new information and communication technologies, but it does not move beyond a more efficient means of capital accumulation. The basic aim of the network enterprise is to 'transform signals into commodities by processing knowledge' (p. 188). But in our view this does not transform the company into something that is beyond or outside the basic parameters of capitalism. The network enterprise is a theoretical construct within the post-Fordist tradition and Castells argues that it has fundamentally altered the tendency within capitalism for monopolies and oligopolies to arise and larger units of capital overrun their less successful competitors. That is, the paradigm of the information economy represents a break with the age of monopoly capitalism based on the concentration and centralisation of capital (Wayne 2003, p. 67). However, the process of capital accumulation, which has not been abandoned by the network enterprise, 'emphasises the continuity of post-Fordism with [the] exploitative, antagonistic social relations' (p. 66) that define monopoly capitalism itself.

All that the network enterprise reveals, in an analytical sense, is that the methods of the assembly line have been transferred—with some success—to the new information and knowledge economy industries. One good example is call centres and IT helpdesks. Millions of low-wage workers in countries on the fringes of global capitalism are now caught up in the web of the information economy. Instead of being chained to a lathe or an automotive assembly line, call centre staff are wired into a mainframe computer via a keyboard, mouse, and headphones. Their work day is not organised along so-called democratic principles of post-Fordist theory; it is highly structured and controlled by the computer-generated list of calls that are dialled automatically. It is not free from surveillance and control; in fact it is very tightly controlled and monitored. Mike Wayne uses the example of the global film industry to make a similar point. Hollywood has been used as a model of the new information economy paradigm by supporters of post-Fordism—the old studio system was disaggregated and smaller independent companies came on the scene in the late 1980s—but Wayne suggests that it is a 'highly misleading' example of post-Fordism in action. The studios—now horizontally and vertically integrated with other media companies—control distribution, the 'key strategic' element 'linking products to audiences' (Wayne 2000, p. 72). The tendency to monopoly and oligopoly is also still a determining force in the social relations of the capitalist economy and we have already outlined how strategic mergers among media companies have reinforced this aspect of the global communication industries.

While for some the debate is not yet closed, we are inclined to agree with those, like Mosco (1996, p. 91), who characterise post-Fordism as 'another cycle in the development of a system that is above all else dynamic and self-transformative', and Wayne (2000, p. 160), who describes capitalism as now being in its 'post-Fordist mode of development'. Rather than being a fundamental break with the relations of production that define capitalism's inexorable march to dominate every available nook and cranny of the world economy, post-Fordism is another stage in the system's 'intensive squeezing out of more surplus value from already commodified domains' (p. 262).

Having said that, we are confident in suggesting that the surveillance economy represents a refinement of the post-Fordist system, which is itself an attempt to keep the crisis-ridden capitalist economy afloat. The surveillance economy will increase the intensity of capital's drive to extract surplus value by effectively commodifying even more of our time, space, and social relations. It will do so by penetrating even the most private aspects of our lives through often hidden, but nonetheless intrusive, methods of digital search, data-mining, and the rapid collation of information to establish our citizen-consumer profile.

Conclusion

We are not yet living in a fully operational surveillance economy, but the signs are there that it is growing in size and appears to be an emerging mode of development within the global capitalist economy. Narrowcasting represents an attempt by global media companies to stay on the crest of this wave. To stretch this metaphor almost to breaking point, our surfing habits—across the Internet and other narrowcast media—will be managed in ways that keep the surveillance economy afloat. Thus, the surveillance economy is not, as some analysts and academics are arguing, something fundamentally different from capitalism; the same laws of value, labour, and capital accumulation apply. Whether we choose to call it the information or the knowledge economy does not alter the basic ground rules of the capitalist mode of production. The digital revolution has already made its mark on the relations of production and the methods of capital accumulation and profit-taking. But the digital revolution and the ongoing process of technological convergence is not a revolution in the same sense as the transition from feudalism to capitalism (for example) was revolutionary. That change was one that radically altered the property and production relations that marked feudalism as a mode of production as distinct from those that had existed before. While profound in many ways, the digital revolution has not displaced capitalism but is a new form of capitalist production relations, perhaps best described as hypercapitalism, or cybercapitalism. The process is an extension of the exploitative and alienating relations of production (and all social relations) that distinguish the epoch of global capitalism. Cyberspace has been tamed; it is still the new frontier, but it is not something separate from the process of accumulation, hegemony, and domination that has characterised capitalism for the past 250 years. In the final chapters we want to turn our attention to the ways in which the surveillance economy is being re-imagined and normalised in politics and how it might be resisted in the future.

KEY POINTS

- In this chapter, we return once more to focus of the political economy of mass communication and new media.
- We have argued that definitions of the global economy as a 'knowledge' or 'information' economy are inadequate and do not take into account the growing importance of both commercial and security surveillance.
- We have suggested that it is more accurate to describe the current formation of global capitalism as a surveillance economy and we have shown how this involves both a 'security' and a 'search' economy.
- We examine ways of explaining what as happening as 'post-Fordist' or as 'hyper-capitalism'.
- We have argued that narrowcasting is a new form of media that is complementary to and helps sustain the emerging surveillance economy.
- While the roots of convergence are deep, it is the pace of change that is characteristic of our time, as the dialectic moves inexorably onwards. Where will it all end? Or is there no end?

CLASS DISCUSSION

Exercise: Go forth and Google

Google yourself. See what the Internet tells anyone who cares to look, about you. Google your parents, other people, you know, perhaps in prominent places in the community. Google and be gobsmacked about the scope and scale of the surveillance society.

Questions

1. Are the distinctions between 'knowledge', 'security', 'search', and 'surveillance' economy meaningful and useful?
2. How comfortable are you with the level of commercial and/or political surveillance that now seems to surround our lives, both online and on the street?

15

POLITICS AND NEW MEDIA

OBJECTIVES

There are two aspects to our discussion of politics and the new media. The first is to interrogate the ways that the new media—particularly the shift towards a narrowcasting media environment—might impact on the way in which what we traditionally call 'politics' might be conducted. Can we make a case that the shift towards narrowcasting and the surveillance economy makes *participation in politics*, or even what we mean by politics, more problematic? The second aspect is to look at the politics of the new media itself as both an institution and a process. This relates to some of the arguments raised in earlier chapters about *reform of the media* system, in particular around ownership and control, but it also raises questions about the level of public involvement in these changes.

Given the constraints of space, in this chapter we will concentrate on the first aspect—the conduct of politics in the world of narrowcasting. Our discussion of media reform will be taken up in the next chapter. As a result of reading this chapter you should increase your understanding of the following:

- how the shift towards narrowcasting and digital media platforms might change the nature of political participation, particularly for people who are today just reaching voting age;

- how online media are creating both a new space and a new set of problems for the conduct of political debate;
- how the shift towards a greater degree of social and political surveillance will alter the broader political landscape;
- how the myths of the digital sublime shape our views of 'electronic democracy'.

KEYWORDS

activist media
democracy
digital citizenship
e-democracy
indymedia
liberalism
populism
vote.com

Have the old ways changed forever? Dick Morris and *Vote.com*

> One of the more persistent myths throughout the development of communication technology is that it would transform politics as we know it by bringing power closer to the people. (Mosco 2004, p. 98)

The supposed democratising influence of the Internet is indeed a powerful myth of the digital sublime. It is attractive, says Vincent Mosco (2004, p. 99), because it implies that the 'fundamental insecurities' deeply embedded in traditional politics can be transcended, just as some believe that the Internet can obliterate the inequities of time and space. Despite the depressing and dystopian dimensions of the digital future we have outlined, there are many analysts, commentators, politicians, and academics who make an argument that the Internet offers citizens the capacity to influence the democratic process in previously unforeseen ways (see, for example, Tsagarousianou et al. 1998). US political consultant Dick Morris, influential in the 1996 re-election of US President Bill Clinton, is one person who pursues this argument with vigour in his book *Vote.com* (1999). The book created a lot of interest within political, academic, media, and IT circles because of its focus on the use of the Internet in empowering voters through direct democracy. We begin this chapter by outlining and critiquing the main points raised by Morris.

The *Vote.com* argument

The premise of Morris's position, that the Internet will become a revolutionary tool for citizens to control their own destiny, is one that has found a lot of support. After all, it creates a higher purpose for a medium that has been dominated so far by pornography, gambling, online shopping, and entertainment. In a similar vein, former Democratic party campaign worker Joe Trippi (2004, p. 225) believes that the 2008 US election will be the first one that is 'waged and won' primarily via the Internet. In *Vote.com* Dick Morris outlines the decline in public perceptions of politicians and the media in the United States over the last two decades, and equates this decline with the increasing distance of the baby-boomer-dominated opinion leaders from the new generations, who have very different ideals and beliefs. This is an idea common to the Internet true-believers (see, for example, Tsagarousianou et al. 1998; Trippi 2004; Flew 2005, pp. 186–90). However, while there is plenty of evidence that young people are turned off by mainstream political bickering (see, for example, Bryan et al. 1998), there is not the same level of evidence to suggest that the concept of e-democracy will attract them back. There is, in modern society, a shrinking of what communication theorists call the public sphere—the open space where politics and debates about social issues are conducted. Within the market capitalist economy there is a fundamental contradiction between the formal equality of political participation and the inequalities of income and opportunity that define the relationships of the market (Schultz 1989, 1994, 1998; Dahlgren 1991). This has a particular impact on the media's relationship with political power—what Julianne Schultz (1998) and others describe as the 'Fourth Estate'. The theory of the Fourth Estate suggests that the media can play an unofficial watchdog role, in effect acting as a series of checks and balances on those who exercise power. But this oversight role has become lost among the 'tensions, cracks and contradictions' within the media and the broader society (Dahlgren 1991, p. 11). Despite the best efforts of writers like Schultz, any revival of the Fourth Estate seems doomed by the dialectic that has created an unbridgeable fault line between the media's public service role and the profit motive that drives the commercial media (Hirst & Patching 2005). It is perhaps too early to predict confidently whether or not digital developments will help or hinder attempts to reconstruct the media as a Fourth Estate. But for people like Dick Morris, the argument has been overtaken by the constant march of convergence.

VOTE.COM

The vision of participatory democracy represented by US political consultant Dick Morris, in which public policy is determined by an ongoing series of electronic referendums. Morris has published a book, and runs a website of the same name.

Morris posits the emergence of what he calls the Fifth Estate—the Internet, which will take over from the Fourth Estate, which is the traditional media—as the major organ for moving and gauging public opinion in the United States and elsewhere. The Fifth Estate, he argues, will finally bring to the United States a utopian model of direct Jeffersonian democracy and will forever move America from the time-honoured model of representative democracy. Ian Kearns (2002, p. 4) make a similar argument in the British context when he argues that the Internet can be used 'creatively' to extend what he calls 'active citizenship' and public commitment to the 'liberal state'. Moves have already been made to institutionalise forms of local e-democracy in various European Union member nations as a means of transforming urban and civic spaces and reconnecting citizens with governments through digital 'civic networks' (Bryan et al. 1998).

Part One of *Vote.com* focuses on the increasing dominance of the Internet in all aspects of modern life in the United States. But Morris's arguments have relevance for all Western capitalist democracies. He begins with a snapshot of his theory of how the Internet will lead to a system of de facto government through instant, online referendums. Rather than petition-based legislation which forces action from incumbent governments, Morris outlines a grander vision for these online referendums, a vision that will fundamentally change the way democracy is conducted. As he states in his précis for chapter 1: 'Soon, tens of millions of people will register their opinions on the Net and compel the attention of elected representatives' (1999, p. xvi). This is indeed a noble sentiment and one that we would be happy to support if there were some chance it might take effect. However, it represents an idealisation of politics and a worldview that denies the centrality of economic power in 'neo-liberal' capitalist states today. This economic power, wielded by the mega-corporations, renders public politics largely ineffectual (see, for example, Tiffen 1989, pp. 178–98). As Robert McChesney points out, a political economy analysis suggests that 'democracy' is fine in principle, and it is tolerated by big business as long as real control is 'off-limits to popular deliberation'. He adds, 'that is, so long as it isn't democracy' (2000b, p.111).

Morris argues that unlike television, which is dominated by three networks, Internet-based election campaigns would be significantly cheaper because of the lack of a dominant player in the medium, and therefore a lack of high advertising revenues. Morris concludes that the Internet forces advertisers to change their tune because Net surfers will only voluntarily view ads, rather than being forced to compulsorily view ads while watching their favourite shows on free-to-air television. However, as we've argued previously, commercial convergence means that advertising and selling are now unremarkable features in any online experience. Furthermore, the evidence for a vibrant non-commercial sector of the Internet is not compelling. Indeed, it seems that activist and civic-minded citizens of the Internet have been relegated to the 'distant margins' of cyberspace (McChesney 2000b, p. 183).

Morris says the so-called establishment will be steamrolled by the sheer numbers of those voting on the Net. Rather than discuss whether those who question the veracity, relevance, and moral fabric behind direct democracy can be successful, he merely reinforces the view that it is inevitable, and therefore has some intrinsic worth. McChesney's view (2000b, p. 183) is quite opposed to this; he argues that those who believe that digital convergence can provide a 'viable [online] public sphere' are 'deluding themselves'.

Leaps in logic?

While much of Morris's view of the political process is insightful, and his vision for Internet-based democracy is, it seems, based on the desire for a better future and a more responsive democratic system, *Vote.com* includes some heroic leaps in logic, and a great deal of wishful thinking. While interesting in its premise, and exciting in its broad vision, *Vote.com* fails in that it draws conclusions that are not necessarily based in reality, nor in fact desirable, at least in the Australian political context. In particular, it fails to account for the stranglehold that entrenched corporate interests have over the American political system. Giant corporations, including all the big media players, bankroll US politicians with millions of dollars in campaign donations and other 'in kind' contributions. In this context, McChesney (2000b, p. 184) suggests that any view of the Internet as being able to cut through this tangle of interconnected self-interest is 'dubious at best'. The single greatest flaw in Morris's reasoning, however, is his belief that citizen-initiated government through instant and constant polling on complex political issues can, and in fact will, replace the existing political system. Like much of the rhetoric underpinning digital myths, this is a flawed premise. It ignores and glosses over historical political realities, such as the following:

- The Internet is no less susceptible to being manipulated by political parties and sectional interest groups than the current system.
- Internet polling, referendums, or elections will be led by those who feel most passionately about a given subject, and will be largely ignored by the general public.
- Results will depend on the phraseology of the question, and the associated 'commentary', and may therefore be unrepresentative of overall public opinion.
- Advertising costs could actually increase for political candidates in the United States and Australia, who will maintain current advertising hits on free-to-air television while expanding their advertising into the Internet.
- The control of sites by sectional interests will greatly diminish the credibility of the polling results within political circles, defeating the purpose of sites like Vote.com in the process.

Vote.com is an important addition to the debate on the future impact of the Internet on the political fabric of Western democracies. But while the author's perceptive views on how Internet advertising, email campaigns, and dedicated candidate-based websites will play an increasingly important role in political campaigning are accurate and prescient, the book is flawed by its premise that polling through websites like Morris's own can play a dominant role in future campaign directions, let alone replace them. To compound these errors, by stating that political campaigns will become cheaper, because candidates will ignore television to focus on the less expensive medium of the Internet, reveals a surprising lack of understanding of the very nature of political campaigning. Instead of replacing television advertising, the Internet and email will be additional to existing campaigns. This will greatly increase the cost, therefore compounding the inherent corruption of the existing, money-based, American political system. These two flawed premises fundamentally undermine much of Morris's subsequent argument on the future dominance of Internet sites like Vote.com.

Agenda-setting online: The Internet as an election campaign tool

> We need to recognise the remarkable changes that the interactive telecommunications age is producing in our political system. We need to understand the consequences of the march toward democratisation. We need to deal with the promise and perils of the electronic republic ... In an electronic republic, it will be essential to look at politics from the bottom up as well as from the top down. (Grossman 1999, p. 282)

How does the Internet—now entrenched in the machinations of the US political parties' campaigns—play a key role in agenda-setting online? The term 'agenda-setting' was coined by McCombs and Shaw (1972) to describe in more general terms a phenomenon that had long been observed and examined in election campaigns (Dearing 1996). In its most basic form, agenda-setting means the transferring of selected or salient issues from and by the media to the public or audiences. Ian Ward (1995, p. 47) defines agenda-setting as the news media's ability to 'shape' what and how we think about the 'political issues of the day'. Takeshita (1997) says that agenda-setting researchers define the word 'agenda' as objects accorded salience in the media context or in people's minds. Agenda-setting is also closely linked to the 'gate-keeper' model of the news media: the exercise of 'selective control' over the types of items that make it onto the news agenda (Ward 1995, p. 99). The electronic medium has adopted both agenda-setting and gate-keeping and refined the process over many decades. If we can see how this control over the selection and placement of politics in the news occurs today, can we sustain an argument that in the digital world things will be 'different', or 'better'? Political reporting in most presidential (US) and parliamentary (UK and Australia) democracies has been reduced to the 'sound bite' and for at least the last twenty years campaign strategies have relied heavily on media management (Tiffen 1989; Gitlin 1991; Franklin 1997, p. 248; Hargreaves 2003). Why should we believe that these same problems won't just migrate online?

In Australia, television has been around for just over fifty years and has long occupied a prominent, albeit contentious, place in shaping the country's most important issues. It has played this role for much of the 20th century and predictably, will continue to do so in the opening decades of this century. Thus it would be fair to claim that the past half-century, by and large, belonged to television in the dispensing and proliferation of information, news, and entertainment. The traditional news media have always been a 'strategic arena' in the 'struggle for power' characterised by political point-scoring and electioneering (Tiffen 1989, p. 7). At the emergence of the 21st century, though, politicians in Australia, following in the footsteps of their American counterparts, have begun to embrace the significance and power of using the Internet to reach their younger constituents. The Internet has become an increasingly necessary tool in Australian mainstream society, not the least because of its cyber-democratic idiosyncratic appeal for many, but largely also because of its immediate and easy accessibility. The Internet's cost-efficiency, lack of regulation control, production simplicity, and swift and active interaction with the individual makes it arguably and potentially the most innovative and powerful medium yet for politicians to communicate directly with their constituents. Clearly, the Internet is here to stay, but so too, it seems, are the digital myths that promote the 'Internet = democracy' line. We have to conclude, then, that there is some grain of 'truth' in these myths that goes some way towards explaining their longevity.

It does not require a great deal of political astuteness to recognise the electoral advantages of catering to the needs of the voters who may eventually become potential 'cyber-voters'. This is not so much a matter of being dictated to by the voting public as it is a case of adapt or perish. Selnow (1998) illustrates this point well when he comments that 'we fear being left behind', which may explain why some campaigns got onto the Web by the mid-1990s. Moreover, not without coincidence, by early 1996 America Online had announced that it had more than 5 million subscribers, a tenfold increase in just two years (Casey 1996).

As Selnow (1998) notes, 1996 was also the year that saw most political campaigns progressing beyond the use of conventional media and, indeed, evolving into real 'media campaigns'. Selnow cites the danger that those who reject or try to resist what is essentially a major telecommunication improvement, in a country as affluent and consumer-driven as America, may well find themselves committing political suicide.

All of these assumptions made by Selnow are valid in that they explain why American politicians so eagerly embraced the adoption of the Internet into their communication channels and political campaigns in the 1990s. But he may have missed a subtler point: that the fear of being left behind may not have been as strong as losing the vote of the youth—the 'X' generation, the growing group of cyber-communicators, or 'netizens' (Katz 1997), who will increasingly turn to the Internet for consumption of products and services, information-gathering, and communication. The ideology of the grassroots cyber-democracy movement is premised on this idea. At the centre of this movement is the belief that new media vectors offer 'new possibilities' of civic engagement, making it easier for citizens to 'respond', 'thereby resolving the crisis of participation' (Bryan et al. 1998, p. 6). Selnow also fails to identify another reason why many American politicians so enthusiastically endorsed the use of the Internet in their campaigns by the mid-1990s. Perhaps it was due to the campaign donations made by the technology companies (see, for example, Mosco 1996, 2004; McChesney 2000b). There are a great deal of vested economic and cultural interests in America that aim to set the world pace in Internet technology. America is, after all, the birthplace of the World Wide Web and the Internet.

Presently, though, the Internet's ability to get in touch with the critical audiences is fast emerging as an important driver of change. Consider the 2000 US presidential election campaign. Both Al Gore and George W. Bush ran what can be described as the first Internet political campaigns since the advent of the medium. To visit their Web home pages was to be flooded with an astonishing array of campaign promotional materials to purchase:

souvenirs, stickers, bumpers, t-shirts. Above all, there was the seemingly endless amount of campaign information offering everything from the latest polling results to the last speech or press conference given by the candidates and directions on where to obtain even more information if you had not already found what they are providing too overwhelming or boring.

Interactivity and power: A strength of the Internet?

For the individual and organisations—public, private, or non-profit—the Internet has created the digital myth that we are empowered with a sense of being in touch with the rest of the community. In other words, it has created an electronic version of Marshall McLuhan's 'global village'. To its supporters, empowerment on the Internet is also about being part of, or having the ability to construct, cultures and shared significances (Reid 1996), and for some, a sense of belonging. If, as McLuhan claims, the printing press is a form of 'hot' media (Stevensen 1995)—that is, newspapers and books do not allow direct interaction or interpretation on the part of the reader—then it must follow that with the advent of the Internet, television has become a 'hot' medium. Television viewing encourages passive reception and interpretation—if any. Therefore, while it may have been a 'cool' medium at the time McLuhan was writing, in the face of the Internet's rise as the new 'cool' medium, television must by comparison be deemed a 'hot' medium.

According to the myths of the digital sublime, what better way is there to change 'old' politics than to communicate directly with the people via the Internet? A press conference means having your issues mediated by journalists, thus leaving traditional media as the 'gate-keeper' to sift through and interpret the information that seems most salient. The Internet is not only a tool that allows you determine which issues on your agenda are most newsworthy, but better still, it also enables you to communicate directly with your voters any time, anywhere. Never before has a medium been so impressive in its ability to accommodate the ideas and needs of its audience (Selnow 1998; Paletz 1999; Parenti 1999).

Like other aspects of cyber-mythology, however, we have to interpret these notions with a certain amount of bubble-bursting scepticism. One of our key arguments throughout *Communication and New Media* has been that narrowcasting further fragments the audience of *consumers* for commercial purposes. We can transpose this disaggregating effect onto our discussion of politics to suggest that far from constituting an active and organised collective, the shift of politics online may further fragment the audience of *citizens*. Some, like Peter Dahlgren (1991, p. 14), have suggested that this is a positive move that creates 'dynamic alternative public spheres' in the vacuum left by the decline of traditional political discourse. Others, such as Neil Postman, argue the opposite: 'bureaucracies, expertise and technical machinery become the principal means by which Technopoly hopes to control information and thereby provide itself with intelligibility and order' (Postman 1993, p. 91).

Vincent Mosco provides an instructive case study that tends to support Postman, based on his analysis of a conservative American think-tank, the Progress and Freedom Foundation

(PFF). According to Mosco (2004, p. 105), the PFF's mission is to reconceptualise politics to regain a lost sense of 'community and public life'. One of the leading figures in the PFF is the ultra-conservative former US Congressman, Newt Gingrich, and his group includes many high-profile names from the right-wing of American politics and public life, including the conservative futurist Alvin Toffler. The PFF vision is, says Mosco (2004, p. 112), based on 'an individualistic populism suffused with elite ideals'. This becomes clear when we examine what the PFF says about itself on its website www.pff.org:

> The Progress & Freedom Foundation is a market-oriented think tank that studies the digital revolution and its implications for public policy. Its mission is to educate policymakers, opinion leaders and the public about issues associated with technological change, based on a philosophy of limited government, free markets and individual sovereignty. (PFF 1993)

One of the most recent (at time of writing) posts on the PFF website in March 2006 highlighted what Mosco (2004, p. 112) calls the 'privatization ethic' of the foundation. A senior fellow at the foundation, Randolph May, appeared before a Congressional committee to argue for further deregulation of the American telecommunication system based on 'rigorous market-oriented competition analysis' (PFF 2006). The founding document of the PFF is its 'Magna Carta for the digital age', published in 1994 and now available on the foundation website. The document is full of flowery rhetoric and contains this interesting (though patently mythic) definition of cyberspace: 'Cyberspace is the land of knowledge, and the exploration of that land can be a civilization's truest, highest calling. The opportunity is now before us to empower every person to pursue that calling in his or her own way' (Dyson et al. 1994).

In order to achieve this 'Golden Age' vision, the PFF is in favour of radically downsizing government and privatising most public services and replacing them with a new version of individualism, which, according to Mosco's interpretation (2004, p. 113), replaces the class struggle of contemporary capitalism with 'the triumph of indeterminate webs of communication'. In the PFF's charter document this is expressed as the sentiment that governments are 'the last great redoubt of bureaucratic power on the face of the planet' (Dyson et al. 1994). This will be replaced in what the PFF refers to as 'third wave' societies based on digital convergence and new 'virtual communities' connected via modems and cables: 'cyberspace will play an important role knitting together ... the diverse communities of tomorrow, facilitating the creation of "electronic neighborhoods" bound together not by geography but by shared interests' (Dyson et al. 1994).

E-democracy: A digital renaissance?

This seems an appealing vision, particularly in a world where people in America and many Western liberal democracies have grown increasingly disillusioned with traditional media and the structures and norms of society, and are increasingly resentful about the way politics and government is conducted in general. In the hands of the PFF's skilled operatives, the new politics appears to be a 'digital renaissance' (Fiorina 2001, p. 1). Carly Fiorina was CEO of the Hewlett Packard corporation when he wrote on the digital renaissance for the PFF's *Future Insight* newsletter. His main focus is on the business opportunities created by digital convergence, but he also mentions a renaissance in government, using technology to 'reinvent' its relationship with the public along the lines of the 'immediacy and relevance' of commercial ties between a business and its consumers (p. 3). The purpose of political leadership in the digital age, says Fiorina, is to create the right conditions for individualism: 'digital leadership', in this idealistic worldview, 'sets guidelines, and parameters, and boundaries, and then sets us free'. This is also a chance—in the land of the free and the home of the brave—to make the 'American dream a universal dream' (p. 5). Is this a desirable future—a global 'marketplace of politics' online? In particular, do we want a completely deregulated market in telecommunications in which the government takes a back seat to the creative (destructive?) interplay of unfettered market forces? This is certainly the view argued the founders of the PFF (Gilder 1995). However, for critics like Robert Jensen (2004) such ideals merely reinforce notions of 'empire' and effectively prevent any genuine engagement with 'citizenship'.

Can e-democracy overcome the tyranny of distantiation? Much like Americans who lament the distance of tyranny between them and Washington, Australians are often heard expressing their cynicism about Canberra's ability, or lack thereof, to relate to the rest of the country. Can the digital myth that the Internet reduces distance to immeasurably small tolerances overcome the tyranny of separation in a vast continent like Australia? The irony is that, according to the myths, in the 'electronic age' the Internet has actually bridged distance and time, thus dramatically bringing us closer to those who govern us (Grossman 1999).

Lawrence Grossman highlights an important incentive for using the Internet as a campaign tool. A growing number of Americans have become more active in contributing to the making of public policy in such key issues as direct state primaries, budget amendments, electing their own presidential candidates, bypassing legislatures, and even allowing for people to make their own laws. Obviously, according to the digital myths, as online participation grows, it follows that ordinary citizens can claim a greater voice and a more direct role in the governing of society. However, progress has been slow at an official level, according to Ian Kearns (2002, p. 11). While there is a certain level of 'transactional' engagement between the British public and the government, for example, there has been less success in making so-called 'e-democracy' work. The UK government's 'e-democracy' website www.edemocracy.gov.uk/default.htm is up and running with more than twenty local government projects under way, including a blog and forum page that was launched in March 2005. The focus of this project is local government, but national government services can be accessed from a one-stop-shop site called 'directgov'. Various experiments in several European cities and neighbourhoods are

E-DEMOCRACY

The use of digital (e = electronic) technologies to enhance the participation of citizens in the democratic process.

outlined in *cyberdemocracy* (Tsagarousianou et al. 1998), including a virtual 'city' that has existed in Amsterdam since 1994—a place that Francissen & Brants (1998, p. 21) describe as a 'telematic euphoria' and a 'breeding ground' for other e-democracy projects.

However, it's not just governments that are playing in the 'e-democracy' sandpit. A group calling itself 'E-democracy.org' (www.e-democracy.org) has set up a site for local activists to get involved in community work and elections with links to mainly American, Canadian, and British issues and organisations. E-democracy.org is a non-partisan group that focuses on politics and the media and appears to be physically located in Minnesota. Another group, 'grassroots.org' (www.grassroots.org), has established an online clearing-house for not-for-profit organisations as diverse as those wanting to save the marine environment to local groups affiliated to the US 'war on drugs'. However, with such a diverse group of interests (some of which appear to be contradictory) it is hard to discern a particular program for change. It appears to be mainly a site where community organisations and other small groups can advertise for business and members.

E-democracy is a new buzz phrase in the lexicon of the digital myth-makers. A Google search in March 2006 returned over 3 million hits—everything from government gateway sites to blogs, forums, and e-democracy home pages started by individuals and groups. The ever-reliable Wikipedia (2006a) suggests that the Minnesota experiment (E-democracy .org) originated the concept in 1994 and adds that today, more than a decade later, it is still in an experimental and largely theoretical phase. Ian Kearns (2002, p. 11) gives a useful short definition: e-democracy is 'the use of web technologies to engage citizens in debate, discussion, consultation and online voting'. Roza Tsagaraousianou (1998, p. 167) defines it as 'a means of improving the responsiveness and accountability of political institutions and enhancing citizen participation in the political process'. However, she says, it also gives politicians an unprecedented level of control over their messages and 'spin'.

Cyberdemocracy: A digital myth?

For a politician, the ability to communicate may be a key criterion in determining political success, but equally important is the access to information (Schwartz 1996). The digital myth suggests that access to and the value of information, hence knowledge, can be equated with power; it then extrapolates from this that the Internet has empowered us both as individuals and organisations (Flew 2005, p. 187). This is seen as an embodied feature of digital technology that can steer us towards an era where an entire global network of resources and freedom of information for many appears on the horizon. The cyber-mythology also states that the digital media have the power to shrink both time and space (see Cassell 1993; Giddens 1995). This implies that the Internet may also become a 'place' where our personal ideology; cultural, ethical, and social identities; political structures; and rules are not dictated by the hegemony of the conventional, mainly unilateral mass media. At the same time, the roll-out of 'e-democracy' trials in several countries may also contribute to the growth of social surveillance. In Europe the existence of a techno-legal time-gap in the regulation of virtual cities and e-democracy projects has been recognised, particularly around privacy and the distribution of 'offensive' material (see Bryan et al. 1998, pp. 14–16). In the British context the government wants to issue 'digital certificates' and 'smart cards' to citizens to enable them to participate in e-democracy, but advocates like Ian Kearns also recognise the digital dialectic and the 'potentially serious political consequences' that come with the deployment of more government surveillance technologies that can potentially 'undermine privacy' and 'threaten equality in new ways'. At the same time, he is forced to concede that they are 'crucial' to the 'security and integrity' of online information (Kearns 2002, p. 3).

Going global, living local: Distanciation of politics on the net

The idea that distance, space, and time are losing their importance is one of the most enduring myths of the Internet. This can be evidenced by the spawning of phrases such as 'global on-line economy', 'e-commerce', 'global information structure', 'wired world', 'cyberspace', and 'multi-user domain (MUD)' (Ludlow 1996; Bangemann 1999; Gore 1999; Leer 1999). The development of cyberspace has created a blurring of geographic and time-related boundaries as the Internet continues to converge with existing forms of mass media. According to the digital mythology, there are numerous advantages to be gained from convergence, not the least of which is the much freer, hence more democratic, dissemination of information. It is more democratic because there is no domination of any one authority in the receiving and sending of information. Democratic media (of which the Internet is undoubtedly a part) have the potential to provide us with immense value in the sharing and distribution of content, products, and services, and of reaching larger audiences (Siochru 1999).

While the Internet is about global access to products and services, websites are becoming increasingly localised—by language, presentation, and offers—with branding and corporate identity standards (Marlow 1997). Politicians can, with the help of political marketing experts and advertising agencies, help voters deal with local issues at the grassroots level by encouraging citizens to use the Internet to bridge the distance—real or imagined—between themselves and their elected representatives. Marlow's suggestions for effective advertising on the Internet for businesses can also be adopted by politicians. In many ways the Internet can be seen as an extension of direct response marketing (Marlow 1997), which allows politicians to localise and tailor their messages and identities directly to voters.

By virtue of its immediacy and interactive nature, the Internet's ability to customise—as opposed to standardise—ideas, issues, and policies is a marketing tool that any politician can employ in their election campaign. Customisation is localisation or, put another way, niche political marketing. Politicians, by using the Internet to construct a local identity, are conveying several important messages to voters: that they are promoting the use of a community-like medium; that the information voters access is not only legitimate and credible but can also be creative and varied; and that this information is linked or is linkable to other networked alliances for additional sources of information. The creation of a local outlook on the Internet in an election campaign serves another critical function: the facilitating of discussion because of the Internet's targeting ability. You only have to look at some of the activist organisations on the Internet in Australia to see that they are becoming very skilled at aiming their sites' messages at their supporters (for examples, refer to www.mediachannel.org and www.green.net.au).

With the current hoopla surrounding the seemingly infinite cataclysmic powers of the Internet and the commercial success of many entrepreneurial start-ups, it is easy to get carried along with the idea that the Internet has, indeed, become the holy grail in our quest for self-determination and empowerment, and thus freed us from the clutches of traditional media—a metaphoric parting of the political sea so that voters and politicians are more directly interactive with each other and that governments at all tiers are much more directly accountable to us. But does the Internet really offer a land of milk and honey—that is, 'true individualism' and greater interactivity?

Interactivity or fragmentation?

With this question in mind then, is it fair to say that the Internet, rather than actually promoting individualism, is instead acting to disaggregate the community? The Internet encourages the individualism and freedom of choice of its audiences but divides those who only visit sites that interest them. For example, during elections, a ritual practised by many is to gather in front of television sets and watch the progressive results as they are tallied. The Internet, however, replaces this ritual by allowing audiences to log onto the election sites that interest them to find out about a particular candidate's results. What is intended to be a socially integrative process involving all forms of community participation risks becoming a segregating instrument (Selnow 1998).

As Nicholas Negroponte, the director of MIT Media Lab and friend of Al Gore, observed, as well as adding flatness to any organisation (business or political), local can also mean the coexistence of individualism and harmony. Negroponte believes that we are experiencing a new kind of localism where we will eventually see neighbourhoods no longer being mere places. Instead, neighbourhoods will become groups that stem from common interests (take mailing lists, for example), newsgroups, or alliances formed by individuals with similar concerns. In Negroponte's words, 'A family stretched far and wide can become a virtual neighbourhood'. Each of us will have many kinds of 'being local'. Being local will be determined by 'what we think and say, when we work and play, where we earn and pay' (Negroponte 1999, pp. 389–90). John Hartley (1996) takes up a similar theme in *Popular Reality* when he talks about the creation of 'virtual' suburbs and 'suburbia' becoming the 'postmodern public sphere'. Hartley's renaissance is to be led by 'telebrities' (media-created celebrities) who will teach 'certain public virtues' within a 'suburban cultural context'. What exactly these second-rate public figures and rejects from *The Biggest Loser* will teach is not clearly spelled out, but Hartley (1996, p. 156) assures us that the message will 'not only [be about] the virtues of suburbia, but also the future of democracy'. The new political agenda of the suburban revolutionaries will be based on 'comfort, privacy and self-building' (p.

157). This might be a winning formula for a reality TV show, but it is hardly a manifesto for radical social change!

Of course, whether or not these visions of localism are viable, it can only be truly possible if every one of us, governments included, wants to be a part of 'being local'. Otherwise, we are merely making an assumption that everyone is happy to jump onto the same bandwagon when not all of us may want to share even if it makes sense to do so. A second criticism is that suburbia is precisely the place where the fragmentation of the citizen-consumer is most evident. Private consumption within the 'household' and keeping one's opinions to oneself are the dominant virtues of most suburban dormitory precincts. Furthermore, we cannot assume that all sections of society have the means, knowledge, freedom, or even the desire to participate in the construction of this envisaged global village. In the face of the very real economic and social inequalities that still separate much of the world's population from the developed nations' technologies, some may find Negroponte and Hartley's views utopian. It is a point not lost on the supporters of e-democracy and, like the digital divide, it is not a question that can be quickly or easily resolved. As Roza Tsargarousianou suggests, it will take much more work in both the real and the virtual worlds for e-democracy to prove itself. The digital dialectic once again asserts itself: 'succumbing to the binary division between optimism and dystopia undermines our ability to comprehend [the] implications and potential [of cyber-democracy]' (Tsagarousianou 1998, p. 176). We agree with Terry Flew who, after surveying several e-democracy initiatives, concludes that to date there is no clear evidence that they are having the desired effect: 'any assessment of the utilisation of the Internet and ICTs for political engagement reveals a decidedly mixed score card' (Flew 2005, p. 188).

Value, speed, and familiarity of format

There is not a great deal to be said about the user-friendly value and immediacy of the Internet that has not already been covered. Suffice to say that these factors may well be the reason why the Internet is fast outstripping traditional media and why narrowcasting is subverting the broadcast paradigm. In spite of his own scathing comments regarding the impact of the Internet on traditional media, even the editor-in-chief of Queensland Newspapers, Chris Mitchell (2000), conceded that the Internet 'is growing exponentially' and that newspapers can, in fact, benefit financially from it. Beyond providing us with information, news, and entertainment as print and broadcast media do, and for a fraction of the cost by comparison, the Internet has also opened up a whole new dimension in the way we communicate with politicians.

Despite the claim that election campaigns provide people with the opportunity to give feedback to their political leaders (Perloff 1998), it is feedback only within a limited set of choices. The preconceived expectations, views, and ideals voters may have about candidates are reinforced and largely guided by the media's limited and limiting coverage during election campaigns in their process of shaping the public agenda (Tiffen 1989; Ward 1991, 1995; Dearing 1996; Kenski 1996; Perloff 1998). In turn, the news media cannot build their news agenda without reflecting and enlarging the agendas of candidates, opinion leaders, and voters. The digital myth states that the Internet facilitates mobilisation of political participation (Paletz 1999) and, above all, that it challenges the status quo in thinking, reliance on conventional media, and how we define the value of information. For all its benefits, it is essential that we examine the weaknesses of the Internet also if we are to grasp its assets better and exploit them fully. One of the most pressing issues would undoubtedly concern the question of access to all sections of society in using the Internet.

Inequality of access

> The question of access is critical to the hopes of the civic networking movement, because, if certain groups either cannot, or simply do not participate in the electronic public sphere—women, the poor, etc.—ICTs will mirror problems of the old media—i.e., exclusion. (Bryan et al. 1998, p. 15)

It is on this basis that the fallacy of the digital mythology is exposed: access to the necessary infrastructure is not available to some social groups. In a capitalist world, based on profit rather than need, this is an almost insurmountable problem. If the experts and the media are to be believed, the current situation in Australia is such that information and communications technologies are pervading every stratum of society, to the point that we cannot seem to escape them. Yet if knowledge were to be equated with power, then there are certainly groups in our society who are powerless, for there are some who are not even aware of such technological innovations, let alone possessing the knowledge or the means necessary to access them.

According to results published by the Australian Bureau of Statistics, despite the strong increases in the growth rates of Internet use in the last few years, there still exists a slower uptake among the regional, female, Indigenous, migrant, and older sectors in Australia. Not surprisingly, the demographics of the Internet-using public are dominated by middle- to upper-class males, and far from becoming evenly distributed, the gender gap is widening in favour of males. What politicians need to be mindful of here is that this situation has resulted in a socio-cultural divide in access to new media technologies. We have already mentioned the impact of this 'digital divide' in other areas (see also Flew 2005, pp. 71–5) and it is no less of a problem in politics. Politically speaking, if political parties are to wage effective election campaigns online, they cannot afford to—nor would they want to—exclude any of the sectors described, especially rural voters.

DEMOCRACY

Rule by the people, as distinct from monarchy (rule by a monarch), plutocracy (rule by the rich), oligarchy (rule by a few), and anarchy (the absence of rulers).

It would seem that online political participation is on the rise in Australia as evidenced by the number of activist organisations hosting their sites on the Internet. The notion of participation may be open to everyone, but is online politicking, in reality, something that is monopolised by city dwellers and privileged groups? How is it truly participatory democracy when not everyone has equal access to the Internet? Central to the creation of a national information service is the issue of access to the information highway. If Australia is a country that depends on an informed citizenry, all sections of society must have equitable access to the information that can help improve their circumstances. This means that the information highway must reach rural areas and other socially and economically disadvantaged groups (Pavlik 1994). Any politician using the Internet as an election campaign tool cannot hope to succeed where there is a predominance of the information-rich over the information-poor. Politicians cannot risk being seen as offering their messages to the technologically affluent, for this would contradict the Internet's core digital myth: its supposed power to deliver 'direct democracy'.

'One culture fits all'

One of the problems facing the Internet in Australia is that it is culture-bound. That is, the Internet's communication arises chiefly from Anglo and, specifically, English-speaking language and cultural traditions to which non-European and non-English-speaking cultures have difficulty adjusting (Kessler 1996). If Australia is to see itself as a multicultural 'melting pot', our political organisations' sites need to reflect this in order to capture a broader base of voters. For example, their Internet communication should accommodate multilingual needs. Both Al Gore and George W. Bush offered Spanish translations on their websites during the 2000 US presidential election.

Once again, this shows that politicians cannot assume all their constituents are proficient in English. The English-speaking population may be the dominant voting sector in Australia but such political parties as the Liberal Party, which prides itself on garnering a large portion of their votes from the Chinese community, should be aware that after Italian, Chinese is the second most commonly spoken language in the country. Likewise, for other political parties, it should be remembered that an emerging generation of 'digital' Australians may no longer be willing to maintain the language divide online. The reasons are the mood of a younger generation, arguably more global in its social and cultural attitudes; the way we do business and interact with people overseas; and the fact that we have increasingly come to understand that Australia's future—politically and economically—lies mostly in Asia.

Implications and strategies for Australian election campaigns

In Australia, there are presently about 6 million adults (44 per cent of Australia's adult population) accessing the Internet, mostly either from home or at work, and this figure is expected to grow. Further, the Internet is fast becoming an omnipresent strategic and tactical medium for marketing, public relations, advertising, and organisational communications throughout Australia. What the Internet is doing to American election campaigns is certainly going to have consequences for Australian elections. Like any business organisation, political parties today need to have a sound communication strategy that enables them to gain optimum results in using and managing all their resources.

What political candidates also need to keep in mind is that they should not use their website solely to promote their image or persona. Personalising messages and the design of the site is a creative way to engage voters but it should not be done at the expense of detracting from the significance of the issues. While it may be common practice for political candidates in America, getting in touch with constituents does not mean that every voter in Australia wants to log online to read about candidates' personal historical ascent in politics or every gossipy detail of their private life. It is doubtful, though, whether Australian politicians will go to the lengths of their American counterparts in offering the entire campaign kit and caboodle—such as personalised badges, t-shirts, and stickers—to online voters. In the present cultural context, Australia's cynical attitude towards politics and politicians in general may not be receptive to that type of election accessory campaigning.

We have become disenchanted with traditional media, sceptical about our authorities, and we often lament about the government in general. As Schwartz (1996) rightly suggests, if you hate politics on television, why would you bother looking for it on the Internet? But that doesn't mean the Internet can't be of any use. The point here is that the Internet could be seen as merely an extension of political broadcasting. For people who do not have the slightest interest in politics, all the efforts on the Internet will not attract their attention. Where the power of the Internet lies is in its ability to act as a resource system for political activism. Now the aim is not to reach the people least interested in politics but rather, the most committed—the people who already have an interest in politics and who vote. The advantage Australia has, compared with America, is that we can usually expect a voter turnout of about 95–96 per cent, due, in part, to Australia's compulsory voting policy. Theoretically at least, this means there is some kind of voter interest in the candidates and the outcome. The Internet merely makes it easier for these people to get information. What candidates need are the people who will go door to door with flyers and policy brochures and information about the campaigns. These are the people who can mobilise the larger population if given the proper support. Candidates need to have the will and support of such people if they are to conduct an effective online election campaign and make the most of their websites.

Perhaps this encapsulates the notion of 'perpetual campaigning'. In light of traditional media's soaring costs, online political campaigning may become the norm in the continual marketing and reinforcement of a party's goals and image branding. More importantly, perpetual online campaigning may prove effective in party policy formation and development because it is subject to the opinion and feedback of constituents. More precisely, because it encourages interactivity, the Internet stimulates involvement in policy-making, thus political participation (Paletz 1999).

According to the digital mythology, Internet campaigning invariably also means greater accountability on the politician's part. But this does not necessarily translate into a compromise of their power. What it might mean, over time, is that voters and other online audiences will morph into a system of checks and balances in a much quicker fashion than was previously possible. Voters may no longer be prepared to receive information via the 'trickle down' mode. With direct democracy at their fingertips, it is possible that online voters could in the future become a political force to be reckoned with, which will challenge certain decision-making processes and powers of their elected representatives. The importance of the Internet as a narrowcasting communication medium also has implications for the way that politics might be reported in the future, including further shifts within what we have described as the 'reportorial community' (see chapter 11).

Online politics and the reportorial community

> There's more opportunity for DIY communication in cyberspace, lending itself to democratic voices finding an audience. Perhaps it's more democratic online because independent media sources who don't have money for printing can make news without hard copy. (Fitzgibbon 2006)

As we discussed in chapter 11, there's no doubt that digital media convergence is shifting the borders of the reportorial community. Blogging has become influential in politics and agenda-setting and, as Bec Fitzgibbon mentions, do-it-yourself journalism appears to be thriving in cyberspace. Undoubtedly, one of the most significant consequences of online political campaigning is that it has the potential to support a new kind of journalism. Not that long ago, a journalist starting to forge a career usually had to decide between print or broadcast. Since the birth of the Internet, the demand for multimedia jobs has blurred such boundaries (Stepp 1999). One trait that all online communication professionals working for political parties (or any organisation) as media specialists need is a multimedia outlook: the ability to integrate text, images, sounds, and video into understandable packages for audiences (Pavlik 2001). Their style of writing will need to be more personal and creative, too. Lengthy, complex reporting of information and data may have to go by the wayside in favour of concise, simple statements. Acting as online political marketing consultants for political parties means coming into contact with voters, often in real time. This two-way process shapes coverage, so 'new' journalists need to both accept and anticipate that interactivity (Stepp 1999). That means journalists will have to predict voter questions, and collect and present information that accommodates them. Ultimately and ironically, this may produce a new kind of power for both the cyber-journalist and the political party.

This prompts questions about how much new material will be strictly voter-driven and how much will reflect the political party's concerns about social responsibility. Will politicians use new media to serve voters (online audiences) with only what they want in order to win the populist vote, or will they devote resources to serious topics that may have less popularity? It also raises questions about the importance and influence of news websites, like *Crikey.com* and others. The reliance on traditional news sources—usually those with some official link to 'power'—may break down further as online journalism takes off. It's also likely that blogging will push this process further still.

Are bloggers the future of democracy?

> Individually they may not have many readers, but when you multiply them by several million weblogs, there is a huge audience out there. (Knobel 2005, p. 54)

While we don't want to underestimate the collective power of 'several million' bloggers, we have to remain a little sceptical about the extent of their influence. If there are, as Lance Knobel says, millions of blogs, there are probably at least hundreds of thousands that are boring, irrelevant, or just plain stupid. There are probably a few hundred that are really influential, and several thousand more that might catch someone's interest, or be focused on politics, but the vast majority will not register with most people. For a start, how much time do we actually have to sit at a computer terminal and chase down more than a handful of blogs? Second, surfing the Internet is a solitary and asocial pastime, so how can reading even the most useful, well-written, and pertinent blogs add to the sum total of political interest and activism in the world?

The potential of blogging to undermine the dominant (hegemonic) power structures is a powerful myth, but is it going to create a social revolution? Probably not in our lifetime. Then there's the problem of self-referential feedback loops; if we only read the news and the blogs that interest us, or reflect our taste, we might end up in what Ranald McDonald (2005, p. 15) calls the 'hall of mirrors' in which the media we access reinforce our beliefs or prejudices and we are never surprised, or shocked out of complacency. McDonald calls it 'media for narcissists'. On the other side of this debate is the respected American media ethicist Jay Rosen. He believes that blogging is another experiment in the ongoing democratisation of the media and the free press: 'the very media tools once commandeered by professionals are falling into public hands' (2005, p. 27). He also argues that blogging makes the reader the editor and reverses the information flow (media to public) into a public to media model (p. 35). Knobel (2005, p. 45) supports this view, arguing that blogs create a 'two-way' medium and are at the centre of 'media democratisation' that makes all of us media 'creators'.

For Eric Beecher, former newspaper editor and now managing director of *Crikey.com*, the advent of blogging represents a major fault line in the world of media, a point where 'two tectonic plates' collide in a grinding dialectic: 'the intersection between the capability of new technology to deliver instantaneous portable information, and the apparent apathy of younger people towards the old idea of what's important in society and life' (2005, p. 66).

If this is the case, can weblogs, wikis, and other forms of do-it-yourself media shift the sensibilities of teenagers and young adults? Certainly it's a big job, particularly when the dominant media discourse is pushing so many advertorial and lifestyle memes into the new media vectors. Eric Beecher recognises the seismic potential of this fault line to create a major shift in both the media and politics, but it's hard to share in any optimistic view that this might somehow reconnect young voters with the political process. Political weblogs have to compete for the attention of young consumers alongside MP3 downloads, SMS messaging, and participation in the digital democracy of evicting housemates from *Big Brother*, or supporting a local hero on *Australian Idol*. For an audience already numbed to politics in the real world, it's a 'no brainer'. This creates what Beecher (2005, p. 71) calls a 'vicious cycle' in media, culture, and politics. A generation of 'digital natives' fed on a diet of 'mobile telephony and the all-singing Internet' that churns out endless hours of entertainment, served in 'snack' format for 'easy digestion', cannot then appreciate anything that exists outside this paradigm. It might be easy to condemn this sentiment as the musings of a grumpy old man, but it would be a mistake to dismiss Beecher's concerns too lightly. Perhaps he's right to describe the blogosphere as an 'insular and largely impenetrable universe' (p. 72).

Beecher's comments on the tug-of-war between the old and the new media are also interesting, He says that while blogs may be more democratic and less autocratic than the 'old' media, digital technology seems to be oriented more to instant gratification than to deep reflection. When it comes to politics, instant gratification tends towards populism and the lowest common denominator, rather than good policy. It also tends to overpower the 'journalism of ideas' that we associate with the more serious side of the media and independent publishing (p. 75).

POPULISM

A policy of doing what is seen to be popular at the lowest common denominator, as distinct from what may best serve the public interest, but be unpopular.

Perhaps it's also instructive here to mention Margo Kingston's 'webdiary', one of the first serious blogs in Australia, and one that was initially supported by her employer, the Fairfax group. Margo was a respected and sharp political reporter who moved to the *Sydney Morning Herald*'s online site to establish her weblog in 2000 as a virtual diary of her work in the Canberra Press Gallery (Kingston 2005a). It was immensely popular and generated some interesting debates fed by her readers, who quickly became contributors and collaborators. In 2004 Margo parted ways with Fairfax and accepted a redundancy package. She moved her webdiary to another server, but within twelve months it had folded, because of lack of commercial support and also because Margo had fought some tough battles and was weary. Her brief but poignant sign-off approaching midnight on 7 December 2005 indicates some of the pressures Margo was under: 'G'day. Webdiary will close at midnight tonight. Thank you to everyone who contributed and helped me try to make it work. Unfortunately I couldn't get funding in time to stop me going broke, and certain events' (Kingston 2005b).

Other journalist-bloggers have had more longevity, but often only with the support of their 'old' media employer. Guy Rundle, though not commenting directly on the demise of Kingston's webdiary, offers some useful insights into the larger issues that might have contributed to its demise. Kingston is a left-of-centre personality and Rundle sees that beneath the seismic 'surface motion' of the dialectic described by Beecher, there has been a profound narrowing of culture and politics. The result is that political debate is also narrowing, becoming 'mono-cultural' and 'one-dimensional' with a focus only on 'key economic and social questions' (Rundle 2005, p. 90). In this climate, perhaps there was no room for an iconoclastic and at times anarchic voice like Kingston's.

Alternative politics on the Internet

> People have access to the media they want to read—and there's a lot of it out there, from serious political blogs to independent open-sourced newsreels. I think news has to be more cutting, more headlining, and ideally, more objectively truthful to gain readership today. (Fitzgibbon 2006)

Bec Fitzgibbon specialises in counter-culture and pop culture and she's also into environmental activism. Her take is that the new medium is not replacing traditional methods of grassroots and activist political organisation, but that it can supplement it:

> I don't know that it's 'taking over' as much as adding to. I also work in environmental activism and music event promotion both online and on the streets, they're complementary as they reach different audiences. The global link-up of the internet community rises above physical isolation, but I still use paper and sticky-tape when I'm outdoors—'old school' propaganda! (Fitzgibbon 2006)

Internet activism is mushrooming at an impressive rate in America (Schwartz 1996) and, to a lesser extent, Australia. The Internet is slowly decentralising the conventional media's power base and structures (Barskdale 1999; Davis 1999; Hiebert 1999; Ogden 1999). As opposed to television and print media, the Internet has elevated us to new heights and perhaps even reshaped our understanding of interactivity. We determine what information is salient and what is not—all at our fingertips, in the office or at home; we choose what to digest and what to reject. Rather than being sponges passively soaking up the products of the television and the newspaper, the luxury of choice the Internet offers empowers both the sender and the receiver—in this case, the politician and the voter, or the activist and the curious seeker of alternative ideas. The types of information we seek and choose to receive are reliant on our subjective perceptions and interpretations. Greater interactivity and direct participation on the Net means that both senders and receivers assume greater accountability for their actions, and see themselves as in charge of setting the agenda.

Today there is a global network of independent media (indymedia) sites with local chapters based in most nations and large cities dedicated to 'the creation of radical, accurate, and passionate tellings of truth' (Indymedia.org 2006). The movement was initially established in Seattle to support protests at the November 1999 World Trade Organization meeting. The news reports and other content hosted on the various indymedia sites is generated by volunteers, some of whom are working journalists or students, but all have an activist orientation. Editorial policies are generally progressive and range from fierce anti-capitalism to mild green. The network is decentralised but does have a structure of sorts that can admit new members and provide some sort of collective overview of editorial policy. This generates some friction within and between various indymedia collectives, but generally relations between individuals and groups are fairly harmonious. There are also other grassroots media sites, such as 'wikinews' that model themselves on the indymedia format (Wikipedia 2006b). While many indymedia sites begin as text-only, most also carry audio and video files and are updated regularly. At various times indymedia reporters have been assaulted by police while covering protests, and in June 2005 a group in Bristol (UK) had some computer equipment seized by police who alleged they had been inciting violence by urging a protest 'action' against a freight train carrying cars during the lead-up to another government–business summit meeting in Genoa (Wikipedia 2006b). In Canada an organisation calling itself Media Alliance for New Activism (MANA) is attempting to establish itself as a national media presence and to challenge the dominance of mainstream media. MANA wants to develop an alternative media structure based on social justice values, but also to create an 'infrastructure of resistance' (ACTivist Magazine 2005).

While indymedia has only a limited appeal outside activist circles, this does not take away from its importance in the digital media world. As a global coalition of mostly average people without access to the vast funds at the disposal of the media barons, indymedia has done well to maintain its presence for nearly a decade. It is not likely to go away, unless there are serious attempts to shut its networks down, and it may build a bigger following over time. Certainly it provides a welcome alternative to what most major media outlets churn out.

ACTIVIST MEDIA

Media outlets with a declared politico-social agenda. Sometimes wrongly described as 'indie-media', or 'indymedia' (that is, independent media), because activist media can have a range of social and political points of view whereas the indymedia tradition seems to have a left-wing or anarchist disposition, as distinct from media outlets owned by corporations whose principal function is to make money for shareholders.

WHAT LINUS RECKONS: DOES INDYMEDIA HAVE A FUTURE?

The increased interest in indymedia in recent years is, I believe, a witness to the fact that alternative mass media have become an integral part of the new protest/progressive movements. The explanation for this ought to be the development and accessibility of media technologies. I'm talking about both people-to-people communications technologies (such as mobile phones and email) and those that adapt the characteristics of a mass medium (such as web pages), and perhaps foremost, the unification of these where a personal communications medium could be used as a mass medium.

Still, I believe that much of indymedia's impact/relevance has been dependent on events situated outside the media, for example when mobilising for major protests and demonstrations. In Sweden, for instance, the Independent Media Center had its most

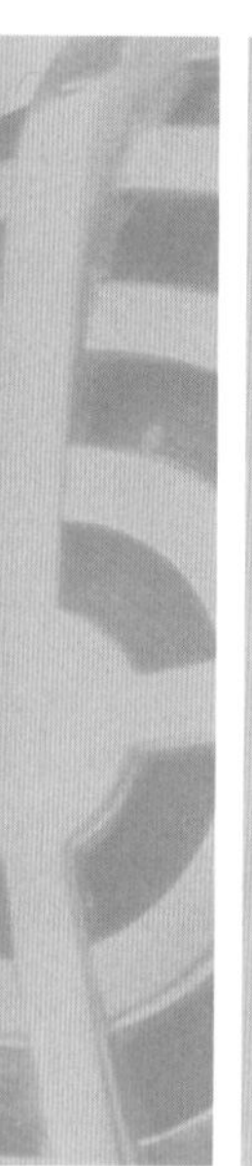

busy days during the June 2001 protests against the EU summit in Gothenburg. Since then the webpage has been more or less on stand-by.

Because of the general trend towards owner concentration in the mainstream media (both global and local), the alternative media will continue to fill a purpose when it comes to contesting the power of representation and information. On the other hand, the divergence logic of new media technology suggests a future where indymedia channels that resemble the mass media will give space for a multitude of voices through personal media such as blogs. In that case, the promises of indymedia in mobilising or unifying progressive movements may fall short and we will see a situation where these groups only address themselves through inward communication. One thing that was unique with Seattle 1999 was that a lot of different movements and groups, who had been struggling for years, found that they shared some concerns. If their common communication channel breaks down into a diversity of specialised communities, then I am afraid that we might witness a decline of the global justice movement(s).

Conclusion

Not since the time of ancient Greece, where the birth of democracy occurred, has political communication been so dramatically altered. If we accept Aristotle's premise that the art of politics is all about persuasion, then the 21st century's politicians will be able to exploit this art to the hilt thanks to the unlimited powers of the Internet. There is no question that the Internet has propelled us into a new era of rapid communication and technological change. However, we must continue—as we've attempted in this chapter—to separate the reality from the mythology. This means we must constantly ask the question: does the Internet promote democracy? This is particularly relevant as we shift from a broadcast to a narrowcast communication paradigm.

On the upside, there is no disputing that the Internet has given people unrivalled opportunities to obtain information and to encounter a whole new range of views and interactions. In the future, the advantages of the medium, as discussed in this chapter, will increasingly reduce our dependence on traditional media and increase our ability to draw our own conclusions about politics and government decisions and actions. People at the grassroots level will not only play a bigger part in political participation but also give the agenda-setting process a whole new dimension. The Internet will make increasingly possible the personalisation of politics and one-on-one courting of voters. As a new generation shifts its focus more towards online politics—of either the electoral, campaigning, or activist type—it may not necessarily spell doom to traditional mass media coverage, as evidenced by the continuing dominance of political and government-related advertising on television; nor will it necessarily affect the large budgets allocated by political candidates to television. But it does raise some important issues that leave room for greater research.

On the downside, there is every possibility that a move towards online voting and polling will only increase political and social surveillance of citizens by governments. It might also lead to further audience fragmentation and withdrawal from active citizenship, as Linus warns in his observations about indymedia. While this may be a fairly benign development at the moment, things could be very different in a time of political crisis, or when a government moves from being open and 'democratic' to being secretive and authoritarian. In this climate it is important that groups like indymedia continue to function. This is particularly relevant if we are to see the real generation of a 'Fifth Estate' in the electronic media that is not beholden to the hegemonic economic and political powers of the day. We can only conclude that our digital future will be determined by the choices we make as engaged citizens, more so than as engorged consumers.

KEY POINTS

The key points made in this chapter are that new media can have a transformative effect on politics, on political philosophy, and on public policy, but that this depends on the play of the digital dialectic. Further, we have argued that present trends by no means indicate a certain outcome. In particular, we examined:

- the digital direct democracy model advocated by US political consultant Dick Morris;
- how the dialectic of convergence and digital myths create a powerful mimetic effect that portrays the Internet as a great force for democratic change;
- the agenda-setting impact of interactivity;
- the impact of the immediacy created by telescoping time and space and the effect of the digital divide;
- netactivism and the function of bloggers as the town criers of cyberspace.

CLASS DISCUSSION

1. Given the conventional wisdom that television is still regarded as the dominant medium, will the Internet eventually reduce the audience share of traditional media?
2. To what extent will the voters who would normally otherwise read newspapers, watch television, and listen to the radio for voting information now use the Internet to replace this activity and other political rituals?
3. What does the Internet's role in agenda-setting suggest for the survival of newspapers and television?
4. In the increasingly electronic-driven society of Australia, traditional media institutions will come to be viewed as 'hot' media. Does this mean that future electioneering and politics in general will be conducted on a bigger scale on the Internet?
5. Check out the indymedia sites in your local area; do they offer a useful and enjoyable alternative news experience when compared with other news sources that you consume?
6. What do you think is the value of weblogs? Do they offer a good range of alternative opinion?

16

CAN WE INFLUENCE THE FUTURE OF NARROWCASTING?

OBJECTIVES

The purpose of this final chapter is to round out our discussion by looking at the issue of media reform and our ability to influence the future of both broadcasting and narrowcasting. Like Robert McChesney, we are not necessarily hopeful; the history of media regulation, government action and inaction, and the overwhelming power of entrenched and monopolistic business interests does not leave advocates of greater media democracy much room to manoeuvre. Like Aldous Huxley, however, we retain a certain optimism that 'education for freedom' may have a cumulative effect—if enough like-minded souls push collectively in the same direction. In particular, our concluding remarks emphasise two important points:

- old technologies rarely die; they usually converge with other technologies to form a hybrid technology that can live on;
- how ongoing reform and change in the narrowcasting media might unfold and what opportunities and obstacles this might create for the concept of digital citizenship.

If video killed the radio stars, will podcasting kill the video stars?

> The significance is not that so many forms of communication have died, but that with each death, the content and significance of communication changes. And therefore society changes. (Simons 2006)

The first section of this book covered the birth of the mass broadcast media from the late 19th to the end of the 20th century. It was never meant to be a comprehensive history—more a series of snapshots that illustrate our themes and help you to piece together both a narrative and a set of ideas (theories) of your own. To complete our journey the age of broadcasting, it is customary to remember the 'dead'; those who didn't make it out. In this case we honour the passing (or at least rumoured demise) of some fine 20th century technologies.

In February 2006, *Crikey*, the cheeky gadfly of electronic journalism in Australia (see case study in chapter 11), ran a series of articles in its daily subscriber email reflecting on the 'dead media' syndrome. This syndrome revolves around the argument that every time a new media technology and/or media form is invented, it kills off—either quickly, or by degrees—the 'old' forms and technology that it replaces. In her contribution, Margaret Simons pointed out that in most cases these claims are overstated, though there are exceptions that prove the rule. For example, most drive-in theatres in Australia are now no more than ghost arenas that get an occasional use as Sunday flea markets, and the wireless radio did seem to kill off that wonderful old-fashioned home entertainment device, the player-piano that played all the vaudeville hits from carefully punched rolls of 'sheet music' (Simons 2006).

We are also seeing audience attention migrate from the traditional mass media (newspapers, radio, and television) towards narrowcasting forms—podcasts and Internet radio, subscription services, news websites, and blogs—which are all marketed as convenience media that no longer tie us to broadcast and publishing schedules. There's no doubt that this is affecting the viability of commercial media, but is it killing them off? And if so, how quickly? As Margaret wrote in her piece for *Crikey*, the list of 'dead' media is quite long and covers a range of technologies. She has kindly given us permission to reprint the list, which was originally compiled from suggestions made by *Crikey* readers (our additional comments are in italics):

- Kodak film and the box Brownie killed forms of wet plate photography and democratised the snapshot. *Digital photography has nearly wiped out the domestic camera film industry and darkrooms belong in the media dark ages.*
- Talkies killed silent movies. *Now it seems some are predicting the obsolescence of the movie theatre*: 'Movie going is an exercise in regimented inconvenience, imposed at premium prices' (Moore 2006).

- Radio killed the player-piano as home entertainer. *Radio is now under threat from the iPod and the Internet.*
- Television slowly killed the illustrated newspaper, most of the general interest magazines, and most of the comic book industry.
- Radio and television slowly killed the afternoon newspapers.
- Television killed old-style radio programming, including almost all radio drama. *Now free-to-air television is under threat from pay-per-view television and digital competitors like TiVo.*
- The video camcorder killed the home movie camera. *Analogue tape has been replaced by digital tape and now the recordable DVD may spell the end of digital tape-recording.*
- Phone calls may soon be a thing of the past thanks to texting and videotexting.
- Semaphore (signalling with flags) was killed by the telegraph, which in turn was killed by the telephone. *The landline-handset is slowly being replaced by mobile-only subscribers.*
- Telex machines were killed by fax machines, and fax machines are now on the way out thanks to email and PDF formats. *Despite this, the paperless office still seems a long way off.*
- PABX telephone exchanges, once the heart of the commercial office, are dead.
- The 78 rpm disc record killed the Edison phonograph cylinder, and was in turn killed by the microgroove vinyl record. The vinyl disc is a relic of the past thanks to CDs and digital music downloads.
- The VHS cassette took over the market for 16 mm non-theatrical films. *Now VHS is being replaced in the domestic market by DVD, TiVo and video-on-demand over the Internet.*
- The main competitor to VHS, the Beta system of video recording, did not last long in the domestic market, but survived for almost thirty years in television news. *Beta tape is slowly being phased out by digital tape and direct-to-disc recording.*
- Super 8 mm killed standard 8 mm, and standard 8 mm killed 16 mm. *Now even major release motion pictures are shot straight to disc.*
- The CD Walkman is being rapidly superseded by the iPod.
- And remember roneo machines and carbon paper? Even in the computer age there have been rapid lives and deaths. The Internet's 'gopher' protocol. And how about 'active desktop channels' and 'push technology' and 'Pointcast'?

It is easy to prepare lists like this one and it's a reminder that some technologies do indeed 'die' when confronted with a more efficient alternative. But it doesn't happen overnight and, more often than not, the old form and the new form can coexist for some time before the old one withers away and the new becomes dominant. This is the dialectic of convergence and technological change at work within the capitalist economy where 'planned' obsolescence is built in to most consumer goods, particularly electronics. One observation that's worth making, though, is that in the digital age the time-frame can be shortened, particularly if there is fierce commercial rivalry around the introduction of similar but competing technologies, even if the differences are not entirely obvious to consumers, or very large. In early 2006 a serious skirmish in the technology wars erupted between Toshiba's HD-DVD format and Sony's Blu-ray. When Microsoft decided that it would support the Toshiba product and not Sony, the decision 'reverberated through the technology industry' (Belson 2006). Microsoft stands to gain from this move because of its strong position in gaming and computing, rather than movies and television. Ken Belson's article in the *New York Times* draws the parallel between the HD-DVD versus Blu-ray contest and the 'format war' between VHS and Betamax video technologies in the 1980s and over the first generation of DVD players between Sony and Philips on one side and Toshiba/Warner Brothers on the other. It is consumers and retailers who get caught in the crossfire when these platform skirmishes erupt, but this does not upset the manufacturers too much because DVD player sales have stagnated and the new product is aimed at getting consumers to upgrade their equipment if they want to view HD movies, or play games with more features. An interesting side issue is that several major Hollywood studios and computer game companies have been dragged into the platform brawl. This issue still has some time to play out, and for now both Toshiba and Sony are committed to introducing their new technologies progressively and they're expected in the stores in time for Christmas 2008 (Belson 2006).

The Toshiba–Sony platform battle confirms that seemingly out-of-date media technologies can indeed persist in the market for some time, often for years if not decades. This is a point that Australian media law academic Jock Given made in his 1998 pamphlet, *The Death of Broadcasting?* The question mark in Given's title is important because, as we've seen, broadcasting is not yet dead, despite a decade of digital convergence. Take-up rates for the new digital television system in Australia have not met government or industry expectations and this has delayed the planned changes to Australian media ownership laws for several years. As Given notes, in the global media world '[w]hether you think broadcasting is dying depends a lot on where you live' (Given 1998, p. 43).

Given supports this claim by showing how the 'death' of broadcasting means different things in different countries. In the United States it is generally taken to mean the demise of the big commercial networks. In Canada and parts of western Europe it means drastic cuts to the public broadcasting system. Given argues that the obituaries for broadcasting in Australia seemed a bit premature in the 1990s because the free-to-air networks and radio stations did well out of the reorganisation of the airwaves that occurred through the process of 'market liberalisation' in that decade (pp. 44–5). We have outlined in chapter 12 how the government's 'digital roadmap' may extend the death rattle of analogue media for a few more years yet. As Given notes, what usually happens is that new technologies 'supplement rather than replace' older forms: 'Radio threatened newspapers but didn't destroy them. Television threatened radio and the cinema, but left them standing. Home video [now DVDs] threatened cinema and television but they're still there' (p. 46).

This is more accurate than bald statements that new media kill off the old media and it was certainly true in the age of analogue. But 'the more difficult question' is what happens to the 'social and cultural practices' when a new technology is introduced, and 'thus what happens to communication' (p. 47). What Given observed in 1998 and what we're now seeing come to pass with increasing rapidity is that digital technologies provide a greater capacity, through convergence of forms, for the concentration of control of 'media distribution' (p. 48). In-house production of program content has all but ceased at all the big free-to-air networks in Australia, including the ABC and the SBS. Most programs are now outsourced to local production companies, or bought in ready-made from giant international distributors, mainly from America and the UK.

Certainly the CEOs of the major television networks don't think that TV is dead—at least not yet. Michael Eisner, former head of the Disney corporation, thinks that while television is 'decreasing in importance', its reported demise 'is not real'. But he does think that the social relations of television are changing. He says that the rise of pay TV in the crowded American free-to-air market is creating an 'underclass' of viewers who cannot afford to pay for content that they previously watched free; 'there's a large population being left out so there's a social issue in the supposed demise of broadcast TV' (quoted in Nguyen 2006). Thus we can see that there's a growing divide between the television 'haves' and 'have-nots' in the narrowcast environment. In a small way this is demonstrated in Australia where the popular weekly wrap of British soccer has been bought by Foxtel and will no longer be shown on the free-to-air SBS network.

Narrowcasting: An audience of one?

Another aspect that's changing is the conglomeration of audiences that is implicit in a broadcast model of media production and distribution, which meant that traditionally, radio and television networks devised their program schedule around content that had a wide appeal (Given 1998, p. 52). Convergence in the digital age has meant that marketers and advertisers are able to test the grounds for this convenient (for broadcasting) model. Questions can now be asked about whether mass audiences are a factor of 'social and cultural choice', or of 'economic and technical necessity' (p. 52). Since the late 1990s the large TV networks around the globe have been able to cross-promote their content (and thus increase its appeal to advertisers) by taking advantage of digital production, storage, and delivery platforms—for example, linking their television programming to websites and specialist magazines.

There's also been a shift in the nature of time constraints around broadcast content. Until the advent of digital time-shifting, the main organising principle of mass media has been the aggregation of what Jock Given calls the 'simultaneous audience' (1998, p. 54). This made sense when advertising was rated and valued according to the size of the audience listening or watching at any one time. This is the genesis of the concept of prime-time viewing in the evenings when most people are home, relaxing in front of the 'box'. But what is prime time when audience units (individuals or family groups) can choose to watch their program of choice at any time thanks to video and digital recording technology and new forms of delivery such as TiVo or video-on-demand over the Internet? There are still landmark program events on television that can command huge audiences and most of them are sporting events—the Olympics, the Commonwealth Games, Grand Slam tennis, and finals in many team sports. Broadcast rights to the 2010 and 2012 summer and winter Olympic games went on sale in June 2005 and were estimated to be worth over $A100 million. The Australian domestic football codes were asking between $A40 and $A70 million a year from the 2007 season (Schulze & Korporaal 2005).

It's easy to understand why the networks will pay these prices when you consider that American companies spent around $US3.3 million for a 30-second spot during the 2006 Super Bowl, shown live on the US ABC network. The benefit of a spot in this traditionally high-rating event is that over 90 million Americans watched the game live: over 40 per cent of US households (Williams 2006). Outside of these landmark events, many commentators are suggesting that the era of 'appointment TV' is coming to an end. This process began with the VCR nearly thirty years ago, but it has been the new digital technologies that really sealed its fate (Moore 2006).

We are now able to look back on Jock Given's perceptive analysis from 1998 and say that he was right in many respects. The 'technical inevitability' that television and computing will be integrated is now a social reality. According to reality television producer Mark Burnett, 'The world is changing and the Internet is about to become the next broadcast network' (quoted in Moore 2006). It is also apparent that media companies have figured out a series of new business models that appear to have tapped into the ways in which audiences choose to interact with the converged digital media. They have worked out how to beat audience timeshifting to their benefit. The implication in this is that advertising dollars will move from traditional broadcast media and gravitate to online, interactive services. Given's prediction that 'advertising may be replaced by direct contact between suppliers and customers' (1998, p. 56) is the new model for electronic commerce and it is predicated on the growth of the surveillance economy. This new trend in tailored online marketing has been described as 'mass target marketing à la Google style' and it is predicted that over the next few years this model will colonise all electronic media spaces, including television, PCs, mobile and car phones, and wireless devices (Sallabank 2006).

Part III looked at how these new technologies, marketing ideas, and cultural forms of narrowcasting are coming together through the process of digital convergence to form a narrowcasting media environment. We discussed how and why telephony, computing, and televisions are slowly morphing into one technology in many convenient sizes, packaging options, and decorative surfaces. Where is the 'digital revolution' at right now and where is it all going to end? These are the themes that occupied the second half of *Communication and New Media*. In the final section we drew together some thoughts about the future of what we are calling the surveillance economy. Our final question is: what can be done to alter this possible digital future that appears to have many dystopian elements?

The surveillance society: Be careful what you wish for

We have argued in this book that the defining characteristic of the digital age is the surveillance society: that society is founded upon, and sustained by, a surveillance economy. That economy is about controlling and directing digital flows of information, resources, and value. In it, regulatory bodies across the globe are focused on the regulation and censorship of media content rather than a careful scrutiny of the regulation of ownership in the greater public interest. In the East, the government of China energetically blocks access to Internet material that promotes freedom of expression and freedom of religious belief. In the West, liberal democracies are just as energetic in proscribing material—all in the name of the fight against terrorism.

The digital divide

> It is one of the great ironies of IT technology … No one said the Internet wasn't a paradox. (Noonan 2006)

We have mentioned the 'digital divide' several times. It is a chasm marked by several social indicators: sex, ethnicity, language, culture, and, perhaps most importantly, age—'just ask most parents with a teenager' (Noonan 2006). According to Brisbane journalist Kathleen Noonan, parents are having a difficult time coping with the techno-savvy lives of their children, particularly Generation Y. Advice to parents, from the experts, is that they must 'get with it' and catch up to their children. According to RMIT researcher Darren Sharp, most adults are 'a million miles behind teens and pre-teens in understanding digital media, both technologically and culturally. Meanwhile, concerned organisations like Relationships Australia warn that many people are avoiding "real" world responsibilities in an idealised "virtual" space' (cited in Noonan 2006).

Can we intervene to 'save' the future?

In *Communication and New Media* we have made an argument that the digital future can be either utopian or dystopian. Throughout this book we have discussed this in relation to science fiction imaginings. A key literary device in utopian literature is the 'time-traveller'. Writing in the 'Prime Space' property pages of the *Australian*, demographer Bernard Salt (2005) adopted this technique in an interesting piece of 'creative' journalism. He imagines a time-traveller from the 1950s who visits our present and our future, but is unimpressed by a number of things—equality for women and our obsession with large infrastructure projects among them. On this visit the traveller explains to Bernard Salt that in 2035 the Generation Y age group is distraught because the rising death toll among baby-boomers meant 'an end to their free and easy lifestyle'. There are elements of both utopia and dystopia apparent in the traveller's tales and Salt's conclusion at the end of this mythic conversation is that the changes of the past fifty years will seem like nothing compared to what will happen in the next fifty. While we cannot take advantage of time travel to predict the future, we can say that it will largely depend on our responses to the intrusions of the surveillance society in our lives. We can choose to do nothing, or we can argue for an alternative.

They say 'sit back'. We say 'fight back'

> Instead of opposing the media, culture jammers and activists become the media, in order to incite change. (Fitzgibbon 2005)

We discussed indymedia in chapter 15 and don't want to cover the same ground here. All we need to add is that culture jamming—using art and performance to 'jam' commercial and ideological memes and disrupt their transmission—is one way to get an alternative point of view across. Like utopian and dystopian literature, culture-jamming holds up 'commercial and mainstream vices' to ridicule and contempt 'in the most well-natured way' to expose the 'quirks of modern culture' (Fitzgibbon 2005).

The business model of electronic commerce was pioneered by the sex industry—pay per view—with the pornography industry arguably the globe's biggest online media business. Now business and government are being encouraged to 'socialise' their websites by engaging with the creations of the cybergypsies: wikis, tikis, and blogs. The commercial application of so-called 'social software' demonstrates the power of corporate and government strategists to cannibalise and re-purpose the tools of the anti-establishment digital pioneers of the Internet's 'Golden Age' (Guenther 2005). There is, in effect, a virtual arms race going on between the hacker and hacktivist communities and Internet business interests: as one develops a new tool or methodology, the other ups the ante by countering with a blocking tactic or product. Privacy activists at the Freenet Project are working on a 'darknet' application to hide their activities and to keep their file-swapping safe from the prying eyes of law enforcement ('Darknet to hide swappers' 2005). The hacktivists won a skirmish in November 2005 when a large multinational soft-drink manufacturer was caught out infiltrating chatrooms and blogs with its commercial messaging and 'social software'. As part of an $A18 million strategy to launch a new product, Coca-Cola Australia began a guerrilla marketing campaign that included setting up an apparently independent website www.thezeromovement.com and then sent anonymous 'viral marketers' into chatrooms to urge traffic to the site. Net activist Tim Longhurst, who set up a counter-site (www.thezeromovement.org), was scathing in his denunciation of Coke's underhanded tactics: '"Presumably someone who has only recently chopped off their ponytail has decided it would be a good idea," Mr Longhurst said' (Mathewson 2006).

Today we are confronted by an Internet that in many respects resembles a strip mall rather than an online global space for democratic expression. Each week, it seems, more and more 'virtual' commodities become available, thanks to the increasing capacity and speed of broadband and thanks also to the ingenuity of marketing and distribution honchos in the movie studios, the media, telcos, and the music business (Griffiths 2006). However, we have continually emphasised the role of the dialectic in determining the outcome of a constant struggle between the forces of the market and competing social forces that seek to express an alternative. This is a battle that has been fought over all media platforms from the earliest printed works to the introduction of electronic broadcast media and now across the digital frontier.

It is our view that eventually, narrowcasting diminishes diversity. Audiences fragmented to an aggregate of one have little in common, and no basis for common discourse and debate around the water cooler. Just as the diffusion of television in the United States brought about what Robert Putnam calls 'the cocooning of America', narrowcasting has the capacity to bring about a new version of social isolation, alienation, and fragmentation. This is characterised as the digital 'thumbing down' of our public and private conversations.

We've also argued that social and cultural divergence is a by-product of technological convergence as we hurtle towards a narrowcasting world. We've documented the impact of this on the reportorial community and shown how the explosion of blog sites has both positive and negative consequences. Blogging may well be a new wave of open expression in cyberspace and certainly everyone, from marketers to academics, is being encouraged to jump on the webdiary bandwagon (Farrell 2005).

Thus the digital divide—traditionally understood as being a factor limiting access to new communications technologies (Parayil 2005)—is also manifest within digitally wealthy societies as a social disconnect that leads to what we have already described as the fetishisation of technology and the online experience, and the further alienation of human beings from personal interactions with each other. This is particularly apparent in teenagers; Stephen Gennaro (2005, p. 133) describes it as an 'epidemic' of 'fabricated youth culture' based on commercially leveraged American ideas, trends, fashions, and embedded in endless commodities.

We can also see similar divisions in the related field of biotechnology (the computer-mediated application of new technologies to medicine and science) where the gap between the medically rich and medically poor spheres of the world is increasing and many scientists appear to be blinded by a 'global myopia' when it comes to ethical thinking (Rose 2006). There is also a danger of greater fragmentation of a user's online experience in the Web2.0 version of browsers released by Google, Yahoo, Wikipedia, and Amazon.com in late 2005. Web2.0 is supposed to offer a richer experience and the ability to personalise tags on pages that can then be shared across networks. According to technology reporter Jack Schofield (2005), Web2.0 is being heavily marketed, but is more hype than new technology. However, it is important to acknowledge the small steps that are being taken to bridge the digital divide, such as the wind-up laptop computer that was unveiled by Nicholas Negroponte and UN Secretary-General Kofi Annan in November 2005. This device, powered by a spring-mechanism, is reported to have the same capabilities as a notebook computer. And the not-for-profit 'One Laptop per Child' project hopes to distribute over 100 million units by the end of 2007 (Agence France Press 2005). This is certainly an innovative adaptation of convergence—the relatively new power of digital computing linked to the age-old power of mechanical springs.

Our close personal, social, and work-related interactions are increasingly mediated by digital technologies that help us to 'interface', but not really connect 'face to face'. While supporters of the digital knowledge economy think this will be tremendous boost to productivity (and the 'bottom line' for business) it also creates a social fault line in the very foundations of a liberal democratic nation-state. As we are 'empowered' as *customers* we are in danger of being simultaneously stripped of our power as *citizens*. We have argued that cyber-democracy is perhaps a poor substitute for real, live, cumbersome, and difficult politics in the real world. Such mediated politics can also lead to greater commercial and state-sanctioned intrusions into our life. The concept of digital 'passports' and identity keys is very clearly on the agenda of both business and government. Once such technologies are in place we will have literally 'no place to hide' from the panoptic surveillance of every move we make.

It's always difficult to make any good predictions about the future, simply because we don't have the benefit (yet) of time travel. But it's clear that the digital revolution has some way to go yet and the pace of change will not slow down any time soon. For example, just a couple of years after the release of the MP3-playing iPod, a new model that allows the viewing of digital video was released on the market. Humourist and columnist Richard Glover (2005) christened it the 'whyPod', 'as in the phrase "Why do we need it?"'. With the screen pressed to our face and the earphones jacked in, Glover says iPod users become 'entirely cocooned', like 'medieval monks' locked away from the real world, and any thoughts that might 'bubble up' are drowned out by aural and visual stimuli (Glover 2005). How can politics compete with 24/7 entertainment? The distracting presence of video screens invades nearly all public and private space these days and Richard Glover's witty vision of the future, like all utopian/dystopian satire, also contains a biting grain of truth: 'Once there's a screen on every packet of chips and bottle of coke, I don't see why all of us can't have one installed in the back of our heads. Stuck in a queue, you could catch up on a few old episodes of *M*A*S*H*, buried within the head of the bloke in front of you' (Glover 2005).

Are we, then, really caught up in what William Connolly (2005) calls the 'evangelical-capitalist resonance machine'? This far-fetched contraption is a potent mix of 'cowboy capitalism' and the 'theocratic ambitions' of conservative American Christian militants, and it is embodied in the administration of US President George W. Bush. According to Connolly, the electronic media serve as an 'echo chamber' that mimetically reverberates with the ideological messages of the machine and by 'market apologism and scandalmongering', stifles any attempt to mobilise a democratic counter-force. In order to begin a process of democratic change, social activists and their supporters must mobilise on both economic and cultural fronts to challenge corporate and political power from 'inside and outside at the same time' (2005, p. 870). This dystopian 'machine' finds a useful doppelganger in what Buckingham and Scanlon (2005) call the 'selling' of learning through a growing 'edutainment media'. The 'logic' of this system reinforces the anti-student culture of testing, which gives producers and distributors 'predictability and security in an increasingly competitive commercial environment' (2005, p. 47). The edutainment commodities in this market create their own 'educational divide' between those who can afford to buy them and those who can't. At the same time it makes the school curriculum 'narrower and more reductive', which in turn creates less motivated and less curious learners (p. 57). There is little or no room, in such a climate, for potentially threatening alternative analysis. While the picture we have captured may appear to be dark, bleak, and dystopian, we are optimistic about the capacity of any powerful medium to be suborned, so that it becomes an instrument of education for democracy. The future of the digital world is in your hands.

Pessimism of the intellect, optimism of the will

To give you some cause to share our optimism and to provide some tools—in case you're inclined to start campaigning—we want to close with some thoughts from experienced agitators for media reform whose ideas and politics are motivated by a democratic instinct and the theory of a dialectically attuned political economy.

Culture-jamming is a new term for a tradition that has a long history among progressive political activists. In the 1970s one of the authors was heavily involved in 'culture-jamming' billboards around the inner suburbs of Sydney. A group calling itself 'Billboard Utilising Graffiti Against Unhealthy Promotions' (BugaUp) regularly defaced and artistically altered beer and cigarette hoardings, transforming slogans like Resch's beer 'Silver Bullet' to 'Liver Bullet' and 'Anyhow have a Winfield' to 'Anyhow have lung cancer'. Culture-jamming is a low level of direct action when used on the streets. In the hands of hacktivists it takes the form of both street journalism and clever send-ups of official websites, and it can also be actual hacking or 'denial of service' attacks on web servers. In one recent Australian example of culture jamming, the anti-war activist and social commentator Richard Neville placed a spoof website on his server that mimicked the Prime Minister's own site, but included a cleverly reworded 'speech' that seemed to indicate John Howard thought the occupation of Iraq was a mistake.

In the United States student groups have taken their protests against President George W. Bush online through emails and petitions, but they haven't forgotten the old techniques of boycotts either. According to a survey of American students by Harvard University's Institute of Politics, about a third of students had signed an online petition or written an email in support of political campaigns. Nearly 20 per cent had contributed comments to a politics blog site. The Harvard study concluded that the students were making good use of the technology available to them in their protests (Reuters 2005).

If culture-jammers are working both inside and outside the mainstream media, what can we say about attempts to reform the media? How do we, in the Information Age, convince governments and corporate interests that it is in everyone's interests to have open, transparent, and accountable decision-making when it comes to allocations of communication infrastructure and resources?

For media lawyer and social progressive Jock Given (1998, p. 71), the answer is partly to convince politicians that they need to take our interests seriously; that there are mechanisms to safeguard Australian interests in international trade agreements and policies in place to distribute communication resources equitably. But he acknowledges that it is often difficult for citizens and consumer groups to be seen, let alone listened to, in the 'dense politics' that tend to hide important decisions about technology from the public gaze (p. 71). There is a chance, Given argues, for societies like Australia to become 'a little fairer, a little freer, more inventive' and even 'more tolerant and curious' as a result of digital convergence and the new media technologies. In the end, he writes: 'All that will matter is whether the chance is lost or taken' (p. 73).

For Trevor Barr (2000, pp. 215–18), the key issues revolve around how well Australia can integrate its digital economy with the global new information order to secure 'our prosperity for the future'. While his focus is mainly on the economic benefits that might flow from the new technology, Barr does argue for a revitalisation of the public sphere, even though he says it should be situated within 'a stronger market-based ideology' (p. 217). But this does not move us beyond the paradigm of capitalism and it is subject to all the same dialectical dilemmas that we've discussed in this book. It gets hung up on the central contradiction, expressed in the duality of media commodities, of how you reconcile the relations of the market with an overriding public interest. We have argued that this is almost impossible to resolve in terms of the capitalist 'free market'. It is an uncrossable fault line in the political economy of the global capitalist system and the stumbling block over which all attempts at 'reform' will trip.

While firmly in the reformist camp, Robert McChesney (2000b, p. 283) at least argues that the foundation principle of any citizen-led resistance to globalisation and the rising surveillance economy must be the subservience of the economy to democratic political decision-making and 'the will of the people'. McChesney (p. 289) even dares to mention an ideologically loaded taboo word, 'socialism', and argues that a fully public socialist economy is one possible solution and an expression of the 'logical full development of the democratic principle', while conceding that this might seem unpalatable to many people at the moment. Finally McChesney, too, falls back onto a 'reform' argument—we can make capitalism more 'humane' if we protest loudly enough.

That this seems all that is possible today is a testament to the strength of mimetic capitalist ideologies—they have all but obliterated any hope that the 'Left', in particular those arguing for a socialist transformation of capitalism, might win a political argument. Some Marxists, like Nick Dyer-Witheford (1999), argue an 'autonomist' line—that is, the 'Left' needs to regenerate its analysis and political program without any of the historical baggage of Stalinism and the failure of previous revolutionary movements. At the centre of the 'autonomist' analysis is the materialist concept of class struggle—the continuous, sometimes hidden, sometimes violent struggle between the power of capital and the power of the working class. Any realistic Marxist who isn't 'on something' will acknowledge that when the class struggle is at a low point—such as in the last twenty years and today—it is hard to see how the working class can emancipate itself from the rule of capital. This is the power of hegemonic ideological memes circulating in vectors that are themselves controlled by capital and their hired gate-keepers. To resist the temptation to 'sit back' and to gain the strength and insight to 'fight back' is a difficult task for most social progressives—even for two old comrades with nearly sixty years' experience in socialist and church politics between us.

However, the dialectic constantly reasserts itself and new spaces—indymedia, blogs, the 'darknet', and others—do open up and prove, for a while at least, to be resistant to the dominant ideology. Certainly the digital revolution contains these spaces and the mythology of cyberspace encourages counter-cultural alternatives to colonise them. The responsibility that rests with all of us is to be awake to the reality and to the mythology of the digital age and to critically assess the information that swirls all around us. If we keep our eyes and ears open and our 'bullshit detectors' switched on we stand a better chance of making up our own minds based on good information and being fully aware of the personal and social consequences of the actions of other individuals, corporate players, and governments (both officials and politicians). Unfortunately this is all too true. In May 2006 the US government admitted that the National Security Agency had secretly collected and analysed tens of millions of phone records on the spurious grounds that this would help 'catch' so-called terrorists. According to US law, such wide scale invasions of privacy are illegal—nobody has been charged over this incident.

You might also like to know that recruitment agencies are now also Googling job applicants to look for any unsavoury digital traces that might indicate that they have a less than pristine past. According to the *NYT*, several recent university graduates have had promising corporate careers derailed when their new employer found embarrassing images posted in chatrooms and websites.

In the age of surveillance and narrowcasting there really is no place to hide. It's not about watching *Big Brother*, Big Brother *is* watching you.

However, we do not have to sit back and allow ourselves to be overwhelmed by the surveillance economy. Through collective action and insight it is possible to make a digital future in the interests of the broad 'public', instead of the narrow 'private' interests of big business. One final note of caution: if you see a light in the tunnel up ahead and it turns out to be a digital road-train barrelling towards you down the information superhighway, take the nearest exit out of cyberspace and see what's really happening out on the street. The view from the pavement is often safer and more revealing than the view from an illuminated video-screen. Besides, you are never really out of touch if your mobile's switched on!

GLOSSARY

activist media

Media outlets with a declared politico-social agenda. Sometimes wrongly described as 'indie-media', or 'indymedia' (that is, independent media), because activist media can have a range of social and political points of view whereas the indymedia tradition seems to have a left-wing or anarchist disposition, as distinct from media outlets owned by corporations whose principal function is to make money for shareholders.

analogue

A mechanical technology used to transmit sound, light, temperature, position, or pressure. Perhaps best described as a wave that is measured by variations in time and amplitude during transmission, rather than by the binary system (zero or one), which is the basis of digital technology.

backpack journalism

The practice of a single journalist taking to the field equipped to report in all media forms: radio, television, print, online. Typically such a journalist would be equipped with a laptop computer, digital camcorder, and satellite phone: all items that can be carried in a backpack. Compare this with the baggage carried by a traditional television crew with lights, tripods, booms, reflector boards, monitors, and a picnic basket of pâté and red wine.

bit, byte, megabyte

A bit is the smallest unit of computerised data, either a zero or one; a byte is usually 8 bits; a megabyte is a million bytes.

blogging

The publication on the Internet of the views and opinions of an individual. The distinctive attribute of blogging is that it is unfiltered by the traditional media 'gatekeepers', although not necessarily unmoderated. Purportedly, blogging has created a new flowering of opinion, and represents the diversity of opinion characteristic of new media.

boom-bust cycle

See **dot.com crash.**

broadcasting

To broadcast means to scatter (cast) widely. In this sense broadcasting is clearly linked to the concept of publishing in the print media. The message (program) is published (broadcast) to a wide audience via electronic signals originating from a single source. Radio stations and free-to-air television services are the most common forms of broadcasting today.

broadsheet

A newspaper format in which each page is approximately A2 size. Traditionally regarded as an upmarket form to distinguish it from tabloid, which is A3, and downmarket.

camera obscura

An ancient form of reprographic technology. Using a pinhole or lens, a lighted image is projected from outside, into a darkened room, allowing the external image to be reproduced on the opposite wall. It is suggested that some of the Old Masters who achieved such fine detail in their paintings were assisted by a camera obscura.

capital

For Marx and political economy, capital refers to the accumulation of value, usually expressed in terms of money, that accrues from the exploitation of labour during the production of commodities in a particular set of production relations. In neo-classical economics the term is stripped of any notion of exploitation and refers to the exclusive right of the monied class to own and control the means of production.

capitalism

An economic system based on private ownership of the means of production (capital) and the private accumulation of profits. Capitalist ideology is based on the idea that an unfettered free market is the best way to deliver increased wealth and prosperity for all. The operation of capitalist systems is often characterised by distortions arising from excessive government regulation and intervention, monopoly and oligopoly, plutocracy, low wages, and hyper-consumerism. Capitalism is a class system in which two contending classes (labour and capital) are engaged in a constant struggle over the distribution of the production surplus (surplus value).

celluloid

Based on the natural polymer cellulose, celluloid is a form of plastic, from which film was originally made in pre-digital times. The word has also become a shorthand way of describing the world of film and its ephemeral character.

citizen-journalist

A person who is not attached to a media organisation, who witnesses an event, and then provides an account of that event, normally using traditional and new journalistic forms. Distinguished from an eyewitness by the nature and form(s) of their account.

commodity or commodification
the process of turning non-commercial material—goods, services, ideas—into saleable products or commodities.

contradiction
A state of tension or conflict between two ideas or social forces that indicates two opposing sides to an issue or idea.

convergence
To converge means to come together. In the context of communications technologies this means the *coming together* of telecommunications, computing, and broadcasting. The key to this modern form of convergence is the microprocessor—the computer chip. Convergence is both a technological and an economic-social process that proceeds dialectically and via a series of contradictions.

creative industries
A collective noun that refers to a range of activities and professions associated with media production in the information or knowledge economy. The creative industries include print, radio, and television production; literature and poetry; theatre and film; public relations; journalism; and marketing and advertising.

cyberia
A play on the word Siberia—the frozen wastes of Russia—suggesting that the digital future is dystopian. See also **cyberpunk**.

cyberpunk
a genre of literary fiction that chronicles the dystopian aspects of cyber society; exemplified by the novels of William Gibson.

democracy
Rule by the people, as distinct from monarchy (rule by a monarch), plutocracy (rule by the rich), oligarchy (rule by a few), and anarchy (the absence of rulers).

dialectic
The idea that history is shaped by opposing forces. The predominant force, idea, movement, or paradigm (the thesis) is challenged by an opposing force, idea, movement, or paradigm (the antithesis), which results in a third new force, idea, movement, or paradigm (the synthesis). The synthesis, in turn, becomes the new predominant force, idea, movement, or paradigm (the new thesis), and the process begins all over again. The dialectic is the process of creation, and resolution of contradictions.

digital

Digital electronic technology works using binary code to store and transmit data using only two states: 'positive' and 'non-positive'. These conditions of either 'on' or 'off' are represented by two numbers (digits), 'one' and 'zero'. Digital technology is primarily used with new communications media, such as mobile phones and satellite and fibre optic transmission.

digital citizenship

see **e-democracy**.

digital mythology

The power of myth is that it contains elements of truth and seems to hold a timeless manifestation of an eternal and powerful entity. Digital mythology is based on the seemingly unstoppable power of technology to do 'good'. See also **dystopia**.

digital revolution

The technological, social, cultural, and economic changes wrought by digital technologies.

'digital sublime'

Vincent Mosco uses the phrase 'digital sublime' to suggest the power of digital computing and digital technologies to apparently transcend the everyday (the 'banal') by seeming to be everywhere and able to satisfy desire or instil fear and to impress with an overwhelming presence.

dot.com crash

In the second half of the 1990s a significant number of computer companies 'went public'; that is, they listed on the stock exchange through a process known as an IPO (Initial Public Offering). In doing so, they created fabulous paper profits for those who owned the shares prior to the IPO. Those who cashed in their shares made huge profits. This was known as the dot.com boom. In late 1999 and early 2000, however, these stocks lost their allure and the market crashed. This is, of course, the traditional manner in which capital markets operate. Speculators push share prices to unsustainable levels, at which point investors deem the stocks to be overpriced, and a correction or a crash occurs.

dystopia

The view that the future is bleak and bad, as distinct from the utopian view that it is bright and good.

e-democracy

The use of digital (e = electronic) technologies to enhance the participation of citizens in the democratic process.

ethico-legal paradox
The confusion that arises when an action is morally right, but legally wrong.

ethics
Asks 'how ought we act?' and 'what is the right thing to do?', as distinct from 'what does the law permit us to do?' A concept little understood by many politicians and business people.

'global village'
A phrase popularised by the Canadian media sociologist Marshall McLuhan to describe the social effect of convergent technologies. In essence a global village would mean that we all get to know each other and interact in some utopian way, as was supposed to be the case in pre-industrial village life.

globalisation
The mistaken and outdated notion that economic development proceeds best on the basis of a single worldwide market dominated by the United States and, to a lesser extent, Europe, who source materials and labour from anywhere in the world at the lowest possible cost.

'golden age'
The idea that in looking back, there was a halcyon period in history in which everything was bright and beautiful.

governance
The rules, principles, and practices by which a corporate entity is constituted, organised, and managed.

half-tone
A series of black and white dots used to simulate grey in the reproduction of black-and-white images. The more dense the black dots, the more dark that section of the image; the more frequent the white dots, the lighter sections of the image would be when printed.

hegemony
A term popularised by Antonio Gramsci to describe the domination of one social class by another.

idealism
The opposite of materialism. Idealism is the worldview in which all manifestations of reality actually stem from the thought process of human beings, rather than from their material circumstances. For example: 'People are greedy, that's just human nature' is idealist thinking.

ideology
A worldview based on principles or intuitions that may or may not be logical or internally consistent.

information society
See **knowledge society**.

killer application
A computer application that revolutionises the use of the computer system and renders redundant (kills off) previous applications. Spreadsheets and word processing were the original killer applications; Internet browsers and search engines are another example. The search is always on for the next 'killer app'.

knowledge society
Also known as the 'information society'. The idea that society is structured around the production of information, as distinct from the industrial society that preceded it, which was structured around the production of goods.

labour
'Labour' and 'labour power' are terms from political economy that refer to the actual process of work that humans undertake in their interactions with technology and nature (the means of production) to produce the means of subsistence and the necessities of life. Within any given social formation or economic system, the forms that this labour takes are determined by the relations of production. Within the capitalist economy of the 20th century (and today), labour takes a commodity form in which its price (wages) is determined not on the principle of a fair day's pay for a fair day's work, but by the power of capital to impose conditions of exploitation on the labouring classes.

liberalism
While this term may have a number of meanings, it is best described as a political philosophy or ideology that emphasises maximum human choice, and promotes diversity and liberty of opinion, including freedom of speech and association. The phrase 'liberal-democratic state' refers to one in which such values are constitutionally enshrined, and expressed through the rule of law. See also **neo-liberalism**.

mainframe
A term used to describe the large refrigerator-size computers that preceded the personal computer. The first commercial mainframe was the Univac, manufactured in 1951. The mainframe made a comeback in the 1990s as electronic commerce took off, and as networks-based systems became subject to hacking and virus attacks, as an efficient and

secure means of performing high-volume transactions. IBM dominates the market for mainframe computers.

materialism

The philosophical mode of thought that suggests that events, situations, and relationships in the real, physical world determine, to the largest degree, human consciousness and thinking. Historical materialism, the method of Marx and Engels, posits the theory that human beings' interaction with nature creates the material conditions for the development of social structures and argues that the social force that drives historical change is the struggle between classes for control of the material world, in particular control over the means of production.

means of production

An ensemble of the available technologies and natural resources that combine with human labour and within specific forms of social relations to form what political economy calls the mode of production.

meme

A small but powerful chunk of ideological 'DNA' that carries ideas, meanings, trends, and fashions through both time and space via the process of mimetic (imitation) transfer. Memes can be generated by hegemonic or subversive social forces and are usually transported via the various communication vectors of the mass media, narrowcasting, and popular culture.

mode of development

The mode of development in any mode of production will determine how the economy is shaped by what Castells (1996, p. 16) calls the 'technical relations of production'.

mode of production

A mode of production is the way that human society organises its productive relationship with nature in order to provide the means of subsistence that allow a society to function and reproduce itself. A mode of production exists historically as the sum total of the relations of production that govern how society is organised economically, socially, and politically. Modes of production are usually named after the dominant social relations of an epoch. For example, slavery, feudalism, capitalism, and socialism are social structures based on particular modes of production.

MP3

A digital audio compression format. MP3 stands for MPEG Audio Layer 3. Just as jpeg is a graphics file format, mpeg is a file format for audio files, standardised in 1991. Just as many other technolgies like ARPAnet were government-funded, mpeg developed out of the EU-funded Eureka research project in Germany.

mutual constitution
Mosco uses this term to describe the state of the dialectic at any given point in its cycle. Contradictory elements are, according to Mosco, held together in a magnetic field of mutual constitution.

narrowcasting
The distribution of media content to increasingly segmented audiences, to the point where the ideal is a mass audience of individual consumers and the advertising or media message can be tailored to fit that person's needs or consumer profile.

neo-liberalism
A political ideology associated with contemporary capitalism, which argues for smaller government, based on the Lochean principle that the two principal functions of the state are to protect citizens from external threats and internal disorder. It is expressed as a mania to privatise every state-owned asset, including infrastructure and utilities. It has been hugely successful in delivering high levels of personal taxation, bloated and inefficient public bureaucracies, and impoverished public services in health, education, and transport.

new media
A catchall phrase used to distinguish digital media forms from 'old media' forms such as newspapers, magazines, radio, and television.

participatory journalism
See **citizen-journalist**.

personal computer
Also called mini-computer, or desktop computer, to distinguish it from mainframe computers and servers. PCs came of age in the 1980s, as a low-cost and accessible means of processing information.

photogravure
A mechanical method of printing images whereby a negative of the image is transferred to a printing plate by means of an acid etching process. This process enabled the widespread publication of photographs in newspapers, magazines, and books.

pixel
A dot that is the smallest single identifiable element of an image or picture. The greater the number of pixels per square inch (PSI), the clearer the image will reproduce.

podcasting
A digital audio technology that enables listeners to download material from the Internet for time-shift listening using a digital media player. Also possible with video.

political economy
A theory of social economics which argues that knowledge and analysis of ownership and control of economic entities is a useful, indeed, essential means of understanding. Political economy can be based on a class analysis or some other taxonomy, such as institutional form.

populism
A policy of doing what is seen to be popular at the lowest common denominator, as distinct from what may best serve the public interest, but be unpopular.

public service broadcasting
A broadcasting regime funded by the citizens—the public—by taxes or other means of public subscription such as licence fees. Such broadcasters, of which the BBC is the definitive model, have a charter obligation to address certain audience needs. The ABC is one such broadcaster; other examples are PBS in the USA and NHK in Japan.

radio
Transmission or broadcast of sound by wireless or a device for receiving such transmissions. An abbreviation of radio broadcasting, which is the intentional and programmatic broadcasting of programs via a radio broadcasting station dedicated to that purpose.

reality television
A genre of television drama that purports to be a 'fly on the wall' rendering of the activities of non-professional actors in contrived situations. More easily understood as a postmodern format of the 'game show' genre.

regulation
The legislative, but more often sub-legislative, subordinate regimes that govern organisations.

relations of production
The social ties that bind together the elements (labour, technology, nature) that constitute a mode of production. The relations of production determine how various technologies and labour processes come together to produce goods and services and to reproduce themselves.

reportorial community

Those who 'report' in a variety of media, old and new, using traditional journalistic genres and forms: the news story (written inside and outside the inverted pyramid); the feature story; the radio news report; the television news report; the 'live cross'; the documentary; the online news story, etc.

search economy

Battelle uses this term to describe the economic relations of production that seem to permeate capitalism in the early years of the 21st century, epitomised by the ubiquitous presence of Google on the World Wide Web. Bartelle coined the term to emphasise how so much of what constitutes commerce today relies on some kind of search function, particularly forms of electronic commerce.

security economy

The OECD uses this term as a polite way of describing what we define as the surveillance economy. The security economy has grown exponentially over the past decade in response to heightened risk assessment, particularly the threat of terrorism on a global scale.

self-regulation

The governance of organisations and professions by those organisations and professionals without recourse to external authorities such as the courts.

SMS

Short messaging service. The electronic equivalent of the telegram. First commercial services date from 1992.

surveillance economy

The idea that the dominant forces in an economy are those to do with surveillance; that research and development in an economy has a focus on surveillance or security technologies; that capital investment in technologies is in the area of surveillance; that recurrent budgets in both the private and public sector make increasing provision for surveillance; that employment growth is related to surveillance and security; and that continuing surveillance of the citizenry and border protection are key imperatives in economic and social discourse.

surveillance society

A society based on the principles of the surveillance economy. A society in which social and political surveillance are the new paradigm for interaction between citizens and the state.

tabloid (compact)

A newspaper format based on a page size approximately A3. Traditionally associated with journalistic practices such as beat-ups, sensationalist reporting, and photographs of semi-naked women on page 3. Also a pejorative term used to describe poor-quality journalism in any medium.

techno-

A prefix meaning 'technological'. Therefore techno-fix, technophobe, technophile, technoclutz, etc.

techno-legal time-gap

The gap between the time a technology reaches the market, and the time it takes for legislators to regulate the socially undesirable aspects of that technology. At a minimum this is usually about two years.

technology

1) An object, or system of connected objects, that can be used in a productive process to provide a practical solution to a problem. 2) A process of incorporating knowledge into the production process; in capitalist systems this takes a distinct commodity form.

telegraphy

The transmission of data over purpose built data lines (copper wires) using Morse code, developed in 1835.

television

An electrically powered box of valves, tubes, vacuums, chips, and wires, used mainly for home entertainment, and occasionally for receiving information from a number of central sources known as television broadcasters.

typeface, font, or typefont

The characteristic styling of the letters of the alphabet, particularly through the ascenders and descenders of individual letters, to create a particular look. Serif (with curly bits) and sans serif (without curly bits) are the two main forms of type. Fonts can also be rendered in bold, italic, condensed, and extended forms.

typography

The study, or the art, of understanding and creating typefonts.

utopia

An imagined place of unremitting happiness.

'video-journalist' (VJ)

See **backpack journalism**.

vector

In medical science a vector is the pathway or pathways open to pathogens to infect a population. For example, infected birds may be a vector for avian bird flu to infect humans. In communication studies a vector is a pathway or pathways open for communication, in particular the transmission of ideology via mimetic transfer and mutation.

vote.com

The vision of participatory democracy represented by US political consultant Dick Morris, in which public policy is determined by an ongoing series of electronic referendums. Morris has published a book and runs a website of the same name.

Wiki

Stands for 'What I Know Is'. A constantly evolving user-edited text. The best known wiki is Wikipedia. The concept was first developed in 1995 by Ward Cunningham in Hawaii.

Zine

An abbreviation of *ezine*. The Internet equivalent of printed maga-zines.

BIBLIOGRAPHY

AAP. 2005. Lachlan Murdoch testifies in One.Tel trial. *New Zealand Herald.*

———. 2006. Changes are 'bad news for diversity'. *Australian*, 15 March, 7.

ABC News Online. 2004a. 2UE escapes 'cash for comment' charges.

———. 2004b. Draft ABA report found Jones breached codes.

ACTivist Magazine. 2005. MANA Overview. *ACTivist Magazine.*

Advertising Federation of Australia. 1 November. *The AFA agency code of ethics* 2001 [cited 1 November]. Available from http://www.afa.org.au/WebStreamer?page_id=46.

Agence France Press. 2005. Free wind-up laptops for world's poor. *Australian*, 18 November, 9.

Alden, Chris. 2005. Looking back on the crash. *Guardian Unlimited*, 10 March [cited 23 March 2006] http://media.guardian.co.uk/newmedia/story/0,1434637,00.html.

Alexander, Mark. 2005. Caught in the act. *Sunday Mail*, 10 July, 11.

Amis, Kingsley. 1960. *New Maps of Hell.* New York: Ballantine Books.

Anderson, Alan. 2005. The last thing a free society needs is a worldwide web of control. *SMH*, 6 May, 13.

Anderson, Tim. 2003. Method in poltical economy. *Journal of Australian Political Economy* 54: 135–45.

Andreas. 2000. *Is the Web Boom Over?* Andreas.com, 1 February 2000 [cited 19 March 2006]. Available from http://www.andreas.com/faq-dotcrash.html.

Andrews, Charles M. 2003. Introduction. In *The New Atlantis and The City of the Sun*. Mineola, NY: Dover.

Anscombe, G. E. M. 1958. Modern Moral Philosophy. *Philospy* 33: 1–19.

Apple. n.d. *Everybody can Edit* [website]. Apple.com n.d. [cited 25 March 2004]. Available from http://www.apple.com/pro/video/ktvx/index2.html.

Archer, Jeffrey. 1996. *The Fourth Estate*. London: HarperCollins.

Armstrong, Mark, David Lindsay & Ray Watterson. 1995. *Media Law in Australia* 3rd edn. Melbourne: Oxford University Press.

ASIO. 2005. *GIO: Generalist Intelligence Officer* [website]. ASIO, 2005 [cited 28 October 2005]. Available from www.asio.gov.au/employment/GIO/what_you_will_do.htm.

Associated Press. 2004. Bush accused of lying over his military record. *Courier-Mail*, 10 September, 18.

Atwood, Margaret. 1996 [1985]. *The Handmaid's Tale*, *Contemporary Classics*. London: Vintage.

Australian Broadcasting Authority. 1998. Australian co-regulation a success says ABA deputy chairman. In Media Release, 11 September.

Australian Press Council. 1996. *Statement of Principles* 1996 [cited 1 June 2002]. Available from www.presscouncil.org.au/pcsite/complaints/sop.html.

Ayres, Chris. 2005. *War Reporting for Cowards: Between Iraq and a hard place*. London: John Murray.

Babbage, Charles. 2005 [1864?]. *Pages from the life of a philosopher* [website]. fourmilab.ch 1864 [cited 6 September 2005]. Available from www.fourmilab.ch/babbage/1pae.html.

Bacon, Francis. 2003 [1627]. The New Atlantis. In *The New Atlantis and The City of the Sun*, ed. C. M. Andrews. Mineola, NY: Dover.

Bagdikian, Ben H. 1997. *The new communications cartel* [website]. Third World Traveller, 1997 [cited 20 November 2003]. Available from www.thirdworldtraveller.com/Media/CommunCartel_Bagdikian.html.

Bangemann, M. 1999. The global on-line economy: private and public sector co-operation in policy development. In *Masters of the Wired World*, ed. A. Leer. London: Financial Times Pitman Publishing.

Barol, Bill. 2002. In My Lifes.What began as an impulse buy became a quest to preserve history. And then there was eBay. *American Journalism Review* 24(10): 18–19.

Barr, Trevor. 2000. *newmedia.com.au: the changing face of Australia's media and communications*. Sydney: Allen & Unwin.

Barrie-Anthony, Steven. 2005. *Following the deleter* [website]. latimes.com, 7 August 2005 [cited 8 August 2005]. Available from www.latimes.com/features/lifestyle/la-ca-evidence7aug07,0,1529488.story?coll=la-home-style.

Barskdale, J. L. 1999. Ramping up for the net economy. In *Masters of the Wired World*, ed. A. Leer. London: Financial Timcs Pitman Publishing.

Battelle, John. 2005. *The Search: How Google and its rivals rewrote the rules of business and transformed our culture*. Boston: Nicholas Brealey.

BBC. 2004. *Online newspapers tempt readers* [website]. BBC, 1 June 2004 [cited 1 June 2004].

Beecher, Eric. 2005. The end of serious journalism? In *Barons to bloggers: confronting media power*, edited by J. Mills. Melbourne: Miegunyah Press.

Beizer, Doug. 2006. Harris inks NSA secure wireless deal. In *Washington Technology*.

Bell, Daniel. 1973. *The Coming of the Post-Industrial Society*. London: Harmondsworth.

Bellis, Mary. 1997. *A brief history of writing instruments* [website]. About.com, 1 October 1997 [cited 6 September 2005]. Available from http://inventors.about.com/library/weekly/aa100197.htm.

———. n.d.-a *Herman Hollerith—punch cards* [website]. About.com n.d. [cited 14 September 2005]. Available from http://inventors.about.com/library/inventors/blhollerith.htm.

———. n.d.-b *Inventors of the modern computer* [website]. About.com n.d. [cited 21 September 2005]. Available from http://inventors.about.com/library/.

Belson, Ken. 2006. *In Sony's stumble, the ghost of Betamax*. NYTimes.com, 26 February 2006 [cited 2 March 2006]. Available from www.nytimes.com/2006/02/26/business/.

Berkowitz, Dan (ed.) 1997. *Social Meanings of News: A text-reader*. Thousand Oaks, Calif.: Sage.

Beware rise of Big Brother stare, warns data watchdog. 2004. *Times*, 16 August, 1, 17.

Birmingham, John. 2004. *Weapons of choice: World War 2.1*. Sydney: Pan Macmillan.

———. 2005. *Designated targets: World War 2.2*. Sydney: Pan Macmillan.

Bivins, Thomas. 1993. Public relations, professionalism, and the public interest. *Journal of Business Ethics* 12(2): 117–26.

Black, Jay. 1985. The case against mass media codes of ethics. *Journal of Mass Media Ethics* 1(1): 27–36.

———, Bob Steele, & Ralph Barney. 1995. *Doing Ethics in Journalism*. Boston: Allyn & Bacon.

Blood, Rebecca. 2006. *the weblog handbook* 2006 [cited 30 March 2006]. Available from www.rebeccablood.net/handbook/index.html.

Boland, Michaela. 2004. Who's dreaming now? Whatever happened to the Australian film industry? *AFR Magazine*, October, 22–6.

Boreham, Tim. 2005. Fairfax shreds magazines. *Weekend Australian*, 23–24 July, 3.

Botan, Carl. 1997. Ethics in strategic communication campaigns: The case for a new approach to public relations. *Journal of Business Communication* 34(2): 188–202.

Boukhari, Sophie. 1998. Cybersnoopers on the prowl. *Unesco Courier*, September, 44–6.

Bourdieu, Pierre. 1998. *On Television and Journalism*. London: Pluto Press.

Bowker, Gordon. 2003. *George Orwell*. London: Little, Brown.

Bowman, David. 1988. *The Captive Press: Our newspapers in crisis and the people responsible*. Melbourne: Penguin.

Bowman, Shayne, & Chris Willis. 2005. The future is here, but do news media companies see it? *Nieman Reports* 59(4): 6–10.

Boyd-Barrett, Oliver. 1998. 'Global' News Agencies. In *The Globalization of News*, ed. O. Boyd-Barrett & T. Rantanen. London: Sage.

Boyd, Tony. 2006a. Policies hold Australia back. *AFR*, 15 March, 50.

———. 2006b. Telstra divident at risk from regulation. *AFR*, 16 March, 15.

———. 2006c. Trujillo looks at Microsoft link. *AFR*, 16 March, 17.

Boyle, Alan. 2005. The human strain. *Weekend Australian*, 14–15 May, 28.

Bradbury, Ray. 1984 [1954]. *Fahrenheit 451: The novels of Ray Bradbury*. London: Granada.

Briet, Rhonda, & Jan Servaes. 2005. Introduction: Background and issues for whom and for what? In *Information Society or Knowledge Societies? UNESCO in the Smart State*, ed. R. Briet & J. Servaes. Penang: Southbound.

Bringhurst, Robert. 1992. *The Elements of Typographic Style*. Vancouver, BC: Hartley & Marks.

Brooks, Leonard J. 1989. Ethical codes of conduct: Deficient in guidance for the Canadian accounting profession. *Journal of Business Ethics* 8(5): 325–35.

Bruk, Tilman. 2004. Assessing the economic trade-offs of the Security Economy. In *The Security Economy*, ed. OECD. Paris: OECD.

Bryan, Cathy, Roza Tsagarousianou & Damien Tambini. 1998. Electronic democracy and the civic networking movement in context. In *cyberdemocracy: technology, cities and civic networks*, ed. R. Tsagarousianou, D. Tambini & C. Bryan. London & New York: Routledge.

Buckingham, David, & Margaret Scanlon. 2005. Selling learning: Towards a political economy of edutainment media. *Media, Culture & Society* 27(1): 41–58.

Bullock, Alan, & Stephen Trombley (eds) 2000 [1977]. *The New Fontana Dictionary of Modern Thought* 3rd edn. London: HarperCollins.

Burchett, Wilfred. 1981. *At the Barricades: Memoirs of a rebel journalist*. Melbourne: Macmillan Australia.

Burns, Alex. 2001. dot.com disaster: the new e-poor. In *Disinformation* January 7 [accessed 19 March 2006] http://www.disinfo.com/archive/pages/dossier/id333/pg1/.

Burton, Tom. 2006. Buyers turned off by digital TVs. *SMH*, 16 March, 6.

Butler, Samuel. 1967 (1872). *Erewhon*. Airmont Classic edn. Clinton, Mass: Airmont Publishing.

Cain, Alexandra. 2006. Only way is up as media sniffs freedom. *AFR*, 15 March, 28.

Callinan, Rory. 2003. Journalists kept in dark. *Weekend Australian*, 22–23 March, 2.

Callinicos, Alex. 1987. *The Revolutionary Ideas of Marx*. London: Bookmarks.

———. 1995. *Theories and Narratives: Reflections on the philosophy of history*. Cambridge: Polity Press.

Campanella, Tomasso. 2003 [*c.* 1626]. The City of the Sun. In *The New Atlantis and The City of the Sun*, ed. C. M. Andrews. Mineola, NY: Dover.

Campbell, John Edward, & Matt Carlson. 2002. Panopticon.com: online surveillance and the commodification of privacy. *Journal of Broadcasting & Electronic Media* 46(4): 586–605.

Canning, Simon. 2005. Blogs and banners strive to coexist. *Australian*, 19 May, 17.

Carey, Benedict. 2005. *Straight, gay or lying? Bisexuality revisited*. nytimes.com, 5 July 2005 [cited 8 July 2005]. Available from www.nytimes.com/2005/07/05/health/05sex.html.

Carlton, Mike. 2005. Big Brother rules the great brown land. *SMH*, 22–23 October, 28.

Carney, Matthew. 2006. *The Ice Age*. Sydney: ABC.

Casey, C. 1996. *The Hill on the Net: Congress enters the information age*. Boston: Academic Press.

Cashmore, Ellis. 1994. *... and there was television*. London & New York: Routledge.

Cassell, Philip (ed.). 1993. *The Giddens Reader*. London: Macmillan.

Castells, Manuel. 1999. *The Information Age: Economy, Society and Culture: End of millennium* rev. edn. 3 vols. Oxford and Malden, Mass.: Blackwell.

———. 2000 [1996]. *The Information Age: Economy, Society and Culture: The rise of the network society* 2nd edn, vol. 1. Oxford and Malden, Mass.: Blackwell.

Centeno, Miguel. 2005. McDonalds, Wienerwald and the Corner Deli. www.princeton.edu/~cenmiga/works/ Global%20Flows%20of%20Information%20for%20draft%20august%202005.doc.

Chalmers, Emma. 2005. Australia's film-making industry still reeling. *Courier-Mail*, 3–4 September, 35.

Chappell, N. C. L. 1967. The vocation of journalism. In *The New Zealand Herald Manual of Journalism*, ed. J. Hardingham. Wellington: A.H & A.W. Reed.

Chenoweth, Neil. 2001. *Virtual Murdoch: Reality wars on the information highway*. London: Secker & Warburg.

———. 2003. Cut! the Australian film industry loses the plot. *AFR*, 13–14 September, 22–3.

Chilcott-Moore, Tanya. 2005. Cameras track youths during rampage. *Courier-Mail*, 13 July, 10.

Childs, Ros. 2006. Govt to change media ownership laws. *7:30 Report*. Australia: ABC.

Chu, Jeff. 2002. A view to a sell. In *TIME*. Posted 3 November 2002, 2.02 p.m. GMT. http://www.time.com/time/europe/bond2002/gadget.html.

Clark, Andrew. 2005. These photos may be illegal. *SMH*, 16 November, 15.

CNN.com. 2002. Bush: Prevail in war, defeat recession. In *CNN.com*.

Coates, Stephen. 2005. Cards on the table. *Courier-Mail*, 19 July, 11.

Collins, I. 1959. *The Government and the Newspaper Press in France 1814–1881*, *Oxford Historical Series*. London: Oxford University Press.

Computer Science and Telecommunications Board. 2006. *Cryptography's Role in Securing the Information Society*. National Research Council 1996 [cited 3 April 2006]. Available from http://newton.nap.edu/html/crisis/.

Conley, David. 2002. *The Daily Miracle: An introduction to journalism* 2nd edn. Melbourne: Oxford University Press.

———. 2006. Journalism tertiary courses force feed a shrinking market. *Australian*, 2 March, 13.

Connolly, P. J. 2000. Privacy as global policy. *Infoworld*, 11 September, 49–50.

Connolly, William E. 2005. The evangelical-capitalist resonance machine. *Political Theory* 33(6): 869–86.

Connors, Emma. 2006. Phishing crackdown reins in fraud. *AFR*, 58.

Coonan, Helen. 2005a. 2005—A Telecommunications Odyssey. In *Address to Deutsche Bank*. Sydney: DCITA.

———. 2005b. Self-regulation and the challenge of new technologies. In *AMTA Annual General Meeting*. Sydney: DCITA.

———. 2006. Meeting the Digital Challenge: Reforming Australia's media in the digital age, ed. DCITA.

Corn, David, & Jeff Goldberg. 2005. *How Deep Throat fooled the FBI* [Internet]. *The Nation*, 4 July 2005 [cited 10 July 2005]. Available from www.thenation.com.

Coultan, Mark. 2004. Big bother. *SMH*, 19–20 June, 29.

Cousins, Mark. 2004. *The Story of Film*. London: Pavillion Books.

Crikey.com. 2006. 2004 [cited 1 April 2006]. Available from http://www.crikey.com.au/articles/2004/01/0-0008.html.

Crofts, Stephen. 1996. The adventures of Barry McKenzie: comedy, satire and nationhood in 1972. *Continuum* 10(2): 123–40.

Crosland, Sydney P. 1965. Journalism as a career. In *The Journalist's Craft: A guide to modern practice*, ed. L. Revill & C. Roderick. Sydney: Angus & Robertson.

Crowe, David. 2006a. Call to prevent merging of newsrooms in the bush. *AFR*, 16 March, 19.

———. 2006b. Enforcers have mergers in their sights. *AFR*, 15 March, 49.

———. 2006c. A matter of definition and clarity. *AFR*, 16 March, 17.

———. 2006d. What's on the phone tonight? *AFR*, 15 March, 50.

Crowe, David, & Neil Shoebridge. 2006a. ACCC to set media merger rules. *AFR*, 16 March, 1, 16.

———. 2006b. Coonan's hardline on media. *AFR*, 15 March, 1, 14.

Cryle, Denis. 1997a. Colonial journalists and journalism: an overview. In *Disreputable Profession: Journalists and journalism in colonial Australia*. Rockhampton, Qld: Central Queensland University Press.

———, ed. 1997b. *Disreputable Profession: Journalists and journalism in colonial Australia*. Rockhampton, Qld: Central Queensland University Press.

———. 1997c. Journalism and status: An historical case study approach. *Australian Journalism Review* 19(1): 171–80.

Cunningham, Stuart. 2006. Local content lost in policy. *Courier Mail*, 16 March, 28.

da Cruz, Frank. 2004. *Herman Hollerith* [website]. da Cruz, Frank, 27 September, 2004 [cited 14 September 2005]. Available from www.columbia.edu/acis/history/hollerith.html.

Dacles, Wilfredo. 2005. *The history of computers* [website]. Dacles 2005 [cited 6 September 2005]. Available from angelfire.com/de3/dacz/index.html.

Dahlgren, Peter. 1991. Introduction. In *Communication and citizenship: journalism and the public sphere in the new media age*, ed. P. Dahlgren & C. Sparks. London & New York: Routledge.

Daly, Mick. 2005. Smile, Big Brother is arresting you. *Courier-Mail*, 11–12 June, 15.

Darknet to hide swappers. 2005. *Australian*, 9 August.

DARPA. 2005. A huge leap forward for robotics R&D. In *News Release: Defense Advanced Research Projects Agency*, ed. T. G. Goodwin & D. Shipley. Arlington, Va.: DARPA.

Davidson, John. 2006. High-tech reality races ahead of reform. *AFR*, 16 March, 16.

Davis, D. K. 1999. Media as public arena: reconceptualizing the role of media for a post-cold war and postmodern world. In *Towards equity in global communication*, Vincent, R. C., Nordenstreng, K. & Traber, M. (eds) (1999), New Jersey: Hampton Press.

Davis, Mark. 2005. Terror laws end customer privacy rights. *AFR*, 18 October, 1.

Dawkins, Richard. 1989 [1976]. *The Selfish Gene* 2nd edn. London: Oxford University Press.

Day, Mark. 2005. Radio set for digital revolution. *Australian*, 13 October, 15.

———. 2006a. After a decade, it's still just talk. *Australian*, 15 March, 7.

———. 2006b. Coonan plan prepares to usher in the digital age. *Australian*, 16 March, 22.

———. 2006c. Making hay while the stars shine. *Australian*, 6 April, 13–14.

DCITA. 2002. Options for structural reform in spectrum management. Discussion Paper. Canberra: DCITA.

———. 2003. Proposal for new institutional arrangements for the Australian Communications Authority and the Australian Broadcasting Authority. Canberra: DCITA.

———. 2004. Australia's Strategic Framework for the Information Economy 2004–2006. Canberra: DCITA.

———. 2005. Film Tax Concession Schemes: 2005 Review of Divisions 10B and 10BA: Call for submissions. Canberra: DCITA.

———. 2006. Meeting the Digital Challenge: Reforming Australia's media in the digital age. Discussion paper on media reform options. Canberra: DCITA.

De Bens, Els, & Gianpietro Mazzoleni. 1998. The media in the age of digital communication. In *Media Policy: Convergence, concentration and commerce*, ed. D. McQuail & K. Siune. London: Sage.

de la Haye, Yves. 1980. Contribution to a materialist analysis of the media. In *Marx and Engels on the Means of Communication (The Movement of Commodities, People, Information and Capital)*, ed. Y. de la Haye. New York & Bagnolet, France: International General & International Mass Media Research Centre.

Dearing, J. W. & E. M. Rogers. 1996. *Agenda Setting*. Thousand Oaks, Calif.: Sage.

Delbridge, Arthur (ed.). 1990. *The Penguin Macquarie Dictionary*. Melbourne: Penguin in association with the Macquarie Library.

Derra, Manuel, n.d. *William Gibson aleph*, cited 15 January 2006. Available from www.antonraubenweiss.com/gibson/gibson1.html.

Diversity is strength. 2006. *Australian*, 15 March, 13.

Do we have a story for you! 2006. *Economist*, 21–27 January, 59.

Doctorow, Cory. 1999. *William Gibson: Globe and Mail story* 1999 [cited 25 February 2006]. Available from www.craphound.com/nonfic/gibson.html.

Dombkins, Margaret. 1993. The impact of technology and environmental factors on newspaper organisational design. *Australian Journalism Review* 5(1): 29–51.

Dowd, Maureen. 2003. *Walk this way*. NYTimes.com, 21 May 2003 [cited 5 November 2005]. Available from www.NYTimes.com.

Draper, John. 2000. Foreword. In *Cybershock: Surviving hackers, phreakers, identity thieves, Internet terrorists and weapons of mass disruption*, ed. W. Schwartau. New York: Thunder's Mouth Press.

Drapes, Michaela, Michael Hayden, & Alex Peguero. 1996. *Bohemian Ink* 1996 [cited 25 February 2006]. Available from www.levity.com/corduroy/gibson.htm.

Drummond, Matt. 2005. Court hears of plot 'to leak policy'. *AFR*, 8 November, 11.

Dudley, Jennifer. 2005a. Dial your own future. *Courier-Mail*, 18–19 June, 27.

———. 2005b. Ears to the groundswell. *Courier-Mail*, 21–22 May, 30.

Dyer-Witheford, Nick. 1999. *Cyber-Marx: Cycles and circuits of struggle in high-technology capitalism*. Urbana and Chicago: University of Illinois Press.

Dyson, Esther, George Gilder, George Keyworth & Alvin Toffler. 1994. *Cyberspace and the American Dream: A Magna Carta for the Knowledge Age*. Progress and Freedom Foundation, August 1994 [cited 5 April 2006]. Available from http://www.pff.org/issues-pubs/futureinsights/fi1.2magnacarta.html.

Earth Island Journal. 2001. The globalization of repression. *Earth Island Journal*.

Ehrlich, Matthew C. 1997. The competitive ethos in television newswork. In *Social Meanings of News: A text-reader*, ed. D. Berkowitz. Thousand Oaks, Calif.: Sage.

Elass, Mateen A. 2006. What Muslims think of America. *Moody Magazine* 21 May 2006 http://www.moodymagazine.com/articles.php?action=view_article&id=357.

Elliott, Geoff. 2005. *I was wrong on net: Murdoch* [Internet]. Australian IT [News Limited], 14 April 2005 [cited 9 May 2005]. Available from australianit.nws.com.au.

Engel, Matthew. 1996. *Tickle the Public: One hundred years of the popular press*. London: Victor Gollancz.

Engels, Friedrick. 1975 [1876]. *The Part Played by Labour in the Transition from Ape to Man*. Peking (Beijing): Foreign Language Press.

———. 1976 [1888]. *Ludwig Feuerbach and the End of Classical German Philosophy*. Peking (Beijing): Foreign Language Press.

Epstein, Jason. 2001. Reading: The digital future. In *New York Review of Books*, 5 July 2001, Vol. 48, No. 11.

Ernst & Young. 1999. *The Knowledge Economy* [Online Government Report]. Ministry of Economic Development (New Zealand), August 1999 [cited 3 April 2006]. Available from http://www.med.govt.nz/templates/MultipageDocumentTOC____17256.aspx.

Espiner, G. 2000a. PR ethics review sidelined. *Sunday Star Times*, 30 July, 4.

———. 2000b. PR industry seeks new image after Timberlands saga. *Sunday Star Times*, 7 May, 5.

Express tollway plan for net. 2006. *Australian*, 14 March, IT Business, 5.

Fairclough, Norman. *c.* 2000. The Dialectics of Discourse. www.ling.lancs.ac.uk/staff/norman/2001a.doc [cited 23 March 2006].

Falvey, Brooke. 2005. Cyber-thieves. *Westside News*, 18 May, 1.

Farmer, Dan, & Charles C. Mann. 2003. Surveillance Nation, Part 1. *Technology Review*, April, 34–43.

Farrell, B. J., & D. M. Cobbin. 1996. A content analysis of codes of ethics in Australian enterprises. *Journal of Managerial Psychology* 11: 37–55.

———. 2000. A content analysis of codes of ethics from fifty-seven national accounting organisations. *Business Ethics* 9(3): 180–90.

Farrell, Henry. 2005. Blogging a carnival of ideas. *Australian*, 26 October, 36–7.

Fels, Allan, & Fred Brenchely. 2006. ACCC's vital role in defence of diversity. *AFR*, 16 March, 17.

Ferguson, Cassie. 1998. Howard Aiken: Makin' a computer wonder [website]. *Harvard University Gazette*, 9 April, 1998 [cited 14 September 2005]. Available from www.news.harvard.edu/gazette;1998/04.09/HowardAiken/Maki.html.

Finberg, Howard I. 2002. Convergence and the Corporate Boardroom: changing the idustry's cultural template. Speech given at the Poynter Institute, 9 January 2002 [cited 17 June 2004]. Available from www.poynter.org/content.

Finnila, Richard. 2005. Staring down the screen test. *Courier-Mail*, 14 June, 17.

Fiorina, Carleton S. 2001. The digital renaissance. In *Future Insight*. 8.1 March http://www.pff.org/issues-pubs/futureinsights/fi8.1digitalrenaissance.pdf [cited 23 March 2006].

Fitzgibbon, Rebecca. 2005. The downloadable future: Australia's culture jamming digital 'Undergrowth'. In *Newtopia Magazine*.

———. 2006. Some thoughts on Indymedia and new journalism. Interview with Martin Hirst via email, 15 March.

Flew, Terry. 2005. *New Media: An introduction* 2nd edn. Melbourne: Oxford University Press.

Forgacs, David (ed.). 2000 [1988]. *The Antonio Gramsci Reader: Selected writings 1916–1935*. New York: New York University Press.

——— & Geoffrey Nowell-Smith (eds). 1985. *Antonio Gramsci: Selections from cultural writings*. Cambridge, Mass: Harvard University Press.

Foucault, Michel. 1979. *Discipline and Punish*. New York: Vintage Books.

———. 1990. *History of Sexuality* vol. 1. New York: Vintage Books.

Francissen, Letty, & Kees Brants. 1998. Virtually going places: Amsterdam. In *cyberdemocracy: technology, cities and civic networks*, ed. R. Tsagarousianou, D. Tambini & C. Bryan. London and New York: Routledge.

Franklin, Bob. 1997. *Newszak and News media*. London: Arnold.

Fraser, Andrew, & Blair Speedy. 2004. Digital boom forces Kodak to shutter up shop. *Weekend Australian*, 18–19 September.

Freeman, Edward H. 2005. Data protection and the commerce clause. *Legally Speaking* (January/February): 5–9.

Frith, David. 2006. Map on the lap for lost road travellers. *Australian*, 14 March, ExecTech, 7.

Frugal e-paper nears reality. 2005. *Courier-Mail*, 16–17 July, 14.

Galvin, Peter. 2004. Mention 'Australian film industry' and he takes on a look of mock surprise: 'is there really an industry?' *Inside Film* 65: 34–5.

Garson, Barbara. 1988. *The Electronic Sweatshop*. New York: Simon & Schuster.

Gennaro, Stephen. 2005. Purchasing the Canadian teenaage identity: ICTs, American media, and brand-name consumption. *International Social Science Review* 80(3/4): 119–36.

Ghosts in the machine. *Weekend Australian*, 23–24 April, 17.

Gibson, Owen. 2006. Citizen Murdoch says end of the mogul is nigh. *SMH*, 15 March, 5.

Gibson, William. 1993. *Virtual Light*. London: Penguin.

———. 1993 [1984]. *Neuromancer*. London: HarperCollins. London: Victor Gollancz.

———. 1995 [1976]. Burning Chrome. In *Burning Chrome*, ed. W. Gibson. London: Voyager.

———. 1995 [1986]. The Gernsback Continuum. In *Burning Chrome*, ed. W. Gibson. London: Voyager.

———. 1995 [1986]. Johnny Mnemonic. In *Burning Chrome*, ed. W. Gibson. London: Voyager.

———. 2001. Modern boys and mobile girls. *Observer*, 1 April. Available from http://books.guardian.co.uk/departments/sciencefiction/story/0,,466421,00.html [cited 23 March 2006].

———. 2003. *Pattern Recognition*. London: Penguin.

Gibson, William, & Bruce Sterling. 2003 [1990]. *The Difference Engine*. London: Victor Gollancz.

Giddens, Anthony. 1995. *A Contemporary Critique of Historical Materialism* 2nd edn. Houndmills, Basingstoke: Macmillan.

Gilder, George. 1995. *The Freedom Model of Telecommunications*. Progress and Freedom Foundation, March, last updated 1995 [cited 5 April 2006]. Available from www.pff.org/issues-pubs/other/950301freedommodel.html.

Gillmor, Dan. 2005. Where citizens and journalists intersect. *Nieman Reports* 59(4): 11–13.

Gitlin, Todd. 1991. Bites and blips: chunk news, savvy talk and the bifurcation of American politics. In *Communication and citizenship: journalism and the public sphere in the new media age*, ed. P. Dahlgren & C. Sparks. London & New York: Routledge.

Given, Jock. 1998. *The Death of Broadcasting? Media's digital future, Frontlines*. Sydney: UNSW Press and the Communications Law Centre.

———. 2006. The signal is clear: do not adjust your sets. *SMH*, 16 March, 13.

Glasner, Joanna. 2000. Why the Bubble's in Trouble. In *Wired*, 14 April 2000. http://www.wired.com/news/business/0,35477-0.html.

Glover, Richard. 2005. My, oh my, from iPod to whyPod in the twinkling of an eye. *SMH*, 22–23 October, 28.

Goff, Peter. 2005. China rues the sound of one hand tapping. *SMH*, 12 October, 15.

Gooch, Liz, & Fleur Leyden. 2004. Kodak sacks 600 workers. *Age*, 17 September, 1.

Goodheart, Eugene. 2000. Marshall McLuhan revisited. *Partisan Review* 61(1).

Gore, A. 1999. Putting people first in the information age. In *Masters of the Wired World*, ed. A. Leer. London: Financial Times Pitman Publishing.

Gottliebsen, Robert. 2006. Technology gurus unveil new corporate paradigm. *Weekend Australian*, 4–5 February, 32.

Graham, Alex. 2006. Reflections on ABC media technology. Interview with Martin Hirst via email, 29 March.

Graham, Katharine 1997. The Watergate watershed: A turning point for a nation and a newspaper. *Washington Post*, 28 January, D01.

Graham, Phil. 1999. *Hypercapitalism: Political economy, electric identity, and authorial alienation*. Northumbria University, Newcastle, UK.

———. 2002. Hypercapitalism: language, new media and social perceptions of value. *Discourse & Society* 13(2): 228–49.

Granato, Len. 1991. *Reporting and Writing News*. Sydney: Prentice Hall.

Griffiths, Chris. 2006. Movies and more slip down the Internet to you. *Courier-Mail*, 14–15 January, 28.

Groombridge, Brian. 1972. *Television and the People: A programme for democratic participation*, ed. W. van der Eyken, *Penguin Education*. Melbourne: Penguin.

Grossman, Lawrence 1999. The electronic republic. In *Impact of mass media: current issues*, ed. R. E. Hiebert. New York: Addison-Wesley Longman.

———. 1999. From Marconi to Murrow to—Drudge? *Columbia Journalism Review*: 17–18.

Guenther, Kim. 2005. Socializing your web site with wikis, twikis and blogs. *Online* (November/December): 51–3.

Gureveitch, Michael, Mark R. Levy, & Itzhak Roeh. 1991. The global newsroom: convergences and diversities in the globalization of television news. In *Communication and Citizenship: Journalism and the public sphere in the new media age*, ed. P. Dahlgren & C. Sparks. London & New York: Routledge.

Gwynne, Beris. 2005. Smoke and Mirrors: a commentary of prospects for success for the WSIS process and the role of the Smart State. In *Information Society or Knowledge Societies? UNESCO in the Smart State*, ed. R. Briet & J. Servaes. Penang: Southbound.

Hafner, Katie, & Matthew Lyon. 2003. *Where Wizards Stay Up Late*. London: Pocket Books.

Hafner, Katie, & John Markoff. 1991. *Cyberpunk: Outlaws and hackers on the computer frontier*. New York: Simon & Schuster.

Hall, Stuart. 1996 [1971]. Technics of the medium. In *Television Times: A reader*, ed. J. Corner & S. Harvey. London: Arnold. Original title: Television as a medium and its relation to culture. Part 4 of a report to UNESCO, *Innovation and Decline in the Treatment of Culture on British Television*. Birmingham: Centre for Contemporary Cultural Studies, pp. 89–97.

Hallin, Daniel. 1989. *The 'Uncensord War': The media and Vietnam*. Berkeley: University of California Press.

Hanks, Patrick (ed.). 1990. *The Collins Concise Dictionary Plus*. London: Collins.

Hansell, Saul. 2006. *Comments push Google down 7%*. nytimes.com, 1 March 2006 [cited 3 March 2006]. Available from www.nytimes.com/2006/03/01/technology.

Hargreaves, Ian. 2003. *Journalism: Truth or Dare?* Oxford: Oxford University Press.

Hartcher, Peter. 2006. Opening the airwaves comes with trade-off. *SMH*, 15 March, 5.

Hartely, John. 1999. What is journalism? The view from under a stubbie cap. *Media International Australia incorporating Culture and Policy* 90: 15–31.

———. 1996. *Popular Reality: Journalism, modernity, popular culture*. London: Arnold.

——— (ed.). 2005. *Creative Industries*. Oxford: Blackwell Publishing.

Harvey, Adam, and AFP. 2005. Watergate figures go for throat. *Courier-Mail*, 2 June, 20.

Hayes, Simon. 2005. Music for a song, quick sharp, or web piracy continues. *Weekend Australian*, 10–11 September.

Hearn, Greg, David Anthony, Leanne Holman, June Dunleavy & Tom Mandeville. 1994. The Information Superhighway and Consumers. In *Research Report*. Brisbane: The Communication Centre, Faculty of Business, Queensland University of Technology.

———, David Rooney, & Thomas Mandeville. 2003. Phenomenological Turbulence and Innovation in Knowledge Systems. *Prometheus* 21(2): 231–45.

Heaton, Terry L. 2003. *TV news in a postmodern world: the rise of the independent video journalist*. The digital journalist, October 2003 [cited 8 November 2003]. Available from ww.digitaljournalist.org.issue0310/tvpomo.html.

Herman, Edward S., & Noam Chomsky. 1988. *Manufacturing Consent: The political economy of the mass media*. New York: Pantheon.

Hewett, Jennifer. 2006. Reforms tempered by caution. *AFR*, 15 March, 48.

Heywood, Lachlan. 2005. Feds plan to block annoying sale calls. *Courier-Mail*, 31 October, 3.

Hiaasen, Carl. 1998. *Team Rodent: How Disney Devours the World, The Library of Contemporary Thought*. New York: Ballantine.

Hickman, Christine. 2003. Shooting stars—Helmut Newton: Autobiography—Book Review. *New Statesman*, 3 November, 52–3.

Hinduja, Sameer. 2004. Theory and policy in online privacy. *Knowledge, Technology, & Policy* 17(1): 38–58.

Hirst, Martin. 1997. MEAA Code of Ethics for journalists: an historical and theoretical overview. *Media International Australia* 83: 63–77.

———. 2001. Journalism in Australia: hard yakka? In *Journalism: Theory in practice*, ed. S. Tapsall & C. Varley. Melbourne: Oxford University Press.

———. 2004. Playtime for Gonzo. *Walkley Magazine*.

Hirst, Martin, & Roger Patching. 2005. *Journalism Ethics: Arguments and Cases*. Melbourne: Oxford University Press.

Hirst, Martin, & Robert Schutze. 2004a. Allies Down Under? The Australian at war and the 'Big Lie'. In *Global Media Goes to War: Role of news and entertainment media during the 2003 Iraq war*, ed. R. D. Berenger. Spokane, WA: Marquette Books.

———. 2004b. Duckspeak Crusader: Greg Sheridan's unique brand of seculo-Christian morality. *Overland* 176: 18–25.

Hollis, P. 1970. *The Pauper Press: A study in working-class radicalism of the 1830s*. Oxford: Oxford University Press.

Holub, Renate. 1992. *Antonio Gramsci: Beyond Marxism and Postmodernism*, ed. C. Norris, *Critics of the Twentieth Century*. London: Routledge.

Hoyle, Michelle, A. 2004. *Computers: From the past to the present* [website and Powerpoint]. Hoyle, Michelle, A., 14 September 2004 [cited 6 September 2005]. Available from http://www.eingang.org/Lecture/.

Hughes, Lucille. 2004. Love's Brother and the state of Australian filmmaking. *Eureka Street* 14(2): 29.

Huxley, Aldous. 1965a [1932]. *Brave New World amd Brave New World Revisited*. New York: HarperPerennial.

———. 1965b [1958]. Brave New World Revisited. In *Brave New World and Brave New World Revisited*, ed. A. Huxley. New York: HaperPerennial. New York, Harper & Row.

Idato, Michael. 2005. Stealing the show. *SMH*, 28 March, 4.

Identity card not part of war on terror. 2005. *Courier-Mail*, 19 July, 10.

IEEE Virtual Museum. 2005. *War as a technological watershed* [website]. IEEE 2005 [cited 14 September 2005]. Available from http://www.ieee-virtual-museum.org/exhibit.

IFEX Communique. 2005. *Is Microsoft aiding internet censorship in China?* [website]. International Freedom of Expression eXchange 2005 [cited 20 June 2005]. Available from www.ifex.org/.

Indymedia.org. 2006. *Independent Media Center*. Indymedia.org 2006 [cited 8 April 2006]. Available from http://www.indymedia.org/en/index.shtml.

Investopedia.com. 2006. *The Dot.Com Crash*. Investopedia.com [cited 19 March 2006]. Available from http://www.investopedia.com/features/crashes/crashes8.asp.

Jackson, Joab, & William Welsh. 2003. *Rise in Commerce's IT spending reflects role in homeland security, economy* (17(21)), 30 March 2003 [cited 4 April 2006]. Available from http://www.washingtontechnology.com/news/17_21/cover-stories/20029-1.html.

Jackson, Sally. 2002. Crikey! 'It's lasted 1000 days'. *Australian*, 17 October, B3.

Jameson, Fredric. 1998. Postmodernism and consumer society. In *The Cultural Turn: Selected writings on the postmodern, 1983–1998*. London and New York: Verso.

Jaspan, Andrew. 2005. *In the internet Age: Speech to the Property Council, October 14 2005.*, 14 October 2005 [cited 1 November 2005]. Available from http://www.theage.com.au/news/creative--media/in-the-internet-age/2005/10/21/1129775943039.html.

Jenkins, Chris. 2006. Blogging the brand. *Austalian*, 14 March, IT Business, 1.

———, & Andrew Colley. 2005. Asian gangs join cyber fraudsters. *Australian*, 24 May, 5.

Jensen, Robert. 2004. *Citizens of the Empire: The struggle to claim our humanity*. San Francisco: City Lights.

Johnson, Rob. 2000. *Cash for Comment: The seduction of journo culture*. Sydney: Pluto Press.

Johnston, George. 1964. *My Brother Jack*. London: Fontana.

Josefsson, Dan. 1995. *'I don't even have a modem'* 1995 [cited 25 February 2006]. Available from http://www.josefsson.net/gibson/.

Jury, Alan. 2006. Valuations in the eye of the beholder. *AFR*, 15 March, 14.

Kakutani, Michiko. 2005. *An aura of mystery still hovers around the man who is Deep Throat* [NYT Online]. NYTimes.com, 6 July 2005 [cited 7 July 2005]. Available from www.nytimes.com/2005/07/06/books/06kaku.html.

Katz, Jon. 1997. Birth of a digital nation. In *Wired*, Vol. 5, No. 4. http://www.wired.com/wired/5.04/netizen.html.

Kearns, Ian. 2002. *Code Red: Progressive politics in the digital age*. London: Institute for Public Policy Research.

Kenski, H. C. 1996. From agenda setting to priming and framing: reflections on theory and method. In *The Theory and Practice of Political Communication Research.*, ed. M. E. Stuckey. New York: State University of New York Press.

Kerr, Joseph, & Kevin Morrison. 2001. Workers tell One.Tel to pay up. *SMH*, June 2001, p. 1.

Kershaw, Alex. 2002. *Blood and Champagne: The life and times of Robert Capa*. London: Pan Books.

Kessler, J. 1996. *Internet Digital Libraries: The international dimension*. Boston: Artech House.

Kilmon, Jack. n.d. *The history of writing* [website]. The Scriptorium n.d. [cited 8 September 2005]. Available from www.historian.net/hxwrite.htm.

King content. 2006. *Economist*, 21–27 January, 11.

Kingston, Margo. 2005a. The future of fair-dinkum journalism. In *Barons to bloggers: confronting media power*, ed. J. Mills. Melbourne: Miegunyah Press.

———. 2005b. *Thank you and goodbye* [weblog]. Margo Kingston's webdiary, 7 December [cited 17 January 2006]. Available from http://margokingston.typepad.com/harry_version_2/2005/12/thank_you_and_g.html.

Kirkpatrick, Rod. 2005. 'Publishers' Circulation Figures', *Australian Newspaper History Group Newsletter*, No. 35, Dec 2005 pp. 4–5.

Kitamura, Hiroshi. 2004. Hollywood and the Wider World: A Review Essay. *American Studies International* 42(2/3): 235–49.

Kjonstad, Bjorn, & Wilmott Hugh. 1995. Business ethics: Restrictive or empowering? *Journal of Business Ethics* 14(6): 445–65.

Knightley, Phillip. 2002 [1975]. *The First Casualty: The war correspondent as hero and myth-maker from the Crimea to Kosovo*. Baltimore: Johns Hopkins University Press.

———. 2003. *The Eye of War: Words and photographs from the front line*. London: Weidenfeld & Nicolson.

Knobel, Lance. 2005. Nullius in verba: Navigating through the new media democracy. In *Barons to Bloggers: confronting media power*, ed. J. Mills. Melbourne: Miegunyah Press.

Kohler, Alan. 2004. No news not good news for super funds. *SMH*, 14 April, 22.

Kovacs, Suzann. 2004. Scam-baiters vs organised criminals. *Independent Monthly*, September, 4.

Krause, Tim. 1999. Goodbye to all that. *Australian*, 29 April, 7.

Kyte, Sue. 2002. A report on Limelight, the dawn of Australian film. *Metro* 133: 246–52.

Langer, John. 1998. *Tabloid Television: Popular journalism and the 'other news'*, ed. J. Curran, *Communication and Society*. London & New York: Routledge.

Laufer, William, & Diana Robertson. 1997. Corporate ethics initiatives as social control. *Journal of Business Ethics* 16(10): 1029–49.

Lebihan, Rachel. 2005a. Big Brother law catches business on hop. *AFR*, 5 October, 3.

———. 2005b. Getting heads together on use of spy cameras. *AFR*, 11 November, 15.

———. 2005c. Telemarketers seek to delay do-not-call list. *AFR*, 23 November.

Lee, J. A. N. 2002. *John Louis von Neumann* [website]. Lee, J. A. N., 9 February, 2002 [cited 6 September 2005]. Available from http://ei.cs.vt.edu./~History/VonNeumann.html.

Lee, Julian. 2005. Thinking outside the box. *SMH*, 22–23 October, 31.

Leer, A. 1999. *Masters of the Wired World*. London: Financial Times Pitman Publishing.

Lehmann, John. 2005a. Courier-Mail turns tabloid. *Australian*, 15 December, 13.

———. 2005b. Gloves off in battle for AFL rights. *Australian*, 10 November, 15.

———. 2006. Digital radio off the dial due to delays: Macquarie. *Australian*, 14 March, 22.

——— & Steve Lewis. 2006. Reforms to spark a media. *Australian*, 15 March, 1.

Lekakis, George. 2005. Banks lose millions in Net fraud. *Courier-Mail*, 19 July, 1.

Leonard, Andrew. 2003. *Nodal point*. Salon.com 2003 [cited 25 February 2006]. Available from http://www.salon.com/tech/books/2003/02/13/gibson/print.html.

Lewis, Peter M., & Jerry Booth. 1989. *The Invisible Medium: Public, commercial and community radio*, ed. R. Brunt, S. Frith, S. Niall & A. McRobbie. *Communications and Culture*. London: Macmillan Education.

Lewis, Steve. 2006. Nats fear for ads, news in bush. *Australian*, 16 March, 2.

Lewis, Tyson. 2003. The surveillance economy of post-Columbine schools. *Review of Education, Pedagogy and Cultural Studies* 25: 335–55.

Lichtblau, Eric. 2005. *Large volume of FBI files alarms US activist groups* [website]. NYTimes.com, 18 July 2005 [cited 19 July 2005].

Lippowicz, Alice. 2006. *Chertoff: Shipping firms need to invest in tracking systems* (30 March), 2006 [cited 4 April 2006]. Available from http://www.washingtontechnology.com/news/1_1/homeland/28301-1.html.

Liu, Melinda. 2005. Big Brother is talking. *Newsweek*, 16 October, 30–1.

Lloyd, Clem. 1985. *Profession: Journalist: A history of the Australian Journalists' Association*. Sydney: Hale & Iremonger.

Lohr, Steve. 2005. *Is Silicon Valley similar to Detroit?* nytimes.com, 28 March 2005 [cited 3 March 2006]. Available from www.nytimes.com/2005/03/28/technology.

Long, Chris, & Clive Sowry. 1994. Australia's first films. Facts and fables [Series of parts]: Part 8: ' Soldiers of the Cross': milestones and myths *Cinema Papers* 99: 60–7, 82–3.

Longstaff, Simon. 1994. Why codes fail. In *Ethics for the public sector*, ed. N. Preston. Sydney: Federation Press.

Lovink, Geert. 2002. McLuhan: The Mechanical Bride. *Mediamatic* 7(3/4).

Ludlow, Peter. 1996. *High Noon on the Electronic Frontier*. Cambridge, Mass.: MIT Press.

MacIntyre, Alisdair. 1984. *After Virtue*. Notre Dame, Ind.: University of Notre Dame Press.

MacKinnon, Rebecca. 2004. The world-wide conversation: Online participatory media and international news. In *Working paper series*. Boston: Joan Shorenstein Center on the Press, Politics and Public Policy.

Mackintosh, Hamish. 2003. Talk time: William Gibson. *Guardian* 2003 [cited 25 February 2006].Availablefromhttp://books.guardian.co.uk/reviews/sciencefiction/0,,946656,00.html.

MacLean, Sheena. 2005a. Better friend to celebs, that's Who. *Australian*, 20 October, 15.

———. 2005b. Print learns to love the web. *Australian*, 28 April, 15.

———. 2005c. Vega fails to register with the over-40s. *Australian*, 3 November, 16.

———. 2006. Triple J makes a multi-platform play. *Australian*, 6 April, 15.

Maguire, Stephen. 1999. The discourse of control. *Journal of Business Ethics* 19(1): 109–15.

Malik, Alex. 2005. Music, music, music—with no copyright troubles. *SMH*, 2 November, 15.

Markhoff, John. 2005. *In a grueling desert race, a winner, but not a driver* [website]. NYTimes.com, 9 October 2005 [cited 10 October 2005]. Available from www.nytimes.com/2005/10/09/national/09robot.html.

Marlow, E. 1997. *Web visions*. New York: Van Nostrand Reinhold.

Marshall, Gordon (ed.). 1998. *Oxford Dictionary of Sociology* 2nd edn. Oxford and New York: Oxford University Press.

Marx, Gary T. 2004. What's new about the 'New Surveillance'?: Classifying for change and continuity. *Knowledge, Technology, & Policy* 17(1): 18–37.

Marx, Karl. 1990 [1867, 1884, 1894]. *Capital*. Penguin Classics edn, 3 vols. London: Penguin.

Marx, Karl, & Friedrich Engels. 1973 [1872]. *Manifesto of the Communist Party*. Moscow: Progress Publishers.

Masterton, Murray, & Roger Patching. 1990. *Now the News in Detail: A guide to broadcast journalism in Australia* 2nd edn. Geelong, Vic.: Deakin University Press.

Mathews, John. 1989. *Tools of Change: Technology and the transformation of work*. Sydney: Pluto Press.

Mathewson, Catriona. 2006. Web stunt sends Coke from hero to zero. *Courier-Mail*, 28 January, 13.

Mathieson, Clive. 2005. Films feature in News surge. *Australian*, 3 February, 21.

———. 2005. Google now largest of the giants. *Australian*, 9 June, 15.

maxmon.com. 2005a. *1000BC to 500BC: The Invention of the Abacus* [website]. maxmon.com n.d. [cited 6 September 2005]. Available from www.maxmon.com/1000bc.htm.

———. 2005b. *1274 AD: Ramon Lull's Ars Magna* [website]. maxmon.com n.d. [cited 21 September 2005]. Available from www.maxmon.com/1274ad.htm.

———. 2005c. *1600 AD: John Napier and Napier's Bones* [website]. maxmon.com n.d. [cited 6 September 2005]. Available from www.maxmon.com/1600ad.htm.

———. 2005d. *1714 AD: The first English typewriter patent* [website]. maxmon.com n.d. [cited 21 September 2005]. Available from www.maxmon.com/1714ad.htm.

———. 2005e. *1867 AD: The first commercial typewriter* [website]. maxmon.com n.d. [cited 21 September 2005]. Available from www.maxmon.com/1867ad.htm.

Maxwell, Richard. 1998. What is a spy to do? *Social Text* 16(3): 125–41.

Mayer, Henry. 1968 [1964]. *The Press in Australia*. Sydney: Landsdowne Press.

Mayne, Stephen. 2006. *Vale Hugo Kelly, Crikey 'madman'* Crikey.com, 16 February 2006 [cited 1 April 2006]. Available from http://www.crikey.com.au/articles/2006/02/16-1526-2424.html.

McChesney, Robert W. 2000a. The political economy of communication and the future of the field. *Media, Culture & Society* 22(1): 109–16.

———. 2000b. *Rich Media, Poor Democracy: Communication politics in dubious times*. Paperback edn. New York: New Press.

McChesney, Robert W., & Dan Schiller. 2003. *The Political Economy of International Communications: Foundations for the emerging global debate about media ownership and regulation*. Geneva: UN Research Institute for Social Development.

McChesney, Robert W. & Ben Scott. 2003 (eds). *The Brass Check: A study of American journalism*. Urbana and Chicago: University of Illinois Press.

McCombs, M. E., & D. L Shaw. 1972. The agenda-setting function of mass media. *Public Opinion Quarterly* 36: 176–87.

McCrann, Terry. 2004. Murdoch follows a 21st century path. News's US listing should be a model not a problem. *Weekend Australian*, 26–27 June, 32.

McDonald, Donald. 2005. Introduction. In *Barons to Bloggers: Confronting media power*, ed. J. Mills. Melbourne: Miegunyah Press.

McGarry, Andrew. 2005a. Adelaide's shock jock keeps rattling cages. *Australian*, 3 November, 16.

———. 2005b. Future will be internet systems. *Australian*, 17 November, 13.

McLean, Sheena. 2006. Broadband to challenge pay. *Australian*, 16 March, 20.

McLuhan, Eric, & Frank Zingrone (eds). 1997. *Essential McLuhan*. London: Routledge.

McLuhan, Marshall. 1951. *The Mechanical Bride: Folklore of industrial man*. New York: Vanguard Press.

———. 1967. *Understanding Media: The extension of man*. London: Sphere Books.

McMahon, Peter. 2002. Early electrical communications technology and structural change in the international political economy: The cases of telegraphy and radio. *Prometheus* 20(4): 379–90.

McQueen, Humphrey. 1977. *Australia's Media Monopolies*. Melbourne: Widescope.

MEAA. 1997. *Ethics in journalism / report of the Ethics Review Committee, Media Entertainment and Arts Alliance, Australian Journalists' Association Section.* Melbourne: Melbourne University Press.

Meade, Amanda. 2005. Books, music score in RN revamp. *Australian*, 6 October, 15.

Meadows, Michael. 2001. A return to practice: reclaiming journalism as public conversation. In *Journalism: Theory in practice*, ed. S. Tapsall & C. Varley. Melbourne: Oxford University Press.

Media options are behind the times. 2006. *Courier-Mail*, 16 March, 26.

Media shackles start to loosen. 2006. *SMH*, 15 March, 12.

Menabrea, Luigi Federico, & Augusta Ada Lovelace. 2005. *Sketch of the Analytical Engine* [website]. fourmilab.ch 1843 [cited 6 September 2005]. Available from http://www.fourmilab.ch/babbage/sketch.html.

Michael in New York. 2005. *Bisexuality Study: NYT gives prominence to disgraced researcher* [newsgroup]. QSTUDY-L, 6 July 2005 [cited 8 July 2005].

Microsoft. n.d. Digital Inclusion: Empowering people through technology: Microsoft Corporation.

Miller, Jonathan. 1971. *McLuhan*. Ed. F. Kermode, *Fontana Modern Masters*. London: Fontana/Collins.

Milner, Andrew. 1993. *Cultural Materialism*. Melbourne: Melbourne University Press.

Mitchell, Chris. 2000. The Future Direction of Queensland Newspapers in the 21st Century. Brisbane, 12 April.

Molitorisz, Sacha. 2005. Slow fade to black. *SMH*, 9 June, 14.

Moore, Dinty W. 1995. *The Emperor's Virtual Clothes: The naked truth about internet culture*. Chapel Hill, NC.: Algonquin Books.

Moore, Frazier. 2006. *Entertainment about me, me, me*. latimes.com & Associated Press 2006 [cited 3 March 2006]. Available from www.latimes.com/enertainment/news.

More, Thomas. 1997 (1516). *Utopia*. Ed. P. Negri. 10th edn. *Dover Thrift Editions*. Mineola, NY: Dover Publications.

Moreville, Peter. 2006. *Lessons Learned from the Dot.Com Crash: A Passenger's Story* Argus Center for Information Architecture 2001 [cited 19 March 2006]. Available from http:/argus-acia.com/strange_connections/strange009.html.

Morgan, Richard 2002. *Altered Carbon*. New York: Del Rey, Ballantine Books.

——. 2004. *Market Forces*. London: Gollancz.

Morris , Dick. 1999. *Vote.Com: How Big-Money Lobbyists and the Media Are Losing Their Influence, and the Internet is Giving Power to the People*. Los Angeles: Renaissance Books.

Mosco, Vincent. 1996. *The Political Economy of Communication: Rethinking and Renewal*. In *The Media, Culture & Society*, ed. J. Corner, N. Garhham, P. Scannell, P. Schlesinger, C. Sparks & N. Wood, . London: Sage.

———. 1999. New York.Com: A Political Economy of the 'Informational' City. *Journal of Media Economics* 12(2): 103–16.

———. 2004. *The Digital Sublime: Myth, power and cyberspace*. Boston: MIT Press.

Move over, Big Brother. 2004. *Economist*, 4 December.

Murdoch, Rupert. 2005. Speech to the American Society of Newspaper Editors, 13 April 2005 [cited 1 November 2005]. Available from http://www.newscorp.com/news/news_247.html.

Murphy, Kerrie. 2006. *TV Land: Australia's obsession with reality television*. Brisbane: John Wiley & Sons.

Murray, Lisa. 2006a. Bring on media law changes, execs say. *SMH*, 16 March, 29.

———. 2006b. Players jockey to grab a slice of the action. *SMH*, 15 March, 5.

Murray, Simone. 2005. Brand loyalties: rethinking content within global corporate media. *Media, Culture & Society* 27(3): 415–35.

Musgrove, Mike. 2005. Secret codes reveal a printout's origin. *SMH*, 22–23 October, 15.

Mystical World Wide Web. 2005. *A Brief History of Clocks* [website]. Mystical World Wide Web 2005 [cited 6 September 2005]. Available from http://www.mystical-www.co.uk/time/clocks.htm.

Nasaw, David. 2000. *The Chief: The Life of William Randolph Hearst*. Boston: Houghton Mifflin.

Needham, Kirsty. 2005. For all Sony's mod cons, technology is still playing games. *SMH*, 7 October, 9.

Negroponte, Nicholas. 1996. *being digital*. First Vintage edn. New York: Vintage Books.

———. 1999. Being digital in the wired world. In *Masters of the Wired World*, ed. A. Leer. London: Financial Times Pitman Publishing.

News to view from Yahoo 2005. LATimes.com, 13 September 2005 [cited 14 September 2005]. Available from http://www.latimes.com/news/opinion/la-ed-yahoo13sep.

Newsinger, John. 1999. *Orwell's Politics*. London: Palgrave.

Nguyen, Maria. 2006. TV not dead: Michael Eisner. *B&T Weekly*, 20 February.

Nobelprize.org. 2005. *Guglielmo Marconi: Biography*. Elsevier Publishing Company 2005 [cited 6 September 2005]. Available from http://nobelprize.org/physics/laureates/1909/marconi-bio.html.

Noonan, Kathleen. 2006. Children of the cyber revolution. *Courier-Mail*, 14–15 January, 28.

Norden, Eric. 1997. *Playboy* Interview: A candid conversation with the high priest of popcult and metaphysician of media. In *Essential McLuhan*, ed. E. McLuhan & F. Zingrone. London: Routledge. Original edition, 1969, March edition of *Playboy* magazine.

Norington, Brad. 2006. Reforms could herald receivership fallout. *Australian*, 16 March, 19.

O'Connor, Angela. 2004. Six children, rent to pay, debt: a less than perfect picture for Kodak workers. *Age*, 18 September, 5.

O'Connor, J. J., & E. F. Robertson. 1996a. *Blaise Pascal* [website]. MacTutor History of Mathematics, December 1996 [cited 6 September 2005]. Available from http://www-groups.dcs.st-andrews.ac.uk/Printonly/Pascal.html.

———. 1996b. *Wilhelm Schickard*. MacTutor History of Mathematics, December 1996 [cited 6 September 2005]. Available from www.history.mcs.st-andrews.ac.uk/Mathematicians/Schickard.html.

———. 1998a. *Charles Babbage* [website]. MacTutor History of Mathematics, October 1998 [cited 6 September 2005]. Available from http://www-groups.dcs.st-and.ac.uk/~history/Printonly/Babbage.html.

———. 1998b. *John Napier* [website]. MacTutor History of Mathematics, April 1998 [cited 6 September 2005]. Available from www-groups.dcs.st-and.ac.uk/~history/Printonly/Napier.html.

———. 1999a. *Howard Hathaway Aiken* [website]. MacTutor History of Mathematics, July 1999 [cited 14 September 2005]. Available from http://www-groups.dcs.st-and.ac.uk/~history/Printonly/Aiken.html.

———. 1999b. *Konrad Zuse* [website]. MacTutor History of Mathematics, July 1999 [cited 14 September 2005]. Available from http://www-groups.dcs.st-and.ac.uk/~history/Printonly/Zuse.html.

———. 2003a. *Alan Mathison Turing* [website]. MacTutor History of Mathematics, October 2003 [cited 6 September 2005]. Available from www.history.mcs.st-andrews.ac.uk/Mathematicians/Turing.html.

———. 2003b. *John von Neumann* [website]. MacTutor History of Mathematics, October 2003 [cited 6 September 2005]. Available from http://www-groups.dcs.st-andrews.ac.uk/~history/Printonly/Von_Neumann.html.

O'Connor, John D. 2005. 'I'm the guy they called deep throat'. *Vanity Fair*, July, 84–7, 127–31.

O'Harrow Jr, Robert. 2005. *No Place to Hide*. New York: Free Press.

O'Malley, Nick. 2005. Memo all: the boss may be watching. *SMH*, 7 October, 3.

Oakham, Katrina Mandy. 2001. Journalism: Beyond the business. In *Journalism: Theory in practice*, ed. S. Tapsall & C. Varley. Melbourne: Oxford University Press.

Odgers, Rosemary, & Renee Viellaris. 2005. Criminals move online. *Courier-Mail*, 10 November, 7.

OECD. 2004. *The Security Economy*. OECD 2004 [cited 4 April 2006]. Available from http://www.brookings.edu/press/books/clientpr/oecd/securityeconomy.htm.

———. 2005. *Double Safe?* (246/247). OECD 2005 [cited 4 April 2006]. Available from http://www.oecdobserver.org/news/fullstory.php/aid/1532/Double_safe_.html.

Ogden, M. R. 1999. Catching up to our digital future? Cyberdemocracy versus virtual mercantilism. In *Towards equity in global communication*, ed. R. C. Vincent, K. Nordenstreng & M. Traber. New Jersey: Hampton Press.

Old mogul, new media. 2006. *Economist*, 21–27 January, 65–6.

Orwell, George. 1984 [1946]. Why I write. In *The Penguin Essays of George Orwell*, ed. S. Orwell & I. Angus. London: Penguin.

———. 1988 [1949]. *Nineteen Eighty-four*. London: Penguin.

———. 2000 [1946]. James Burnham and the Managerial Revolution. In *In Front of Your Nose 1945–1950*, ed. S. Orwell & I. Angus. Boston: Nonpareil Books.

Ostergaard, Bernte Stubbe. 1998. Convergence: Legislative dilemmas. In *Media Policy: Convergence, concentration and commerce*, ed. D. McQuail & K. Siune. London: Sage.

Paletz, D. L. 1999. *The Media in American Politics*. New York: Addison-Wesley Educational.

Parayil, Govindan. 2005. The digital divide and increasing returns: Contradictions of informational capitalism. *The Information Society* 21: 41–51.

Parenti, Michael. 1999. Methods of media manipulation. In *Impact of Mass Media: Current issues*, ed. R. E. Hiebert. New York: Addison-Wesley Longman.

Partington, Angela (ed.). 1997. *The Concise Oxford Dictionary of Quotations*, ed. E. Knowles. Rev. 3rd edn, *Oxford Quotation Dictionaries*. London: Oxford University Press.

Pavlik, John V. 2001. *Journalism and New Media*. New York: Columbia University Press.

———. 1994. Citizen access, involvement, and freedom of expression in an electronic environment. In *People's Right to Know: Media, democracy, and the information highway*, ed. J. V. Pavlik. New Jersey: Lawrence Erlbaum.

——— & Steven K. Feiner. 1998. *Implications of the Mobile Journalist Workstation for Print Media* [website]. Institute for Cyberinformation, Fall 1998 [cited 25 March 2004]. Available from http://www.futureprint.kent.edu/articles/pavlik01.htm.

Pearl, Cyril. 1977 [1959]. *Wild Men of Sydney*. Sydney: Angus & Robertson.

Pearson, Mark. 2004. *The Journalist's Guide to Media Law: Dealing with legal and ethical issues* 2nd edn. Sydney: Allen & Unwin.

Pelly, Michael. 2006. If the truth be told … *SMH*, 20 January, p. 13.

Perloff, R.M. 1998. *Political Communication: Politics, press, and public in America*. New Jersey: Lawrence Erlbaum.

Pesola, Maija, Sundeep Tucker, & Mark Odell. 2005. Marconi Plunges after BT bid fails. *Weekend Australian*, 30 April–1 May, 43.

Petersen, Neville. 2006. Recollections of a career at the ABC. Interview with Martin Hirst via email, 30 March.

Petre, Daniel, & David Harrington. 1996. *The Clever Country? Australia's Digital Future*. Sydney: Lansdowne & Pan Macmillan.

Pew Research Center for the People and the Press. 2004. *Media Consumption and Believability Study*. Pew Centre 2004 [cited 1 November 2005].

Pfanner, Eric. 2006. *Publicis acts to surf the marketing waves of the future*. nytimes.com, 1 March 2006 [cited 3 March 2006]. Available from www.nytimes.com/2006/03/01/business/media.

PFF. 1993. *Our Mission*. The Progress and Freedom Foundation, 1993 [cited 5 April 2006]. Available from http://www.pff.org/about/.

———. 2006. *Incorporate Competition Standard in 'Net Neutrality'*. The Progess and Freedom Foundation, 30 March 2006 [cited 5 April 2006]. Available from http://www.pff.org/news/news/2006/033006mayhousetestimony.html.

Phelan, John M. 1991. Selling consent: the public sphere as a televisual market-place. In *Communication and Citizenship: Journalism and the public sphere in the new media age*, ed. P. Dahlgren & C. Sparks. London & New York: Routledge.

Place and Time. 2005. Did you buy your mobile phone because of the gadgets on it? *Courier-Mail*, 18–19 June, 34.

Police use videotape in search for gang. 2005. *Courier-Mail*, 12 July, 3.

Postman, Neil. 1993. *Technopoly: The surrender of culture to technology*. New York: Vintage Books.

Pratt, Cornelius. 1997. The 40-year tobacco wars: Giving public relations a black eye? *Public Relations Quarterly* 42(4): 5–10.

Priest, Marcus, & David Crowe. 2005. Copyright ruling runs foul of free-trade pact. *AFR*, 7 October, 3.

Quiggin, John. 2006. Public missing out, again. *AFR*, 16 March, 62.

Quinlivan, Beth. 2003. Reel trouble: The Australian film industry is increasingly dependent on foreign money, and it is getting harder to make a profit. *Business Review Weekly*, 13–19 February, 38–41.

Quinn, Stephen. 1998. Newsgathering and the Internet. In *Journalism: Theory and Practice*, ed. M. Breen. Sydney: Macleay Press.

Reaves, Jessica. 2005. *Anorexia goes hi-tech* [website]. TIME.com, 31 July, 2005 [cited 20 September 2005]. Available from http://www.time.com/time/health/article/0,8599,169660,00.html.

Redshaw, Kerry. 1996. *Konrad Zuse* [website]. Redshaw, Kerry, 5 October, last update 1996 [cited 14 September 2005]. Available from http://www.kerryr.net/pioneers/zuse.htm.

Reed, Rosslyn. 1999. Journalism and technology practice since the Second World War. In *Journalism: Print, politics and popular culture*, ed. A. Curthoys & J. Schultz. Brisbane: Queensland University Press.

Reid, E. M. 1996. Communication and community on internet relay chat: constructing communities. In *High Noon on the Electronic Frontier*, ed. P. Ludlow. Cambridge Mass.: MIT Press.

Reuters. 2005. Students putting it all online against Bush. *Australian*, 18 November, 9.

Reynolds, Glenn Harlan. 2004. Media dinosaurs, your game is up. *Australian*, 24 September, 15.

Rivett, Rohan. 1965. The press today. In *The Journalist's Craft: A guide to modern practice*, ed. L. Revill & C. Roderick. Sydney: Angus & Robertson.

Roberts, Peter. 2004. Snap decision in cruel world. *AFR*, 17 September.

Robinson, Renae. 2005. Cyber sting: How to secure your cash from online thieves. *Sunday Mail*, 27 March, 61.

Roget, Peter Mark. 1979. *Roget's Thesaurus*. Classic American edn. New York: Avenel Books.

Rolled by Net piracy. 2005. *Sunday Herald Sun*, 4 September, 32.

Roosevelt, Franklin D. 1941. On the declaration of war with Japan. In *Fireside Chats of Franklin D. Roosevelt*. United States. http://www.mhric.org/fdr/chat19.html.

Rose, Nik. 2006. A dose of high-tech scepticism. *SMH*, 17.

Rosen, Danny. 2005. Online curbs in China. *Australian*, 4 October, 12.

Rosen, Jay. 2005. Each nation its own press. In *Barons to Bloggers: Confronting media power*, ed. J. Mills. Melbourne: Miegunyah Press.

Rosenberg, Nathan. 1997. *Babbage: Pioneer economist* [website]. The Babbage Pages, 8 January 1997 [cited 6 September 2005]. Available from http://www.exeter.ac.uk/BABBAGE/rosenb.html.

Rothstein, Edward. 2003. Utopia and its discontents. In *Visions of Utopia*, ed. E. Rothstein, H. Muschamp & M. E. Marty. New York: Oxford University Press.

Rowley, William. 2002. 'Surveillance society' and 'transparent society': New challenges for society. *Spectrum: The Journal of State Government*, 75: 16–17.

Roy, Michelle. 2000. *The phoenix: Back from the ashes of the dot.com Crashes*. Expiry Corporation, November 2000 [cited 19 March 2006]. Available from http://www.expiry.com/enet/archive/2000/11-nov-2000-dotcomcrashes.shtml.

Ruehl, Peter. 2006. Want a media treat? You'll get a snack. *AFR*, 16 March, 64.

Rundle, Guy. 2005. Frontier tales: The hype and the reality of the online transformation of news. In *Barons to Bloggers: Confronting media power*, ed. J. Mills. Melbourne: Miegunyah Press.

———. 2006. Message to wounded bloggers: Less is more. In *Crikey*, ed. Misha Ketchell. Private Media (accessed 18 May 2006).

Rushkoff, Douglas. 1994. *Cyberia: Life in the trenches of hyperspace*. London: Flamingo.

———. 2006. *www.rushkoff.com* 2006 [cited 26 March 2006]. Available from www.rushkoff.com.

Rutherford Smith, Robert. 1997. Mythic elements in television news. In *Social meanings of news: A text-reader*, ed. D. Berkowitz. Thousand Oaks, Calif.: Sage.

Sainsbury, Michael. 2006. Technology racing ahead of the changes. *Australian*, 15 March, 1.

Sallabank, Cameron. 2006. Online advertising—but not as you know it. *B&T Weekly*, 16 February.

Salt, Bernard. 2005. Strange new world in 50 years. *Australian*, 10 November, 26.

Salter, David. 2006. Gesture politics a cynical way to admonish Aunty. *Australian*, 6 April, 14.

Sambrook, Richard. 2005. Citizen journalism and the BBC. *Nieman Reports* 59(4): 13–16.

Sanchanta, Mariko. 2006. Vultures hunt for Livedoor assets. *Weekend Australian*, 4–5 February, 39.

Sanders, Karen. 2003. *Ethics and Journalism*. London: Sage.

Schiller, Dan. 1999. The legacy of Robert A. Brady: Antifascist origins of the political economy of communications. *Journal of Media Economics* 12(2): 89–101.

Schofield, Jack. 2005. Coming to a screen near you: Web2.0. *SMH*, 21 November, 15.

Schultz, Julianne. 1989. Failing the public: The media marketplace. In *Communications and the Public Sphere: Essays in memory of Bill Bonney*, ed. H. Wilson. Melbourne: Macmillan.

———. 1998. *Reviving the Fourth Estate: Democracy, Accountability and the Media*. Cambridge: Cambridge University Press.

——— (ed.). 1994. *Not just another business: Journalists, citizens and the media*. Sydney: Pluto Press.

Schulze, Jane. 2004. It's GOOD NEWS week. *Australian*, 8 April, 17.

———. 2005. News rethinks web. *Australian*, 17 February, 27.

———. 2006. Cashed-up regionals look to buy. *Australian*, 15 March, 6.

——— & Glenda Korporaal. 2005. Sports rights in $200m carve-up. *Australian*, 9 June, 15, 18.

——— & Steve Lewis. 2006. Media silent on changes. *Australian*, 17 March, 2.

Schwartau, Winn. 2000. *Cybershock: Surviving hackers, phreakers, indentity thieves, Internet terrorists and weapons of mass disruption*. New York: Thunder's Mouth Press.

Schwartz, E. 1996. *Netactivism: How citizens use the internet.* Thousand Oaks, Calif.: Songline Studios.

Schwartz, Michael. 2000. Why ethical codes constitute an unconscionable regression. *Journal of Business Ethics* 23(2): 173–85.

Searle, Adrian. 2002. The sordid and the sublime: Ansel Adams composed elegant images of America's awe-inspiring landscapes. *Guardian*, 9 July, 12.

Seelye, Katherine Q. 2005. Felt is praised as a hero and condemned as a traitor. *New York Times*, 2 June, 18.

Sekuless, Peter. 1999. *A Handful of Hacks*. Sydney: Allen & Unwin.

Selnow, Gary W. 1998. *Electronic Whistle-stops*. New York: Praeger.

Shainblum, Mark, & Matthew Friedman. 1993. *William Gibson*. Lost Pages 1993 [cited 25 February 2006]. Available from http://lostpages.net/lostpages2gibson.html.

Shaw, Martin. 1988. *The dialectics of war: An essay in the social theory of war and peace*. London: Pluto Press.

Shedden, Ian. 2004. Download a track as you wait for a train. *Weekend Australian*, 20–21 November, 8.

Sherwin, Adam. 2006. Police shut down file-sharing server. *Times*, 23 February, 57.

Shoebridge, Neil. 2006a. Insiders tune in to rumour of a shake-up. *AFR*, 15 March, 48.

———. 2006b. Pay TV appeals turned down. *AFR*, 16 March, 19.

———. 2006c. Scramble to bulk up or be swallowed. *AFR*, 15 March, 48.

Simons, Margaret. 2006. A long list of dead media. *crikey.com*, 28 February 2006 [cited 28 February 2006]. Available from www.crikey.com.au.

Sinclair, Lara. 2005. Booming sectors to lead advertising growth in '06. *Australian*, 17 November, 13.

———. 2006. Advertisers urge faster pace for change. *Australian*, 16 March, 19.

——— & Sheena MacLean. 2005. Celebrity gossip drives sales battle. *Australian*, 24 November, 13.

Sinclair, Upton. 2000 [1924]. *The Millennium: A comedy of the year 2000*. New York: Seven Stories Press.

Sinha, Indra. 1999. *The Cybergypsies: Love, life and travels on the electronic frontier*. London: Scribner.

Siochru, S. O. 1999. Democratic media: the case for getting organised. In *Towards equity in global communication*, ed. R. Vincent, K. Nordenstreng, M. Traber. New Jersey: Hampton Press.

Skulley, Mark. 2004. Digital kills Kodak: 600 jobs axed. *AFR*, 17 September 2004, 1, 8.

Smith, Anthony. 1980. *Goodbye Gutenberg: The newspaper revolution of the 1980s*. New York: Oxford University Press.

Smith, David C. 1986. *H.G. Wells: Desparately Mortal*. New Haven & London: Yale University Press.

Smith, Steve. 2005. *The Emerging Search Economy* (January/February 2005) 2005 [cited 4 April 2006]. Available from http://www.econtentmag.com/Articles/ArticleReader.aspx?ArticleID=7625.

Snoddy, Raymond. 1992. *The Good, the Bad and the Unacceptable*. London: Faber & Faber.

Snow, Deborah. 2005. The future is running too fast towards us. *SMH*, 1–2 January, 35.

Sparrow, Geoff. 1960. *Crusade for Journalism*. Melbourne: Australian Journalists' Association.

Spence, Edward. 2006. Stranger than fiction: the fabrication of fact. *SMH*, 16 January, 9.

Stanley, Jay, & Barry Steinhardt. 2003. *Bigger Monster, Weaker Chains: The growth of an American surveillance society*. New York: American Civil Liberties Union.

Steinberg, Don. 2001. Surveillance Society. *Smartbusinessmag.Com*, December 2001–January 2002, 60.

Steinberg, Sigfrid Henry. 1961. *Five Hundred Years of Printing* 2nd edn. Harmondsworth: Pelican.

Stephenson, Neal. 1992. *Snow Crash*. London: Penguin.

———. 1999. *In the Beginning …, Was the Command Line*. New York: Avon Books.

———. 2002. *Cryptonomicon*. New York: Avon Books.

Stepp, C. S. 1999. The new journalist. In *Impact of Mass Media: Current issues*, ed. R. E. Hiebert. New York: Addison-Wesley Longman.

Stevens, Barrie. 2004. The emerging security economy: An introduction. In *The Security Economy*, ed. OECD. Paris: OECD.

Stevens, Jane. 2002. *Backpack journalism is here to stay*, April 2002 [cited 20 November 2003]. Available from http://www.ojr.org/ojr/workplace/1017771575.php.

Stevensen, Nick. 1995. *Understanding Media Cultures: Social theory and mass communication*. London: Sage.

Stock Market Crash! Net. 2005. *The Nasdaq Bubble*. Stock Market Crash! Net 2005 [cited 19 March 2006]. Available from http://www.stock-market-crash.net/nasdaq.htm.

Stone, Martha. 2002. *The Backpack Journalist is a 'Mush of Mediocrity'* [website]. Online Journalism Review, 2 April 2002 [cited 20 November 2003]. Available from http://www.ojr.org.ojr/workplace/1017771634.php.

Stonehouse, David. 2005. Damn that spam. *SMH*, 29–30 October, icon, 6–7.

Sussman, Gerald. 1999. Special Issue on the Political Economy of Communications. *Journal of Media Economics* 12(2): 85–7.

Swanberg, W. A. 1961. *Citizen Hearst: A biography of William Randolph Hearst*. New York: Scribner, 1961.

Tacket, Michael. 2005. Revealed: Man who ended a presidency. *Daily Telegraph*, 2 June, 25.

Takeshita, T. 1997. Exploring the media's roles in defining reality: From issue-agenda setting to attribute-agenda setting. In *Communication and democracy*, ed. M. McCombs, D. L. Shaw, D. Shaw & D. Weaver. New Jersey: Lawrence Erlbaum.

Talking to the world. 1999. *Economist*, 31 December, 83–5.

Tapsall, Suellen, & Carolyn Varley. 2001. What is a journalist? In *Journalism Theory in Practice*, ed. S. Tapsall & C. Varley. Melbourne: Oxford University Press.

Taylor, Peter. 1980. *An End to Silence. The building of the Overland Telegraph Line from Adelaide to Darwin*. Sydney: Methuen.

Tedmanson, Sophie. 2005. Web diaries of movies in the making. *Australian*, 23 March, 3.

Teichmann, Max. 2004. The answer is a lemon. *Quadrant*, 72–73.

The Jobs Letter. 2002. *The Dot.Com Crash ... after Wall St's biggest fall in history* (No 123). The Jobs Research Trust, 12 May, 2000 [cited 19 March 2006]. Available from http://www.jobslcttcr.org.nz/jbl12310.htm.

Thompson, John B. 1995. *The Media and Modernity: A social theory of the media*. Oxford: Polity Press.

Thompson, Tuck. 2005. Sex-spy cameras capture lovers. *Courier-Mail*, 29–30 October, 5.

Threapleton, Mary M. 1967. Introduction. In *Erewhon*. Clinton, Mass.: Airmont Classic.

Tide turns against digital piracy. 2006. *Townsville Bulletin*, 21 January, 21.

Tiffen, Rod. 1989. *News and Power*. Sydney: Allen & Unwin.

Toffler, Alvin. 1981. *The Third Wave*. London: Pan.

Tomlinson, Sue. 1998. *History of writing* [website]. Tomlinson, Sue, 25 January 1998 [cited 6 September 2005]. Available from www.delmar.edu/engl/instruct/stomline/1301int/lessons;language/history.htm.

Toohey, Brian, & Matt Drummond. 2005. Economists charged over cybercrimes. *AFR*, 27 October, 1, 6.

Trippi, Joe. 2004. *The revolution will not be televised: Democracy, the Internet, and the overthrow of everything*. New York: Regan Books.

Tsagarousianou, Roza. 1998. Electronic democracy and the public sphere: Opportunities and challenges. In *cyberdemocracy: technology, cities and civic networks*, ed. R. Tsagarousianou, D. Tambini & C. Bryan. London & New York: Routledge.

Tsagarousianou, Roza, Damien Tambini, & Cathy Bryan, eds. 1998. *cyberdemocracy: technology, cities and civic networks*. London & New York: Routledge.

Tulloch, Sara (ed.). 1992. *The Oxford Dictionary of New Words: A popular guide to words in the news*. Oxford and New York: Oxford University Press.

Turner, David, & Adam Jones. 2006. Vivendi pays $1.5 billion to call the tune at Universal. *Weekend Australian*, 4–5 February, 39.

Twight, Charlotte. 2001. Watching you: Systematic federal surveillance of ordinary Americans. In *Cato Institute Briefing Papers (No.69)*. Washington DC: Cato Institute.

Vaile, David. 2005. Worst privacy invaders named at Big Brother Awards [Media Release]. *Australian Privacy Foundation*, 8 November.

Villeneuve, Nart. 2006. *The filtering matrix: Integrated mechanisms of information control and the demarcation of borders in cyberspace* 2006 [cited 19 January 2006]. Available from http://firstmonday.org/issues/issue11_1/villeneuve.

Vnuk, Helen. 2003. *Snatched: Sex and censorship in Australia*. Sydney: Vintage.

Von Drehle, David. 2005. *FBI's No. 2 was 'Deep Throat'* [Internet]. wasinghtonpost.com, 1 June 2005 [cited 10 July 2005]. Available from www.washingtonpost.com.

Walker, Jamie. 2002. Harsh light shone on secret passion. *Australian*, 4 July, 1.

Walker, Robin B. 1976. *The Newspaper Press in New South Wales, 1803–1920*. Sydney: Sydney University Press.

Walker, Sally. 1989. *The Law of Journalism in Australia*. Sydney: Law Book Company.

Walle, Monica. 2003. Commentary: What happened to public responsibility? The lack of society in public relations codes of ethics. In *Prism*, Vol. 1. http://www.praxis.bond.edu.au/prism/papers/commentary/paper1.pdf.

Ward, Ian. 1991. Who writes the news? Journalists as hunters or harvesters. *Australian Journalism Review* 13(1/2): 52–8.

———. 1995. *Politics of the Media*. Melbourne: Macmillan.

Wardill, Steven, & Lachlan Heywood. 2005. Privacy advocate tips card to fail. *Courier-Mail*, 19 July, 4.

Wark, McKenzie. 1994. *Virtual Geography: Living with global media events*. Bloomington, Ind.: Indiana University Press.

Washington Post, Newsday. 2005. Accidental Journalists: Close and personal with camera phones. *SMH*, 9–10 July, 17.

Waugh, Evelyn. 1943. *Scoop*. Harmondsworth: Penguin.

Wayne, Mike. 2003. *Marxism and Media Studies: Key concepts and contemporary trends*, ed. M. Wayne & E. Leslie, *Marxism and Culture*. London: Pluto Press.

Weekend Australian. 2004. A photo opportunity that did not develop. *Weekend Australian*, 18–19 September 2004, 18.

Weightman, Gavin. 2003. *Signor Marconi's Magic Box: How an amateur inventor defied scientists and began the radio revolution*. London: HarperCollins.

Welch, Michael, Erica A. Price & Nana Yankey. 2002. Moral panic over youth violence: Wilding and the manufacture of menace in the media. *Youth & Society* 34(1): 3–30.

Wells, H. G. 1976 [1914]. *The World Set Free*. London: Corgi.

———. 2002. *A Modern Utopia* [e-book], 2002 (1905) [cited 24 February 2006]. Available from http://www.gutenberg.org/etext/6424.

wikipedia. 2005a. *History of Computing Hardware* [website]. Wikipedia.org, 4 September, 2005 [cited 6 September 2005]. Available from http://en.wikipedia.org/wiki/Arithmometer.

———. 2005b. *Von Neumann architecture* [website]. Wikipedia.org, 1 September, 2005 [cited 6 September 2005]. Available from http://en.wikipedia.org/wiki/Von_Neumann_architecture.

Wikipedia. 2006a. *E-democracy*. Wikipedia.org, 28 March 2006 [cited 5 April 2006]. Available from http://en.wikipedia.org/wiki/E-democracy.

———. 2006b. *Google Economy*. Wikipedia.org, 23 March 2006 [cited 4 April 2006]. Available from http://en.wikipedia.org/wiki/Google_economy.

———. 2006c. *Independent Media Center*. Wikipedia.org, 4 April 2006 [cited 8 April 2006]. Available from http://en.wikipedia.org/wiki/Indymedia.

———. 2006d. *Knowledge Economy*. Wikipedia, 1 April 2006 [cited 3 April 2006]. Available from http://en.wikipedia.org/wiki/Knowledge_Economy.

Wikipedia. 2005. *meme* [website]. Wikipedia [cited 1 June 2005]. Available from http://en.wikipedia.org/wiki/meme.

Williams, Felicia. 2006. $3.3m for a 30sec spot—who said TV was dead? *B&T Weekly*, 16 February.

Williams, Kevin. 1997. *Get Me a Murder a Day! A history of mass communication in Britain*. London: Arnold.

Williams, Louise. 2006. Every move they make, mum's watching. *SMH*, 11–12 February, 1, 2.

Williams, Rachel. 2006. 'Stalker' map riles stars. *Courier-Mail*, 16 March, 33.

Williams, Raymond. 1978. *Television: technology and cultural form*, ed. J. Benthall, *Technosphere*. London: Fontana.

———. 1980. Base and superstructure in Marxist cultural theory. In *Problems in Materialism and Culture: Selected essays*. London: Verso.

———. 1983. *Towards 2000*. London: Chatto & Windus.

———. 1989 [1976]. *Keywords: A vocabulary of culture and society* 3rd edn. London: Fontana Press.

Williams, Robyn. 1996. *Normal Service Won't be Resumed: The future of public broadcasting*. Sydney: Allen & Unwin.

Wilson, Ashleigh, & Ian Gerard. 2006. Worry over loss of media outlets in far north. *Australian*, 16 March, 2.

Wilson, Peter. 2005. Five police bullets end it all for train bomber who tried again. *Weekend Australian*, 23–24 July, 1, 11.

Winston, Brian. 1993. The CBS Evening News, 7 April 1949: creating an ineffable television format. In *Getting the message; news, truth and power*, ed. J. Eldridge. London and New York: Routledge.

Workman, Chuck 1993. Lasting impressions *Modern Maturity* 36(1): 36–39.

Worldwide but Homegrown. 2005. *New York Times*, 30 October.

Wray, Richard. 2005. *Marconi dealt fatal blow as BT shuts it out of the 21st century* (online) [Internet]. The Guardian, 29 April 2005 [cited 3 May 2005]. Available from http://www.guardian.co.uk/print/0,3858,5182276-111163,00.html.

Wren, Christopher. 1997. Clinton calls fashion ads' 'heroin chic' deplorable. *New York Times*, 22 May, A22.

Wright, Donald K. 1993. Enforcement dilemma:Voluntary nature of public relations codes. *Public Relations Review* 19(1): 13–21.

Young, Richard & Sally Moulsdale. 1989. *Paparazzo: The photographs of Richard Young*. London: Virgin.

Zamyatin, Yevgeny. 1999 [1923]. *We*. Transl. M. Ginsburg. New York: EOS An imprint of HarperCollins.

Zawawi, Clare. 1994. Source of news: Who feeds the watchdogs? *Australian Journalism Review* 16(1): 67–72.

Zion, Lawrie. 2005. Bright light on the horizon. *Weekend Australian*, 15–16 October, 23.

Zuel, Bernard. 1999. Trouble Shooters. *SMH*, 5–11 July, 4–5.

INDEX